Notes From A
DEFEATIST

Notes From A
DEFEATIST

Joe Sacco

JONATHAN CAPE
LONDON

"THE TIME MIGHT WELL COME IN THE NOT TOO DISTANT FUTURE WHEN AN ALL-OUT ATTACK BY EVERY MEANS AT OUR DISPOSAL ON GERMAN CIVILIAN MORALE MIGHT BE DECISIVE." –BRITISH CHIEF OF STAFF TO CHURCHILL, JULY '44
"IF WE ASSUME THAT THE DAYTIME POPULATION OF THE AREA ATTACKED IS 300,000, WE MAY EXPECT 220,000 CASUALTIES. 50 PERCENT OF THESE OR 110,000 MAY EXPECT TO BE KILLED. IT IS SUGGESTED THAT SUCH AN ATTACK RESULTING IN SO MANY DEATHS, THE GREAT PROPORTION OF WHICH WILL BE KEY PERSONNEL, CANNOT HELP BUT HAVE A SHATTERING EFFECT ON POLITICAL AND CIVILIAN MORALE ALL OVER GERMANY..." –DIRECTORATE OF BOMBER OPERATIONS, SUMMER '44
"IN BOMBER COMMAND WE HAVE ALWAYS WORKED ON THE ASSUMPTION THAT BOMBING ANYTHING IN GERMANY IS BETTER THAN BOMBING NOTHING." –HARRIS, FALL '44
"I DID NOT ASK YOU LAST NIGHT ABOUT PLANS FOR HARRYING THE GERMAN RETREAT FROM BRESLAU. ON THE CONTRARY, I ASKED WHETHER BERLIN, AND NO DOUBT OTHER LARGE CITIES IN EAST GERMANY, SHOULD NOT NOW BE CONSIDERED ESPECIALLY ATTRACTIVE TARGETS. I AM GLAD THIS IS UNDER EXAMINATION. PRAY REPORT TO ME TOMORROW WHAT IS GOING TO BE DONE." –CHURCHILL TO SEC. OF STATE IN THE AIR, JAN. '45

Published by Jonathan Cape 2003

First published in the United States by Fantagraphics Books

8 10 9

"Cartoon Genius," "Alessio Easelsmear," "Stanton K. Pragmatron," "Mr. Nit", "Edward L. Warren," "The Truth Hurtz," and all of Parts Four through Nine were originally published in *Yahoo.* "On My Day Off" was originally published in *Drawn & Quarterly* magazine. "The Industrial Revolution" and "Zachary Mindbiscuit" were originally published in *Prime Cuts.* "The Empire," "Apocalypse Then," and "Johnny Sentence" were originally published in *Spotlight on the Genius That Is Joe Sacco.* "The Arnold Homecastle Story" was originally published in *Centrifugal Bumble-Puppy.* "Oliver Limpdingle's Search For Love" was originally published in *Weirdo.* "Edwin Smallcabbage" was originally published in *Suburban High Life.* "Meat" and "Tales of the Office" were originally published in *Neener-Ploy.* "Mark Victorystooge" was originally published in *PDXS.* Much of this volume was already collected in *Spotlight on the Genius That Is Joe Sacco* (Fantagraphics Books, 1994) and *War Junkie* (Fantagraphics Books, 1995).

First published in Great Britain in 2003 by
Jonathan Cape
Random House, 20 Vauxhall Bridge Road, London SW1V 2SA

The Random House Group Limited Reg. No. 954009
www.randomhouse.co.uk

A CIP catalogue record for this book is available from the British Library

ISBN 978-0-224-07270-0

MIX
Paper from
responsible sources
FSC® C016779

Printed and bound in India by
Replika Press Pvt. Ltd.

7 Introduction

9 Part One: Cartoon Genius

17 Part Two: Eight Characters

51 Part Three: Social Studies

63 Part Four: In The Company Of Long Hair

95 Part Five: A Disgusting Experience

109 Part Six: Voyage To The End Of The Library

NOTES FROM A DEFEATIST:

TABLE OF CONTENTS

119 Part Seven: When Good Bombs Happen To Bad People

131 Part Eight: More Women, More Children, More Quickly

155 Part Nine: How I Loved The War

191 Part Ten: Epilogue, On My Day Off

201 Apocrypha

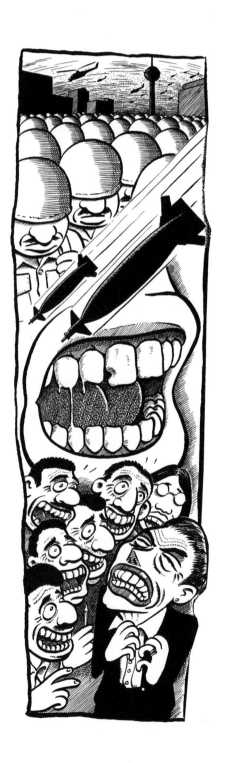

I can hear them scoffing already. All those who are out for my blood. They're saying this is another shameless repackaging of my oft repackaged oeuvre. They've seen it all before in *War Junkie* and in *Spotlight On the Genius That Is Joe Sacco*. And, anyway, they'll tell you this is not up to the standard of my more overtly political work, *Palestine* and *Safe Area Gorazde*. Or they'll tell you that my more overtly political work is a fraud, and that this collection is even more despicable. I can hear them sending their instant messages and logging on to their chat rooms. They're sharpening their virtual knives. They think I'm a sell-out, that I'm milking the same tired substandard pages for all they're worth. No, sir, they don't like the fact that my pockets are now weighed down with money and that I can afford the best escorts in town.

That's right, ladies and gentlemen, after years of struggle, some of them documented in these pages, after years of prying bread crumbs from the beaks of pigeons, my ship finally came in. My career is a roaring success! It was a surprise to me, too. I didn't know so much gold existed. But one day I answered the door and found myself face to face with the driver of a Brink's truck. "Where do you want us to put it?" he said, and I kissed him on both cheeks. I quickly divorced the woman who had stuck by me all those years and got myself a personal trainer. I'm looking ten years younger. Things are just great. In fact, I'm not sure why this collection is called *Notes From A Defeatist*. I think a focus group came up with the title. These petty decisions are no longer in my hands. I don't do much more than read my royalty statements. I'm not even writing this introduction. I'm actually a cute intern who'll sign the name of the cartoonist Joe Sacco and hopes he picks me next time he wants a companion in Paris. That's where he is now. He's going through a mid-life crisis and has joined a few French sex clubs.

NOTES FROM A DEFEATIST:

INTRODUCTION

Please do buy *Notes From A Defeatist*. It's not such a bad overview of the old man's early career. There's a few laughs in here, a few poignant moments. A little sex, a little rock 'n' roll. A little autobiography, a little satire. A little war, a little politics. Anyway, it'll add even more to the plus column of his bank account, and that will suit me just fine. I intend to exploit the weaknesses he can now afford and squeeze him for a few hundred thousand. He's gotta be good for that. Unless he drops it all on those costly hair transplants he keeps talking about.

Joe Sacco
Oct. 2002

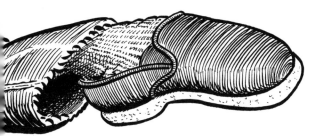

PART ONE:
CARTOON GENIUS

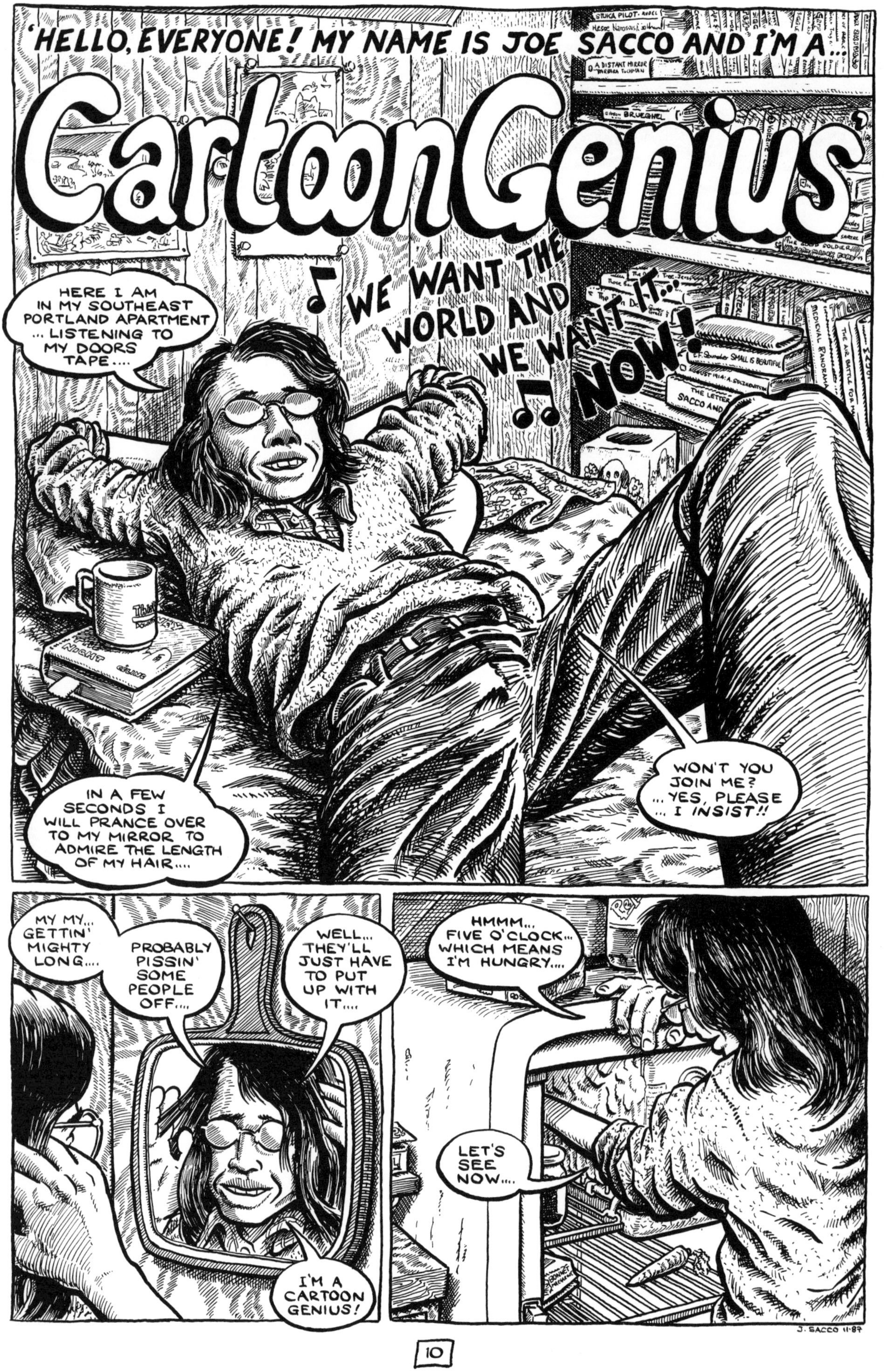
'HELLO, EVERYONE! MY NAME IS JOE SACCO AND I'M A...
CartoonGenius'
HERE I AM IN MY SOUTHEAST PORTLAND APARTMENT ... LISTENING TO MY DOORS TAPE....
WE WANT THE WORLD AND WE WANT IT... WE WANT IT... NOW!
WON'T YOU JOIN ME? ... YES, PLEASE ... I INSIST!!
IN A FEW SECONDS I WILL PRANCE OVER TO MY MIRROR TO ADMIRE THE LENGTH OF MY HAIR....
MY MY... GETTIN' MIGHTY LONG....
PROBABLY PISSIN' SOME PEOPLE OFF....
WELL... THEY'LL JUST HAVE TO PUT UP WITH IT....
I'M A CARTOON GENIUS!
HMMM... FIVE O'CLOCK... WHICH MEANS I'M HUNGRY....
LET'S SEE NOW....
J. SACCO 11·87

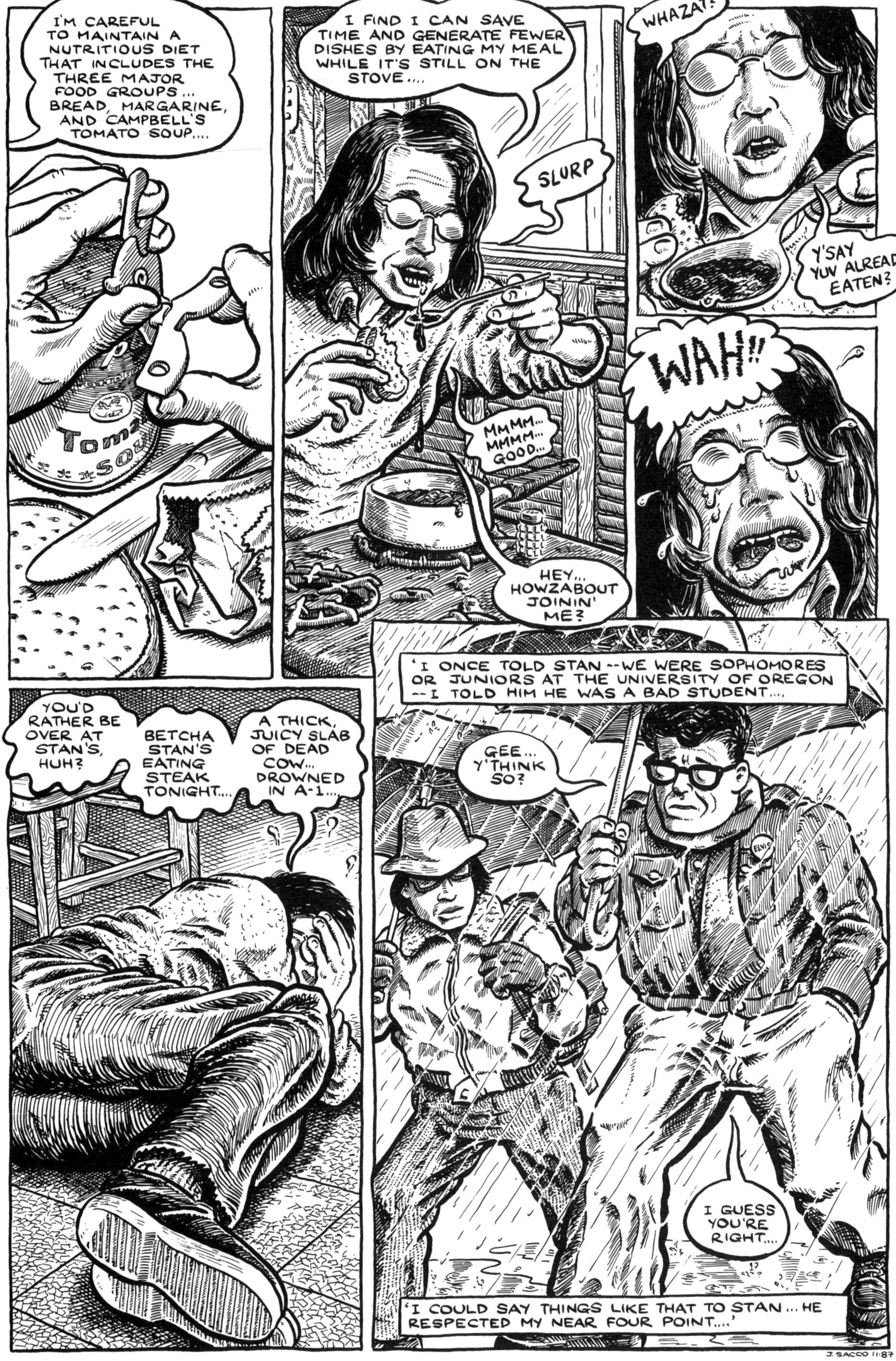
I'M CAREFUL TO MAINTAIN A NUTRITIOUS DIET THAT INCLUDES THE THREE MAJOR FOOD GROUPS... BREAD, MARGARINE, AND CAMPBELL'S TOMATO SOUP....
I FIND I CAN SAVE TIME AND GENERATE FEWER DISHES BY EATING MY MEAL WHILE IT'S STILL ON THE STOVE....
SLURP
MMMM... MMMM... GOOD...
HEY... HOWZABOUT JOININ' ME?
WHAZAT?
Y'SAY YUV ALREADY EATEN?
WAH!!
YOU'D RATHER BE OVER AT STAN'S, HUH?
BETCHA STAN'S EATING STEAK TONIGHT....
A THICK, JUICY SLAB OF DEAD COW... DROWNED IN A-1...
'I ONCE TOLD STAN --WE WERE SOPHOMORES OR JUNIORS AT THE UNIVERSITY OF OREGON --I TOLD HIM HE WAS A BAD STUDENT....
GEE... Y'THINK SO?
I GUESS YOU'RE RIGHT...
'I COULD SAY THINGS LIKE THAT TO STAN... HE RESPECTED MY NEAR FOUR POINT....'
J. SACCO 11·87

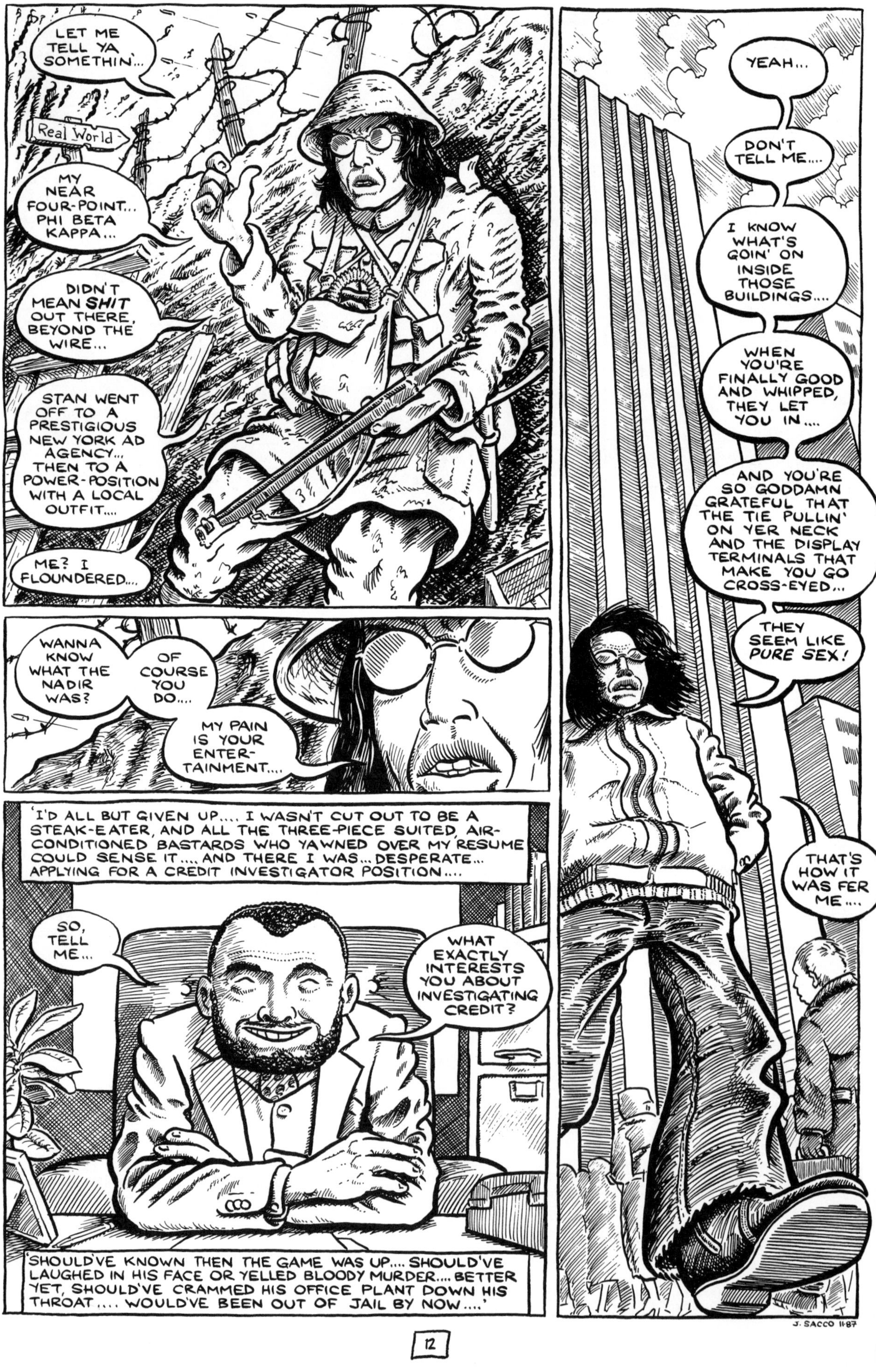

LET ME TELL YA SOMETHIN'...
Real World
MY NEAR FOUR-POINT... PHI BETA KAPPA...
DIDN'T MEAN SHIT OUT THERE, BEYOND THE WIRE...
STAN WENT OFF TO A PRESTIGIOUS NEW YORK AD AGENCY... THEN TO A POWER-POSITION WITH A LOCAL OUTFIT....
ME? I FLOUNDERED....
WANNA KNOW WHAT THE NADIR WAS?
OF COURSE YOU DO....
MY PAIN IS YOUR ENTERTAINMENT....
'I'D ALL BUT GIVEN UP.... I WASN'T CUT OUT TO BE A STEAK-EATER, AND ALL THE THREE-PIECE SUITED, AIR-CONDITIONED BASTARDS WHO YAWNED OVER MY RESUME COULD SENSE IT.... AND THERE I WAS... DESPERATE... APPLYING FOR A CREDIT INVESTIGATOR POSITION....
SO, TELL ME...
WHAT EXACTLY INTERESTS YOU ABOUT INVESTIGATING CREDIT?
'SHOULD'VE KNOWN THEN THE GAME WAS UP.... SHOULD'VE LAUGHED IN HIS FACE OR YELLED BLOODY MURDER.... BETTER YET, SHOULD'VE CRAMMED HIS OFFICE PLANT DOWN HIS THROAT.... WOULD'VE BEEN OUT OF JAIL BY NOW....'
YEAH...
DON'T TELL ME....
I KNOW WHAT'S GOIN' ON INSIDE THOSE BUILDINGS....
WHEN YOU'RE FINALLY GOOD AND WHIPPED, THEY LET YOU IN....
AND YOU'RE SO GODDAMN GRATEFUL THAT THE TIE PULLIN' ON YER NECK AND THE DISPLAY TERMINALS THAT MAKE YOU GO CROSS-EYED...
THEY SEEM LIKE PURE SEX!
THAT'S HOW IT WAS FER ME....
J. SACCO 11-87

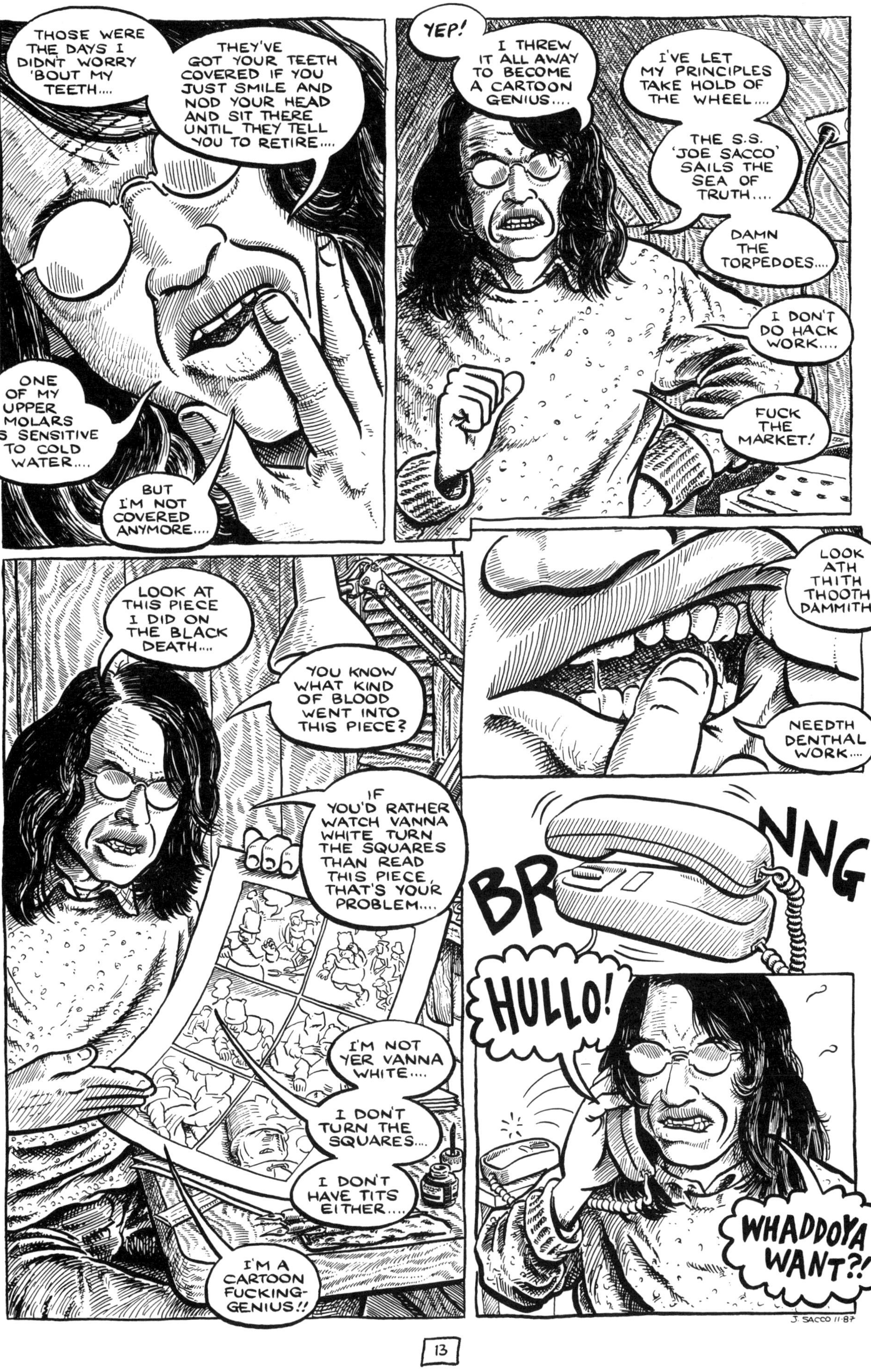

THOSE WERE THE DAYS I DIDN'T WORRY 'BOUT MY TEETH....
THEY'VE GOT YOUR TEETH COVERED IF YOU JUST SMILE AND NOD YOUR HEAD AND SIT THERE UNTIL THEY TELL YOU TO RETIRE....
ONE OF MY UPPER MOLARS IS SENSITIVE TO COLD WATER....
BUT I'M NOT COVERED ANYMORE....
YEP!
I THREW IT ALL AWAY TO BECOME A CARTOON GENIUS....
I'VE LET MY PRINCIPLES TAKE HOLD OF THE WHEEL....
THE S.S. 'JOE SACCO' SAILS THE SEA OF TRUTH....
DAMN THE TORPEDOES....
I DON'T DO HACK WORK....
FUCK THE MARKET!
LOOK AT THIS PIECE I DID ON THE BLACK DEATH....
YOU KNOW WHAT KIND OF BLOOD WENT INTO THIS PIECE?
IF YOU'D RATHER WATCH VANNA WHITE TURN THE SQUARES THAN READ THIS PIECE, THAT'S YOUR PROBLEM....
I'M NOT YER VANNA WHITE....
I DON'T TURN THE SQUARES....
I DON'T HAVE TITS EITHER....
I'M A CARTOON FUCKING-GENIUS!!
LOOK ATH THITH THOOTH, DAMMITH....
NEEDTH DENTHAL WORK....
BRRNNG
HULLO!
WHADDOYA WANT?!
J. SACCO 11·87

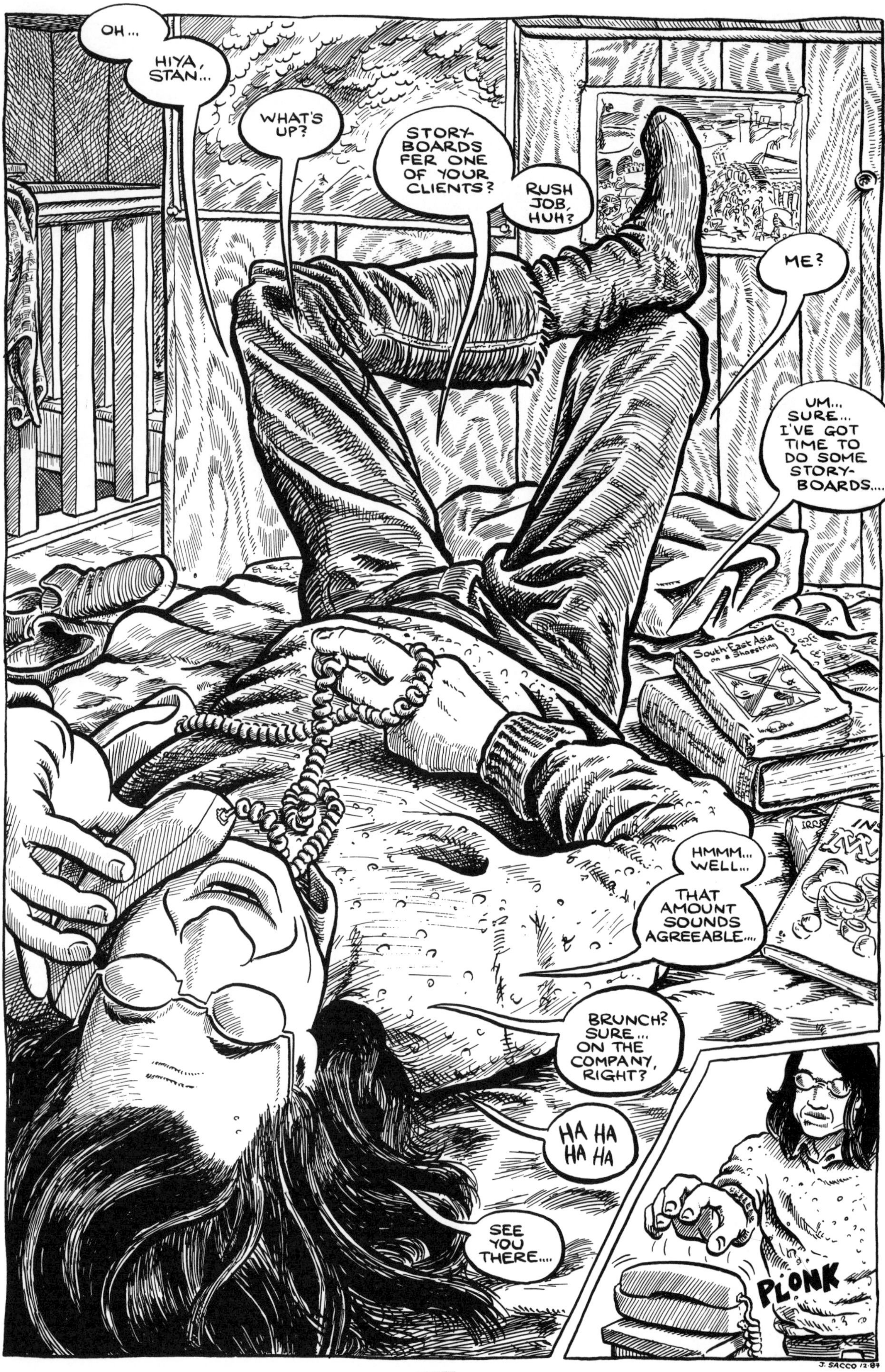
OH...
HIYA, STAN...
WHAT'S UP?
STORY-BOARDS FER ONE OF YOUR CLIENTS?
RUSH JOB, HUH?
ME?
UM... SURE... I'VE GOT TIME TO DO SOME STORY-BOARDS....
South-East Asia on a Shoestring
HMMM... WELL...
THAT AMOUNT SOUNDS AGREEABLE....
BRUNCH? SURE... ON THE COMPANY, RIGHT?
HA HA HA HA
SEE YOU THERE....
PLONK
J. SACCO 12·87

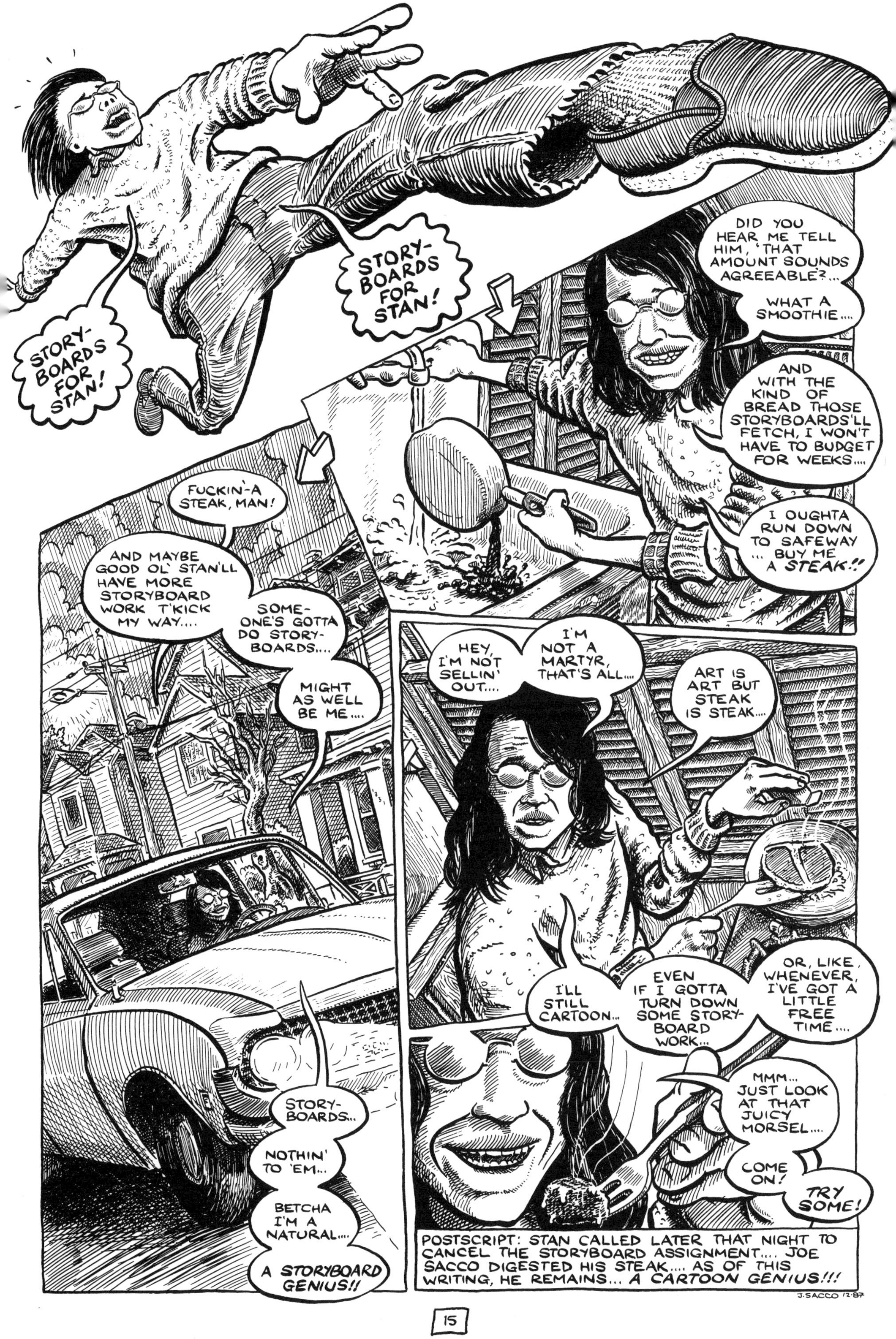
STORY-BOARDS FOR STAN!
STORY-BOARDS FOR STAN!
DID YOU HEAR ME TELL HIM, 'THAT AMOUNT SOUNDS AGREEABLE'?...
WHAT A SMOOTHIE....
AND WITH THE KIND OF BREAD THOSE STORYBOARDS'LL FETCH, I WON'T HAVE TO BUDGET FOR WEEKS....
I OUGHTA RUN DOWN TO SAFEWAY ... BUY ME A STEAK!!
FUCKIN'-A STEAK, MAN!
AND MAYBE GOOD OL' STAN'LL HAVE MORE STORYBOARD WORK T'KICK MY WAY....
SOME-ONE'S GOTTA DO STORY-BOARDS....
MIGHT AS WELL BE ME....
STORY-BOARDS...
NOTHIN' TO 'EM...
BETCHA I'M A NATURAL....
A STORYBOARD GENIUS!!
HEY, I'M NOT SELLIN' OUT....
I'M NOT A MARTYR, THAT'S ALL....
ART IS ART BUT STEAK IS STEAK....
I'LL STILL CARTOON...
EVEN IF I GOTTA TURN DOWN SOME STORY-BOARD WORK...
OR, LIKE, WHENEVER, I'VE GOT A LITTLE FREE TIME....
MMM... JUST LOOK AT THAT JUICY MORSEL....
COME ON!
TRY SOME!
POSTSCRIPT: STAN CALLED LATER THAT NIGHT TO CANCEL THE STORYBOARD ASSIGNMENT.... JOE SACCO DIGESTED HIS STEAK.... AS OF THIS WRITING, HE REMAINS... A CARTOON GENIUS!!!
J. SACCO 12·87

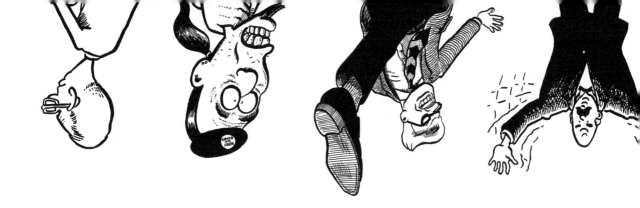

PART TWO:

EIGHT CHARACTERS

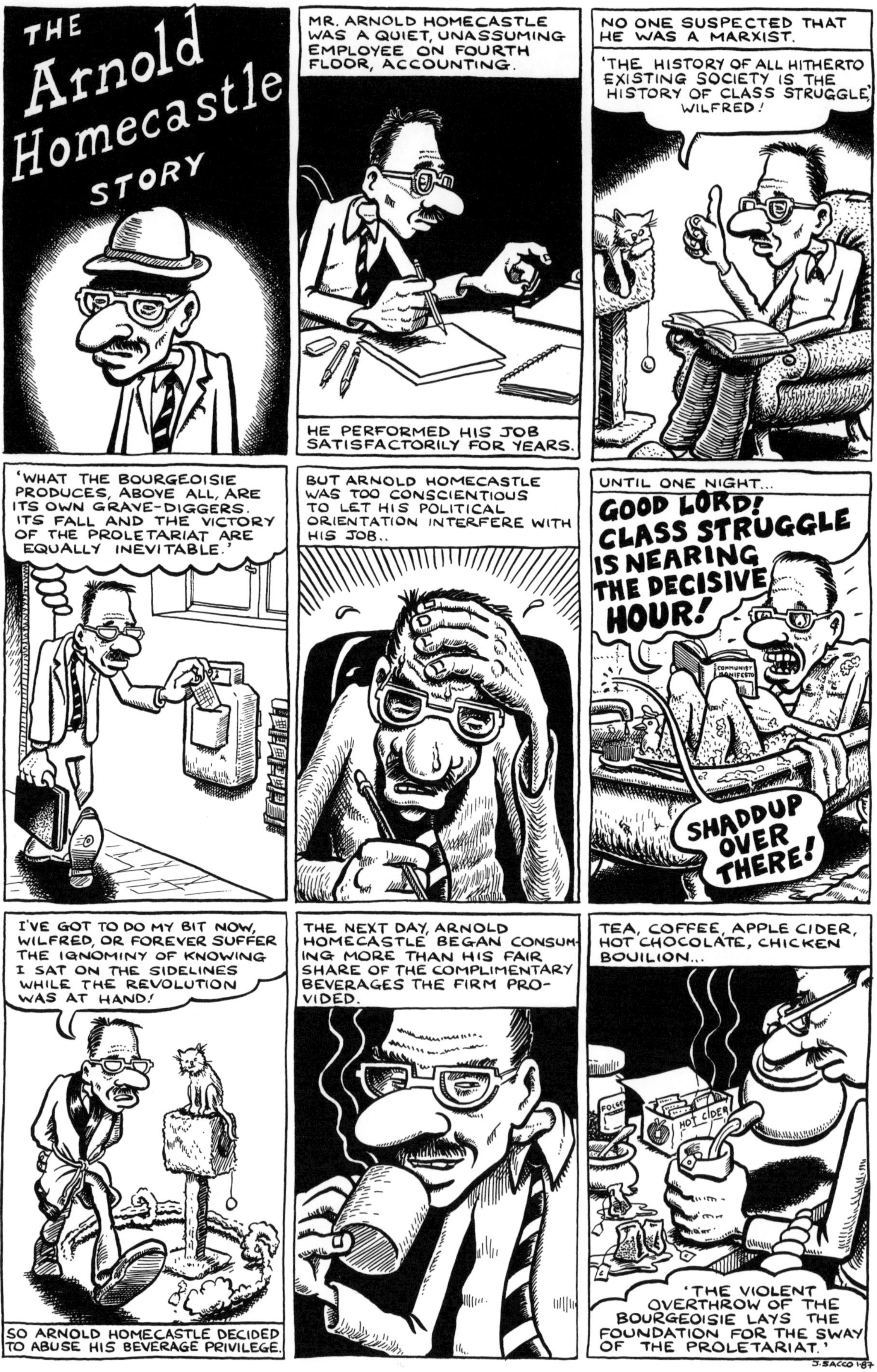
THE Arnold Homecastle STORY
MR. ARNOLD HOMECASTLE WAS A QUIET, UNASSUMING EMPLOYEE ON FOURTH FLOOR, ACCOUNTING.
HE PERFORMED HIS JOB SATISFACTORILY FOR YEARS.
NO ONE SUSPECTED THAT HE WAS A MARXIST.
'THE HISTORY OF ALL HITHERTO EXISTING SOCIETY IS THE HISTORY OF CLASS STRUGGLE,' WILFRED!
'WHAT THE BOURGEOISIE PRODUCES, ABOVE ALL, ARE ITS OWN GRAVE-DIGGERS. ITS FALL AND THE VICTORY OF THE PROLETARIAT ARE EQUALLY INEVITABLE.'
BUT ARNOLD HOMECASTLE WAS TOO CONSCIENTIOUS TO LET HIS POLITICAL ORIENTATION INTERFERE WITH HIS JOB..
UNTIL ONE NIGHT...
GOOD LORD! CLASS STRUGGLE IS NEARING THE DECISIVE HOUR!
COMMUNIST MANIFESTO
SHADDUP OVER THERE!
I'VE GOT TO DO MY BIT NOW, WILFRED, OR FOREVER SUFFER THE IGNOMINY OF KNOWING I SAT ON THE SIDELINES WHILE THE REVOLUTION WAS AT HAND!
SO ARNOLD HOMECASTLE DECIDED TO ABUSE HIS BEVERAGE PRIVILEGE.
THE NEXT DAY, ARNOLD HOMECASTLE BEGAN CONSUMING MORE THAN HIS FAIR SHARE OF THE COMPLIMENTARY BEVERAGES THE FIRM PROVIDED.
TEA, COFFEE, APPLE CIDER, HOT CHOCOLATE, CHICKEN BOUILION...
FOLGE
HOT CIDER
'THE VIOLENT OVERTHROW OF THE BOURGEOISIE LAYS THE FOUNDATION FOR THE SWAY OF THE PROLETARIAT.'
J. SACCO 1-87

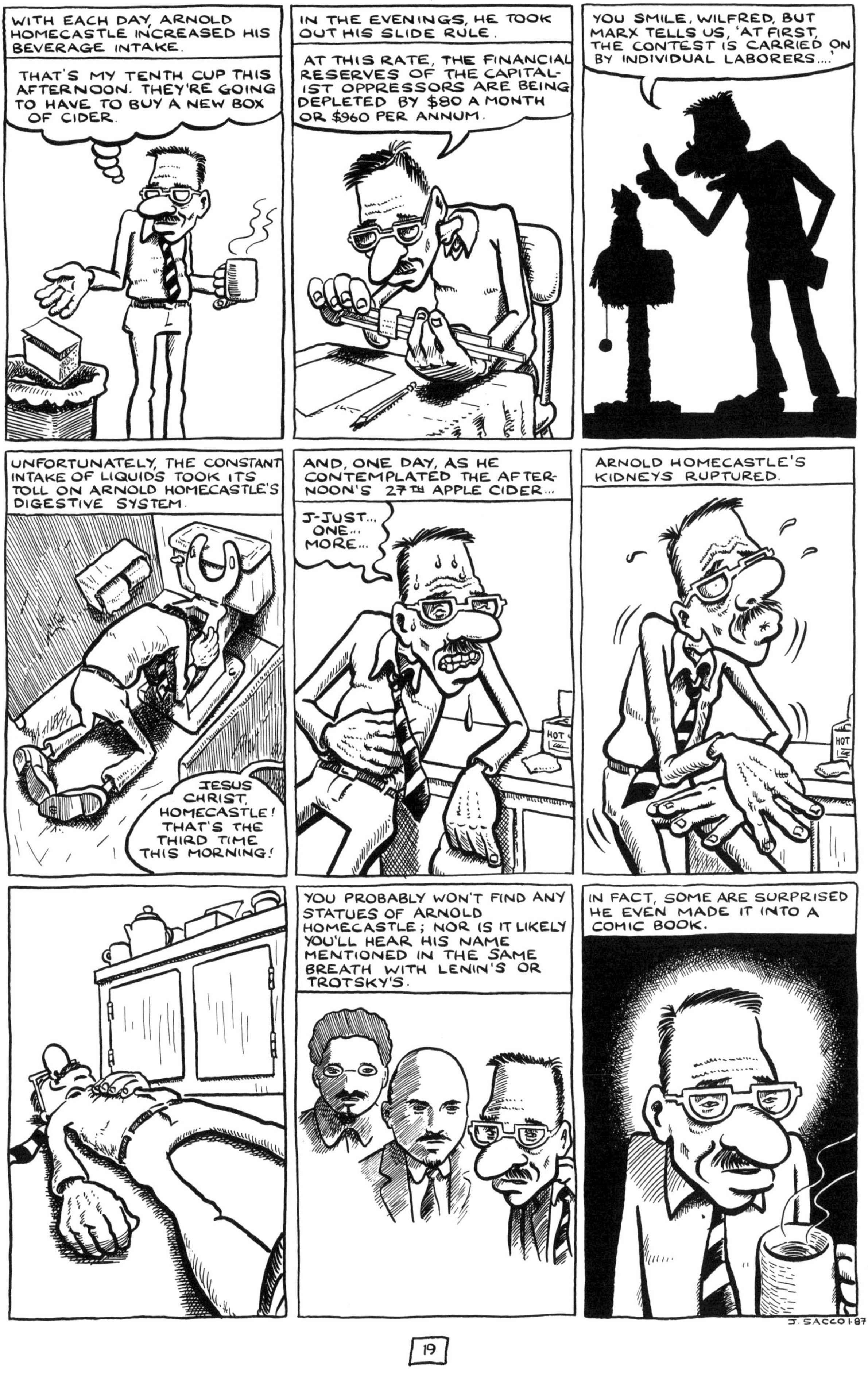
WITH EACH DAY, ARNOLD HOMECASTLE INCREASED HIS BEVERAGE INTAKE.
THAT'S MY TENTH CUP THIS AFTERNOON. THEY'RE GOING TO HAVE TO BUY A NEW BOX OF CIDER.
IN THE EVENINGS, HE TOOK OUT HIS SLIDE RULE.
AT THIS RATE, THE FINANCIAL RESERVES OF THE CAPITALIST OPPRESSORS ARE BEING DEPLETED BY $80 A MONTH OR $960 PER ANNUM.
YOU SMILE, WILFRED, BUT MARX TELLS US, 'AT FIRST, THE CONTEST IS CARRIED ON BY INDIVIDUAL LABORERS....'
UNFORTUNATELY, THE CONSTANT INTAKE OF LIQUIDS TOOK ITS TOLL ON ARNOLD HOMECASTLE'S DIGESTIVE SYSTEM.
JESUS CHRIST, HOMECASTLE! THAT'S THE THIRD TIME THIS MORNING!
AND, ONE DAY, AS HE CONTEMPLATED THE AFTERNOON'S 27TH APPLE CIDER...
J-JUST... ONE... MORE...
HOT
ARNOLD HOMECASTLE'S KIDNEYS RUPTURED.
HOT
YOU PROBABLY WON'T FIND ANY STATUES OF ARNOLD HOMECASTLE; NOR IS IT LIKELY YOU'LL HEAR HIS NAME MENTIONED IN THE SAME BREATH WITH LENIN'S OR TROTSKY'S.
IN FACT, SOME ARE SURPRISED HE EVEN MADE IT INTO A COMIC BOOK.
J. SACCO 1-87

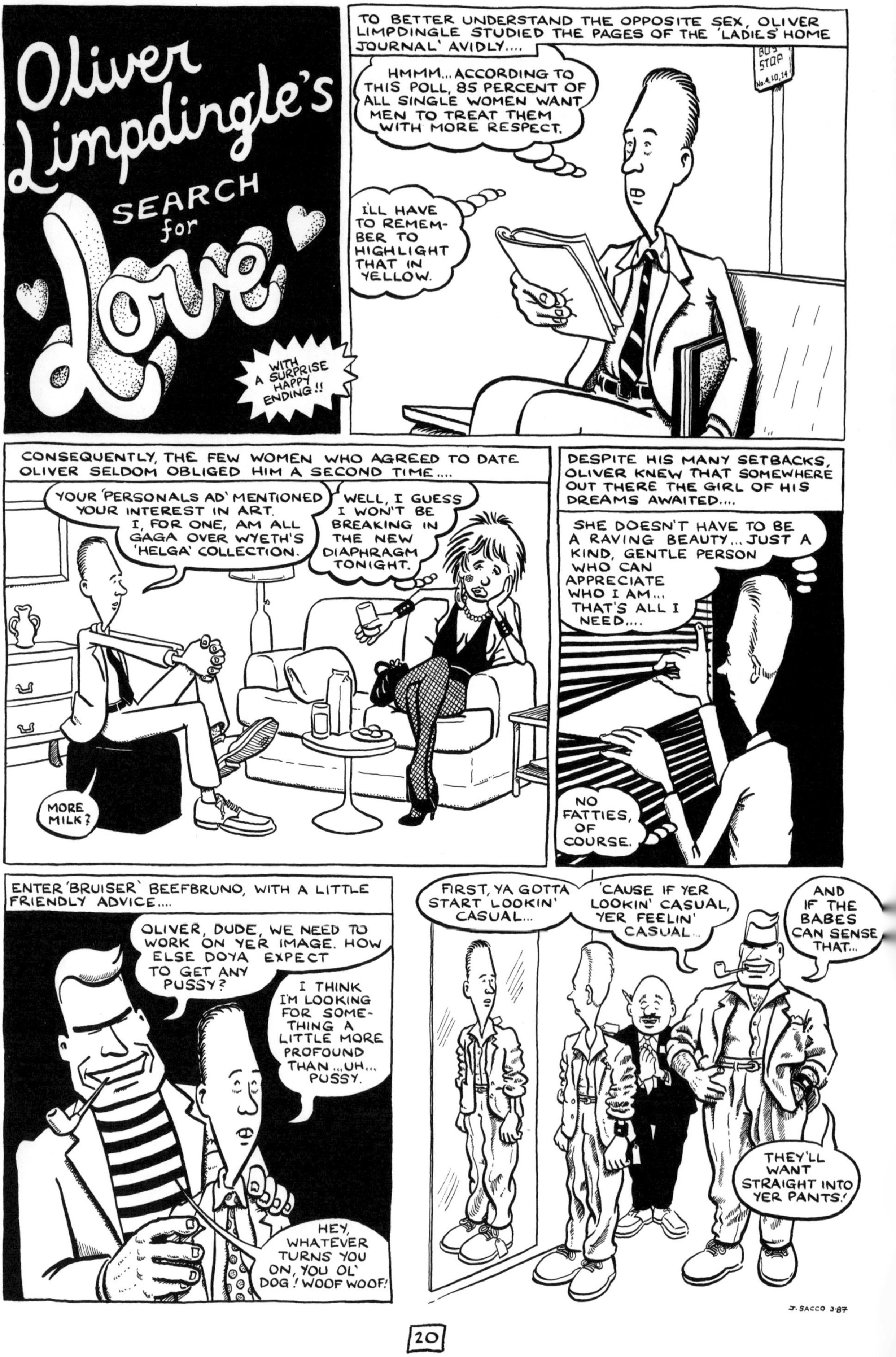
Oliver Limpdingle's SEARCH for Love
WITH A SURPRISE HAPPY ENDING!!
TO BETTER UNDERSTAND THE OPPOSITE SEX, OLIVER LIMPDINGLE STUDIED THE PAGES OF THE 'LADIES' HOME JOURNAL' AVIDLY....
BUS STOP No. 4, 10, 14
HMMM... ACCORDING TO THIS POLL, 85 PERCENT OF ALL SINGLE WOMEN WANT MEN TO TREAT THEM WITH MORE RESPECT.
I'LL HAVE TO REMEMBER TO HIGHLIGHT THAT IN YELLOW.
CONSEQUENTLY, THE FEW WOMEN WHO AGREED TO DATE OLIVER SELDOM OBLIGED HIM A SECOND TIME....
YOUR 'PERSONALS AD' MENTIONED YOUR INTEREST IN ART. I, FOR ONE, AM ALL GAGA OVER WYETH'S 'HELGA' COLLECTION.
WELL, I GUESS I WON'T BE BREAKING IN THE NEW DIAPHRAGM TONIGHT.
MORE MILK?
DESPITE HIS MANY SETBACKS, OLIVER KNEW THAT SOMEWHERE OUT THERE THE GIRL OF HIS DREAMS AWAITED....
SHE DOESN'T HAVE TO BE A RAVING BEAUTY... JUST A KIND, GENTLE PERSON WHO CAN APPRECIATE WHO I AM... THAT'S ALL I NEED....
NO FATTIES, OF COURSE.
ENTER 'BRUISER' BEEFBRUNO, WITH A LITTLE FRIENDLY ADVICE....
OLIVER, DUDE, WE NEED TO WORK ON YER IMAGE. HOW ELSE DOYA EXPECT TO GET ANY PUSSY?
I THINK I'M LOOKING FOR SOMETHING A LITTLE MORE PROFOUND THAN ...UH... PUSSY.
HEY, WHATEVER TURNS YOU ON, YOU OL' DOG! WOOF WOOF!
FIRST, YA GOTTA START LOOKIN' CASUAL...
'CAUSE IF YER LOOKIN' CASUAL, YER FEELIN' CASUAL...
AND IF THE BABES CAN SENSE THAT...
THEY'LL WANT STRAIGHT INTO YER PANTS!
J. SACCO 3·87

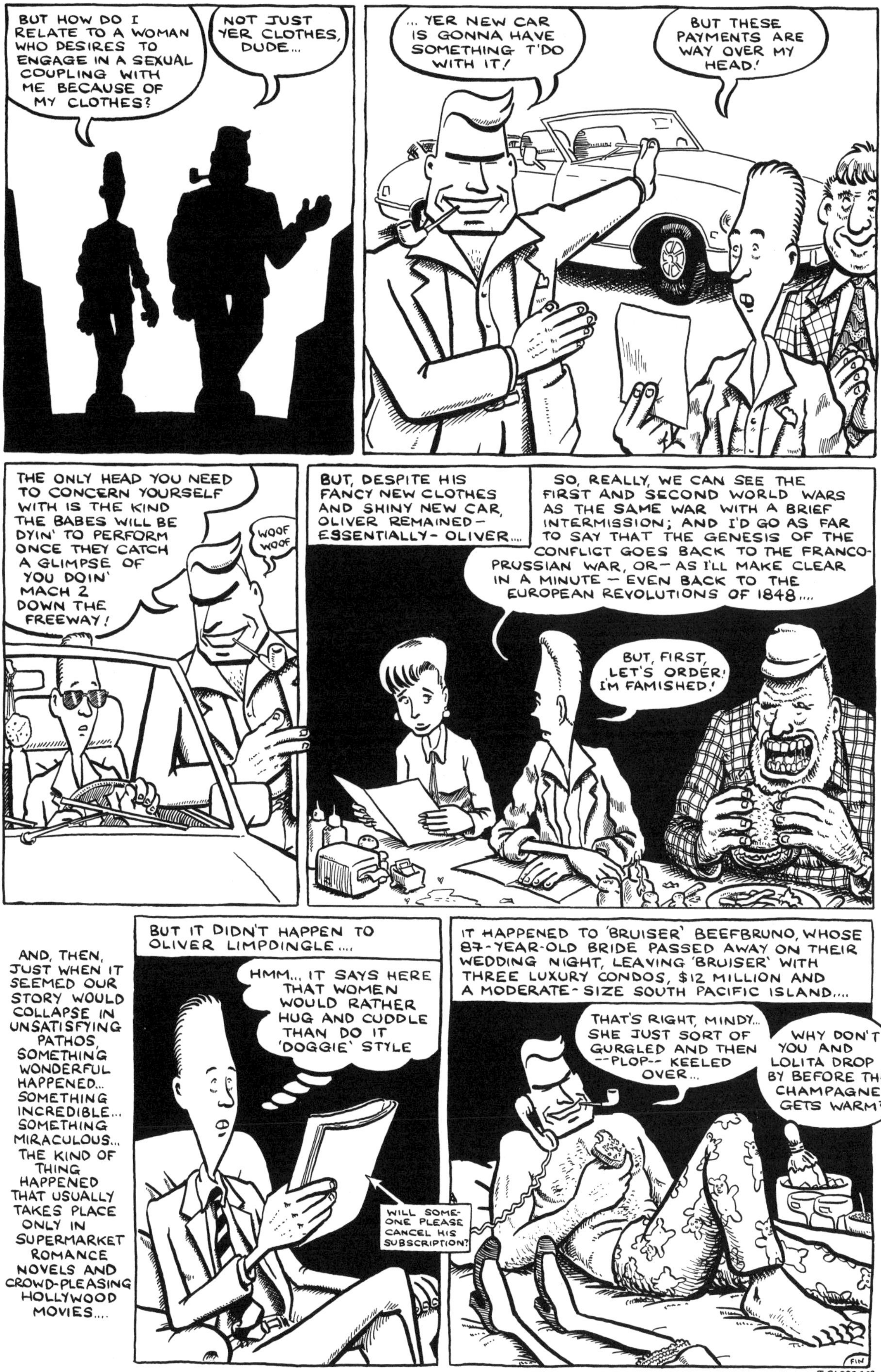
BUT HOW DO I RELATE TO A WOMAN WHO DESIRES TO ENGAGE IN A SEXUAL COUPLING WITH ME BECAUSE OF MY CLOTHES?
NOT JUST YER CLOTHES, DUDE...
...YER NEW CAR IS GONNA HAVE SOMETHING T'DO WITH IT!
BUT THESE PAYMENTS ARE WAY OVER MY HEAD!
THE ONLY HEAD YOU NEED TO CONCERN YOURSELF WITH IS THE KIND THE BABES WILL BE DYIN' TO PERFORM ONCE THEY CATCH A GLIMPSE OF YOU DOIN' MACH 2 DOWN THE FREEWAY!
WOOF WOOF
BUT, DESPITE HIS FANCY NEW CLOTHES AND SHINY NEW CAR, OLIVER REMAINED—ESSENTIALLY—OLIVER....
SO, REALLY, WE CAN SEE THE FIRST AND SECOND WORLD WARS AS THE SAME WAR WITH A BRIEF INTERMISSION; AND I'D GO AS FAR TO SAY THAT THE GENESIS OF THE CONFLICT GOES BACK TO THE FRANCO-PRUSSIAN WAR, OR—AS I'LL MAKE CLEAR IN A MINUTE—EVEN BACK TO THE EUROPEAN REVOLUTIONS OF 1848....
BUT, FIRST, LET'S ORDER! I'M FAMISHED!
AND, THEN, JUST WHEN IT SEEMED OUR STORY WOULD COLLAPSE IN UNSATISFYING PATHOS, SOMETHING WONDERFUL HAPPENED... SOMETHING INCREDIBLE... SOMETHING MIRACULOUS... THE KIND OF THING HAPPENED THAT USUALLY TAKES PLACE ONLY IN SUPERMARKET ROMANCE NOVELS AND CROWD-PLEASING HOLLYWOOD MOVIES....
BUT IT DIDN'T HAPPEN TO OLIVER LIMPDINGLE....
HMM... IT SAYS HERE THAT WOMEN WOULD RATHER HUG AND CUDDLE THAN DO IT 'DOGGIE' STYLE
WILL SOMEONE PLEASE CANCEL HIS SUBSCRIPTION?
IT HAPPENED TO 'BRUISER' BEEFBRUNO, WHOSE 87-YEAR-OLD BRIDE PASSED AWAY ON THEIR WEDDING NIGHT, LEAVING 'BRUISER' WITH THREE LUXURY CONDOS, $12 MILLION AND A MODERATE-SIZE SOUTH PACIFIC ISLAND....
THAT'S RIGHT, MINDY... SHE JUST SORT OF GURGLED AND THEN --PLOP-- KEELED OVER...
WHY DON'T YOU AND LOLITA DROP BY BEFORE THE CHAMPAGNE GETS WARM?
FIN
J. SACCO 3-87

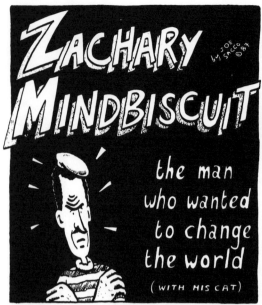

ZACHARY MINDBISCUIT

by JOE SACCO ©87

the man
who wanted
to change
the world

(WITH HIS CAT)

ZACHARY MINDBISCUIT READ THE PAPERS EVERY MORNING, AND EVERY MORNING ZACHARY MINDBISCUIT'S OUTRAGE DEEPENED....

MOPPY! DID YOU READ THIS? A NUCLEAR POWER PLANT ON THE EDGE OF THE CITY!

IT'S MADNESS! MADNESS!

SOMETIMES ZACHARY MINDBISCUIT WOULD BURST INTO TEARS JUST THINKING ABOUT THE POTENTIAL FOR CATASTROPHE....

THERE'S NO SUCH THING AS SAFE NUCLEAR POWER! THE FOOLS ARE DECEIVING THEMSELVES! THEY'RE DECEIVING THE PEOPLE ...AND THE CHILDREN! WHAT ABOUT THE CHILDREN?

THEN, ONE DAY....

MOPPY, WE CAN'T LET THIS INSANITY PROCEED! YOU AND I ARE GOING TO DO SOMETHING! WE'RE GOING TO SHAKE PEOPLE UNTIL THEY AWAKEN FROM THE DEADLY SLUMBER OF APATHY!

AND SO ZACHARY MINDBISCUIT ISSUED A PUBLIC STATEMENT....

FOR EVERY DAY CONSTRUCTION CONTINUES ON THE NUCLEAR PLANT, I SHALL WITHHOLD FOOD FROM MOPPY, MY PET CAT!

AND THUS BEGAN THE HUNGER STRIKE THAT SHAMED A CITY....

LOOK, MOPPY! WE'RE ON T.V.!

...MR. MINDBISCUIT SAID HIS CAT MOPPY WON'T BE FED – NOT EVEN A SINGLE 'TENDER VITTLE' – UNTIL THE CITY COUNCIL HALTS WORK ON THE NUCLEAR FACILITY...

J. SACCO 4-87

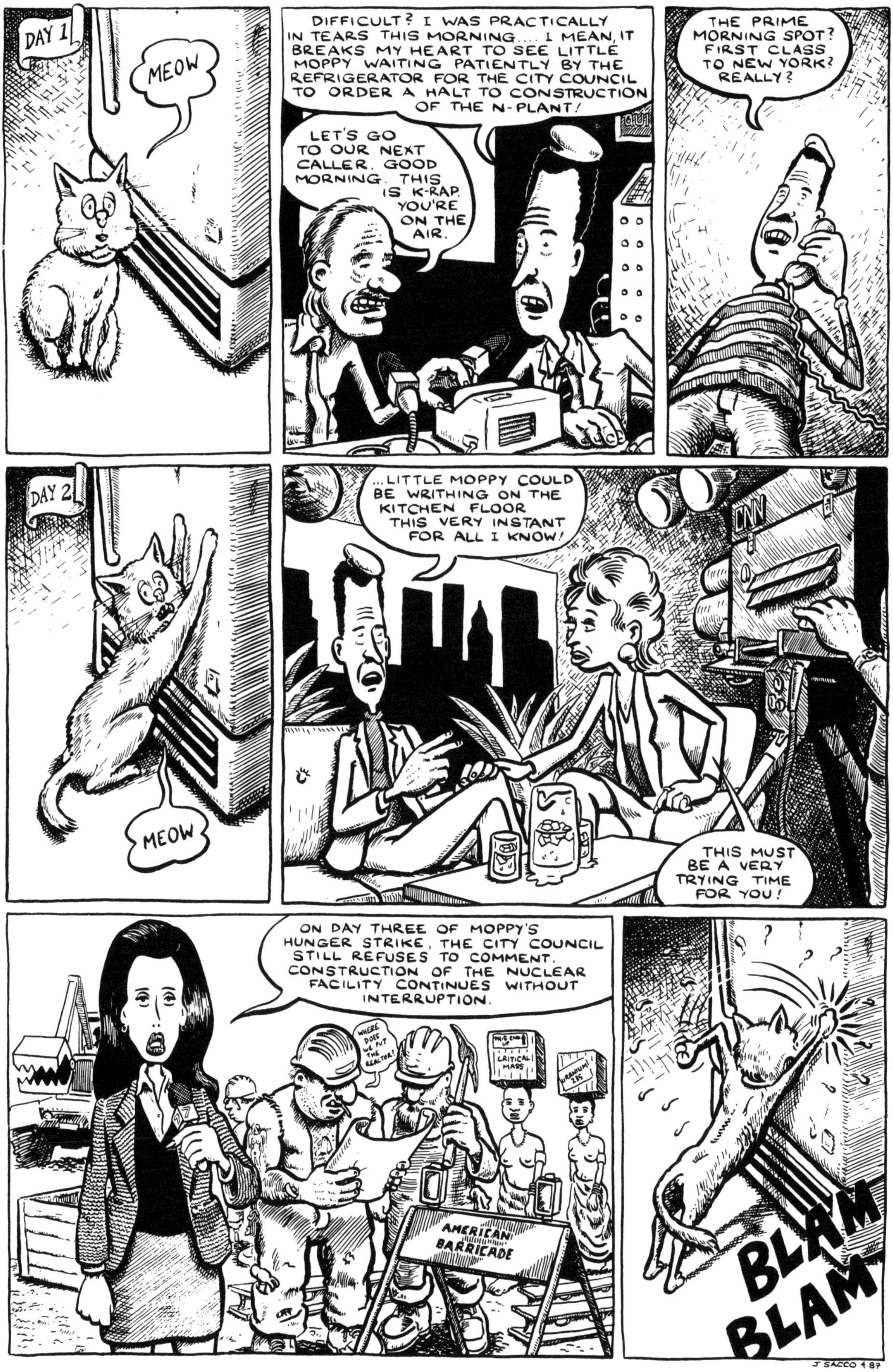
DAY 1
MEOW
DIFFICULT? I WAS PRACTICALLY IN TEARS THIS MORNING.... I MEAN, IT BREAKS MY HEART TO SEE LITTLE MOPPY WAITING PATIENTLY BY THE REFRIGERATOR FOR THE CITY COUNCIL TO ORDER A HALT TO CONSTRUCTION OF THE N-PLANT!
LET'S GO TO OUR NEXT CALLER. GOOD MORNING. THIS IS K-RAP. YOU'RE ON THE AIR.
THE PRIME MORNING SPOT? FIRST CLASS TO NEW YORK? REALLY?
DAY 2
MEOW
...LITTLE MOPPY COULD BE WRITHING ON THE KITCHEN FLOOR THIS VERY INSTANT FOR ALL I KNOW!
CNN
THIS MUST BE A VERY TRYING TIME FOR YOU!
ON DAY THREE OF MOPPY'S HUNGER STRIKE, THE CITY COUNCIL STILL REFUSES TO COMMENT. CONSTRUCTION OF THE NUCLEAR FACILITY CONTINUES WITHOUT INTERRUPTION.
WHERE DOES WE PUT THE REALTOR?
THIS END UP
CRITICAL MASS
URANIUM 235
AMERICAN BARRICADE
BLAM
BLAM

J SACCO 4·87

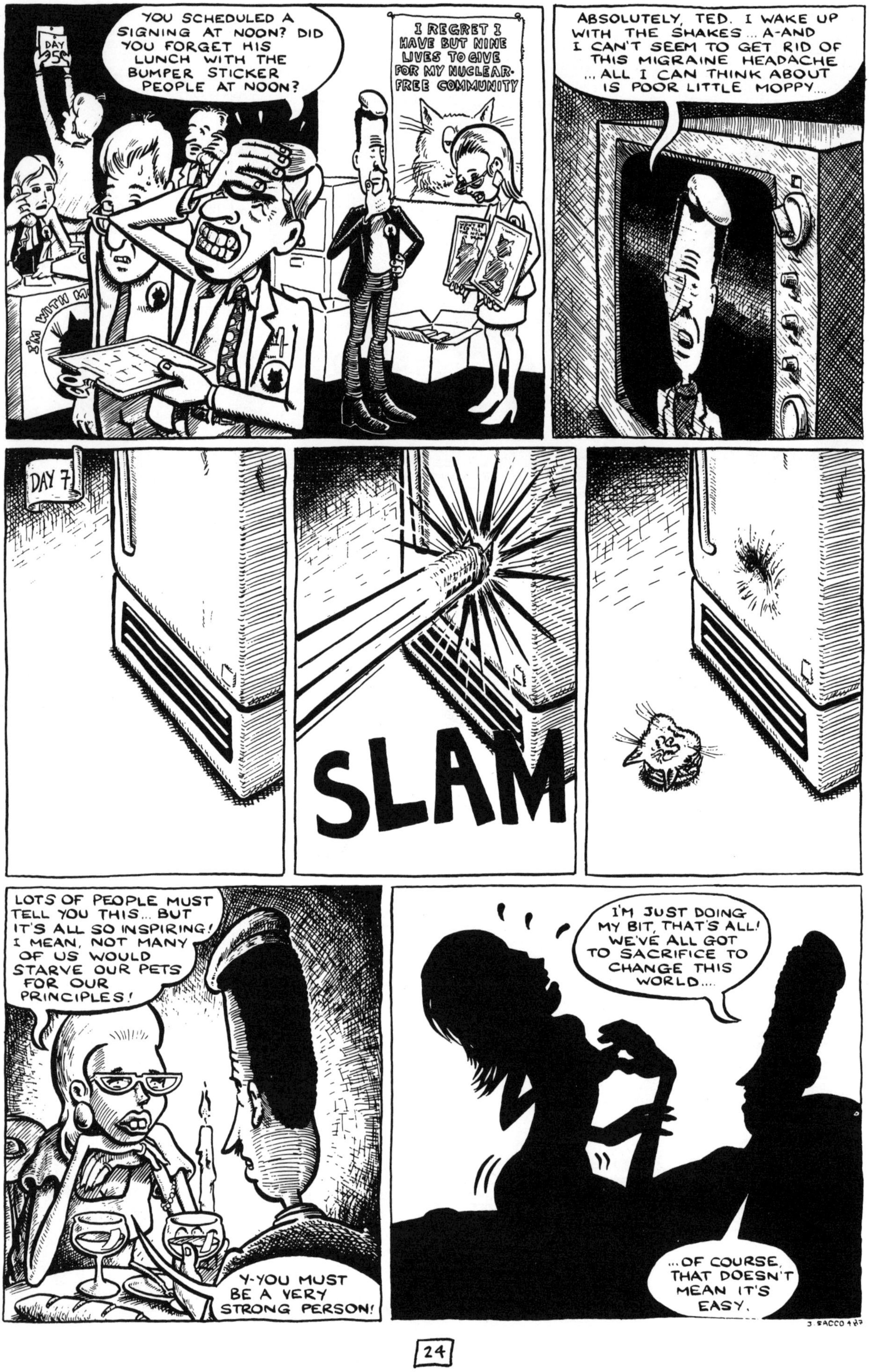
DAY 5
YOU SCHEDULED A SIGNING AT NOON? DID YOU FORGET HIS LUNCH WITH THE BUMPER STICKER PEOPLE AT NOON?
I'M WITH M
I REGRET I HAVE BUT NINE LIVES TO GIVE FOR MY NUCLEAR-FREE COMMUNITY
ABSOLUTELY, TED. I WAKE UP WITH THE SHAKES... A-AND I CAN'T SEEM TO GET RID OF THIS MIGRAINE HEADACHE ... ALL I CAN THINK ABOUT IS POOR LITTLE MOPPY....
DAY 7
SLAM
LOTS OF PEOPLE MUST TELL YOU THIS... BUT IT'S ALL SO INSPIRING! I MEAN, NOT MANY OF US WOULD STARVE OUR PETS FOR OUR PRINCIPLES!
Y-YOU MUST BE A VERY STRONG PERSON!
I'M JUST DOING MY BIT, THAT'S ALL! WE'VE ALL GOT TO SACRIFICE TO CHANGE THIS WORLD....
...OF COURSE, THAT DOESN'T MEAN IT'S EASY.
J. SACCO 4.87

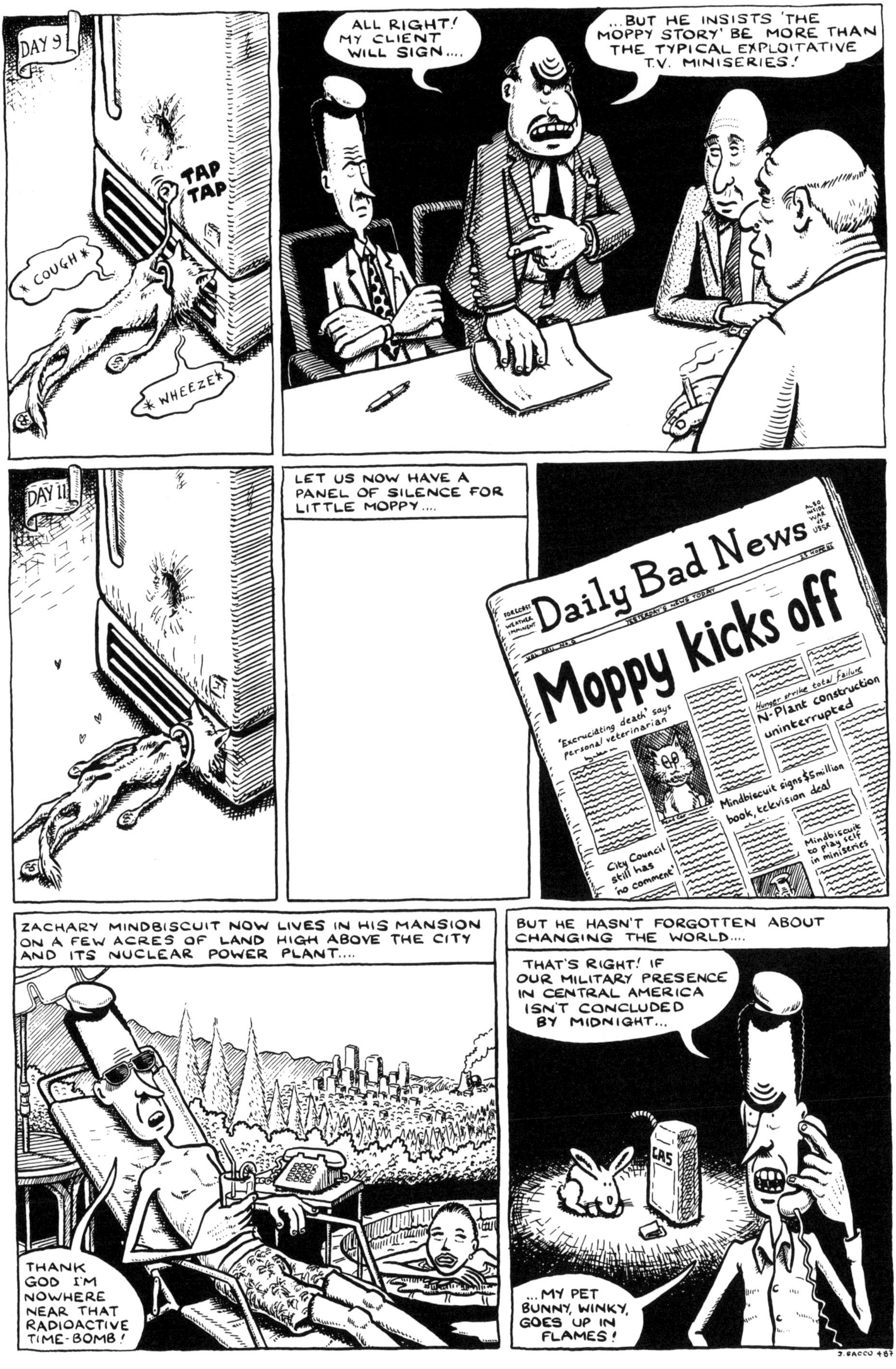
DAY 9
TAP TAP
COUGH
WHEEZE
ALL RIGHT! MY CLIENT WILL SIGN....
...BUT HE INSISTS 'THE MOPPY STORY' BE MORE THAN THE TYPICAL EXPLOITATIVE T.V. MINISERIES!
DAY 11
LET US NOW HAVE A PANEL OF SILENCE FOR LITTLE MOPPY....
Daily Bad News
FORECAST WEATHER IMMINENT
YESTERDAY'S NEWS TODAY
ALSO INSIDE WAR VS USSR
25 KOPECKS
Moppy kicks off
'Excruciating death' says personal veterinarian
Hunger strike total failure
N-Plant construction uninterrupted
Mindbiscuit signs $5 million book, television deal
City Council still has 'no comment'
Mindbiscuit to play self in miniseries
ZACHARY MINDBISCUIT NOW LIVES IN HIS MANSION ON A FEW ACRES OF LAND HIGH ABOVE THE CITY AND ITS NUCLEAR POWER PLANT....
THANK GOD I'M NOWHERE NEAR THAT RADIOACTIVE TIME-BOMB!
BUT HE HASN'T FORGOTTEN ABOUT CHANGING THE WORLD....
THAT'S RIGHT! IF OUR MILITARY PRESENCE IN CENTRAL AMERICA ISN'T CONCLUDED BY MIDNIGHT...
GAS
...MY PET BUNNY, WINKY, GOES UP IN FLAMES!
J. SACCO 4 87

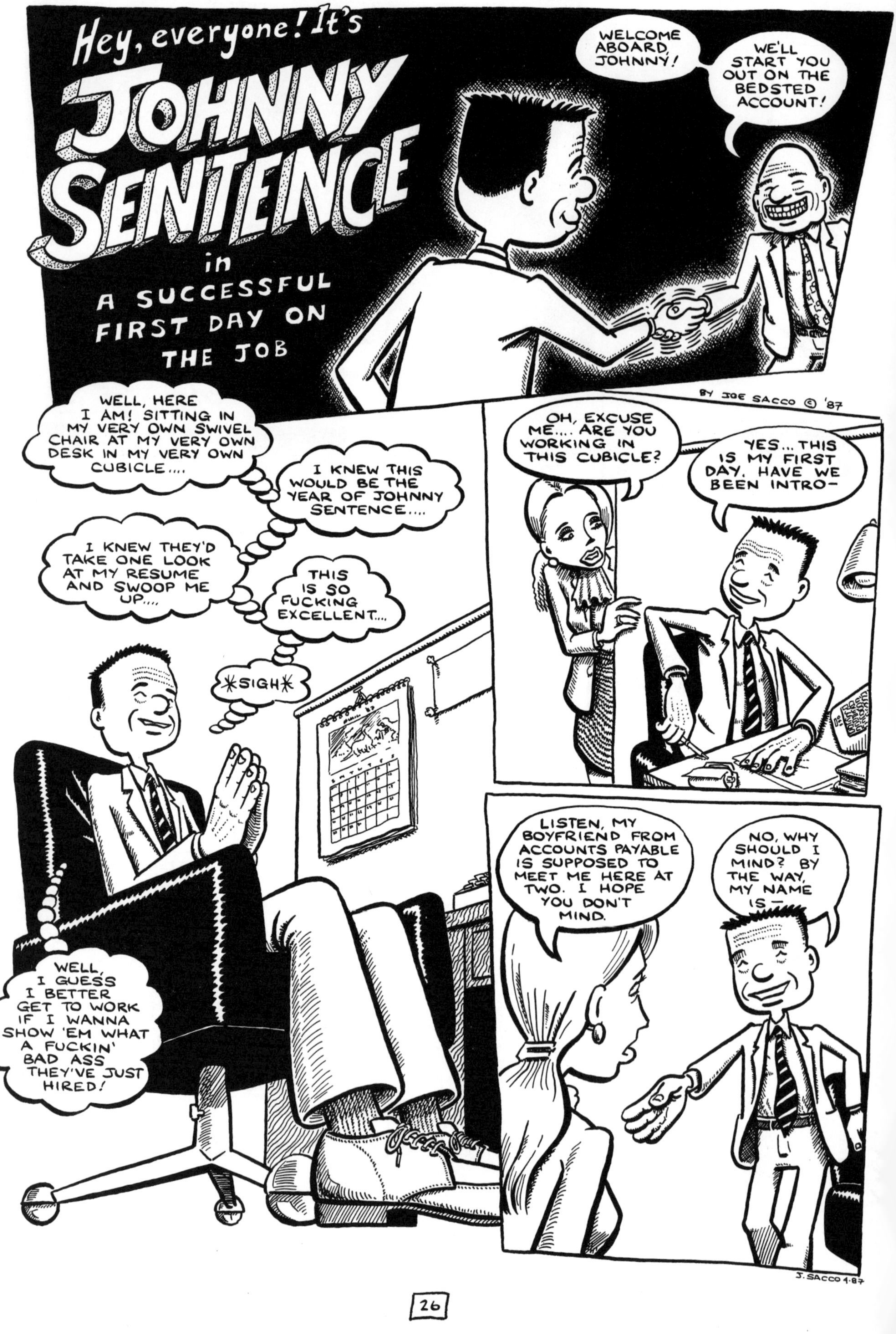
Hey, everyone! It's
JOHNNY SENTENCE
in
A SUCCESSFUL FIRST DAY ON THE JOB
WELCOME ABOARD, JOHNNY!
WE'LL START YOU OUT ON THE BEDSTED ACCOUNT!
BY JOE SACCO © '87
WELL, HERE I AM! SITTING IN MY VERY OWN SWIVEL CHAIR AT MY VERY OWN DESK IN MY VERY OWN CUBICLE....
I KNEW THIS WOULD BE THE YEAR OF JOHNNY SENTENCE....
I KNEW THEY'D TAKE ONE LOOK AT MY RESUME AND SWOOP ME UP....
THIS IS SO FUCKING EXCELLENT....
SIGH
WELL, I GUESS I BETTER GET TO WORK IF I WANNA SHOW 'EM WHAT A FUCKIN' BAD ASS THEY'VE JUST HIRED!
OH, EXCUSE ME.... ARE YOU WORKING IN THIS CUBICLE?
YES... THIS IS MY FIRST DAY. HAVE WE BEEN INTRO-
LISTEN, MY BOYFRIEND FROM ACCOUNTS PAYABLE IS SUPPOSED TO MEET ME HERE AT TWO. I HOPE YOU DON'T MIND.
NO, WHY SHOULD I MIND? BY THE WAY, MY NAME IS—
J. SACCO 4·87

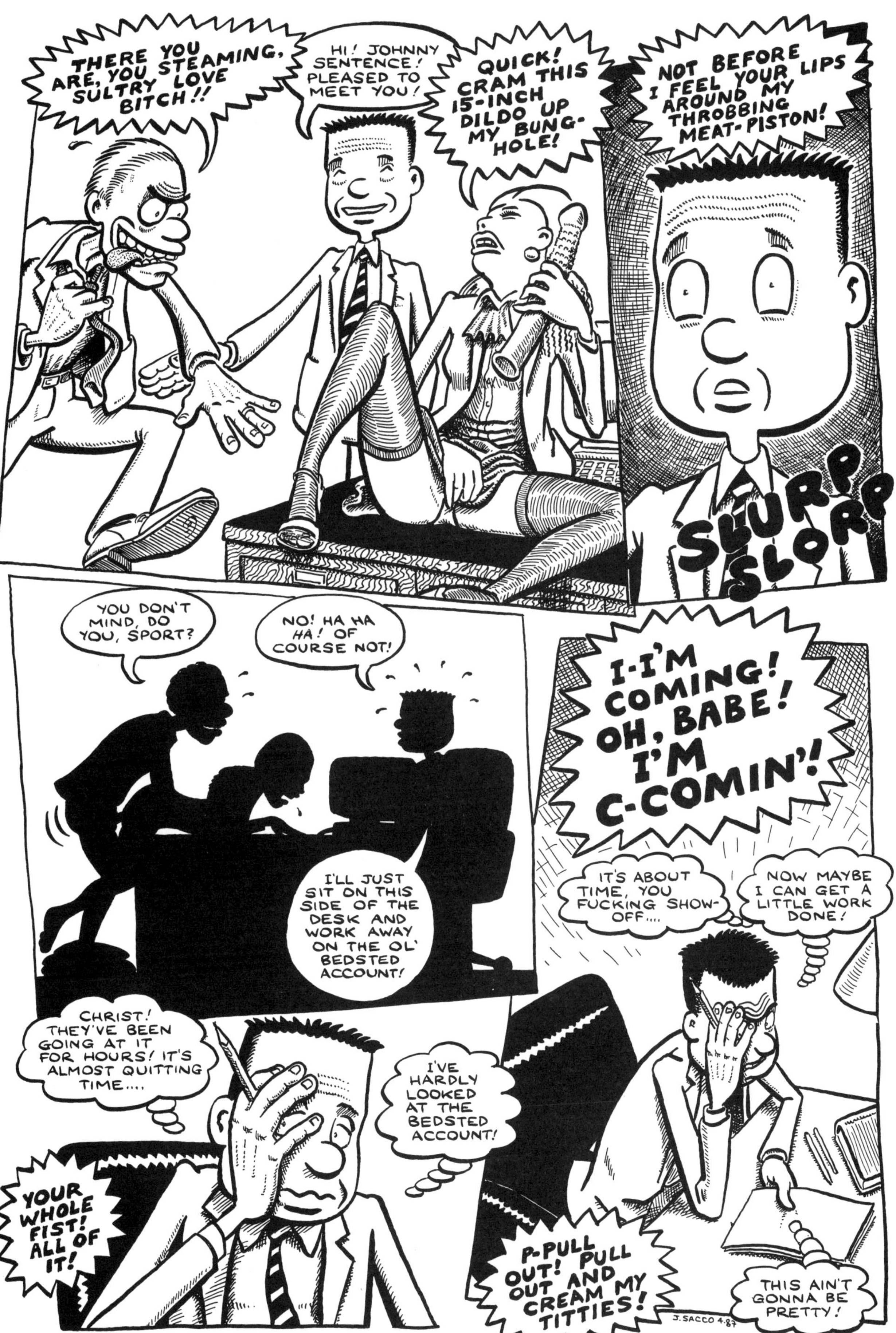
THERE YOU ARE, YOU STEAMING, SULTRY LOVE BITCH!!
HI! JOHNNY SENTENCE! PLEASED TO MEET YOU!
QUICK! CRAM THIS 15-INCH DILDO UP MY BUNG-HOLE!
NOT BEFORE I FEEL YOUR LIPS AROUND MY THROBBING MEAT-PISTON!
SLURPP SLORPP
YOU DON'T MIND, DO YOU, SPORT?
NO! HA HA HA! OF COURSE NOT!
I'LL JUST SIT ON THIS SIDE OF THE DESK AND WORK AWAY ON THE OL' BEDSTED ACCOUNT!
I-I'M COMING! OH, BABE! I'M C-COMIN'!
IT'S ABOUT TIME, YOU FUCKING SHOW-OFF....
NOW MAYBE I CAN GET A LITTLE WORK DONE!
CHRIST! THEY'VE BEEN GOING AT IT FOR HOURS! IT'S ALMOST QUITTING TIME....
I'VE HARDLY LOOKED AT THE BEDSTED ACCOUNT!
YOUR WHOLE FIST! ALL OF IT!
P-PULL OUT! PULL OUT AND CREAM MY TITTIES!
THIS AIN'T GONNA BE PRETTY!
J. SACCO 4.87

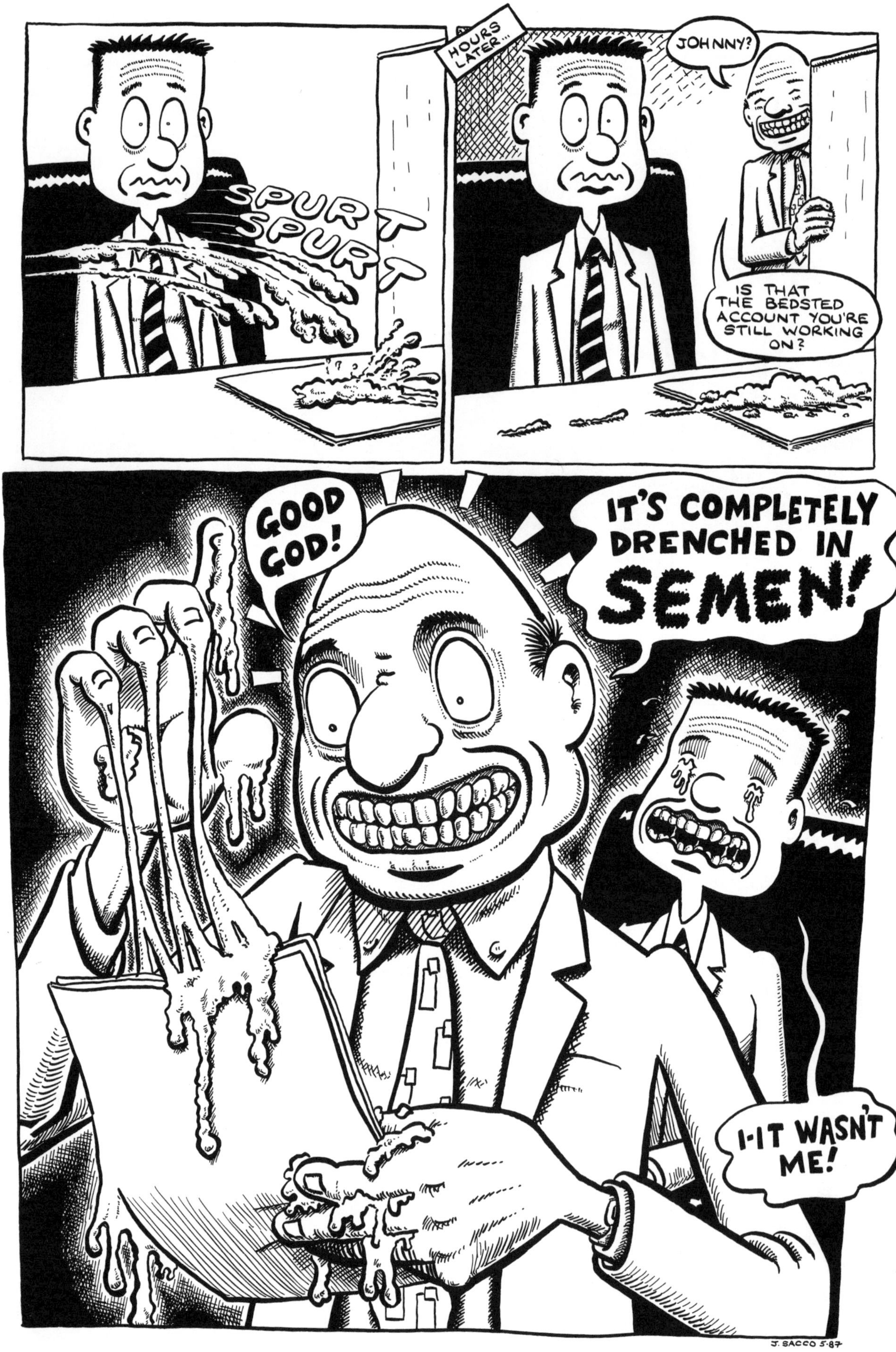
SPURT SPURT
HOURS LATER...
JOHNNY?
IS THAT THE BEDSTED ACCOUNT YOU'RE STILL WORKING ON?
GOOD GOD!
IT'S COMPLETELY DRENCHED IN SEMEN!
I-IT WASN'T ME!
J. SACCO 5-87

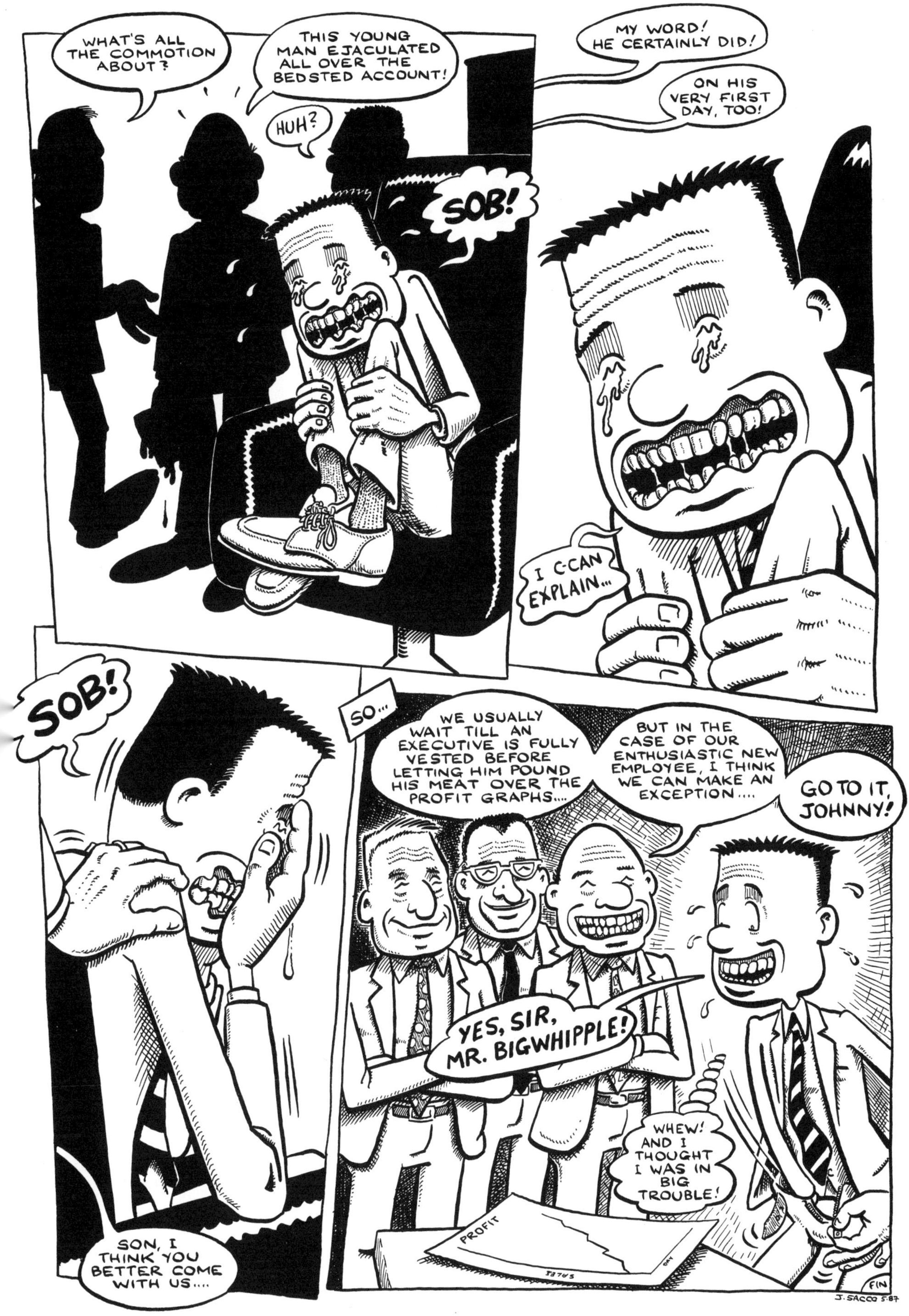
WHAT'S ALL THE COMMOTION ABOUT?
THIS YOUNG MAN EJACULATED ALL OVER THE BEDSTED ACCOUNT!
HUH?
MY WORD! HE CERTAINLY DID!
ON HIS VERY FIRST DAY, TOO!
SOB!
I C-CAN EXPLAIN...
SOB!
SON, I THINK YOU BETTER COME WITH US....
SO...
WE USUALLY WAIT TILL AN EXECUTIVE IS FULLY VESTED BEFORE LETTING HIM POUND HIS MEAT OVER THE PROFIT GRAPHS....
BUT IN THE CASE OF OUR ENTHUSIASTIC NEW EMPLOYEE, I THINK WE CAN MAKE AN EXCEPTION....
GO TO IT, JOHNNY!
YES, SIR, MR. BIGWHIPPLE!
WHEW! AND I THOUGHT I WAS IN BIG TROUBLE!
PROFIT
SALES
FIN
J. SACCO 5.87

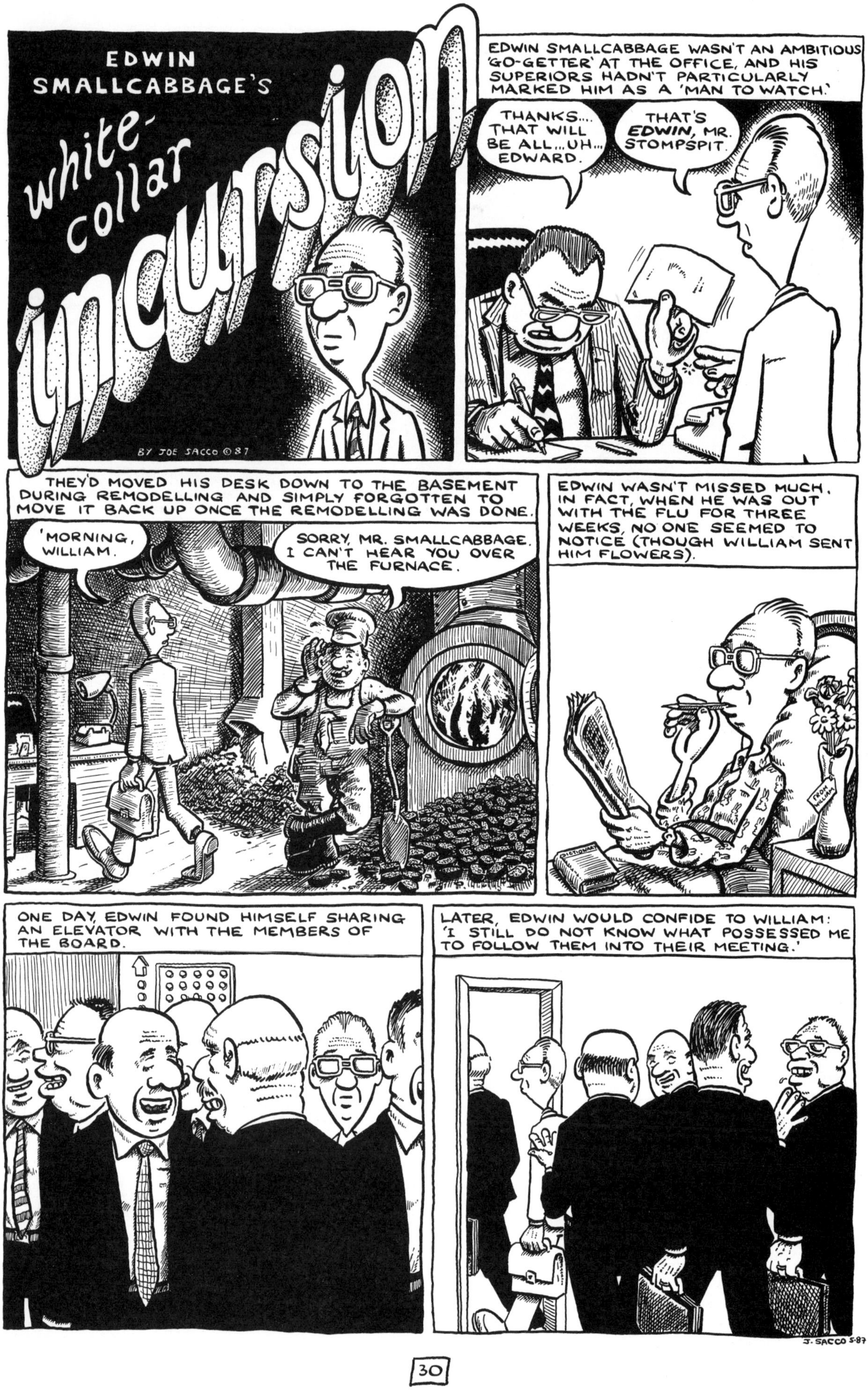
EDWIN SMALLCABBAGE'S
white-collar incursion
BY JOE SACCO ©87
EDWIN SMALLCABBAGE WASN'T AN AMBITIOUS 'GO-GETTER' AT THE OFFICE, AND HIS SUPERIORS HADN'T PARTICULARLY MARKED HIM AS A 'MAN TO WATCH.'
THANKS... THAT WILL BE ALL... UH... EDWARD.
THAT'S EDWIN, MR. STOMPSPIT.
THEY'D MOVED HIS DESK DOWN TO THE BASEMENT DURING REMODELLING AND SIMPLY FORGOTTEN TO MOVE IT BACK UP ONCE THE REMODELLING WAS DONE.
'MORNING, WILLIAM.
SORRY, MR. SMALLCABBAGE. I CAN'T HEAR YOU OVER THE FURNACE.
EDWIN WASN'T MISSED MUCH. IN FACT, WHEN HE WAS OUT WITH THE FLU FOR THREE WEEKS, NO ONE SEEMED TO NOTICE (THOUGH WILLIAM SENT HIM FLOWERS).
FROM WILLIAM
DICTIONARY
ONE DAY, EDWIN FOUND HIMSELF SHARING AN ELEVATOR WITH THE MEMBERS OF THE BOARD.
LATER, EDWIN WOULD CONFIDE TO WILLIAM: 'I STILL DO NOT KNOW WHAT POSSESSED ME TO FOLLOW THEM INTO THEIR MEETING.'
J. SACCO 5-87

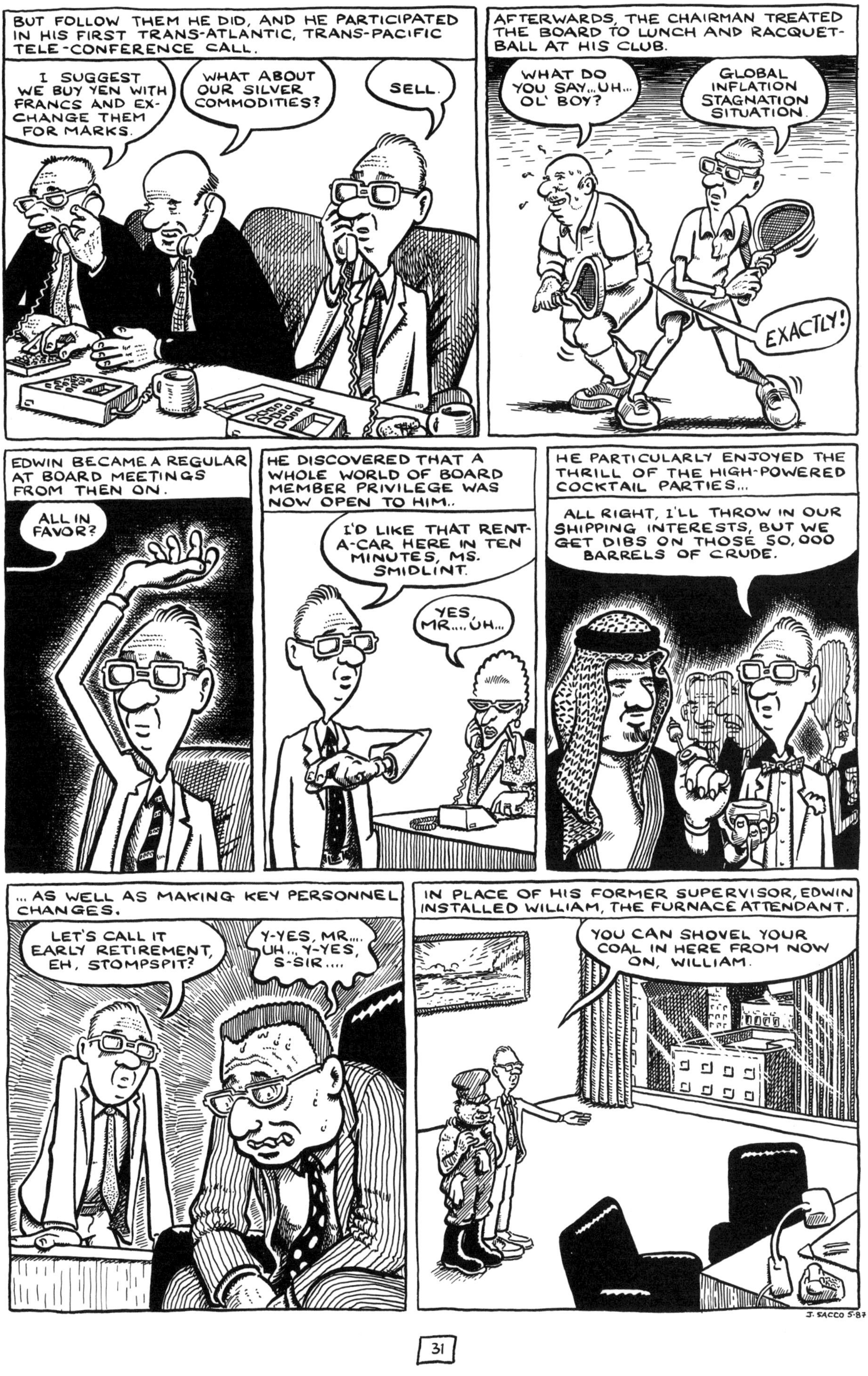
BUT FOLLOW THEM HE DID, AND HE PARTICIPATED IN HIS FIRST TRANS-ATLANTIC, TRANS-PACIFIC TELE-CONFERENCE CALL.
I SUGGEST WE BUY YEN WITH FRANCS AND EX-CHANGE THEM FOR MARKS.
WHAT ABOUT OUR SILVER COMMODITIES?
SELL.
AFTERWARDS, THE CHAIRMAN TREATED THE BOARD TO LUNCH AND RACQUET-BALL AT HIS CLUB.
WHAT DO YOU SAY...UH... OL' BOY?
GLOBAL INFLATION STAGNATION SITUATION.
EXACTLY!
EDWIN BECAME A REGULAR AT BOARD MEETINGS FROM THEN ON.
ALL IN FAVOR?
HE DISCOVERED THAT A WHOLE WORLD OF BOARD MEMBER PRIVILEGE WAS NOW OPEN TO HIM..
I'D LIKE THAT RENT-A-CAR HERE IN TEN MINUTES, MS. SMIDLINT.
YES, MR....UH...
HE PARTICULARLY ENJOYED THE THRILL OF THE HIGH-POWERED COCKTAIL PARTIES...
ALL RIGHT, I'LL THROW IN OUR SHIPPING INTERESTS, BUT WE GET DIBS ON THOSE 50,000 BARRELS OF CRUDE.
...AS WELL AS MAKING KEY PERSONNEL CHANGES.
LET'S CALL IT EARLY RETIREMENT, EH, STOMPSPIT?
Y-YES, MR.... UH... Y-YES, S-SIR....
IN PLACE OF HIS FORMER SUPERVISOR, EDWIN INSTALLED WILLIAM, THE FURNACE ATTENDANT.
YOU CAN SHOVEL YOUR COAL IN HERE FROM NOW ON, WILLIAM.
J. SACCO 5·87

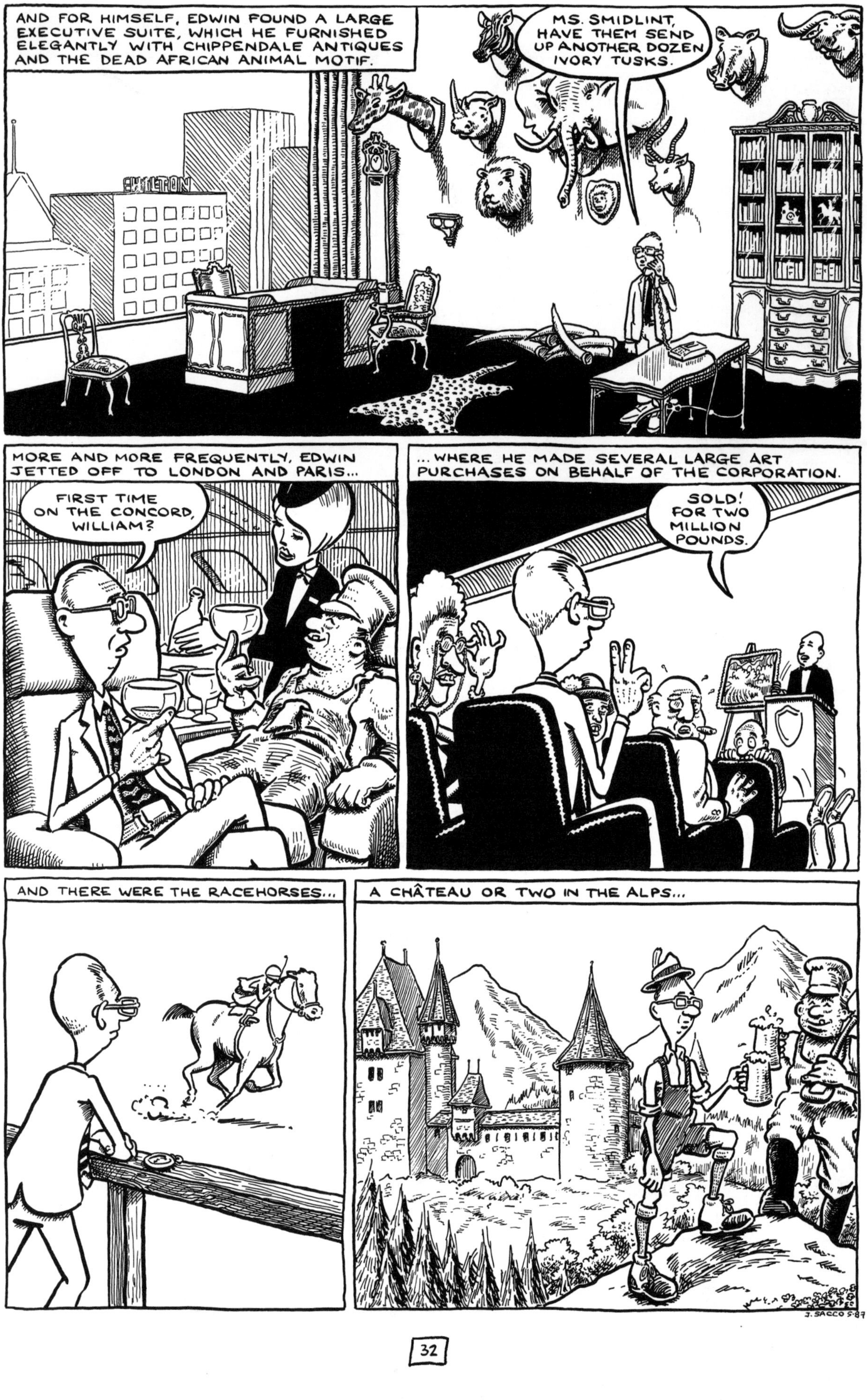
AND FOR HIMSELF, EDWIN FOUND A LARGE EXECUTIVE SUITE, WHICH HE FURNISHED ELEGANTLY WITH CHIPPENDALE ANTIQUES AND THE DEAD AFRICAN ANIMAL MOTIF.
MS. SMIDLINT, HAVE THEM SEND UP ANOTHER DOZEN IVORY TUSKS.
MORE AND MORE FREQUENTLY, EDWIN JETTED OFF TO LONDON AND PARIS...
FIRST TIME ON THE CONCORD, WILLIAM?
...WHERE HE MADE SEVERAL LARGE ART PURCHASES ON BEHALF OF THE CORPORATION.
SOLD! FOR TWO MILLION POUNDS.
AND THERE WERE THE RACEHORSES...
A CHÂTEAU OR TWO IN THE ALPS...
J. SACCO 5·87

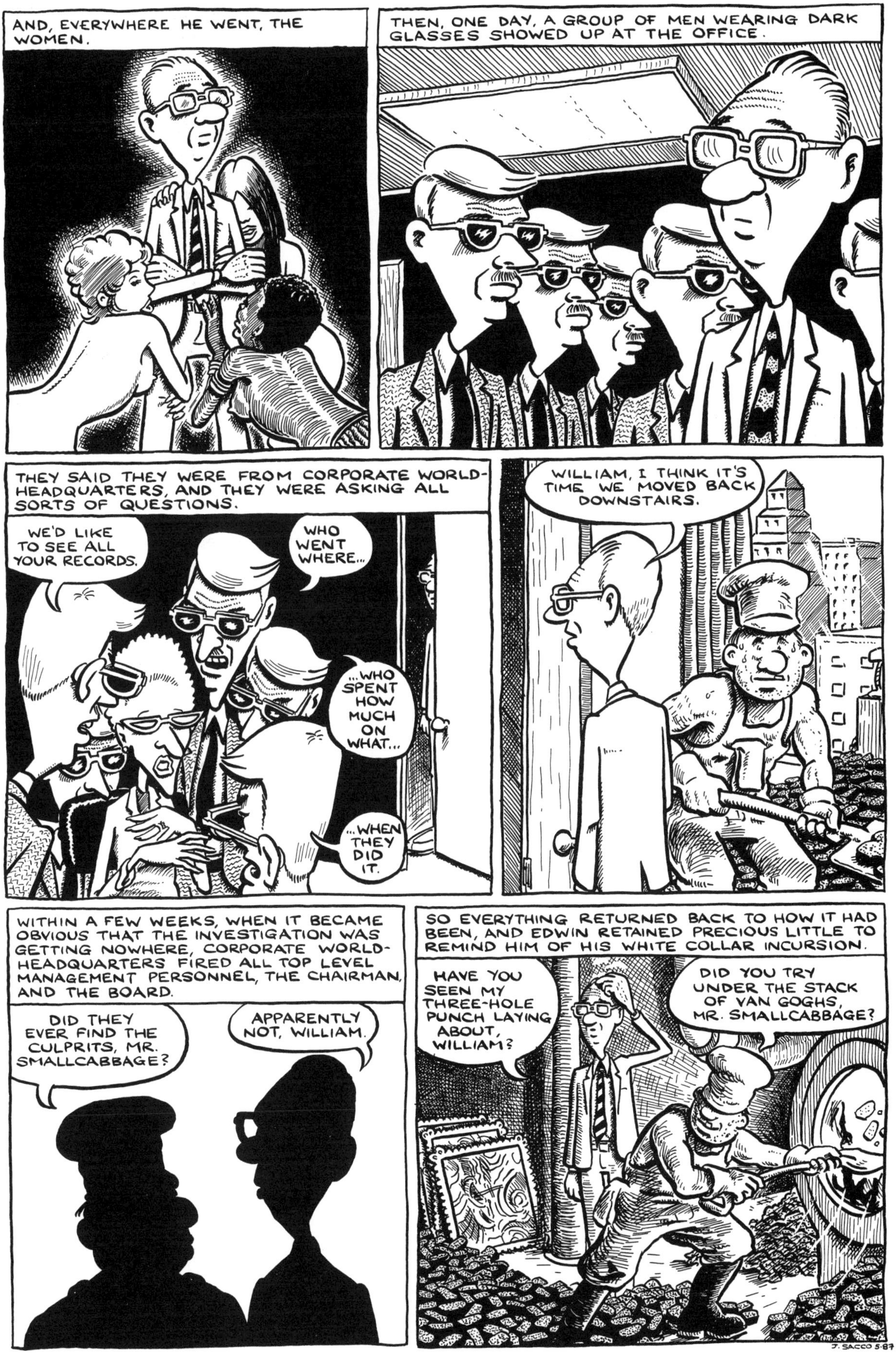
AND, EVERYWHERE HE WENT, THE WOMEN.
THEN, ONE DAY, A GROUP OF MEN WEARING DARK GLASSES SHOWED UP AT THE OFFICE.
THEY SAID THEY WERE FROM CORPORATE WORLD-HEADQUARTERS, AND THEY WERE ASKING ALL SORTS OF QUESTIONS.
WE'D LIKE TO SEE ALL YOUR RECORDS.
WHO WENT WHERE...
...WHO SPENT HOW MUCH ON WHAT...
...WHEN THEY DID IT.
WILLIAM, I THINK IT'S TIME WE MOVED BACK DOWNSTAIRS.
WITHIN A FEW WEEKS, WHEN IT BECAME OBVIOUS THAT THE INVESTIGATION WAS GETTING NOWHERE, CORPORATE WORLD-HEADQUARTERS FIRED ALL TOP LEVEL MANAGEMENT PERSONNEL, THE CHAIRMAN, AND THE BOARD.
DID THEY EVER FIND THE CULPRITS, MR. SMALLCABBAGE?
APPARENTLY NOT, WILLIAM.
SO EVERYTHING RETURNED BACK TO HOW IT HAD BEEN, AND EDWIN RETAINED PRECIOUS LITTLE TO REMIND HIM OF HIS WHITE COLLAR INCURSION.
HAVE YOU SEEN MY THREE-HOLE PUNCH LAYING ABOUT, WILLIAM?
DID YOU TRY UNDER THE STACK OF VAN GOGHS, MR. SMALLCABBAGE?
J. SACCO 5·87

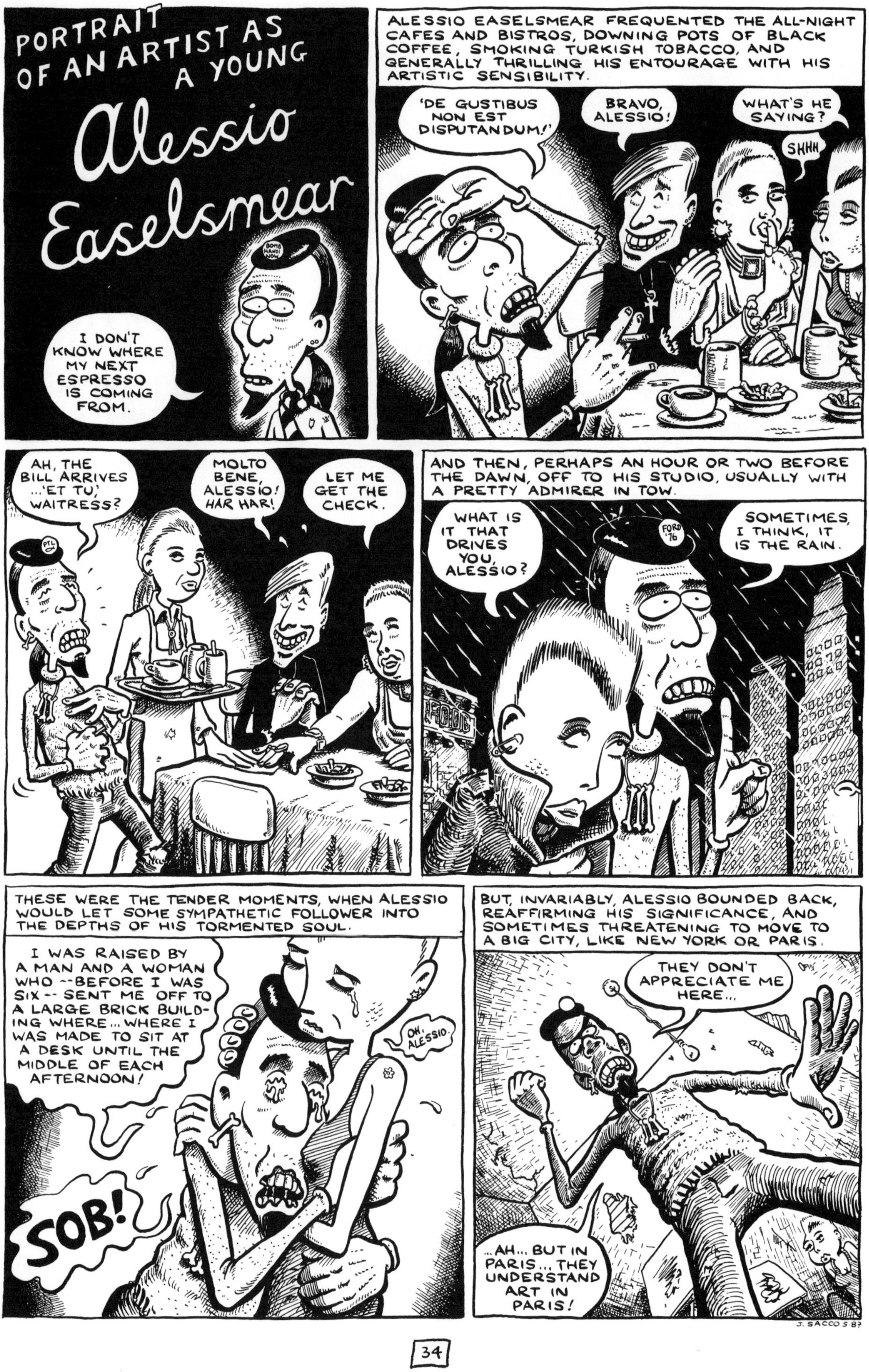
PORTRAIT OF AN ARTIST AS A YOUNG
Alessio Easelsmear
BOMB HANOI NOW
I DON'T KNOW WHERE MY NEXT ESPRESSO IS COMING FROM.
ALESSIO EASELSMEAR FREQUENTED THE ALL-NIGHT CAFES AND BISTROS, DOWNING POTS OF BLACK COFFEE, SMOKING TURKISH TOBACCO, AND GENERALLY THRILLING HIS ENTOURAGE WITH HIS ARTISTIC SENSIBILITY.
'DE GUSTIBUS NON EST DISPUTANDUM!'
BRAVO, ALESSIO!
WHAT'S HE SAYING?
SHHH
AH, THE BILL ARRIVES ...'ET TU,' WAITRESS?
PTL
MOLTO BENE, ALESSIO! HAR HAR!
LET ME GET THE CHECK.
AND THEN, PERHAPS AN HOUR OR TWO BEFORE THE DAWN, OFF TO HIS STUDIO, USUALLY WITH A PRETTY ADMIRER IN TOW.
WHAT IS IT THAT DRIVES YOU, ALESSIO?
FORD '76
SOMETIMES, I THINK, IT IS THE RAIN.
THESE WERE THE TENDER MOMENTS, WHEN ALESSIO WOULD LET SOME SYMPATHETIC FOLLOWER INTO THE DEPTHS OF HIS TORMENTED SOUL.
I WAS RAISED BY A MAN AND A WOMAN WHO --BEFORE I WAS SIX-- SENT ME OFF TO A LARGE BRICK BUILDING WHERE... WHERE I WAS MADE TO SIT AT A DESK UNTIL THE MIDDLE OF EACH AFTERNOON!
OH, ALESSIO.
SOB!
BUT, INVARIABLY, ALESSIO BOUNDED BACK, REAFFIRMING HIS SIGNIFICANCE, AND SOMETIMES THREATENING TO MOVE TO A BIG CITY, LIKE NEW YORK OR PARIS.
THEY DON'T APPRECIATE ME HERE...
...AH... BUT IN PARIS... THEY UNDERSTAND ART IN PARIS!
J. SACCO 5.87

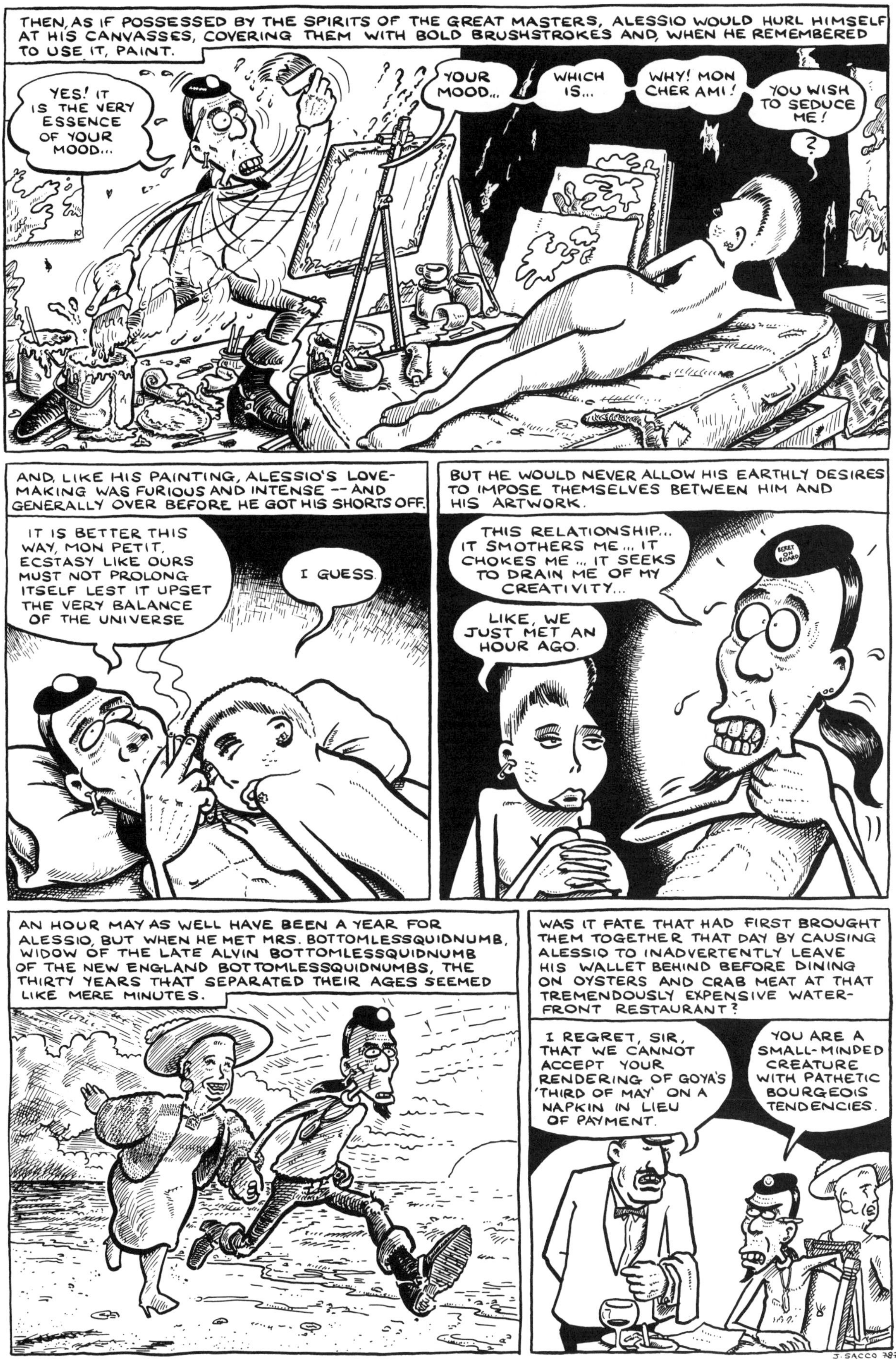
THEN, AS IF POSSESSED BY THE SPIRITS OF THE GREAT MASTERS, ALESSIO WOULD HURL HIMSELF AT HIS CANVASSES, COVERING THEM WITH BOLD BRUSHSTROKES AND, WHEN HE REMEMBERED TO USE IT, PAINT.
YES! IT IS THE VERY ESSENCE OF YOUR MOOD...
YOUR MOOD...
WHICH IS...
WHY! MON CHER AMI!
YOU WISH TO SEDUCE ME!
?
AND, LIKE HIS PAINTING, ALESSIO'S LOVE-MAKING WAS FURIOUS AND INTENSE -- AND GENERALLY OVER BEFORE HE GOT HIS SHORTS OFF.
IT IS BETTER THIS WAY, MON PETIT. ECSTASY LIKE OURS MUST NOT PROLONG ITSELF LEST IT UPSET THE VERY BALANCE OF THE UNIVERSE
I GUESS.
BUT HE WOULD NEVER ALLOW HIS EARTHLY DESIRES TO IMPOSE THEMSELVES BETWEEN HIM AND HIS ARTWORK.
THIS RELATIONSHIP... IT SMOTHERS ME... IT CHOKES ME... IT SEEKS TO DRAIN ME OF MY CREATIVITY...
BERET ON BOARD
LIKE, WE JUST MET AN HOUR AGO.
AN HOUR MAY AS WELL HAVE BEEN A YEAR FOR ALESSIO, BUT WHEN HE MET MRS. BOTTOMLESSQUIDNUMB, WIDOW OF THE LATE ALVIN BOTTOMLESSQUIDNUMB OF THE NEW ENGLAND BOTTOMLESSQUIDNUMBS, THE THIRTY YEARS THAT SEPARATED THEIR AGES SEEMED LIKE MERE MINUTES.
WAS IT FATE THAT HAD FIRST BROUGHT THEM TOGETHER THAT DAY BY CAUSING ALESSIO TO INADVERTENTLY LEAVE HIS WALLET BEHIND BEFORE DINING ON OYSTERS AND CRAB MEAT AT THAT TREMENDOUSLY EXPENSIVE WATER-FRONT RESTAURANT?
I REGRET, SIR, THAT WE CANNOT ACCEPT YOUR RENDERING OF GOYA'S 'THIRD OF MAY' ON A NAPKIN IN LIEU OF PAYMENT.
YOU ARE A SMALL-MINDED CREATURE WITH PATHETIC BOURGEOIS TENDENCIES.
J. SACCO 7'87

THE QUICK INTERVENTION OF MRS. BOTTOMLESSQUIDNUMB (AND HER CHECKBOOK) HAD PREVENTED AN UGLY SCENE...

...AND AN INSTANT ATTRACTION DEVELOPED BETWEEN HER AND ALESSIO.

YOUR FACE....I MUST PAINT IT! I MUST PAINT IT NOW!

I DIDN'T THINK THIS IS WHAT YOU HAD IN MIND.

ALESSIO MOVED IN WITH THE WIDOW THAT EVENING.

FOR THE FIRST FEW DAYS, THE UNLIKELY MATCH-UP BETWEEN THE WEALTHY HEIR TO THE BOTTOMLESSSQUIDNUMB FORTUNE AND THE PAINTER OF SUCH WORKS AS 'THE TEMPTATION OF SAINT ANTHONY DESCENDING A STAIRCASE' AND 'GUERNICA ON A HALF-SHELL' SEEMED IDEAL.

MORE ICED TEA, ALESSIO?

YOU CAN LEAVE IT ON THE TRAY, SNOOGUMS.

BUT, AFTER A WEEK, THINGS RAPIDLY CHANGED.

A HUG?

WHEN I AM AT THE CRUCIAL POINT THAT SEPARATES A BRILLIANT CANVAS FROM A MASTERPIECE, YOU NEED A HUG?!

HAVE YOU GONE CRAZY!??

MORE COFFEE! MORE CIGARETTES!

'NON COMPOS MENTIS'

YES, YOU HEARD ME CORRECTLY: A 1,000 SQUARE FOOT CANVAS! OF COURSE I CAN PAY FOR IT!

WHAT DO YOU THINK YOU CAN GET FOR YOUR FURS!

EVENTUALLY, MRS. BOTTOMLESSSQUIDNUMB, PROMPTED BY CONCERNED SOCIETY FRIENDS, CONFRONTED ALESSIO WITH HIS EXTRAVAGANT BEHAVIOR.

YOU THINK I CARE ABOUT YOUR MONEY?

I LAUGH AT YOUR MONEY!

HA HA HA

I BURN YOUR MONEY!

J. SACCO 7-87

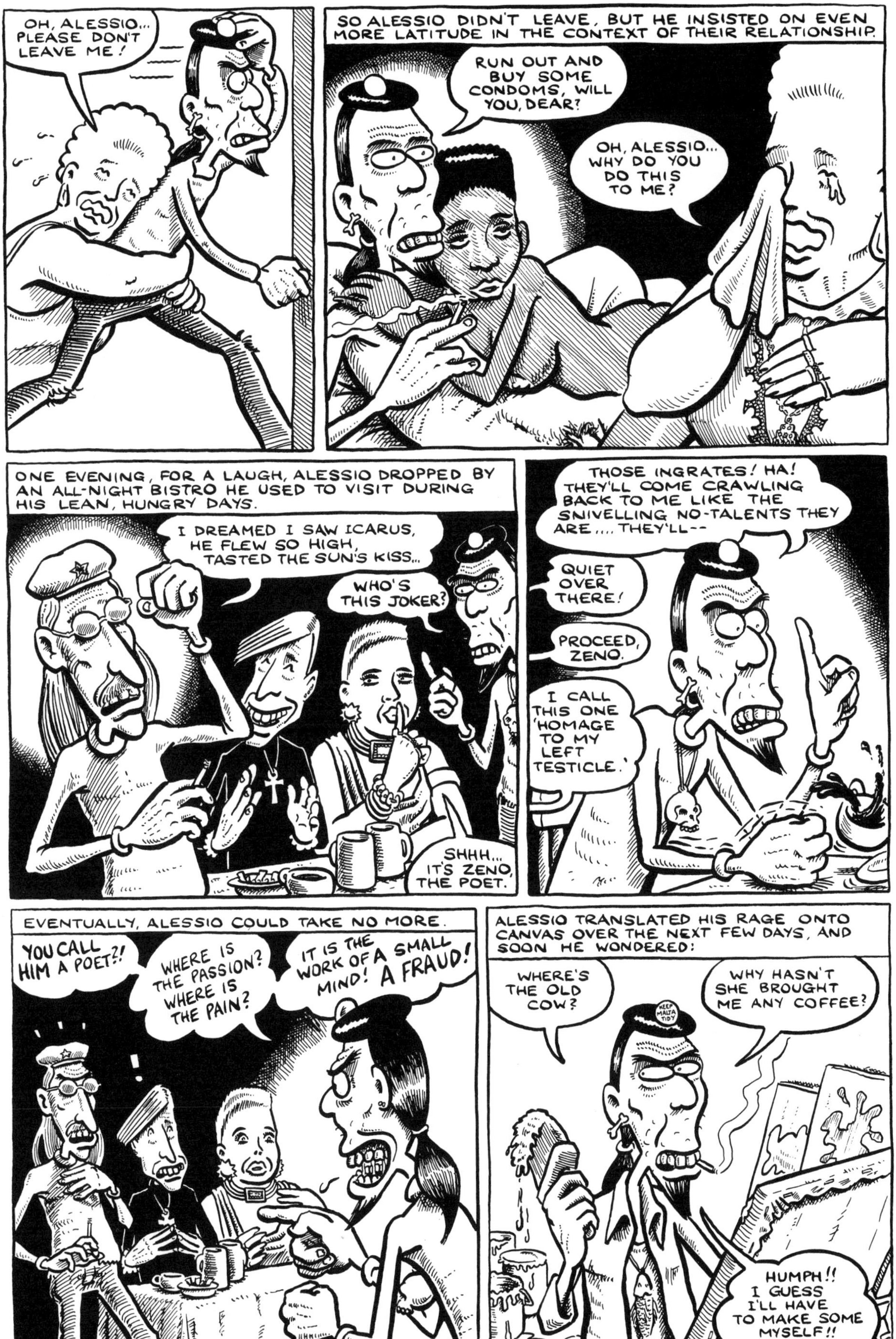
OH, ALESSIO... PLEASE DON'T LEAVE ME!
SO ALESSIO DIDN'T LEAVE, BUT HE INSISTED ON EVEN MORE LATITUDE IN THE CONTEXT OF THEIR RELATIONSHIP.
RUN OUT AND BUY SOME CONDOMS, WILL YOU, DEAR?
OH, ALESSIO... WHY DO YOU DO THIS TO ME?
ONE EVENING, FOR A LAUGH, ALESSIO DROPPED BY AN ALL-NIGHT BISTRO HE USED TO VISIT DURING HIS LEAN, HUNGRY DAYS.
I DREAMED I SAW ICARUS, HE FLEW SO HIGH, TASTED THE SUN'S KISS...
WHO'S THIS JOKER?
SHHH... IT'S ZENO, THE POET.
THOSE INGRATES! HA! THEY'LL COME CRAWLING BACK TO ME LIKE THE SNIVELLING NO-TALENTS THEY ARE.... THEY'LL--
QUIET OVER THERE!
PROCEED, ZENO.
I CALL THIS ONE 'HOMAGE TO MY LEFT TESTICLE.'
EVENTUALLY, ALESSIO COULD TAKE NO MORE.
YOU CALL HIM A POET?!
WHERE IS THE PASSION? WHERE IS THE PAIN?
IT IS THE WORK OF A SMALL MIND! A FRAUD!
ALESSIO TRANSLATED HIS RAGE ONTO CANVAS OVER THE NEXT FEW DAYS, AND SOON HE WONDERED:
WHERE'S THE OLD COW?
WHY HASN'T SHE BROUGHT ME ANY COFFEE?
KEEP MALTA TIDY
HUMPH!! I GUESS I'LL HAVE TO MAKE SOME MYSELF!!
J. SACCO 7·87

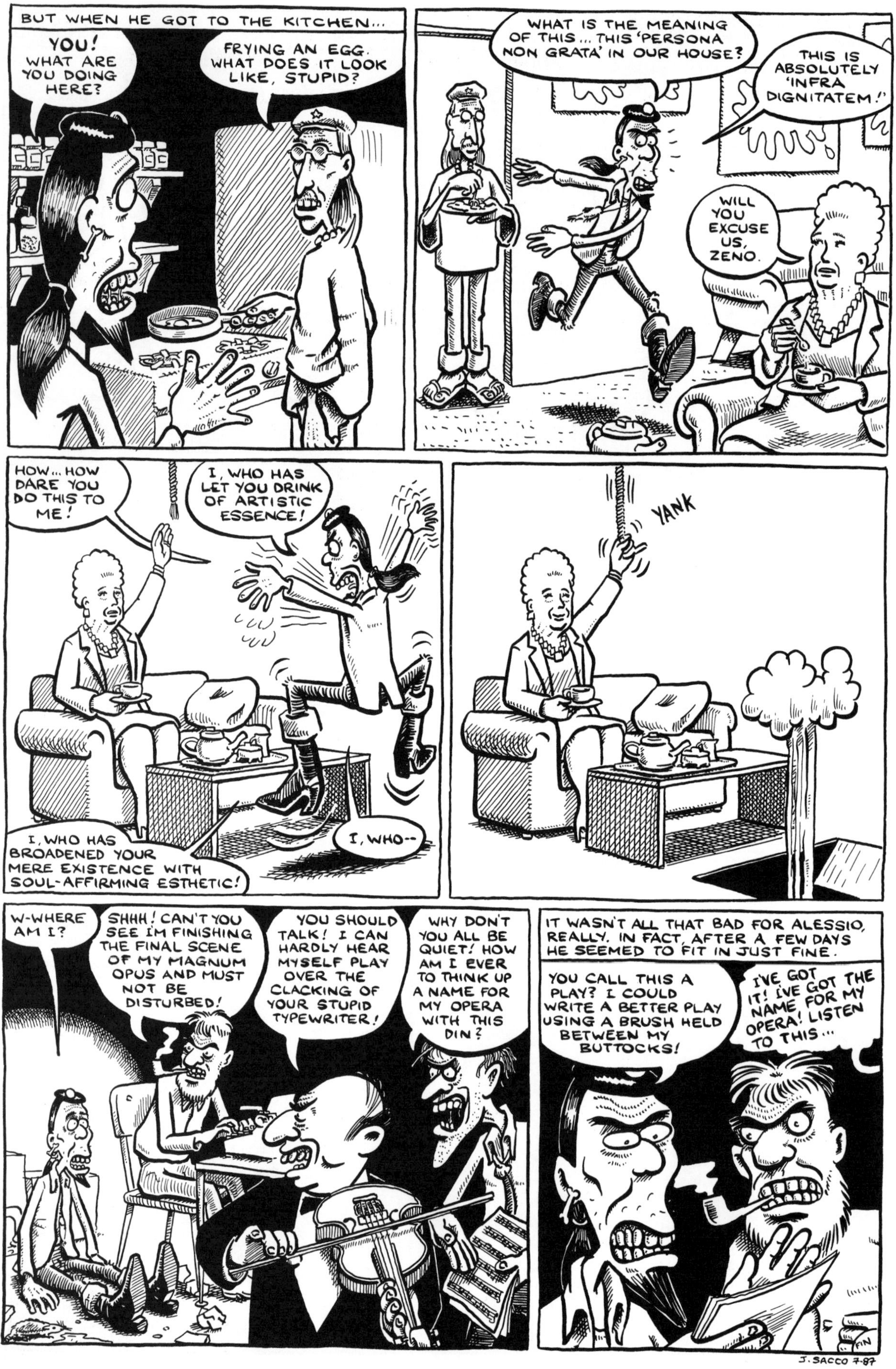

BUT WHEN HE GOT TO THE KITCHEN...
YOU! WHAT ARE YOU DOING HERE?
FRYING AN EGG. WHAT DOES IT LOOK LIKE, STUPID?
WHAT IS THE MEANING OF THIS... THIS 'PERSONA NON GRATA' IN OUR HOUSE?
THIS IS ABSOLUTELY 'INFRA DIGNITATEM!'
WILL YOU EXCUSE US, ZENO.
HOW... HOW DARE YOU DO THIS TO ME!
I, WHO HAS LET YOU DRINK OF ARTISTIC ESSENCE!
I, WHO HAS BROADENED YOUR MERE EXISTENCE WITH SOUL-AFFIRMING ESTHETIC!
I, WHO--
YANK
W-WHERE AM I?
SHHH! CAN'T YOU SEE I'M FINISHING THE FINAL SCENE OF MY MAGNUM OPUS AND MUST NOT BE DISTURBED!
YOU SHOULD TALK! I CAN HARDLY HEAR MYSELF PLAY OVER THE CLACKING OF YOUR STUPID TYPEWRITER!
WHY DON'T YOU ALL BE QUIET! HOW AM I EVER TO THINK UP A NAME FOR MY OPERA WITH THIS DIN?
IT WASN'T ALL THAT BAD FOR ALESSIO, REALLY. IN FACT, AFTER A FEW DAYS HE SEEMED TO FIT IN JUST FINE.
YOU CALL THIS A PLAY? I COULD WRITE A BETTER PLAY USING A BRUSH HELD BETWEEN MY BUTTOCKS!
I'VE GOT IT! I'VE GOT THE NAME FOR MY OPERA! LISTEN TO THIS...
FIN
J. SACCO 7-87

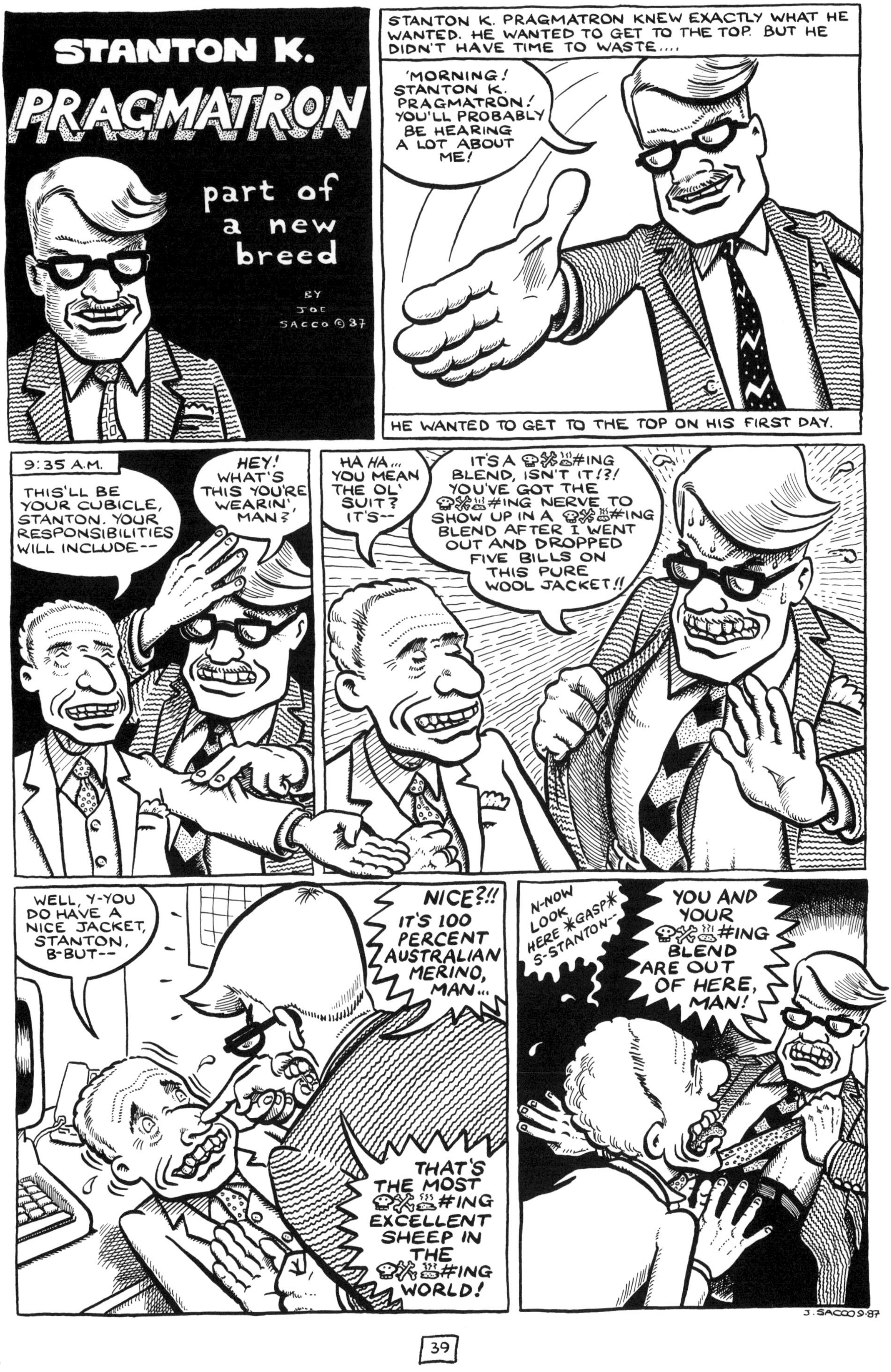
STANTON K. PRAGMATRON
part of a new breed
BY JOE SACCO ©87
STANTON K. PRAGMATRON KNEW EXACTLY WHAT HE WANTED. HE WANTED TO GET TO THE TOP. BUT HE DIDN'T HAVE TIME TO WASTE....
'MORNING! STANTON K. PRAGMATRON! YOU'LL PROBABLY BE HEARING A LOT ABOUT ME!
HE WANTED TO GET TO THE TOP ON HIS FIRST DAY.
9:35 A.M.
THIS'LL BE YOUR CUBICLE, STANTON. YOUR RESPONSIBILITIES WILL INCLUDE--
HEY! WHAT'S THIS YOU'RE WEARIN', MAN?
HA HA... YOU MEAN THE OL' SUIT? IT'S--
IT'S A #ING BLEND, ISN'T IT!?! YOU'VE GOT THE #ING NERVE TO SHOW UP IN A #ING BLEND AFTER I WENT OUT AND DROPPED FIVE BILLS ON THIS PURE WOOL JACKET!!
WELL, Y-YOU DO HAVE A NICE JACKET, STANTON, B-BUT--
NICE?!! IT'S 100 PERCENT AUSTRALIAN MERINO, MAN...
THAT'S THE MOST #ING EXCELLENT SHEEP IN THE #ING WORLD!
N-NOW LOOK HERE *GASP* S-STANTON--
YOU AND YOUR #ING BLEND ARE OUT OF HERE, MAN!
J. SACCO 9·87

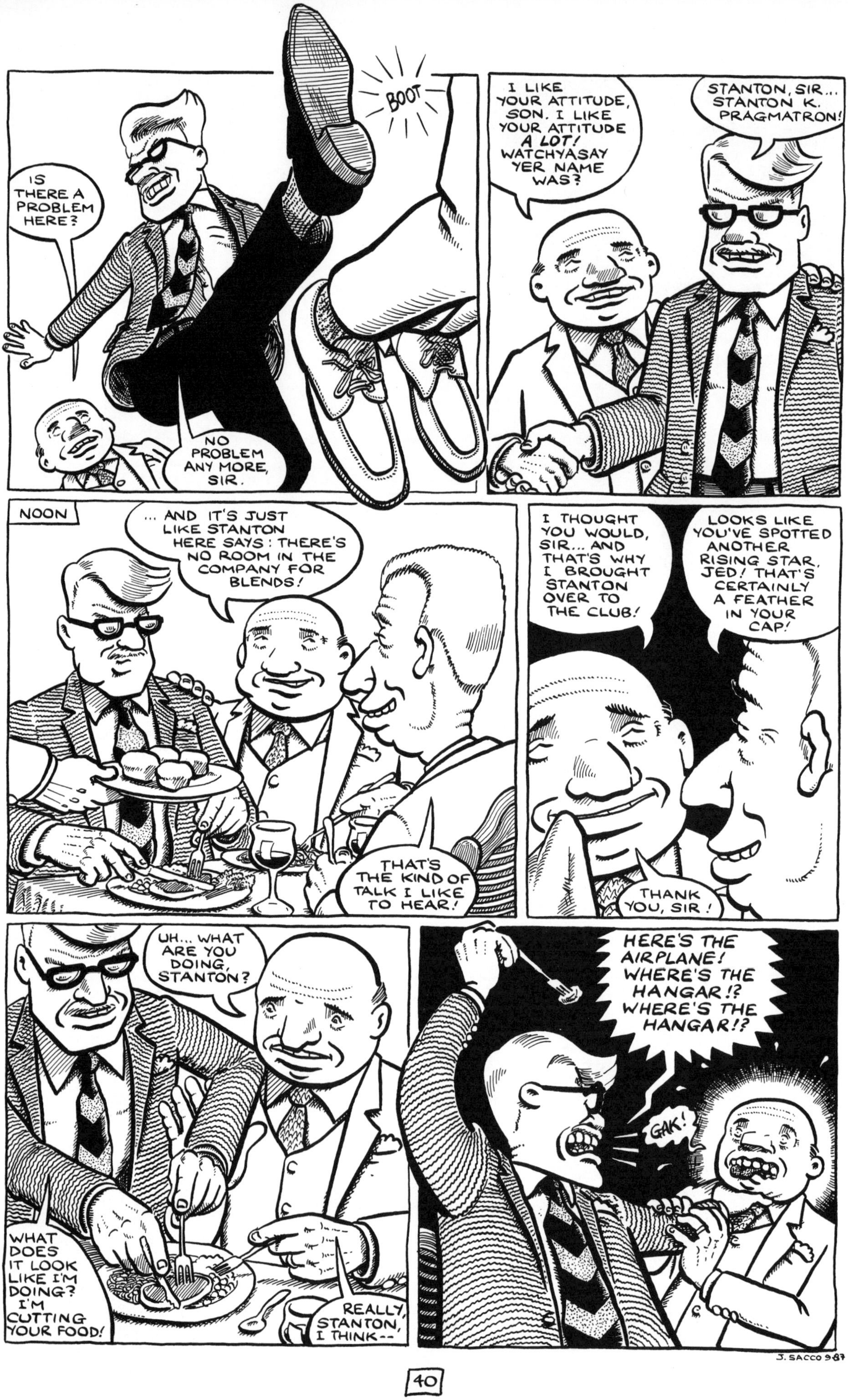
BOOT
IS THERE A PROBLEM HERE?
NO PROBLEM ANY MORE, SIR.
I LIKE YOUR ATTITUDE, SON. I LIKE YOUR ATTITUDE A LOT! WATCHYASAY YER NAME WAS?
STANTON, SIR... STANTON K. PRAGMATRON!
NOON
... AND IT'S JUST LIKE STANTON HERE SAYS: THERE'S NO ROOM IN THE COMPANY FOR BLENDS!
THAT'S THE KIND OF TALK I LIKE TO HEAR!
I THOUGHT YOU WOULD, SIR... AND THAT'S WHY I BROUGHT STANTON OVER TO THE CLUB!
LOOKS LIKE YOU'VE SPOTTED ANOTHER RISING STAR, JED! THAT'S CERTAINLY A FEATHER IN YOUR CAP!
THANK YOU, SIR!
UH... WHAT ARE YOU DOING, STANTON?
WHAT DOES IT LOOK LIKE I'M DOING? I'M CUTTING YOUR FOOD!
REALLY, STANTON, I THINK--
HERE'S THE AIRPLANE! WHERE'S THE HANGAR!? WHERE'S THE HANGAR!?
GAK!

J. SACCO 9-87

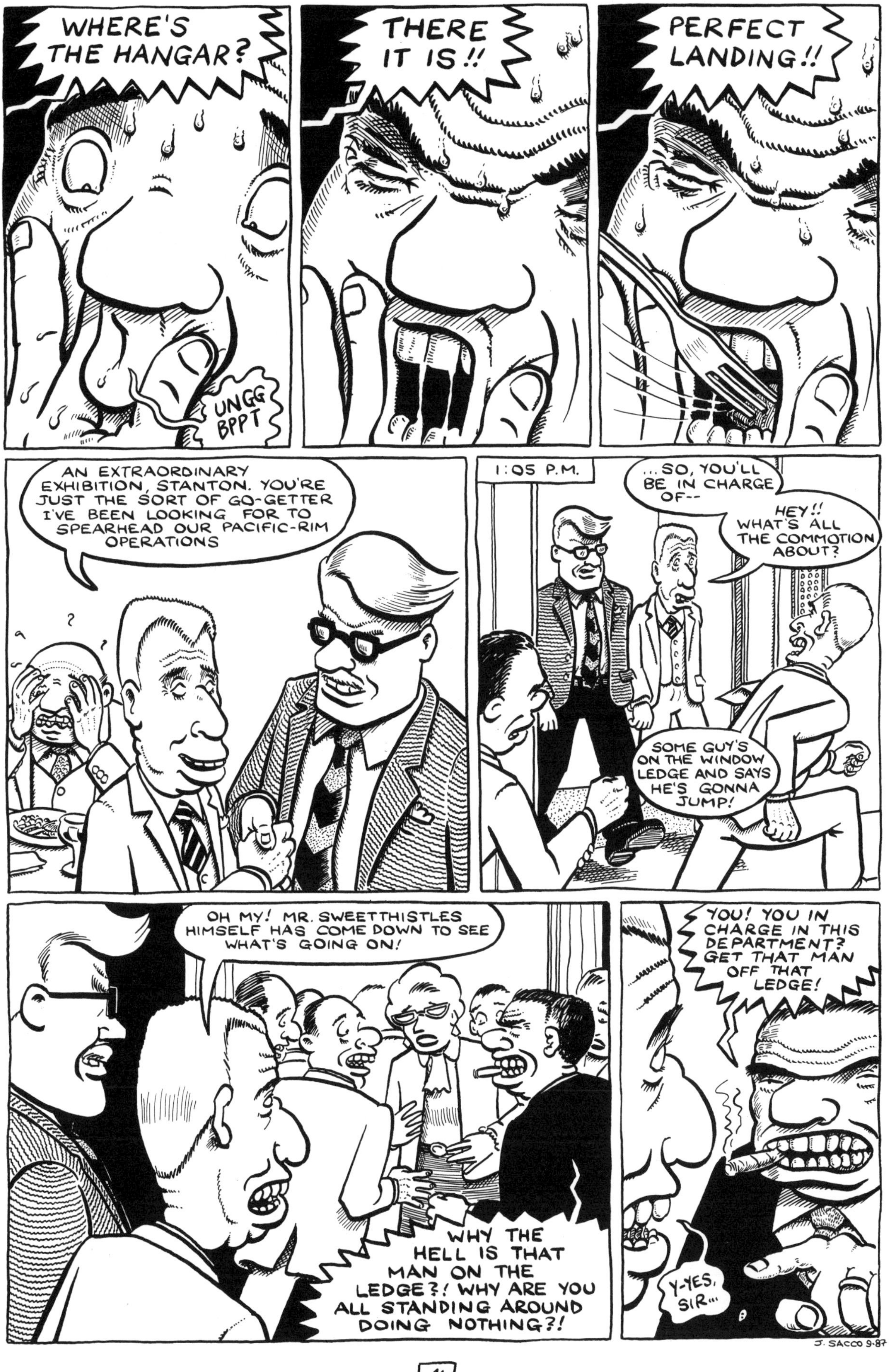
WHERE'S THE HANGAR?
UNGG BPPT
THERE IT IS!!
PERFECT LANDING!!
AN EXTRAORDINARY EXHIBITION, STANTON. YOU'RE JUST THE SORT OF GO-GETTER I'VE BEEN LOOKING FOR TO SPEARHEAD OUR PACIFIC-RIM OPERATIONS
1:05 P.M.
...SO, YOU'LL BE IN CHARGE OF--
HEY!! WHAT'S ALL THE COMMOTION ABOUT?
SOME GUY'S ON THE WINDOW LEDGE AND SAYS HE'S GONNA JUMP!
OH MY! MR. SWEETTHISTLES HIMSELF HAS COME DOWN TO SEE WHAT'S GOING ON!
WHY THE HELL IS THAT MAN ON THE LEDGE?! WHY ARE YOU ALL STANDING AROUND DOING NOTHING?!
YOU! YOU IN CHARGE IN THIS DEPARTMENT? GET THAT MAN OFF THAT LEDGE!
Y-YES, SIR...
J. SACCO 9-87

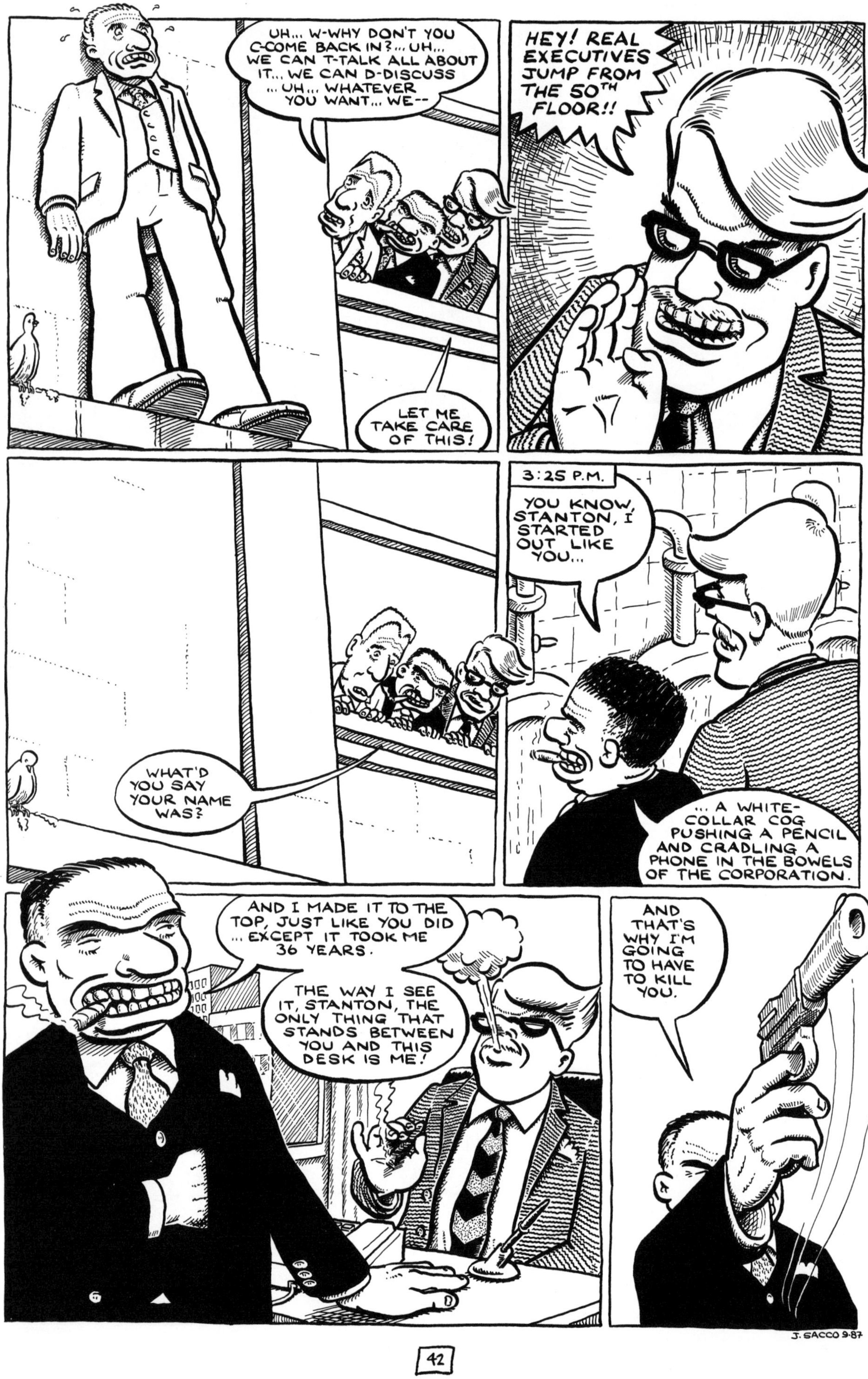
UH... W-WHY DON'T YOU C-COME BACK IN?... UH... WE CAN T-TALK ALL ABOUT IT... WE CAN D-DISCUSS ... UH... WHATEVER YOU WANT... WE--
LET ME TAKE CARE OF THIS!
HEY! REAL EXECUTIVES JUMP FROM THE 50TH FLOOR!!
WHAT'D YOU SAY YOUR NAME WAS?
3:25 P.M.
YOU KNOW, STANTON, I STARTED OUT LIKE YOU...
... A WHITE-COLLAR COG PUSHING A PENCIL AND CRADLING A PHONE IN THE BOWELS OF THE CORPORATION.
AND I MADE IT TO THE TOP, JUST LIKE YOU DID ... EXCEPT IT TOOK ME 36 YEARS.
THE WAY I SEE IT, STANTON, THE ONLY THING THAT STANDS BETWEEN YOU AND THIS DESK IS ME!
AND THAT'S WHY I'M GOING TO HAVE TO KILL YOU.
J. SACCO 9·87

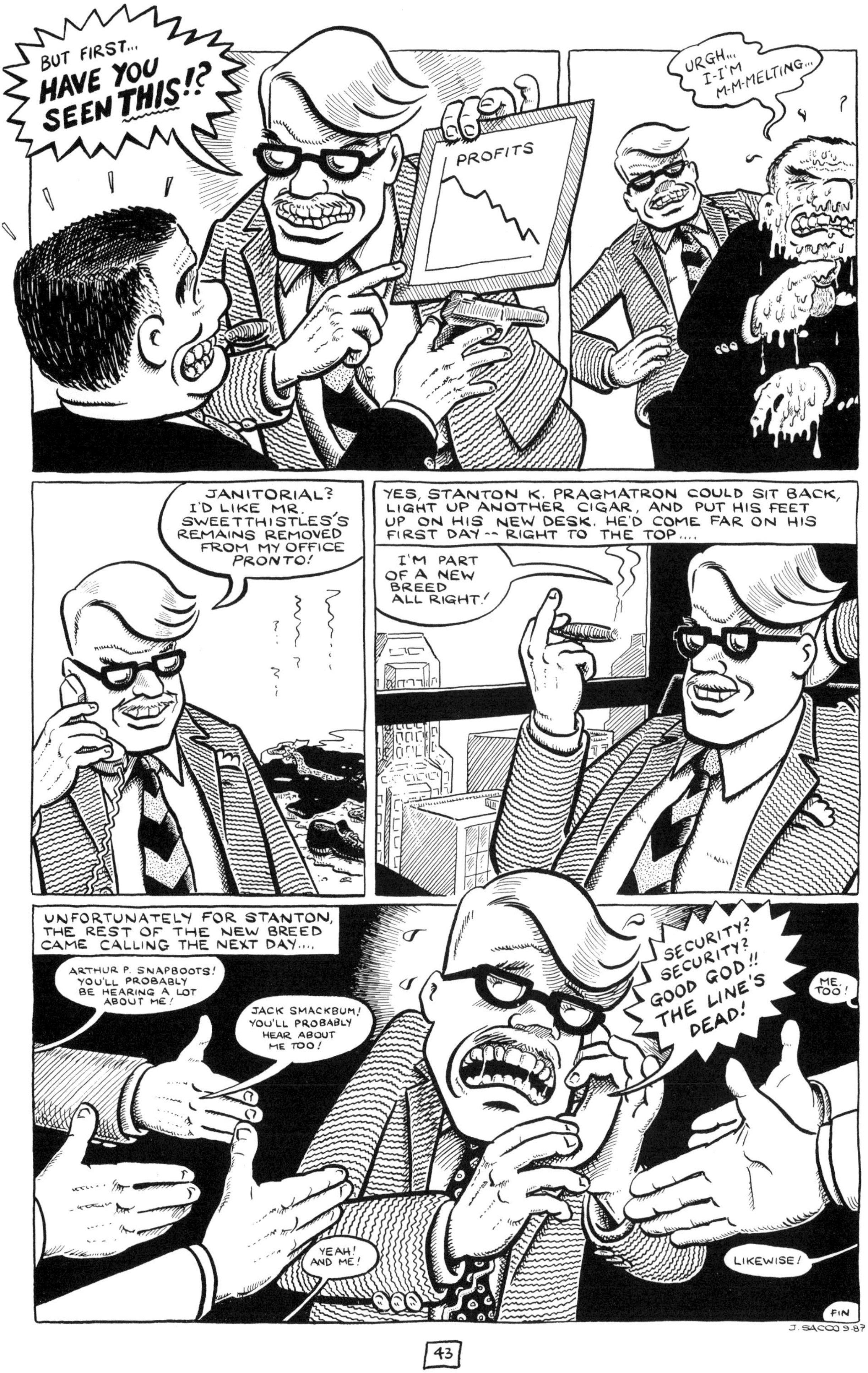
BUT FIRST... HAVE YOU SEEN THIS!?
PROFITS
URGH... I-I'M M-M-MELTING...
JANITORIAL? I'D LIKE MR. SWEETTHISTLES'S REMAINS REMOVED FROM MY OFFICE PRONTO!
YES, STANTON K. PRAGMATRON COULD SIT BACK, LIGHT UP ANOTHER CIGAR, AND PUT HIS FEET UP ON HIS NEW DESK. HE'D COME FAR ON HIS FIRST DAY -- RIGHT TO THE TOP....
I'M PART OF A NEW BREED ALL RIGHT!
UNFORTUNATELY FOR STANTON, THE REST OF THE NEW BREED CAME CALLING THE NEXT DAY....
ARTHUR P. SNAPBOOTS! YOU'LL PROBABLY BE HEARING A LOT ABOUT ME!
JACK SMACKBUM! YOU'LL PROBABLY HEAR ABOUT ME TOO!
SECURITY? SECURITY? GOOD GOD!! THE LINE'S DEAD!
ME, TOO!
YEAH! AND ME!
LIKEWISE!
FIN
J. SACCO 9-87

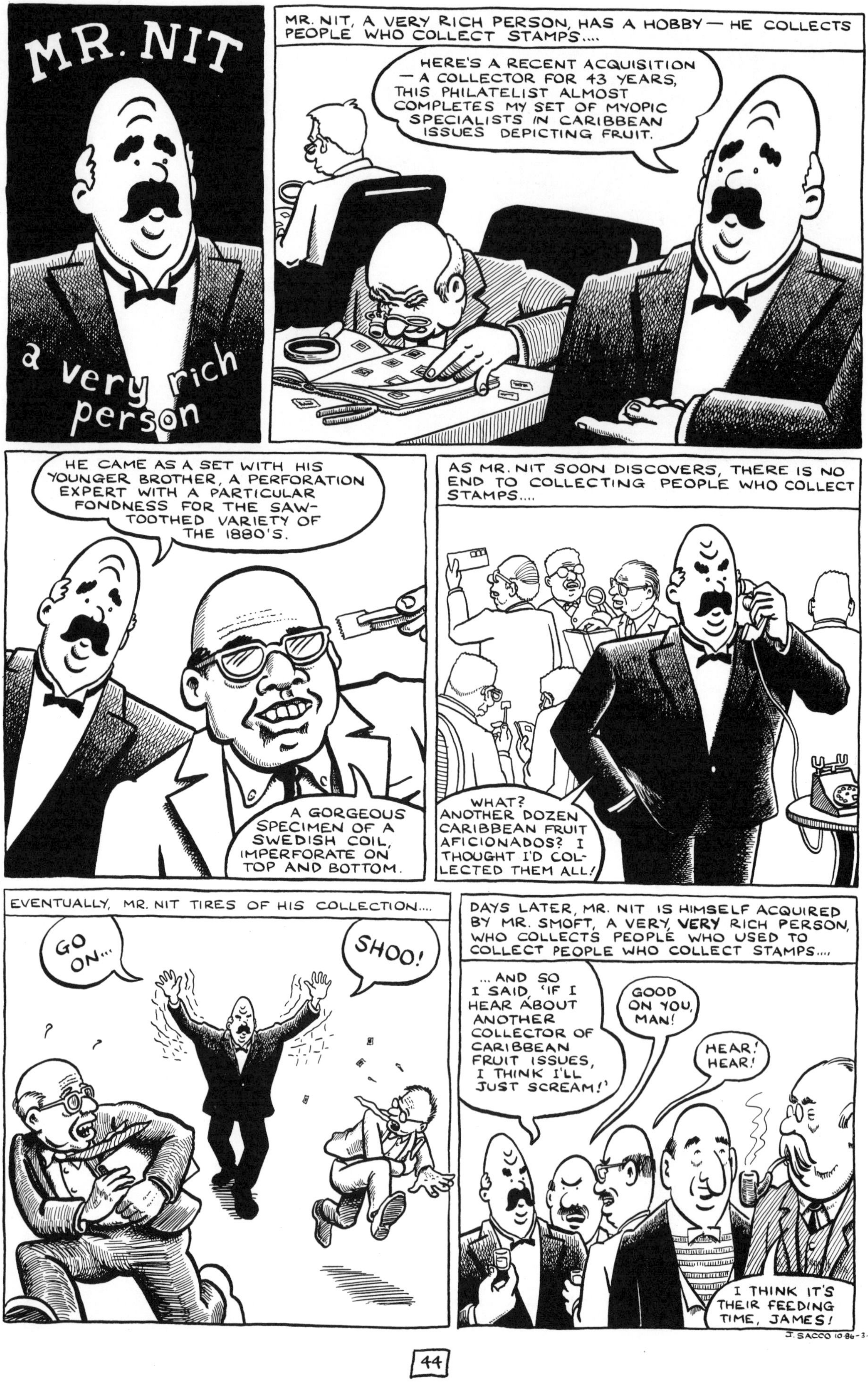
MR. NIT
a very rich person
MR. NIT, A VERY RICH PERSON, HAS A HOBBY — HE COLLECTS PEOPLE WHO COLLECT STAMPS....
HERE'S A RECENT ACQUISITION — A COLLECTOR FOR 43 YEARS, THIS PHILATELIST ALMOST COMPLETES MY SET OF MYOPIC SPECIALISTS IN CARIBBEAN ISSUES DEPICTING FRUIT.
HE CAME AS A SET WITH HIS YOUNGER BROTHER, A PERFORATION EXPERT WITH A PARTICULAR FONDNESS FOR THE SAW-TOOTHED VARIETY OF THE 1880'S.
A GORGEOUS SPECIMEN OF A SWEDISH COIL, IMPERFORATE ON TOP AND BOTTOM.
AS MR. NIT SOON DISCOVERS, THERE IS NO END TO COLLECTING PEOPLE WHO COLLECT STAMPS....
WHAT? ANOTHER DOZEN CARIBBEAN FRUIT AFICIONADOS? I THOUGHT I'D COLLECTED THEM ALL!
EVENTUALLY, MR. NIT TIRES OF HIS COLLECTION....
GO ON...
SHOO!
DAYS LATER, MR. NIT IS HIMSELF ACQUIRED BY MR. SMOFT, A VERY, VERY RICH PERSON, WHO COLLECTS PEOPLE WHO USED TO COLLECT PEOPLE WHO COLLECT STAMPS....
...AND SO I SAID, 'IF I HEAR ABOUT ANOTHER COLLECTOR OF CARIBBEAN FRUIT ISSUES, I THINK I'LL JUST SCREAM!'
GOOD ON YOU, MAN!
HEAR! HEAR!
I THINK IT'S THEIR FEEDING TIME, JAMES!
J. SACCO 10.86-3.87

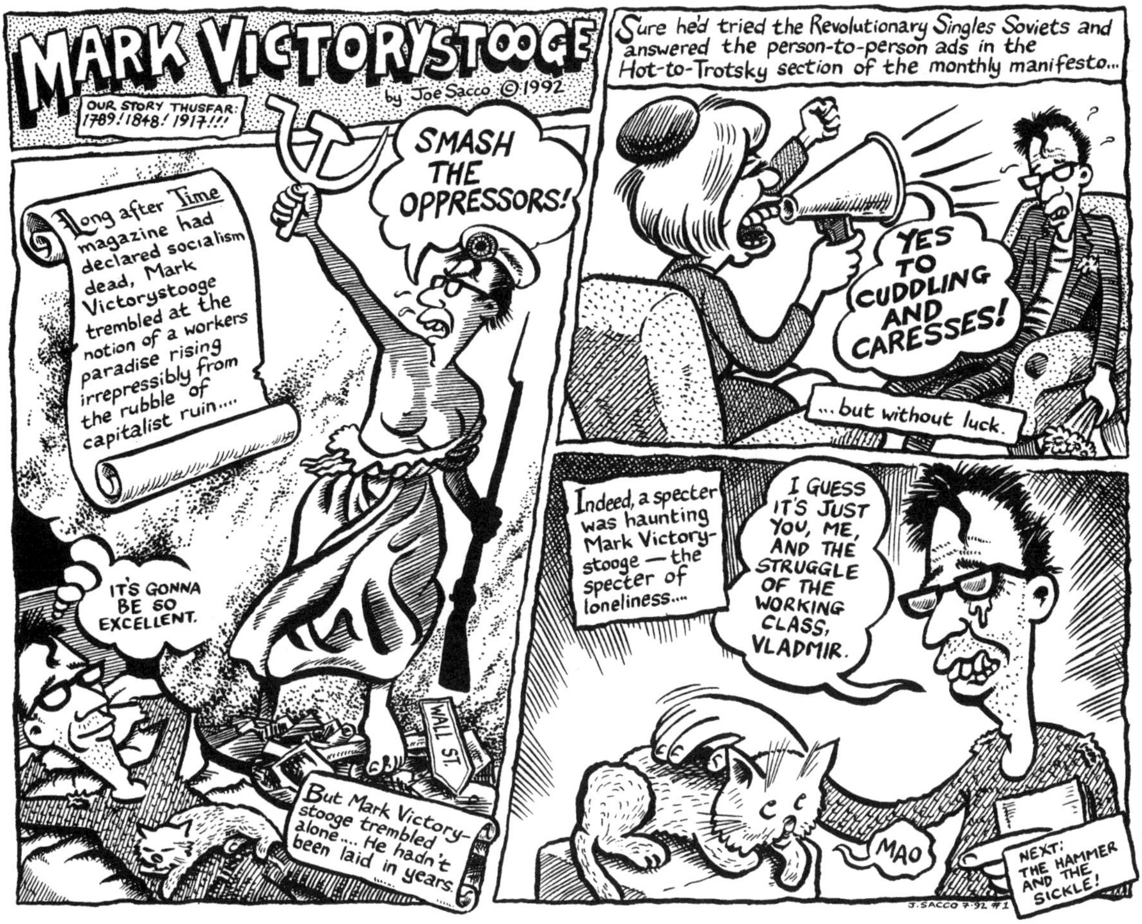
MARK VICTORYSTOOGE
by Joe Sacco ©1992
OUR STORY THUSFAR: 1789! 1848! 1917!!!
Long after Time magazine had declared socialism dead, Mark Victorystooge trembled at the notion of a workers paradise rising irrepressibly from the rubble of capitalist ruin....
SMASH THE OPPRESSORS!
IT'S GONNA BE SO EXCELLENT.
WALL ST.
But Mark Victorystooge trembled alone.... He hadn't been laid in years.
Sure he'd tried the Revolutionary Singles Soviets and answered the person-to-person ads in the Hot-to-Trotsky section of the monthly manifesto...
YES TO CUDDLING AND CARESSES!
...but without luck.
Indeed, a specter was haunting Mark Victorystooge — the specter of loneliness....
I GUESS IT'S JUST YOU, ME, AND THE STRUGGLE OF THE WORKING CLASS, VLADMIR.
MAO
NEXT: THE HAMMER AND THE SICKLE!
J. SACCO 7·92 #1

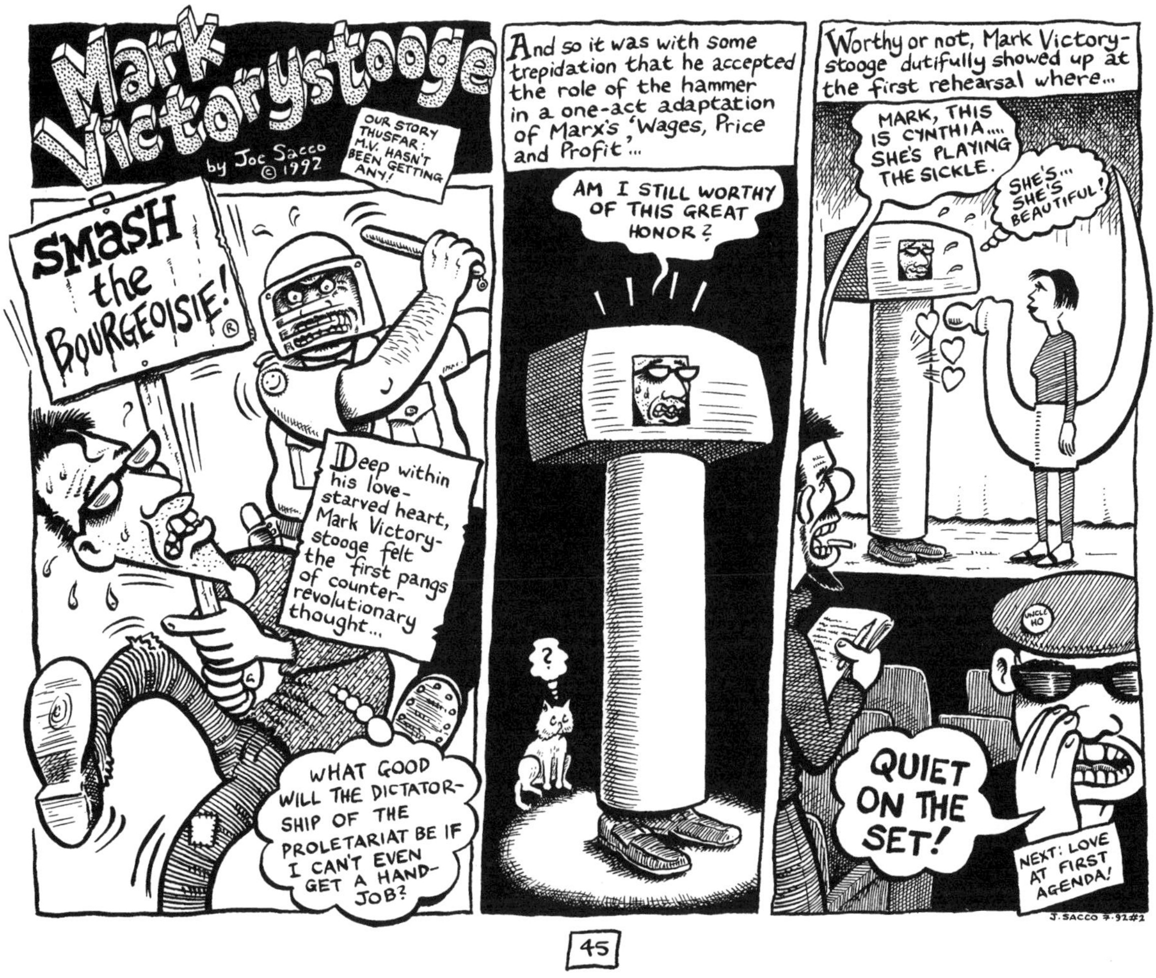
Mark Victorystooge
by Joe Sacco ©1992
OUR STORY THUSFAR: M.V. HASN'T BEEN GETTING ANY!
SMASH the BOURGEOISIE!®
Deep within his love-starved heart, Mark Victorystooge felt the first pangs of counter-revolutionary thought...
WHAT GOOD WILL THE DICTATORSHIP OF THE PROLETARIAT BE IF I CAN'T EVEN GET A HAND-JOB?
And so it was with some trepidation that he accepted the role of the hammer in a one-act adaptation of Marx's 'Wages, Price and Profit'...
AM I STILL WORTHY OF THIS GREAT HONOR?
Worthy or not, Mark Victorystooge dutifully showed up at the first rehearsal where...
MARK, THIS IS CYNTHIA.... SHE'S PLAYING THE SICKLE.
SHE'S... SHE'S BEAUTIFUL!
UNCLE HO
QUIET ON THE SET!
NEXT: LOVE AT FIRST AGENDA!
J. SACCO 7·92 #2

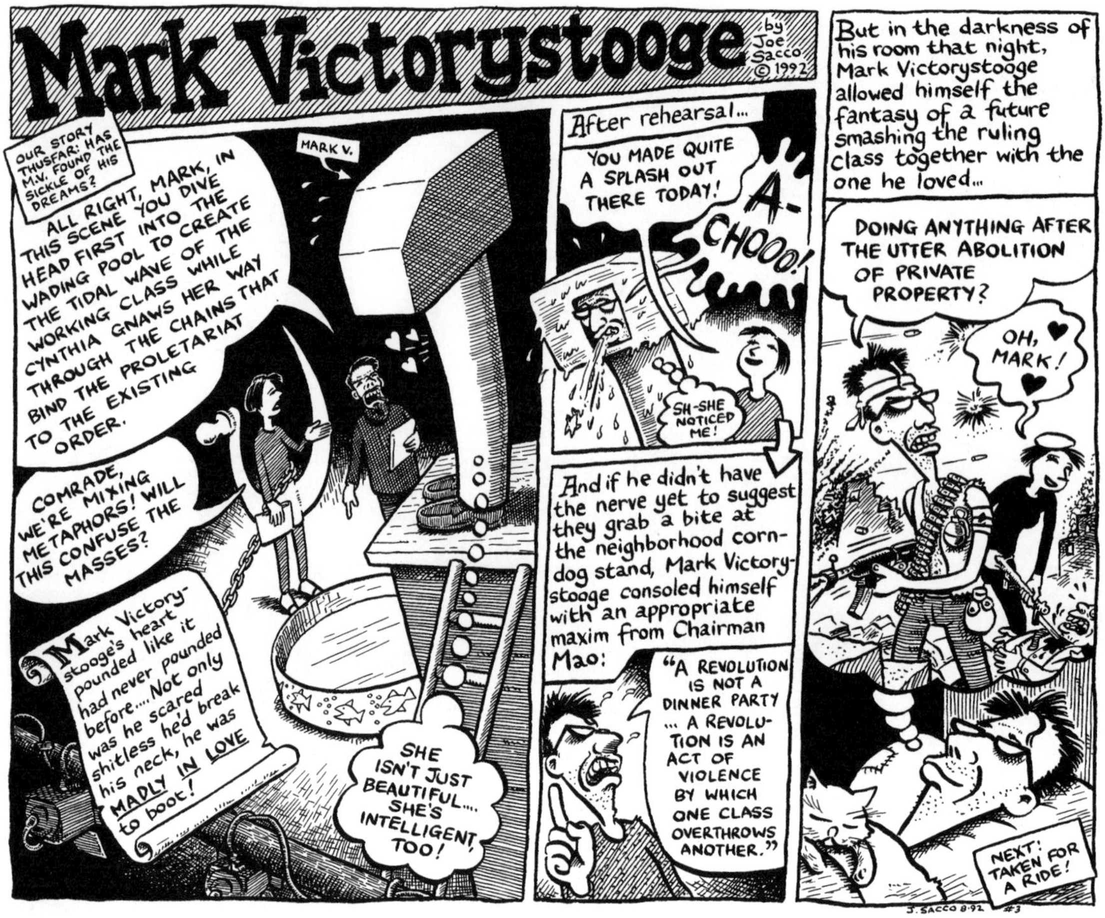
Mark Victorystooge
by Joe Sacco © 1992
OUR STORY THUSFAR: HAS M.V. FOUND THE SICKLE OF HIS DREAMS?
MARK V.
ALL RIGHT, MARK, IN THIS SCENE YOU DIVE HEAD FIRST INTO THE WADING POOL TO CREATE THE TIDAL WAVE OF THE WORKING CLASS WHILE CYNTHIA GNAWS HER WAY THROUGH THE CHAINS THAT BIND THE PROLETARIAT TO THE EXISTING ORDER.
COMRADE, WE'RE MIXING METAPHORS! WILL THIS CONFUSE THE MASSES?
Mark Victorystooge's heart pounded like it had never pounded before.... Not only was he scared shitless he'd break his neck, he was MADLY IN LOVE to boot!
SHE ISN'T JUST BEAUTIFUL.... SHE'S INTELLIGENT, TOO!
After rehearsal...
YOU MADE QUITE A SPLASH OUT THERE TODAY!
A-CHOOO!
SH-SHE NOTICED ME!
And if he didn't have the nerve yet to suggest they grab a bite at the neighborhood corn-dog stand, Mark Victorystooge consoled himself with an appropriate maxim from Chairman Mao:
"A REVOLUTION IS NOT A DINNER PARTY ... A REVOLUTION IS AN ACT OF VIOLENCE BY WHICH ONE CLASS OVERTHROWS ANOTHER."
But in the darkness of his room that night, Mark Victorystooge allowed himself the fantasy of a future smashing the ruling class together with the one he loved...
DOING ANYTHING AFTER THE UTTER ABOLITION OF PRIVATE PROPERTY?
OH, MARK!
NEXT: TAKEN FOR A RIDE!
J. SACCO 8-92 #3

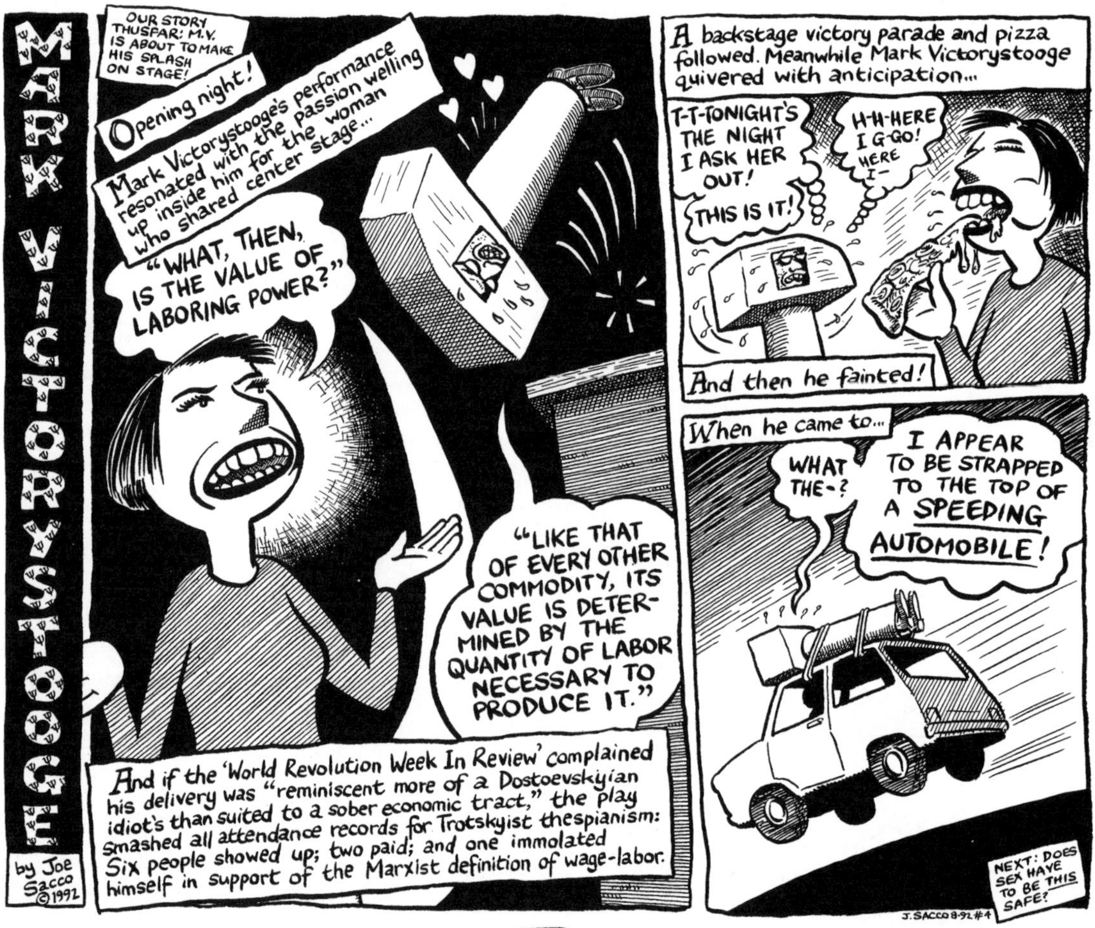
MARK VICTORYSTOOGE
by Joe Sacco ©1992
OUR STORY THUSFAR: M.V. IS ABOUT TO MAKE HIS SPLASH ON STAGE!
Opening night!
Mark Victorystooge's performance resonated with the passion welling up inside him for the woman who shared center stage...
"WHAT, THEN, IS THE VALUE OF LABORING POWER?"
"LIKE THAT OF EVERY OTHER COMMODITY, ITS VALUE IS DETERMINED BY THE QUANTITY OF LABOR NECESSARY TO PRODUCE IT."
And if the 'World Revolution Week In Review' complained his delivery was "reminiscent more of a Dostoevskyian idiot's than suited to a sober economic tract," the play smashed all attendance records for Trotskyist thespianism: Six people showed up; two paid; and one immolated himself in support of the Marxist definition of wage-labor.
A backstage victory parade and pizza followed. Meanwhile Mark Victorystooge quivered with anticipation...
T-T-TONIGHT'S THE NIGHT I ASK HER OUT!
THIS IS IT!
H-H-HERE I G-GO! HERE I-
And then he fainted!
When he came to...
WHAT THE-?
I APPEAR TO BE STRAPPED TO THE TOP OF A SPEEDING AUTOMOBILE!
NEXT: DOES SEX HAVE TO BE THIS SAFE?
J. SACCO 8-92 #4

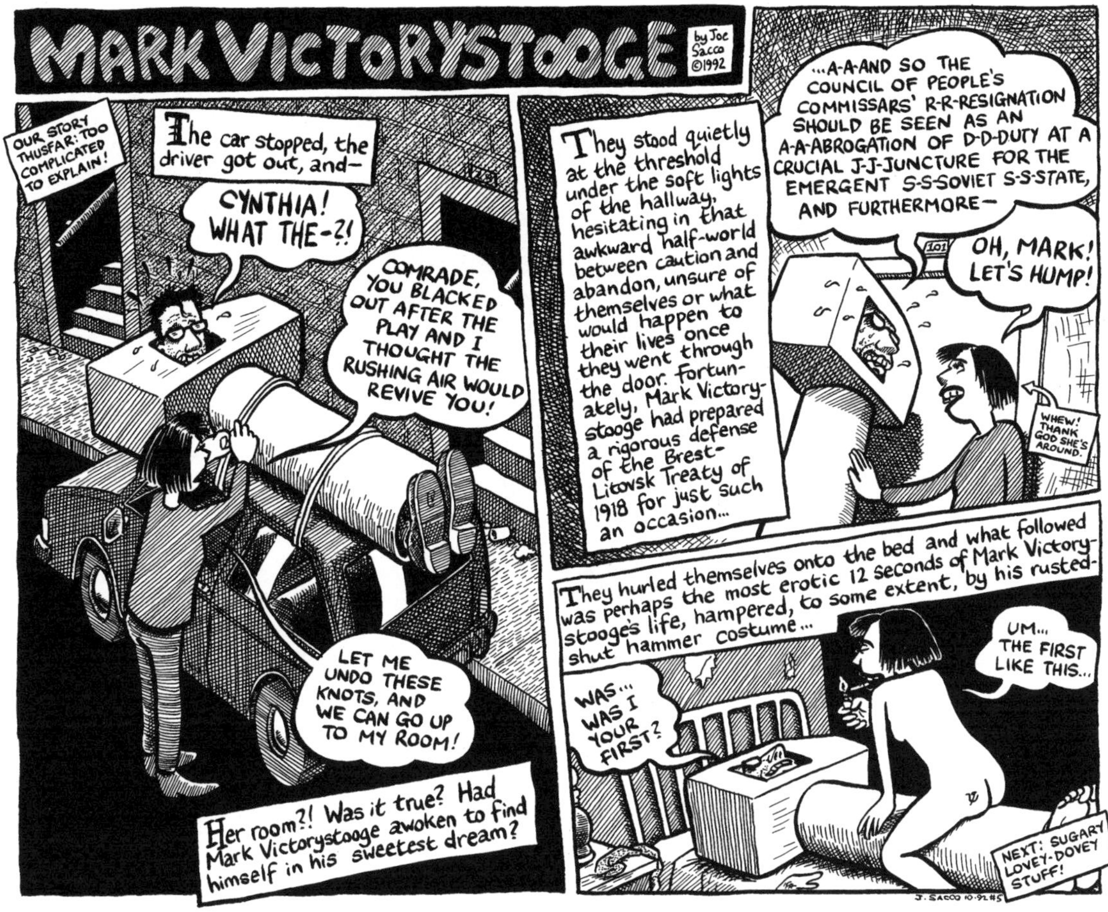
MARK VICTORYSTOOGE
by Joe Sacco ©1992
OUR STORY THUSFAR: TOO COMPLICATED TO EXPLAIN!
The car stopped, the driver got out, and—
CYNTHIA! WHAT THE-?!
COMRADE, YOU BLACKED OUT AFTER THE PLAY AND I THOUGHT THE RUSHING AIR WOULD REVIVE YOU!
LET ME UNDO THESE KNOTS, AND WE CAN GO UP TO MY ROOM!
Her room?! Was it true? Had Mark Victorystooge awoken to find himself in his sweetest dream?
They stood quietly at the threshold under the soft lights of the hallway, hesitating in that awkward half-world between caution and abandon, unsure of themselves or what would happen to their lives once they went through the door. Fortunately, Mark Victorystooge had prepared a rigorous defense of the Brest-Litovsk Treaty of 1918 for just such an occasion...
...A-A-AND SO THE COUNCIL OF PEOPLE'S COMMISSARS' R-R-RESIGNATION SHOULD BE SEEN AS AN A-A-ABROGATION OF D-D-DUTY AT A CRUCIAL J-J-JUNCTURE FOR THE EMERGENT S-S-SOVIET S-S-STATE, AND FURTHERMORE—
OH, MARK! LET'S HUMP!
WHEW! THANK GOD SHE'S AROUND.
They hurled themselves onto the bed and what followed was perhaps the most erotic 12 seconds of Mark Victorystooge's life, hampered, to some extent, by his rusted-shut hammer costume...
WAS... WAS I YOUR FIRST?
UM... THE FIRST LIKE THIS...
NEXT: SUGARY LOVEY-DOVEY STUFF!
J. SACCO 10-92 #5

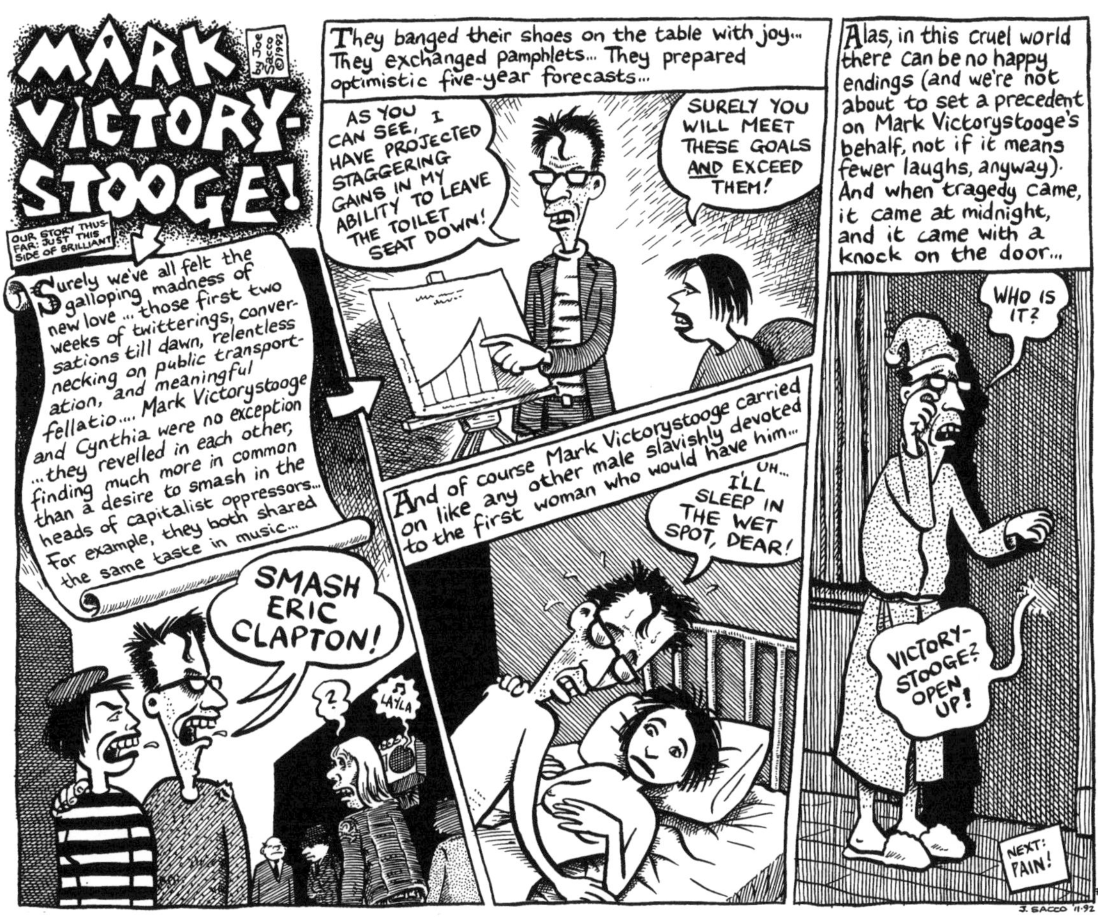
MARK VICTORY-STOOGE!
by Joe Sacco ©1992
OUR STORY THUSFAR: JUST THIS SIDE OF BRILLIANT
Surely we've all felt the galloping madness of new love ... those first two weeks of twitterings, conversations till dawn, relentless necking on public transportation, and meaningful fellatio.... Mark Victorystooge and Cynthia were no exception ...they revelled in each other, finding much more in common than a desire to smash in the heads of capitalist oppressors... For example, they both shared the same taste in music...
SMASH ERIC CLAPTON!
?
LAYLA
They banged their shoes on the table with joy... They exchanged pamphlets... They prepared optimistic five-year forecasts...
AS YOU CAN SEE, I HAVE PROJECTED STAGGERING GAINS IN MY ABILITY TO LEAVE THE TOILET SEAT DOWN!
SURELY YOU WILL MEET THESE GOALS AND EXCEED THEM!
And of course Mark Victorystooge carried on like any other male slavishly devoted to the first woman who would have him...
UH... I'LL SLEEP IN THE WET SPOT, DEAR!
Alas, in this cruel world there can be no happy endings (and we're not about to set a precedent on Mark Victorystooge's behalf, not if it means fewer laughs, anyway). And when tragedy came, it came at midnight, and it came with a knock on the door...
WHO IS IT?
VICTORY-STOOGE? OPEN UP!
NEXT: PAIN!
#6
J. SACCO 11-92

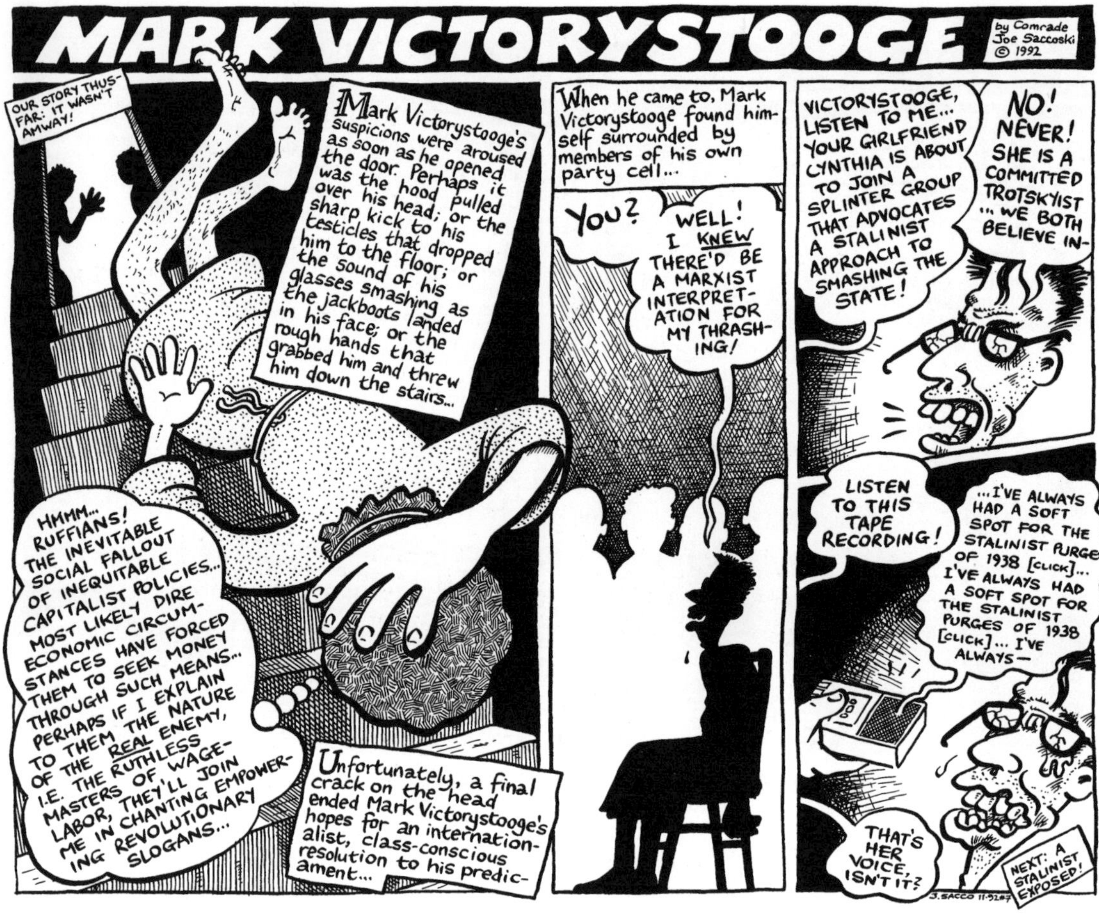
MARK VICTORYSTOOGE
by Comrade Joe Saccoski © 1992
OUR STORY THUS-FAR: IT WASN'T AMWAY!
Mark Victorystooge's suspicions were aroused as soon as he opened the door. Perhaps it was the hood pulled over his head; or the sharp kick to his testicles that dropped him to the floor; or the sound of his glasses smashing as the jackboots landed in his face; or the rough hands that grabbed him and threw him down the stairs...
HMMM... RUFFIANS! THE INEVITABLE SOCIAL FALLOUT OF INEQUITABLE CAPITALIST POLICIES... MOST LIKELY DIRE ECONOMIC CIRCUMSTANCES HAVE FORCED THEM TO SEEK MONEY THROUGH SUCH MEANS... PERHAPS IF I EXPLAIN TO THEM THE NATURE OF THE REAL ENEMY, I.E. THE RUTHLESS MASTERS OF WAGE-LABOR, THEY'LL JOIN ME IN CHANTING EMPOWERING REVOLUTIONARY SLOGANS...
Unfortunately, a final crack on the head ended Mark Victorystooge's hopes for an internationalist, class-conscious resolution to his predicament...
When he came to, Mark Victorystooge found himself surrounded by members of his own party cell...
YOU?
WELL! I KNEW THERE'D BE A MARXIST INTERPRETATION FOR MY THRASHING!
VICTORYSTOOGE, LISTEN TO ME... YOUR GIRLFRIEND CYNTHIA IS ABOUT TO JOIN A SPLINTER GROUP THAT ADVOCATES A STALINIST APPROACH TO SMASHING THE STATE!
NO! NEVER! SHE IS A COMMITTED TROTSKYIST ... WE BOTH BELIEVE IN-
LISTEN TO THIS TAPE RECORDING!
...I'VE ALWAYS HAD A SOFT SPOT FOR THE STALINIST PURGES OF 1938 [CLICK]... I'VE ALWAYS HAD A SOFT SPOT FOR THE STALINIST PURGES OF 1938 [CLICK]... I'VE ALWAYS—
THAT'S HER VOICE, ISN'T IT?
NEXT: A STALINIST EXPOSED!
J. SACCO 11-92 #7

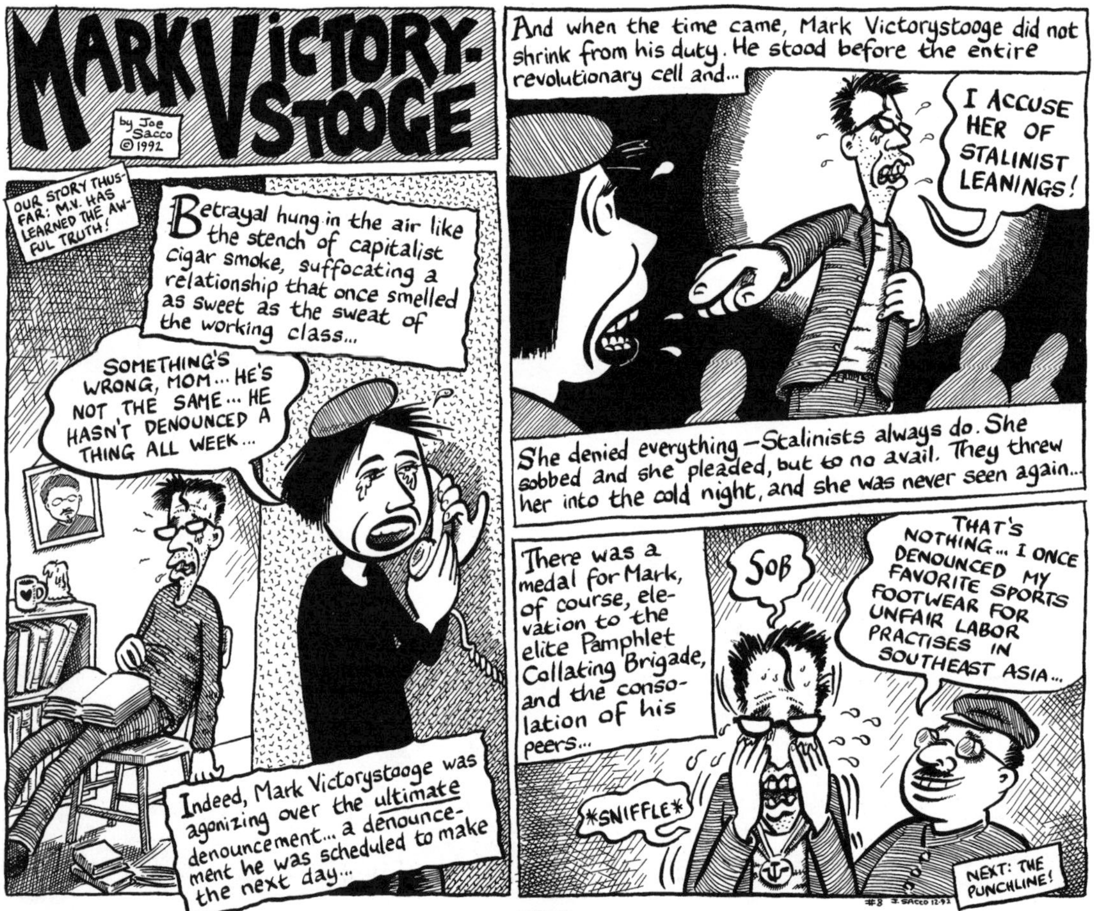
MARK VICTORYSTOOGE
by Joe Sacco ©1992
OUR STORY THUS-FAR: M.V. HAS LEARNED THE AWFUL TRUTH!
Betrayal hung in the air like the stench of capitalist cigar smoke, suffocating a relationship that once smelled as sweet as the sweat of the working class...
SOMETHING'S WRONG, MOM... HE'S NOT THE SAME... HE HASN'T DENOUNCED A THING ALL WEEK...
Indeed, Mark Victorystooge was agonizing over the ultimate denouncement... a denouncement he was scheduled to make the next day...
And when the time came, Mark Victorystooge did not shrink from his duty. He stood before the entire revolutionary cell and...
I ACCUSE HER OF STALINIST LEANINGS!
She denied everything—Stalinists always do. She sobbed and she pleaded, but to no avail. They threw her into the cold night, and she was never seen again...
There was a medal for Mark, of course, elevation to the elite Pamphlet Collating Brigade, and the consolation of his peers...
SOB
THAT'S NOTHING... I ONCE DENOUNCED MY FAVORITE SPORTS FOOTWEAR FOR UNFAIR LABOR PRACTISES IN SOUTHEAST ASIA...
SNIFFLE
NEXT: THE PUNCHLINE!
#8 J. SACCO 12-92

Mark Victorystooge

by Joe Sacco © 1991

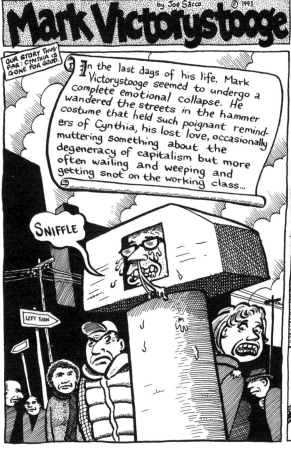

OUR STORY THUS FAR: CYNTHIA IS GONE FOR GOOD.

In the last days of his life, Mark Victorystooge seemed to undergo a complete emotional collapse. He wandered the streets in the hammer costume that held such poignant reminders of Cynthia, his lost love, occasionally muttering something about the degeneracy of capitalism but more often wailing and weeping and getting snot on the working class...

SNIFFLE

LEFT TURN

And when the workers finally rose up and smashed the state, Mark Victorystooge hardly warmed to the violent overthrow of all he had despised...

COMING ALONG, MARK? WE'RE KICKING IN THE HEADS OF INDUSTRIALIST OPPRESSORS LIKE THEY WERE SO MANY PUMPKINS.

HUH?

His lack of enthusiasm did not go unnoticed. He was promptly arrested and declared an Enemy of the People and an Element of the Reaction...

He seemed disinterested at his trial and during his sentencing, though some say he regained something of his former lucidity in the final moments...

WAS I JUST A TOOL OF THE REVOLUTION?

TAKE AIM!

THE END!

J. SACCO ©'91 #3

49

PART THREE:
SOCIAL STUDIES

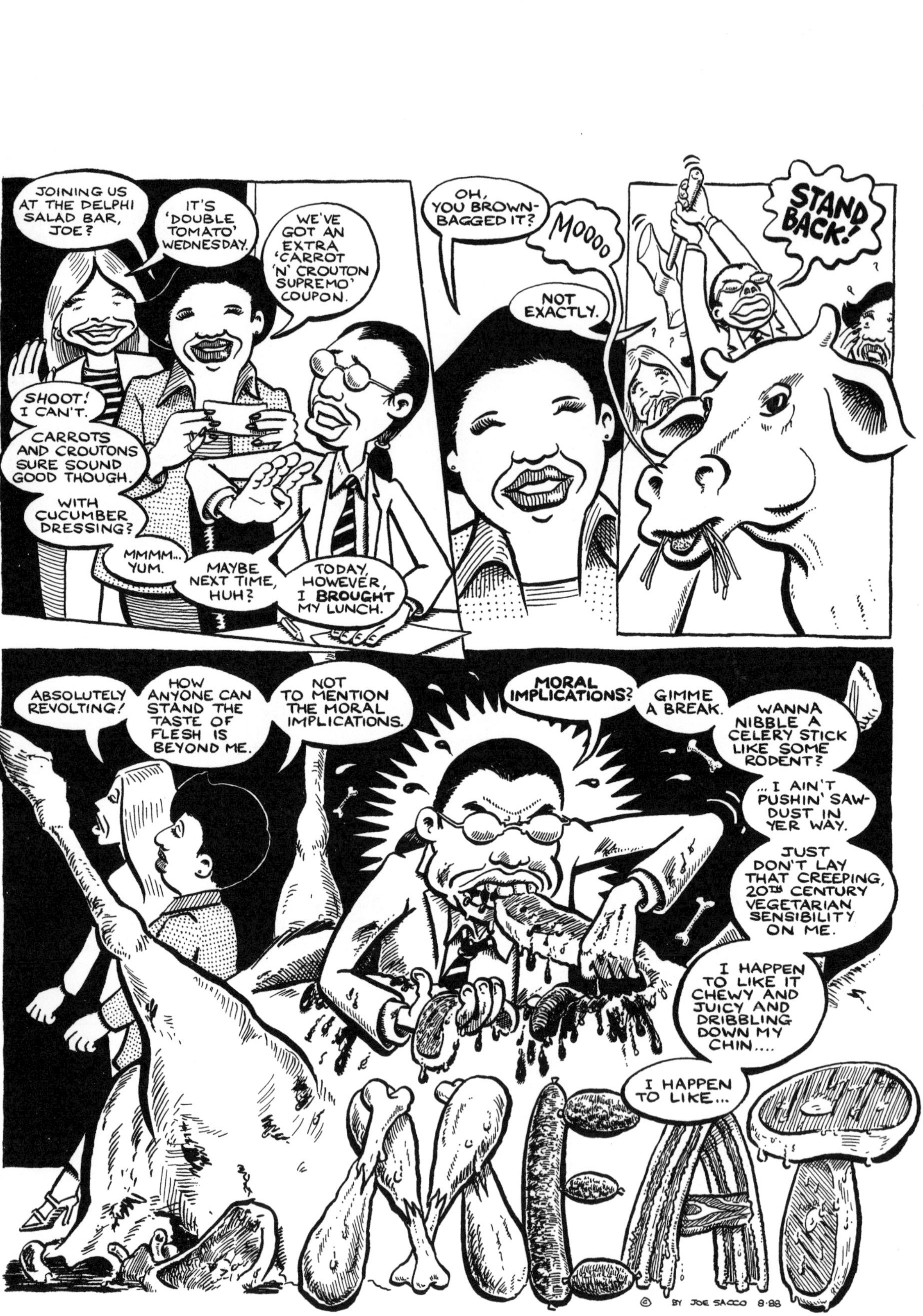
JOINING US AT THE DELPHI SALAD BAR, JOE?
IT'S 'DOUBLE TOMATO' WEDNESDAY.
WE'VE GOT AN EXTRA 'CARROT 'N' CROUTON SUPREMO' COUPON.
SHOOT! I CAN'T.
CARROTS AND CROUTONS SURE SOUND GOOD THOUGH.
WITH CUCUMBER DRESSING?
MMMM... YUM.
MAYBE NEXT TIME, HUH?
TODAY, HOWEVER, I BROUGHT MY LUNCH.
OH, YOU BROWN-BAGGED IT?
MOOOO
NOT EXACTLY.
STAND BACK!
ABSOLUTELY REVOLTING!
HOW ANYONE CAN STAND THE TASTE OF FLESH IS BEYOND ME.
NOT TO MENTION THE MORAL IMPLICATIONS.
MORAL IMPLICATIONS? GIMME A BREAK.
WANNA NIBBLE A CELERY STICK LIKE SOME RODENT?
... I AIN'T PUSHIN' SAWDUST IN YER WAY.
JUST DON'T LAY THAT CREEPING, 20TH CENTURY VEGETARIAN SENSIBILITY ON ME.
I HAPPEN TO LIKE IT CHEWY AND JUICY AND DRIBBLING DOWN MY CHIN....
I HAPPEN TO LIKE...
MEAT
© BY JOE SACCO 8·88

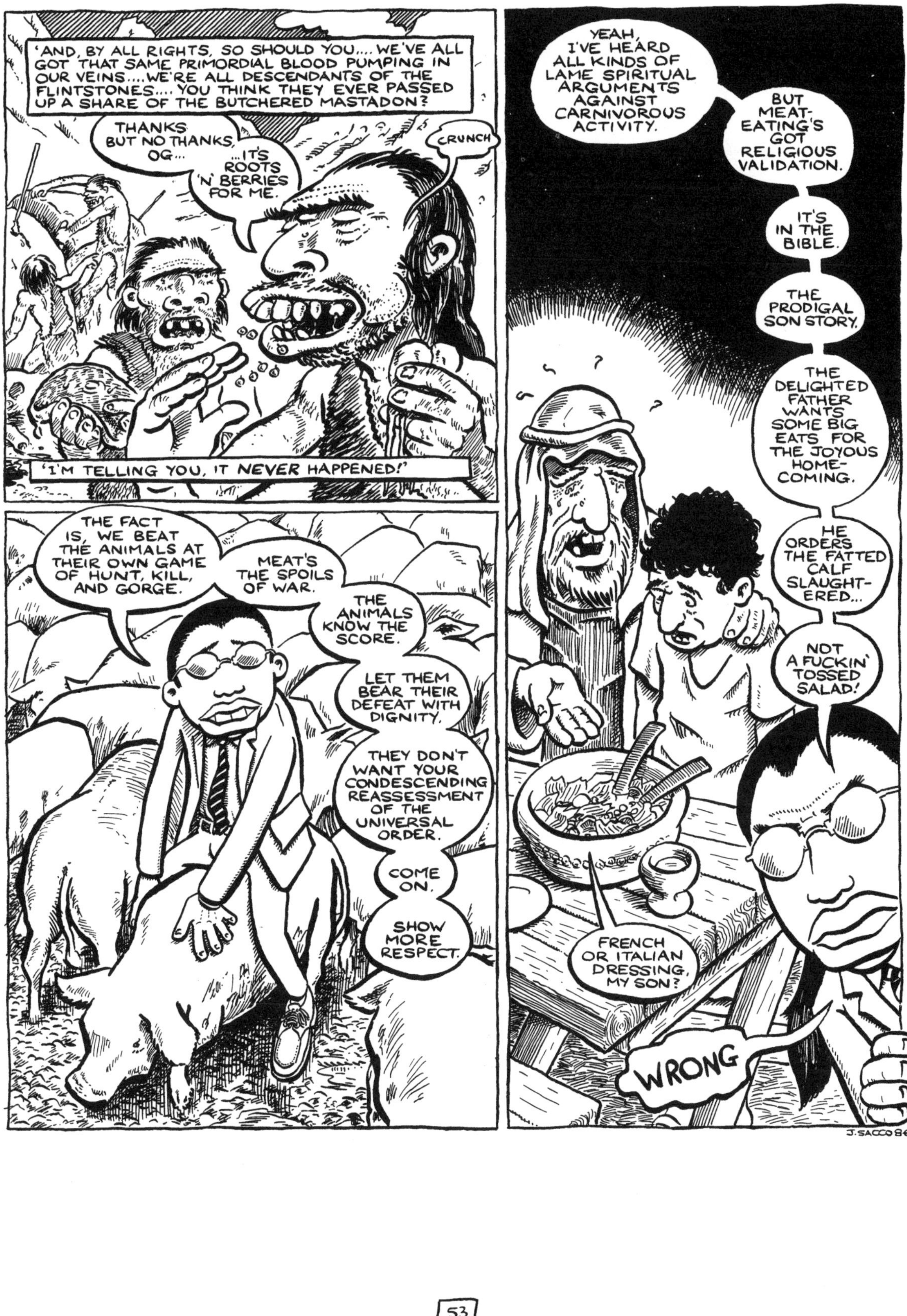
'AND, BY ALL RIGHTS, SO SHOULD YOU.... WE'VE ALL GOT THAT SAME PRIMORDIAL BLOOD PUMPING IN OUR VEINS.... WE'RE ALL DESCENDANTS OF THE FLINTSTONES.... YOU THINK THEY EVER PASSED UP A SHARE OF THE BUTCHERED MASTADON?
THANKS BUT NO THANKS, OG...
...IT'S ROOTS 'N' BERRIES FOR ME.
CRUNCH
'I'M TELLING YOU, IT NEVER HAPPENED!'
THE FACT IS, WE BEAT THE ANIMALS AT THEIR OWN GAME OF HUNT, KILL, AND GORGE.
MEAT'S THE SPOILS OF WAR.
THE ANIMALS KNOW THE SCORE.
LET THEM BEAR THEIR DEFEAT WITH DIGNITY.
THEY DON'T WANT YOUR CONDESCENDING REASSESSMENT OF THE UNIVERSAL ORDER.
COME ON.
SHOW MORE RESPECT.
YEAH, I'VE HEARD ALL KINDS OF LAME SPIRITUAL ARGUMENTS AGAINST CARNIVOROUS ACTIVITY.
BUT MEAT-EATING'S GOT RELIGIOUS VALIDATION.
IT'S IN THE BIBLE.
THE PRODIGAL SON STORY.
THE DELIGHTED FATHER WANTS SOME BIG EATS FOR THE JOYOUS HOMECOMING.
HE ORDERS THE FATTED CALF SLAUGHTERED...
NOT A FUCKIN' TOSSED SALAD!
FRENCH OR ITALIAN DRESSING, MY SON?
WRONG
J. SACCO 8-88

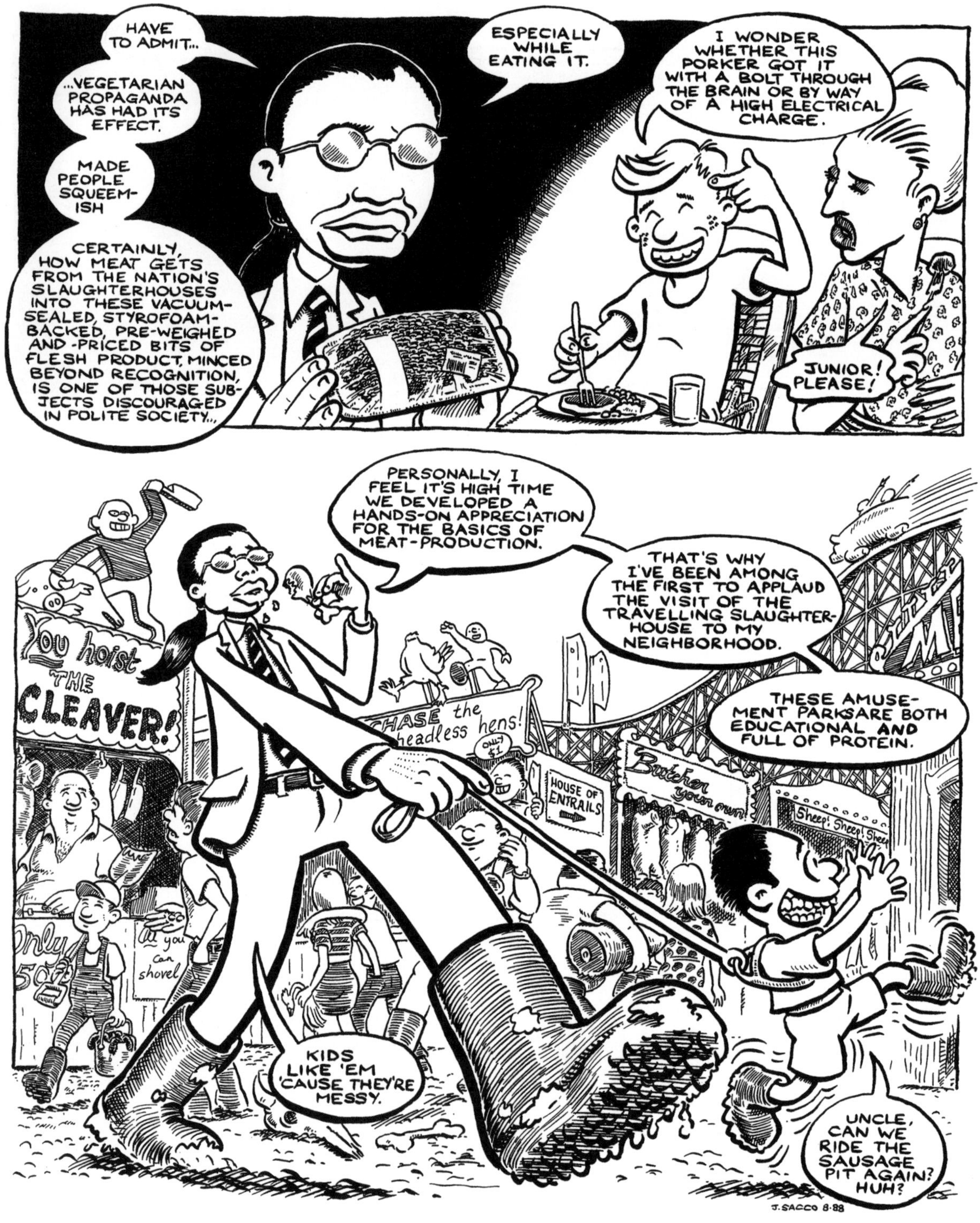
HAVE TO ADMIT...
...VEGETARIAN PROPAGANDA HAS HAD ITS EFFECT.
MADE PEOPLE SQUEEM-ISH
CERTAINLY, HOW MEAT GETS FROM THE NATION'S SLAUGHTERHOUSES INTO THESE VACUUM-SEALED, STYROFOAM-BACKED, PRE-WEIGHED AND -PRICED BITS OF FLESH PRODUCT, MINCED BEYOND RECOGNITION, IS ONE OF THOSE SUBJECTS DISCOURAGED IN POLITE SOCIETY...
ESPECIALLY WHILE EATING IT.
I WONDER WHETHER THIS PORKER GOT IT WITH A BOLT THROUGH THE BRAIN OR BY WAY OF A HIGH ELECTRICAL CHARGE.
JUNIOR! PLEASE!
PERSONALLY, I FEEL IT'S HIGH TIME WE DEVELOPED A HANDS-ON APPRECIATION FOR THE BASICS OF MEAT-PRODUCTION.
THAT'S WHY I'VE BEEN AMONG THE FIRST TO APPLAUD THE VISIT OF THE TRAVELLING SLAUGHTER-HOUSE TO MY NEIGHBORHOOD.
THESE AMUSEMENT PARKS ARE BOTH EDUCATIONAL AND FULL OF PROTEIN.
KIDS LIKE 'EM 'CAUSE THEY'RE MESSY.
UNCLE, CAN WE RIDE THE SAUSAGE PIT AGAIN? HUH?
You hoist THE CLEAVER!
CHASE the headless hens!
ONLY $1
HOUSE OF ENTRAILS
Butcher your own
Sheep! Sheep! Shee
All you can shovel
J. SACCO 8-88

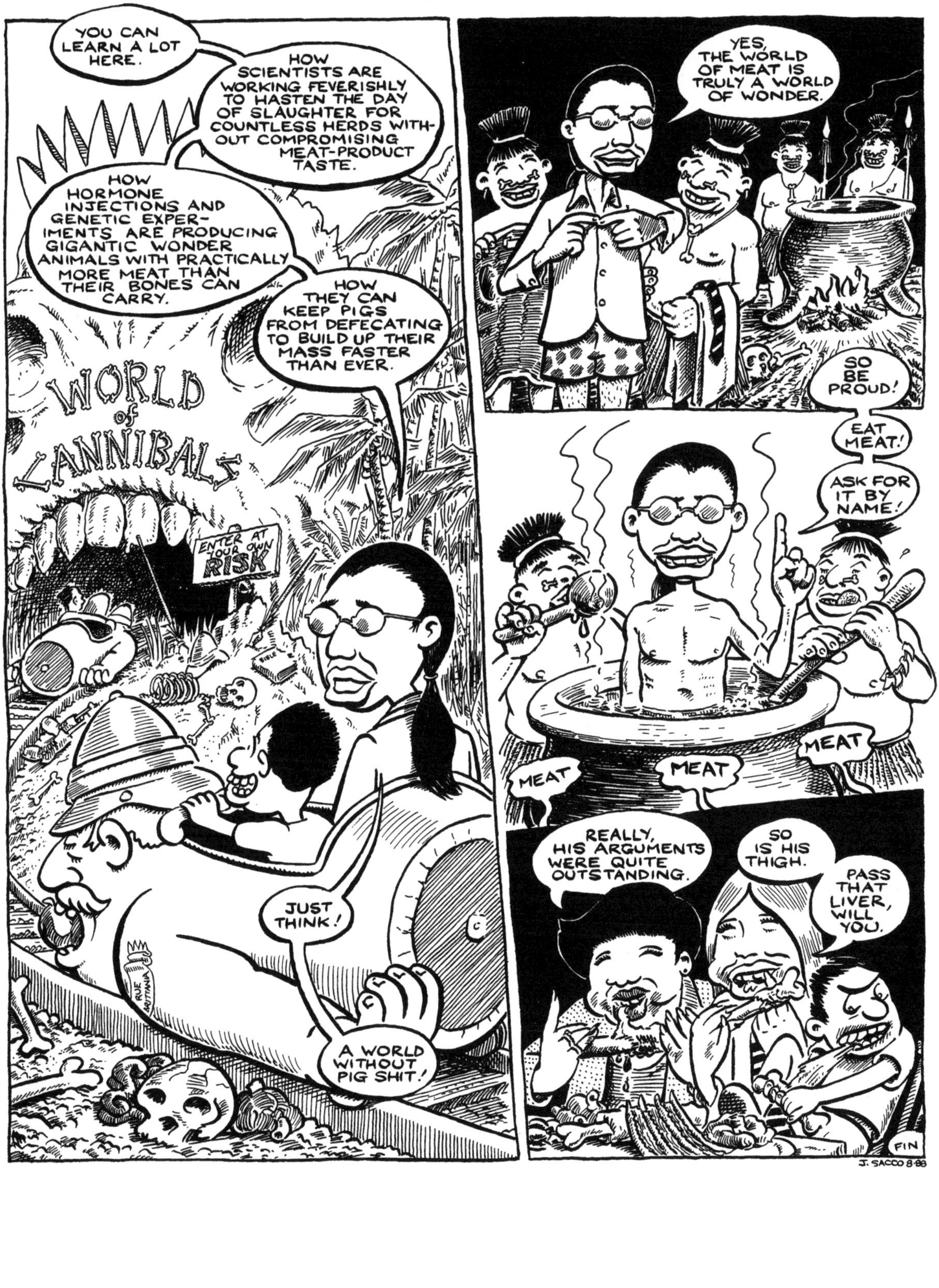
YOU CAN LEARN A LOT HERE.
HOW SCIENTISTS ARE WORKING FEVERISHLY TO HASTEN THE DAY OF SLAUGHTER FOR COUNTLESS HERDS WITHOUT COMPROMISING MEAT-PRODUCT TASTE.
HOW HORMONE INJECTIONS AND GENETIC EXPERIMENTS ARE PRODUCING GIGANTIC WONDER ANIMALS WITH PRACTICALLY MORE MEAT THAN THEIR BONES CAN CARRY.
HOW THEY CAN KEEP PIGS FROM DEFECATING TO BUILD UP THEIR MASS FASTER THAN EVER.
WORLD of CANNIBALS
ENTER AT YOUR OWN RISK
BIBLE
RUE BRITANNIA
JUST THINK!
A WORLD WITHOUT PIG SHIT!
YES, THE WORLD OF MEAT IS TRULY A WORLD OF WONDER.
SO BE PROUD!
EAT MEAT!
ASK FOR IT BY NAME!
MEAT
MEAT
MEAT
REALLY, HIS ARGUMENTS WERE QUITE OUTSTANDING.
SO IS HIS THIGH.
PASS THAT LIVER, WILL YOU.
FIN
J. SACCO 8-88

OKAY... I'LL ADMIT I'M A CYNICAL, HEARTLESS BASTARD WITH MISANTHROPIC TENDENCIES, BUT EVEN I HAVE A SOFT SPOT AND CAN WAX NOSTALGIC ABOUT FRIENDS OF YESTERYEAR, OL' PALS LIKE...

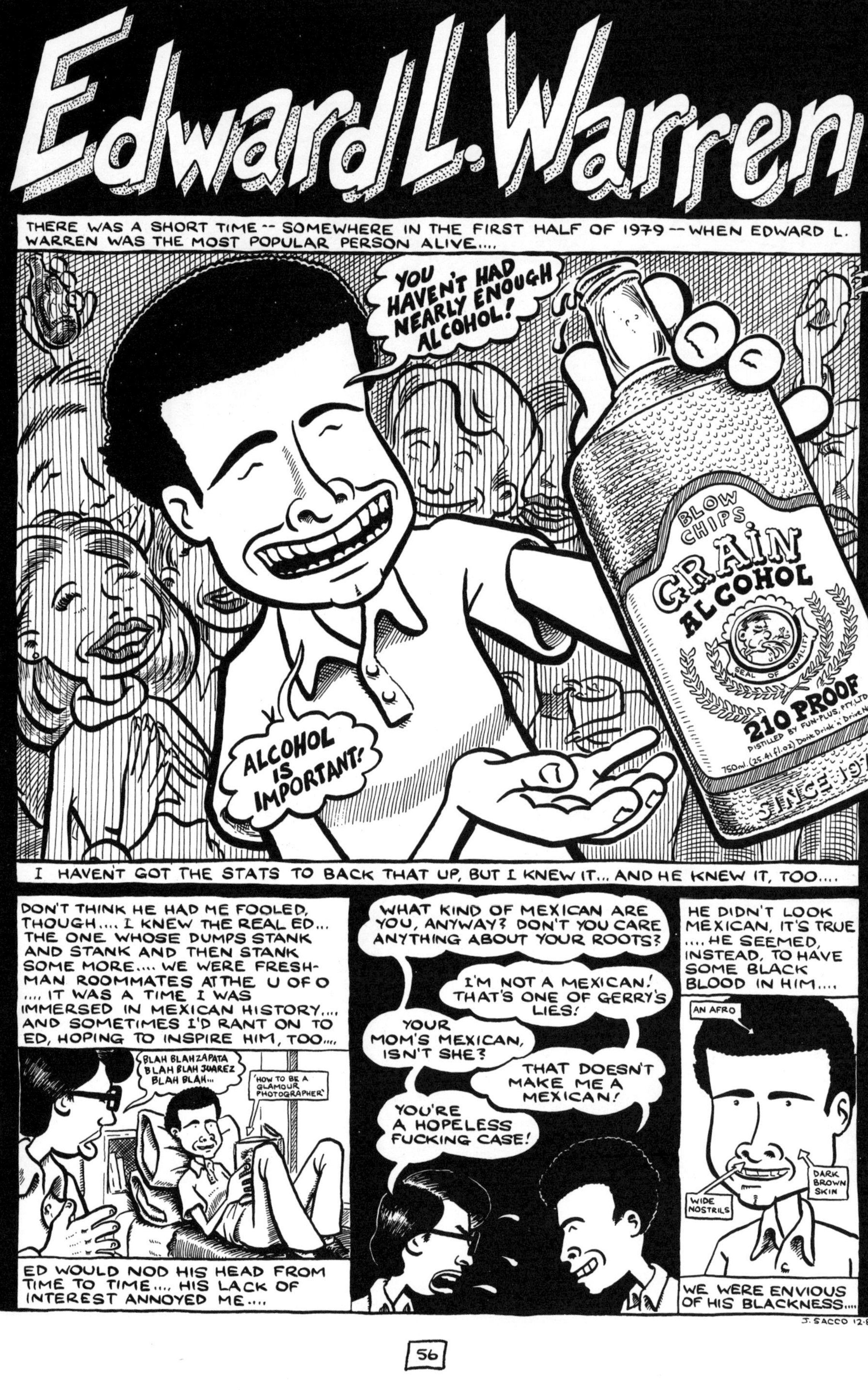
Edward L. Warren
THERE WAS A SHORT TIME -- SOMEWHERE IN THE FIRST HALF OF 1979 -- WHEN EDWARD L. WARREN WAS THE MOST POPULAR PERSON ALIVE....
YOU HAVEN'T HAD NEARLY ENOUGH ALCOHOL!
ALCOHOL IS IMPORTANT!
BLOW CHIPS
GRAIN ALCOHOL
SEAL OF QUALITY
210 PROOF
DISTILLED BY FUN-PLUS, PTY. LTD.
SINCE 1975
I HAVEN'T GOT THE STATS TO BACK THAT UP, BUT I KNEW IT... AND HE KNEW IT, TOO....
DON'T THINK HE HAD ME FOOLED, THOUGH.... I KNEW THE REAL ED... THE ONE WHOSE DUMPS STANK AND STANK AND THEN STANK SOME MORE.... WE WERE FRESHMAN ROOMMATES AT THE U OF O .... IT WAS A TIME I WAS IMMERSED IN MEXICAN HISTORY.... AND SOMETIMES I'D RANT ON TO ED, HOPING TO INSPIRE HIM, TOO....
BLAH BLAH ZAPATA BLAH BLAH JUAREZ BLAH BLAH...
'HOW TO BE A GLAMOUR PHOTOGRAPHER'
ED WOULD NOD HIS HEAD FROM TIME TO TIME.... HIS LACK OF INTEREST ANNOYED ME....
WHAT KIND OF MEXICAN ARE YOU, ANYWAY? DON'T YOU CARE ANYTHING ABOUT YOUR ROOTS?
I'M NOT A MEXICAN! THAT'S ONE OF GERRY'S LIES!
YOUR MOM'S MEXICAN, ISN'T SHE?
THAT DOESN'T MAKE ME A MEXICAN!
YOU'RE A HOPELESS FUCKING CASE!
HE DIDN'T LOOK MEXICAN, IT'S TRUE .... HE SEEMED, INSTEAD, TO HAVE SOME BLACK BLOOD IN HIM....
AN AFRO
DARK BROWN SKIN
WIDE NOSTRILS
WE WERE ENVIOUS OF HIS BLACKNESS....

J. SACCO 12·87

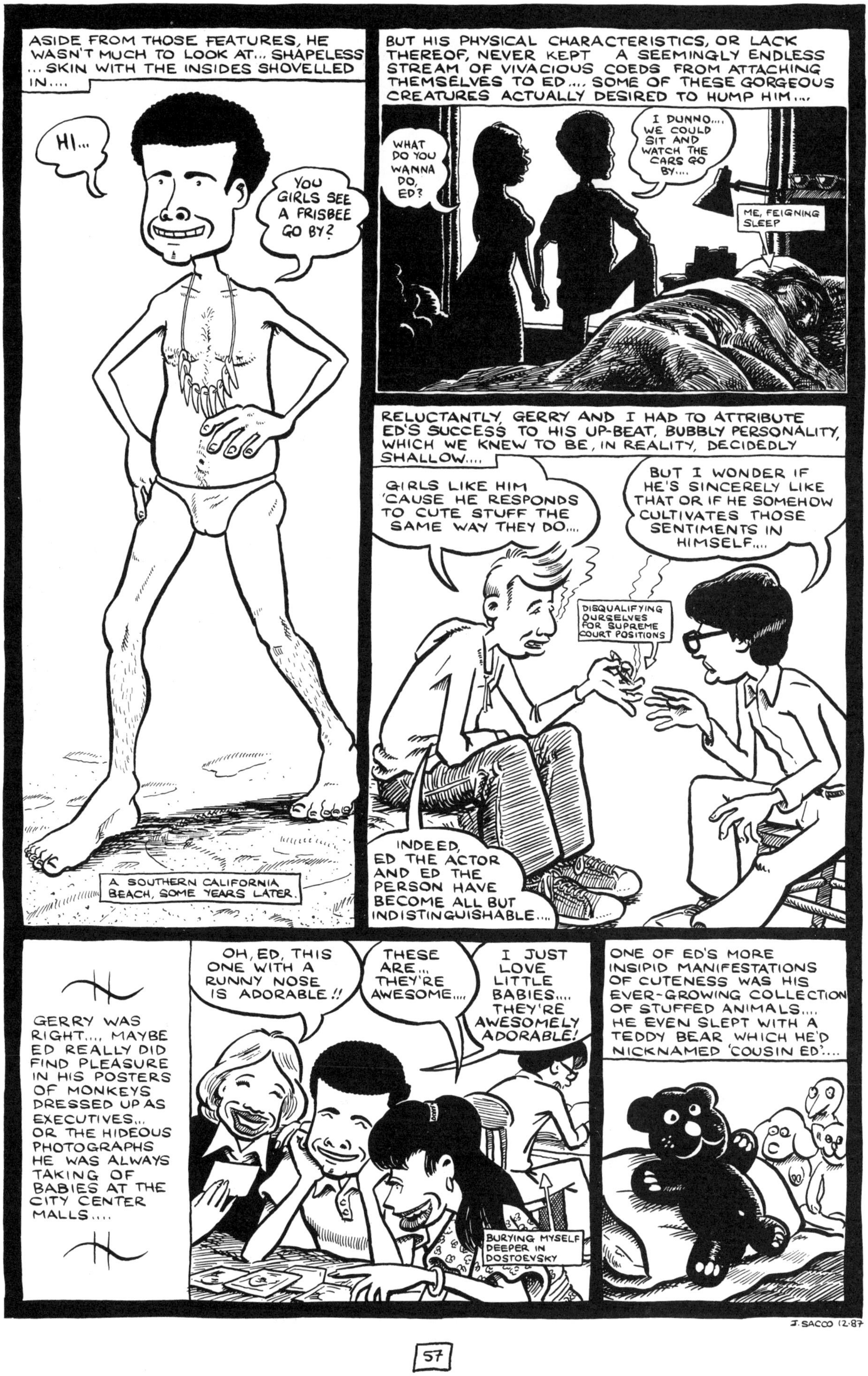

ASIDE FROM THOSE FEATURES, HE WASN'T MUCH TO LOOK AT... SHAPELESS ...SKIN WITH THE INSIDES SHOVELLED IN....
HI...
YOU GIRLS SEE A FRISBEE GO BY?
A SOUTHERN CALIFORNIA BEACH, SOME YEARS LATER.
BUT HIS PHYSICAL CHARACTERISTICS, OR LACK THEREOF, NEVER KEPT A SEEMINGLY ENDLESS STREAM OF VIVACIOUS COEDS FROM ATTACHING THEMSELVES TO ED.... SOME OF THESE GORGEOUS CREATURES ACTUALLY DESIRED TO HUMP HIM....
WHAT DO YOU WANNA DO, ED?
I DUNNO.... WE COULD SIT AND WATCH THE CARS GO BY....
ME, FEIGNING SLEEP
RELUCTANTLY, GERRY AND I HAD TO ATTRIBUTE ED'S SUCCESS TO HIS UP-BEAT, BUBBLY PERSONALITY, WHICH WE KNEW TO BE, IN REALITY, DECIDEDLY SHALLOW....
GIRLS LIKE HIM 'CAUSE HE RESPONDS TO CUTE STUFF THE SAME WAY THEY DO....
BUT I WONDER IF HE'S SINCERELY LIKE THAT OR IF HE SOMEHOW CULTIVATES THOSE SENTIMENTS IN HIMSELF....
DISQUALIFYING OURSELVES FOR SUPREME COURT POSITIONS
INDEED, ED THE ACTOR AND ED THE PERSON HAVE BECOME ALL BUT INDISTINGUISHABLE....
GERRY WAS RIGHT...., MAYBE ED REALLY DID FIND PLEASURE IN HIS POSTERS OF MONKEYS DRESSED UP AS EXECUTIVES... OR THE HIDEOUS PHOTOGRAPHS HE WAS ALWAYS TAKING OF BABIES AT THE CITY CENTER MALLS....
OH, ED, THIS ONE WITH A RUNNY NOSE IS ADORABLE!!
THESE ARE... THEY'RE AWESOME....
I JUST LOVE LITTLE BABIES.... THEY'RE AWESOMELY ADORABLE!
BURYING MYSELF DEEPER IN DOSTOEVSKY
ONE OF ED'S MORE INSIPID MANIFESTATIONS OF CUTENESS WAS HIS EVER-GROWING COLLECTION OF STUFFED ANIMALS.... HE EVEN SLEPT WITH A TEDDY BEAR WHICH HE'D NICKNAMED 'COUSIN ED'....
J. SACCO 12·87

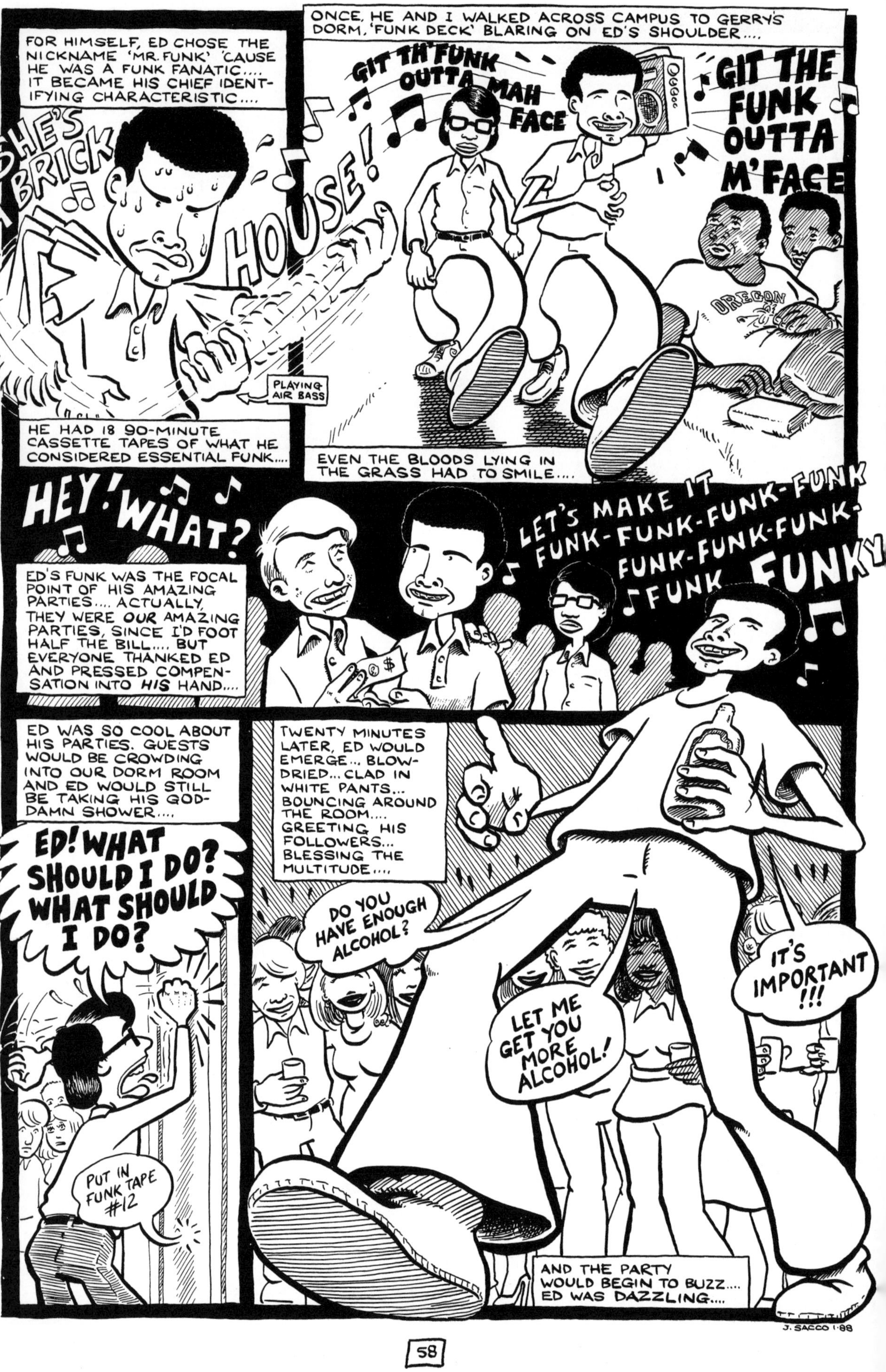
FOR HIMSELF, ED CHOSE THE NICKNAME 'MR. FUNK' 'CAUSE HE WAS A FUNK FANATIC.... IT BECAME HIS CHIEF IDENTIFYING CHARACTERISTIC....
SHE'S A BRICK HOUSE!
PLAYING AIR BASS
HE HAD 18 90-MINUTE CASSETTE TAPES OF WHAT HE CONSIDERED ESSENTIAL FUNK....
ONCE, HE AND I WALKED ACROSS CAMPUS TO GERRY'S DORM, 'FUNK DECK' BLARING ON ED'S SHOULDER....
GIT TH' FUNK OUTTA MAH FACE
GIT THE FUNK OUTTA M'FACE
OREGON
EVEN THE BLOODS LYING IN THE GRASS HAD TO SMILE....
HEY! WHAT?
LET'S MAKE IT FUNK-FUNK-FUNK-FUNK FUNK-FUNK-FUNK-FUNK-FUNK FUNK-FUNK FUNKY
ED'S FUNK WAS THE FOCAL POINT OF HIS AMAZING PARTIES.... ACTUALLY, THEY WERE OUR AMAZING PARTIES, SINCE I'D FOOT HALF THE BILL.... BUT EVERYONE THANKED ED AND PRESSED COMPENSATION INTO HIS HAND....
ED WAS SO COOL ABOUT HIS PARTIES. GUESTS WOULD BE CROWDING INTO OUR DORM ROOM AND ED WOULD STILL BE TAKING HIS GOD-DAMN SHOWER....
ED! WHAT SHOULD I DO? WHAT SHOULD I DO?
PUT IN FUNK TAPE #12
TWENTY MINUTES LATER, ED WOULD EMERGE... BLOW-DRIED... CLAD IN WHITE PANTS... BOUNCING AROUND THE ROOM... GREETING HIS FOLLOWERS... BLESSING THE MULTITUDE....
DO YOU HAVE ENOUGH ALCOHOL?
LET ME GET YOU MORE ALCOHOL!
IT'S IMPORTANT!!!
AND THE PARTY WOULD BEGIN TO BUZZ.... ED WAS DAZZLING....
J. SACCO 1·88

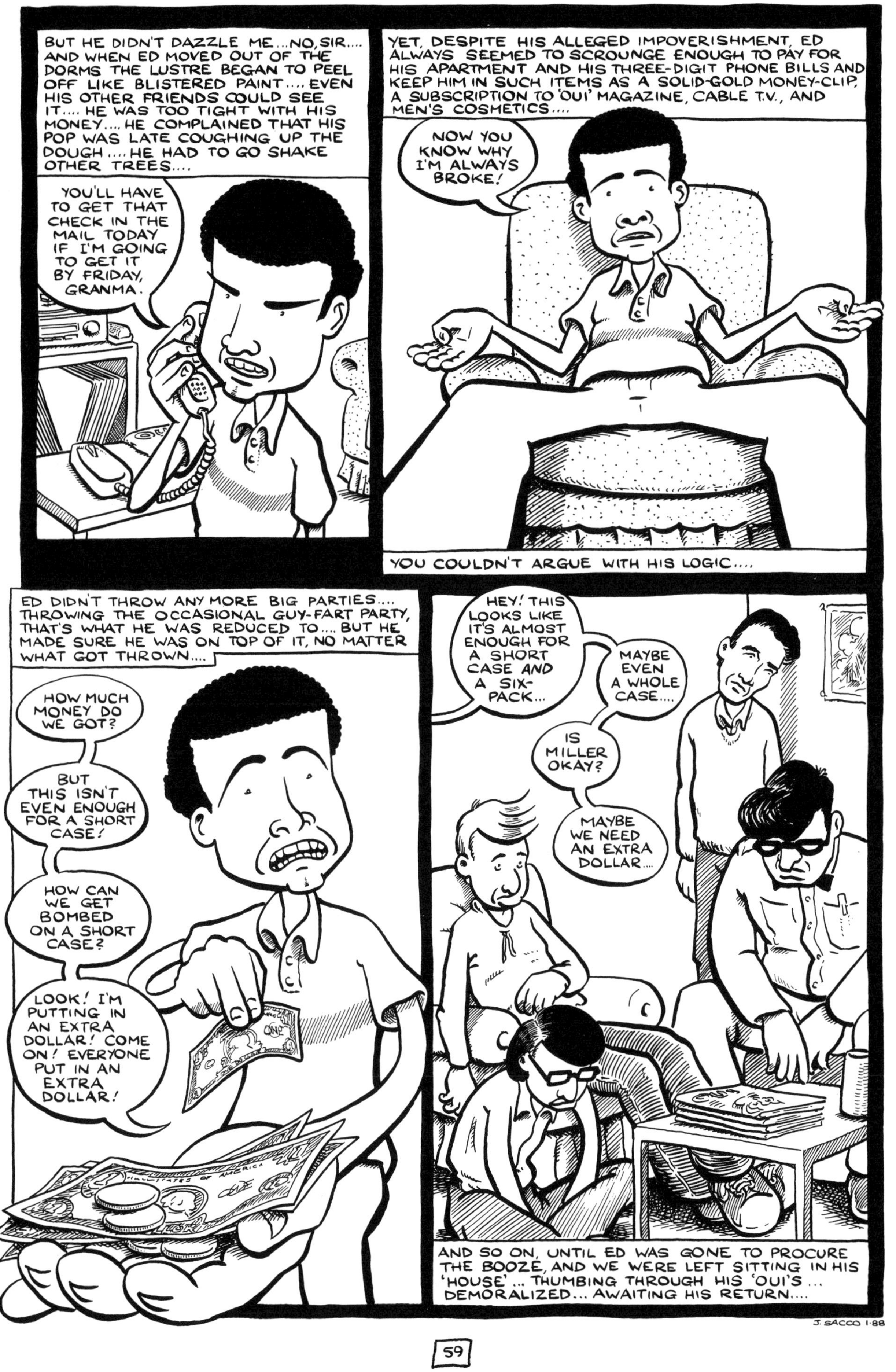

BUT HE DIDN'T DAZZLE ME...NO, SIR.... AND WHEN ED MOVED OUT OF THE DORMS THE LUSTRE BEGAN TO PEEL OFF LIKE BLISTERED PAINT.... EVEN HIS OTHER FRIENDS COULD SEE IT.... HE WAS TOO TIGHT WITH HIS MONEY.... HE COMPLAINED THAT HIS POP WAS LATE COUGHING UP THE DOUGH.... HE HAD TO GO SHAKE OTHER TREES....
YOU'LL HAVE TO GET THAT CHECK IN THE MAIL TODAY IF I'M GOING TO GET IT BY FRIDAY, GRANMA.
YET, DESPITE HIS ALLEGED IMPOVERISHMENT, ED ALWAYS SEEMED TO SCROUNGE ENOUGH TO PAY FOR HIS APARTMENT AND HIS THREE-DIGIT PHONE BILLS AND KEEP HIM IN SUCH ITEMS AS A SOLID-GOLD MONEY-CLIP, A SUBSCRIPTION TO 'OUI' MAGAZINE, CABLE T.V., AND MEN'S COSMETICS....
NOW YOU KNOW WHY I'M ALWAYS BROKE!
YOU COULDN'T ARGUE WITH HIS LOGIC....
ED DIDN'T THROW ANY MORE BIG PARTIES.... THROWING THE OCCASIONAL GUY-FART PARTY, THAT'S WHAT HE WAS REDUCED TO.... BUT HE MADE SURE HE WAS ON TOP OF IT, NO MATTER WHAT GOT THROWN....
HOW MUCH MONEY DO WE GOT?
BUT THIS ISN'T EVEN ENOUGH FOR A SHORT CASE!
HOW CAN WE GET BOMBED ON A SHORT CASE?
LOOK! I'M PUTTING IN AN EXTRA DOLLAR! COME ON! EVERYONE PUT IN AN EXTRA DOLLAR!
HEY! THIS LOOKS LIKE IT'S ALMOST ENOUGH FOR A SHORT CASE AND A SIX-PACK...
MAYBE EVEN A WHOLE CASE....
IS MILLER OKAY?
MAYBE WE NEED AN EXTRA DOLLAR....
AND SO ON, UNTIL ED WAS GONE TO PROCURE THE BOOZE, AND WE WERE LEFT SITTING IN HIS 'HOUSE'... THUMBING THROUGH HIS 'OUI'S... DEMORALIZED... AWAITING HIS RETURN....
J. SACCO 1·88

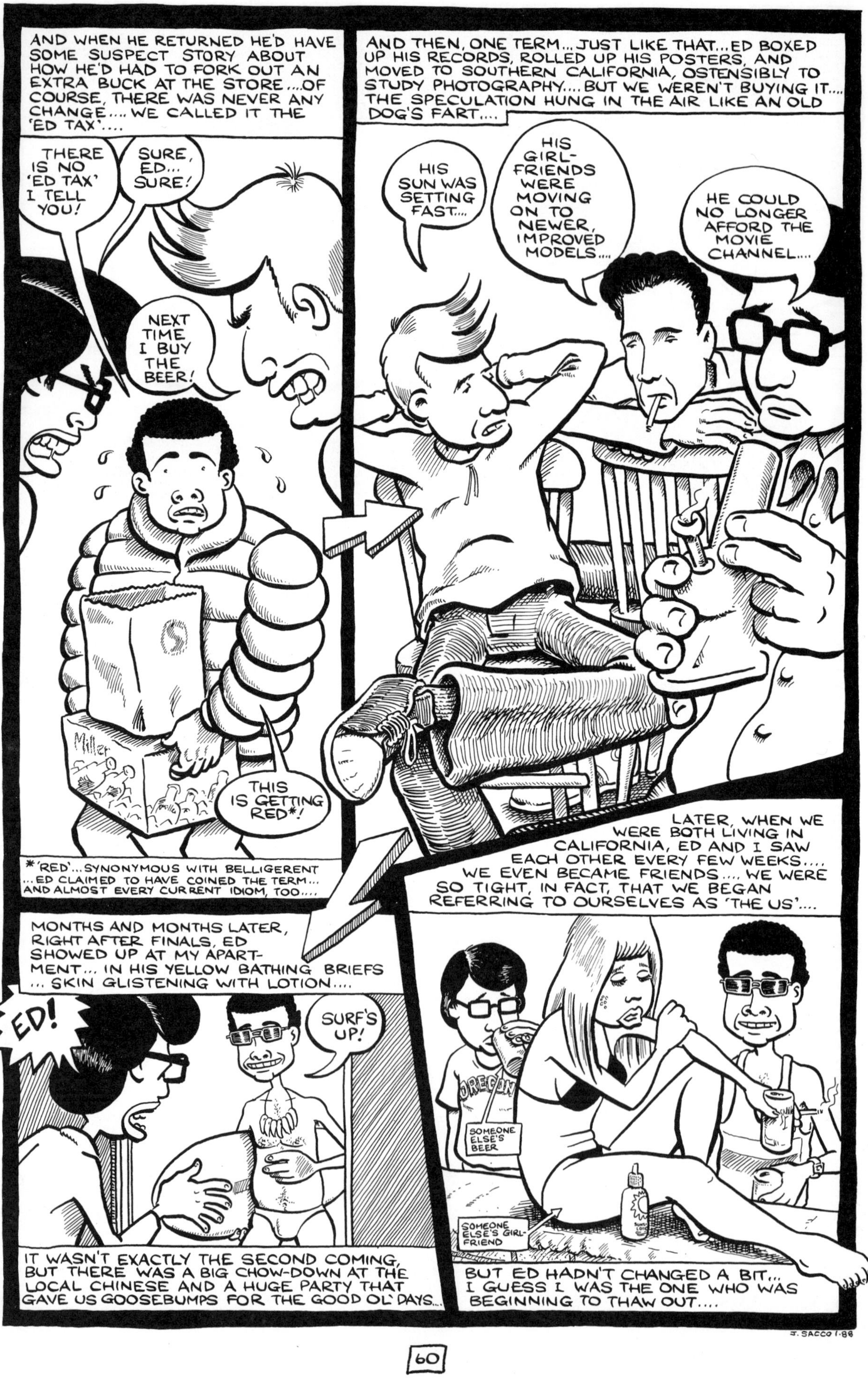
AND WHEN HE RETURNED HE'D HAVE SOME SUSPECT STORY ABOUT HOW HE'D HAD TO FORK OUT AN EXTRA BUCK AT THE STORE....OF COURSE, THERE WAS NEVER ANY CHANGE.... WE CALLED IT THE 'ED TAX'....
THERE IS NO 'ED TAX' I TELL YOU!
SURE, ED... SURE!
NEXT TIME I BUY THE BEER!
THIS IS GETTING RED*!
Miller
*'RED'...SYNONYMOUS WITH BELLIGERENT ...ED CLAIMED TO HAVE COINED THE TERM... AND ALMOST EVERY CURRENT IDIOM, TOO....
AND THEN, ONE TERM... JUST LIKE THAT...ED BOXED UP HIS RECORDS, ROLLED UP HIS POSTERS, AND MOVED TO SOUTHERN CALIFORNIA, OSTENSIBLY TO STUDY PHOTOGRAPHY.... BUT WE WEREN'T BUYING IT.... THE SPECULATION HUNG IN THE AIR LIKE AN OLD DOG'S FART....
HIS SUN WAS SETTING FAST....
HIS GIRL-FRIENDS WERE MOVING ON TO NEWER, IMPROVED MODELS....
HE COULD NO LONGER AFFORD THE MOVIE CHANNEL....
MONTHS AND MONTHS LATER, RIGHT AFTER FINALS, ED SHOWED UP AT MY APART-MENT... IN HIS YELLOW BATHING BRIEFS ... SKIN GLISTENING WITH LOTION....
ED!
SURF'S UP!
IT WASN'T EXACTLY THE SECOND COMING, BUT THERE WAS A BIG CHOW-DOWN AT THE LOCAL CHINESE AND A HUGE PARTY THAT GAVE US GOOSEBUMPS FOR THE GOOD OL' DAYS...
LATER, WHEN WE WERE BOTH LIVING IN CALIFORNIA, ED AND I SAW EACH OTHER EVERY FEW WEEKS.... WE EVEN BECAME FRIENDS.... WE WERE SO TIGHT, IN FACT, THAT WE BEGAN REFERRING TO OURSELVES AS 'THE US'....
OREGON
SOMEONE ELSE'S BEER
SOMEONE ELSE'S GIRL-FRIEND
BUT ED HADN'T CHANGED A BIT... I GUESS I WAS THE ONE WHO WAS BEGINNING TO THAW OUT....
J. SACCO 1·88

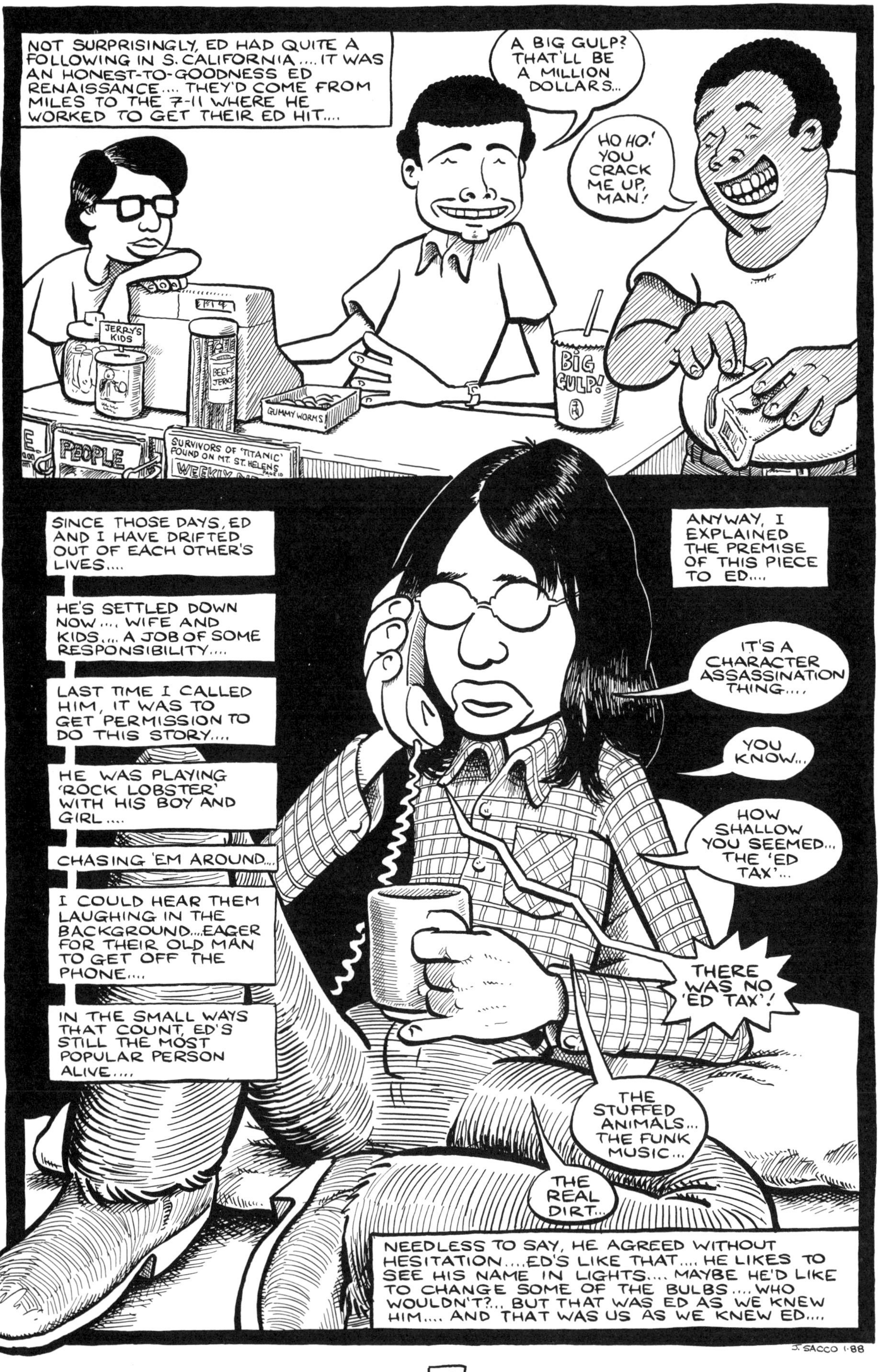
NOT SURPRISINGLY, ED HAD QUITE A FOLLOWING IN S. CALIFORNIA.... IT WAS AN HONEST-TO-GOODNESS ED RENAISSANCE.... THEY'D COME FROM MILES TO THE 7-11 WHERE HE WORKED TO GET THEIR ED HIT....
A BIG GULP? THAT'LL BE A MILLION DOLLARS...
HO HO! YOU CRACK ME UP, MAN!
JERRY'S KIDS
BEEF JERKY
GUMMY WORMS
BIG GULP!
PEOPLE
SURVIVORS OF 'TITANIC' FOUND ON MT. ST. HELENS
SINCE THOSE DAYS, ED AND I HAVE DRIFTED OUT OF EACH OTHER'S LIVES....
HE'S SETTLED DOWN NOW.... WIFE AND KIDS.... A JOB OF SOME RESPONSIBILITY....
LAST TIME I CALLED HIM, IT WAS TO GET PERMISSION TO DO THIS STORY....
HE WAS PLAYING 'ROCK LOBSTER' WITH HIS BOY AND GIRL....
CHASING 'EM AROUND...
I COULD HEAR THEM LAUGHING IN THE BACKGROUND.... EAGER FOR THEIR OLD MAN TO GET OFF THE PHONE....
IN THE SMALL WAYS THAT COUNT, ED'S STILL THE MOST POPULAR PERSON ALIVE....
ANYWAY, I EXPLAINED THE PREMISE OF THIS PIECE TO ED....
IT'S A CHARACTER ASSASSINATION THING....
YOU KNOW...
HOW SHALLOW YOU SEEMED... THE 'ED TAX'...
THERE WAS NO 'ED TAX'!
THE STUFFED ANIMALS... THE FUNK MUSIC...
THE REAL DIRT...
NEEDLESS TO SAY, HE AGREED WITHOUT HESITATION.... ED'S LIKE THAT.... HE LIKES TO SEE HIS NAME IN LIGHTS.... MAYBE HE'D LIKE TO CHANGE SOME OF THE BULBS.... WHO WOULDN'T?... BUT THAT WAS ED AS WE KNEW HIM.... AND THAT WAS US AS WE KNEW ED....
J. SACCO 1-88

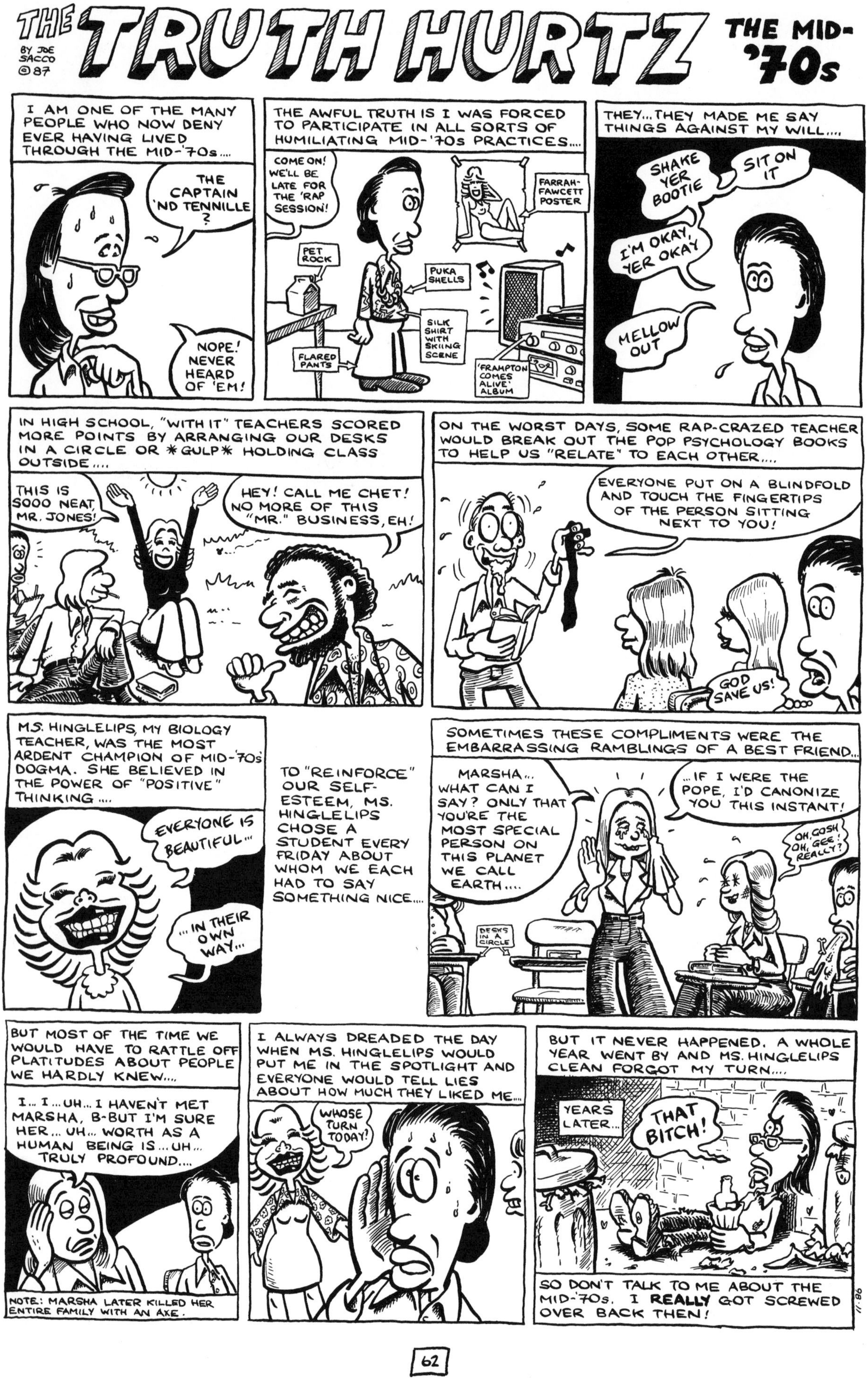
THE TRUTH HURTZ
BY JOE SACCO ©87
THE MID-'70s
I AM ONE OF THE MANY PEOPLE WHO NOW DENY EVER HAVING LIVED THROUGH THE MID-'70s....
THE CAPTAIN 'ND TENNILLE?
NOPE! NEVER HEARD OF 'EM!
THE AWFUL TRUTH IS I WAS FORCED TO PARTICIPATE IN ALL SORTS OF HUMILIATING MID-'70s PRACTICES....
COME ON! WE'LL BE LATE FOR THE 'RAP SESSION'!
FARRAH-FAWCETT POSTER
PET ROCK
PUKA SHELLS
SILK SHIRT WITH SKIING SCENE
FLARED PANTS
'FRAMPTON COMES ALIVE' ALBUM
THEY... THEY MADE ME SAY THINGS AGAINST MY WILL....
SHAKE YER BOOTIE
SIT ON IT
I'M OKAY, YER OKAY
MELLOW OUT
IN HIGH SCHOOL, "WITH IT" TEACHERS SCORED MORE POINTS BY ARRANGING OUR DESKS IN A CIRCLE OR *GULP* HOLDING CLASS OUTSIDE....
THIS IS SOOO NEAT, MR. JONES!
HEY! CALL ME CHET! NO MORE OF THIS "MR." BUSINESS, EH!
ON THE WORST DAYS, SOME RAP-CRAZED TEACHER WOULD BREAK OUT THE POP PSYCHOLOGY BOOKS TO HELP US "RELATE" TO EACH OTHER....
EVERYONE PUT ON A BLINDFOLD AND TOUCH THE FINGERTIPS OF THE PERSON SITTING NEXT TO YOU!
GOD SAVE US!
MS. HINGLELIPS, MY BIOLOGY TEACHER, WAS THE MOST ARDENT CHAMPION OF MID-'70s DOGMA. SHE BELIEVED IN THE POWER OF "POSITIVE" THINKING....
EVERYONE IS BEAUTIFUL...
...IN THEIR OWN WAY...
TO "REINFORCE" OUR SELF-ESTEEM, MS. HINGLELIPS CHOSE A STUDENT EVERY FRIDAY ABOUT WHOM WE EACH HAD TO SAY SOMETHING NICE....
SOMETIMES THESE COMPLIMENTS WERE THE EMBARRASSING RAMBLINGS OF A BEST FRIEND...
MARSHA... WHAT CAN I SAY? ONLY THAT YOU'RE THE MOST SPECIAL PERSON ON THIS PLANET WE CALL EARTH....
...IF I WERE THE POPE, I'D CANONIZE YOU THIS INSTANT!
OH, GOSH! OH, GEE! REALLY?
DESKS IN A CIRCLE
BUT MOST OF THE TIME WE WOULD HAVE TO RATTLE OFF PLATITUDES ABOUT PEOPLE WE HARDLY KNEW....
I... I... UH... I HAVEN'T MET MARSHA, B-BUT I'M SURE HER... UH... WORTH AS A HUMAN BEING IS... UH... TRULY PROFOUND....
NOTE: MARSHA LATER KILLED HER ENTIRE FAMILY WITH AN AXE.
I ALWAYS DREADED THE DAY WHEN MS. HINGLELIPS WOULD PUT ME IN THE SPOTLIGHT AND EVERYONE WOULD TELL LIES ABOUT HOW MUCH THEY LIKED ME....
WHOSE TURN TODAY?
BUT IT NEVER HAPPENED. A WHOLE YEAR WENT BY AND MS. HINGLELIPS CLEAN FORGOT MY TURN....
YEARS LATER...
THAT BITCH!
SO DON'T TALK TO ME ABOUT THE MID-'70s. I REALLY GOT SCREWED OVER BACK THEN!
11/86

PART FOUR:

IN THE COMPANY OF LONG HAIR

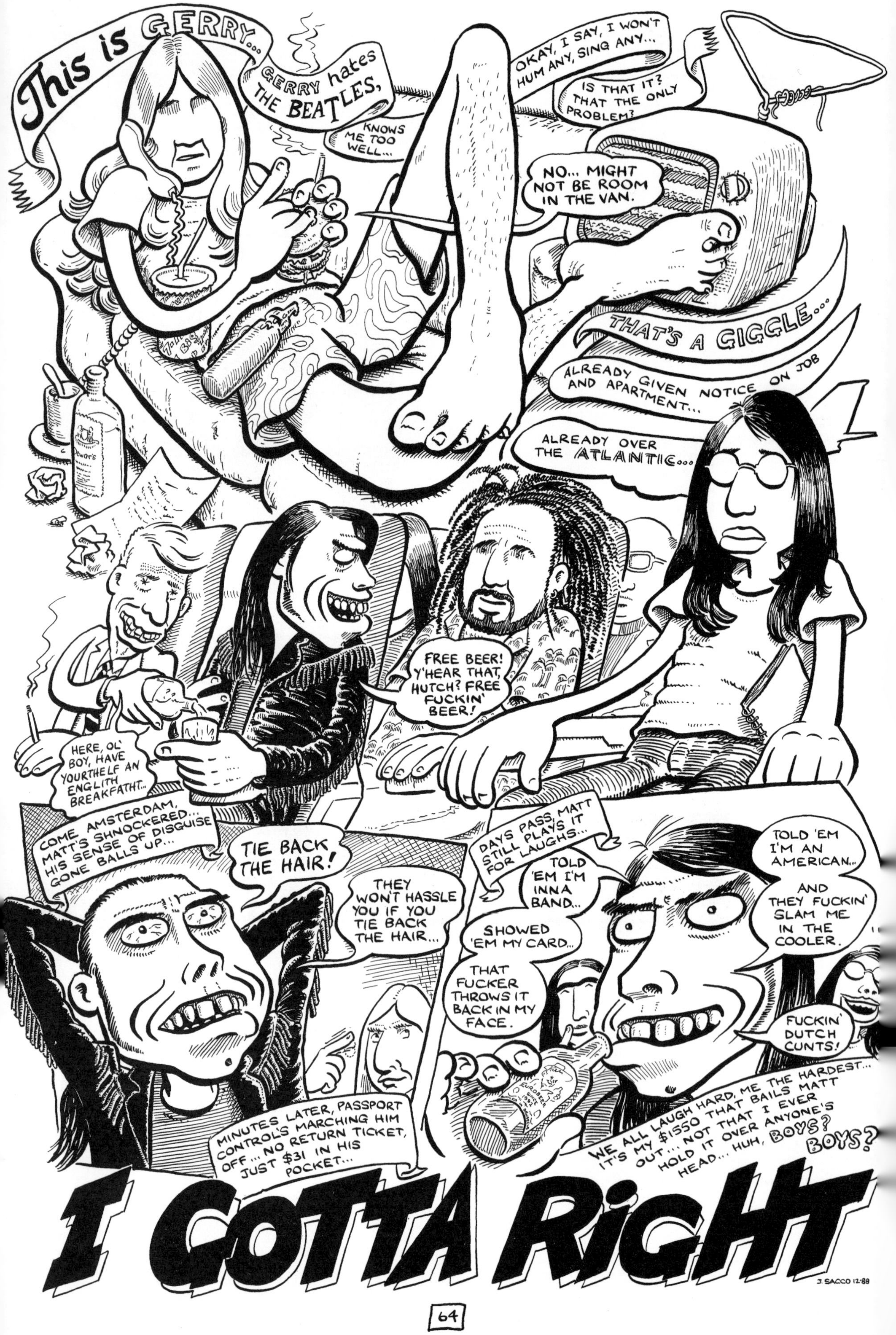
This is GERRY...
GERRY hates THE BEATLES,
KNOWS ME TOO WELL...
OKAY, I SAY, I WON'T HUM ANY, SING ANY...
IS THAT IT? THAT THE ONLY PROBLEM?
NO... MIGHT NOT BE ROOM IN THE VAN.
THAT'S A GIGGLE...
ALREADY GIVEN NOTICE ON JOB AND APARTMENT...
ALREADY OVER THE ATLANTIC...
FREE BEER! Y'HEAR THAT, HUTCH? FREE FUCKIN' BEER!
HERE, OL' BOY, HAVE YOURTHELF AN ENGLITH BREAKFATHT...
COME AMSTERDAM, MATT'S SHNOCKERED... HIS SENSE OF DISGUISE GONE BALLS UP...
TIE BACK THE HAIR!
THEY WON'T HASSLE YOU IF YOU TIE BACK THE HAIR...
MINUTES LATER, PASSPORT CONTROL'S MARCHING HIM OFF... NO RETURN TICKET, JUST $31 IN HIS POCKET...
DAYS PASS, MATT STILL PLAYS IT FOR LAUGHS...
TOLD 'EM I'M INNA BAND...
SHOWED 'EM MY CARD...
THAT FUCKER THROWS IT BACK IN MY FACE.
TOLD 'EM I'M AN AMERICAN...
AND THEY FUCKIN' SLAM ME IN THE COOLER.
FUCKIN' DUTCH CUNTS!
WE ALL LAUGH HARD, ME THE HARDEST... IT'S MY $1550 THAT BAILS MATT OUT... NOT THAT I EVER HOLD IT OVER ANYONE'S HEAD... HUH, BOYS? BOYS?
I GOTTA RIGHT
J. SACCO 12-88

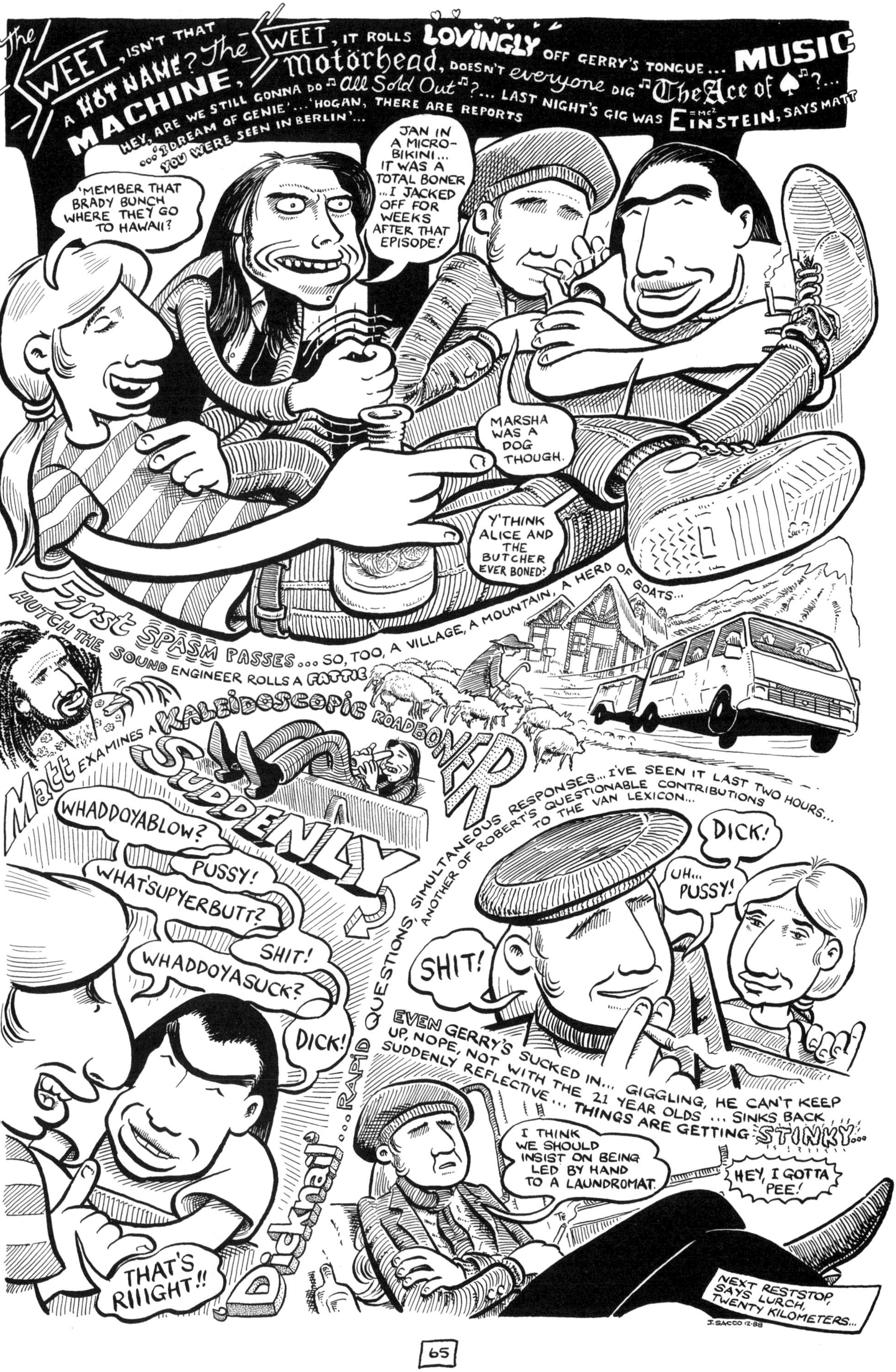
The SWEET, isn't that a HOT NAME? The SWEET, it rolls LOVINGLY off Gerry's tongue... MUSIC MACHINE, motörhead, doesn't everyone dig ♫The Ace of ♠♫?... Hey, are we still gonna do ♫All Sold Out♫?... Last night's gig was E=mc² EINSTEIN, says Matt
...'I Dream of Genie'...'Hogan, there are reports you were seen in Berlin'...
'MEMBER THAT BRADY BUNCH WHERE THEY GO TO HAWAII?
JAN IN A MICRO-BIKINI... IT WAS A TOTAL BONER ...I JACKED OFF FOR WEEKS AFTER THAT EPISODE!
MARSHA WAS A DOG THOUGH.
Y'THINK ALICE AND THE BUTCHER EVER BONED?
First SPASM passes... so, too, a village, a mountain, a herd of goats...
Hutch the sound engineer rolls a FATTIE
Matt examines a KALEIDOSCOPIC ROADBONER
SUDDENLY
WHADDOYABLOW?
PUSSY!
WHAT'SUPYERBUTT?
SHIT!
WHADDOYASUCK?
DICK!
...Rapid questions, simultaneous responses... I've seen it last two hours... another of Robert's questionable contributions to the van lexicon...
DICK!
UH... PUSSY!
SHIT!
Even Gerry's sucked in... giggling, he can't keep up, nope, not with the 21 year olds... sinks back, suddenly reflective... things are getting STINKY...
Dickmail
THAT'S RIIIGHT!!
I THINK WE SHOULD INSIST ON BEING LED BY HAND TO A LAUNDROMAT.
HEY, I GOTTA PEE!
Next reststop, says Lurch, twenty kilometers...
J. SACCO 12.88

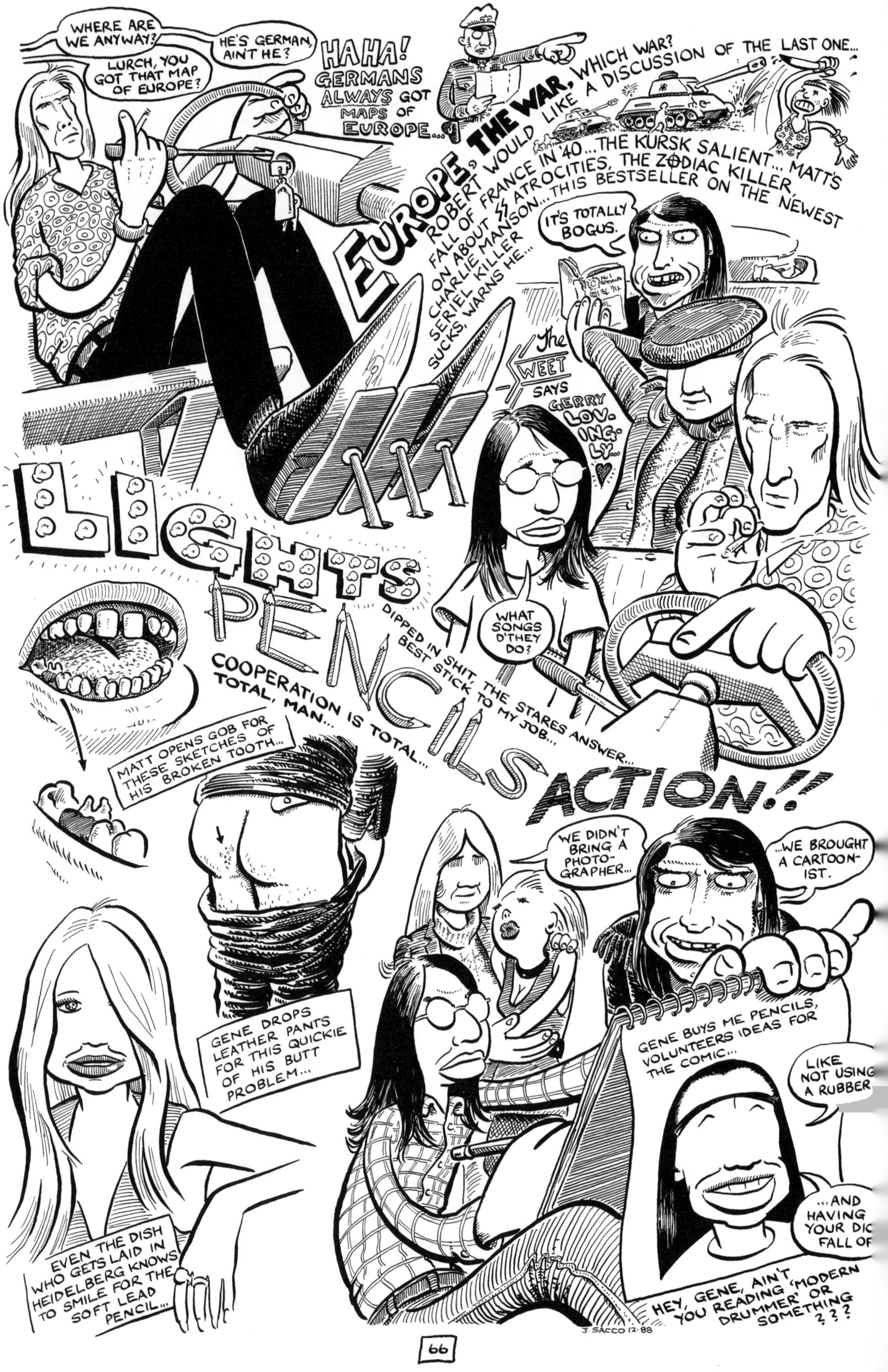
WHERE ARE WE ANYWAY?
LURCH, YOU GOT THAT MAP OF EUROPE?
HE'S GERMAN, AIN'T HE?
HAHA! GERMANS ALWAYS GOT MAPS OF EUROPE...
EUROPE, THE WAR, WHICH WAR? ROBERT WOULD LIKE A DISCUSSION OF THE LAST ONE... FALL OF FRANCE IN '40... THE KURSK SALIENT... MATT'S ON ABOUT SS ATROCITIES, THE ZODIAC KILLER, CHARLIE MANSON... THIS BESTSELLER ON THE NEWEST SERIEL KILLER SUCKS, WARNS HE...
IT'S TOTALLY BOGUS.
The SWEET SAYS GERRY LOV-ING-LY...
LIGHTS
PENCILS
ACTION!!
WHAT SONGS D'THEY DO?
DIPPED IN SHIT, THE STARES ANSWER... BEST STICK TO MY JOB...
COOPERATION IS TOTAL... TOTAL, MAN...
MATT OPENS GOB FOR THESE SKETCHES OF HIS BROKEN TOOTH...
GENE DROPS LEATHER PANTS FOR THIS QUICKIE OF HIS BUTT PROBLEM...
EVEN THE DISH WHO GETS LAID IN HEIDELBERG KNOWS TO SMILE FOR THE SOFT LEAD PENCIL...
WE DIDN'T BRING A PHOTO-GRAPHER...
...WE BROUGHT A CARTOON-IST.
GENE BUYS ME PENCILS, VOLUNTEERS IDEAS FOR THE COMIC...
LIKE NOT USING A RUBBER
...AND HAVING YOUR DIC FALL OF
HEY, GENE, AIN'T YOU READING 'MODERN DRUMMER' OR SOMETHING ???
J. SACCO 12·88

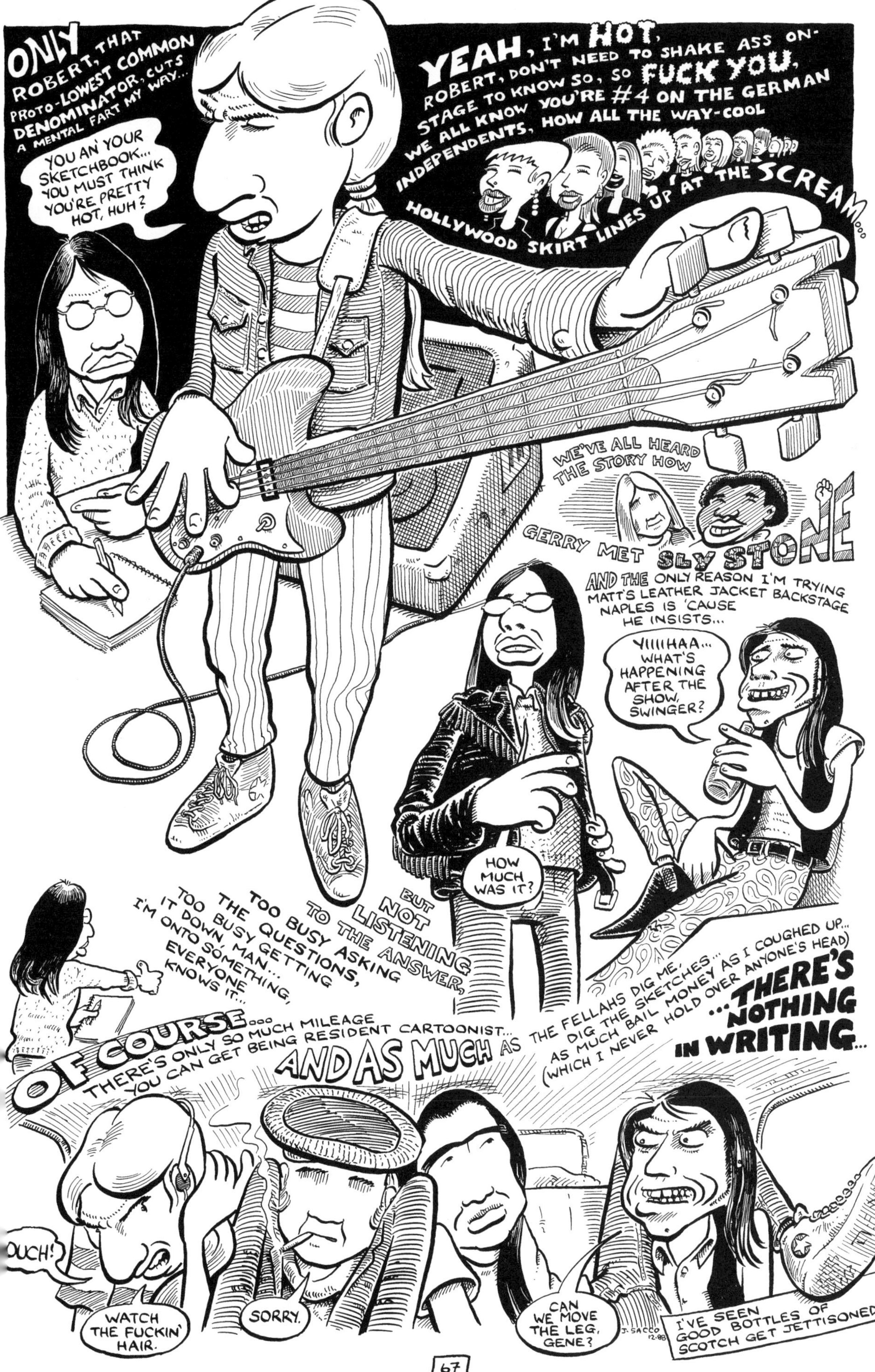
ONLY ROBERT, THAT PROTO-LOWEST COMMON DENOMINATOR, CUTS A MENTAL FART MY WAY...
YOU AN' YOUR SKETCHBOOK... YOU MUST THINK YOU'RE PRETTY HOT, HUH?
YEAH, I'M HOT, ROBERT, DON'T NEED TO SHAKE ASS ON-STAGE TO KNOW SO, SO FUCK YOU, WE ALL KNOW YOU'RE #4 ON THE GERMAN INDEPENDENTS, HOW ALL THE WAY-COOL HOLLYWOOD SKIRT LINES UP AT THE SCREAM...
WE'VE ALL HEARD THE STORY HOW GERRY MET SLY STONE
AND THE ONLY REASON I'M TRYING MATT'S LEATHER JACKET BACKSTAGE NAPLES IS 'CAUSE HE INSISTS...
YIIIIHAA... WHAT'S HAPPENING AFTER THE SHOW, SWINGER?
HOW MUCH WAS IT?
BUT NOT LISTENING TO THE ANSWER, TOO BUSY ASKING THE QUESTIONS, TOO BUSY GETTING IT DOWN, MAN... I'M ONTO SOMETHING, EVERYONE KNOWS IT...
OF COURSE... THERE'S ONLY SO MUCH MILEAGE YOU CAN GET BEING RESIDENT CARTOONIST...
AND AS MUCH AS THE FELLAHS DIG ME, DIG THE SKETCHES... AS MUCH BAIL MONEY AS I COUGHED UP... (WHICH I NEVER HOLD OVER ANYONE'S HEAD)
...THERE'S NOTHING IN WRITING...
OUCH!
WATCH THE FUCKIN' HAIR.
SORRY.
CAN WE MOVE THE LEG, GENE?
I'VE SEEN GOOD BOTTLES OF SCOTCH GET JETTISONED...
J. SACCO 12·88

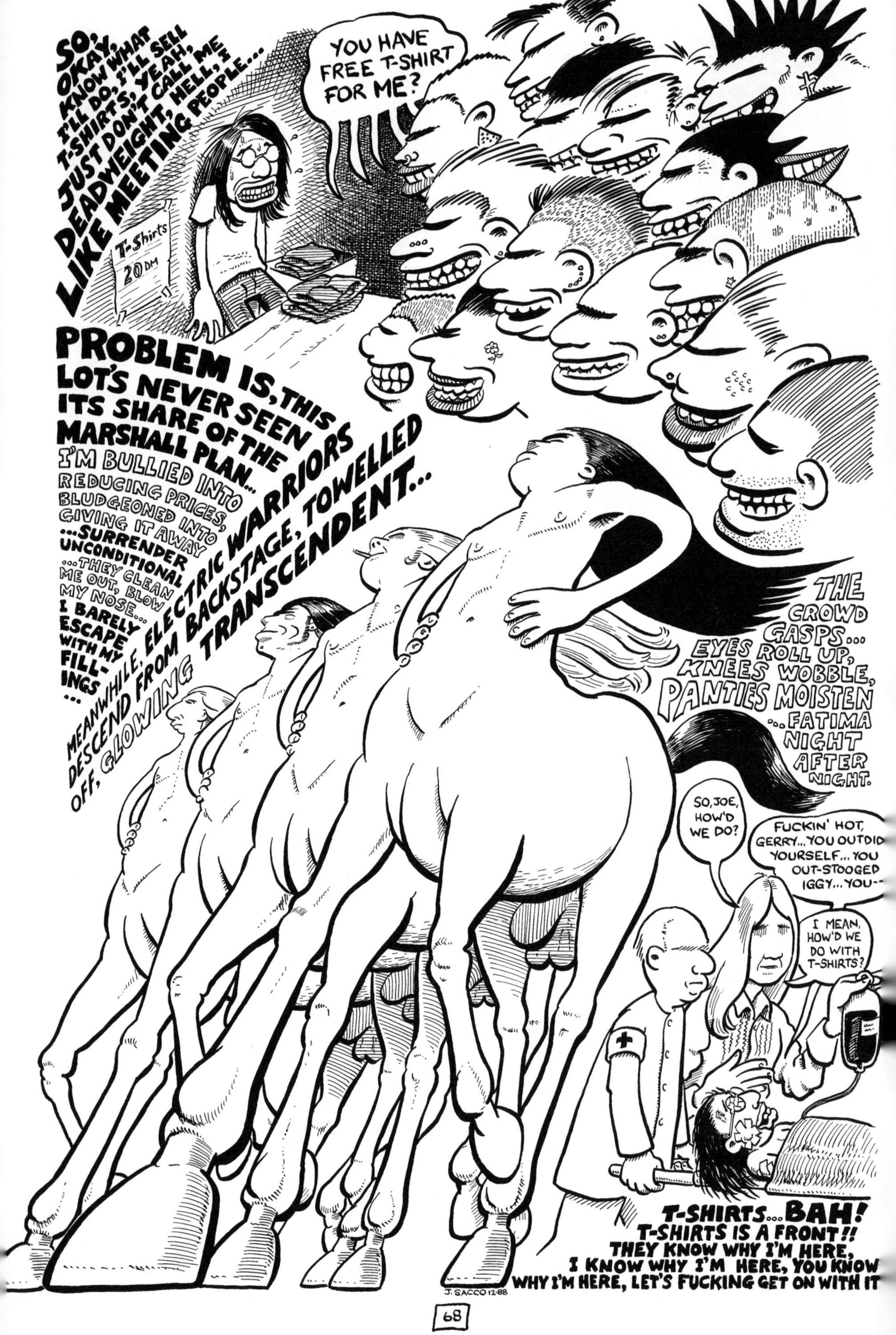
SO, OKAY, KNOW WHAT I'LL DO, I'LL SELL T-SHIRTS, YEAH, JUST DON'T CALL ME DEADWEIGHT, HELL, I LIKE MEETING PEOPLE...
T-Shirts 20 DM
YOU HAVE FREE T-SHIRT FOR ME?
PROBLEM IS, THIS LOT'S NEVER SEEN ITS SHARE OF THE MARSHALL PLAN...
I'M BULLIED INTO REDUCING PRICES, BLUDGEONED INTO GIVING IT AWAY ...SURRENDER UNCONDITIONAL ...THEY CLEAN ME OUT, BLOW MY NOSE... I BARELY ESCAPE WITH MY FILL-INGS...
MEANWHILE, ELECTRIC WARRIORS DESCEND FROM BACKSTAGE, TOWELLED OFF, GLOWING TRANSCENDENT...
THE CROWD GASPS... EYES ROLL UP, KNEES WOBBLE, PANTIES MOISTEN ...FATIMA NIGHT AFTER NIGHT.
SO, JOE, HOW'D WE DO?
FUCKIN' HOT, GERRY... YOU OUTDID YOURSELF... YOU OUT-STOOGED IGGY... YOU--
I MEAN, HOW'D WE DO WITH T-SHIRTS?
T-SHIRTS... BAH! T-SHIRTS IS A FRONT!! THEY KNOW WHY I'M HERE, I KNOW WHY I'M HERE, YOU KNOW WHY I'M HERE, LET'S FUCKING GET ON WITH IT
J. SACCO 12-88

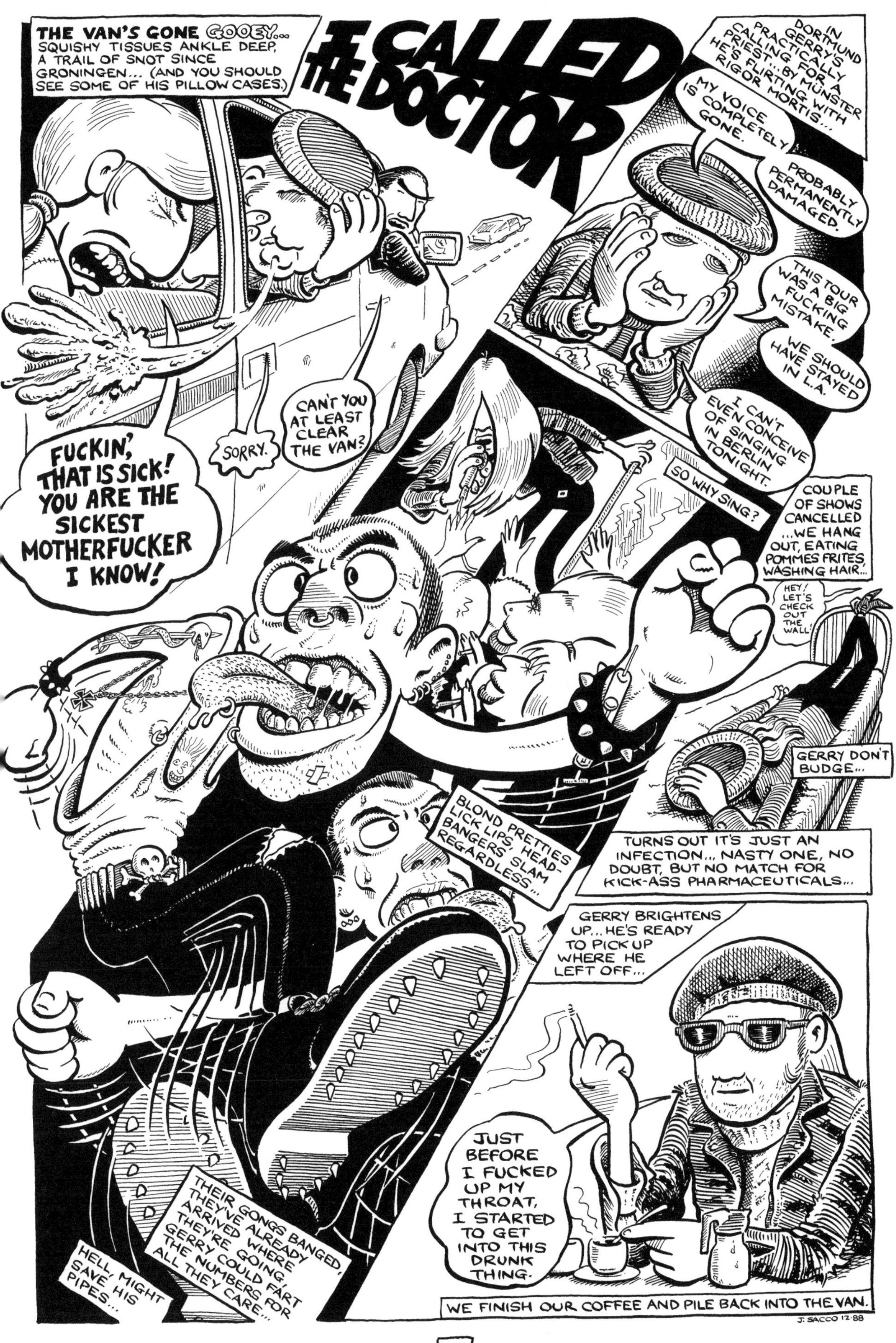
THE VAN'S GONE GOOEY... SQUISHY TISSUES ANKLE DEEP, A TRAIL OF SNOT SINCE GRONINGEN... (AND YOU SHOULD SEE SOME OF HIS PILLOW CASES.)
HE CALLED THE DOCTOR
FUCKIN', THAT IS SICK! YOU ARE THE SICKEST MOTHERFUCKER I KNOW!
SORRY.
CAN'T YOU AT LEAST CLEAR THE VAN?
DORTMUND IN PRAGUE... GERRY'S PRACTICALLY CALLING FOR A PRIEST... BY MÜNSTER HE'S FLIRTING WITH RIGOR MORTIS...
MY VOICE IS COMPLETELY GONE.
PROBABLY PERMANENTLY DAMAGED.
THIS TOUR WAS A BIG FUCKING MISTAKE.
WE SHOULD HAVE STAYED IN L.A.
I CAN'T EVEN CONCEIVE OF SINGING IN BERLIN TONIGHT.
SO WHY SING?
COUPLE OF SHOWS CANCELLED ...WE HANG OUT, EATING POMMES FRITES, WASHING HAIR...
HEY! LET'S CHECK OUT THE WALL!
GERRY DON'T BUDGE...
BLOND PRETTIES LICK LIPS, HEAD-BANGERS SLAM REGARDLESS...
TURNS OUT IT'S JUST AN INFECTION... NASTY ONE, NO DOUBT, BUT NO MATCH FOR KICK-ASS PHARMACEUTICALS...
THEIR GONGS BANGED, THEY'VE ALREADY ARRIVED WHERE THEY'RE GOING. GERRY COULD FART THE NUMBERS FOR ALL THEY CARE...
HELL, MIGHT SAVE HIS PIPES...
GERRY BRIGHTENS UP... HE'S READY TO PICK UP WHERE HE LEFT OFF...
JUST BEFORE I FUCKED UP MY THROAT, I STARTED TO GET INTO THIS DRUNK THING.
WE FINISH OUR COFFEE AND PILE BACK INTO THE VAN.
J. SACCO 12·88

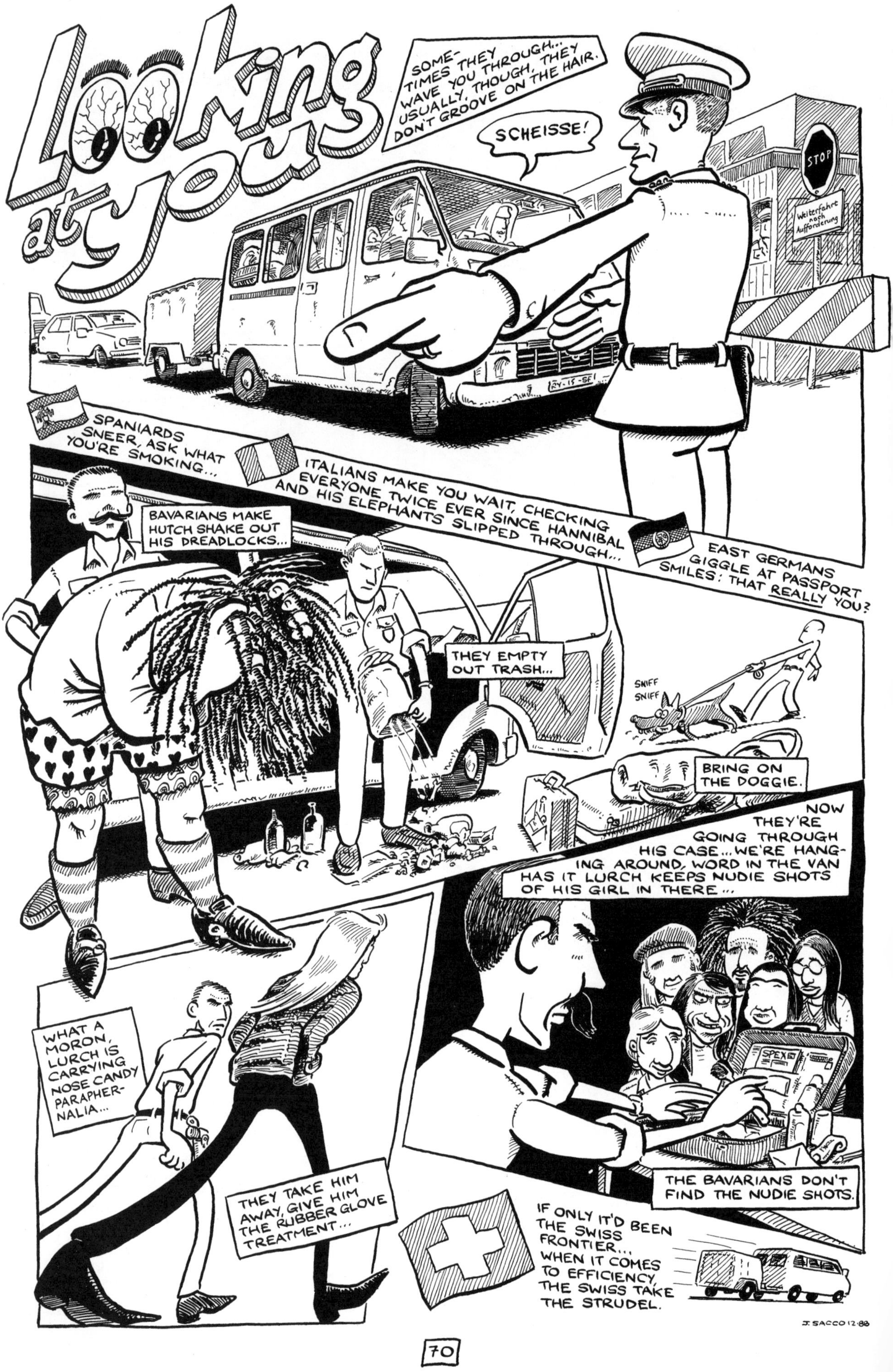
Looking at you
SOMETIMES THEY WAVE YOU THROUGH... USUALLY, THOUGH, THEY DON'T GROOVE ON THE HAIR.
SCHEISSE!
STOP
Weiterfahrt nach Aufforderung
SPANIARDS SNEER, ASK WHAT YOU'RE SMOKING...
ITALIANS MAKE YOU WAIT, CHECKING EVERYONE TWICE EVER SINCE HANNIBAL AND HIS ELEPHANTS SLIPPED THROUGH...
EAST GERMANS GIGGLE AT PASSPORT SMILES: THAT REALLY YOU?
BAVARIANS MAKE HUTCH SHAKE OUT HIS DREADLOCKS...
THEY EMPTY OUT TRASH...
SNIFF
SNIFF
BRING ON THE DOGGIE.
NOW THEY'RE GOING THROUGH HIS CASE... WE'RE HANGING AROUND, WORD IN THE VAN HAS IT LURCH KEEPS NUDIE SHOTS OF HIS GIRL IN THERE...
SPEX
WHAT A MORON, LURCH IS CARRYING NOSE CANDY PARAPHERNALIA...
THEY TAKE HIM AWAY, GIVE HIM THE RUBBER GLOVE TREATMENT...
THE BAVARIANS DON'T FIND THE NUDIE SHOTS.
IF ONLY IT'D BEEN THE SWISS FRONTIER... WHEN IT COMES TO EFFICIENCY, THE SWISS TAKE THE STRUDEL.
J. SACCO 12-88

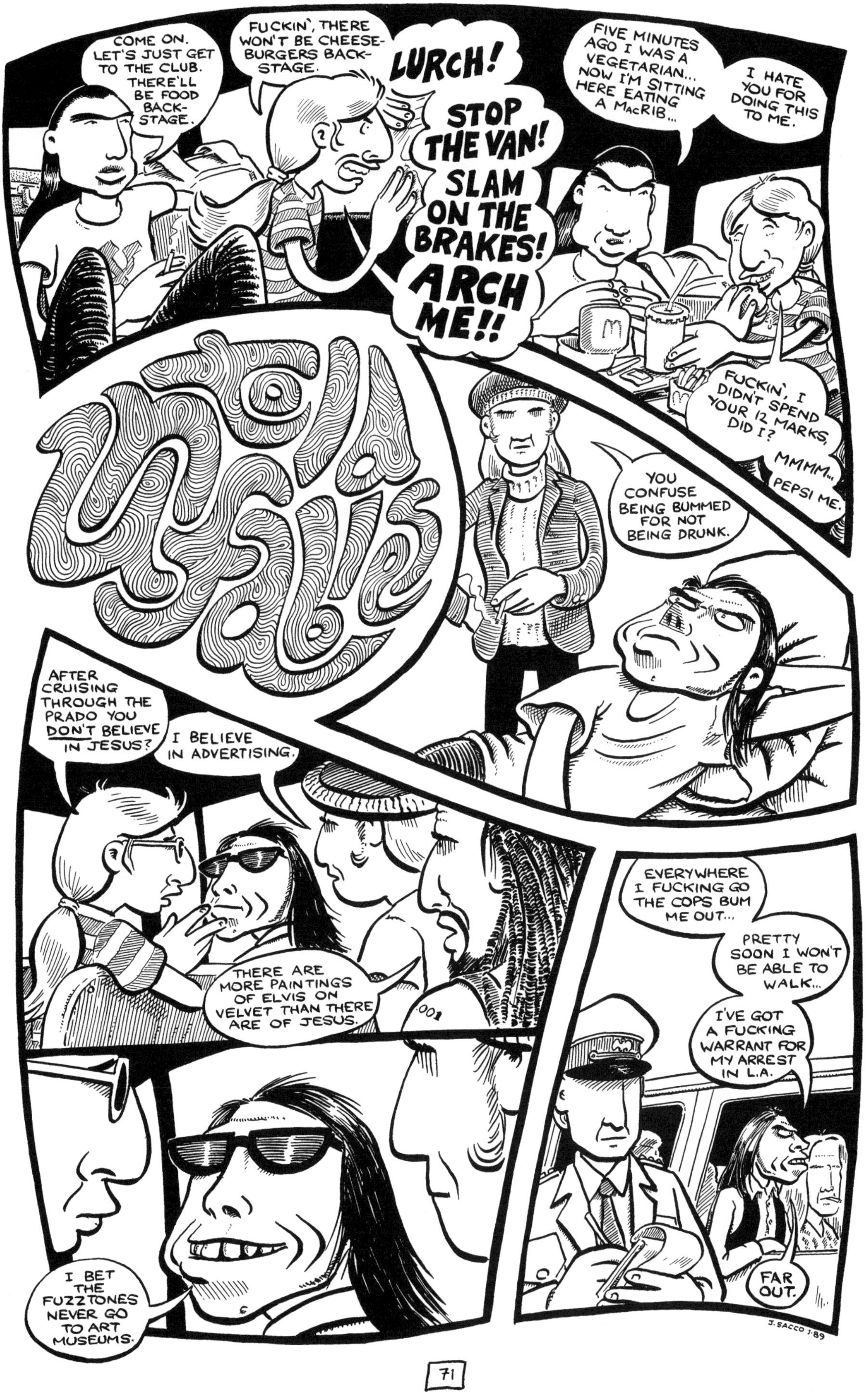
COME ON. LET'S JUST GET TO THE CLUB. THERE'LL BE FOOD BACK-STAGE.
FUCKIN', THERE WON'T BE CHEESE-BURGERS BACK-STAGE.
LURCH!
STOP THE VAN! SLAM ON THE BRAKES! ARCH ME!!
FIVE MINUTES AGO I WAS A VEGETARIAN... NOW I'M SITTING HERE EATING A MacRIB...
I HATE YOU FOR DOING THIS TO ME.
FUCKIN', I DIDN'T SPEND YOUR 12 MARKS, DID I?
MMMM... PEPSI ME.
YOU CONFUSE BEING BUMMED FOR NOT BEING DRUNK.
AFTER CRUISING THROUGH THE PRADO YOU DON'T BELIEVE IN JESUS?
I BELIEVE IN ADVERTISING.
THERE ARE MORE PAINTINGS OF ELVIS ON VELVET THAN THERE ARE OF JESUS.
I BET THE FUZZTONES NEVER GO TO ART MUSEUMS.
EVERYWHERE I FUCKING GO THE COPS BUM ME OUT...
PRETTY SOON I WON'T BE ABLE TO WALK...
I'VE GOT A FUCKING WARRANT FOR MY ARREST IN L.A.
FAR OUT.
J. SACCO 1·89

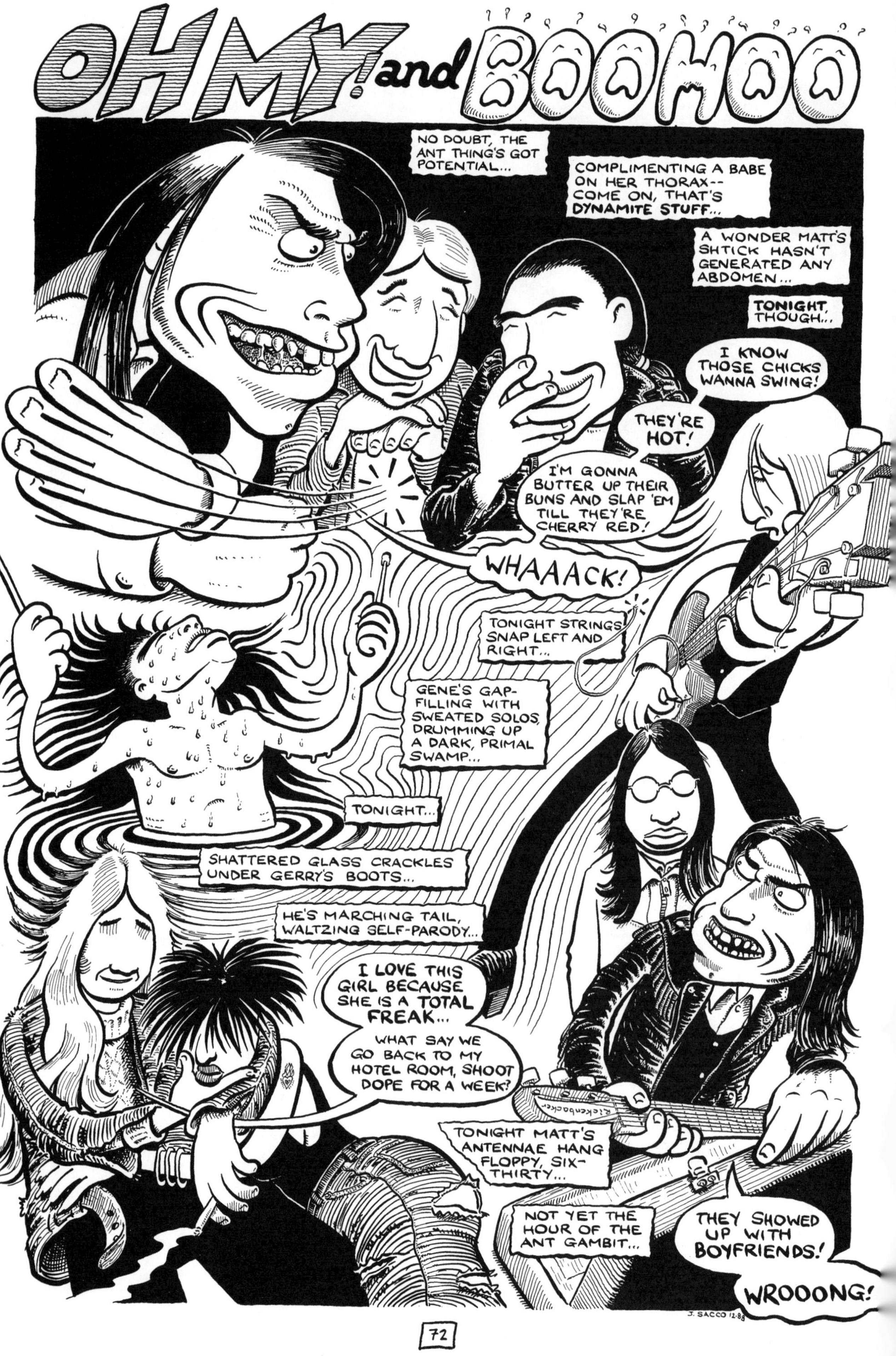
OHMY! and BOOHOO
NO DOUBT, THE ANT THING'S GOT POTENTIAL...
COMPLIMENTING A BABE ON HER THORAX-- COME ON, THAT'S DYNAMITE STUFF...
A WONDER MATT'S SHTICK HASN'T GENERATED ANY ABDOMEN...
TONIGHT, THOUGH...
I KNOW THOSE CHICKS WANNA SWING!
THEY'RE HOT!
I'M GONNA BUTTER UP THEIR BUNS AND SLAP 'EM TILL THEY'RE CHERRY RED!
WHAAACK!
TONIGHT STRINGS SNAP LEFT AND RIGHT...
GENE'S GAP-FILLING WITH SWEATED SOLOS, DRUMMING UP A DARK, PRIMAL SWAMP...
TONIGHT...
SHATTERED GLASS CRACKLES UNDER GERRY'S BOOTS...
HE'S MARCHING TAIL, WALTZING SELF-PARODY...
I LOVE THIS GIRL BECAUSE SHE IS A TOTAL FREAK...
WHAT SAY WE GO BACK TO MY HOTEL ROOM, SHOOT DOPE FOR A WEEK?
TONIGHT MATT'S ANTENNAE HANG FLOPPY, SIX-THIRTY...
NOT YET THE HOUR OF THE ANT GAMBIT...
THEY SHOWED UP WITH BOYFRIENDS!
WROOONG!
Rickenbacker
J. SACCO 12.88

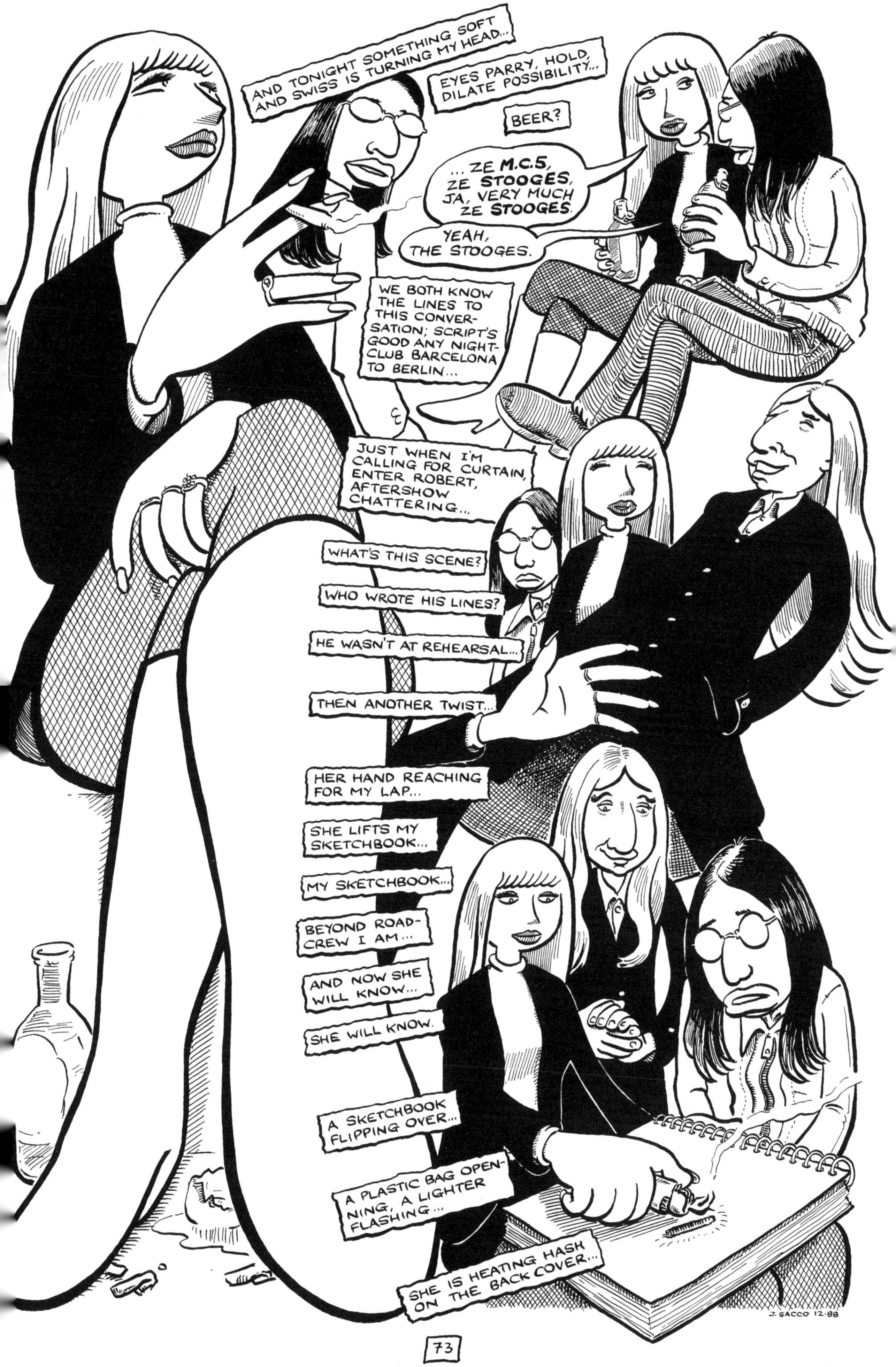

AND TONIGHT SOMETHING SOFT AND SWISS IS TURNING MY HEAD...
EYES PARRY, HOLD, DILATE POSSIBILITY...
BEER?
...ZE M.C.5, ZE STOOGES, JA, VERY MUCH ZE STOOGES.
YEAH, THE STOOGES.
WE BOTH KNOW THE LINES TO THIS CONVERSATION; SCRIPT'S GOOD ANY NIGHT-CLUB BARCELONA TO BERLIN...
JUST WHEN I'M CALLING FOR CURTAIN, ENTER ROBERT, AFTERSHOW CHATTERING...
WHAT'S THIS SCENE?
WHO WROTE HIS LINES?
HE WASN'T AT REHEARSAL...
THEN ANOTHER TWIST...
HER HAND REACHING FOR MY LAP...
SHE LIFTS MY SKETCHBOOK...
MY SKETCHBOOK...
BEYOND ROAD-CREW I AM...
AND NOW SHE WILL KNOW...
SHE WILL KNOW.
A SKETCHBOOK FLIPPING OVER...
A PLASTIC BAG OPEN-NING, A LIGHTER FLASHING...
SHE IS HEATING HASH ON THE BACK COVER...
J. SACCO 12·88

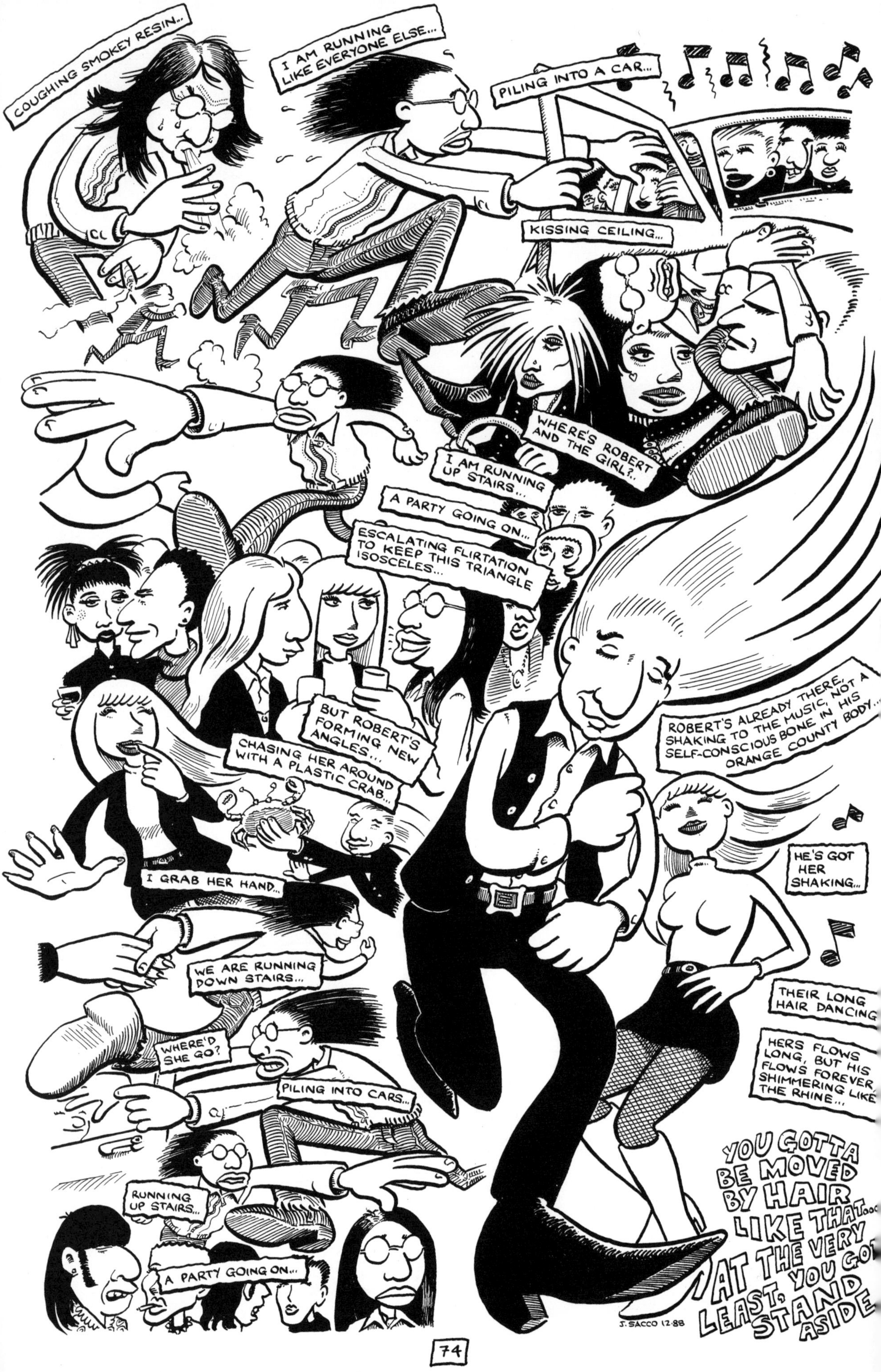
COUGHING SMOKEY RESIN...
I AM RUNNING LIKE EVERYONE ELSE...
PILING INTO A CAR...
KISSING CEILING...
WHERE'S ROBERT AND THE GIRL?..
I AM RUNNING UP STAIRS...
A PARTY GOING ON...
ESCALATING FLIRTATION TO KEEP THIS TRIANGLE ISOSCELES...
BUT ROBERT'S FORMING NEW ANGLES...
CHASING HER AROUND WITH A PLASTIC CRAB...
ROBERT'S ALREADY THERE, SHAKING TO THE MUSIC, NOT A SELF-CONSCIOUS BONE IN HIS ORANGE COUNTY BODY...
HE'S GOT HER SHAKING...
I GRAB HER HAND...
WE ARE RUNNING DOWN STAIRS...
WHERE'D SHE GO?
PILING INTO CARS...
THEIR LONG HAIR DANCING
HERS FLOWS LONG, BUT HIS FLOWS FOREVER, SHIMMERING LIKE THE RHINE...
RUNNING UP STAIRS...
A PARTY GOING ON...
YOU GOTTA BE MOVED BY HAIR LIKE THAT...
AT THE VERY LEAST, YOU GOT STAND ASIDE
J. SACCO 12·88

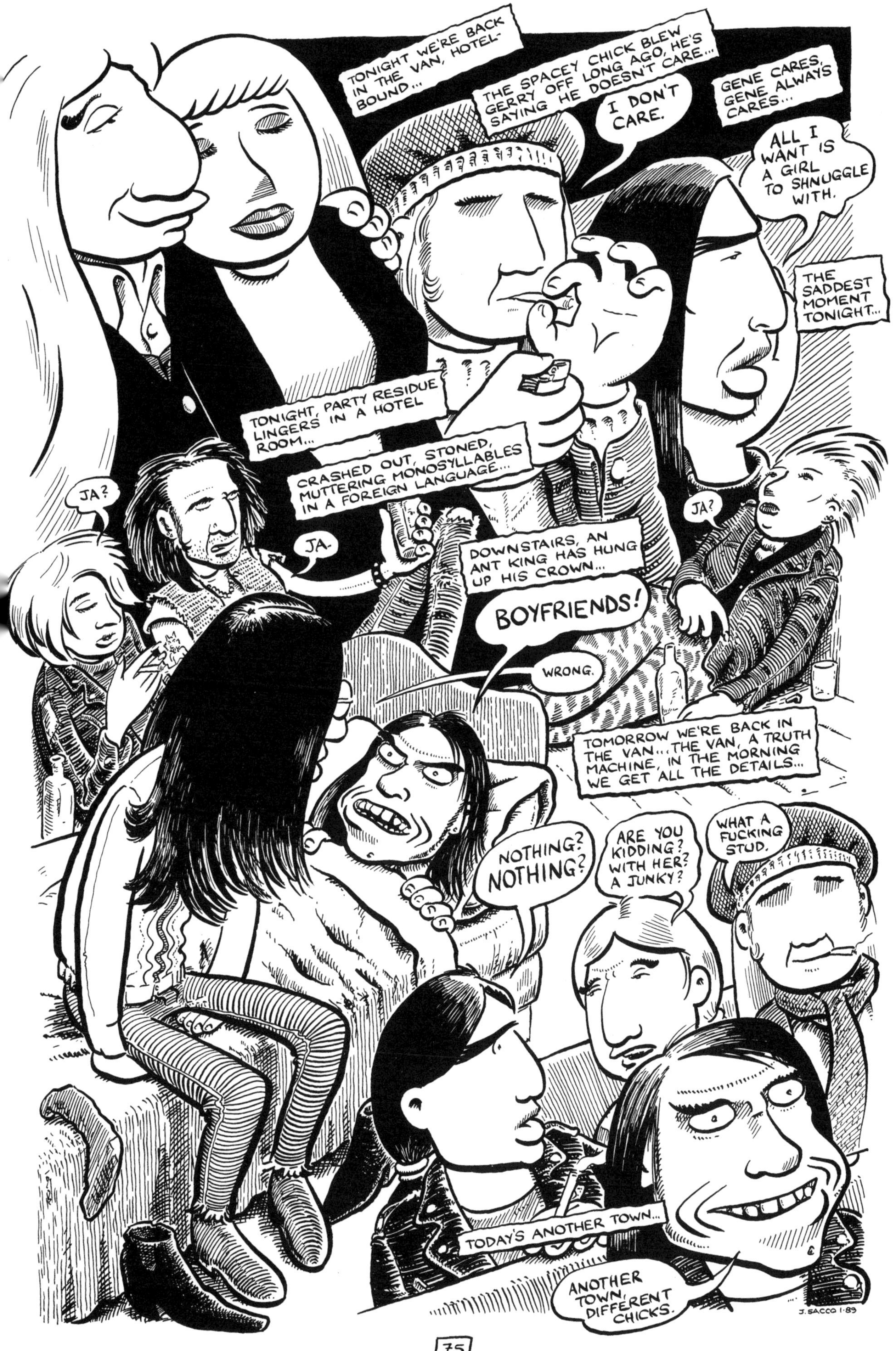
TONIGHT WE'RE BACK IN THE VAN, HOTEL-BOUND...
THE SPACEY CHICK BLEW GERRY OFF LONG AGO, HE'S SAYING HE DOESN'T CARE...
I DON'T CARE.
GENE CARES, GENE ALWAYS CARES...
ALL I WANT IS A GIRL TO SHNUGGLE WITH.
THE SADDEST MOMENT TONIGHT...
TONIGHT, PARTY RESIDUE LINGERS IN A HOTEL ROOM...
CRASHED OUT, STONED, MUTTERING MONOSYLLABLES IN A FOREIGN LANGUAGE...
JA?
JA.
JA?
DOWNSTAIRS, AN ANT KING HAS HUNG UP HIS CROWN...
BOYFRIENDS!
WRONG.
TOMORROW WE'RE BACK IN THE VAN... THE VAN, A TRUTH MACHINE, IN THE MORNING WE GET ALL THE DETAILS...
NOTHING? NOTHING?
ARE YOU KIDDING? WITH HER? A JUNKY?
WHAT A FUCKING STUD.
TODAY'S ANOTHER TOWN...
ANOTHER TOWN, DIFFERENT CHICKS.
J. SACCO 1·89

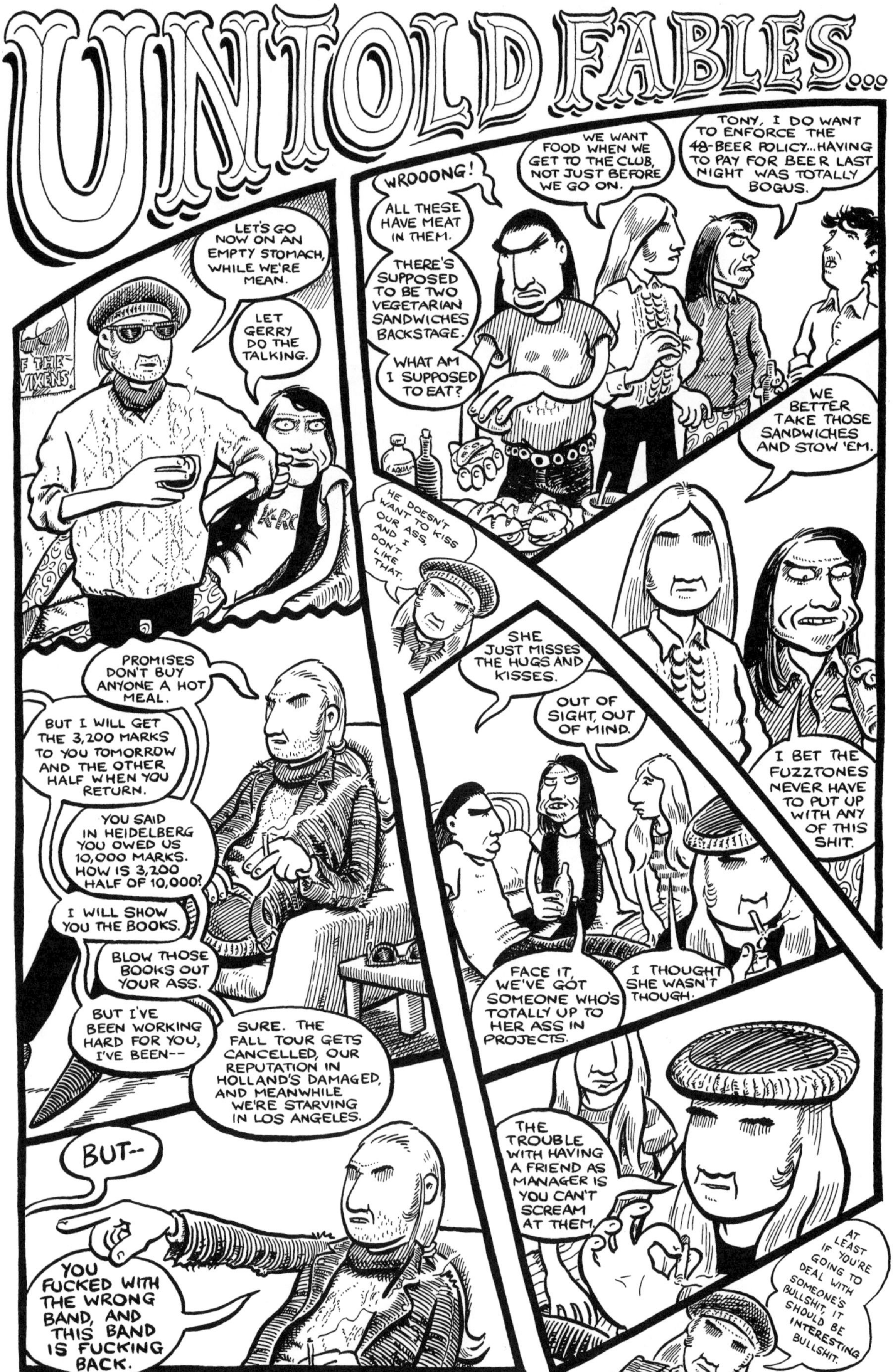
UNTOLD FABLES...
LET'S GO NOW ON AN EMPTY STOMACH, WHILE WE'RE MEAN.
LET GERRY DO THE TALKING.
VIXENS
WROOONG!
ALL THESE HAVE MEAT IN THEM.
THERE'S SUPPOSED TO BE TWO VEGETARIAN SANDWICHES BACKSTAGE.
WHAT AM I SUPPOSED TO EAT?
WE WANT FOOD WHEN WE GET TO THE CLUB, NOT JUST BEFORE WE GO ON.
TONY, I DO WANT TO ENFORCE THE 48-BEER POLICY...HAVING TO PAY FOR BEER LAST NIGHT WAS TOTALLY BOGUS.
HE DOESN'T WANT TO KISS OUR ASS, AND I DON'T LIKE THAT.
WE BETTER TAKE THOSE SANDWICHES AND STOW 'EM.
PROMISES DON'T BUY ANYONE A HOT MEAL.
BUT I WILL GET THE 3,200 MARKS TO YOU TOMORROW AND THE OTHER HALF WHEN YOU RETURN.
YOU SAID IN HEIDELBERG YOU OWED US 10,000 MARKS. HOW IS 3,200 HALF OF 10,000?
I WILL SHOW YOU THE BOOKS.
BLOW THOSE BOOKS OUT YOUR ASS.
BUT I'VE BEEN WORKING HARD FOR YOU, I'VE BEEN--
SURE. THE FALL TOUR GETS CANCELLED, OUR REPUTATION IN HOLLAND'S DAMAGED, AND MEANWHILE WE'RE STARVING IN LOS ANGELES.
SHE JUST MISSES THE HUGS AND KISSES.
OUT OF SIGHT, OUT OF MIND.
I BET THE FUZZTONES NEVER HAVE TO PUT UP WITH ANY OF THIS SHIT.
FACE IT, WE'VE GOT SOMEONE WHO'S TOTALLY UP TO HER ASS IN PROJECTS.
I THOUGHT SHE WASN'T THOUGH.
BUT--
YOU FUCKED WITH THE WRONG BAND, AND THIS BAND IS FUCKING BACK.
THE TROUBLE WITH HAVING A FRIEND AS MANAGER IS YOU CAN'T SCREAM AT THEM.
AT LEAST IF YOU'RE GOING TO DEAL WITH SOMEONE'S BULLSHIT, IT SHOULD BE INTERESTING BULLSHIT.
J. SACCO 1-89

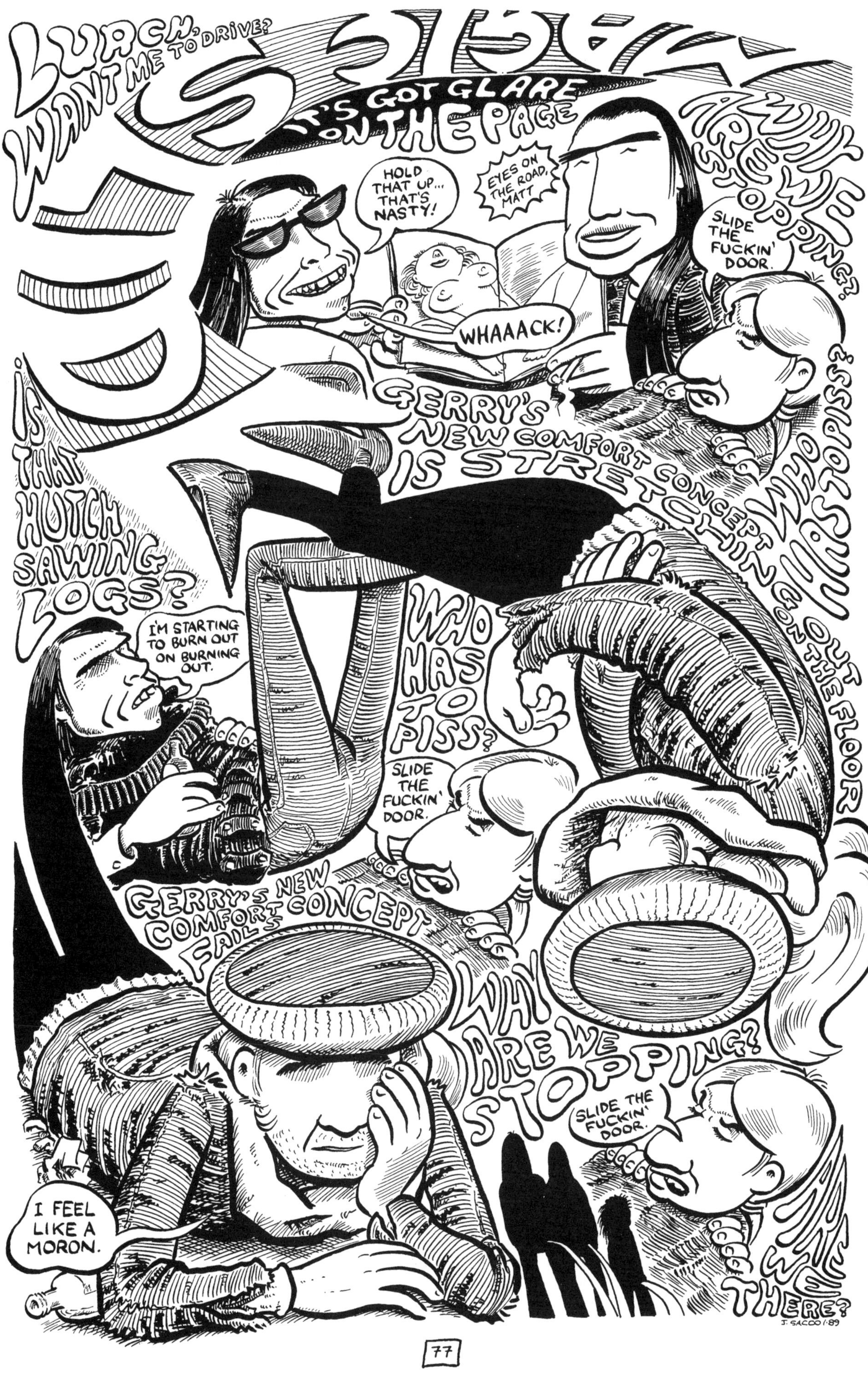
LURCH, WANT ME TO DRIVE?
IT'S GOT GLARE ON THE PAGE
HOLD THAT UP... THAT'S NASTY!
EYES ON THE ROAD, MATT
WHY ARE WE STOPPING?
SLIDE THE FUCKIN' DOOR.
WHAAACK!
IS THAT HUTCH SAWING LOGS?
GERRY'S NEW COMFORT CONCEPT IS STRETCHING OUT ON THE FLOOR
WHO HAS TO PISS?
I'M STARTING TO BURN OUT ON BURNING OUT.
WHO HAS TO PISS?
SLIDE THE FUCKIN' DOOR.
GERRY'S NEW COMFORT CONCEPT FAILS
WHY ARE WE STOPPING?
SLIDE THE FUCKIN' DOOR.
ARE WE THERE?
I FEEL LIKE A MORON.
J. SACCO 1·89

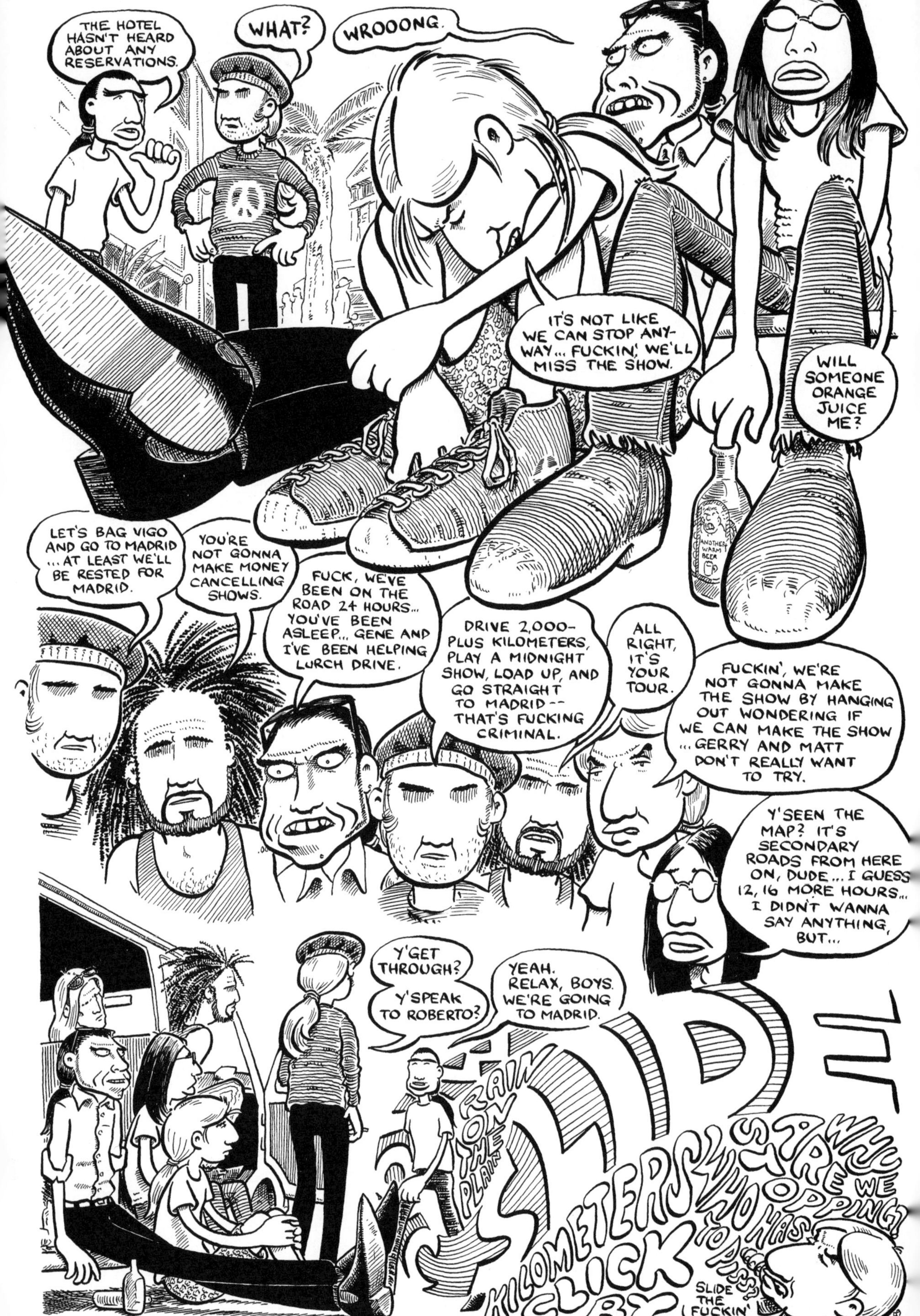

THE HOTEL HASN'T HEARD ABOUT ANY RESERVATIONS.
WHAT?
WROOONG.
IT'S NOT LIKE WE CAN STOP ANYWAY... FUCKIN', WE'LL MISS THE SHOW.
WILL SOMEONE ORANGE JUICE ME?
ANOTHER WARM BEER
LET'S BAG VIGO AND GO TO MADRID ...AT LEAST WE'LL BE RESTED FOR MADRID.
YOU'RE NOT GONNA MAKE MONEY CANCELLING SHOWS.
FUCK, WE'VE BEEN ON THE ROAD 24 HOURS... YOU'VE BEEN ASLEEP... GENE AND I'VE BEEN HELPING LURCH DRIVE.
DRIVE 2,000-PLUS KILOMETERS, PLAY A MIDNIGHT SHOW, LOAD UP, AND GO STRAIGHT TO MADRID -- THAT'S FUCKING CRIMINAL.
ALL RIGHT, IT'S YOUR TOUR.
FUCKIN', WE'RE NOT GONNA MAKE THE SHOW BY HANGING OUT WONDERING IF WE CAN MAKE THE SHOW ...GERRY AND MATT DON'T REALLY WANT TO TRY.
Y'SEEN THE MAP? IT'S SECONDARY ROADS FROM HERE ON, DUDE... I GUESS 12, 16 MORE HOURS... I DIDN'T WANNA SAY ANYTHING, BUT...
Y'GET THROUGH?
Y'SPEAK TO ROBERTO?
YEAH. RELAX, BOYS. WE'RE GOING TO MADRID.
RAIN ON THE PLAIN
KILOMETERS
WHO HAS TO PISS?
WHY ARE WE STOPPING?
CLICK
BY
SLIDE THE FUCKIN' DOOR.
J. SACCO 1-89

you've got your head on BACKWARDS

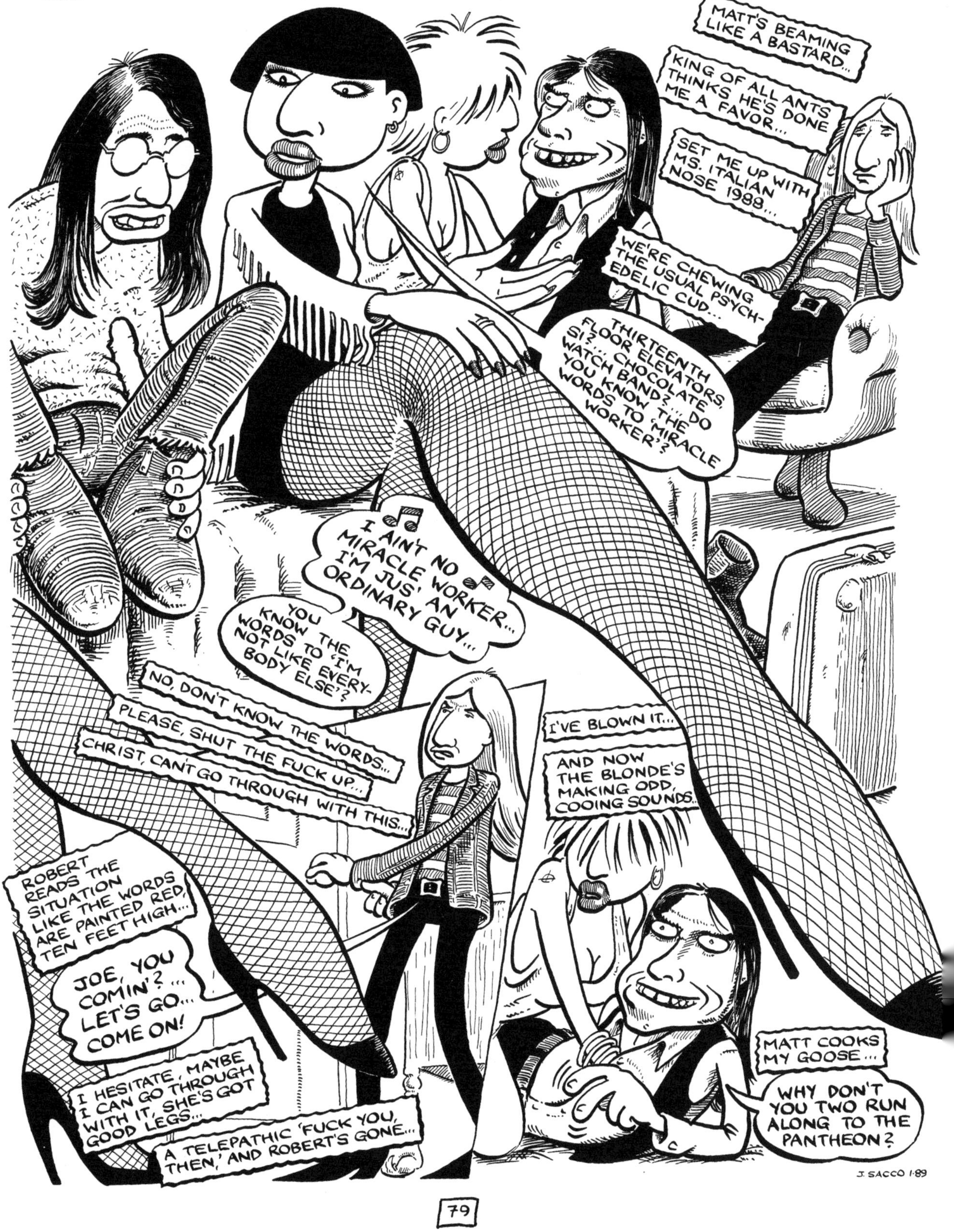
MATT'S BEAMING LIKE A BASTARD...
KING OF ALL ANTS THINKS HE'S DONE ME A FAVOR...
SET ME UP WITH MS. ITALIAN NOSE 1988...
WE'RE CHEWING THE USUAL PSYCH-EDELIC CUD...
THIRTEENTH FLOOR ELEVATORS, SI?... CHOCOLATE WATCH BAND?... DO YOU KNOW THE WORDS TO 'MIRACLE WORKER'?
I AIN'T NO MIRACLE WORKER... I'M JUS' AN ORDINARY GUY...
YOU KNOW THE WORDS TO 'I'M NOT LIKE EVERY-BODY ELSE'?
NO, DON'T KNOW THE WORDS...
PLEASE, SHUT THE FUCK UP...
CHRIST, CAN'T GO THROUGH WITH THIS...
I'VE BLOWN IT...
AND NOW THE BLONDE'S MAKING ODD, COOING SOUNDS...
ROBERT READS THE SITUATION LIKE THE WORDS ARE PAINTED RED, TEN FEET HIGH...
JOE, YOU COMIN'?... LET'S GO... COME ON!
I HESITATE, MAYBE I CAN GO THROUGH WITH IT, SHE'S GOT GOOD LEGS...
A TELEPATHIC 'FUCK YOU, THEN,' AND ROBERT'S GONE...
MATT COOKS MY GOOSE...
WHY DON'T YOU TWO RUN ALONG TO THE PANTHEON?
J. SACCO 1.89

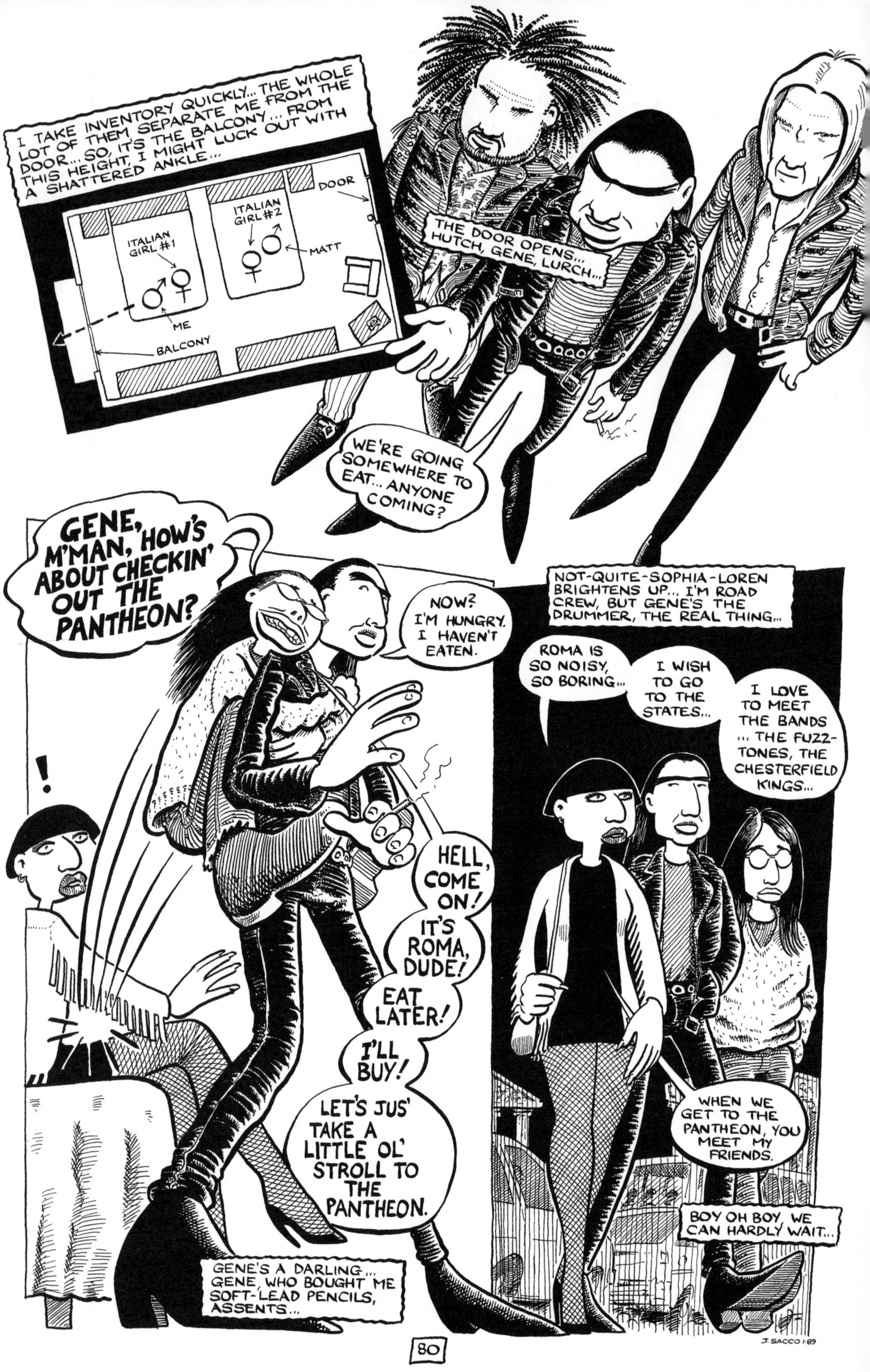
I TAKE INVENTORY QUICKLY... THE WHOLE LOT OF THEM SEPARATE ME FROM THE DOOR... SO, IT'S THE BALCONY... FROM THIS HEIGHT, I MIGHT LUCK OUT WITH A SHATTERED ANKLE...
DOOR
ITALIAN GIRL #2
ITALIAN GIRL #1
MATT
ME
BALCONY
THE DOOR OPENS... HUTCH, GENE, LURCH...
WE'RE GOING SOMEWHERE TO EAT... ANYONE COMING?
GENE, M'MAN, HOW'S ABOUT CHECKIN' OUT THE PANTHEON?
NOW? I'M HUNGRY. I HAVEN'T EATEN.
!
HELL, COME ON!
IT'S ROMA, DUDE!
EAT LATER!
I'LL BUY!
LET'S JUS' TAKE A LITTLE OL' STROLL TO THE PANTHEON.
GENE'S A DARLING... GENE, WHO BOUGHT ME SOFT-LEAD PENCILS, ASSENTS...
NOT-QUITE-SOPHIA-LOREN BRIGHTENS UP... I'M ROAD CREW, BUT GENE'S THE DRUMMER, THE REAL THING...
ROMA IS SO NOISY, SO BORING...
I WISH TO GO TO THE STATES...
I LOVE TO MEET THE BANDS ... THE FUZZ-TONES, THE CHESTERFIELD KINGS...
WHEN WE GET TO THE PANTHEON, YOU MEET MY FRIENDS.
BOY OH BOY, WE CAN HARDLY WAIT...
J. SACCO 1-89

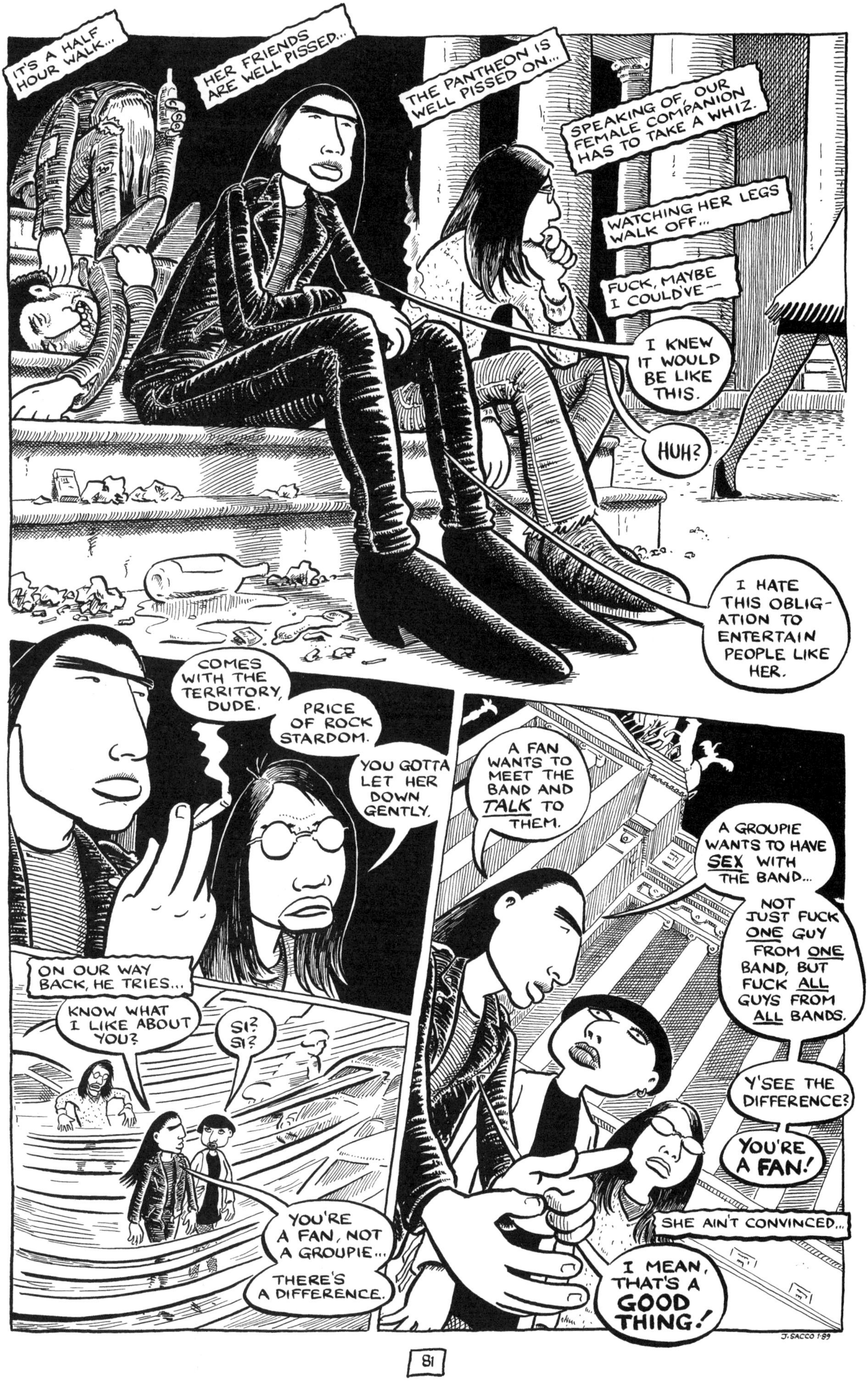
IT'S A HALF HOUR WALK...
HER FRIENDS ARE WELL PISSED...
THE PANTHEON IS WELL PISSED ON...
SPEAKING OF, OUR FEMALE COMPANION HAS TO TAKE A WHIZ.
WATCHING HER LEGS WALK OFF...
FUCK, MAYBE I COULD'VE--
I KNEW IT WOULD BE LIKE THIS.
HUH?
I HATE THIS OBLIG-ATION TO ENTERTAIN PEOPLE LIKE HER.
COMES WITH THE TERRITORY, DUDE.
PRICE OF ROCK STARDOM.
YOU GOTTA LET HER DOWN GENTLY.
ON OUR WAY BACK, HE TRIES...
KNOW WHAT I LIKE ABOUT YOU?
SI? SI?
YOU'RE A FAN, NOT A GROUPIE...
THERE'S A DIFFERENCE.
A FAN WANTS TO MEET THE BAND AND TALK TO THEM.
A GROUPIE WANTS TO HAVE SEX WITH THE BAND...
NOT JUST FUCK ONE GUY FROM ONE BAND, BUT FUCK ALL GUYS FROM ALL BANDS.
Y'SEE THE DIFFERENCE?
YOU'RE A FAN!
SHE AIN'T CONVINCED...
I MEAN, THAT'S A GOOD THING!
J. SACCO 1-89

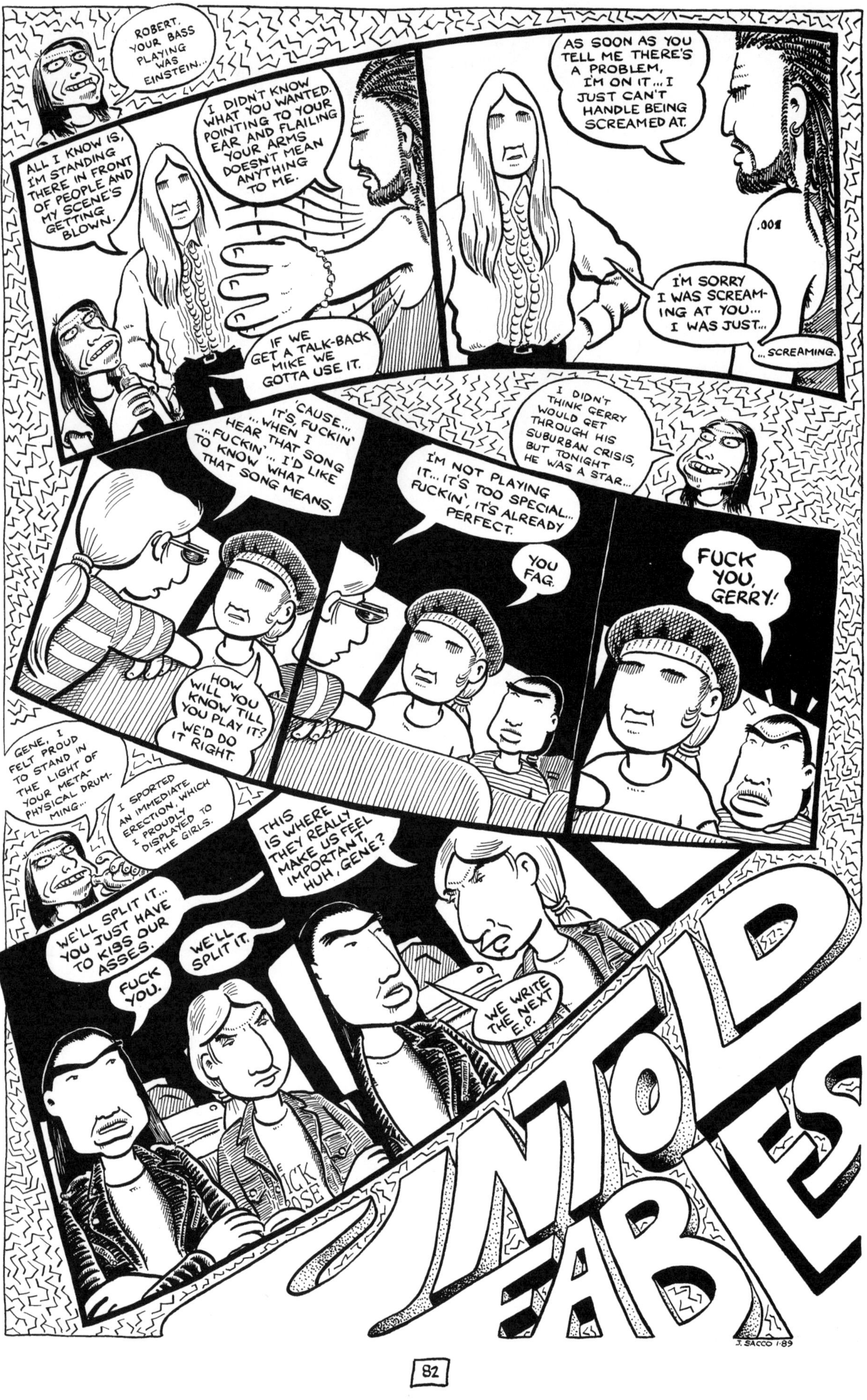
ROBERT, YOUR BASS PLAYING WAS EINSTEIN...
ALL I KNOW IS, I'M STANDING THERE IN FRONT OF PEOPLE AND MY SCENE'S GETTING BLOWN.
I DIDN'T KNOW WHAT YOU WANTED. POINTING TO YOUR EAR AND FLAILING YOUR ARMS DOESN'T MEAN ANYTHING TO ME.
IF WE GET A TALK-BACK MIKE WE GOTTA USE IT.
AS SOON AS YOU TELL ME THERE'S A PROBLEM, I'M ON IT... I JUST CAN'T HANDLE BEING SCREAMED AT.
I'M SORRY I WAS SCREAMING AT YOU... I WAS JUST...
...SCREAMING.
I DIDN'T THINK GERRY WOULD GET THROUGH HIS SUBURBAN CRISIS, BUT TONIGHT HE WAS A STAR...
'CAUSE... IT'S, FUCKIN' ...WHEN I HEAR THAT SONG ...FUCKIN'... I'D LIKE TO KNOW WHAT THAT SONG MEANS.
HOW WILL YOU KNOW TILL YOU PLAY IT? WE'D DO IT RIGHT.
I'M NOT PLAYING IT... IT'S TOO SPECIAL... FUCKIN', IT'S ALREADY PERFECT.
YOU FAG.
FUCK YOU, GERRY!
GENE, I FELT PROUD TO STAND IN THE LIGHT OF YOUR METAPHYSICAL DRUMMING...
I SPORTED AN IMMEDIATE ERECTION, WHICH I PROUDLY DISPLAYED TO THE GIRLS.
THIS IS WHERE THEY REALLY MAKE US FEEL IMPORTANT, HUH, GENE?
WE'LL SPLIT IT... YOU JUST HAVE TO KISS OUR ASSES.
WE'LL SPLIT IT.
FUCK YOU.
WE WRITE THE NEXT E.P.
UNTOLD TALES
J. SACCO 1·89

NO FUN TO HANG AROUND

I DIDN'T COME 10,000 MILES TO BE LEFT IN A HOTEL ROOM WHEN THERE'S FUN T'BE HAD.

WRONG WRONG WRONG WRONG

Y'THINK THEY TOOK THE VAN TO FRANKFURT?

NO DOUBT. WHERE THERE'S A U.S. AIR FORCE BASE, THERE'S PUSSY.

OH, YOU SPELL THAT OUT FOR THEM?

I BLAME LURCH FOR THIS. HE KNOWS WE'RE LEAVING AT MIDNIGHT.

THE VAN'S HIS RESPONS- IBILITY.

WHAT'S THE STORY ABOUT LEAVING AT MID- NIGHT?

WE SKIPPING OUT ON THE HOTEL BILL?

IT'S MATT'S FAULT. HE CONTROLS LURCH.

I'M HORNY.

I'M BORED.

YOU'RE BORED??! I'M DRINKING WINE!!!

I KNOW OF ZIS BAR VE CAN VALK TO.

GROOVY.

WALL-TO- WALL STONE- WASH.

PRETTY SOON WE'RE GONNA GET INTO A CONVERSATION ABOUT GARFIELD.

THIS IS SORT OF AN INTERESTING LITTLE TOWN, GERRY...

YOU KNOW THAT GUY WHO WROTE THAT BOOK ABOUT THE THIRTY YEARS WAR? 'THE ADVENTURES OF SOMEONEOROTHER?

NO.

WELL, HE WAS BORN HERE.

J. SACCO 1·83

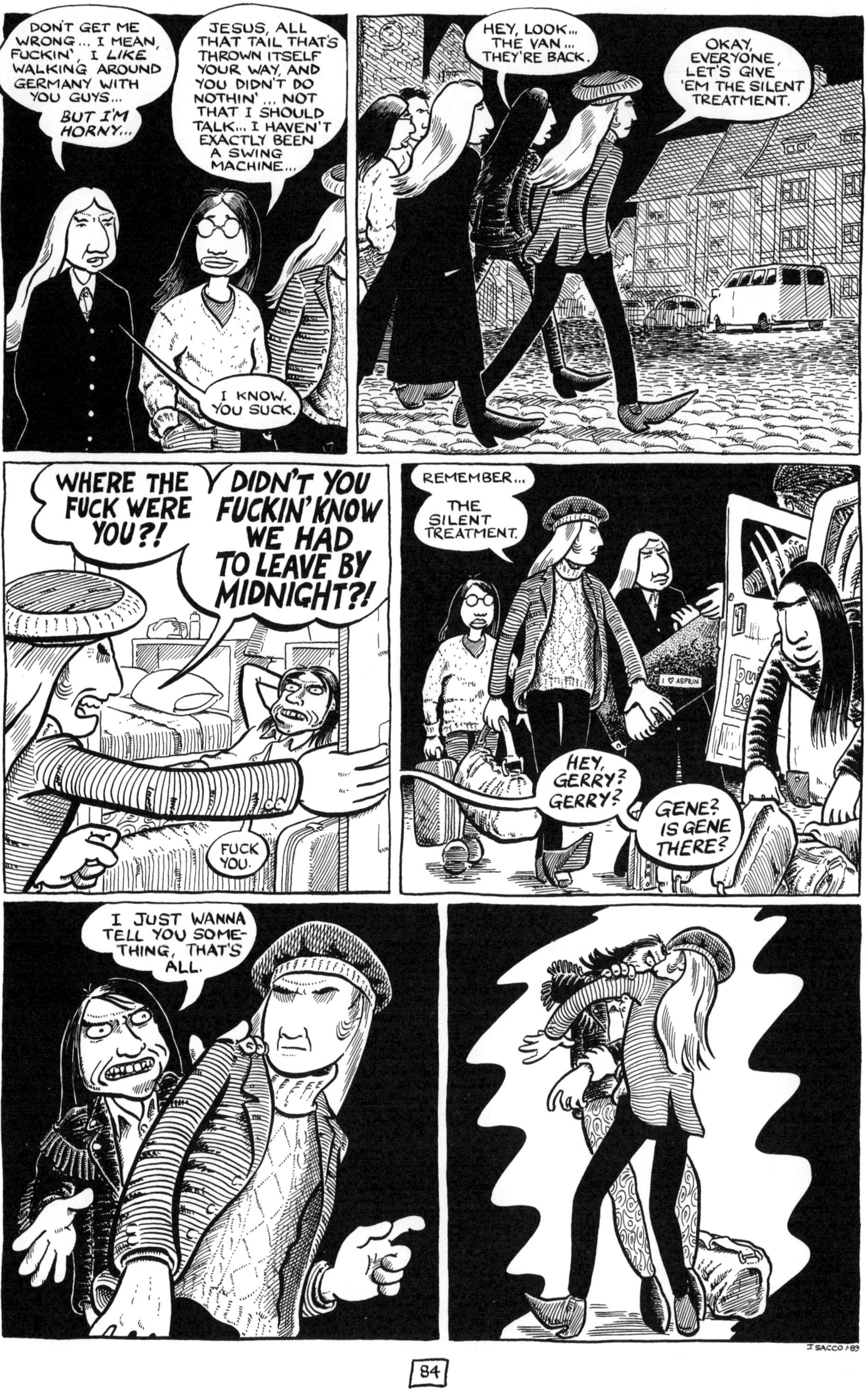
DON'T GET ME WRONG... I MEAN, FUCKIN', I LIKE WALKING AROUND GERMANY WITH YOU GUYS... BUT I'M HORNY...
JESUS, ALL THAT TAIL THAT'S THROWN ITSELF YOUR WAY, AND YOU DIDN'T DO NOTHIN'... NOT THAT I SHOULD TALK... I HAVEN'T EXACTLY BEEN A SWING MACHINE...
I KNOW. YOU SUCK.
HEY, LOOK... THE VAN... THEY'RE BACK.
OKAY, EVERYONE, LET'S GIVE 'EM THE SILENT TREATMENT.
WHERE THE FUCK WERE YOU?!
DIDN'T YOU FUCKIN' KNOW WE HAD TO LEAVE BY MIDNIGHT?!
FUCK YOU.
REMEMBER...
THE SILENT TREATMENT.
I ♡ ASPRIN
HEY, GERRY? GERRY?
GENE? IS GENE THERE?
I JUST WANNA TELL YOU SOMETHING, THAT'S ALL.
J SACCO '89

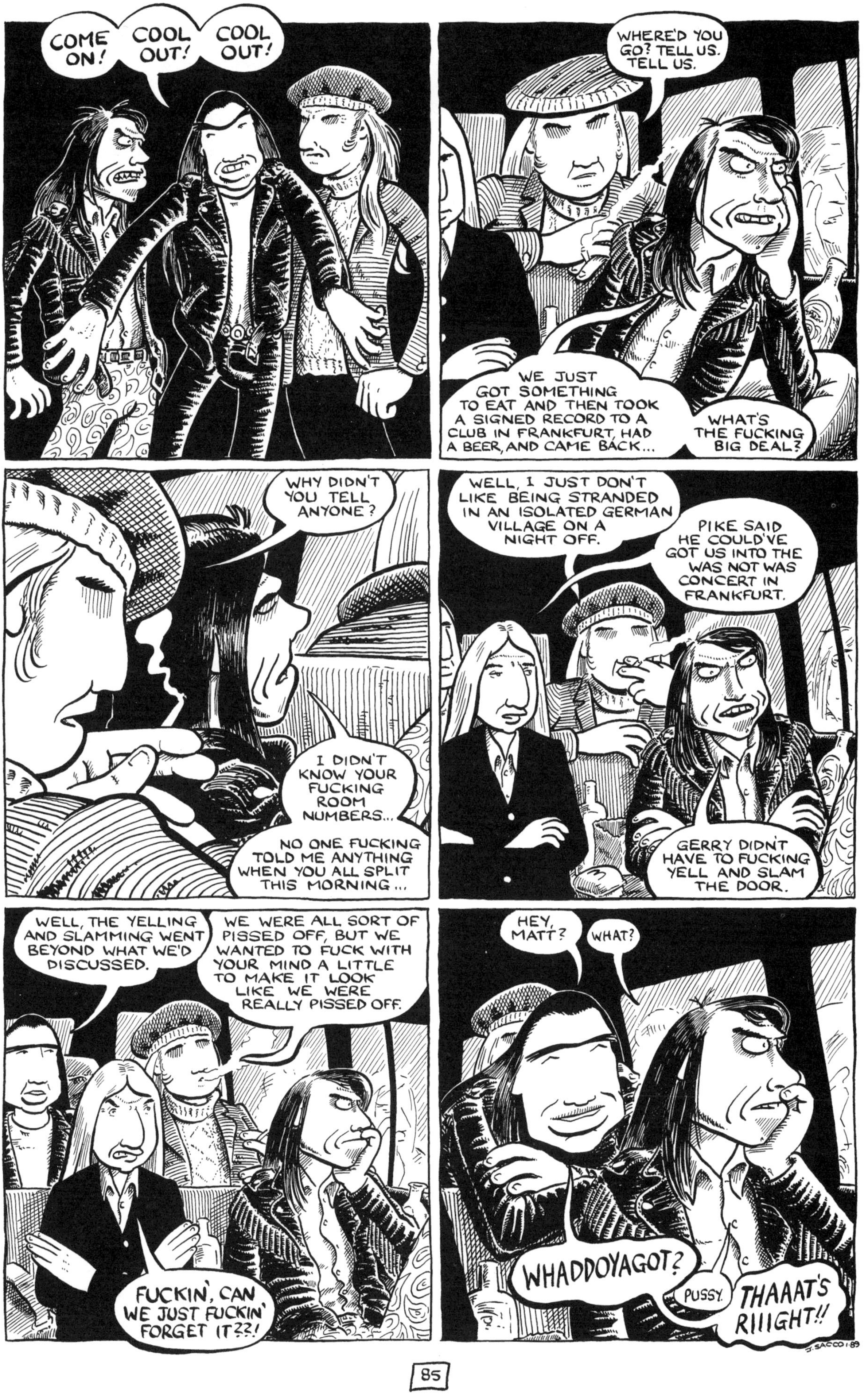
COME ON!
COOL OUT!
COOL OUT!
WHERE'D YOU GO? TELL US. TELL US.
WE JUST GOT SOMETHING TO EAT AND THEN TOOK A SIGNED RECORD TO A CLUB IN FRANKFURT, HAD A BEER, AND CAME BACK...
WHAT'S THE FUCKING BIG DEAL?
WHY DIDN'T YOU TELL ANYONE?
I DIDN'T KNOW YOUR FUCKING ROOM NUMBERS...
NO ONE FUCKING TOLD ME ANYTHING WHEN YOU ALL SPLIT THIS MORNING...
WELL, I JUST DON'T LIKE BEING STRANDED IN AN ISOLATED GERMAN VILLAGE ON A NIGHT OFF.
PIKE SAID HE COULD'VE GOT US INTO THE WAS NOT WAS CONCERT IN FRANKFURT.
GERRY DIDN'T HAVE TO FUCKING YELL AND SLAM THE DOOR.
WELL, THE YELLING AND SLAMMING WENT BEYOND WHAT WE'D DISCUSSED.
WE WERE ALL SORT OF PISSED OFF, BUT WE WANTED TO FUCK WITH YOUR MIND A LITTLE TO MAKE IT LOOK LIKE WE WERE REALLY PISSED OFF.
FUCKIN', CAN WE JUST FUCKIN' FORGET IT??!
HEY, MATT?
WHAT?
WHADDOYAGOT?
PUSSY.
THAAAT'S RIIIGHT!!
J. SACCO 1-89

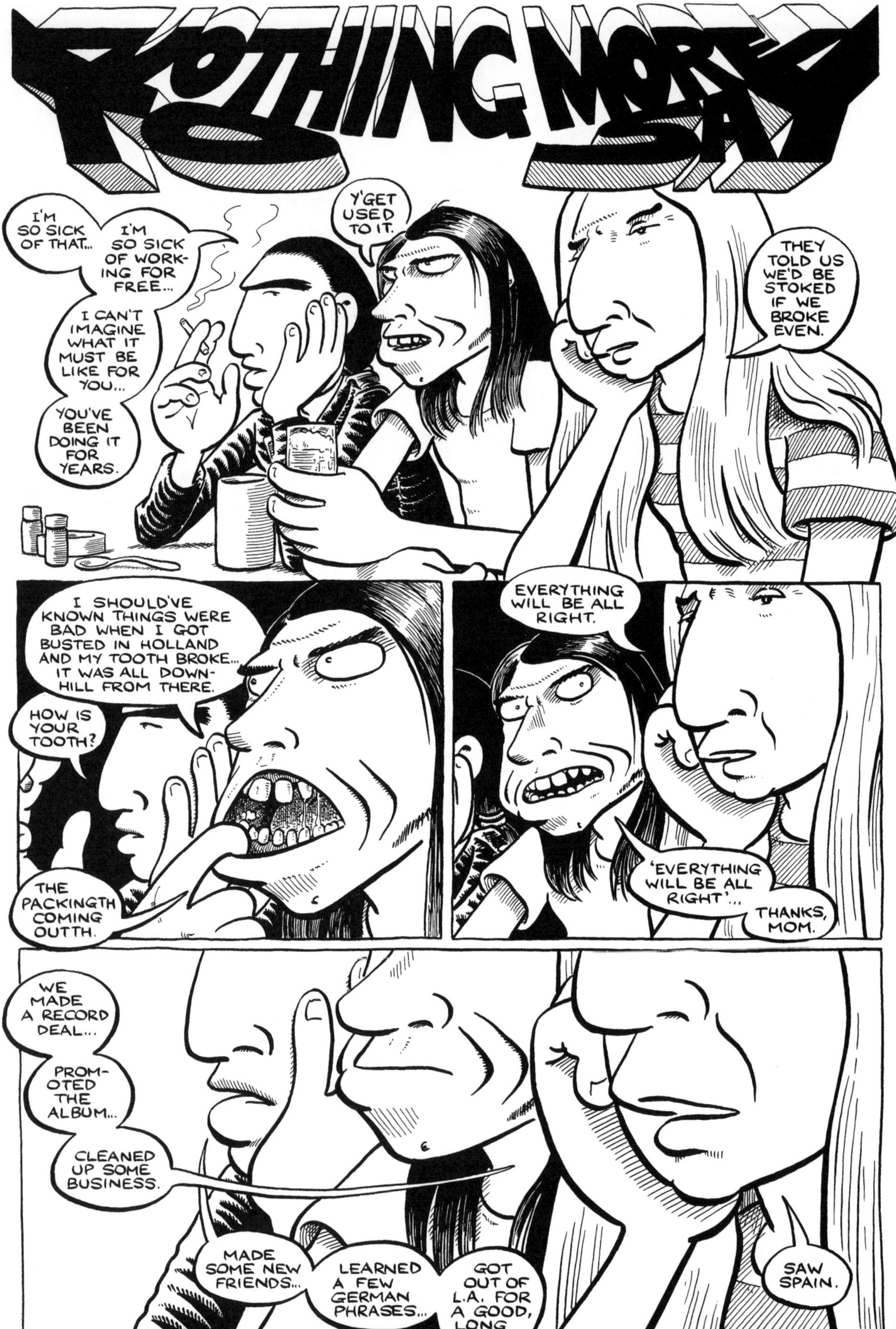
NOTHING MORE TO SAY
I'M SO SICK OF THAT...
I'M SO SICK OF WORKING FOR FREE...
I CAN'T IMAGINE WHAT IT MUST BE LIKE FOR YOU...
YOU'VE BEEN DOING IT FOR YEARS.
Y'GET USED TO IT.
THEY TOLD US WE'D BE STOKED IF WE BROKE EVEN.
I SHOULD'VE KNOWN THINGS WERE BAD WHEN I GOT BUSTED IN HOLLAND AND MY TOOTH BROKE... IT WAS ALL DOWNHILL FROM THERE.
HOW IS YOUR TOOTH?
THE PACKINGTH COMING OUTTH.
EVERYTHING WILL BE ALL RIGHT.
'EVERYTHING WILL BE ALL RIGHT'...
THANKS, MOM.
WE MADE A RECORD DEAL...
PROMOTED THE ALBUM...
CLEANED UP SOME BUSINESS.
MADE SOME NEW FRIENDS...
LEARNED A FEW GERMAN PHRASES...
GOT OUT OF L.A. FOR A GOOD, LONG TIME.
SAW SPAIN.
J. SACCO 1-89

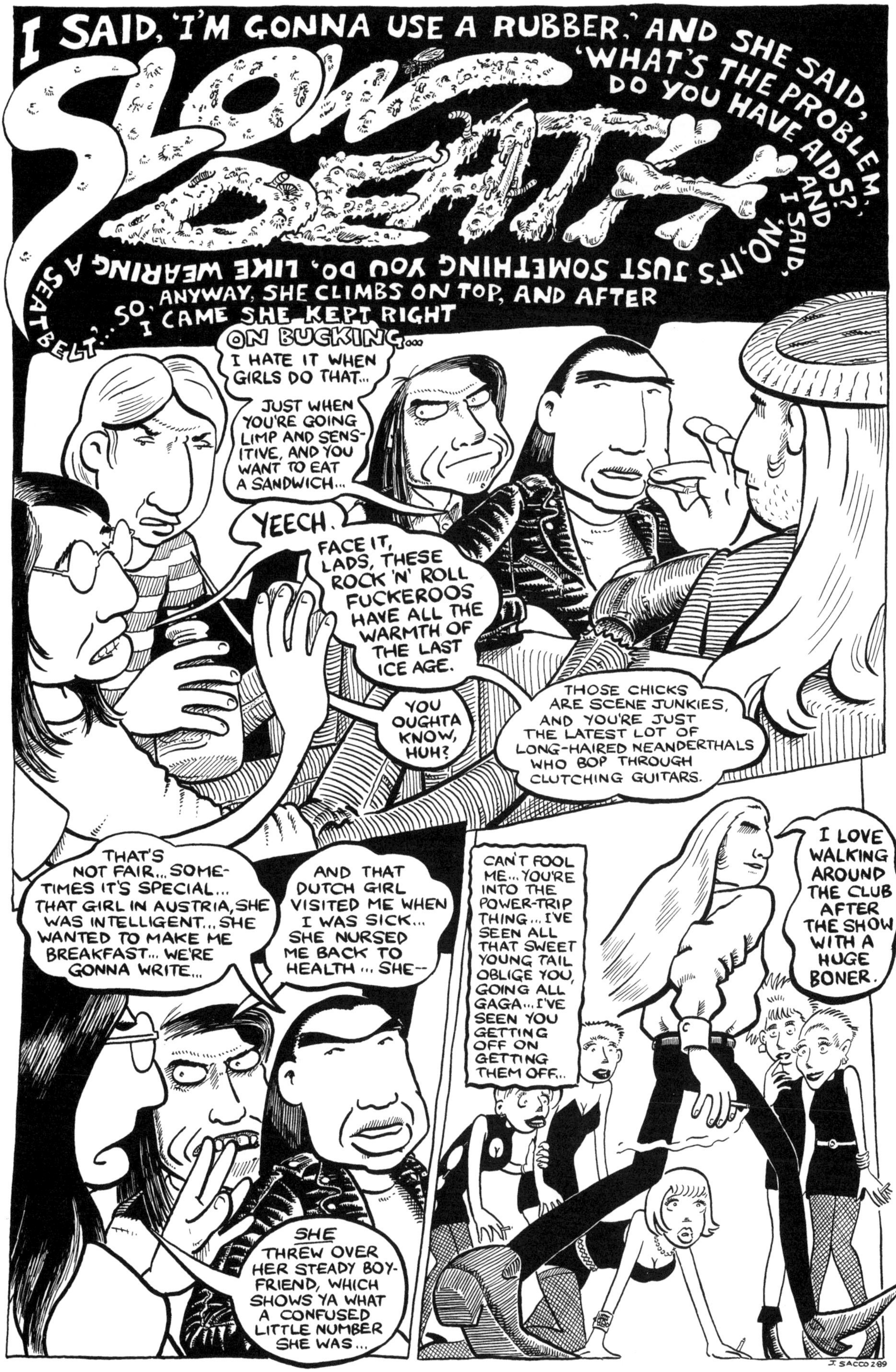

SLOW DEATH
I SAID, 'I'M GONNA USE A RUBBER,' AND SHE SAID, 'WHAT'S THE PROBLEM, DO YOU HAVE AIDS?,' AND I SAID, 'NO, IT'S JUST SOMETHING YOU DO, LIKE WEARING A SEATBELT'... SO, ANYWAY, SHE CLIMBS ON TOP, AND AFTER I CAME SHE KEPT RIGHT ON BUCKING...
I HATE IT WHEN GIRLS DO THAT... JUST WHEN YOU'RE GOING LIMP AND SENSITIVE, AND YOU WANT TO EAT A SANDWICH...
YEECH.
FACE IT, LADS, THESE ROCK 'N' ROLL FUCKEROOS HAVE ALL THE WARMTH OF THE LAST ICE AGE.
YOU OUGHTA KNOW, HUH?
THOSE CHICKS ARE SCENE JUNKIES, AND YOU'RE JUST THE LATEST LOT OF LONG-HAIRED NEANDERTHALS WHO BOP THROUGH CLUTCHING GUITARS.
THAT'S NOT FAIR... SOMETIMES IT'S SPECIAL... THAT GIRL IN AUSTRIA, SHE WAS INTELLIGENT... SHE WANTED TO MAKE ME BREAKFAST... WE'RE GONNA WRITE...
AND THAT DUTCH GIRL VISITED ME WHEN I WAS SICK... SHE NURSED ME BACK TO HEALTH ... SHE--
SHE THREW OVER HER STEADY BOYFRIEND, WHICH SHOWS YA WHAT A CONFUSED LITTLE NUMBER SHE WAS...
CAN'T FOOL ME... YOU'RE INTO THE POWER-TRIP THING... I'VE SEEN ALL THAT SWEET YOUNG TAIL OBLIGE YOU, GOING ALL GAGA... I'VE SEEN YOU GETTING OFF ON GETTING THEM OFF...
I LOVE WALKING AROUND THE CLUB AFTER THE SHOW WITH A HUGE BONER.
J. SACCO 2-89

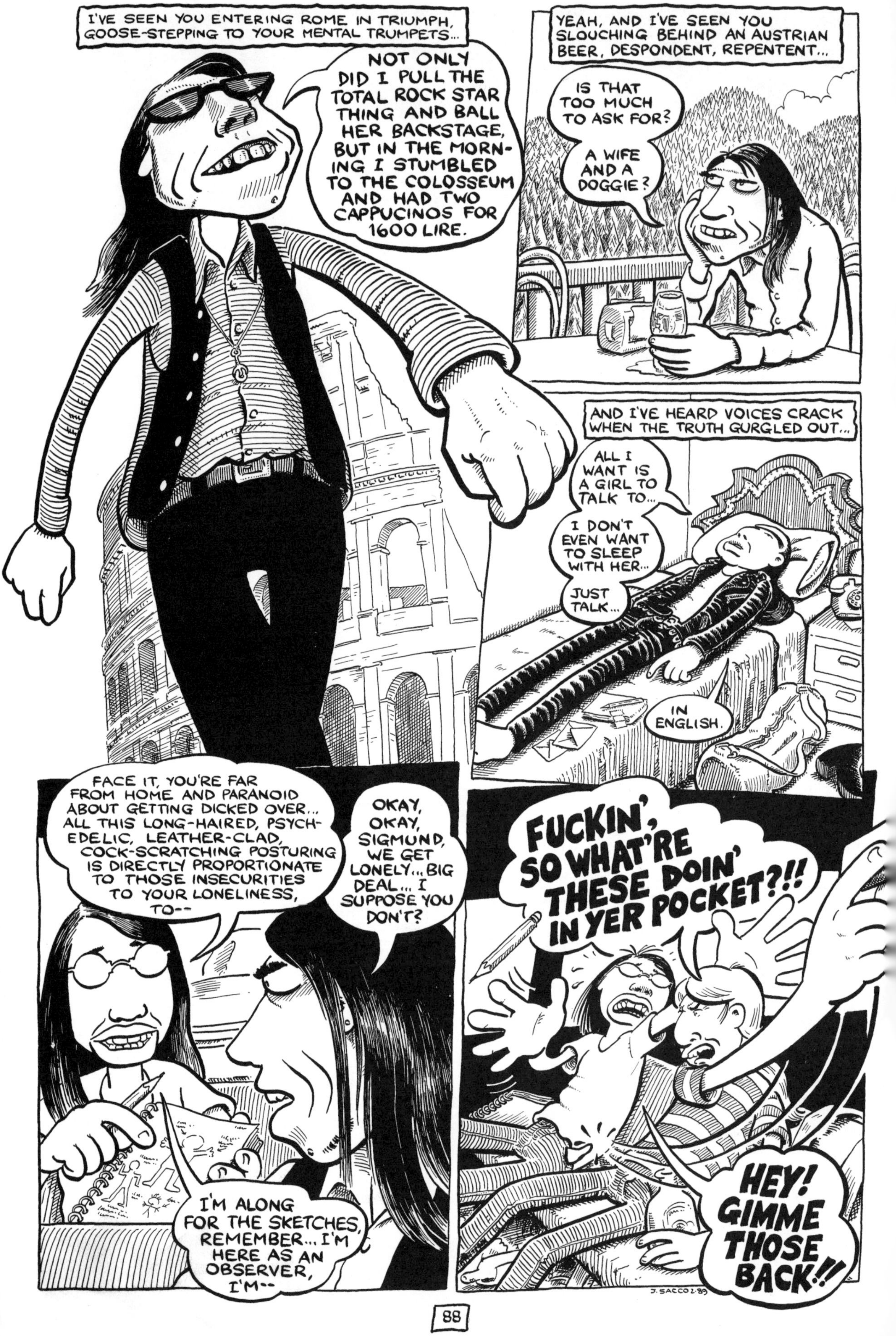

I'VE SEEN YOU ENTERING ROME IN TRIUMPH, GOOSE-STEPPING TO YOUR MENTAL TRUMPETS...
NOT ONLY DID I PULL THE TOTAL ROCK STAR THING AND BALL HER BACKSTAGE, BUT IN THE MORNING I STUMBLED TO THE COLOSSEUM AND HAD TWO CAPPUCINOS FOR 1600 LIRE.
YEAH, AND I'VE SEEN YOU SLOUCHING BEHIND AN AUSTRIAN BEER, DESPONDENT, REPENTENT...
IS THAT TOO MUCH TO ASK FOR?
A WIFE AND A DOGGIE?
AND I'VE HEARD VOICES CRACK WHEN THE TRUTH GURGLED OUT...
ALL I WANT IS A GIRL TO TALK TO...
I DON'T EVEN WANT TO SLEEP WITH HER...
JUST TALK...
IN ENGLISH.
FACE IT, YOU'RE FAR FROM HOME AND PARANOID ABOUT GETTING DICKED OVER... ALL THIS LONG-HAIRED, PSYCHEDELIC, LEATHER-CLAD, COCK-SCRATCHING POSTURING IS DIRECTLY PROPORTIONATE TO THOSE INSECURITIES TO YOUR LONELINESS, TO--
OKAY, OKAY, SIGMUND, WE GET LONELY... BIG DEAL... I SUPPOSE YOU DON'T?
I'M ALONG FOR THE SKETCHES, REMEMBER... I'M HERE AS AN OBSERVER, I'M--
FUCKIN', SO WHAT'RE THESE DOIN' IN YER POCKET?!!
HEY! GIMME THOSE BACK!!
J. SACCO 2·89

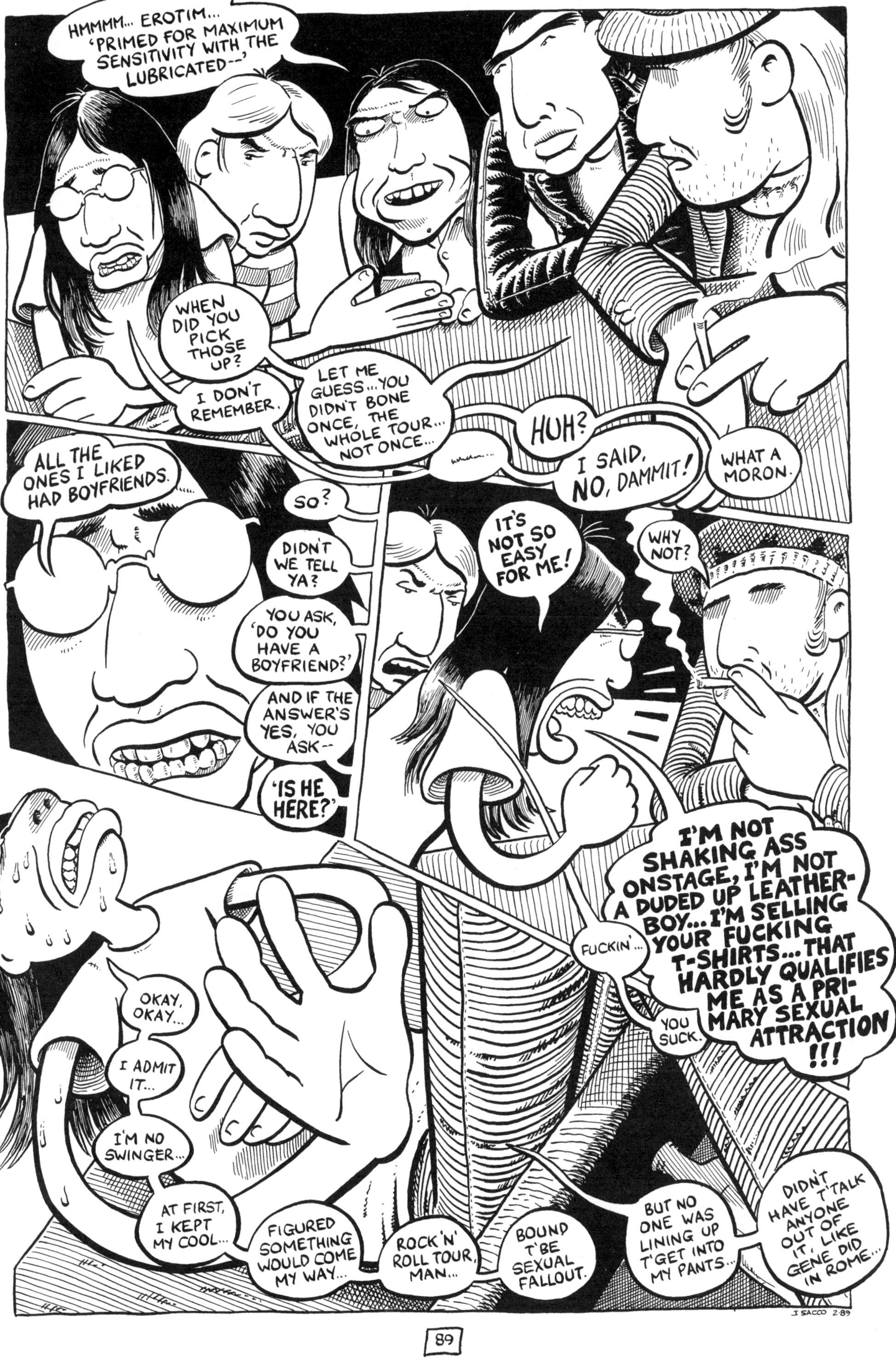
HMMMM... EROTIM... 'PRIMED FOR MAXIMUM SENSITIVITY WITH THE LUBRICATED--'
WHEN DID YOU PICK THOSE UP?
I DON'T REMEMBER.
LET ME GUESS... YOU DIDN'T BONE ONCE, THE WHOLE TOUR... NOT ONCE...
HUH?
I SAID, NO, DAMMIT!
WHAT A MORON.
ALL THE ONES I LIKED HAD BOYFRIENDS.
SO?
DIDN'T WE TELL YA?
YOU ASK, 'DO YOU HAVE A BOYFRIEND?'
AND IF THE ANSWER'S YES, YOU ASK--
'IS HE HERE?'
IT'S NOT SO EASY FOR ME!
WHY NOT?
I'M NOT SHAKING ASS ONSTAGE, I'M NOT A DUDED UP LEATHER-BOY... I'M SELLING YOUR FUCKING T-SHIRTS... THAT HARDLY QUALIFIES ME AS A PRIMARY SEXUAL ATTRACTION!!!
FUCKIN'...
YOU SUCK.
OKAY, OKAY...
I ADMIT IT...
I'M NO SWINGER...
AT FIRST, I KEPT MY COOL...
FIGURED SOMETHING WOULD COME MY WAY...
ROCK 'N' ROLL TOUR, MAN...
BOUND T'BE SEXUAL FALLOUT.
BUT NO ONE WAS LINING UP T'GET INTO MY PANTS...
DIDN'T HAVE T'TALK ANYONE OUT OF IT, LIKE GENE DID IN ROME...
J SACCO 2·89

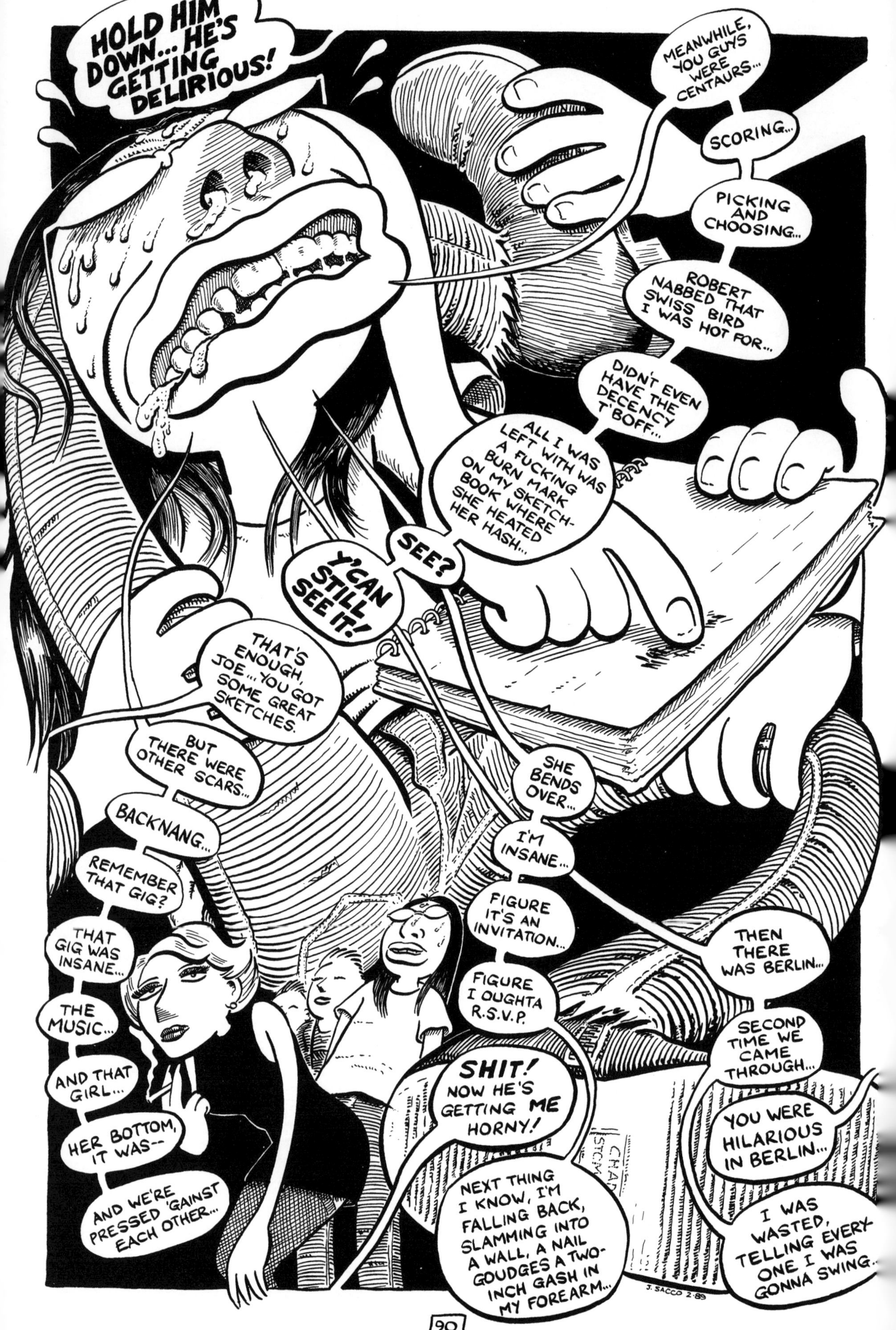
HOLD HIM DOWN... HE'S GETTING DELIRIOUS!
MEANWHILE, YOU GUYS WERE CENTAURS...
SCORING...
PICKING AND CHOOSING...
ROBERT NABBED THAT SWISS BIRD I WAS HOT FOR...
DIDN'T EVEN HAVE THE DECENCY T'BOFF...
ALL I WAS LEFT WITH WAS A FUCKING BURN MARK ON MY SKETCH-BOOK WHERE SHE HEATED HER HASH...
SEE?
Y'CAN STILL SEE IT!
THAT'S ENOUGH, JOE... YOU GOT SOME GREAT SKETCHES.
BUT THERE WERE OTHER SCARS...
BACKNANG...
REMEMBER THAT GIG?
THAT GIG WAS INSANE...
THE MUSIC...
AND THAT GIRL...
HER BOTTOM, IT WAS--
AND WE'RE PRESSED 'GAINST EACH OTHER...
SHE BENDS OVER...
I'M INSANE...
FIGURE IT'S AN INVITATION...
FIGURE I OUGHTA R.S.V.P.
SHIT! NOW HE'S GETTING ME HORNY!
NEXT THING I KNOW, I'M FALLING BACK, SLAMMING INTO A WALL, A NAIL GOUDGES A TWO-INCH GASH IN MY FOREARM...
THEN THERE WAS BERLIN...
SECOND TIME WE CAME THROUGH...
YOU WERE HILARIOUS IN BERLIN...
I WAS WASTED, TELLING EVERY-ONE I WAS GONNA SWING...
J. SACCO 2.89

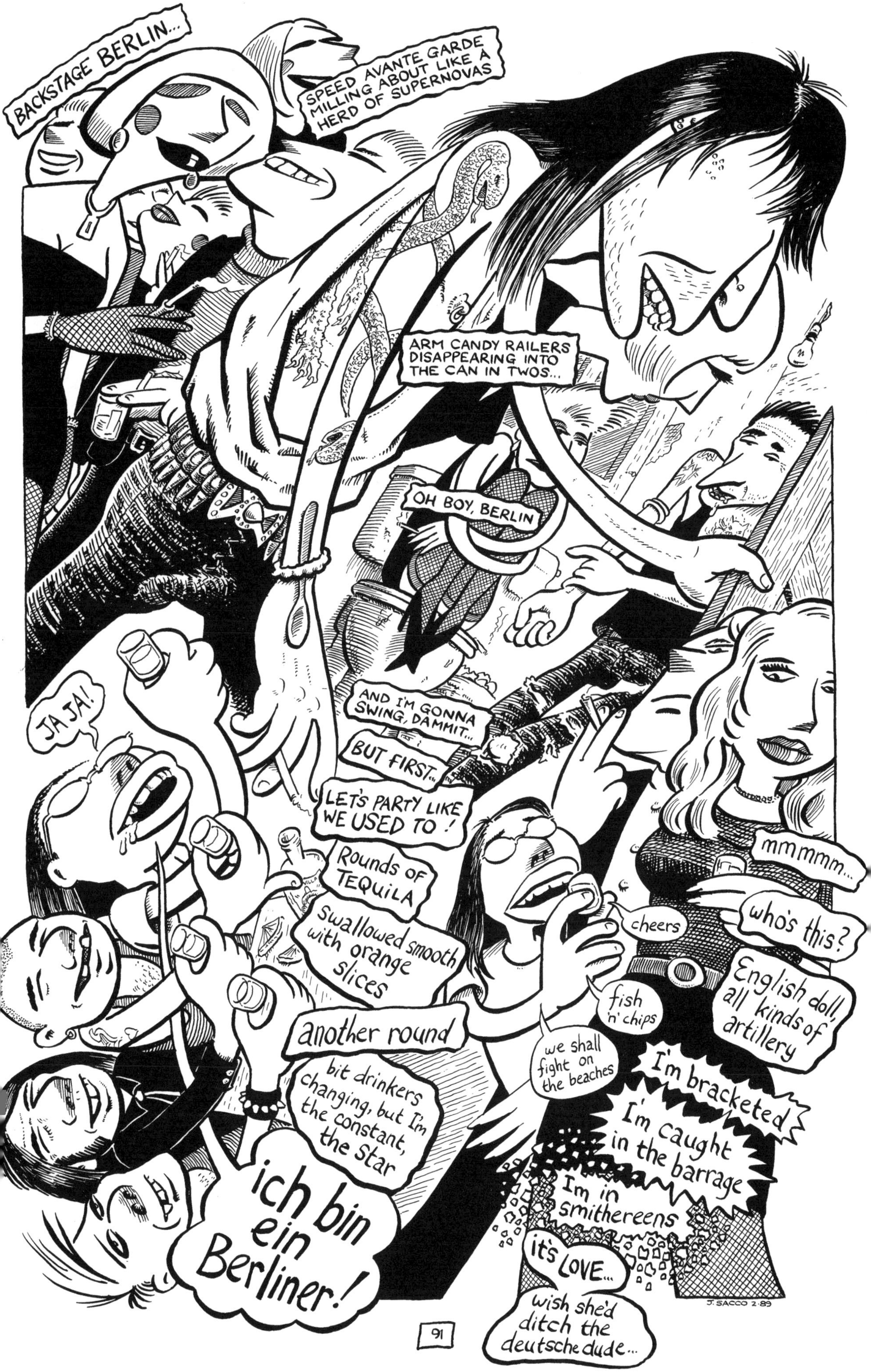
BACKSTAGE BERLIN...
SPEED AVANTE GARDE MILLING ABOUT LIKE A HERD OF SUPERNOVAS
ARM CANDY RAILERS DISAPPEARING INTO THE CAN IN TWOS...
OH BOY, BERLIN
AND I'M GONNA SWING, DAMMIT...
BUT FIRST...
LET'S PARTY LIKE WE USED TO!
JA JA!
Rounds of TEQUILA
Swallowed smooth with orange slices
another round
bit drinkers changing, but I'm the constant, the Star
ich bin ein Berliner!
mmmmm...
cheers
who's this?
English doll, all kinds of artillery
fish 'n' chips
we shall fight on the beaches
I'm bracketed
I'm caught in the barrage
I'm in smithereens
it's LOVE...
wish she'd ditch the deutsche dude...
J. SACCO 2·89

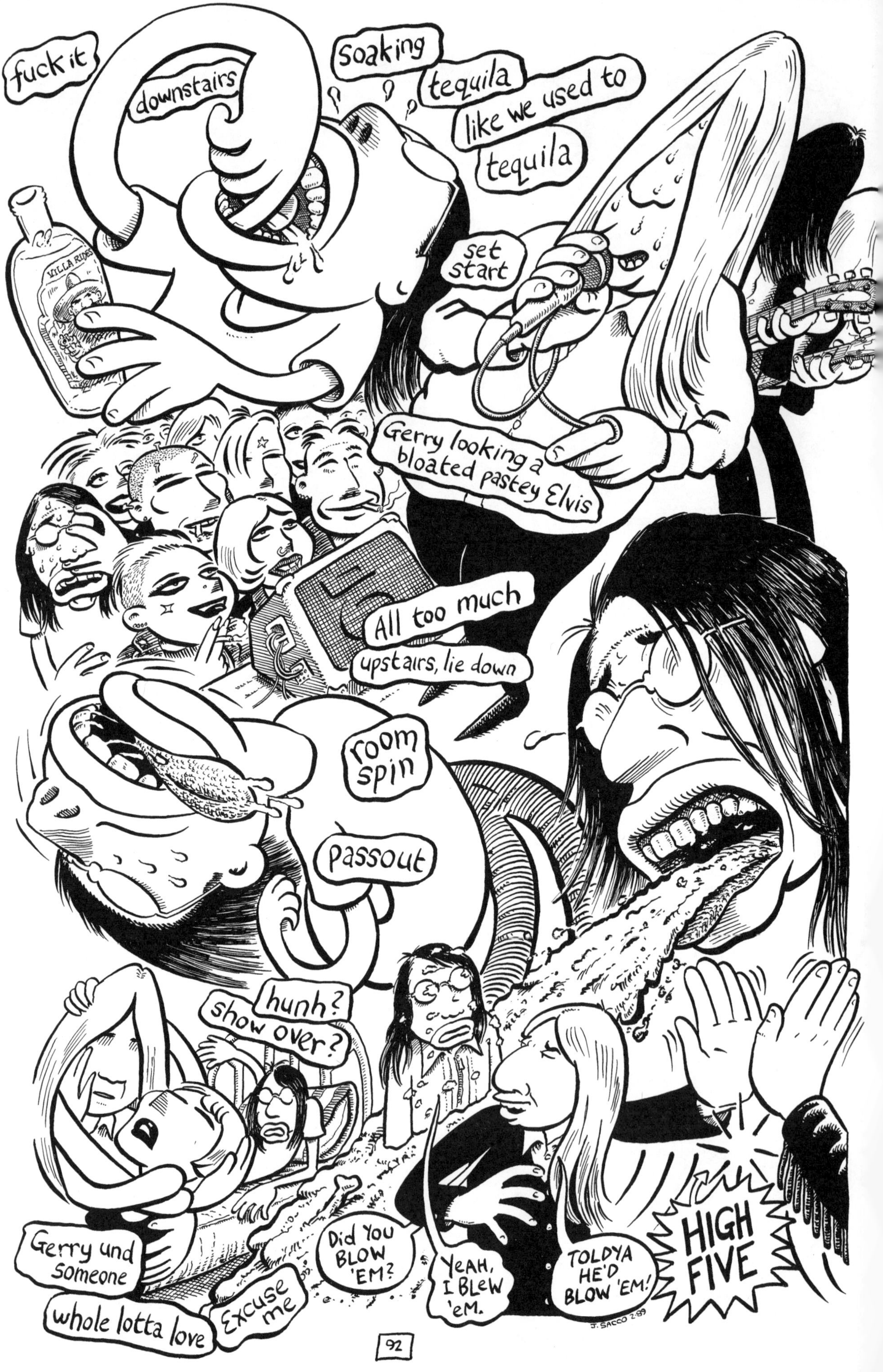
fuck it
downstairs
soaking
tequila
like we used to
tequila
VILLA RIDES
set start
Gerry looking a bloated pastey Elvis
All too much
upstairs, lie down
room spin
passout
hunh?
show over?
Gerry und someone
whole lotta love
Excuse me
Did You BLOW 'EM?
YeAH, I BLEW 'eM.
TOLDYA HE'D BLOW 'EM!
HIGH FIVE
J. SACCO 2-89

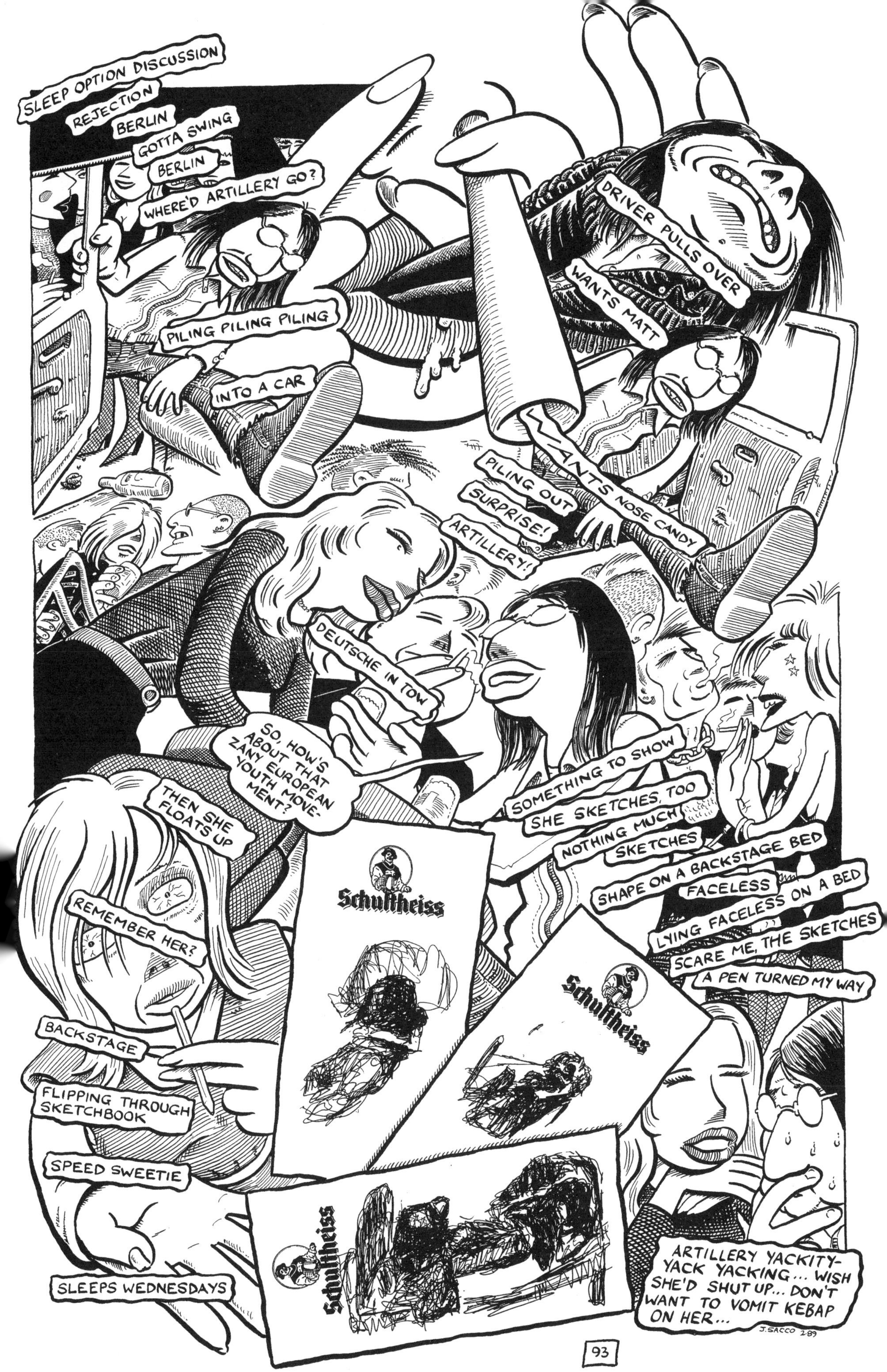

SLEEP OPTION DISCUSSION
REJECTION
BERLIN
GOTTA SWING
BERLIN
WHERE'D ARTILLERY GO?
PILING PILING PILING
INTO A CAR
DRIVER PULLS OVER
WANTS MATT
WANTS NOSE CANDY
PILING OUT
SURPRISE!
ARTILLERY!
DEUTSCHE IN TOW
SO, HOW'S ABOUT THAT ZANY EUROPEAN YOUTH MOVE-MENT?
THEN SHE FLOATS UP
SOMETHING TO SHOW
SHE SKETCHES, TOO
NOTHING MUCH
SKETCHES
SHAPE ON A BACKSTAGE BED
FACELESS
LYING FACELESS ON A BED
SCARE ME, THE SKETCHES
A PEN TURNED MY WAY
REMEMBER HER?
Schultheiss
Schultheiss
BACKSTAGE
FLIPPING THROUGH SKETCHBOOK
SPEED SWEETIE
Schultheiss
SLEEPS WEDNESDAYS
ARTILLERY YACKITY-YACK YACKING... WISH SHE'D SHUT UP... DON'T WANT TO VOMIT KEBAP ON HER...
J. SACCO 2.89

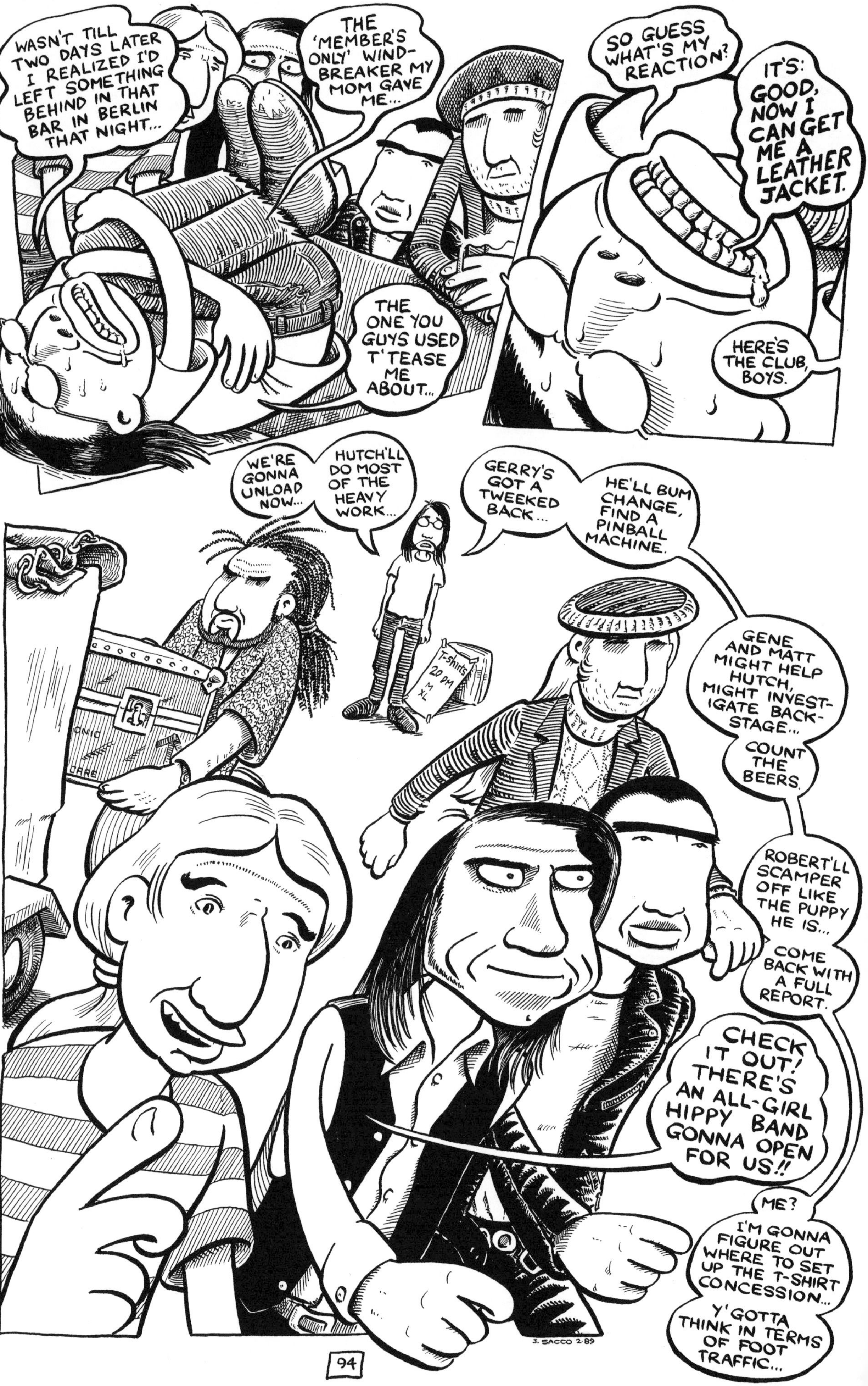
WASN'T TILL TWO DAYS LATER I REALIZED I'D LEFT SOMETHING BEHIND IN THAT BAR IN BERLIN THAT NIGHT...
THE 'MEMBER'S ONLY' WIND-BREAKER MY MOM GAVE ME...
THE ONE YOU GUYS USED T'TEASE ME ABOUT...
SO GUESS WHAT'S MY REACTION?
IT'S: GOOD, NOW I CAN GET ME A LEATHER JACKET.
HERE'S THE CLUB, BOYS.
WE'RE GONNA UNLOAD NOW...
HUTCH'LL DO MOST OF THE HEAVY WORK...
GERRY'S GOT A TWEEKED BACK...
HE'LL BUM CHANGE, FIND A PINBALL MACHINE.
GENE AND MATT MIGHT HELP HUTCH, MIGHT INVEST-IGATE BACK-STAGE...
COUNT THE BEERS.
ROBERT'LL SCAMPER OFF LIKE THE PUPPY HE IS...
COME BACK WITH A FULL REPORT.
CHECK IT OUT! THERE'S AN ALL-GIRL HIPPY BAND GONNA OPEN FOR US!!
ME?
I'M GONNA FIGURE OUT WHERE TO SET UP THE T-SHIRT CONCESSION...
Y'GOTTA THINK IN TERMS OF FOOT TRAFFIC...
T-Shirts 20 PM M XL
J. SACCO 2·89

PART FIVE:

A DISGUSTING
EXPERIENCE

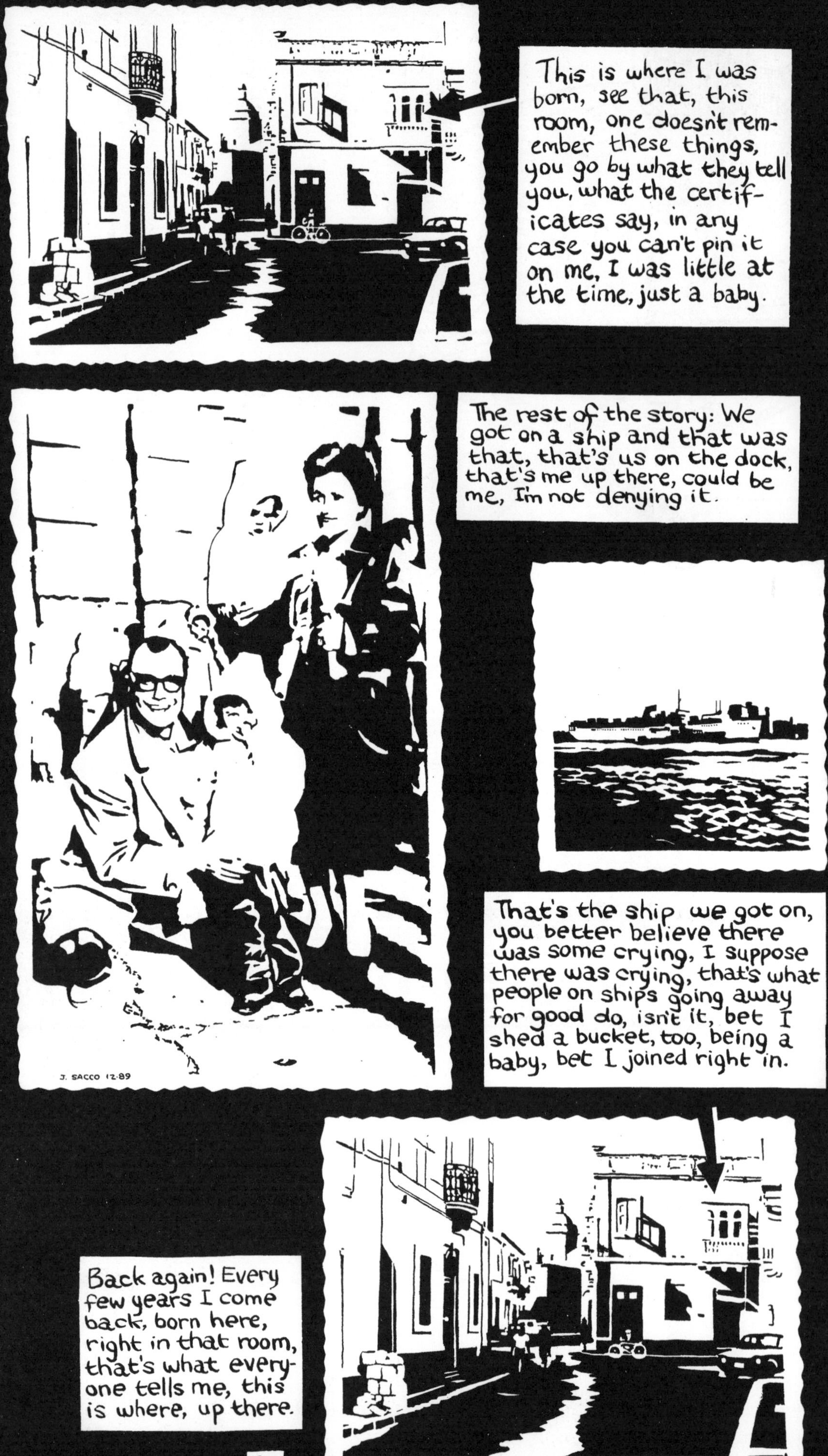
This is where I was born, see that, this room, one doesn't remember these things, you go by what they tell you, what the certificates say, in any case you can't pin it on me, I was little at the time, just a baby.
The rest of the story: We got on a ship and that was that, that's us on the dock, that's me up there, could be me, I'm not denying it.
J. SACCO 12·89
That's the ship we got on, you better believe there was some crying, I suppose there was crying, that's what people on ships going away for good do, isn't it, bet I shed a bucket, too, being a baby, bet I joined right in.
Back again! Every few years I come back, born here, right in that room, that's what everyone tells me, this is where, up there.

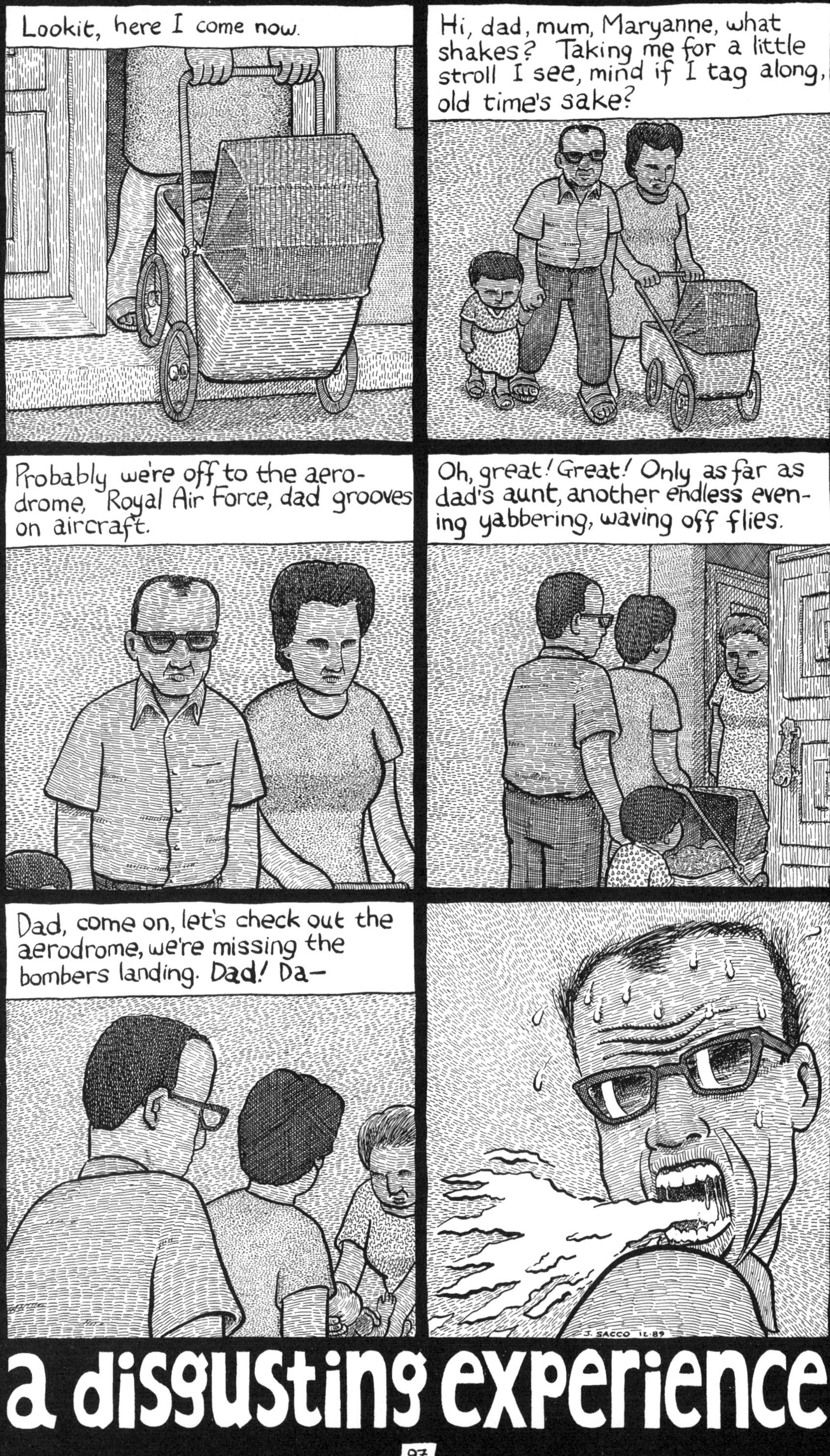
Lookit, here I come now.
Hi, dad, mum, Maryanne, what shakes? Taking me for a little stroll I see, mind if I tag along, old time's sake?
Probably we're off to the aerodrome, Royal Air Force, dad grooves on aircraft.
Oh, great! Great! Only as far as dad's aunt, another endless evening yabbering, waving off flies.
Dad, come on, let's check out the aerodrome, we're missing the bombers landing. Dad! Da—
J. SACCO 12·89
a disgusting experience

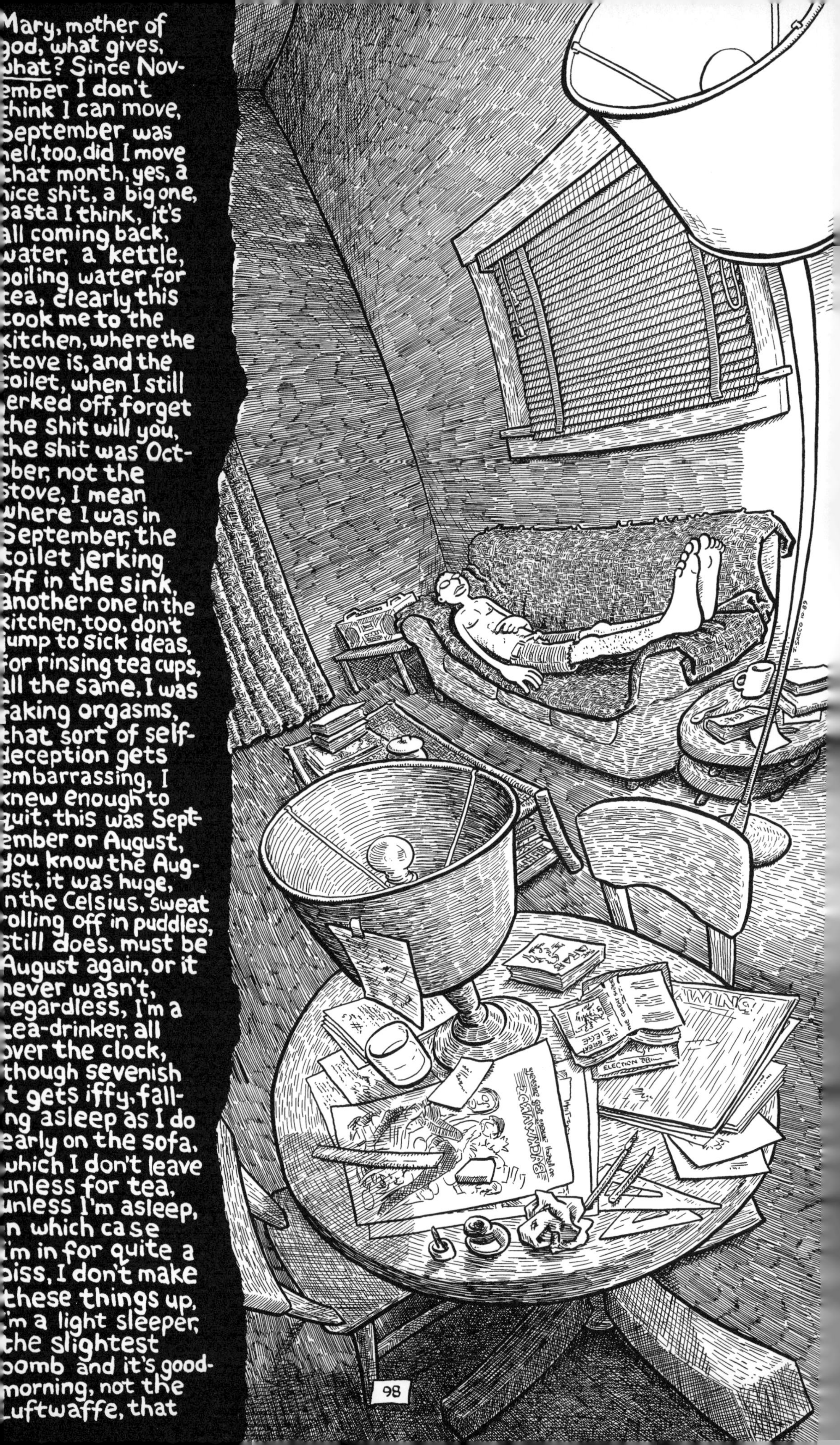

Mary, mother of god, what gives, what? Since November I don't think I can move, September was hell, too, did I move that month, yes, a nice shit, a big one, pasta I think, it's all coming back, water, a kettle, boiling water for tea, clearly this took me to the kitchen, where the stove is, and the toilet, when I still jerked off, forget the shit will you, the shit was October, not the stove, I mean where I was in September, the toilet jerking off in the sink, another one in the kitchen, too, don't jump to sick ideas, for rinsing tea cups, all the same, I was faking orgasms, that sort of self-deception gets embarrassing, I knew enough to quit, this was September or August, you know the August, it was huge, in the Celsius, sweat rolling off in puddles, still does, must be August again, or it never wasn't, regardless, I'm a tea-drinker, all over the clock, though sevenish it gets iffy, falling asleep as I do early on the sofa, which I don't leave unless for tea, unless I'm asleep, in which case I'm in for quite a piss, I don't make these things up, I'm a light sleeper, the slightest bomb and it's good-morning, not the Luftwaffe, that
ELECTION '88

was '42, good guess, I mean now, outside, blam! hear that? There's a religion going on, blam-blam-blam! fireworks! color! an inferno in the sky! coach-loads of English on the roundtrip oohing and ahhing, they're clapping, on their tiptoes, they've never seen anything like it! tourists take to sulfur, I take it personally, this is my snooze we're talking about, blam-blam-blam! culture I suppose, priests making signs of the cross, bell-ringing, tran-substantiation, statues hoisted in and out of churches, two or three bands march through the whole works, it's in the Berlitz, blam-blam-blam! two millenniums of soot coming down, it leaves a pious gunk, everyone wears a layer, I'm not so fashion con-scious, I'm quite content on my sofa thank you, blam-blam-blam! okay, a confession, who am I joshing, this is first-class sour grapes, then, years ago, I oohed, I ahhed, my cousin and I, we followed our noses to the sulfur, we buzzed around, chased girls, nights we reeked of whiskey, 'Slow down! you'll get us killed! har har!' I've got stories, then, now he'd tear my head off, let's skip it, it's simple, I've changed, everyone's the first to notice, my hair, but let's

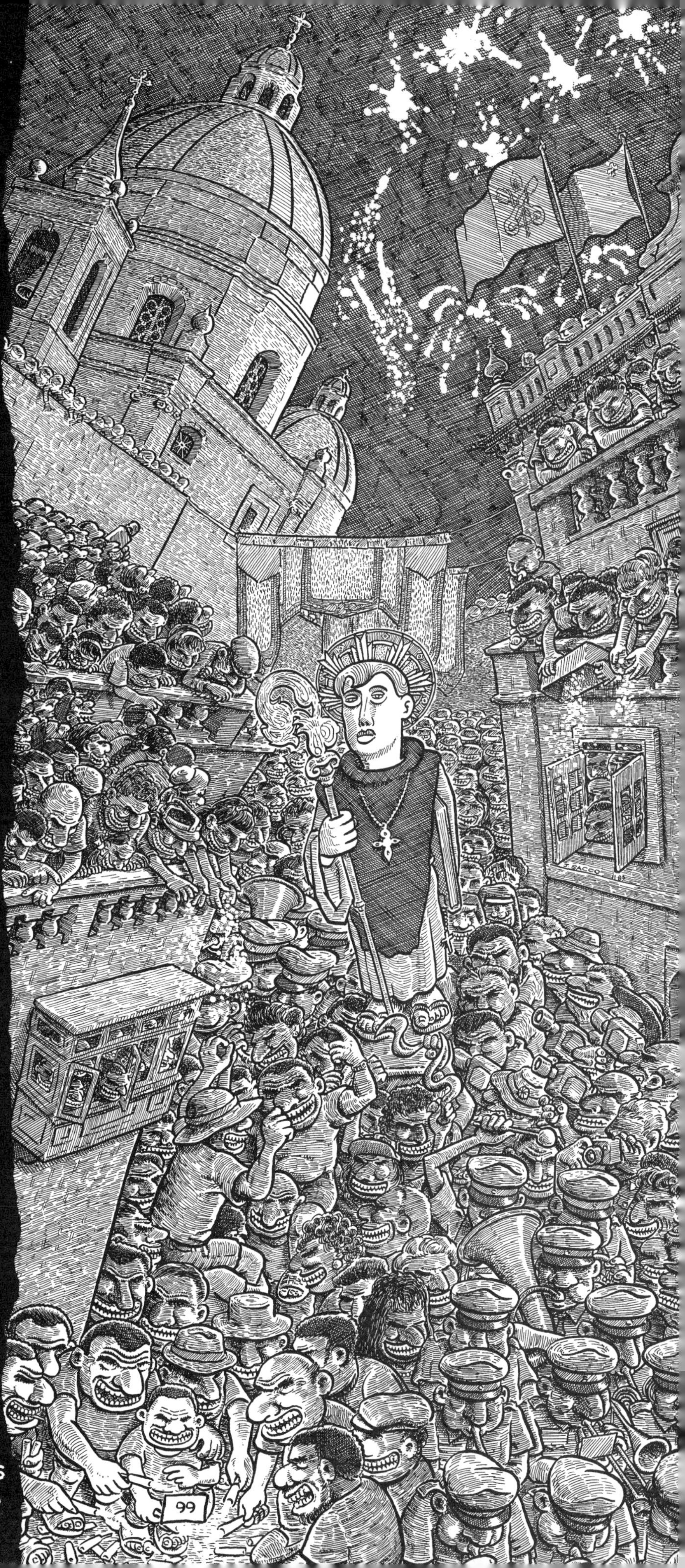

skip it, I haven't changed a bit, 'You're still running around, having fun, that's the life', they smell a rat, something's queer, my hair, I'm not kidding, my forearms, too, a girl's forearms, my dick if they could see that, my hands, you get the picture, the entire checklist, it's <u>me</u>, me not leaving a ring of quarry slime round the tub, me without an honest pair of stinking feet, me who's never worked in a factory, and my uncle says if I've never worked in a factory in his book I've never worked, he started with the English forces bashing rats, ended up cooking for the Americans, not the rats, he can set me up spray-painting cars, do I want the job, yes or no, let's skip it, I keep my trap shut, I zip up, loose lips sink ships, they try, they ply me with tea, they lay a heavy verbal minefield—'What are you cooking tonight?'—hard to port! I'm weaving a zigzag—'Seriously, what about your hair?'—shudders! straining at the bulkheads!—'Found a girl yet?'—a flash of her blue eyes and the sea's gushing in! bridge to engineroom: on the pumps chop-chop! a near miss! the kettle whistles, another cup, steaming, a real soother, I take a sip, I sigh,

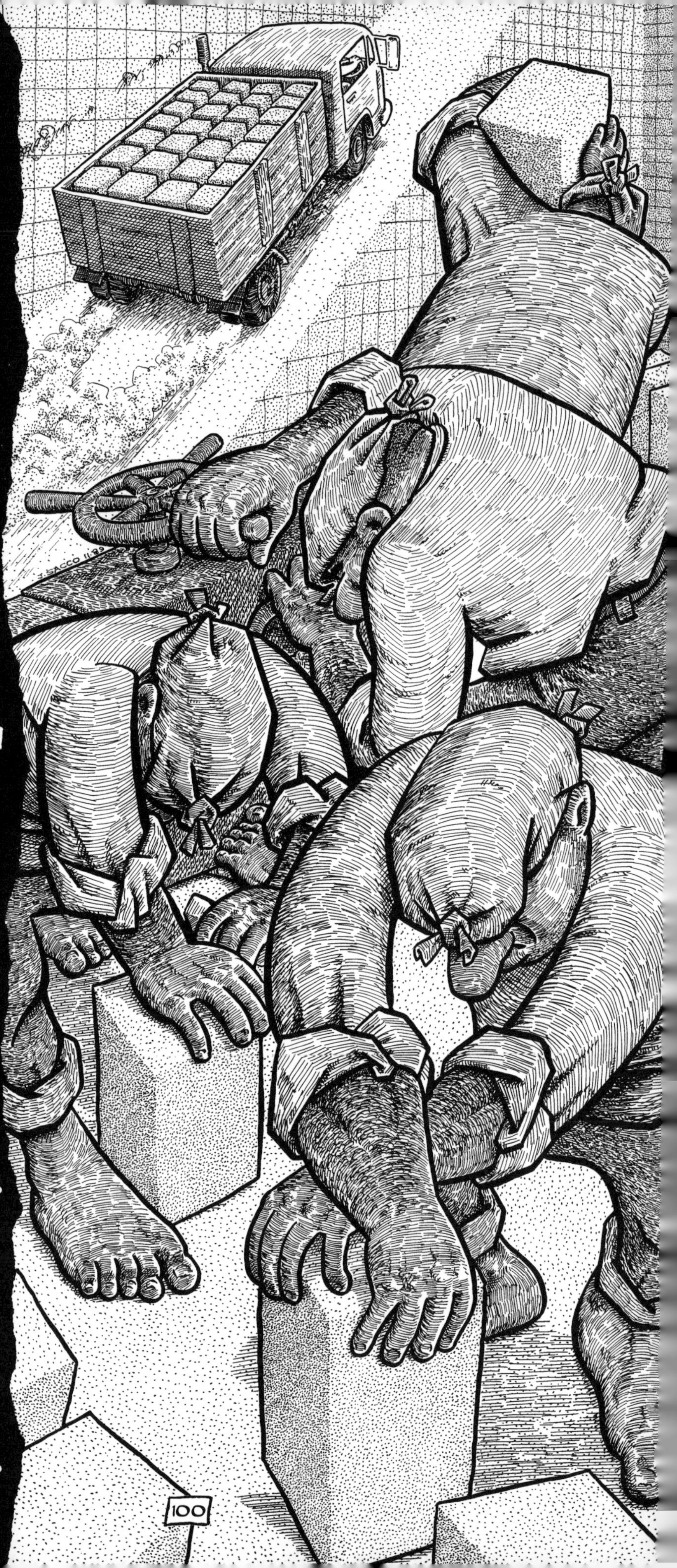

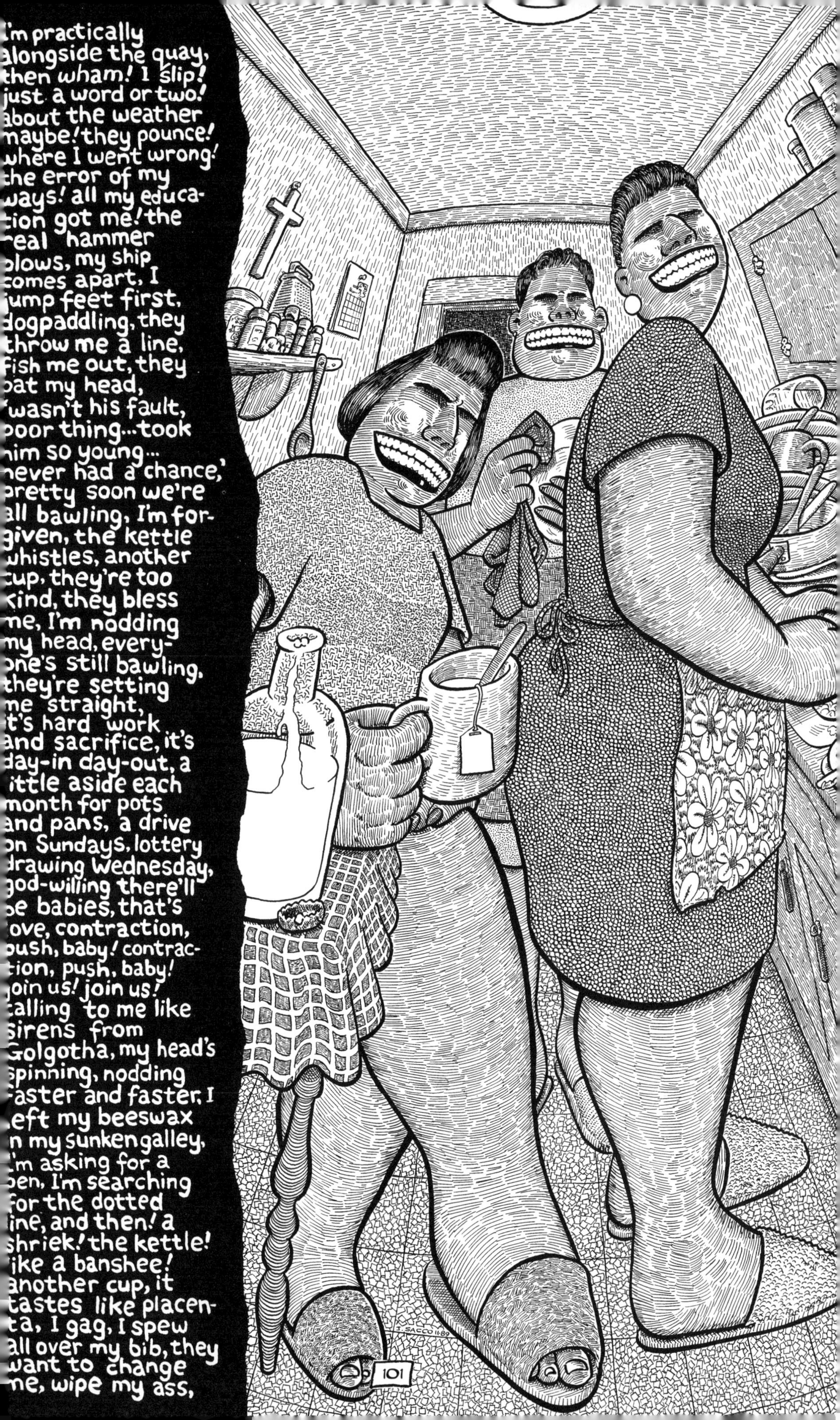

I'm practically alongside the quay, then wham! I slip! just a word or two! about the weather maybe! they pounce! where I went wrong! the error of my ways! all my education got me! the real hammer blows, my ship comes apart, I jump feet first, dogpaddling, they throw me a line, fish me out, they pat my head, 'wasn't his fault, poor thing...took him so young... never had a chance,' pretty soon we're all bawling, I'm forgiven, the kettle whistles, another cup, they're too kind, they bless me, I'm nodding my head, everyone's still bawling, they're setting me straight, it's hard work and sacrifice, it's day-in day-out, a little aside each month for pots and pans, a drive on Sundays, lottery drawing Wednesday, god-willing there'll be babies, that's love, contraction, push, baby! contraction, push, baby! join us! join us! calling to me like sirens from Golgotha, my head's spinning, nodding faster and faster, I left my beeswax in my sunken galley, I'm asking for a pen, I'm searching for the dotted line, and then! a shriek! the kettle! like a banshee! another cup, it tastes like placenta, I gag, I spew all over my bib, they want to change me, wipe my ass,
T. SACCO 11-89

give me the
nipple, I crawl off,
I'm out of there,
back on my sofa,
I piece together
a jigsaw, missing
a piece, probably
came off on the
bus, those things
have no suspension,
a national disgrace,
but back on my
sofa, relief hardly
a comfort, wool-
covered, smells
when you sweat
into it, I sleep
with the lights on,
it's easier to read
that way, I close
the blinds early,
it's symbolic, they
know I'm home, I
know, too, so we're
even steven, ha ha
ha, goddamn her, I'll
be better when
she loves me, but
don't bring her into
it, her blue eyes,
shut up! when
was the last time
I jerked off, where
is it? there it is!
is that it? well
forget it all over
again, skip it, un-
less Sergio, nah,
he hasn't come by
since— unless
Sergio roars up on
his motorbike, the
nosey parkers will
crack blinds for
that, they like to
know what's up,
head out on the
highway, whatever
comes our way, if
he borrowed the
spare helmet, that
rocker bar, those
rocker chicks, yeh!
we'll reek of whis-
key, I'll buy, Bon
Jovi? Sure! me and
Bon Jovi are like
this if you know
what I mean, I'll
send you a video,
har har, what a
fucking pip, those
rocker chicks loved
my ass, though
Sergio hasn't come

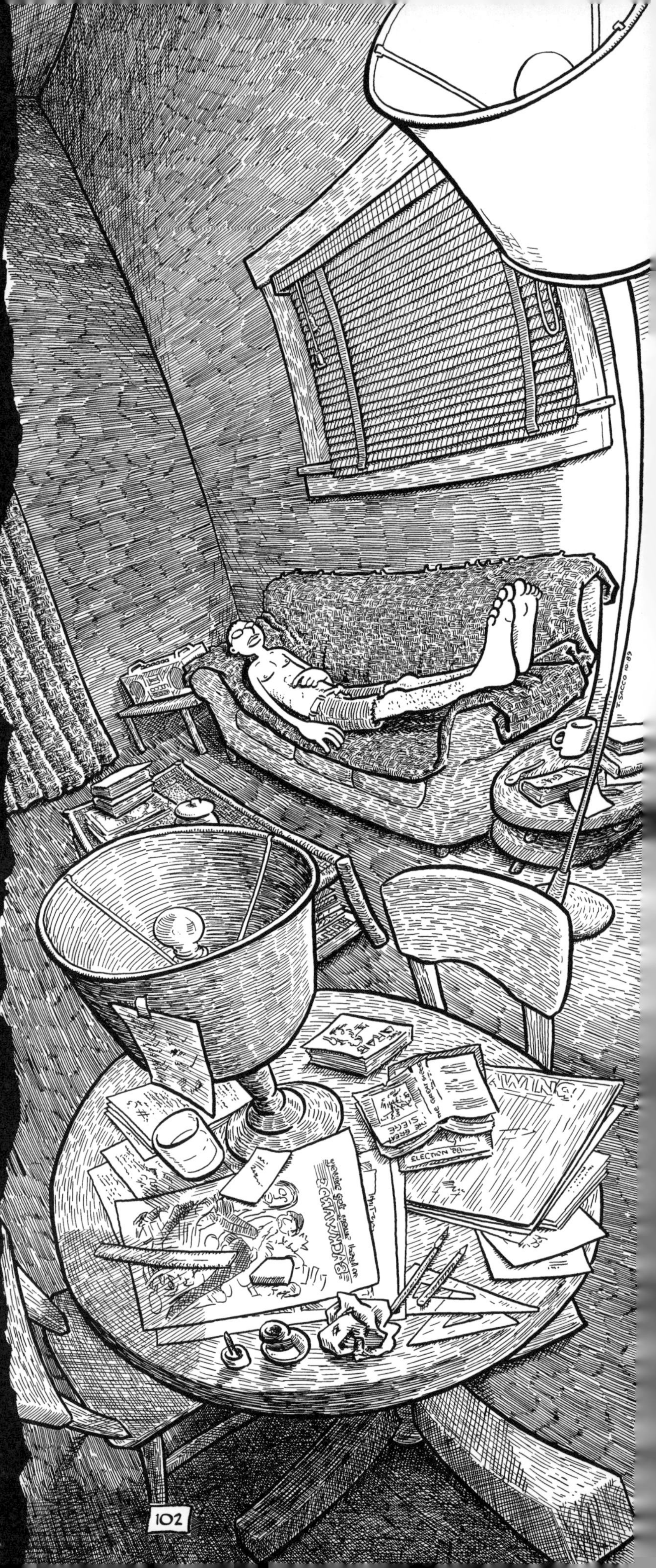
ELECTION '88

by since I don't know when, so I'll stay on my sofa, I'll read till he doesn't get here, I hope with the spare helmet— I wake! shrieks! nightmare? yes, no, oh fuck, the fishmonger screaming her balls off, 'Still alive! They're still alive!' are they, cunt, go park your pram on the moon, 'Still alive!' I cover my head, where are my sheep, 62, 63, 64, 65, but fuck me, corrugated garage doors scrape open, engines backfire, 64, 63, 62, chained dogs yelp and howl, woman upstairs brains her child, shotguns extinguish all hope, pretty soon the schoolkids are at it, they're jamming on my doorbell, tearing up and down the street, their mommas tearing after 'em, 'You fall and hurt yourself, I'll smash you,' forget the sheep, fill the kettle, boil baby boil, after tea more tea, then I go on the roof, watch wash getting hung, it's all there, they really put themselves on the line, smallest to largest, lightest to darkest, societies live by certain conventions, don't go pegging a sock between two blouses, don't give it the raspberries, this is a dangerous place, bam-bam-bam! not '42, shotguns, feathers, another migrating bird that should never have bothered, stuffed with the others in my

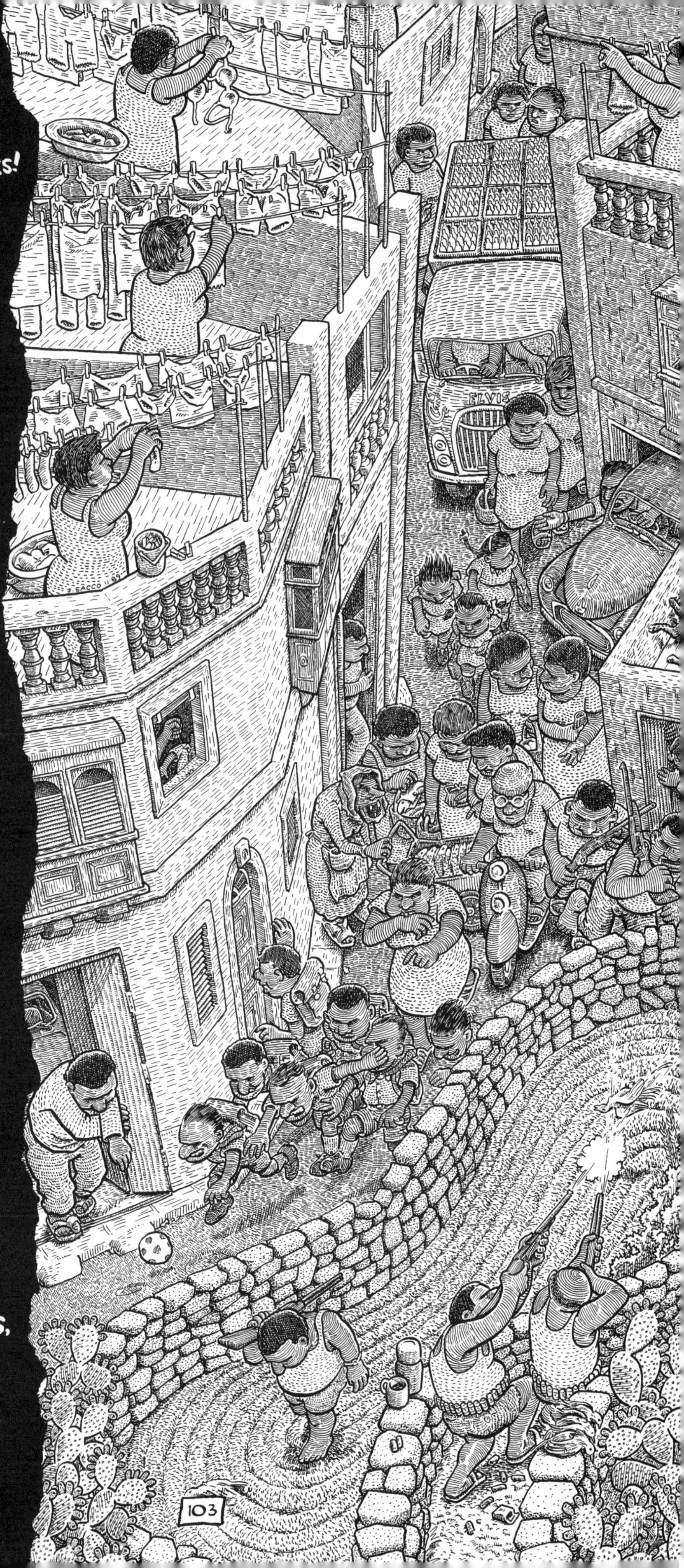
ELVIS
J. SACCO

cousin's showcase, my cousin, one look at me, just off the boat, I'd taken a taxi, the fuck charges me what it cost to get half down Italy, anyway, my cousin, I've got long hair, one look at me, I'm just off from Sicily you understand and: 'There's those that'll tear your head off,' he says that, would've done it himself, too, my mother and his mother came through the same hole, that's what gives him pause, blood's thicker than water, thank the Virgin for that, years ago to the sulfur we followed our noses, and it burns burns burns, the sun, the roof bakes, and something happens to a day, an hour or two hearing mailmen stop out front, tea comes and goes and comes, sharpening pencils, not thinking about her blue eyes, a cough the next time I see her, she's drenched, never forgives me for the weather, you'd be surprised, something happens to a day, later there's a strip show, an Italian channel, give me a break, but maybe I'm getting ahead of myself, though probably not, about the weather I mean, maybe it was me, but she laughed at those jokes, I always put my best foot forward, an awkward way to

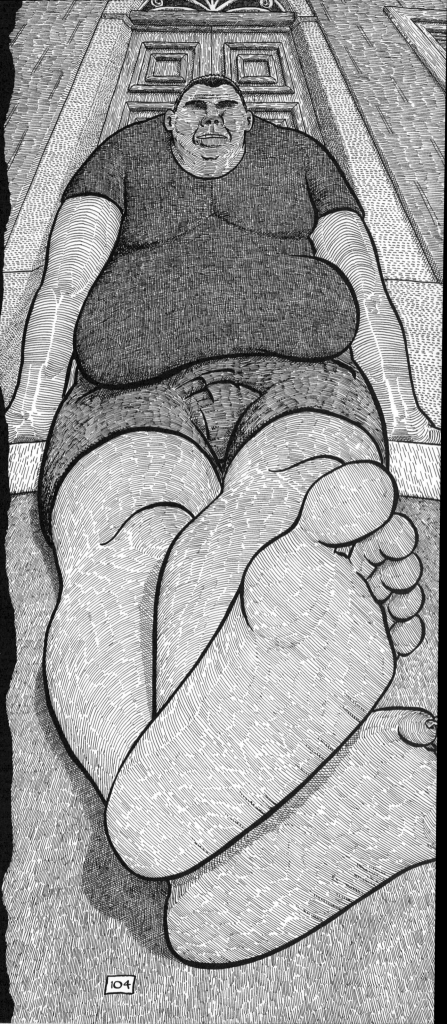

104

walk, screw it, I close the blinds early, and that's what happens to a day, I need a rest, some Alps, a butterfly net, I know, I should get out more, I do when there's no tea, the minimart, my aunt's, I've tried a wider tack, museums, cathedrals, I've read the pamphlets, circled spots of interest, tilted my head to one side for a chiaroscuro, half a pound for one lousy Caravaggio, no thanks, and the guide telling me it's Czechoslovakian glass and getting another half quid for it, you can keep it, the whole ball of wax, and, hell, the Grand Harbor, too, this hallowed ground, years ago, here, where you'd find me, where doped janissaries charged, dive-bombing Stukas wailed, here, even this, take it, go on, out of my sight, and for the love of god don't you think I tried, eyes shut tight, forcing so hard I thought I'd brown my emotional underpants, where once, here, I dissolved into something (what?), here, nothing, nada, and if ever a spell there was, and there is no spell, gone, irretrievable, when, don't rush me, the old man, I am hoping for an ex-stevedore, a sweeping story to dissolve me like years ago, he shuffles up and offers me his hand, ahem, his hand on my cock, do I make myself clear, a hand job, and here the janissaries were mown down, the Stukas smash-

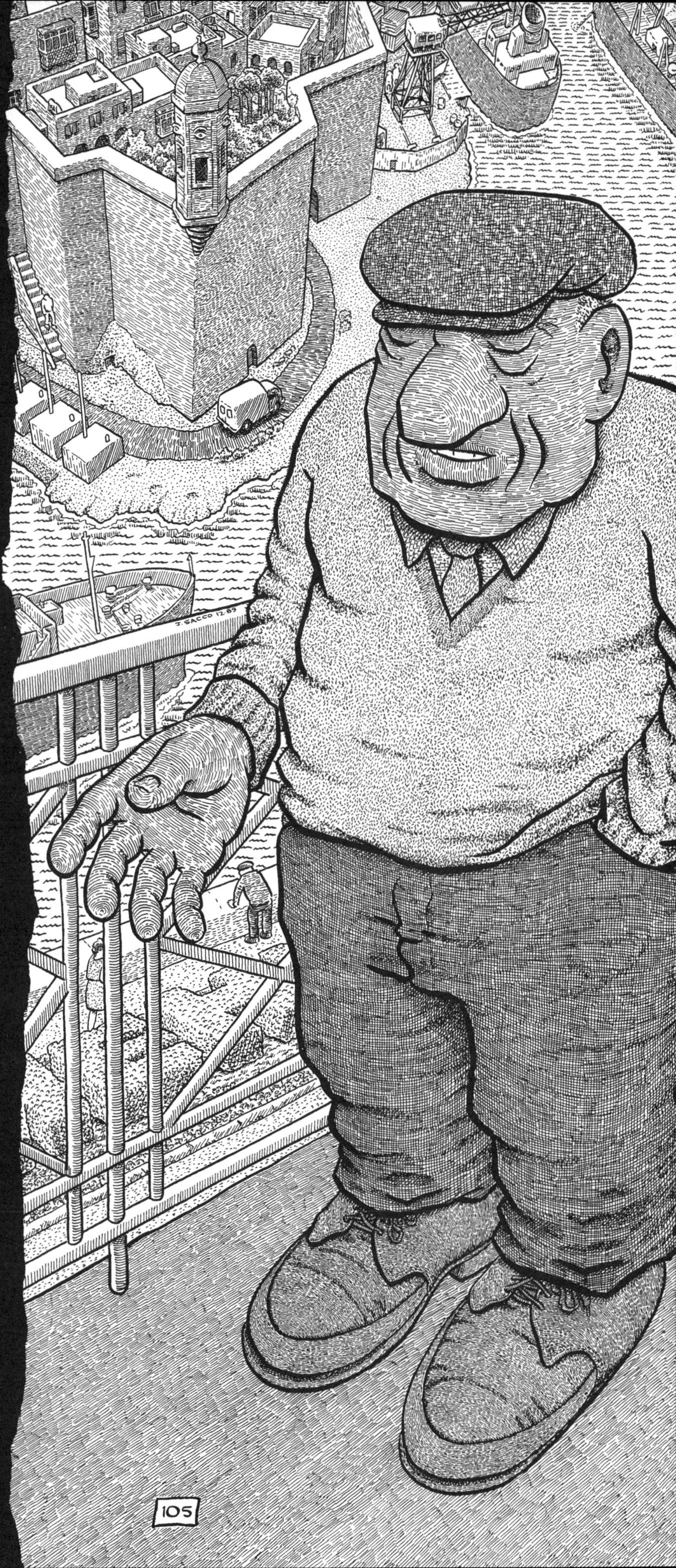
J. SACCO 12.89

ed in scores, and I stumble from something (what?) I had years ago, forever, to the bus, the bus that rattles, drops into potholes, deficiting the jig-saw by one more piece, I tumble off, and then, then—oh, Christ, I've told you nothing yet, <u>nothing</u>—them, between you and your sofa, here they are, you are amongst them, beware! they look good on the evening stoop, half-slapping at mosquitoes, working rosary beads, Mediterranean tip to toe, the whole National Geographic shebang, and, as you pass, they will nod, beware! for this is no salutation wishing for your good health, it is awareness, it is awareness, it is, awareness, and they'll flatten you in a second and kick your balls, in if it gets any darker, for good measure if you were born here, again if your poppa played clarinet in the band club, they've separated the wheat from the chaff, and on my sofa, relief! I pant like a dog, and my eyes close, and her blue eyes open, she got drenched, and I am drenched, I blame it on the weather, August? it smells when you sweat into it, I close the blinds early, switch the lights off, too, a new tactic, no one will know I'm home, no one

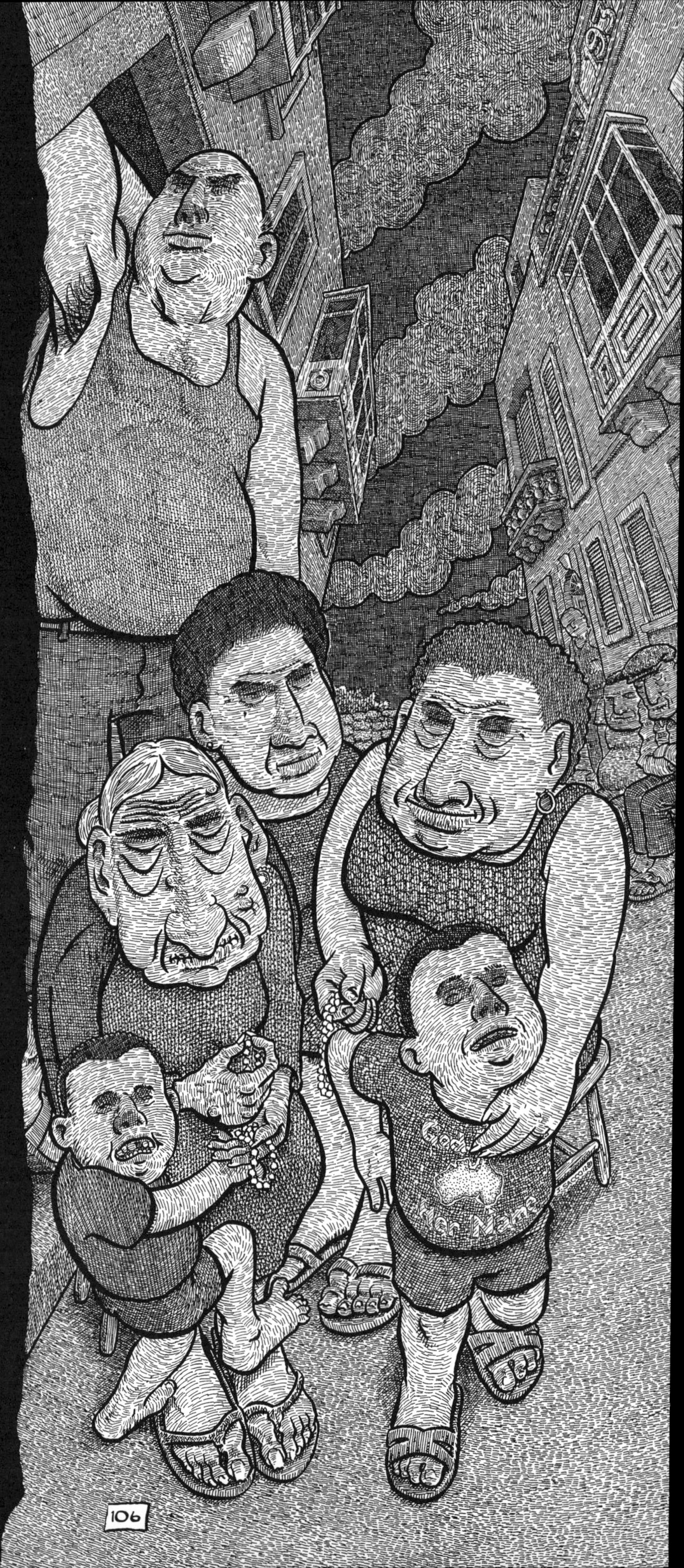

but Sergio, will he know, he should know to try the doorbell, but he might not think of it, I turn the lights back on, and he won't show up, but he will know I am home, I hope with the spare helmet.

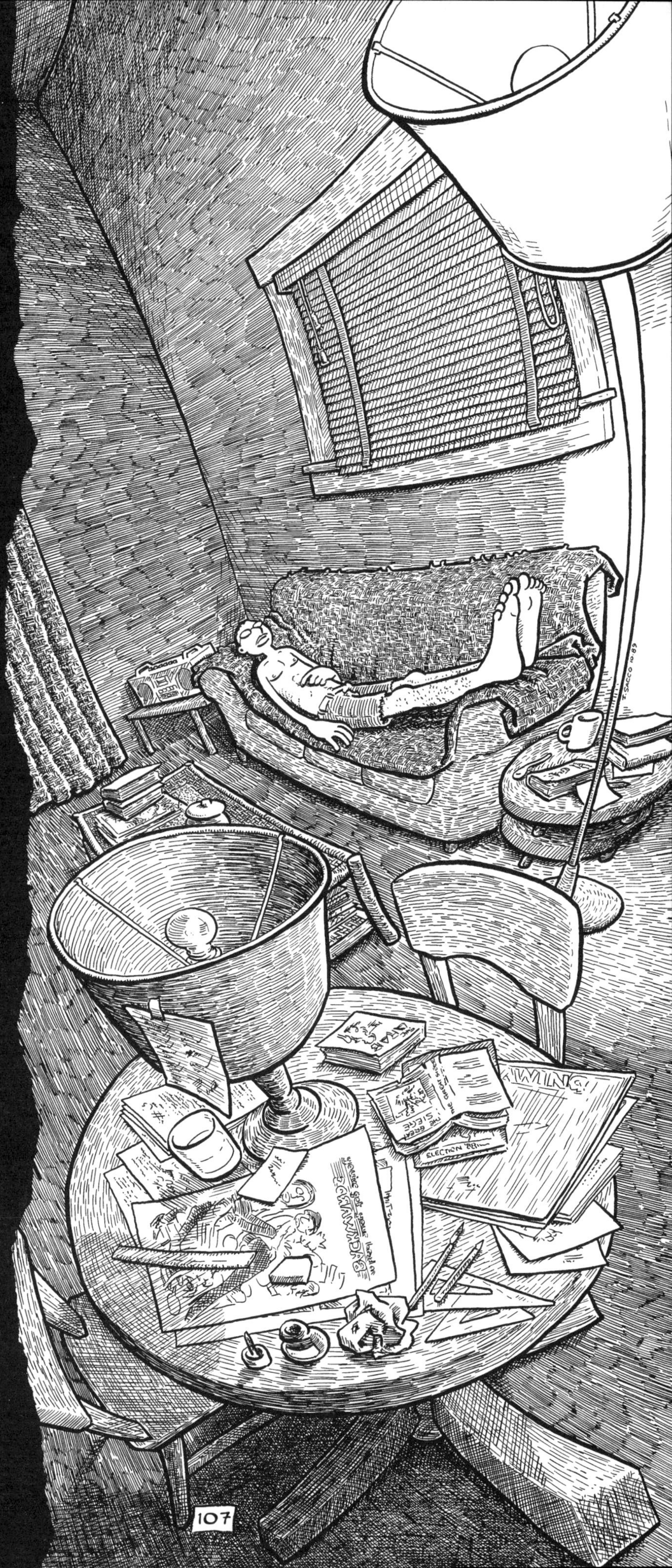

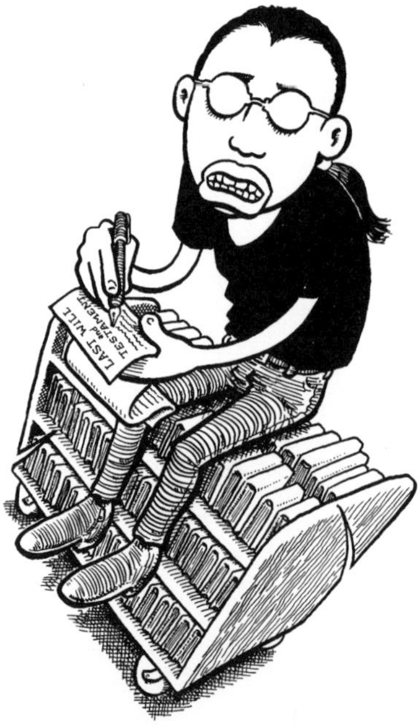
LAST WILL and TESTAMENT

Part Six:

Voyage To The End Of The Library

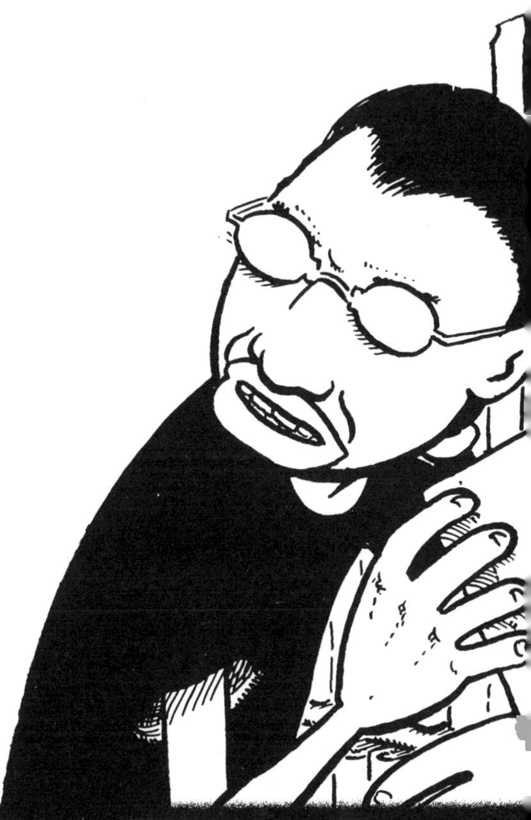

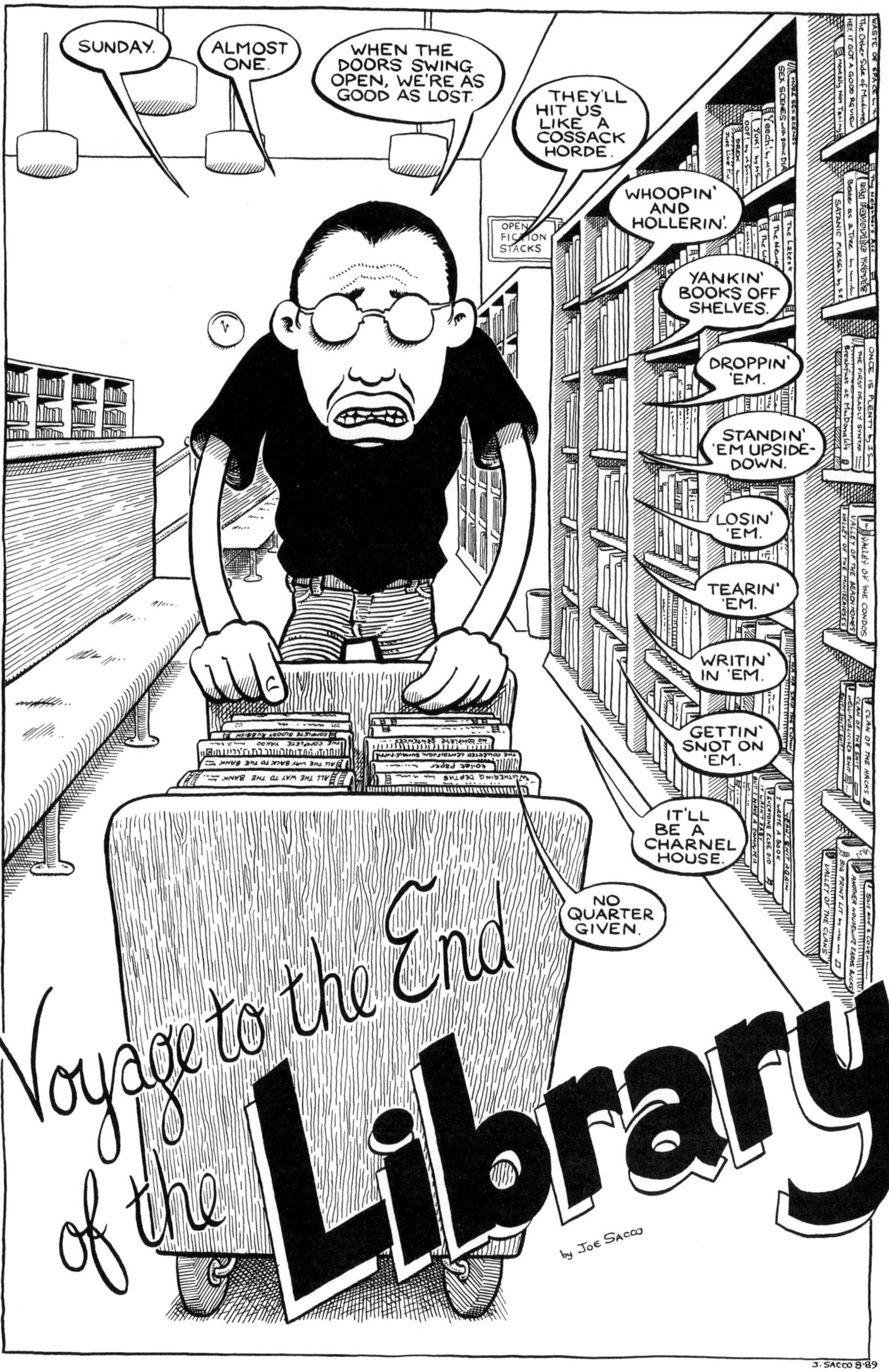
SUNDAY.
ALMOST ONE.
WHEN THE DOORS SWING OPEN, WE'RE AS GOOD AS LOST.
THEY'LL HIT US LIKE A COSSACK HORDE.
WHOOPIN' AND HOLLERIN'.
YANKIN' BOOKS OFF SHELVES.
DROPPIN' 'EM.
STANDIN' 'EM UPSIDE-DOWN.
LOSIN' 'EM.
TEARIN' 'EM.
WRITIN' IN 'EM.
GETTIN' SNOT ON 'EM.
IT'LL BE A CHARNEL HOUSE.
NO QUARTER GIVEN.
OPEN FICTION STACKS
Voyage to the End of the Library
by JOE SACCO
J. SACCO 8·89

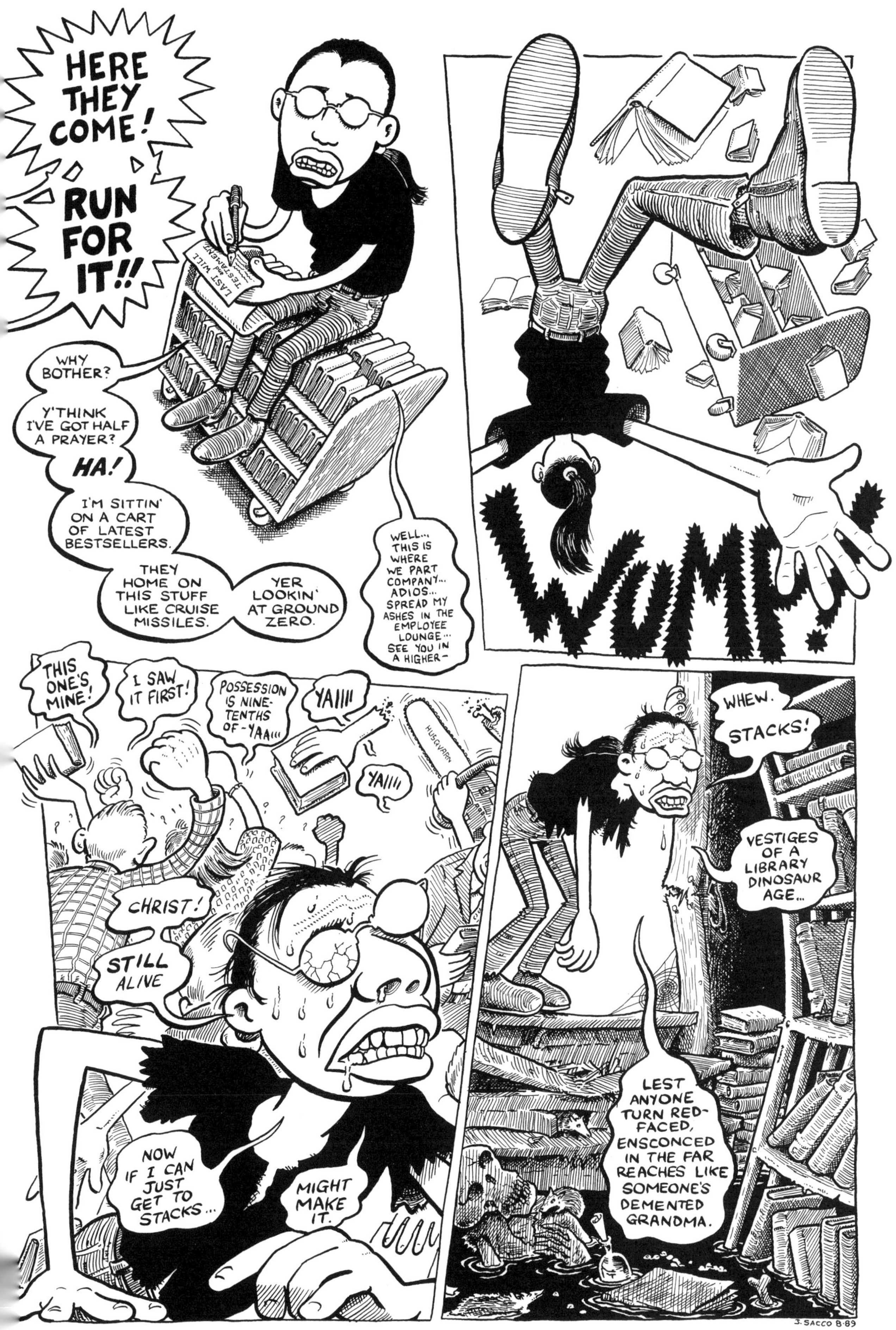
HERE THEY COME!
RUN FOR IT!!
LAST WILL TESTAMENT
WHY BOTHER?
Y'THINK I'VE GOT HALF A PRAYER?
HA!
I'M SITTIN' ON A CART OF LATEST BESTSELLERS.
THEY HOME ON THIS STUFF LIKE CRUISE MISSILES.
YER LOOKIN' AT GROUND ZERO.
WELL... THIS IS WHERE WE PART COMPANY... ADIOS... SPREAD MY ASHES IN THE EMPLOYEE LOUNGE... SEE YOU IN A HIGHER-
WUMP!
THIS ONE'S MINE!
I SAW IT FIRST!
POSSESSION IS NINE-TENTHS OF-YAA
YAIII
YAIII
HUSQVARNA
CHRIST!
STILL ALIVE
NOW IF I CAN JUST GET TO STACKS...
MIGHT MAKE IT.
WHEW.
STACKS!
VESTIGES OF A LIBRARY DINOSAUR AGE...
LEST ANYONE TURN RED-FACED, ENSCONCED IN THE FAR REACHES LIKE SOMEONE'S DEMENTED GRANDMA.
J. SACCO 8-89

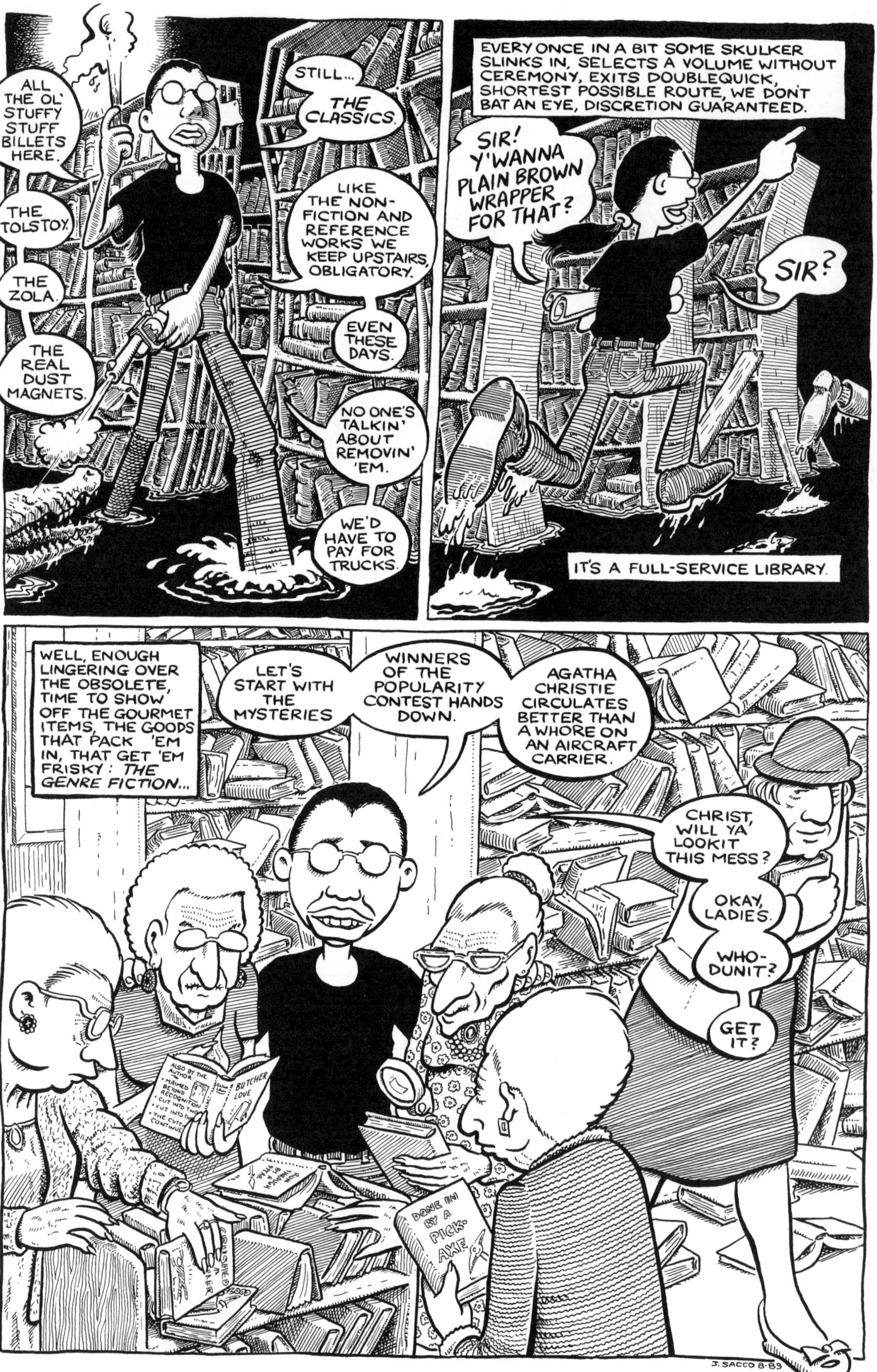
ALL THE OL' STUFFY STUFF BILLETS HERE.
THE TOLSTOY.
THE ZOLA.
THE REAL DUST MAGNETS.
STILL... *THE CLASSICS.*
LIKE THE NON-FICTION AND REFERENCE WORKS WE KEEP UPSTAIRS, OBLIGATORY.
EVEN THESE DAYS.
NO ONE'S TALKIN' ABOUT REMOVIN' 'EM.
WE'D HAVE TO PAY FOR TRUCKS.
EVERY ONCE IN A BIT SOME SKULKER SLINKS IN, SELECTS A VOLUME WITHOUT CEREMONY, EXITS DOUBLEQUICK, SHORTEST POSSIBLE ROUTE, WE DON'T BAT AN EYE, DISCRETION GUARANTEED.
SIR! Y'WANNA PLAIN BROWN WRAPPER FOR THAT?
SIR?
IT'S A FULL-SERVICE LIBRARY.
WELL, ENOUGH LINGERING OVER THE OBSOLETE, TIME TO SHOW OFF THE GOURMET ITEMS, THE GOODS THAT PACK 'EM IN, THAT GET 'EM FRISKY: *THE GENRE FICTION...*
LET'S START WITH THE MYSTERIES
WINNERS OF THE POPULARITY CONTEST HANDS DOWN.
AGATHA CHRISTIE CIRCULATES BETTER THAN A WHORE ON AN AIRCRAFT CARRIER.
CHRIST, WILL YA LOOKIT THIS MESS?
OKAY, LADIES.
WHO-DUNIT?
GET IT?
BUTCHER LOVE
DONE IN BY A PICK-AXE
J. SACCO 8-89

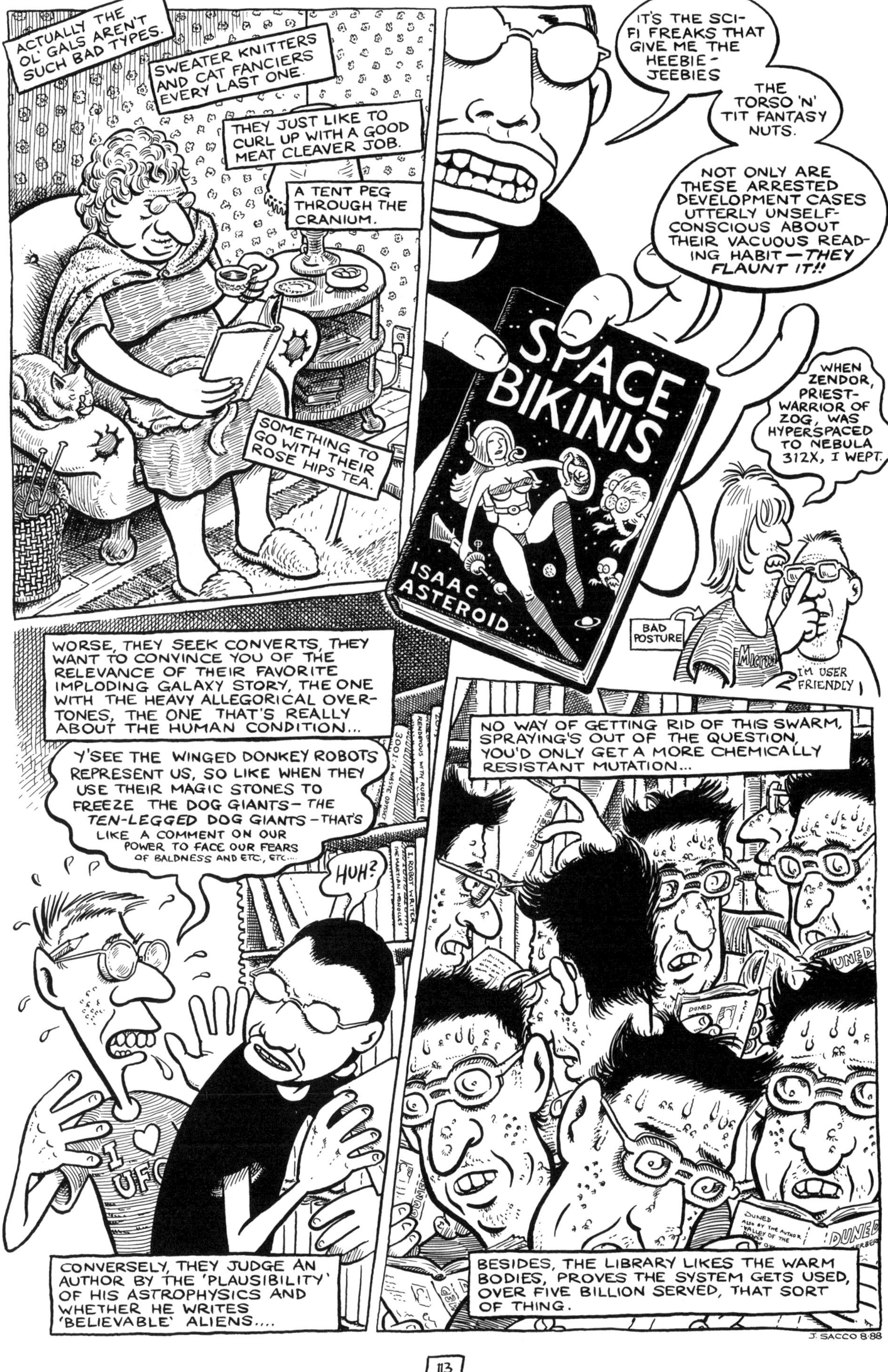
ACTUALLY THE OL' GALS AREN'T SUCH BAD TYPES.
SWEATER KNITTERS AND CAT FANCIERS EVERY LAST ONE.
THEY JUST LIKE TO CURL UP WITH A GOOD MEAT CLEAVER JOB.
A TENT PEG THROUGH THE CRANIUM.
SOMETHING TO GO WITH THEIR ROSE HIPS TEA.
IT'S THE SCI-FI FREAKS THAT GIVE ME THE HEEBIE-JEEBIES
THE TORSO 'N' TIT FANTASY NUTS.
NOT ONLY ARE THESE ARRESTED DEVELOPMENT CASES UTTERLY UNSELF-CONSCIOUS ABOUT THEIR VACUOUS READING HABIT—THEY FLAUNT IT!!
SPACE BIKINIS
ISAAC ASTEROID
WHEN ZENDOR, PRIEST-WARRIOR OF ZOG, WAS HYPERSPACED TO NEBULA 312X, I WEPT.
BAD POSTURE
Microsoft
I'M USER FRIENDLY
WORSE, THEY SEEK CONVERTS, THEY WANT TO CONVINCE YOU OF THE RELEVANCE OF THEIR FAVORITE IMPLODING GALAXY STORY, THE ONE WITH THE HEAVY ALLEGORICAL OVERTONES, THE ONE THAT'S REALLY ABOUT THE HUMAN CONDITION...
Y'SEE THE WINGED DONKEY ROBOTS REPRESENT US, SO LIKE WHEN THEY USE THEIR MAGIC STONES TO FREEZE THE DOG GIANTS—THE TEN-LEGGED DOG GIANTS—THAT'S LIKE A COMMENT ON OUR POWER TO FACE OUR FEARS OF BALDNESS AND ETC., ETC....
HUH?
3001: A WASTE ODYSSEY
I, ROBOT WRITER
I ♥ UFO
CONVERSELY, THEY JUDGE AN AUTHOR BY THE 'PLAUSIBILITY' OF HIS ASTROPHYSICS AND WHETHER HE WRITES 'BELIEVABLE' ALIENS....
NO WAY OF GETTING RID OF THIS SWARM, SPRAYING'S OUT OF THE QUESTION, YOU'D ONLY GET A MORE CHEMICALLY RESISTANT MUTATION...
DUNED
BESIDES, THE LIBRARY LIKES THE WARM BODIES, PROVES THE SYSTEM GETS USED, OVER FIVE BILLION SERVED, THAT SORT OF THING.
J. SACCO 8·88

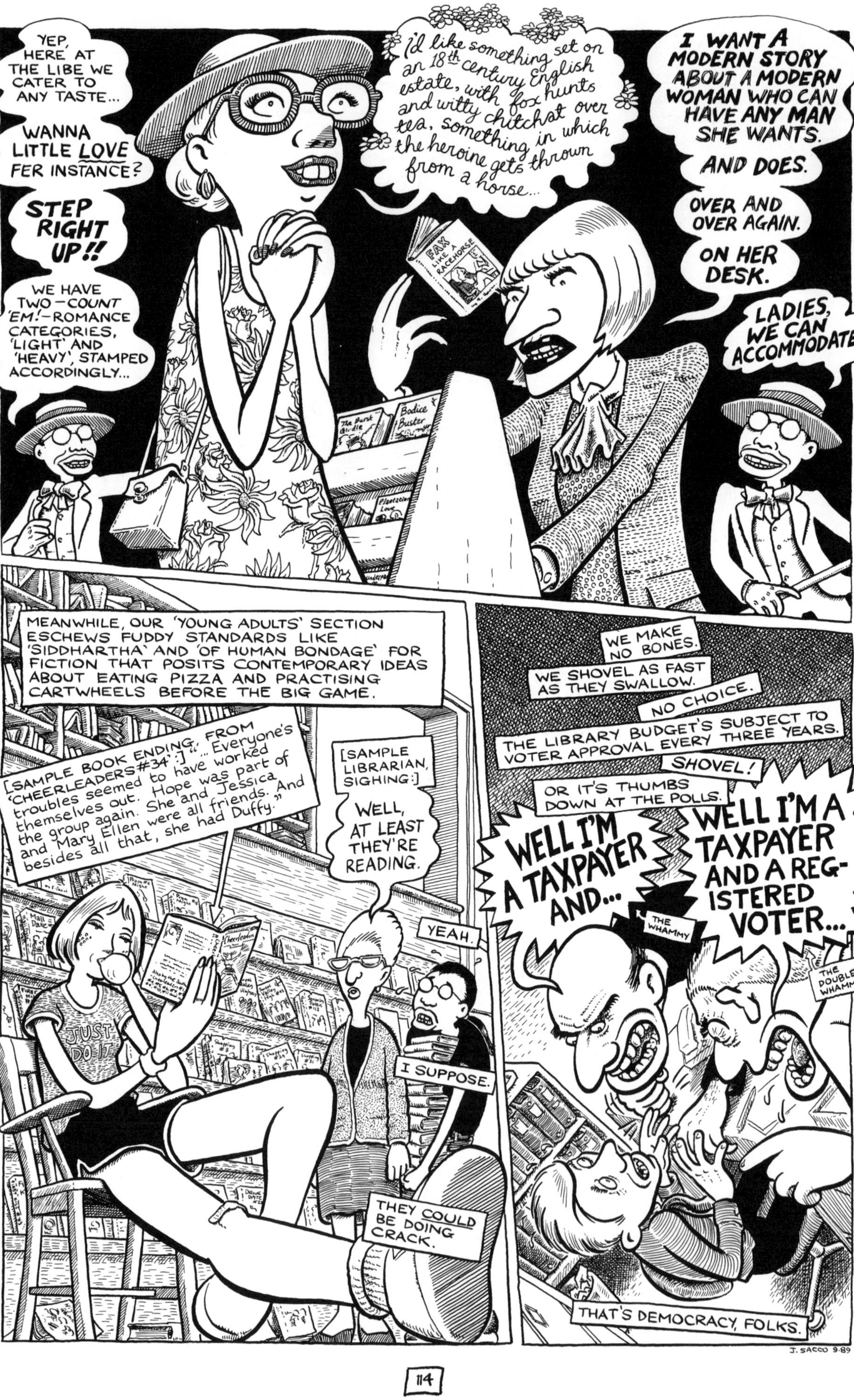
YEP, HERE AT THE LIBE WE CATER TO ANY TASTE...
WANNA LITTLE LOVE FER INSTANCE?
STEP RIGHT UP!!
WE HAVE TWO—COUNT 'EM!—ROMANCE CATEGORIES, 'LIGHT' AND 'HEAVY', STAMPED ACCORDINGLY...
I'd like something set on an 18th century English estate, with fox hunts and witty chitchat over tea, something in which the heroine gets thrown from a horse...
I WANT A MODERN STORY ABOUT A MODERN WOMAN WHO CAN HAVE ANY MAN SHE WANTS.
AND DOES.
OVER AND OVER AGAIN.
ON HER DESK.
LADIES, WE CAN ACCOMMODATE!
FAX LIKE A RACEHORSE
Bodice Buster
MEANWHILE, OUR 'YOUNG ADULTS' SECTION ESCHEWS FUDDY STANDARDS LIKE 'SIDDHARTHA' AND 'OF HUMAN BONDAGE' FOR FICTION THAT POSITS CONTEMPORARY IDEAS ABOUT EATING PIZZA AND PRACTISING CARTWHEELS BEFORE THE BIG GAME.
[SAMPLE BOOK ENDING FROM 'CHEERLEADERS #34':] "...Everyone's troubles seemed to have worked themselves out. Hope was part of the group again. She and Jessica and Mary Ellen were all friends. And besides all that, she had Duffy."
[SAMPLE LIBRARIAN, SIGHING:]
WELL, AT LEAST THEY'RE READING.
YEAH.
I SUPPOSE.
THEY COULD BE DOING CRACK.
Cheerleaders
JUST DO IT
WE MAKE NO BONES.
WE SHOVEL AS FAST AS THEY SWALLOW.
NO CHOICE.
THE LIBRARY BUDGET'S SUBJECT TO VOTER APPROVAL EVERY THREE YEARS.
SHOVEL!
OR IT'S THUMBS DOWN AT THE POLLS.
WELL I'M A TAXPAYER AND...
WELL I'M A TAXPAYER AND A REGISTERED VOTER...
THE WHAMMY
THE DOUBLE WHAMMY
THAT'S DEMOCRACY, FOLKS.
J. SACCO 9·89

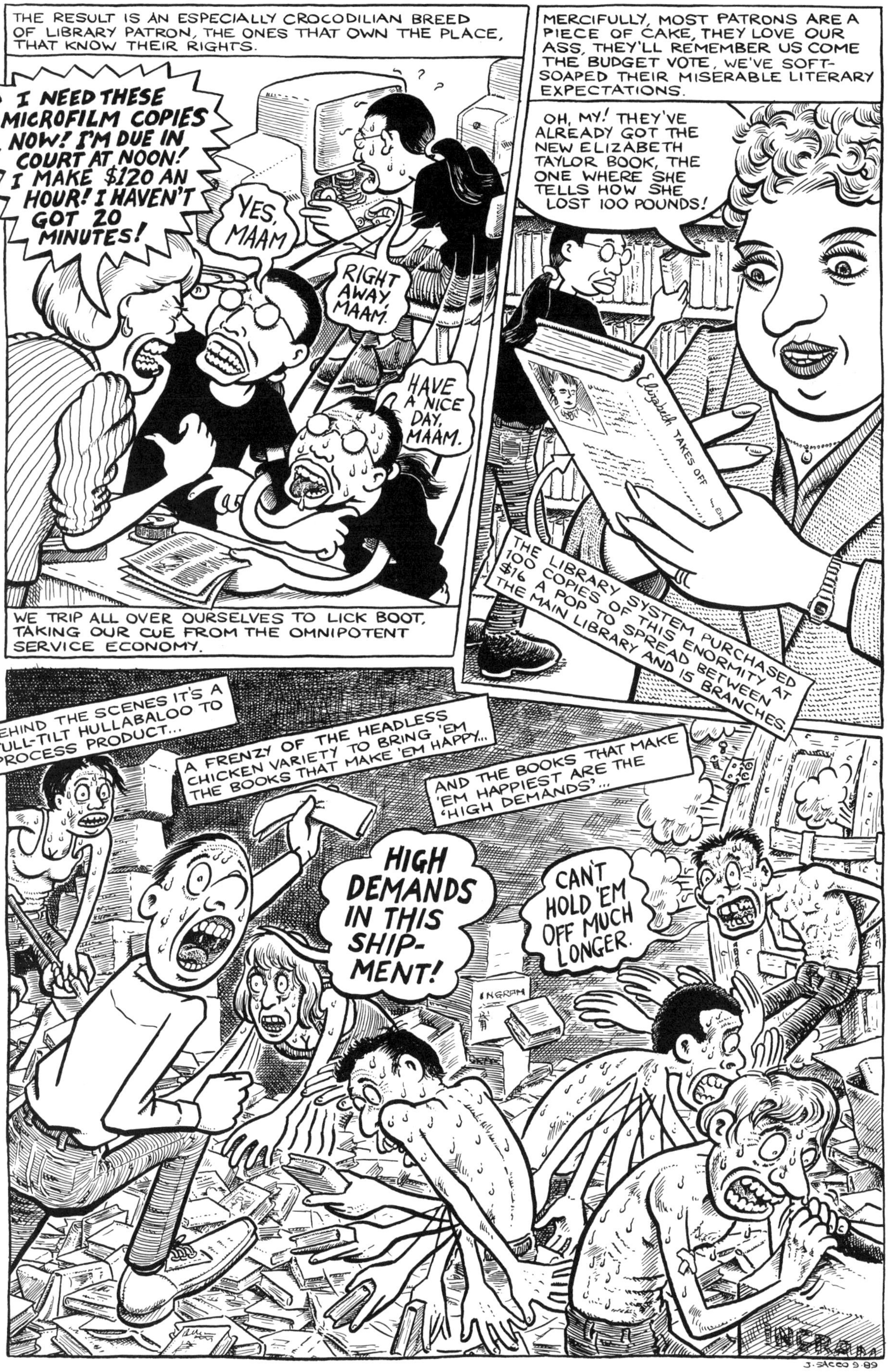
THE RESULT IS AN ESPECIALLY CROCODILIAN BREED OF LIBRARY PATRON, THE ONES THAT OWN THE PLACE, THAT KNOW THEIR RIGHTS.
I NEED THESE MICROFILM COPIES NOW! I'M DUE IN COURT AT NOON! I MAKE $120 AN HOUR! I HAVEN'T GOT 20 MINUTES!
YES, MAAM
RIGHT AWAY, MAAM.
HAVE A NICE DAY, MAAM.
WE TRIP ALL OVER OURSELVES TO LICK BOOT, TAKING OUR CUE FROM THE OMNIPOTENT SERVICE ECONOMY.
MERCIFULLY, MOST PATRONS ARE A PIECE OF CAKE, THEY LOVE OUR ASS, THEY'LL REMEMBER US COME THE BUDGET VOTE, WE'VE SOFT-SOAPED THEIR MISERABLE LITERARY EXPECTATIONS.
OH, MY! THEY'VE ALREADY GOT THE NEW ELIZABETH TAYLOR BOOK, THE ONE WHERE SHE TELLS HOW SHE LOST 100 POUNDS!
Elizabeth TAKES OFF
THE LIBRARY SYSTEM PURCHASED 100 COPIES OF THIS ENORMITY AT $16 A POP TO SPREAD BETWEEN THE MAIN LIBRARY AND 15 BRANCHES.
BEHIND THE SCENES IT'S A FULL-TILT HULLABALOO TO PROCESS PRODUCT...
A FRENZY OF THE HEADLESS CHICKEN VARIETY TO BRING 'EM THE BOOKS THAT MAKE 'EM HAPPY...
AND THE BOOKS THAT MAKE 'EM HAPPIEST ARE THE 'HIGH DEMANDS'...
HIGH DEMANDS IN THIS SHIP-MENT!
CAN'T HOLD 'EM OFF MUCH LONGER.
INGRAM
INGRAM
J. SACCO 9.89

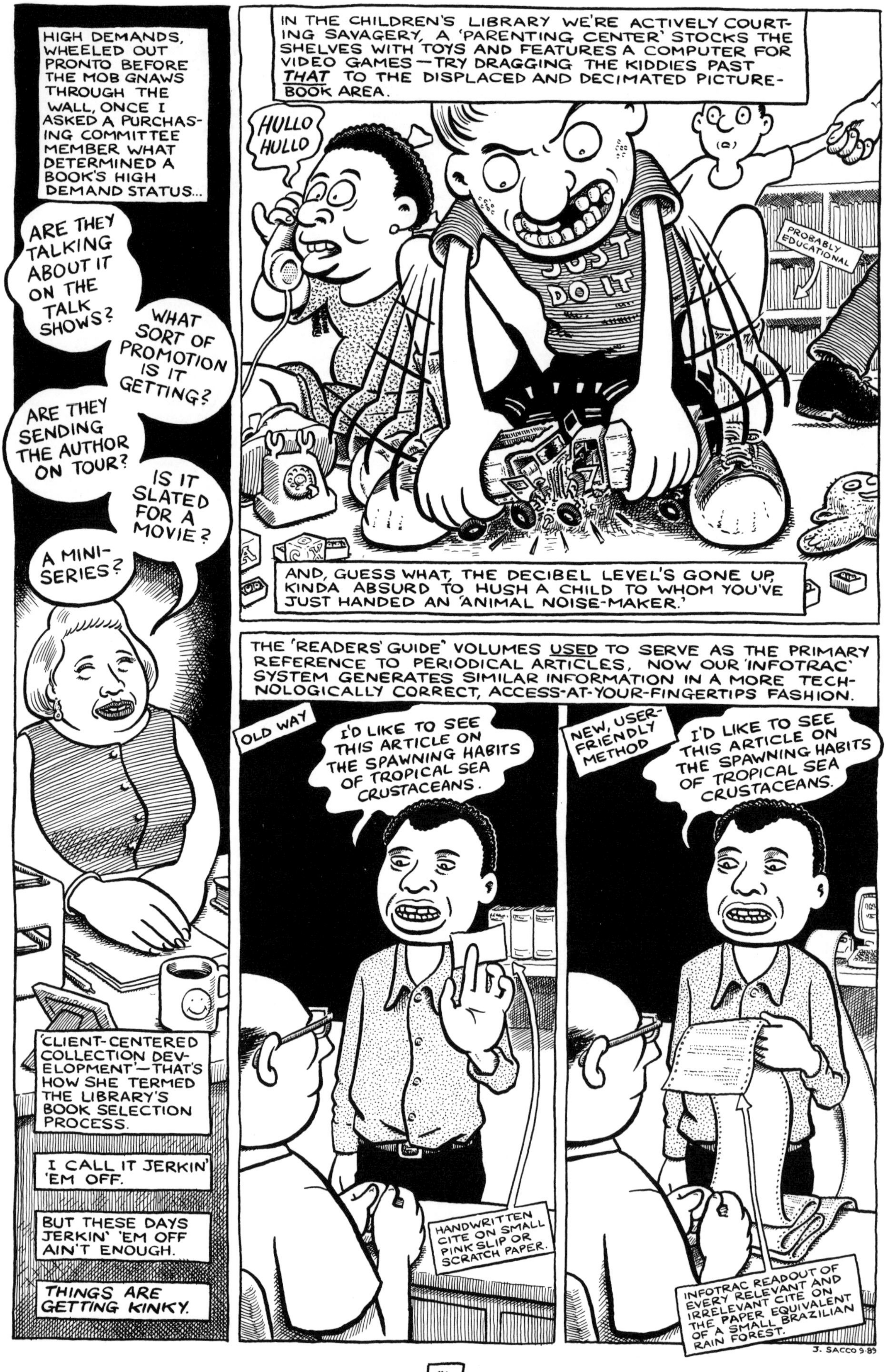
HIGH DEMANDS, WHEELED OUT PRONTO BEFORE THE MOB GNAWS THROUGH THE WALL, ONCE I ASKED A PURCHASING COMMITTEE MEMBER WHAT DETERMINED A BOOK'S HIGH DEMAND STATUS...
ARE THEY TALKING ABOUT IT ON THE TALK SHOWS?
WHAT SORT OF PROMOTION IS IT GETTING?
ARE THEY SENDING THE AUTHOR ON TOUR?
IS IT SLATED FOR A MOVIE?
A MINI-SERIES?
'CLIENT-CENTERED COLLECTION DEVELOPMENT'—THAT'S HOW SHE TERMED THE LIBRARY'S BOOK SELECTION PROCESS.
I CALL IT JERKIN' 'EM OFF.
BUT THESE DAYS JERKIN' 'EM OFF AIN'T ENOUGH.
THINGS ARE GETTING KINKY.
IN THE CHILDREN'S LIBRARY WE'RE ACTIVELY COURTING SAVAGERY, A 'PARENTING CENTER' STOCKS THE SHELVES WITH TOYS AND FEATURES A COMPUTER FOR VIDEO GAMES—TRY DRAGGING THE KIDDIES PAST THAT TO THE DISPLACED AND DECIMATED PICTURE-BOOK AREA.
HULLO HULLO
JUST DO IT
PROBABLY EDUCATIONAL
AND, GUESS WHAT, THE DECIBEL LEVEL'S GONE UP, KINDA ABSURD TO HUSH A CHILD TO WHOM YOU'VE JUST HANDED AN 'ANIMAL NOISE-MAKER.'
THE 'READERS' GUIDE' VOLUMES USED TO SERVE AS THE PRIMARY REFERENCE TO PERIODICAL ARTICLES, NOW OUR 'INFOTRAC' SYSTEM GENERATES SIMILAR INFORMATION IN A MORE TECHNOLOGICALLY CORRECT, ACCESS-AT-YOUR-FINGERTIPS FASHION.
OLD WAY
I'D LIKE TO SEE THIS ARTICLE ON THE SPAWNING HABITS OF TROPICAL SEA CRUSTACEANS.
HANDWRITTEN CITE ON SMALL PINK SLIP OR SCRATCH PAPER.
NEW, USER-FRIENDLY METHOD
I'D LIKE TO SEE THIS ARTICLE ON THE SPAWNING HABITS OF TROPICAL SEA CRUSTACEANS.
INFOTRAC READOUT OF EVERY RELEVANT AND IRRELEVANT CITE ON THE PAPER EQUIVALENT OF A SMALL BRAZILIAN RAIN FOREST.
J. SACCO 9-89

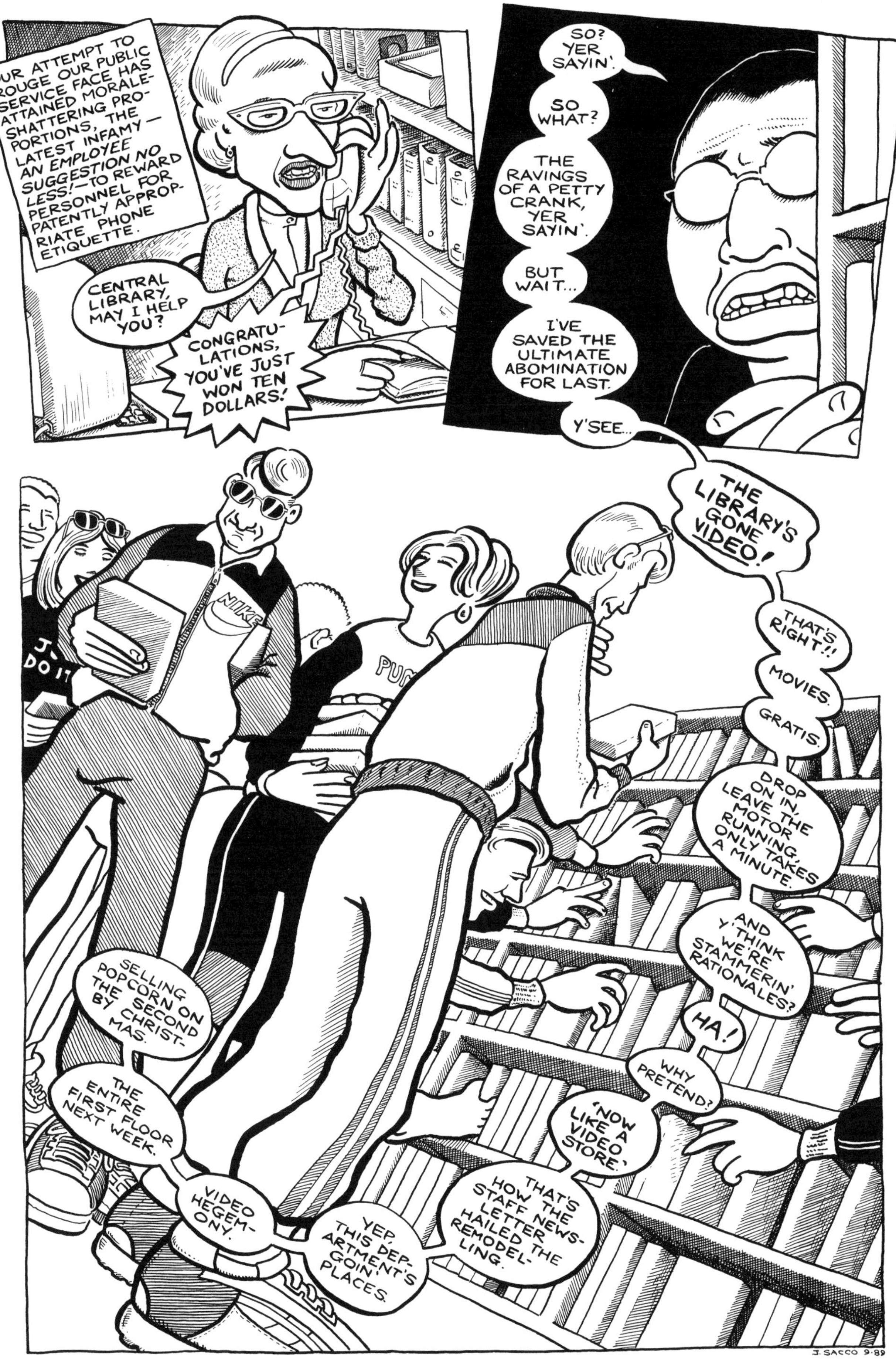
OUR ATTEMPT TO ROUGE OUR PUBLIC SERVICE FACE HAS ATTAINED MORALE-SHATTERING PROPORTIONS, THE LATEST INFAMY — AN *EMPLOYEE SUGGESTION NO LESS!* — TO REWARD PERSONNEL FOR PATENTLY APPROPRIATE PHONE ETIQUETTE.
CENTRAL LIBRARY, MAY I HELP YOU?
CONGRATULATIONS, YOU'VE JUST WON TEN DOLLARS!
SO? YER SAYIN'.
SO WHAT?
THE RAVINGS OF A PETTY CRANK, YER SAYIN'.
BUT WAIT...
I'VE SAVED THE ULTIMATE ABOMINATION FOR LAST.
Y'SEE...
THE LIBRARY'S GONE VIDEO!
THAT'S RIGHT!!
MOVIES.
GRATIS.
DROP ON IN, LEAVE THE MOTOR RUNNING, ONLY TAKES A MINUTE.
AND Y'THINK WE'RE STAMMERIN' RATIONALES?
HA!
WHY PRETEND?
'NOW LIKE A VIDEO STORE,'
THAT'S HOW THE STAFF NEWSLETTER HAILED THE REMODELLING.
YEP, THIS DEPARTMENT'S GOIN' PLACES.
VIDEO HEGEMONY.
THE ENTIRE FIRST FLOOR NEXT WEEK.
SELLING POPCORN ON THE SECOND BY CHRISTMAS.
NIKE
J. SACCO 9·89

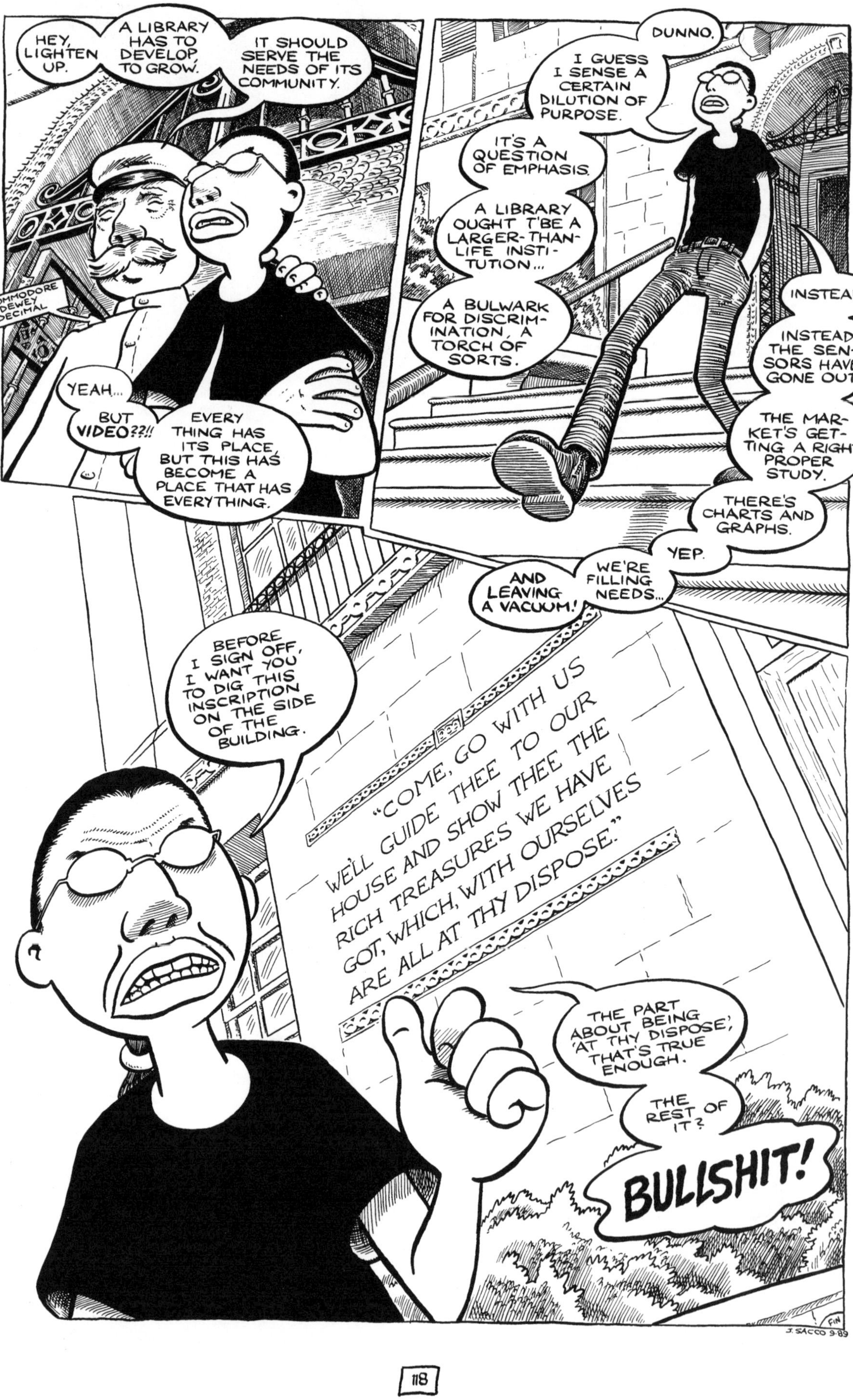
HEY, LIGHTEN UP.
A LIBRARY HAS TO DEVELOP, TO GROW.
IT SHOULD SERVE THE NEEDS OF ITS COMMUNITY.
COMMODORE DEWEY DECIMAL
YEAH...
BUT VIDEO??!!
EVERY THING HAS ITS PLACE, BUT THIS HAS BECOME A PLACE THAT HAS EVERYTHING.
DUNNO.
I GUESS I SENSE A CERTAIN DILUTION OF PURPOSE.
IT'S A QUESTION OF EMPHASIS.
A LIBRARY OUGHT T'BE A LARGER-THAN-LIFE INSTI-TUTION...
A BULWARK FOR DISCRIM-INATION, A TORCH OF SORTS.
INSTEAD?
INSTEAD THE SEN-SORS HAVE GONE OUT.
THE MAR-KET'S GET-TING A RIGHT-PROPER STUDY.
THERE'S CHARTS AND GRAPHS.
YEP.
WE'RE FILLING NEEDS...
AND LEAVING A VACUUM!
BEFORE I SIGN OFF, I WANT YOU TO DIG THIS INSCRIPTION ON THE SIDE OF THE BUILDING.
"COME, GO WITH US WE'LL GUIDE THEE TO OUR HOUSE AND SHOW THEE THE RICH TREASURES WE HAVE GOT, WHICH, WITH OURSELVES ARE ALL AT THY DISPOSE."
THE PART ABOUT BEING 'AT THY DISPOSE,' THAT'S TRUE ENOUGH.
THE REST OF IT?
BULLSHIT!
FIN
J. SACCO 9·89

PART SEVEN:

WHEN GOOD BOMBS HAPPEN TO BAD PEOPLE

introduction

The following two chapters, "When Good Bombs Happen to Bad People" and "More Women, More Children, More Quickly," are about the use of conventional airpower as it relates to civilians. Coincidentally, as I was completing these pages, pilots in the Persian Gulf were readying themselves for missions that proved to add to the unhappy story of non-combatants under aerial attack.

When Air Force Chief of Staff Michael J. Dugan was fired in September of 1990 for inappropriate candor about targeting Saddam Hussein, his family, and his mistress, he also engaged in a bit of speculation that all but escaped mainstream commentary. Military targets, Dugan said, are "not enough... what is unique about Iraqi culture that they put a very high value on? What is it that psychologically would make an impact on the population and regime in Iraq?" (*Los Angeles Times*, Sept. 16, 1990) One hopes these remarks were his alone and not part of any official White House contingency debate, but one should have no such illusions. Today we may have "no quarrel" with a people; tomorrow we may be bombing them to break them, bombing them to kill them in as large numbers as possible.

Historical examples speak for themselves, and in "When Good Bombs Happen to Bad People" I am letting them speak through the mouths and pens of military men, politicians, scientists, bureaucrats, and the U.S. popular media. I have portrayed aerial attacks on our past and present enemies, Germany, Japan, and Libya. I make no attempt to frame this work in the context of German and Japanese outrages, including their use of terror bombing in Warsaw, Rotterdam, London, Chungking, et al. I make no examination of the broader U.S. claims about Libya and terrorism. I add nothing to the ongoing debate about airpower's ability to win wars.

Basically, I am concerned with those who help shape the use of the aerial weapon—their tone, their detachment, their propensity to escalate. My approach, with no narrative to link one quote to the next, leaves historical gaps which are, to some extent, addressed in the comments on page 65 and the following brief introductions:

BRITISH BOMBING OF GERMANY, 1940-45: For most of the war, the Royal Air Force's bomber offensive was the primary means by which Britain carried the fight to Germany. To cut losses, the British bombed at night, and an overwhelming percentage of bombs dropped wide of specific targets. The idea of area bombing developed: if hundreds of bombers could be placed over a city in a short time, where individual bombs landed would be of little consequence—the cumulative effect would be devastating. Through area bombing, the British aimed to kill, "dehouse," or otherwise disrupt German industrial workers. The target was German civilian morale. (By contrast, in the European war the U.S. targeted strategic sites in daylight precision raids, though terror was adopted selectively—on Germany's Balkan allies and Dresden, for example.)

U.S. BOMBING OF JAPAN, 1944-45: High-altitude B-29 raids did not produce the desired result on Japan's industries, which relied to some extent on home workshops. The tinderbox nature of Japanese homes and population density made Japanese cities extremely vulnerable targets. In March, 1945, General Curtis Le May (George Wallace's vice-presidential candidate in 1968) perfected low-level incendiary raids that burned out entire sections of cities. Tokyo was only the first and most dramatic example of the campaign. The atomic bombings have overshadowed the scale of the incendiary raids, which in some cases killed more people outright and more completely eliminated cities. (The racial dimension of the Pacific War is well covered in John W. Dower's *War Without Mercy*.)

U.S. BOMBING OF LIBYA, APRIL 14, 1986: On April 5, 1986, a bomb wrecked a West German disco, killing two U.S. servicemen and a Turkish woman and injuring many others. The U.S. administration blamed Qaddafi and launched air attacks on Tripoli and Benghazi (killing some 37 Libyans), officially to deter further Libyan terrorism. The "irrefutable" U.S. case against Libya has since been questioned.

"More Women, More Children, More Quickly," which begins on page 68, recounts my mother's experiences on Malta during Italian and German aerial attacks in World War II. For a long while Malta was the only British base between Gibraltar and Egypt and was a serious threat to Axis operations in the central Mediterranean and North Africa.

—Joe Sacco

When GOOD BOMBS *happen to* BAD PEOPLE

by Joe Sacco 1990

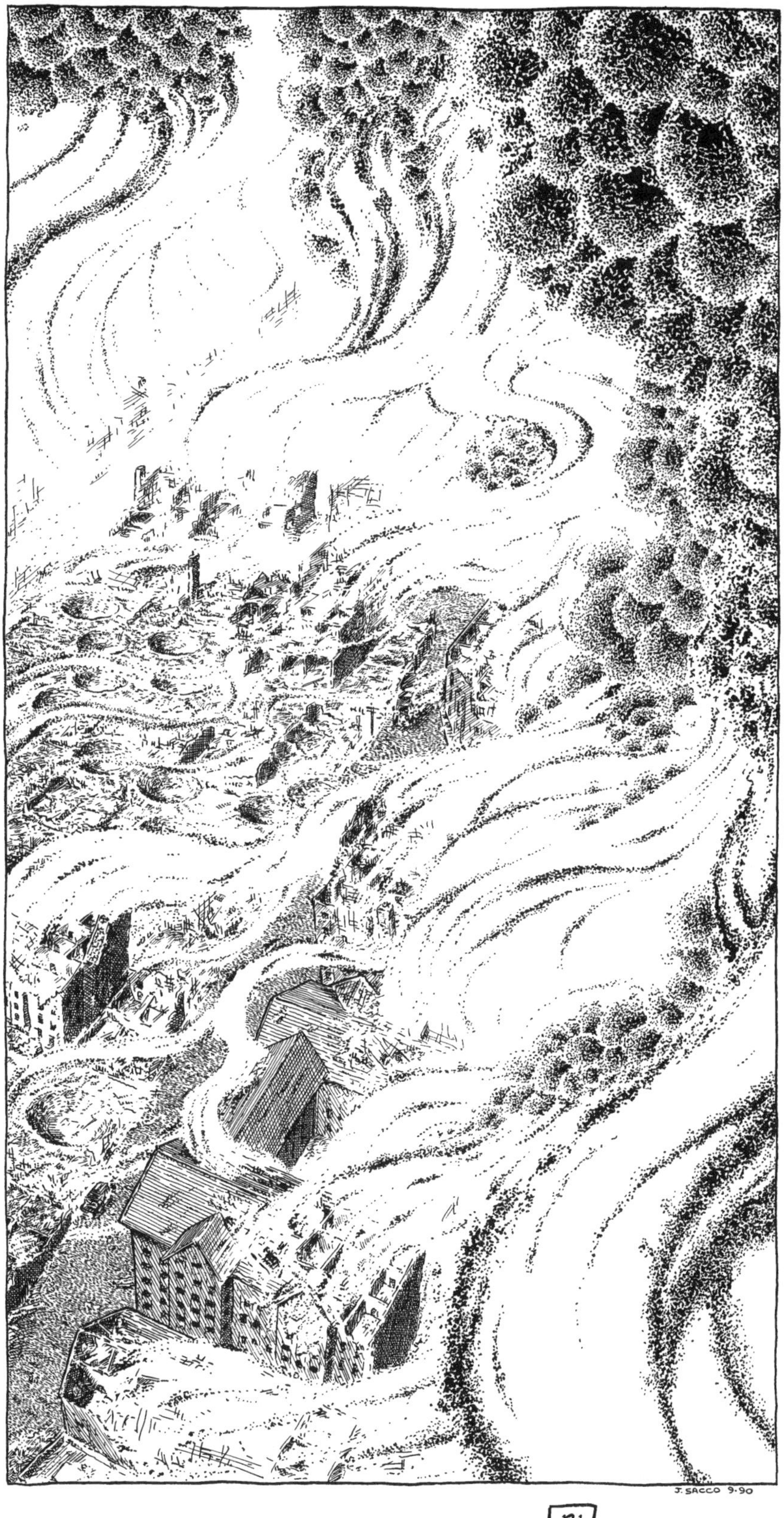
J. SACCO 9-90

BRITISH BOMBING OF GERMANY, 1940-45

"BOMBS ARE NOT TO BE DROPPED INDISCRIMINATELY."
-BOMBER COMMAND, JUNE '40 (1)

"THE ATTACK MUST BE MADE WITH REASONABLE CARE TO AVOID UNDUE LOSS OF CIVIL LIFE IN THE VICINITY OF THE TARGET."
-REVISED INSTRUCTION TO AIR MINISTRY, JUNE '40 (2)

"WE HAVE SEEN WHAT INCONVENIENCE THE ATTACK ON THE BRITISH POPULATION HAS CAUSED US, AND THERE IS NO REASON WHY THE ENEMY SHOULD BE FREE FROM ALL SUCH EMBARRASSMENTS."
-PRIME MINISTER CHURCHILL TO AIR MINISTRY, NOV. '40 (3)

"YOU ARE ACCORDINGLY AUTHORIZED TO EMPLOY YOUR FORCES WITHOUT RESTRICTION. OPERATIONS... SHOULD NOW BE FOCUSED ON THE MORALE OF THE ENEMY CIVIL POPULATION AND IN PARTICULAR OF THE INDUSTRIAL WORKER."
-AIR MINISTRY, FEB. '42 (4)

"REF THE NEW BOMBING DIRECTIVE: I SUPPOSE IT IS CLEAR THAT THE AIMING-POINTS ARE TO BE THE BUILT-UP AREAS, NOT, FOR INSTANCE, THE DOCKYARDS AND AIRCRAFT FACTORIES.... THIS MUST BE MADE QUITE CLEAR IF IT IS NOT ALREADY UNDERSTOOD."
-AIR CHIEF-MARSHAL PORTAL, FEB. '42 (5)

"... ONE TON OF BOMBS DROPPED ON A BUILT-UP AREA DEMOLISHES 20-40 DWELLINGS AND TURNS 100-200 PEOPLE OUT OF HOUSE AND HOME.... WE CAN COUNT ON NEARLY 14 OPERATIONAL SORTIES PER BOMBER PRODUCED. THE AVERAGE LIFT OF THE BOMBERS ... WILL BE ABOUT THREE TONS. IT FOLLOWS THAT EACH OF THESE BOMBERS WILL IN ITS LIFETIME DROP ABOUT FORTY TONS OF BOMBS. IF THESE ARE DROPPED ON BUILT-UP AREAS THEY WILL MAKE 4,000-8,000 PEOPLE HOMELESS...."
-LORD CHERWELL, SCIENTIFIC ADVISER TO CHURCHILL, MAR. '42 (6)

"SLOWLY HIS FOREFINGER MOVED ACROSS THE MAP, OVER THE CONTINENT OF EUROPE UNTIL IT CAME TO REST ON A TOWN IN GERMANY .... HE TURNED TO SAUNDBY, HIS FACE STILL EXPRESSIONLESS.
"'THE THOUSAND-PLAN — TONIGHT.'
"HIS FINGER PRESSED ON COLOGNE AS HE SPOKE."
-ON BOMBER COMMAND C-IN-C ARTHUR HARRIS, MAY 30, '42 (7)

"... AN HOUR AND A HALF AS NO CITY ON EARTH HAD EVER BEFORE UNDERGONE. EVERY SIX SECONDS ANOTHER BRITISH BOMBER ROARED OVER THE DOOMED RHINELAND CENTER."
-NEWSWEEK, JUNE '42 (8)

"WE ARE GOING TO SCOURGE THE THIRD REICH FROM END TO END. WE ARE BOMBING GERMANY CITY BY CITY AND EVER MORE TERRIBLY IN ORDER TO MAKE IT IMPOSSIBLE FOR HER TO GO ON WITH THE WAR. THAT IS OUR OBJECTIVE; WE WILL PURSUE IT RELENTLESSLY."
-HARRIS (9)

"USE OF THESE NEW BOMBS UNDERLINED THE LARGELY UNPUBLICIZED BUT IMMENSELY IMPORTANT ROLE THAT INCENDIARIES ARE PLAYING IN RAF* RAIDS ON THE REICH.... IT MAY BE THAT GERMANY'S FATE IS TO BE BURNED DOWN RATHER THAN BLOWN UP."
-NEWSWEEK, JULY '43 (10)

"OPERATION GOMORRAH."
-CODE NAME FOR RAIDS ON HAMBURG, JULY 24-AUG. 2, '43 (11)

"NEUTRAL EUROPEAN NEWSPAPERS PRINTED STORIES OF THE HORROR AND DESOLATION OF THE CHARNEL STENCH THAT WAS HAMBURG. THESE STORIES OF WIDESPREAD DESTRUCTION WERE PROBABLY INSPIRED BY BERLIN IN THE HOPE OF MISLEADING THE ALLIES INTO THINKING THAT THEY HAD DESTROYED MORE THAN THEY REALLY HAD AND THAT HAMBURG NEEDED NO FURTHER ATTENTION FROM THE AIR."
-LIFE, AUG. '43 (12)

KILLED IN HAMBURG RAIDS: 31-50,000 (13)

"... 2,400,000,000 [ENEMY] MAN-HOURS HAVE BEEN LOST FOR THE EXPENDITURE OF 116,500 TONS OF BOMBS CLAIMED DROPPED, AND THIS AMOUNTS TO AN AVERAGE RETURN FOR EVERY TON OF BOMBS DROPPED OF 20,500 LOST MAN-HOURS, OR RATHER MORE THAN ONE QUARTER OF THE TIME SPENT IN BUILDING A LANCASTER [BOMBER].... THIS BEING SO, A LANCASTER HAS ONLY TO GO TO A GERMAN CITY ONCE TO WIPE OFF ITS OWN CAPITAL COST, AND THE RESULT OF ALL SUBSEQUENT SORTIES WILL BE CLEAR PROFIT."
-AIR STAFF INTELLIGENCE REPORT, FEB. '44 (14)

"NOT INCLUDING THE SUBURBS, A DESTRUCTION OF LESS THAN 40 PER CENT OF BUILT-UP AREA IS ENOUGH TO MAKE A CITY UNPRODUCTIVE."
-HARRIS (15)

"THESE BOMBINGS ARE NOT A SAVAGE RETALIATION.... IT IS A CONSIDERED POLICY WITH ONE AIM IN VIEW: TO FORCE THE SURRENDER OF THE GERMAN GOVERNMENT AT THE EARLIEST POSSIBLE MOMENT AND HENCE WITH THE LEAST POSSIBLE TOTAL LOSS OF LIFE.... TOTAL WAR MEANS JUST THAT. UNIFORMS NO LONGER MASK COMBATANTS. THERE ARE NO NON-COMBATANTS."
-SENIOR SCHOLASTIC, APRIL '44 (16)

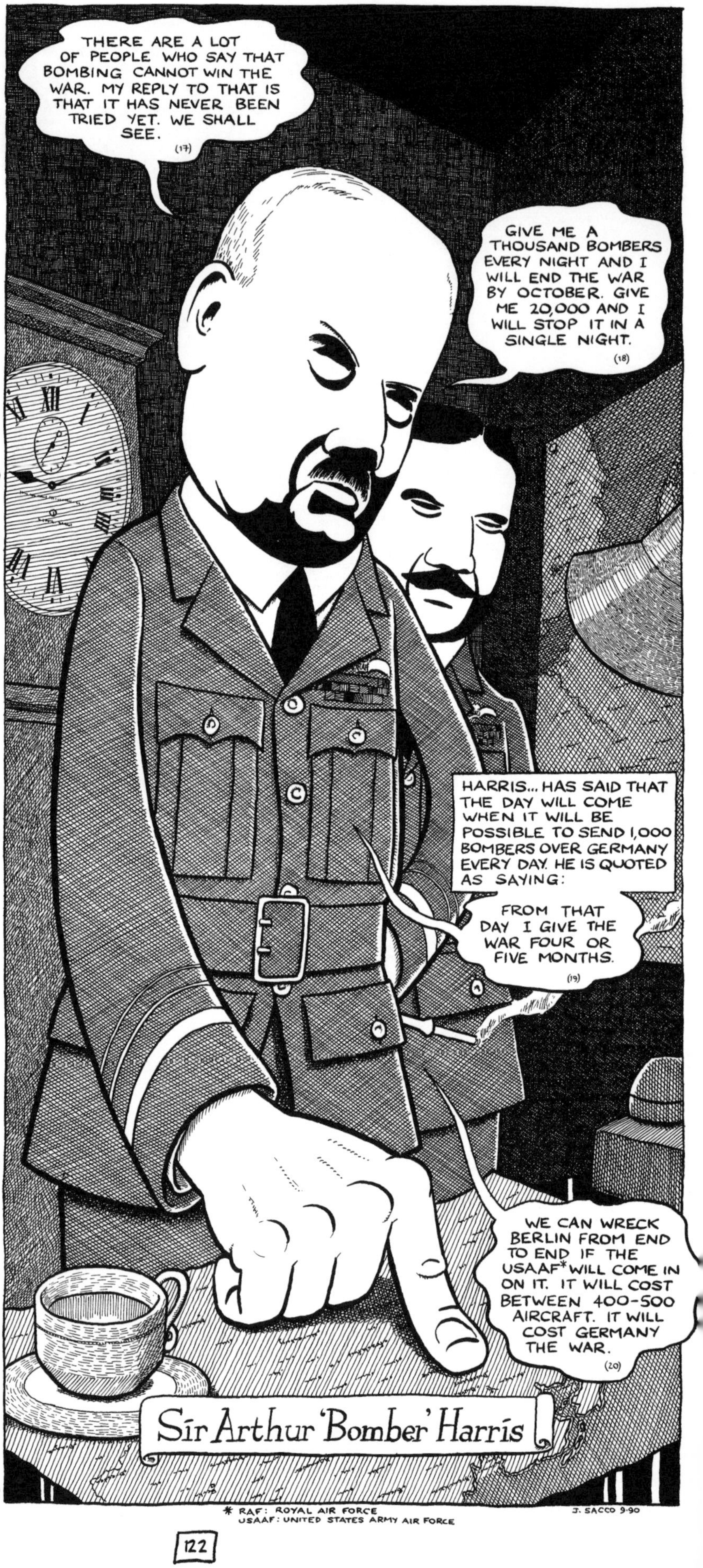
THERE ARE A LOT OF PEOPLE WHO SAY THAT BOMBING CANNOT WIN THE WAR. MY REPLY TO THAT IS THAT IT HAS NEVER BEEN TRIED YET. WE SHALL SEE. (17)
GIVE ME A THOUSAND BOMBERS EVERY NIGHT AND I WILL END THE WAR BY OCTOBER. GIVE ME 20,000 AND I WILL STOP IT IN A SINGLE NIGHT. (18)
HARRIS... HAS SAID THAT THE DAY WILL COME WHEN IT WILL BE POSSIBLE TO SEND 1,000 BOMBERS OVER GERMANY EVERY DAY. HE IS QUOTED AS SAYING:
FROM THAT DAY I GIVE THE WAR FOUR OR FIVE MONTHS. (19)
WE CAN WRECK BERLIN FROM END TO END IF THE USAAF* WILL COME IN ON IT. IT WILL COST BETWEEN 400-500 AIRCRAFT. IT WILL COST GERMANY THE WAR. (20)
Sir Arthur 'Bomber' Harris

* RAF: ROYAL AIR FORCE
USAAF: UNITED STATES ARMY AIR FORCE

J. SACCO 9-90

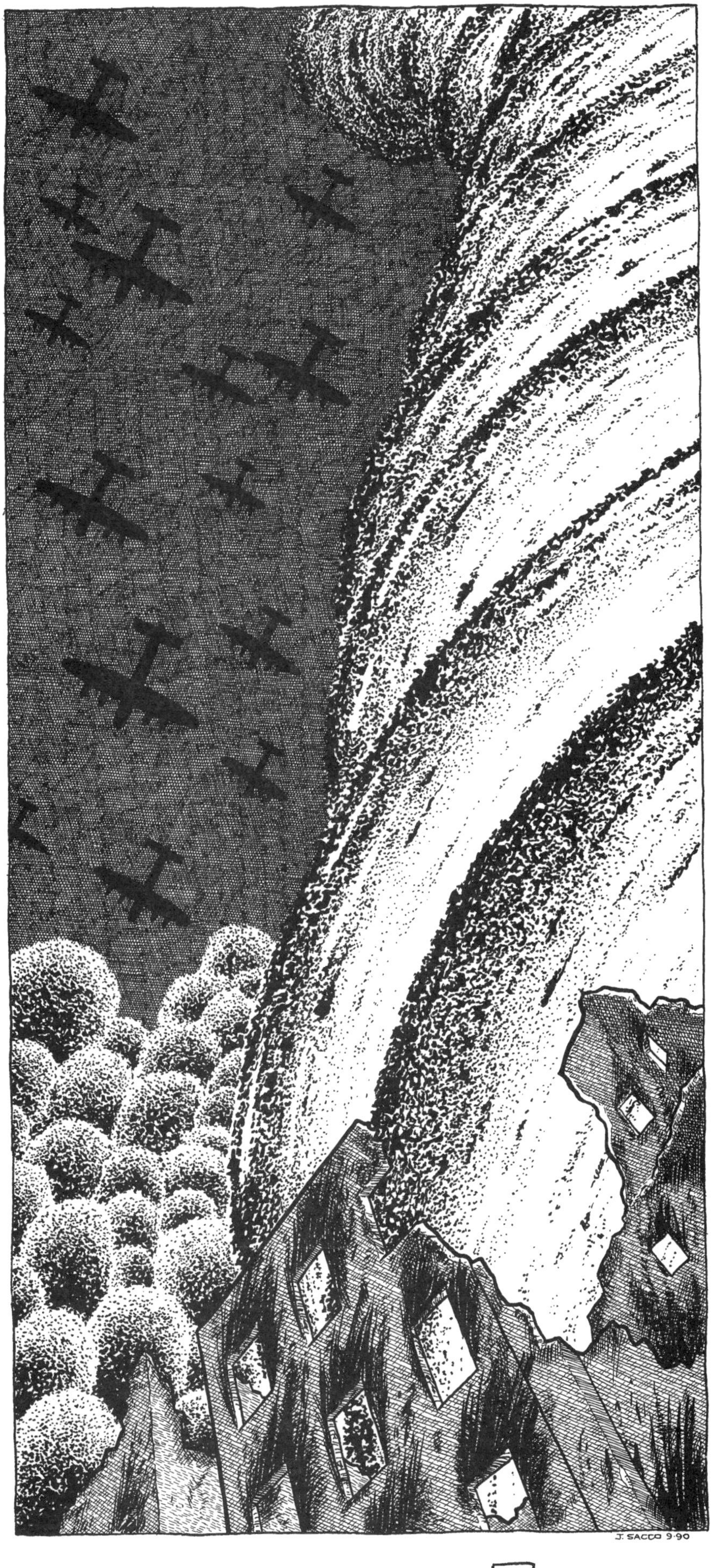
J. SACCO 9·90

"...IN THE PAST EIGHTEEN MONTHS, BOMBER COMMAND HAS VIRTUALLY DESTROYED FORTY-FIVE OUT OF THE LEADING SIXTY GERMAN CITIES. IN SPITE OF INVASION DIVERSIONS WE HAVE SO FAR MANAGED TO KEEP UP AND EVEN EXCEED OUR AVERAGE OF TWO AND A HALF CITIES DEVASTATED A MONTH... THERE ARE NOT MANY INDUSTRIAL CENTERS OF POPULATION NOW LEFT INTACT."

-HARRIS, NOV. '44 [21]

"THE TIME MIGHT WELL COME IN THE NOT TOO DISTANT FUTURE WHEN AN ALL-OUT ATTACK BY EVERY MEANS AT OUR DISPOSAL ON GERMAN CIVILIAN MORALE MIGHT BE DECISIVE."

- BRITISH CHIEF OF STAFF TO CHURCHILL, JULY '44 [22]

"IF WE ASSUME THAT THE DAYTIME POPULATION OF THE AREA ATTACKED IS 300,000, WE MAY EXPECT 220,000 CASUALTIES. 50 PERCENT OF THESE OR 110,000 MAY EXPECT TO BE KILLED. IT IS SUGGESTED THAT SUCH AN ATTACK RESULTING IN SO MANY DEATHS, THE GREAT PROPORTION OF WHICH WILL BE KEY PERSONNEL, CANNOT HELP BUT HAVE A SHATTERING EFFECT ON POLITICAL AND CIVILIAN MORALE ALL OVER GERMANY...."

-DIRECTORATE OF BOMBER OPERATIONS, SUMMER '44 [23]

"IN BOMBER COMMAND WE HAVE ALWAYS WORKED ON THE ASSUMPTION THAT BOMBING ANYTHING IN GERMANY IS BETTER THAN BOMBING NOTHING."

-HARRIS, FALL '44 [24]

"I DID NOT ASK YOU LAST NIGHT ABOUT PLANS FOR HARRYING THE GERMAN RETREAT FROM BRESLAU. ON THE CONTRARY, I ASKED WHETHER BERLIN, AND NO DOUBT OTHER LARGE CITIES IN EAST GERMANY, SHOULD NOT NOW BE CONSIDERED ESPECIALLY ATTRACTIVE TARGETS. I AM GLAD THIS IS 'UNDER EXAMINATION.' PRAY REPORT TO ME TOMORROW WHAT IS GOING TO BE DONE."

-CHURCHILL TO SEC. OF STATE IN THE AIR, JAN. '45 [25]

"... 2250 UNITED STATES HEAVY BOMBERS AND FIGHTERS RANGED OVER GERMANY IN WIDESPREAD RAIDS, DELIVERING THEIR MAIN ATTACK ON THIS REFUGEE-PACKED CAPITAL OF SAXONY.

"THE AMERICAN AIR STRIKES CAME IN THE WAKE OF BLOWS BY 1400 RAF BOMBERS DURING THE NIGHT....[DRESDEN] WAS STILL BURNING WHEN AMERICAN PLANES ARRIVED LATER IN THE DAY."

-ASSOCIATED PRESS, FEB. 15, '45 [26]

KILLED IN DRESDEN RAIDS: 25-135,000 [27]

"THE ALLIED AIR BOSSES HAVE MADE THE LONG-AWAITED DECISION TO ADOPT DELIBERATE TERROR BOMBING OF THE GERMAN POPULATION CENTERS AS A RUTHLESS EXPEDIENT TO HASTEN HITLER'S DOOM."

-ASSOCIATED PRESS, FEB.18, '45 [28]

U.S. BOMBING OF JAPAN, 1944-45

"...ANY GENERAL BOMBING OF AN EXTENSIVE AREA WHERIN THERE RESIDES A LARGE POPULATION ENGAGED IN PEACEFUL PURSUITS IS UNWARRANTED AND CONTRARY TO PRINCIPLES OF LAW AND OF HUMANITY."
-U.S. DEPT. OF STATE, SEPT. '37 (1)

"[I] RECALL WITH PRIDE THAT THE UNITED STATES CONSISTENTLY HAS TAKEN THE LEAD IN URGING THAT THIS INHUMAN PRACTICE BE PROHIBITED."
-PRESIDENT ROOSEVELT, '40 (2)

"[THE USE] OF INCENDIARIES AGAINST CITIES WAS CONTRARY TO OUR NATIONAL POLICY OF ATTACKING ONLY MILITARY OBJECTIVES."
-GENERAL 'HAP' ARNOLD, '40 (3)

"[JAPANESE] TOWNS ARE BUILT LARGELY OF WOOD AND PAPER TO RESIST THE DEVASTATIONS OF EARTHQUAKES AND FORM THE GREATEST AERIAL TARGETS THE WORLD HAS EVER SEEN.... INCENDIARY PROJECTILES WOULD BURN THE CITIES TO THE GROUND IN SHORT ORDER."
-GENERAL 'BILLY' MITCHELL, '31 (4)

"THE JAPANESE LITERALLY LIVE IN A HOUSE OF TINDER.... INCENDIARY BOMBS ARE NIPPON'S NIGHTMARE. FEAR OF FIRE IS BRED IN THE PEOPLE.... IN A GREAT CONGESTED CITY LIKE TOKYO, WITH ITS 7,000,000 PEOPLE ... GREAT SECTIONS... ARE LIKE KINDLING WOOD."
-NY TIMES MAG., APRIL '42 (5)

"THE POSSIBILITIES INHERENT IN INCENDIARY BOMBING HAVE GREATLY BRIGHTENED IN RECENT MONTHS....BETTER AND BETTER INCENDIARIES ARE BECOMING AVAILABLE."
-V.P. OF STANDARD OIL DEVELOPMENT, SEPT. '42 (6)

"ESTIMATES OF ECONOMIC DAMAGE EXPECTED INDICATE THAT INCENDIARY ATTACK OF JAPANESE CITIES MAY BE AT LEAST FIVE TIMES AS EFFECTIVE, TON FOR TON, AS PRECISION BOMBING.... HOWEVER, THE DRY ECONOMIC STATISTICS, IMPRESSIVE AS THEY MAY BE, STILL DO NOT TAKE ACCOUNT OF THE FURTHER AND UNPREDICTABLE EFFECT ON THE JAPANESE WAR EFFORT OF A NATIONAL CATASTROPHE OF SUCH MAGNITUDE—ENTIRELY UNPRECEDENTED IN HISTORY."
-OFFICE OF SCIENTIFIC RESEARCH AND DEVELOPMENT RECOMMENDATION, FALL '44 (7)

"THE SUBCOMMITTEE CONSIDERED AN OPTIMUM RESULT OF COMPLETE CHAOS IN SIX [JAPANESE] CITIES KILLING 584,000 PEOPLE."
-COLONEL JOHN F. TURNER, INCENDIARY SUBCOMMITTEE, COMMITTEE OF OPERATIONS ANALYSTS. (8)

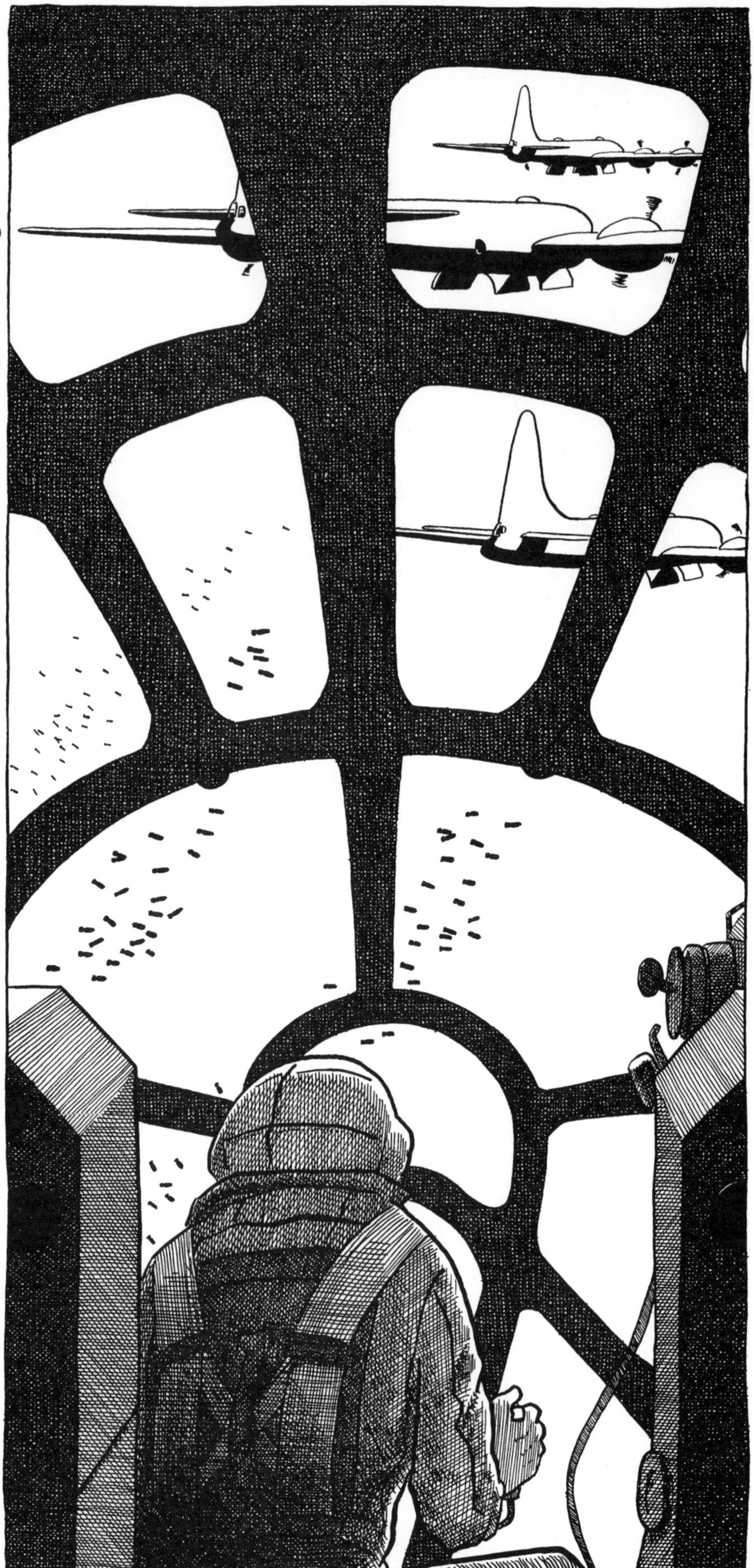

J. SACCO 9·90

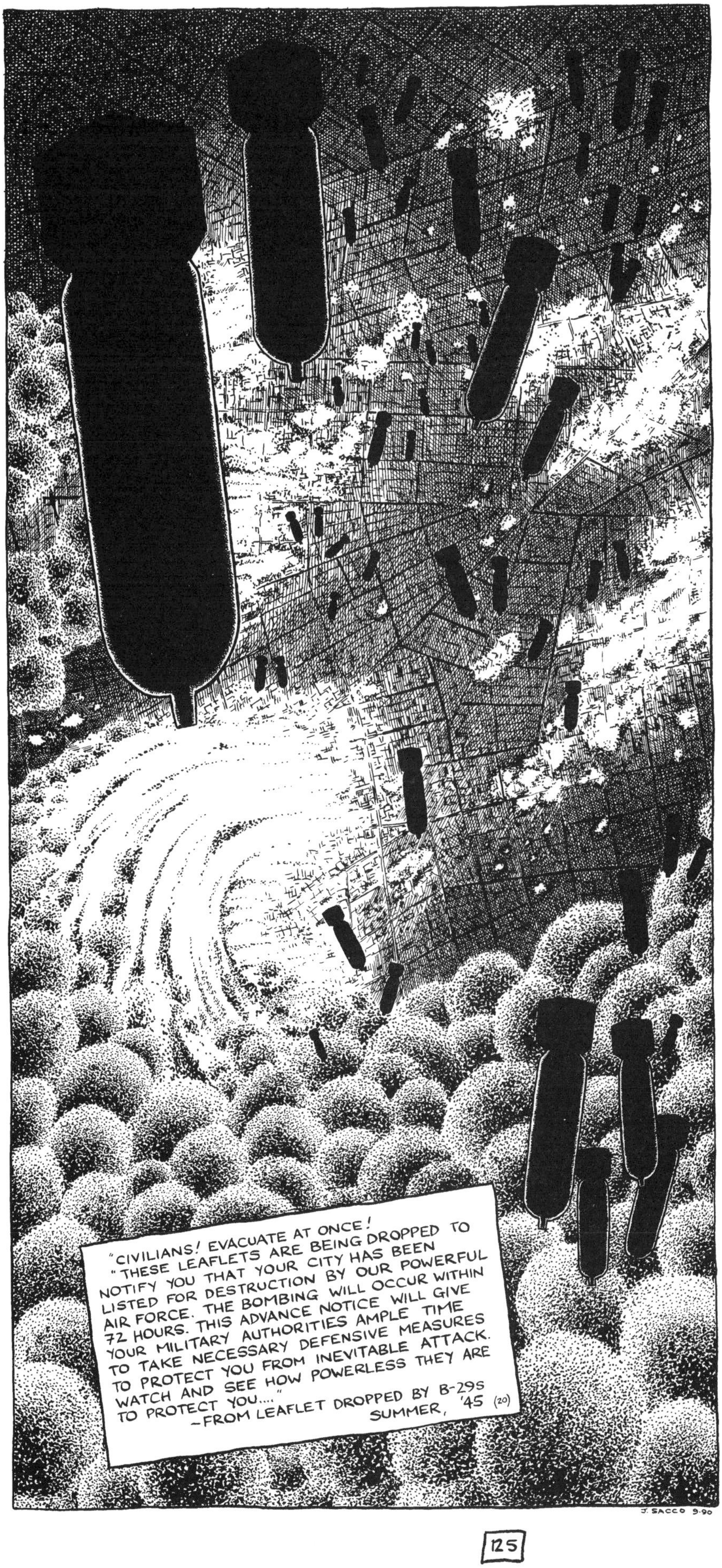
"CIVILIANS! EVACUATE AT ONCE!
"THESE LEAFLETS ARE BEING DROPPED TO NOTIFY YOU THAT YOUR CITY HAS BEEN LISTED FOR DESTRUCTION BY OUR POWERFUL AIR FORCE. THE BOMBING WILL OCCUR WITHIN 72 HOURS. THIS ADVANCE NOTICE WILL GIVE YOUR MILITARY AUTHORITIES AMPLE TIME TO TAKE NECESSARY DEFENSIVE MEASURES TO PROTECT YOU FROM INEVITABLE ATTACK. WATCH AND SEE HOW POWERLESS THEY ARE TO PROTECT YOU...."
-FROM LEAFLET DROPPED BY B-29s SUMMER, '45 [20]
J. SACCO 9.90

"IF THIS RAID WORKS THE WAY I THINK IT WILL, WE CAN SHORTEN THE WAR."
-GEN. CURTIS LEMAY, MAR. '45 [9]

"A BLANKET OF FIRE WAS THROWN OVER AN AREA OF FIFTEEN SQUARE MILES IN THE HEART OF TOKYO EARLY TODAY BY A FLEET OF 300 B-29'S IN THE LARGEST AND MOST INTENSIFIED RAID ON THAT CITY TO DATE."
-NY TIMES, MAR. 10, '45 [10]

"... I CAN SAY WITH CONSERVATISM THAT THIS LOOKS GOOD FROM OUR POINT OF VIEW AND GRIM FROM THE POINT OF VIEW OF THE ENEMY. THERE IS A CONFLAGRATION IN TOKYO TONIGHT."
-GEN. LEMAY, MAR. 10, '45 [11]

"BY NOON LEMAY WAS SURE HE HAD WHAT HE LIKES TO CALL A 'DILLER'."
-FORTUNE, OCT. '45 [12]

"A DREAM CAME TRUE LAST WEEK FOR U.S. ARMY AVIATORS; THEY GOT THEIR CHANCE TO LOOSE AVALANCHES OF FIRE BOMBS ON TOKYO AND NOGOYA, AND THEY PROVED THAT, PROPERLY KINDLED, JAPANESE CITIES WILL BURN LIKE AUTUMN LEAVES."
-TIME, MAR. '45 [13]

RESULT OF MARCH 10, 1945, TOKYO RAID:
80-130,000 KILLED
41,000 INJURED
1,000,000 HOMELESS [14]

"SMALL, INEFFECTIVE RAIDS, SPACED ABOUT TWO WEEKS APART AT FIRST, HAD GROWN TO 400-PLANE RAIDS AT TWO-DAY INTERVALS.... NEW U.S. FIRE BOMBS HAVE PROVED TO BE A WHITE-HOT SUCCESS."
-TIME, MAY '45 [15]

"AT THE END OF JULY ONLY FOUR BOMBERS HAD BEEN LOST IN THE LAST THREE THOUSAND SORTIES. THIS IS AIR WAR ACCORDING TO THE TEXTBOOKS—THE PROGRESSIVE ANNIHILATION OF ONE NATION WITHOUT MUCH AIR POWER BY ANOTHER WITH PRACTICALLY UNLIMITED STRENGTH."
-FORTUNE, SEPT. '45 [16]

"WE DIDN'T HEAR ANY COMPLAINTS FROM THE AMERICAN PEOPLE ABOUT MASS BOMBING OF JAPAN; AS A MATTER OF FACT, I THINK THEY FELT THE MORE WE DID THE BETTER."
-GENERAL CARL SPAATZ [17]

"THERE ARE NO INNOCENT CIVILIANS. IT IS THEIR GOVERNMENT AND YOU ARE FIGHTING A PEOPLE, YOU ARE NOT TRYING TO FIGHT AN ARMED FORCE ANYMORE. SO IT DOESN'T BOTHER ME SO MUCH TO BE KILLING INNOCENT BYSTANDERS."
-GENERAL LEMAY [18]

"THE ENTIRE POPULATION OF JAPAN IS A PROPER MILITARY TARGET....THERE ARE NO CIVILIANS IN JAPAN."
-5TH AIR FORCE WEEKLY INTELLIGENCE REVIEW, JULY '45 [19]

U.S. BOMBING OF LIBYA, APRIL 14, 1986

"TOM, TRIPOLI IS UNDER ATTACK."
-STEVE DELANEY TO TOM BROKAW, ABC NEWS, 7:02 EST (1)

"PUT YOUR MICROPHONE OUT THAT WINDOW AND LET US HEAR IT."
-DAN RATHER TO JEFFREY FAGER, CBS NEWS (2)

"THE RAID BEGAN AROUND 7 P.M. MONDAY WASHINGTON TIME... AND WAS OVER IN TIME FOR A WHITE HOUSE ANNOUNCEMENT TO CATCH EVENING T.V. NEWS SHOWS."
-TIME (3)

"MY FELLOW AMERICANS, AT 7 O'CLOCK THIS EVENING EASTERN TIME, AIR AND NAVAL FORCES OF THE UNITED STATES LAUNCHED STRIKES AGAINST THE HEADQUARTERS, TERRORIST FACILITIES AND MILITARY ASSETS THAT SUPPORT MUAMMAR QADDAFI'S SUBVERSIVE ACTIVITIES....
"THE EVIDENCE IS NOW CONCLUSIVE THAT THE TERRORIST BOMBING OF THE LA BELLE DISCOTHEQUE WAS PLANNED AND EXECUTED UNDER DIRECT ORDERS OF THE LIBYAN REGIME...."
-PRESIDENT RONALD REAGAN (4)

"LIBYA BEARS DIRECT RESPONSIBILITY FOR THE [DISCO] BOMBING IN WEST BERLIN ON APRIL 5 THAT RESULTED IN THE DEATH OF ARMY SGT. KENNETH FORD AND INJURY TO A NUMBER OF AMERICAN SERVICEMEN AND OTHERS...."
-WHITEHOUSE SPOKESPERSON LARRY SPEAKES (5)

"VERY, VERY CLEAR EVIDENCE THAT THERE IS LIBYAN INVOLVEMENT."
-U.S. AMBASSADOR TO W. GERMANY RICHARD BURT (6)

"THE AMERICAN REPRESENTATIVE WAS UNABLE TO CITE ANY FACTUAL EVIDENCE IN SUPPORT OF HIS ALLEGATIONS."
-SOVIET FOREIGN MINISTRY SPOKESPERSON V. LOMEIKO (7)

"OUR EVIDENCE IS DIRECT, IT IS PRECISE, IT IS IRREFUTABLE...."
-PRESIDENT REAGAN (8)

"I HAVE NO MORE EVIDENCE THAT LIBYA WAS CONNECTED TO THE [DISCO] BOMBING THAN I HAD WHEN YOU FIRST CALLED ME TWO DAYS AFTER THE ACT. WHICH IS NONE."
-MANFRED GANSCHOW, HEAD OF 100-MAN TEAM INVESTIGATING THE DISCO BOMBING (9)

"WE ARE BEYOND THE POINT WHERE WE HAVE TO PRODUCE COURTROOM MATERIALS ON QADDAFI."
-UNNAMED "SENIOR OFFICIAL" (10)

Q: "WAS THERE AN EFFORT, SIR, TO GET QADDAFI PERSONALLY?"
SEC. OF DEFENSE CASPAR WEINBERGER: "NO THERE WAS NOT." (11)

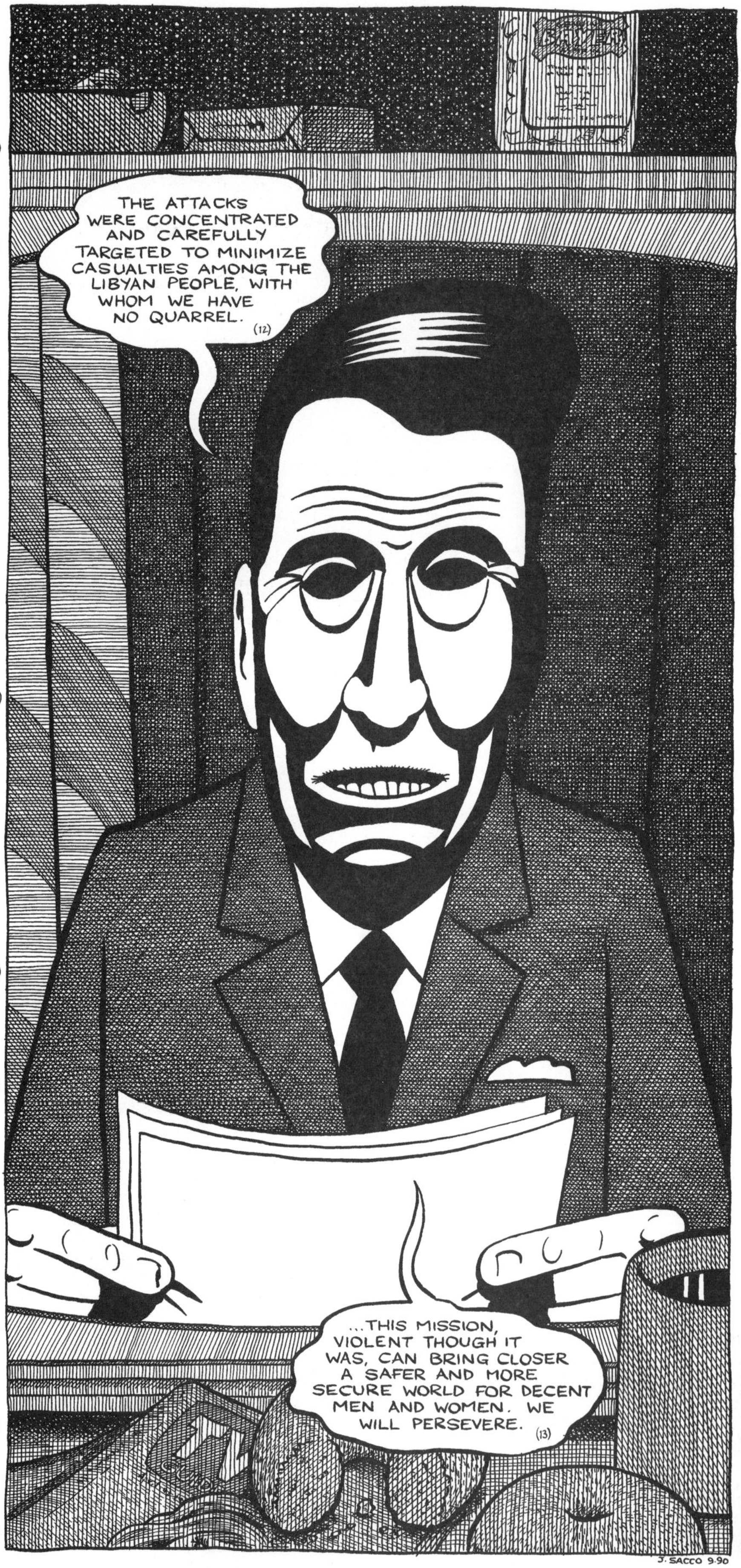
THE ATTACKS WERE CONCENTRATED AND CAREFULLY TARGETED TO MINIMIZE CASUALTIES AMONG THE LIBYAN PEOPLE, WITH WHOM WE HAVE NO QUARREL. (12)
...THIS MISSION, VIOLENT THOUGH IT WAS, CAN BRING CLOSER A SAFER AND MORE SECURE WORLD FOR DECENT MEN AND WOMEN. WE WILL PERSEVERE. (13)
J. SACCO 9.90

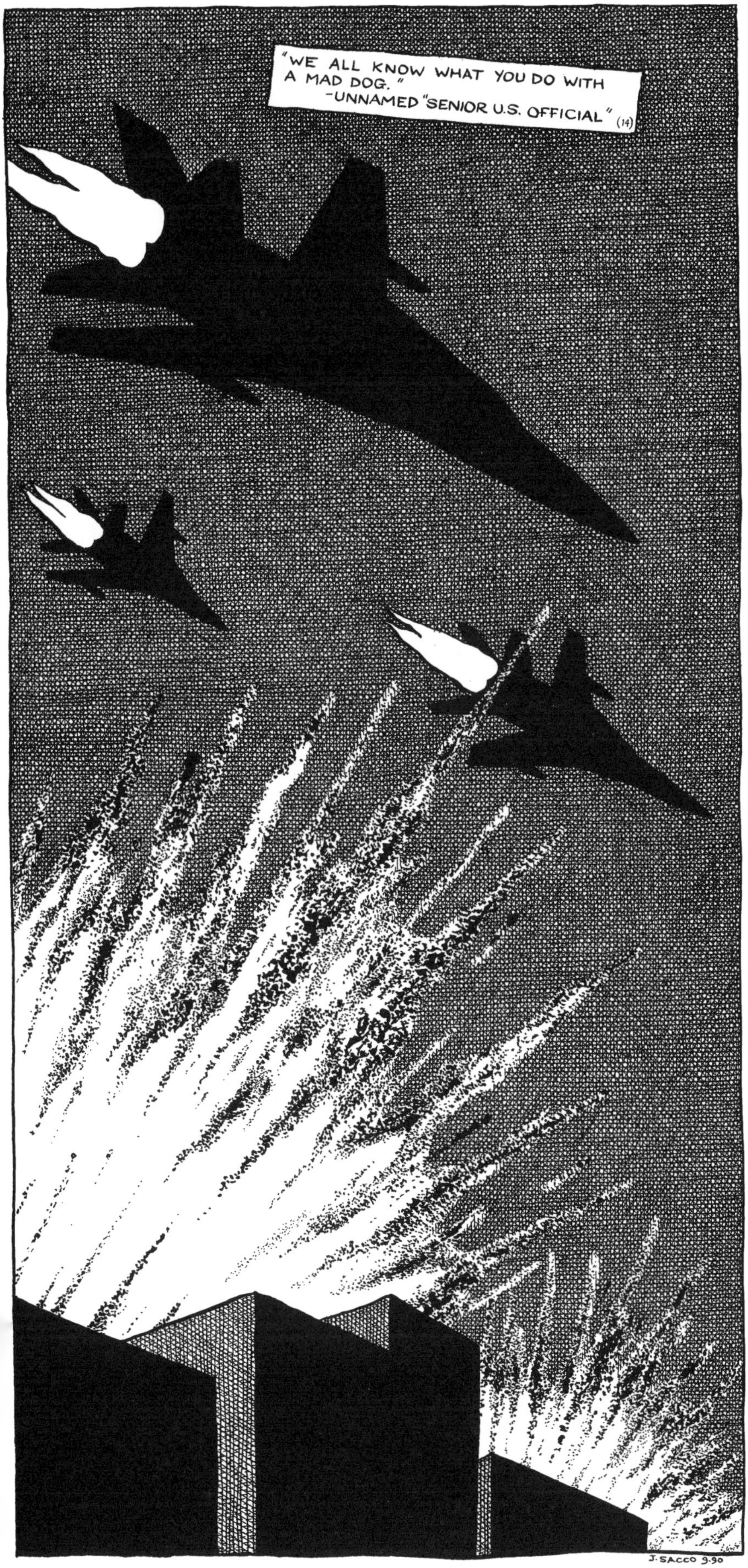
"WE ALL KNOW WHAT YOU DO WITH A MAD DOG."
-UNNAMED "SENIOR U.S. OFFICIAL" (14)
J. SACCO 9.90

"... THERE APPEARED TO BE EIGHT BOMB CRATERS ALONG A 300-YARD ROW EXTENDING FROM IMMEDIATELY IN FRONT OF THE COLONEL'S HOUSE TO AN ADMINISTRATIVE BUILDING UNDER WHICH HE WORKS IN A FORTIFIED BUNKER. THE ROW PASSED WITHIN 50 YARDS OF A CAMOUFLAGED BEDOUIN TENT IN WHICH THE COLONEL ALSO WORKS."
-NY TIMES (15)

"WE ARE NOT TRYING TO GO AFTER QADDAFI AS SUCH, ALTHOUGH WE THINK HE IS A RULER THAT IS BETTER OUT OF HIS COUNTRY."
-SEC. OF STATE GEORGE SHULTZ (16)

"NO FEWER THAN FIVE F-111S WERE ASSIGNED TO HIT QADDAFI'S COMPOUND."
-TIME (17)

"THE UNITED STATES IS NEITHER TRYING TO KILL QADDAFI NOR REPLACE HIS REGIME WITH A GOVERNMENT MORE FAVORABLE TO THE UNITED STATES."
-STATE DEPT. SPOKESPERSON BERNARD KALB (18)

"AMONG THOSE REPORTED DEAD WAS COLONEL QADDAFI'S 15-MONTH-OLD ADOPTED DAUGHTER.... HIS DAUGHTER, HANA, DIED TWO AND A HALF HOURS AFTER SUFFERING A CONCUSSION AND INTERNAL INJURIES FROM AN EXPLOSION NEXT TO THE COLONEL'S HOME.... THE TWO INJURED SONS OF COLONEL QADDAFI'S SEVEN SURVIVING CHILDREN WERE LISTED IN SERIOUS CONDITION.... QADDAFI'S WIFE 'WAS IN A BAD STATE OF SHOCK.'"
-NY TIMES (19)

"ACCORDING TO ONE OF HIS INTIMATES, THE PRESIDENT WAS UPSET WHEN U.S. INTELLIGENCE INDICATED THAT THE RAID ON TRIPOLI HAD KILLED ONE OF QADDAFI'S CHILDREN. 'THE ONE THING THAT GETS TO HIM IS CARNAGE,' THE SOURCE SAYS."
-NEWSWEEK (20)

"WE WEREN'T OUT TO KILL ANYBODY."
-PRESIDENT REAGAN (21)

"WE WERE STRIKING AT HIM PERSONALLY, NOT THAT HE WAS THE TARGET.... WE KNEW THAT THAT WAS HIS RESIDENCE AND THAT HE PERHAPS MIGHT BE THERE AND MEMBERS OF HIS FAMILY."
-UNNAMED "SENIOR WHITE HOUSE AIDE" (22)

"[SHULTZ] NOTED THAT AMERICAN REGULATIONS BAR ASSASSINATIONS OF FOREIGN LEADERS."
-NY TIMES (23)

"A BILL AUTHORIZING THE PRESIDENT TO RESPOND TO FOREIGN TERRORISM WITHOUT CONSULTING CONGRESS IN ADVANCE WAS INTRODUCED BY REPUBLICANS... TODAY.... THE BILL WOULD APPARENTLY PERMIT THE

PRESIDENT TO ORDER THE ASSASSINATION OF A FOREIGN LEADER UNDER SOME CIRCUMSTANCES.... SENATOR DENTON SAID THAT IF COL. MUAMMAR EL-QADDAFI 'BECAME DECEASED AS A RESULT OF OUR COUNTERSTRIKE, THAT WOULD HAVE BEEN WITHIN THE INTENT OF THE BILL.'"
-NY TIMES (24)

"A TONE OF RELIEF AND REVENGE RAN THROUGH MANY COMMENTS, AS CONGRESSMEN COMPETED WITH ONE ANOTHER TO DENOUNCE LIBYA AND ITS LEADER...."
-NY TIMES (25)

"A GREEK DOCTOR, HIS FACE AND WRIST PATCHED UP WITH BAND-AIDS, LIMPED DOWN THE STREET, SAYING HIS WIFE WAS STILL IN THE HOSPITAL AND MUMBLING PROFANITIES ABOUT THE UNITED STATES."
-NY TIMES (26)

"WE'RE JUST NOT GOING TO LET AMERICANS BE TERRORIZED AROUND THE WORLD."
-HOUSE SPEAKER 'TIP' O'NEILL (27)

"TAHER MOHAMMED GUBBIA, HIS VOICE SHAKING IN RAGE, CALLED IT TERRORISM. HE SAID THE AMERICAN FIGHTER BOMBERS DESTROYED HIS HOME EARLY THIS MORNING. HIS WIFE'S ARM WAS BROKEN IN THE ATTACK.... AT LEAST 15 OF MR. GUBBIA'S NEIGHBORS WERE KILLED...."
-NY TIMES (28)

"... A BRAVE, BALANCED AND BOLD DECISION TO RETALIATE IN THE DEFENSE OF FREEDOM AGAINST THE ONSLAUGHT OF A HOSTILE TOTALITARIAN REGIME THAT IS A PARIAH IN THE WORLD COMMUNITY."
-SENATOR DAN QUAYLE (29)

"AT THE DOOR LAY THE BODY OF A LITTLE GIRL.... BESIDE HER WAS AN INFANT IN A PINK PLAYSUIT. BETWEEN THEM LAY TWO SMALL HANDS, SEVERED JUST BELOW THE WRIST."
-NEWSWEEK (30)

"... EVEN THE MOST SCRUPULOUS CITIZEN CAN ONLY APPROVE AND APPLAUD THE AMERICAN ATTACKS ON LIBYA.... IF THERE WERE SUCH A THING AS DUE PROCESS IN THE COURT OF WORLD OPINION, THE UNITED STATES HAS OBSERVED IT...."
-NY TIMES EDITORIAL (31)

"AS FAR AS WHAT WE CALL THE BOMBING OPTION IS CONCERNED, THAT CANNOT BE USED AGAIN UNLESS IT IS MASSIVE.... WITH QADDAFI I THINK WE DID THE RIGHT THING AT THAT TIME, BUT FROM NOW ON WE'VE GOT TO THINK IN BIGGER TERMS."
-FORMER PRESIDENT NIXON (32)

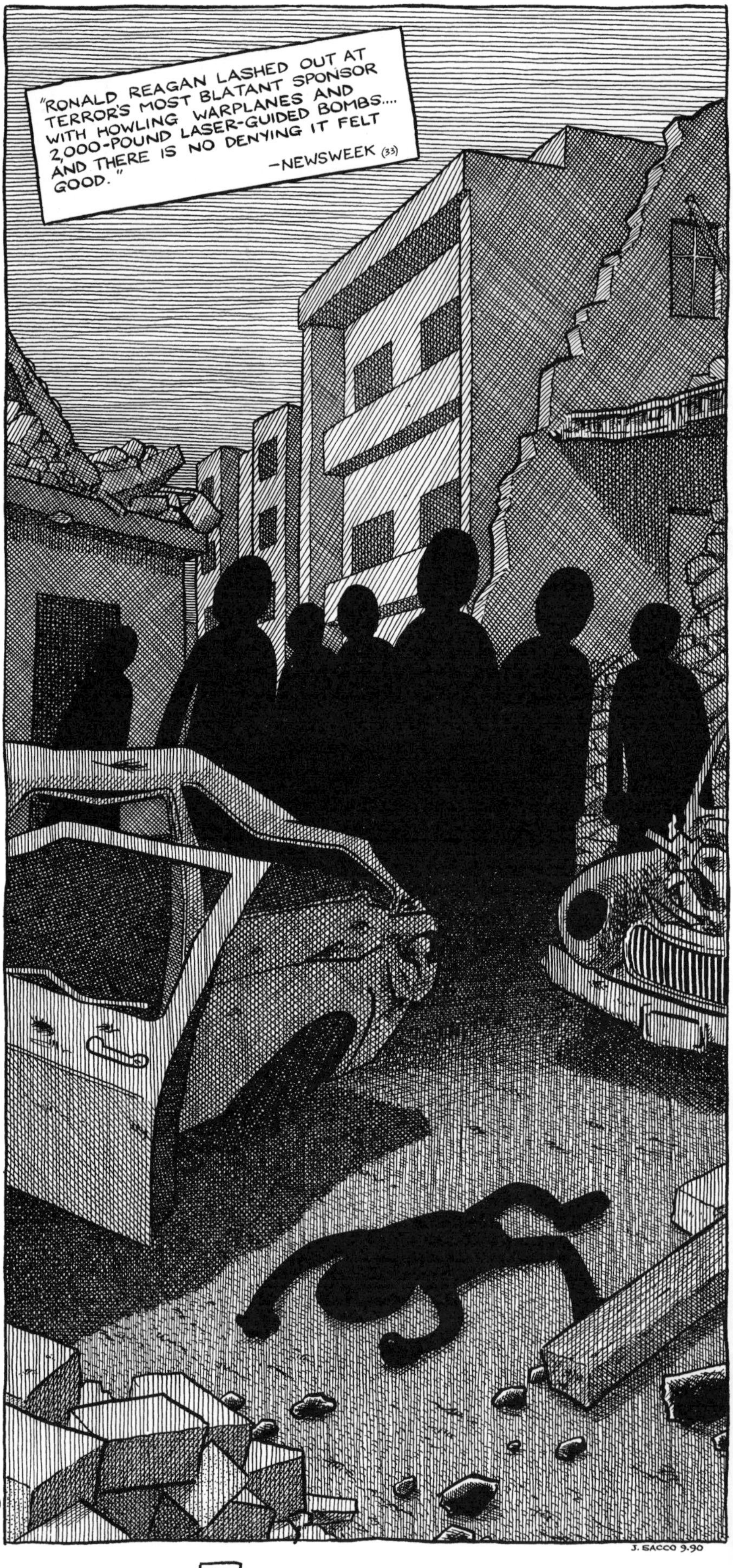
"RONALD REAGAN LASHED OUT AT TERROR'S MOST BLATANT SPONSOR WITH HOWLING WARPLANES AND 2,000-POUND LASER-GUIDED BOMBS.... AND THERE IS NO DENYING IT FELT GOOD."
-NEWSWEEK (33)
J. SACCO 9.90

BIBLIOGRAPHY

- CARL BERGER, 'B29, THE SUPERFORTRESS' (MACDONALD & CO., LONDON, 1970)
- NOAM CHOMSKY, 'PIRATES & EMPERORS: INTERNATIONAL TERRORISM IN THE REAL WORLD' (CLAREMONT RESEARCH & PUBLICATIONS, NEW YORK, 1986)
- JOHN W. DOWER, 'WAR WITHOUT MERCY: RACE AND POWER IN THE PACIFIC WAR' (PANTHEON BOOKS, NEW YORK, 1986)
- MAX HASTINGS, 'BOMBER COMMAND' (DIAL PRESS/JAMES WADE, NEW YORK, 1979)
- EDWARD JABLONSKI, 'WINGS OF FIRE' (DOUBLEDAY & CO., GARDEN CITY, NY, 1972)
- DUDLEY SAWARD, 'VICTORY DENIED' (FRANKLIN WATTS, NEW YORK, 1987)
- RONALD SCHAFFER, 'WINGS OF JUDGMENT: AMERICAN BOMBING IN WORLD WAR II' (OXFORD UNIVERSITY PRESS, NEW YORK, 1985)
- MICHAEL SHERRY, 'THE RISE OF AMERICAN AIRPOWER' (YALE UNIVERSITY PRESS, NEW HAVEN, CONN., 1987)
- VARIOUS PUBLICATIONS AS INDICATED

FOOTNOTES & COMMENTS

BRITISH BOMBING OF GERMANY, 1940-45:

(1) HASTINGS.

(2) HASTINGS.

(3) HASTINGS. HOWEVER, IN RESPONSE TO GERMAN RAIDS ON LONDON DURING THE FIRST WORLD WAR, CHURCHILL ARGUED AGAINST AERIAL RETALIATION. HE FELT THE GERMANS COULD NOT BE "COWED INTO SUBMISSION BY SUCH METHODS." HE WONDERED IF "THEY WOULD NOT BE RENDERED MORE DESPERATELY RESOLVED BY THEM...." (HASTINGS)

(4) HASTINGS.

(5) HASTINGS. SAID BOMBER COMMAND C-IN-C HARRIS AFTER THE WAR: "THE DESTRUCTION OF FACTORIES, WHICH WAS NEVERTHELESS ON AN ENORMOUS SCALE, COULD BE REGARDED AS A BONUS. THE AIMING POINTS WERE USUALLY RIGHT IN THE CENTER OF TOWN." (HASTINGS)

(6) HASTINGS. THE PRACTICE OF TURNING GERMANS "OUT OF HOUSE AND HOME" WAS EUPHEMISTICALLY TERMED "DE-HOUSING."

(7) SAWARD. THE AUTHOR WORKED PERSONALLY WITH HARRIS AT BOMBER COMMAND HEADQUARTERS. AN APOLOGIST THROUGH AND THROUGH.

(8) NEWSWEEK, JUNE 8, 1942. HARRIS MUSTERED MORE THAN 1000 BOMBERS FOR THE COLOGNE RAID. 469 PEOPLE WERE KILLED, 5027 WOUNDED, AND MORE THAN 45,000 "DE-HOUSED." SMALL POTATOES BY LATER STANDARDS.

(9) HASTINGS. HARRIS'S COMMENT SUMS UP THE CONCEPT OF AREA BOMBING: DEFEAT A NATION BY PULVERIZING ITS POPULATION CENTERS.

(10) NEWSWEEK, JULY 12, 1943.

(11) FOR AN EXCELLENT ACCOUNT OF THE HAMBURG RAIDS, SEE MARTIN MIDDLEBROOK'S 'THE BATTLE OF HAMBURG.'

(12) LIFE, AUG. 23, 1943.

(13) DURING THE HAMBURG FIRESTORM TEMPERATURES REACHED 600-1000 DEGREES CENTIGRADE. ALBERT SPEER, HITLER'S MINISTER OF ARMAMENTS, INFORMED HITLER THAT SIX MORE SUCH ATTACKS WOULD END THE WAR. HITLER'S VIEW: "TERROR CAN ONLY BE BROKEN BY TERROR.... THE BRITISH WILL ONLY BE HALTED WHEN THEIR OWN CITIES ARE DESTROYED."

(14) HASTINGS.

(15) NY TIMES MAGAZINE, APRIL 16, 1944: AN ARTICLE WRITTEN BY HARRIS FOR THE AMERICAN PUBLIC.

(16) SENIOR SCHOLASTIC, APRIL 3, 1944:
AN EXPLANATION TO AMERICAN STUDENTS TITLED, "WHY WE BOMB GERMANY."

(17) HASTINGS. THIS COMMENT DATES FROM EARLY 1942.

(18) TIME, JUNE 8, 1942.

(19) NY TIMES MAGAZINE, JUNE 6, 1943.

(20) HASTINGS. COMMENT FROM NOV. '43. HARRIS FELT THE UNITED STATES ARMY AIR FORCE, WHICH (IN THE EUROPEAN WAR) WAS MORE OR LESS COMMITTED TO PRECISION BOMBING OF FACTORIES AND INDUSTRIAL TARGETS ("PANACEA TARGETS" TO HARRIS), SHOULD JOIN THE ROYAL AIR FORCE IN AREA BOMBING.

(21) HASTINGS. HARRIS WAS ARGUING TO AIR CHIEF-MARSHAL PORTAL AGAINST A SWITCH FROM AREA BOMBING TO ATTACKS ON GERMANY'S OIL INDUSTRY. "INVASION DIVERSIONS" REFERS TO BOMBER COMMAND RAIDS IN DIRECT SUPPORT OF ALLIED GROUND FORCES.

(22) HASTINGS.

(23) HASTINGS. "KEY PERSONNEL"? THE MILKMAN, PERHAPS?

(24) HASTINGS. IN MARCH '45, HARRIS STATED, "I WOULD NOT REGARD THE WHOLE OF GERMANY AS WORTH THE BONES OF ONE BRITISH GRENADIER." (HASTINGS)

(25) HASTINGS. CHURCHILL'S ADMONITION TO SEC. OF STATE FOR AIR, SIR ARCHIBALD SINCLAIR, SET THE INFAMOUS DRESDEN RAID INTO MOTION. SINCLAIR HAD FELT THE GERMAN RETREAT FROM THE SOVIETS COULD BEST BE DISRUPTED BY SOVIET TACTICAL AIRCRAFT, NOT BRITISH AND U.S. HEAVY BOMBERS. ACCORDING TO BOMBER COMMAND'S BRIEFING NOTES, PART OF THE JUSTIFICATION FOR ATTACKING DRESDEN ("FAR THE LARGEST UNBOMBED BUILT-UP AREA THE ENEMY HAS GOT") WAS "INCIDENTALLY TO SHOW THE RUSSIANS WHEN THEY ARRIVE WHAT BOMBER COMMAND CAN DO." (HASTINGS) WHEN DRESDEN BECAME A SYMBOL OF UNJUSTIFIED BOMBING OF CIVILIANS, CHURCHILL TRIED TO DISASSOCIATE HIMSELF FROM THE RAID. THOUGH HE AND OTHERS WERE RESPONSIBLE FOR BRITAIN'S RUTHLESS AIR STRATEGY, THE OUTSPOKEN HARRIS WAS LEFT TO HOLD THE HISTORICAL BAG ALONE.

(26) A.P., FEB. 15, 1945. THE U.S. JOINED IN THE DRESDEN BOMBING.

(27) WHO COULD COUNT? LIKE MOST FIGURES RELATING TO CASUALTIES OF AERIAL BOMBING, GUESSES VARY WIDELY AND ARE FREQUENTLY REVISED.

(28) A.P., FEB. 18, 1945. U.S. SEC. OF WAR STIMSON ATTRIBUTED THE REPORT TO "AN EXCUSABLE BUT INCORRECT INTERPRETATION OF SOME REMARK BY A BRIEFING OFFICER AT ALLIED HEADQUARTERS." (SCHAFFER)

U.S. BOMBING OF JAPAN, 1944-45

(1) DOWER. COMMENTS MADE IN CONDEMNING JAPANESE BOMBING OF CHINESE CITIES.

(2) DOWER. ROOSEVELT WAS REFERRING TO CIVILIAN BOMBING AND CALLING FOR RESTRAINT FROM ALL COMBATANTS.

(3) BERGER. ARNOLD'S REPLY TO GENERAL CHENNAULT, WHO HAD URGED THE DEVELOPMENT OF FIRE BOMBS FOR POSSIBLE USE AGAINST JAPAN.

(4) SHERRY. MITCHELL ALSO POINTED OUT THAT A GAS ATTACK WOULD "COMPLETELY BLOCK THEM OUT."

(5) NY TIMES MAGAZINE, APRIL 26, 1942. THE POSSIBILITY OF FIRE RAIDS ON JAPAN WAS POINTED OUT IN A NUMBER OF POPULAR U.S. PUBLICATIONS BEFORE AND AT THE EARLY STAGES OF THE WAR.

(6) SCHAFFER.

(7) SHERRY.

(8) SCHAFFER.

(9) SCHAFFER.

(10) NY TIMES, MARCH 10, 1945.

(11) NY TIMES, MARCH 10, 1945.

(12) FORTUNE, OCT. '45.

(13) TIME, MARCH 19, 1945

(14) "SCORCHED AND BOILED AND BAKED
TO DEATH" IS HOW LE MAY DESCRIBED THE CASUALTIES. (DOWER) FOR A GRISLY (AND UNNECESSARILY OVERSTATED) ACCOUNT OF THE TOKYO RAID, SEE MARTIN CAIDIN'S 'A TORCH TO THE ENEMY.'

(15) TIME, MAY 7, 1945.

(16) FORTUNE, SEPT. '45.

(17) SHERRY.

(18) SHERRY.

(19) SHERRY.

(20) JABLONSKI. THE LEAFLETS CALLED FOR THE JAPANESE TO OVERTHROW THEIR MILITARY GOVERNMENT TO "SAVE WHAT IS LEFT OF YOUR BEAUTIFUL COUNTRY."

U.S. BOMBING OF LIBYA, APR. 14, 1986

(1) TIME, APRIL 28, 1986.

(2) TIME, APRIL 28, 1986.

(3) TIME, APRIL 28, 1986. TIME REFERRED TO THE ATTACK AS "A BATTLE THAT SEEMED TO BE ORCHESTRATED FOR THE 7 O'CLOCK NEWS."

(4) NY TIMES, APRIL 15, 1986. FROM REAGAN'S T.V. ADDRESS THE NIGHT OF THE ATTACK.

(5) NY TIMES, APRIL 15, 1986.

(6) NY TIMES, APRIL 15, 1986.

(7) NY TIMES, APRIL 18, 1986.

(8) NY TIMES, APRIL 15, 1986. FROM REAGAN'S T.V. ADDRESS. PART OF THE "IRREFUTABLE" EVIDENCE OF LIBYAN DIRECTION IN THE BERLIN DISCO BOMBING RELATES TO CERTAIN TELEPHONE INTERCEPTS BETWEEN EAST BERLIN AND TRIPOLI. DER SPIEGEL, A GERMAN WEEKLY, REPORTED ON APRIL 21, 1986, THAT THE INTERCEPTS APPARENTLY DID NOT EXIST. (CHOMSKY) NATURALLY, THE INTERCEPTS HAVE NEVER BEEN RELEASED. WEEKS LATER, SYRIA WAS IMPLICATED, BUT "CRACKING DOWN ON SYRIA IS FAR MORE DIFFICULT... GIVEN DAMASCUS'S FORMIDABLE DEFENSES." (TIME, MAY 12, '86)

(9) CHOMSKY. A STATEMENT TO A STARS AND STRIPES REPORTER, APRIL 28, 1986.

(10) NEWSWEEK, APRIL 28, 1986.

(11) NY TIMES, APRIL 15, 1986. FROM A NEWS CONFERENCE.

(12) AND (13) NY TIMES, APRIL 15, 1986. FROM REAGAN'S T.V. ADDRESS.

(14) NEWSWEEK, APRIL 21, 1986. A COMMENT MADE BEFORE THE RAID. "MAD DOG" WAS REAGAN'S PET NAME FOR QADDAFI.

(15) NY TIMES, APRIL 17, 1986.

(16) NY TIMES, APRIL 16, 1986.

(17) TIME, APRIL 28, 1986.

(18) NY TIMES, APRIL 16, 1986.

(19) NY TIMES, APRIL 16, 1986.

(20) NEWSWEEK, APRIL 28, 1986.

(21) NY TIMES, APRIL 19, 1986.

(22) NY TIMES, APRIL 17, 1986.

(23) NY TIMES, APRIL 18, 1986.

(24) NY TIMES, APRIL 18, 1986. REP. JOE BARTON, A CO-SPONSOR OF THE BILL, DISAGREED: "WE CERTAINLY DON'T WANT TO PUT THE GOVERNMENT ON RECORD AS CONDONING ASSASSINATION." THE BILL FAILED.

(25) NY TIMES, APRIL 16, 1986. CRITICISM FROM CONGRESSMEN WAS MOSTLY CONFINED TO THE FACT THAT THEY HAD NOT BEEN CONSULTED, THOUGH CONGRESSIONAL LEADERS WERE NOTIFIED JUST PRIOR TO THE RAID.

(26) NY TIMES, APRIL 16, 1986. THE MEDIA GAVE SERIOUS CONSIDERATION TO THE SUGGESTION THAT ANTI-AIRCRAFT MISSILES FALLING BACK TO EARTH CAUSED CIVILIAN CASUALTIES. YEP, LIBYAN TERRORISM EVEN IN TRIPOLI!

(27) NY TIMES, APRIL 16, 1986.

(28) NY TIMES, APRIL 16, 1986.

(29) NY TIMES, APRIL 16, 1986.

(30) NEWSWEEK, APRIL 28, 1986.

(31) NY TIMES, APRIL 15, 1986. IN FACT, THE "COURT OF WORLD OPINION" WAS ARRAYED AGAINST THE U.S. RAID. EXCEPT FOR BRITAIN, FROM WHERE THE F-111s WERE LAUNCHED, W. EUROPEAN NATIONS ADVISED AGAINST MILITARY ACTION. FRANCE DISALLOWED OVERFLIGHT. THE NON-ALIGNED MOVEMENT EXPRESSED SOLIDARITY WITH LIBYA. ARAB NATIONS WERE ALMOST UNIVERSAL IN CONDEMNATION. TASS CALLED THE RAID "STATE TERRORISM," ETC.

(32) NEWSWEEK, MAY 19, 1986.

(33) NEWSWEEK, APRIL 28, 1986.

PART EIGHT:

MORE WOMEN, MORE CHILDREN, MORE QUICKLY

"I think it is well for the man in the street to realize that there is no power on earth that can protect him from being bombed....The bomber will always get through. The only defense is offense, which means that you have to kill more women and children more quickly than the enemy if you want to save yourselves. I just mention that... so that people may realize what is waiting for them when the next war comes."

– Stanley Baldwin, former British Prime Minister, 1932

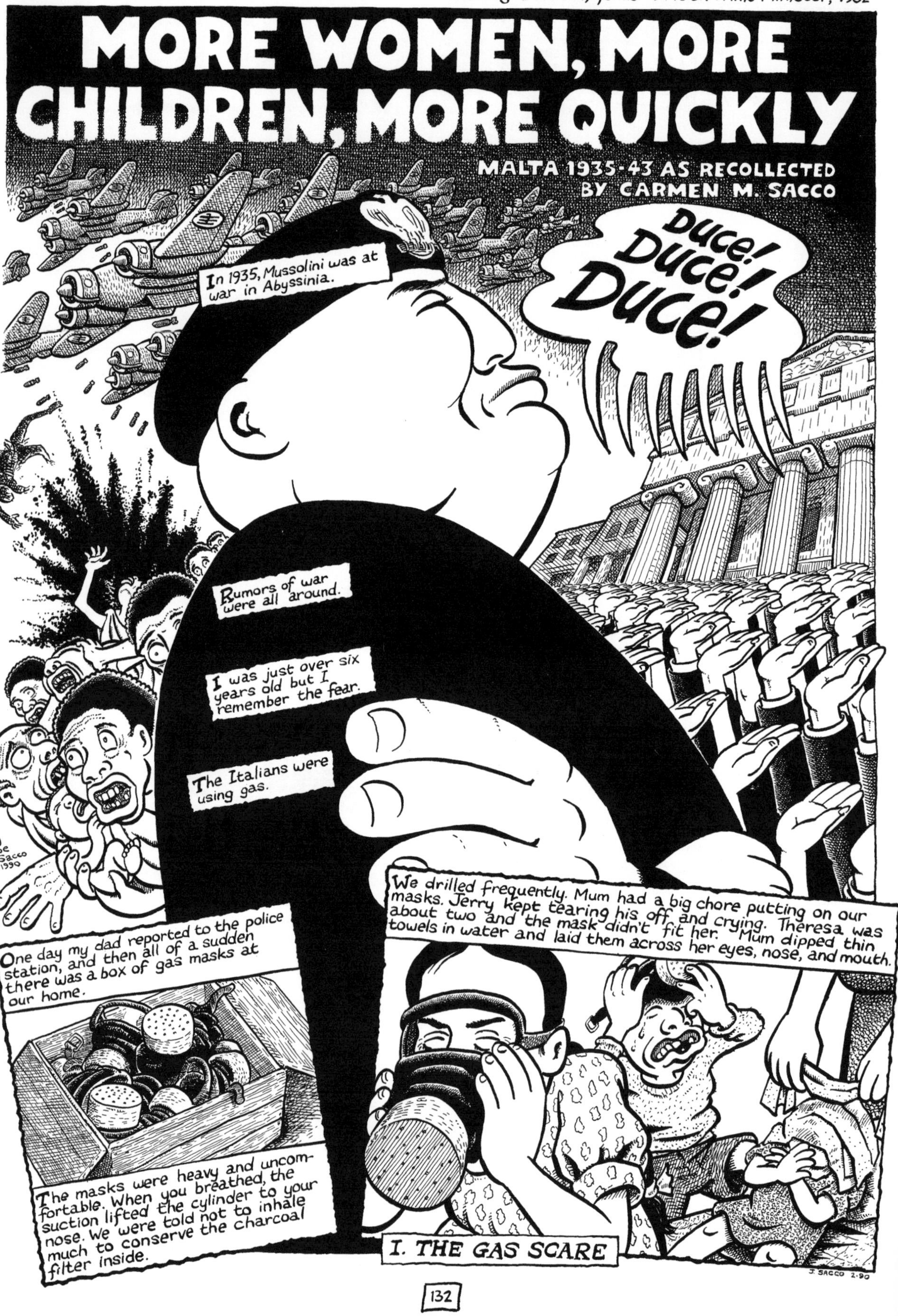

MORE WOMEN, MORE CHILDREN, MORE QUICKLY
MALTA 1935-43 AS RECOLLECTED BY CARMEN M. SACCO
Duce! Duce! Duce!
In 1935, Mussolini was at war in Abyssinia.
Rumors of war were all around.
I was just over six years old but I remember the fear.
The Italians were using gas.
by Joe Sacco 1990
We drilled frequently. Mum had a big chore putting on our masks. Jerry kept tearing his off and crying. Theresa was about two and the mask didn't fit her. Mum dipped thin towels in water and laid them across her eyes, nose, and mouth.
One day my dad reported to the police station, and then all of a sudden there was a box of gas masks at our home.
The masks were heavy and uncomfortable. When you breathed, the suction lifted the cylinder to your nose. We were told not to inhale much to conserve the charcoal filter inside.
I. THE GAS SCARE
J. SACCO 2-90

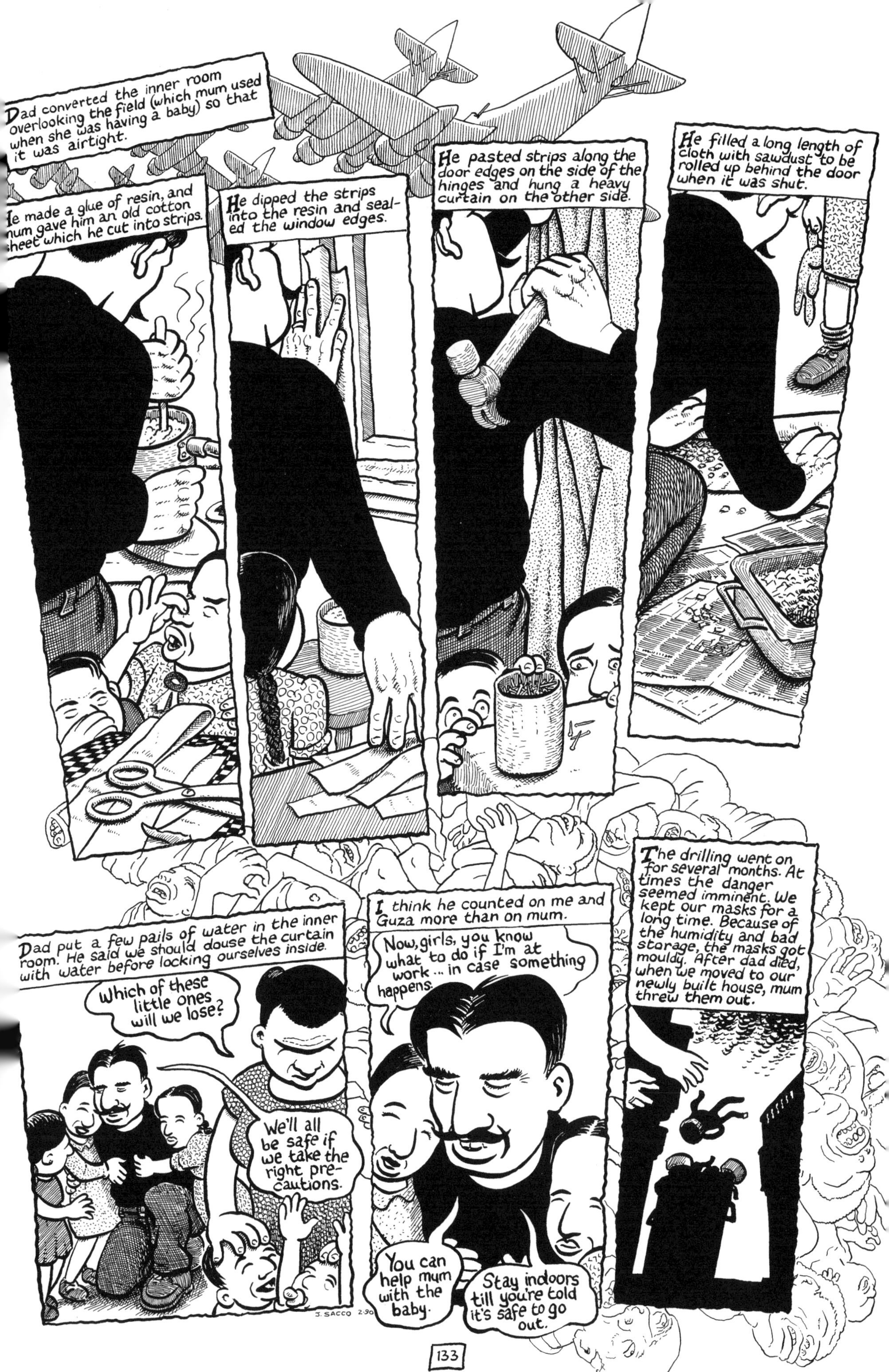
Dad converted the inner room overlooking the field (which mum used when she was having a baby) so that it was airtight.
He made a glue of resin, and mum gave him an old cotton sheet which he cut into strips.
He dipped the strips into the resin and sealed the window edges.
He pasted strips along the door edges on the side of the hinges and hung a heavy curtain on the other side.
He filled a long length of cloth with sawdust to be rolled up behind the door when it was shut.
Dad put a few pails of water in the inner room. He said we should douse the curtain with water before locking ourselves inside.
Which of these little ones will we lose?
We'll all be safe if we take the right precautions.
J. SACCO 2-90
I think he counted on me and Guza more than on mum.
Now, girls, you know what to do if I'm at work ... in case something happens.
You can help mum with the baby.
Stay indoors till you're told it's safe to go out.
The drilling went on for several months. At times the danger seemed imminent. We kept our masks for a long time. Because of the humidity and bad storage, the masks got mouldy. After dad died, when we moved to our newly built house, mum threw them out.

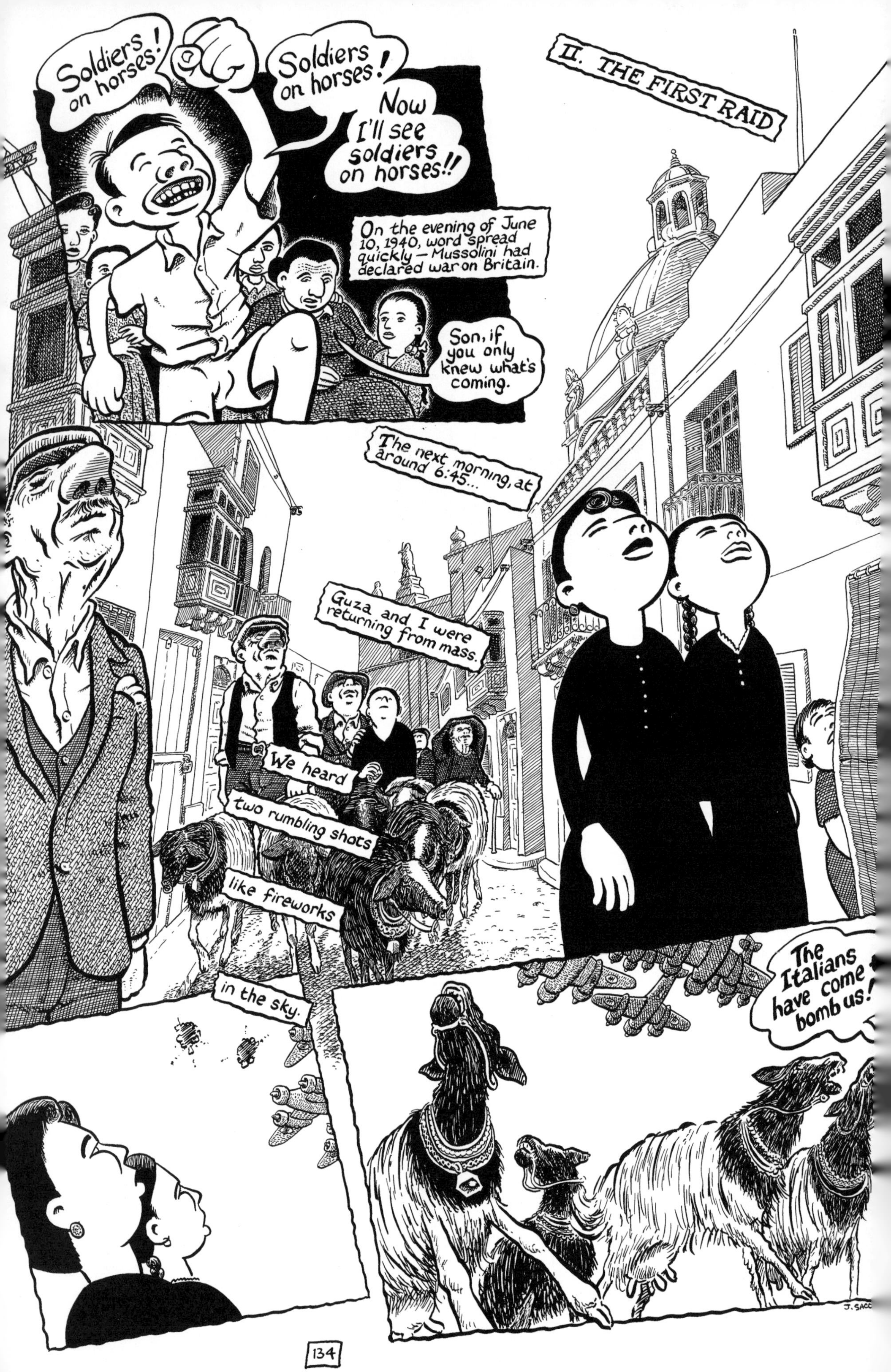
II. THE FIRST RAID
Soldiers on horses!
Soldiers on horses!
Now I'll see soldiers on horses!!
On the evening of June 10, 1940, word spread quickly — Mussolini had declared war on Britain.
Son, if you only knew what's coming.
The next morning, at around 6:45...
Guza and I were returning from mass.
We heard
two rumbling shots
like fireworks
in the sky.
The Italians have come bomb us!
J. SACCO

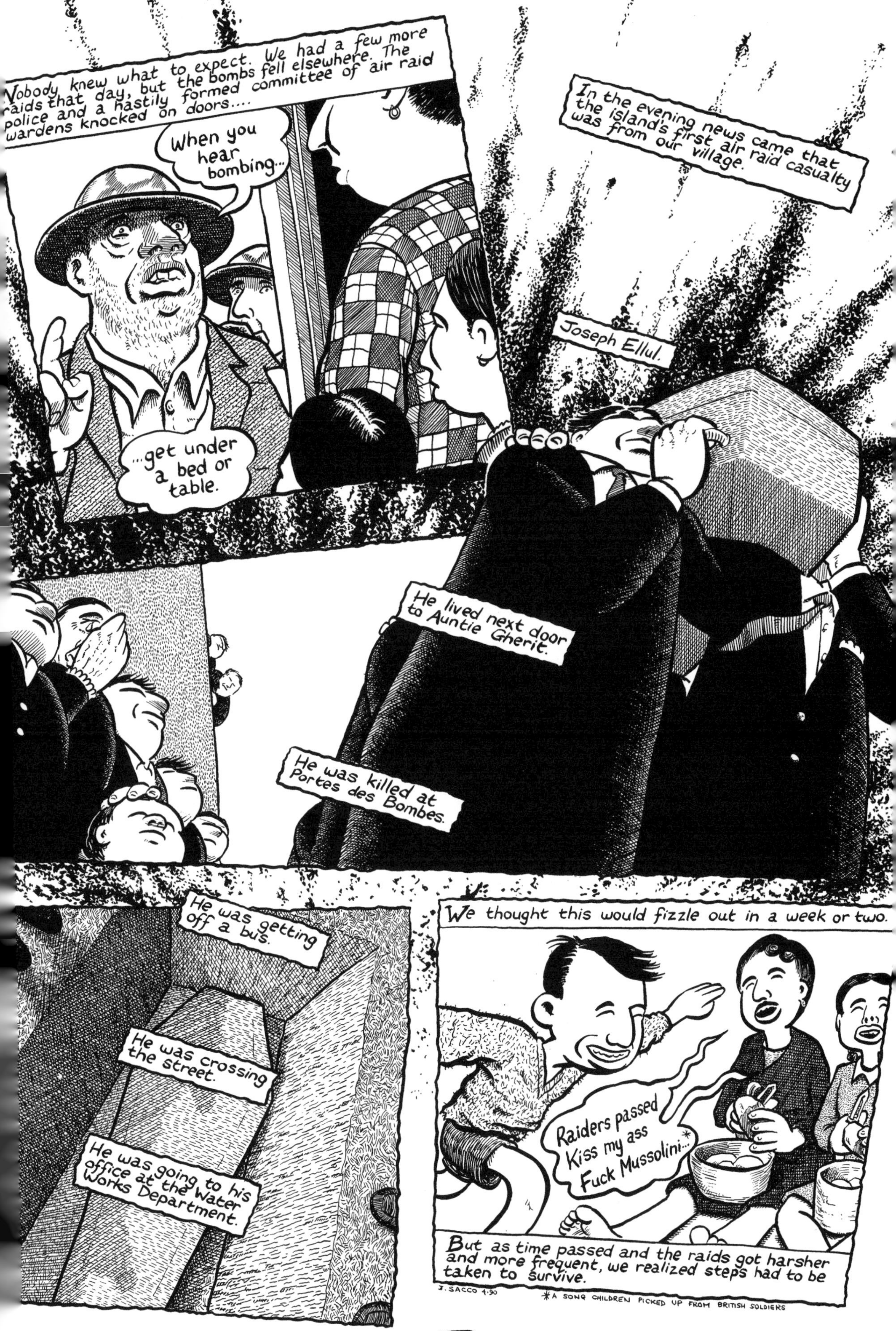
Nobody knew what to expect. We had a few more raids that day, but the bombs fell elsewhere. The police and a hastily formed committee of air raid wardens knocked on doors....
When you hear bombing...
...get under a bed or table.
In the evening news came that the island's first air raid casualty was from our village.
Joseph Ellul.
He lived next door to Auntie Gherit.
He was killed at Portes des Bombes.
He was getting off a bus.
He was crossing the street.
He was going to his office at the Water Works Department.
We thought this would fizzle out in a week or two.
Raiders passed Kiss my ass Fuck Mussolini...*
But as time passed and the raids got harsher and more frequent, we realized steps had to be taken to survive.
J. SACCO 4·90
*A SONG CHILDREN PICKED UP FROM BRITISH SOLDIERS

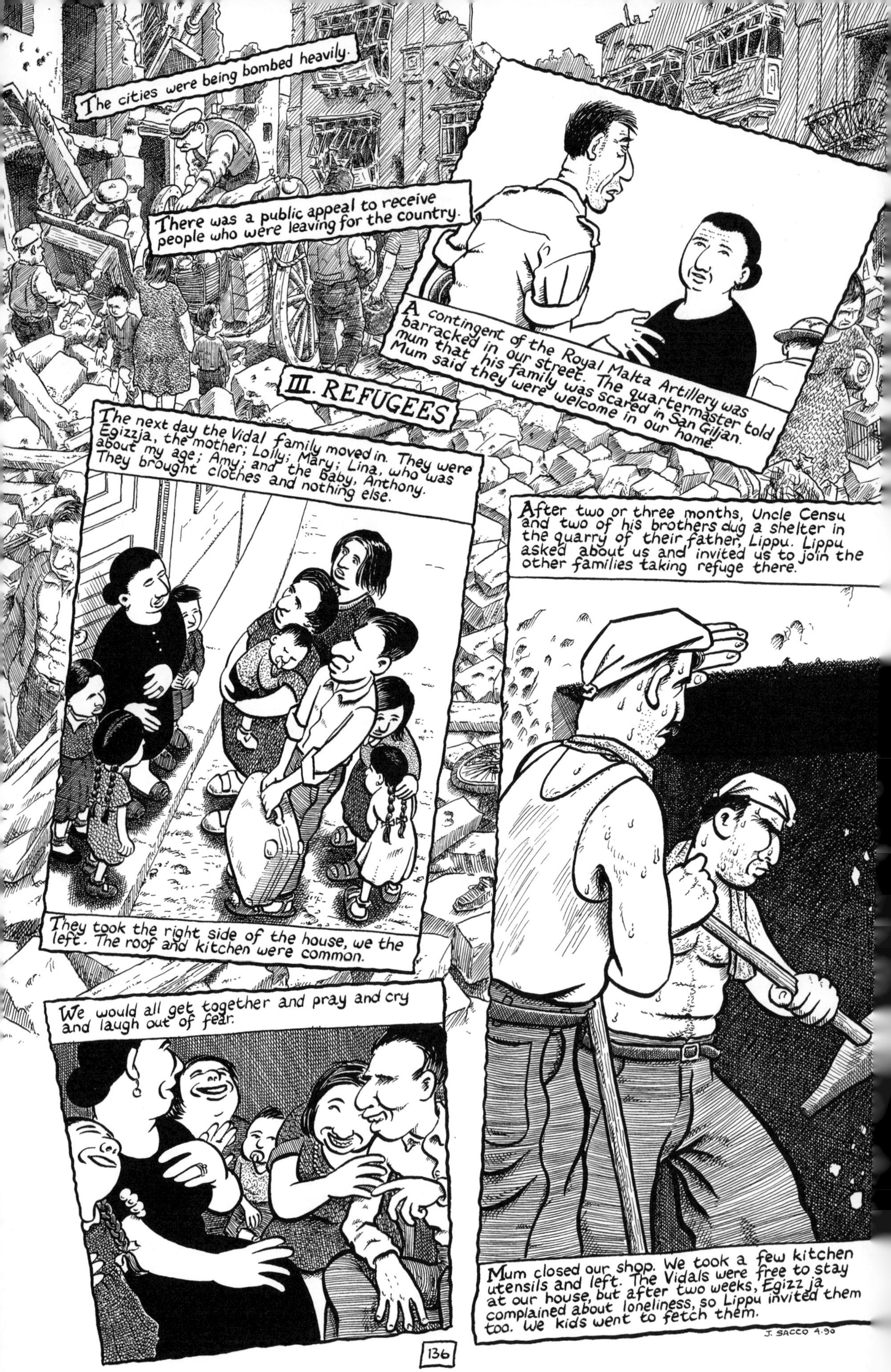

The cities were being bombed heavily.
There was a public appeal to receive people who were leaving for the country.
A contingent of the Royal Malta Artillery was barracked in our street. The quartermaster told mum that his family was scared in San Giljan. Mum said they were welcome in our home.
III. REFUGEES
The next day the Vidal family moved in. They were Egizzja, the mother; Lolly; Mary; Lina, who was about my age; Amy; and the baby, Anthony. They brought clothes and nothing else.
They took the right side of the house, we the left. The roof and kitchen were common.
After two or three months, Uncle Censu and two of his brothers dug a shelter in the quarry of their father, Lippu. Lippu asked about us and invited us to join the other families taking refuge there.
We would all get together and pray and cry and laugh out of fear.
Mum closed our shop. We took a few kitchen utensils and left. The Vidals were free to stay at our house, but after two weeks, Egizzja complained about loneliness, so Lippu invited them too. We kids went to fetch them.
J. SACCO 4.90

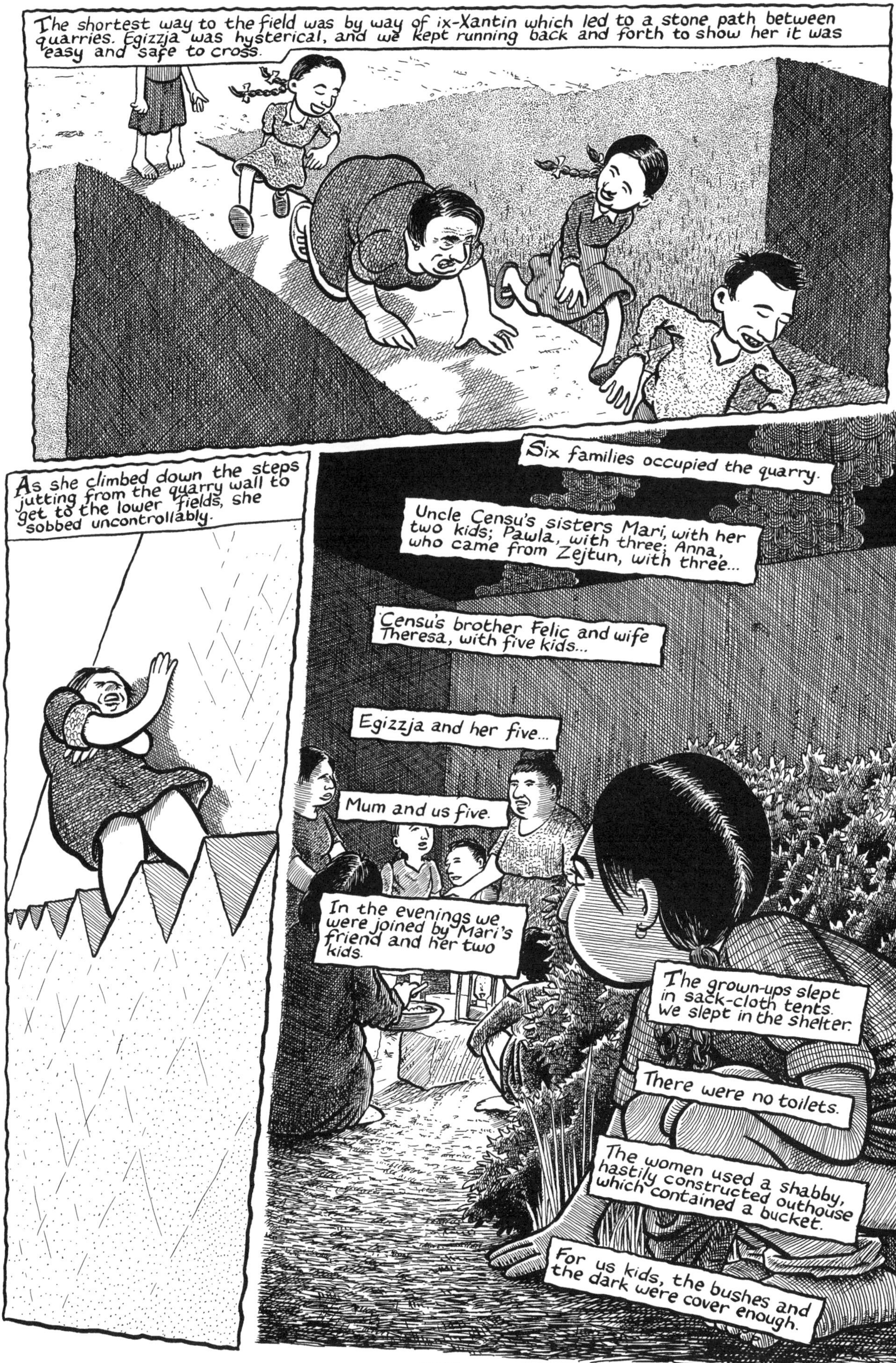

The shortest way to the field was by way of ix-Xantin which led to a stone path between quarries. Egizzja was hysterical, and we kept running back and forth to show her it was easy and safe to cross.
As she climbed down the steps jutting from the quarry wall to get to the lower fields, she sobbed uncontrollably.
Six families occupied the quarry.
Uncle Censu's sisters Mari, with her two kids; Pawla, with three; Anna, who came from Zejtun, with three...
Censu's brother Felic and wife Theresa, with five kids...
Egizzja and her five...
Mum and us five.
In the evenings we were joined by Mari's friend and her two kids.
The grown-ups slept in sack-cloth tents. We slept in the shelter.
There were no toilets.
The women used a shabby, hastily constructed outhouse which contained a bucket.
For us kids, the bushes and the dark were cover enough.
J. SACCO 4.90

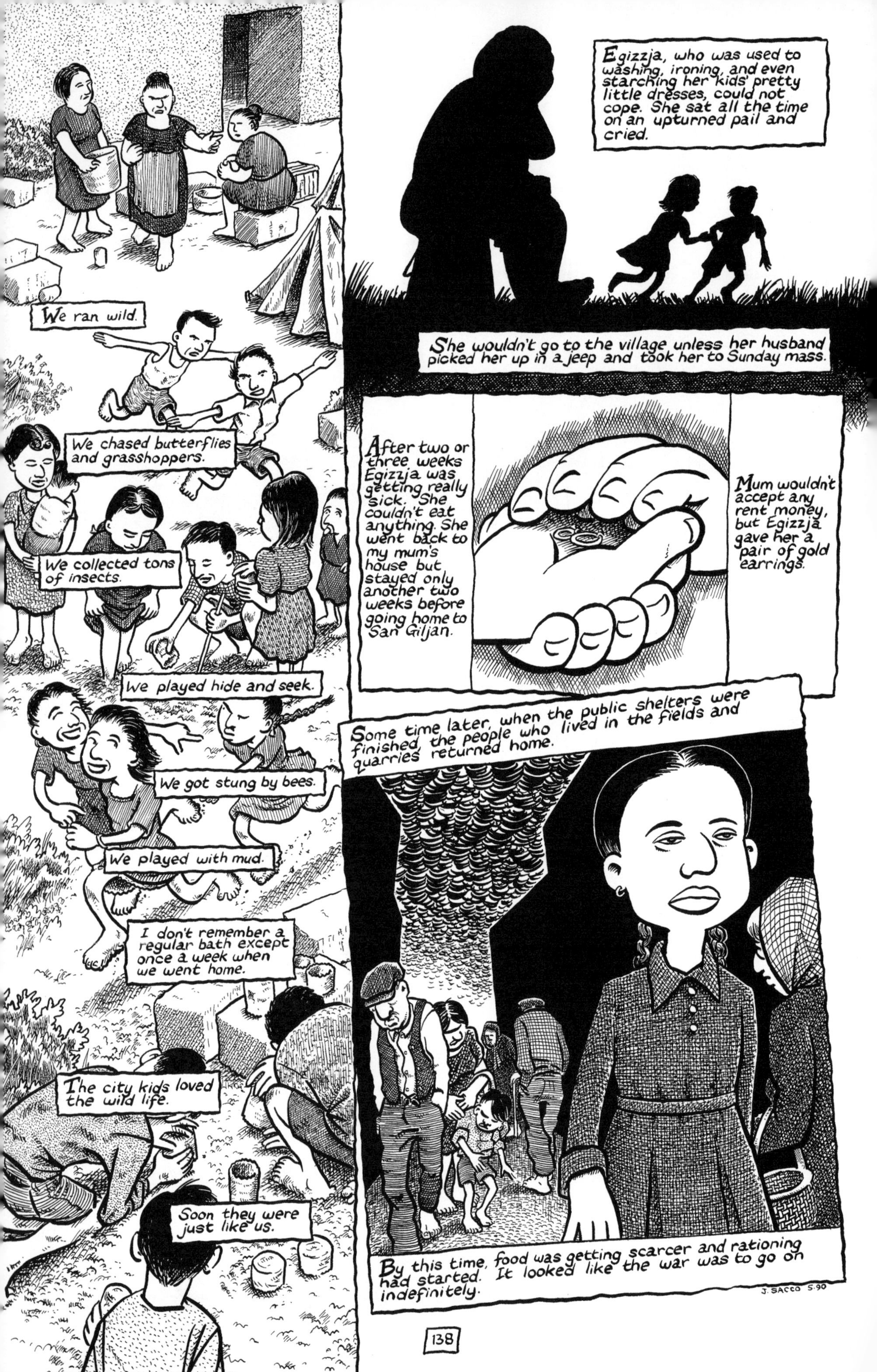
We ran wild.
We chased butterflies and grasshoppers.
We collected tons of insects.
We played hide and seek.
We got stung by bees.
We played with mud.
I don't remember a regular bath except once a week when we went home.
The city kids loved the wild life.
Soon they were just like us.
Egizzja, who was used to washing, ironing, and even starching her kids' pretty little dresses, could not cope. She sat all the time on an upturned pail and cried.
She wouldn't go to the village unless her husband picked her up in a jeep and took her to Sunday mass.
After two or three weeks Egizzja was getting really sick. She couldn't eat anything. She went back to my mum's house but stayed only another two weeks before going home to San Giljan.
Mum wouldn't accept any rent money, but Egizzja gave her a pair of gold earrings.
Some time later, when the public shelters were finished, the people who lived in the fields and quarries returned home.
By this time, food was getting scarcer and rationing had started. It looked like the war was to go on indefinitely.
J. SACCO 5.90

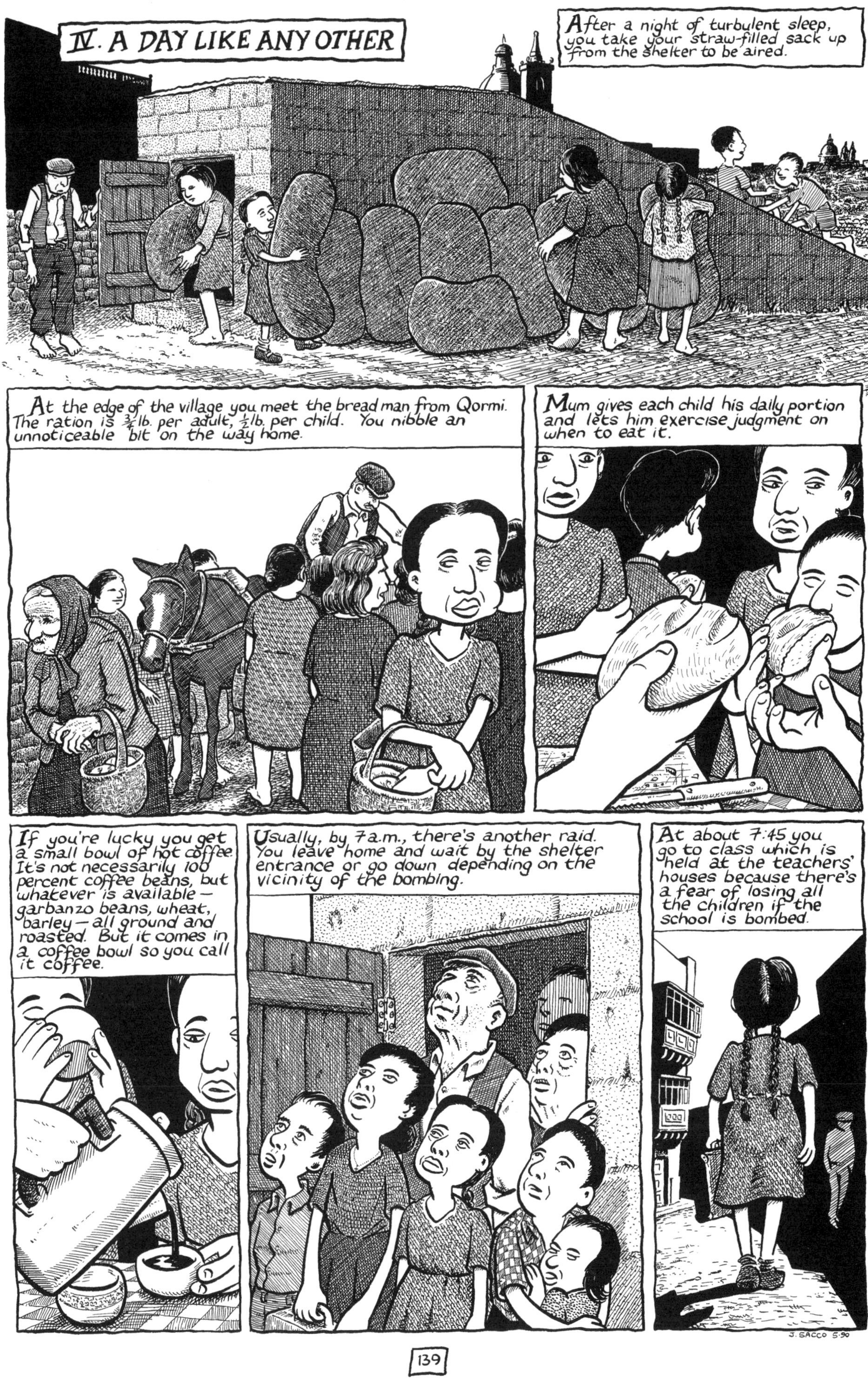

IV. A DAY LIKE ANY OTHER
After a night of turbulent sleep, you take your straw-filled sack up from the shelter to be aired.
At the edge of the village you meet the bread man from Qormi. The ration is ¾ lb. per adult, ½ lb. per child. You nibble an unnoticeable bit on the way home.
Mum gives each child his daily portion and lets him exercise judgment on when to eat it.
If you're lucky you get a small bowl of hot coffee. It's not necessarily 100 percent coffee beans, but whatever is available — garbanzo beans, wheat, barley — all ground and roasted. But it comes in a coffee bowl so you call it coffee.
Usually, by 7 a.m., there's another raid. You leave home and wait by the shelter entrance or go down depending on the vicinity of the bombing.
At about 7:45 you go to class which is held at the teachers' houses because there's a fear of losing all the children if the school is bombed.
J. SACCO 5·90

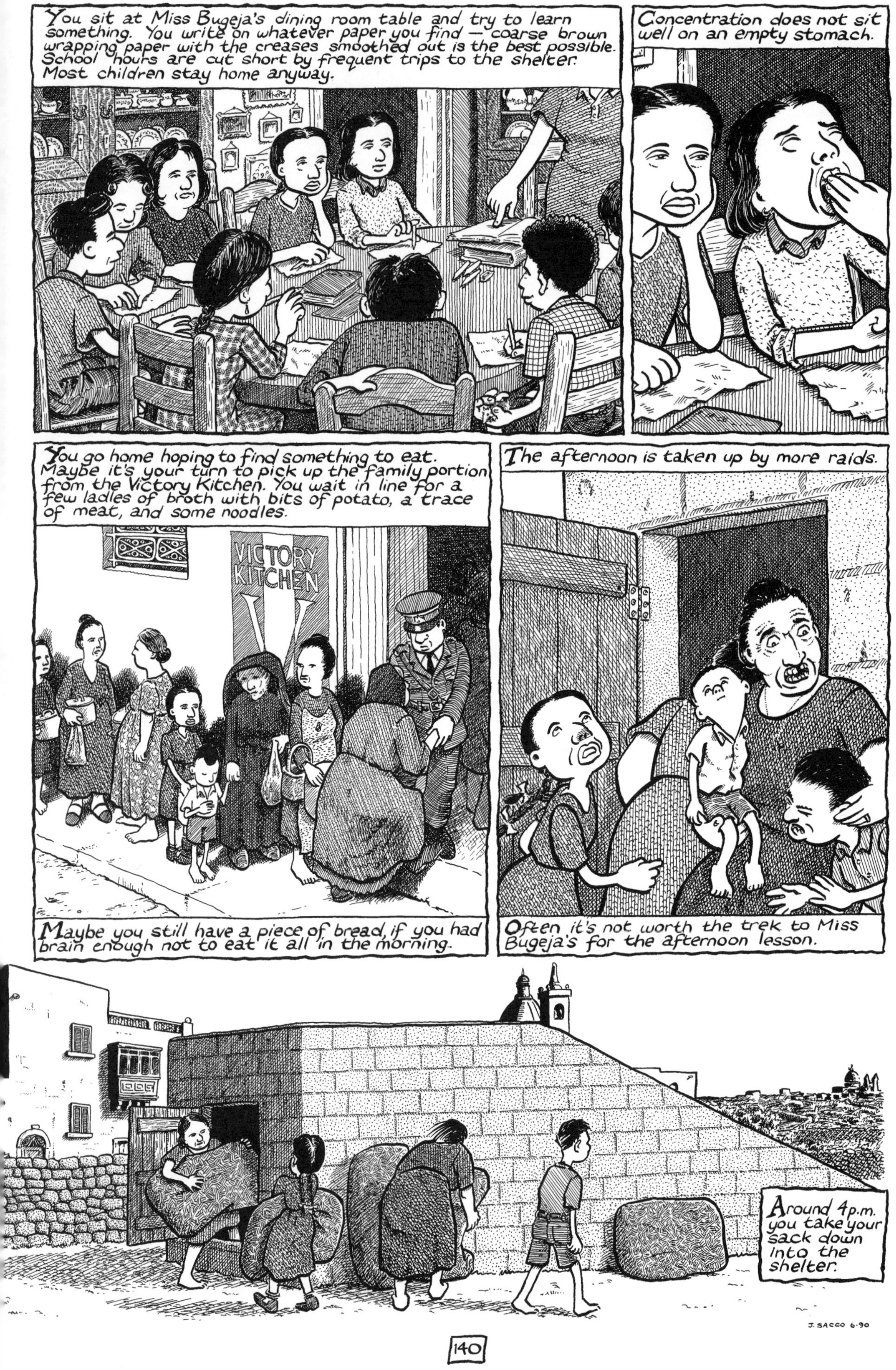
You sit at Miss Bugeja's dining room table and try to learn something. You write on whatever paper you find — coarse brown wrapping paper with the creases smoothed out is the best possible. School hours are cut short by frequent trips to the shelter. Most children stay home anyway.
Concentration does not sit well on an empty stomach.
You go home hoping to find something to eat. Maybe it's your turn to pick up the family portion from the Victory Kitchen. You wait in line for a few ladles of broth with bits of potato, a trace of meat, and some noodles.
VICTORY KITCHEN
V
Maybe you still have a piece of bread, if you had brain enough not to eat it all in the morning.
The afternoon is taken up by more raids.
Often it's not worth the trek to Miss Bugeja's for the afternoon lesson.
Around 4p.m. you take your sack down into the shelter.
J. SACCO 6·90

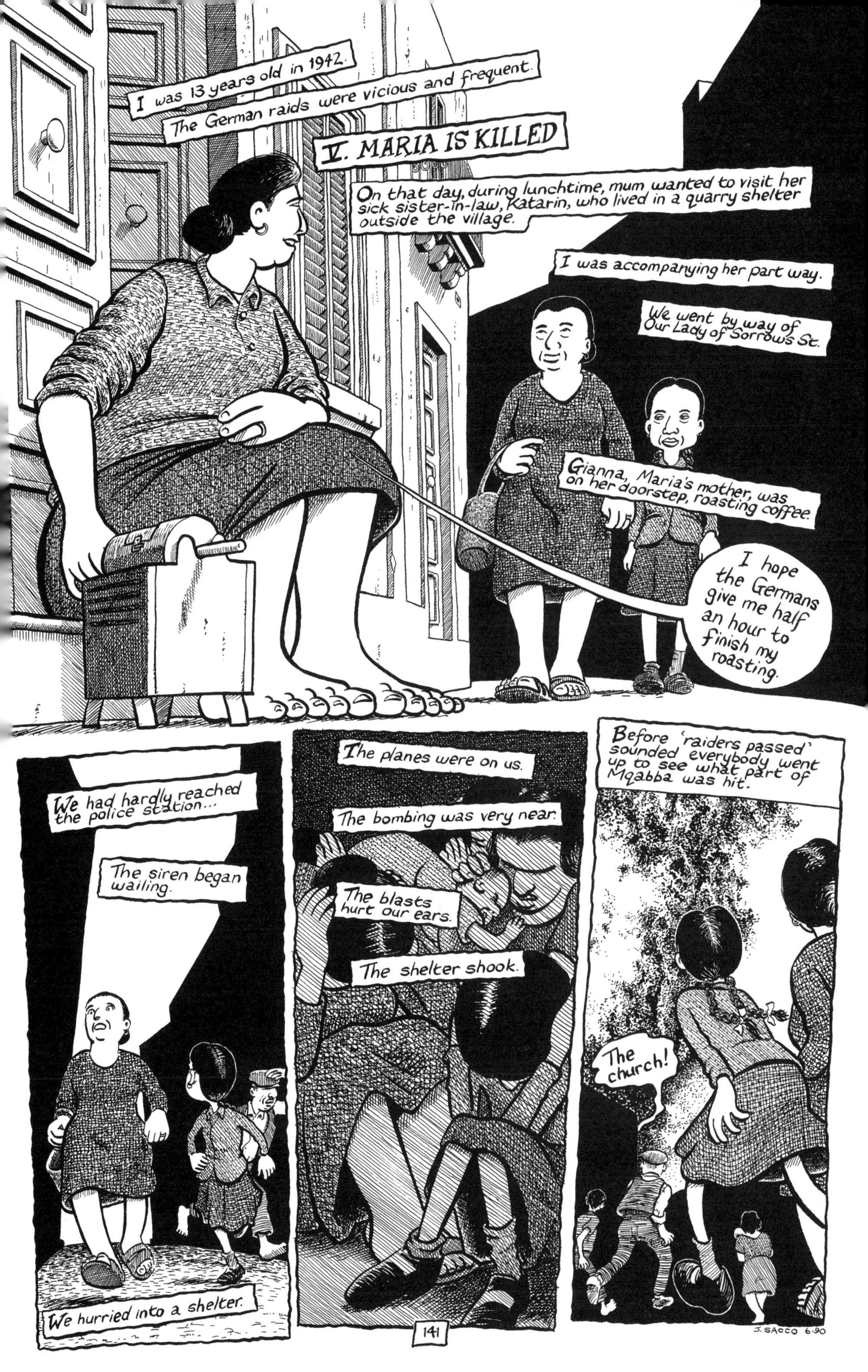
I was 13 years old in 1942.
The German raids were vicious and frequent.
V. MARIA IS KILLED
On that day, during lunchtime, mum wanted to visit her sick sister-in-law, Katarin, who lived in a quarry shelter outside the village.
I was accompanying her part way.
We went by way of Our Lady of Sorrows St.
Gianna, Maria's mother, was on her doorstep, roasting coffee.
I hope the Germans give me half an hour to finish my roasting.
We had hardly reached the police station...
The siren began wailing.
We hurried into a shelter.
The planes were on us.
The bombing was very near.
The blasts hurt our ears.
The shelter shook.
Before 'raiders passed' sounded everybody went up to see what part of Mqabba was hit.
The church!
J. SACCO 6·90

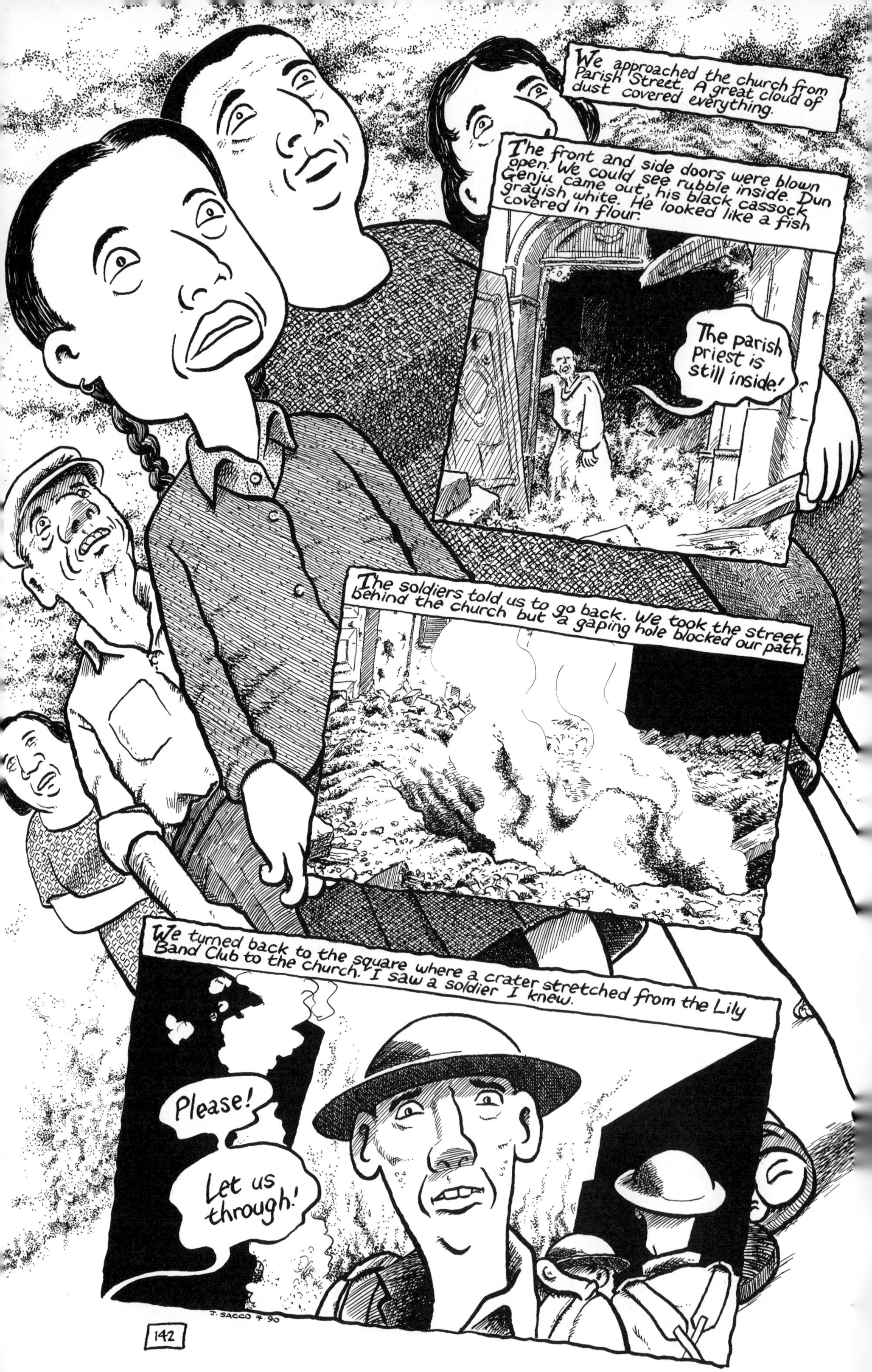
We approached the church from Parish Street. A great cloud of dust covered everything.
The front and side doors were blown open. We could see rubble inside. Dun Genju came out, his black cassock grayish white. He looked like a fish covered in flour.
The parish priest is still inside!
The soldiers told us to go back. We took the street behind the church but a gaping hole blocked our path.
We turned back to the square where a crater stretched from the Lily Band Club to the church. I saw a soldier I knew.
Please!
Let us through!
J. SACCO 7·90

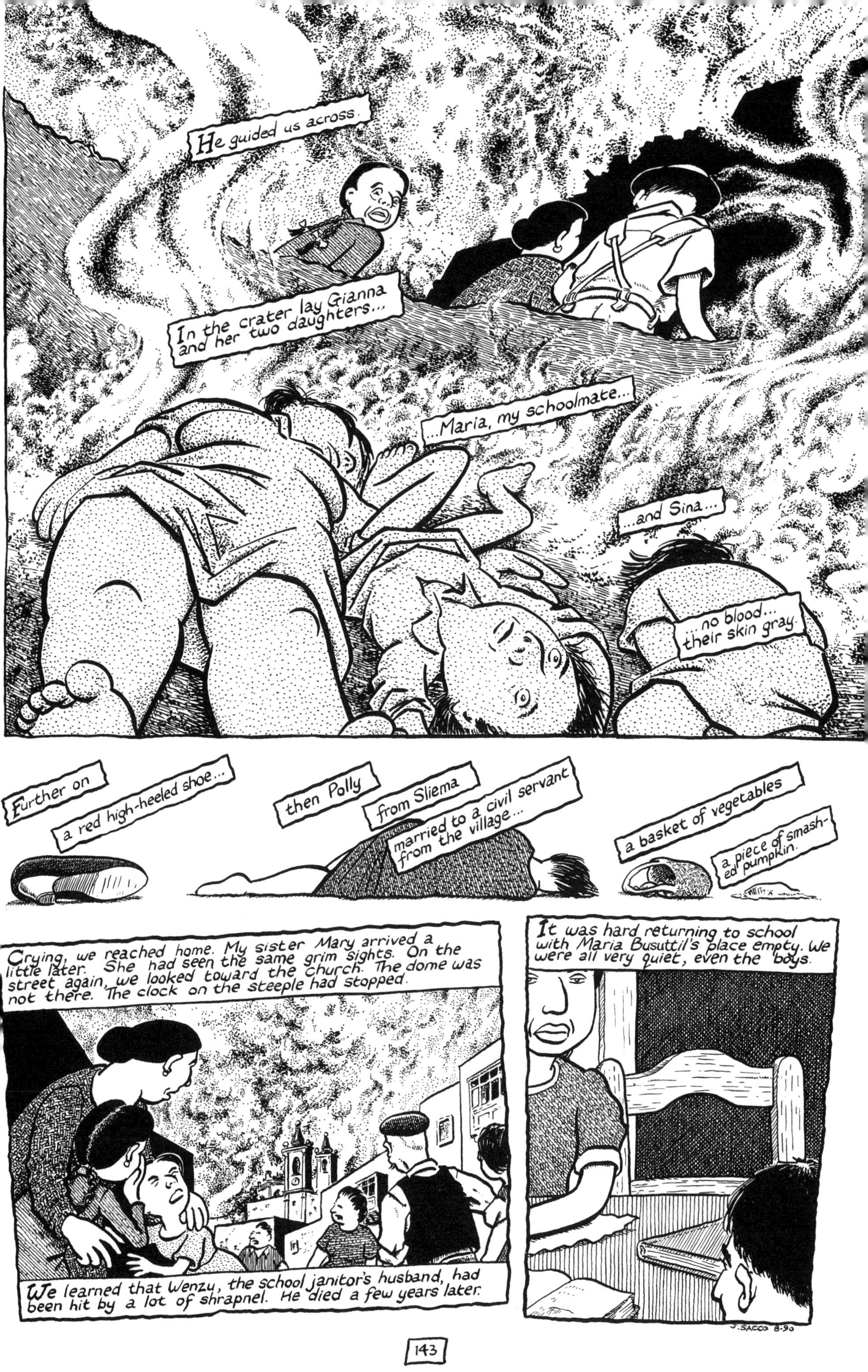
He guided us across.
In the crater lay Gianna and her two daughters...
...Maria, my schoolmate...
...and Sina...
...no blood... their skin gray.
Further on
a red high-heeled shoe...
then Polly
from Sliema
married to a civil servant from the village...
a basket of vegetables
a piece of smashed pumpkin.
Crying, we reached home. My sister Mary arrived a little later. She had seen the same grim sights. On the street again, we looked toward the church. The dome was not there. The clock on the steeple had stopped.
We learned that Wenzu, the school janitor's husband, had been hit by a lot of shrapnel. He died a few years later.
It was hard returning to school with Maria Busuttil's place empty. We were all very quiet, even the boys.
J. SACCO 8-90

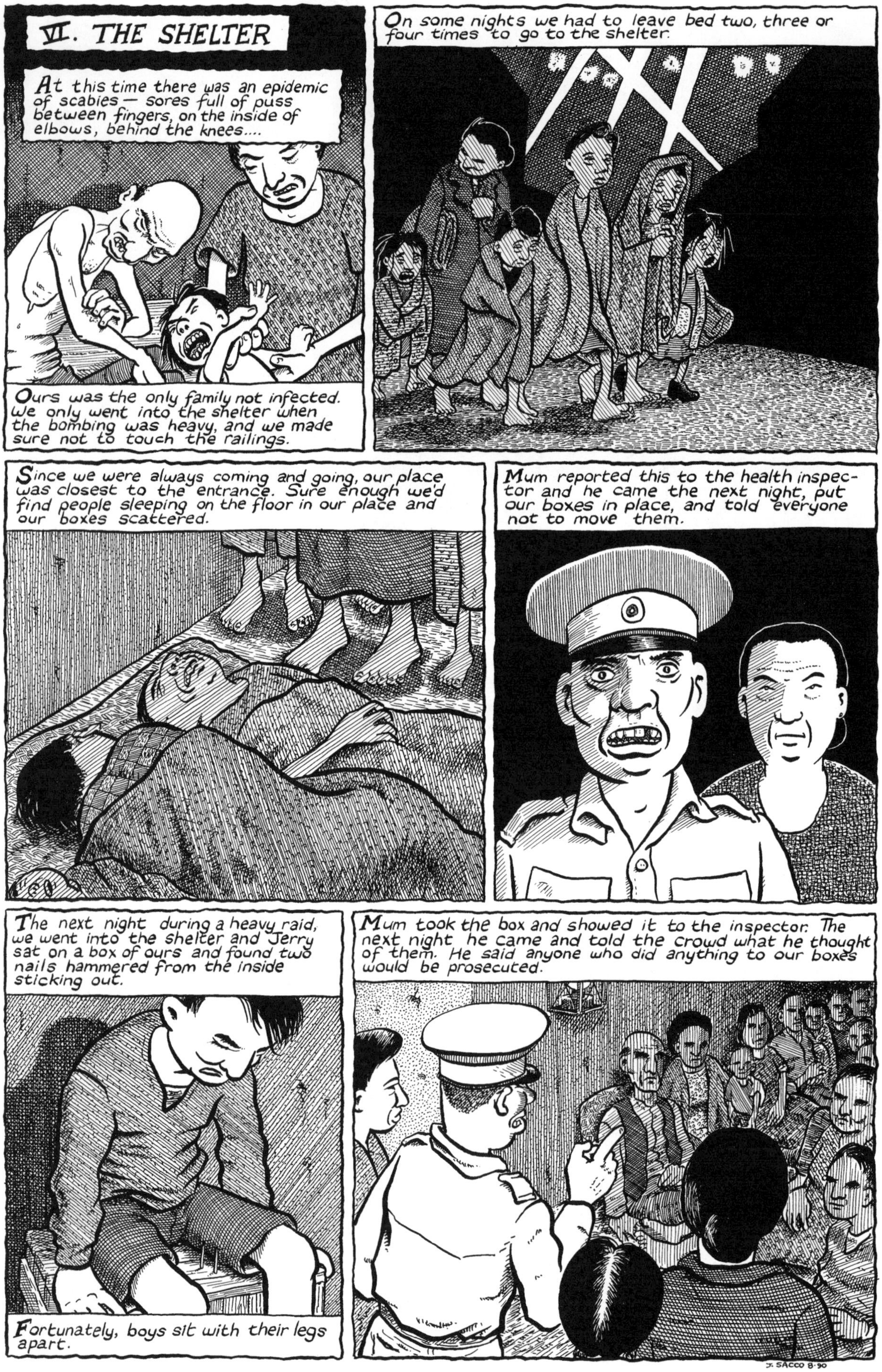
VI. THE SHELTER
At this time there was an epidemic of scabies — sores full of puss between fingers, on the inside of elbows, behind the knees....
Ours was the only family not infected. We only went into the shelter when the bombing was heavy, and we made sure not to touch the railings.
On some nights we had to leave bed two, three or four times to go to the shelter.
Since we were always coming and going, our place was closest to the entrance. Sure enough we'd find people sleeping on the floor in our place and our boxes scattered.
Mum reported this to the health inspector and he came the next night, put our boxes in place, and told everyone not to move them.
The next night during a heavy raid, we went into the shelter and Jerry sat on a box of ours and found two nails hammered from the inside sticking out.
Fortunately, boys sit with their legs apart.
Mum took the box and showed it to the inspector. The next night he came and told the crowd what he thought of them. He said anyone who did anything to our boxes would be prosecuted.
J. SACCO 8·90

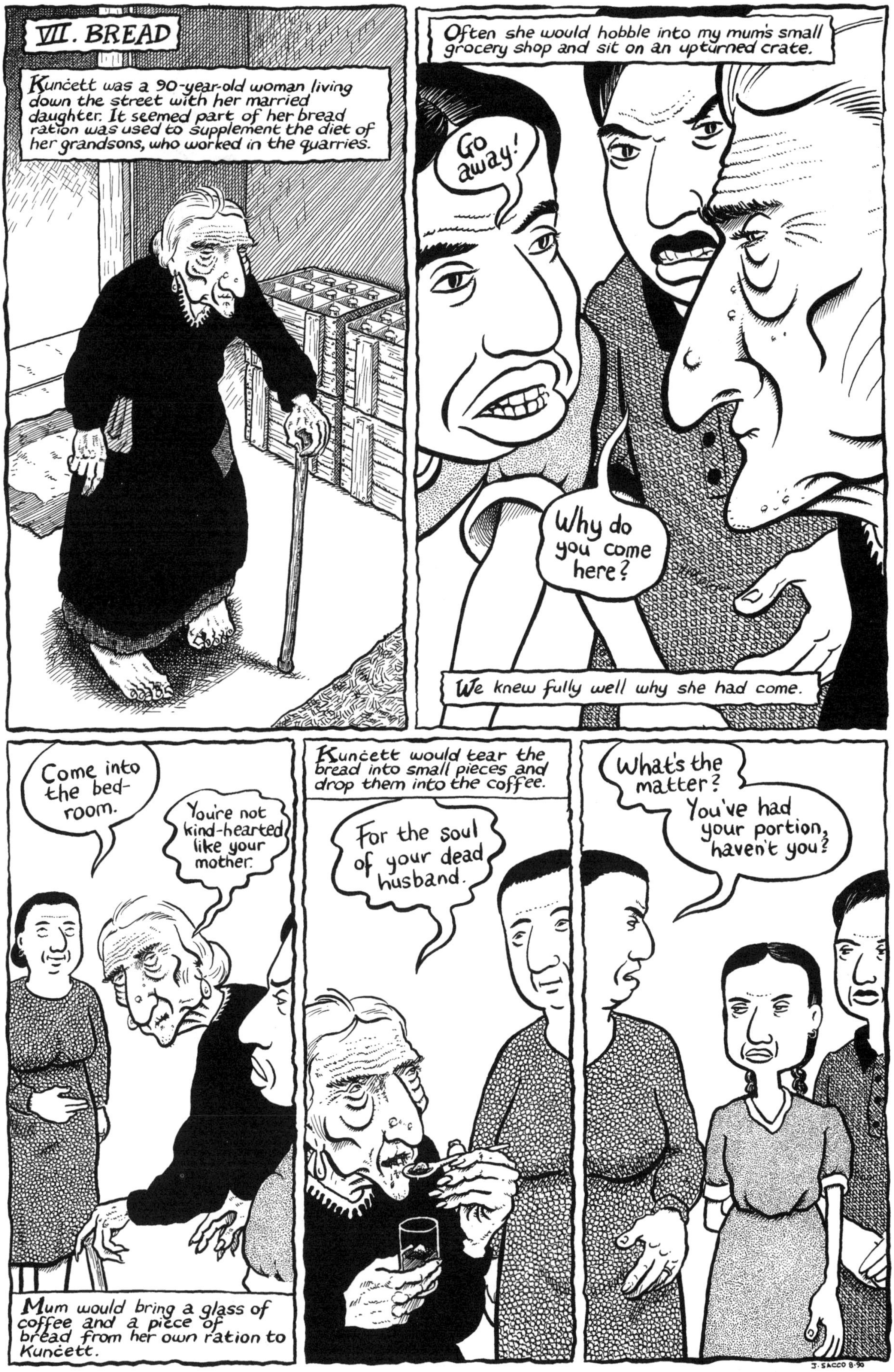
VII. BREAD
Kunċett was a 90-year-old woman living down the street with her married daughter. It seemed part of her bread ration was used to supplement the diet of her grandsons, who worked in the quarries.
Often she would hobble into my mum's small grocery shop and sit on an upturned crate.
Go away!
Why do you come here?
We knew fully well why she had come.
Come into the bed-room.
You're not kind-hearted like your mother.
Mum would bring a glass of coffee and a piece of bread from her own ration to Kunċett.
Kunċett would tear the bread into small pieces and drop them into the coffee.
For the soul of your dead husband.
What's the matter?
You've had your portion, haven't you?
J. SACCO 8·90

The raid had started around 4:30 p.m.

We could tell the village had been hit.

As the bombing subsided, we came out of the shelters.

VIII. FROZEN BLOOD

I wonder who got it this time.

Suddenly, Dun Gużepp ran by toward the western end of the village, which almost reached to the runway.

As he passed he grabbed a bicycle from a teenager and pedalled away.

The news spread...

a truck with some workers from Ta Kandja

a direct hit?

four or five

blown to bits?

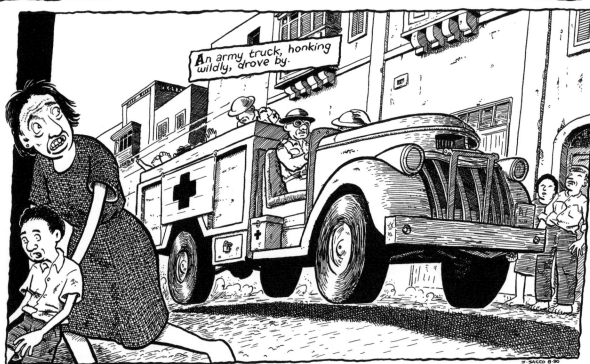

An army truck, honking wildly, drove by.

J. SACCO 8-90

146

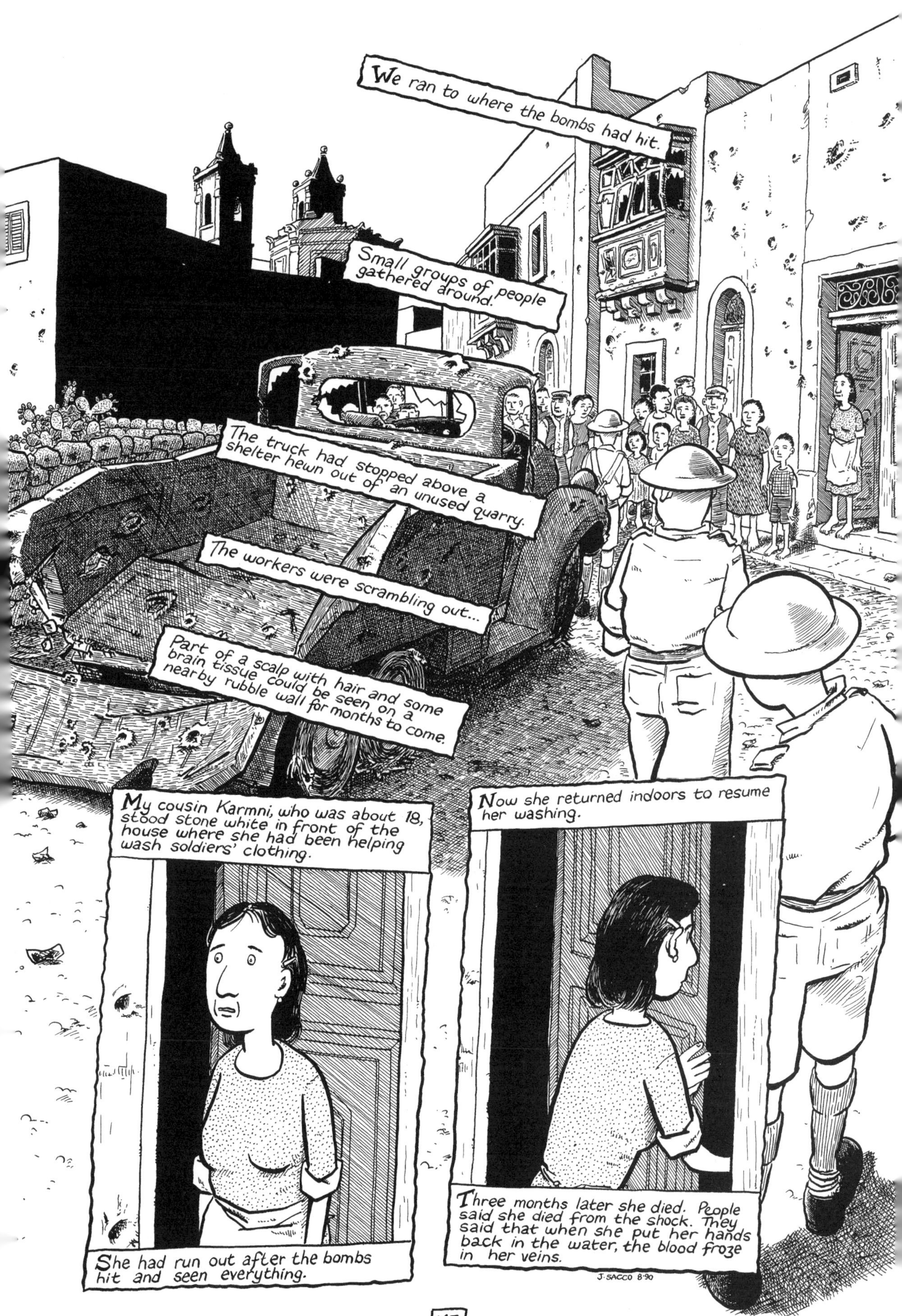
We ran to where the bombs had hit.
Small groups of people gathered around.
The truck had stopped above a shelter hewn out of an unused quarry.
The workers were scrambling out...
Part of a scalp with hair and some brain tissue could be seen on a nearby rubble wall for months to come.
My cousin Karmni, who was about 18, stood stone white in front of the house where she had been helping wash soldiers' clothing.
She had run out after the bombs hit and seen everything.
Now she returned indoors to resume her washing.
Three months later she died. People said she died from the shock. They said that when she put her hands back in the water, the blood froze in her veins.
J. SACCO 8·90

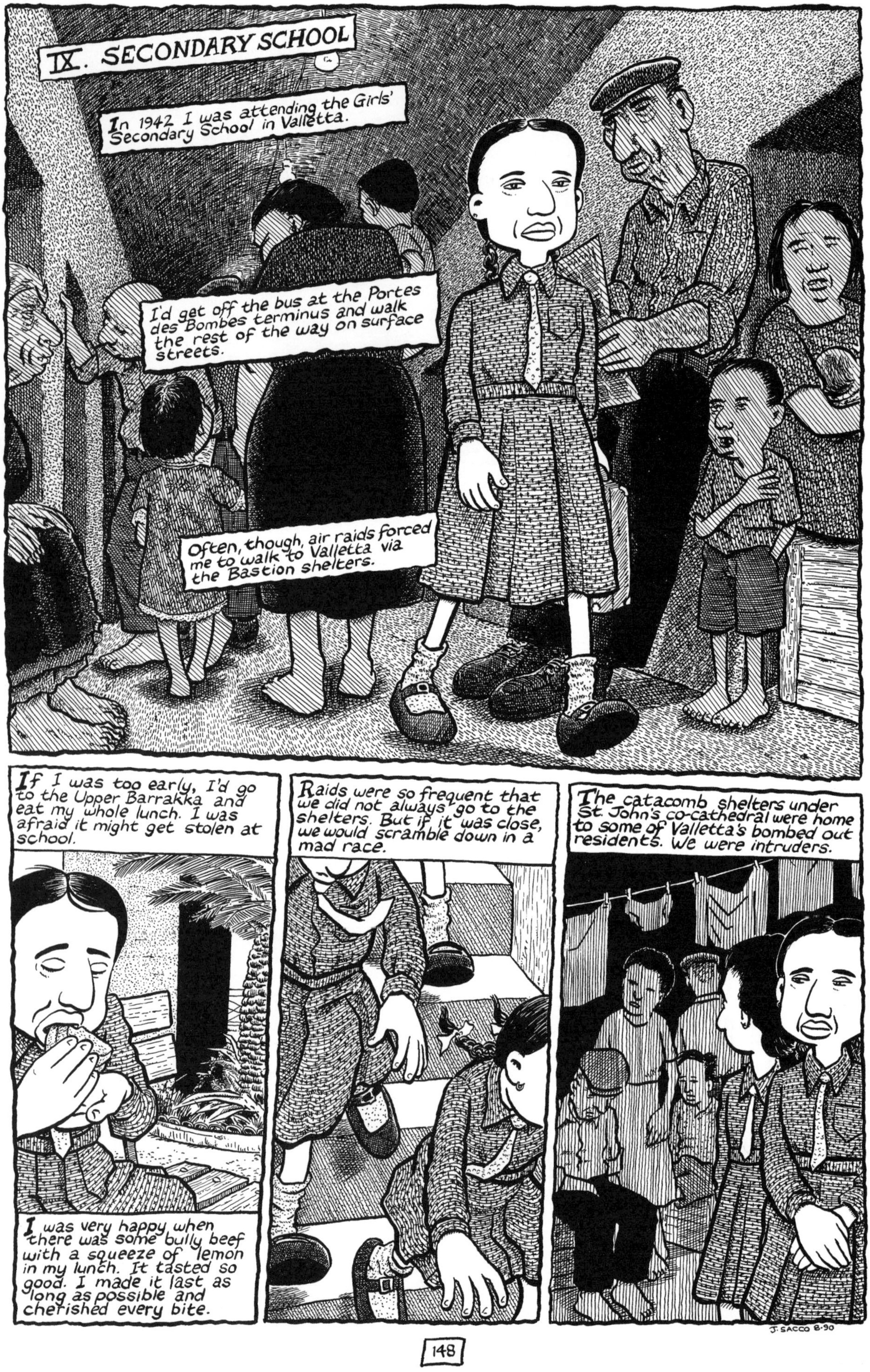
IX. SECONDARY SCHOOL
In 1942 I was attending the Girls' Secondary School in Valletta.
I'd get off the bus at the Portes des Bombes terminus and walk the rest of the way on surface streets.
Often, though, air raids forced me to walk to Valletta via the Bastion shelters.
If I was too early, I'd go to the Upper Barrakka and eat my whole lunch. I was afraid it might get stolen at school.
I was very happy when there was some bully beef with a squeeze of lemon in my lunch. It tasted so good. I made it last as long as possible and cherished every bite.
Raids were so frequent that we did not always go to the shelters. But if it was close, we would scramble down in a mad race.
The catacomb shelters under St John's co-cathedral were home to some of Valletta's bombed out residents. We were intruders.
J. SACCO 8·90

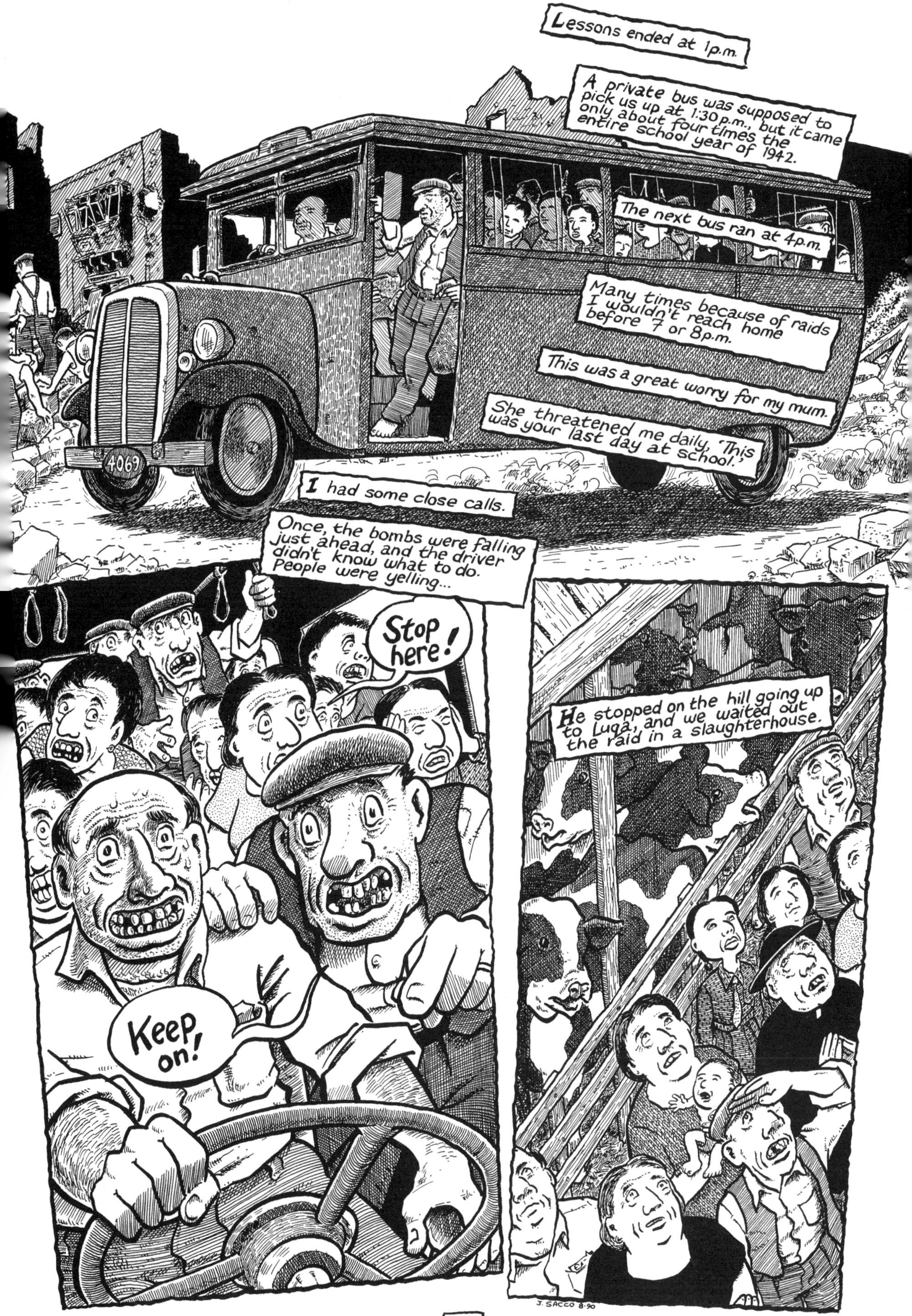
Lessons ended at 1p.m.
A private bus was supposed to pick us up at 1:30 p.m., but it came only about four times the entire school year of 1942.
4069
The next bus ran at 4p.m.
Many times because of raids I wouldn't reach home before 7 or 8p.m.
This was a great worry for my mum.
She threatened me daily, 'This was your last day at school.'
I had some close calls.
Once, the bombs were falling just ahead, and the driver didn't know what to do. People were yelling...
Stop here!
Keep on!
He stopped on the hill going up to Luqa, and we waited out the raid in a slaughterhouse.
J. SACCO 8-90

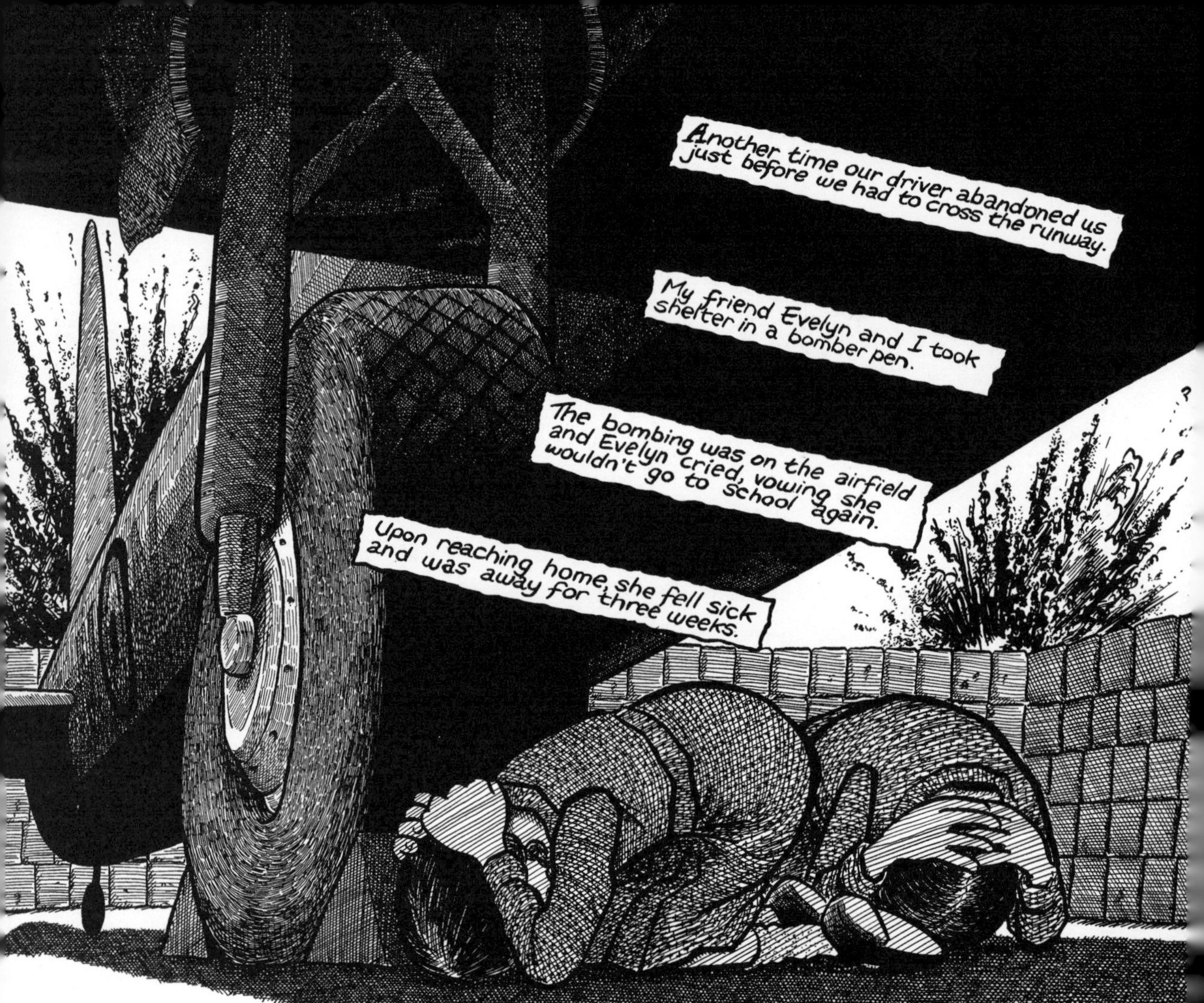
Another time our driver abandoned us just before we had to cross the runway.
My friend Evelyn and I took shelter in a bomber pen.
The bombing was on the airfield and Evelyn cried, vowing she wouldn't go to school again.
Upon reaching home, she fell sick and was away for three weeks.

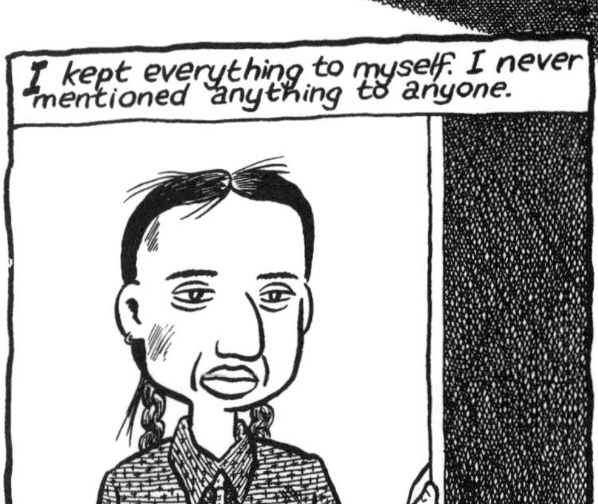
I kept everything to myself. I never mentioned anything to anyone.

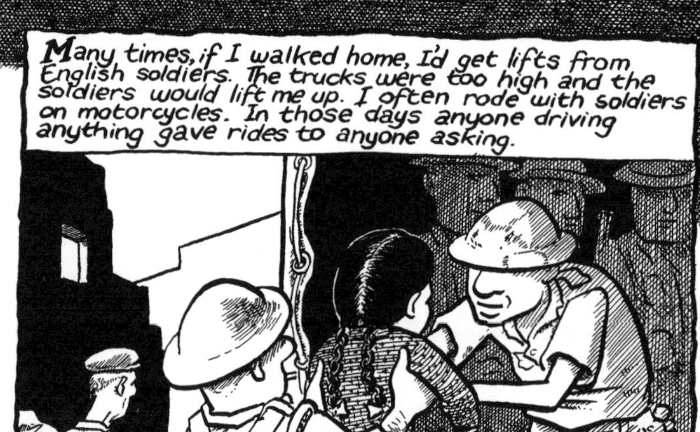
Many times, if I walked home, I'd get lifts from English soldiers. The trucks were too high and the soldiers would lift me up. I often rode with soldiers on motorcycles. In those days anyone driving anything gave rides to anyone asking.
I think it was 1943 when our school was half demolished in a night raid. For a while there was no school, and then we were transferred to Hamrun.
J. SACCO 8.90

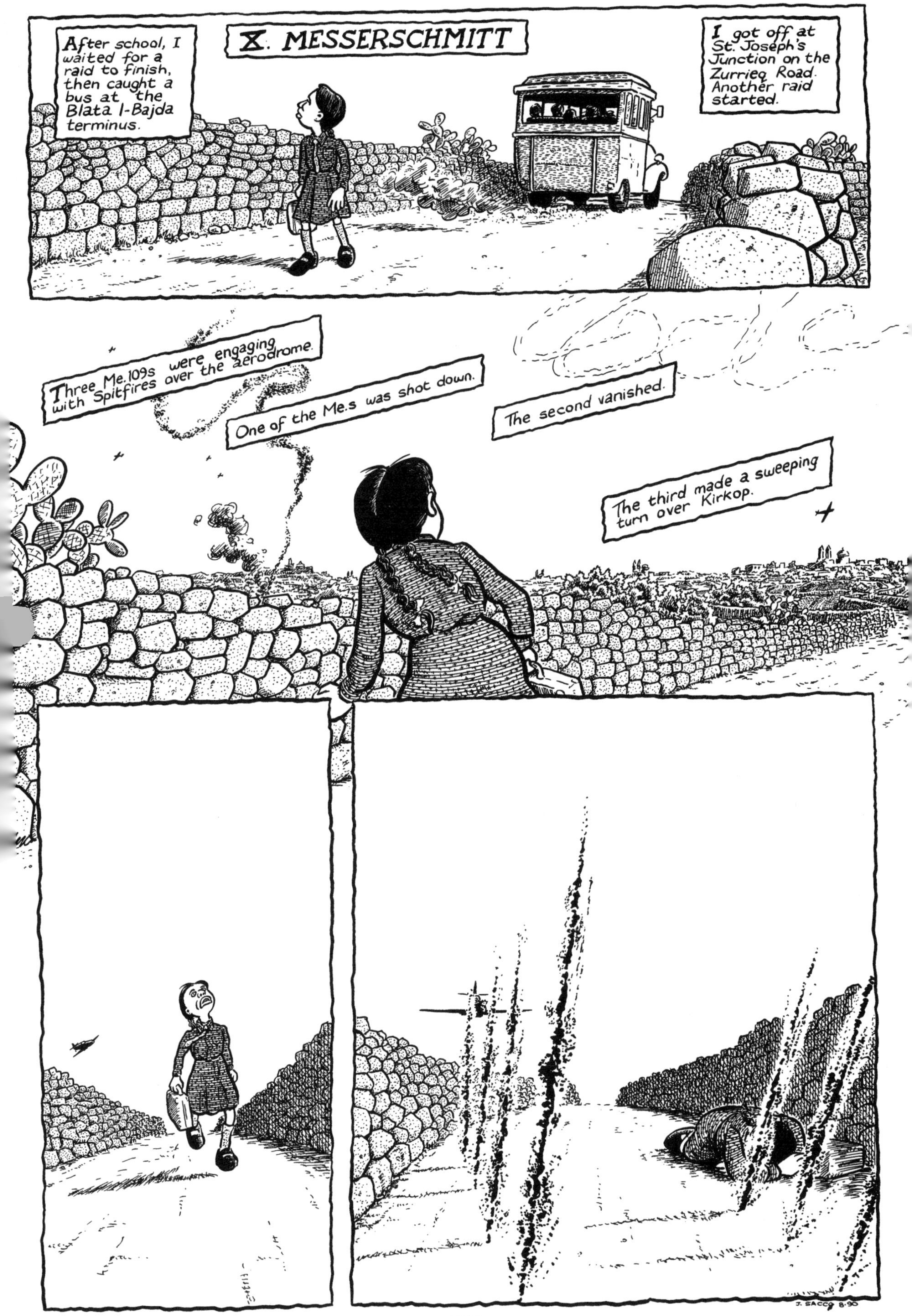
X. MESSERSCHMITT
After school, I waited for a raid to finish, then caught a bus at the Blata l-Bajda terminus.
I got off at St. Joseph's Junction on the Zurrieq Road. Another raid started.
Three Me.109s were engaging with Spitfires over the aerodrome.
One of the Me.s was shot down.
The second vanished.
The third made a sweeping turn over Kirkop.
J. SACCO 8·90

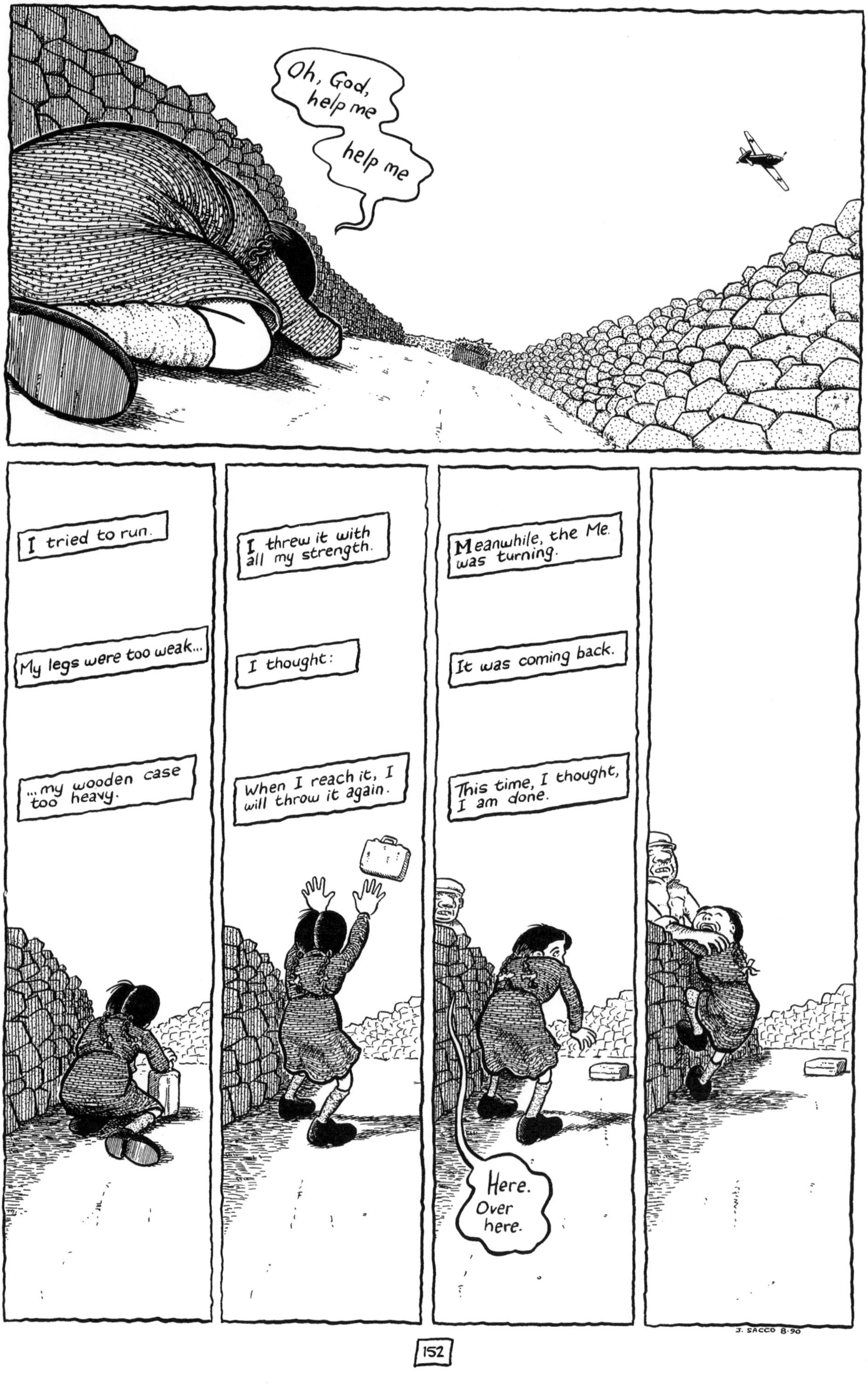

Oh, God, help me
help me
I tried to run.
My legs were too weak...
...my wooden case too heavy.
I threw it with all my strength.
I thought:
When I reach it, I will throw it again.
Meanwhile, the Me. was turning.
It was coming back.
This time, I thought, I am done.
Here. Over here.
J. SACCO 8·90

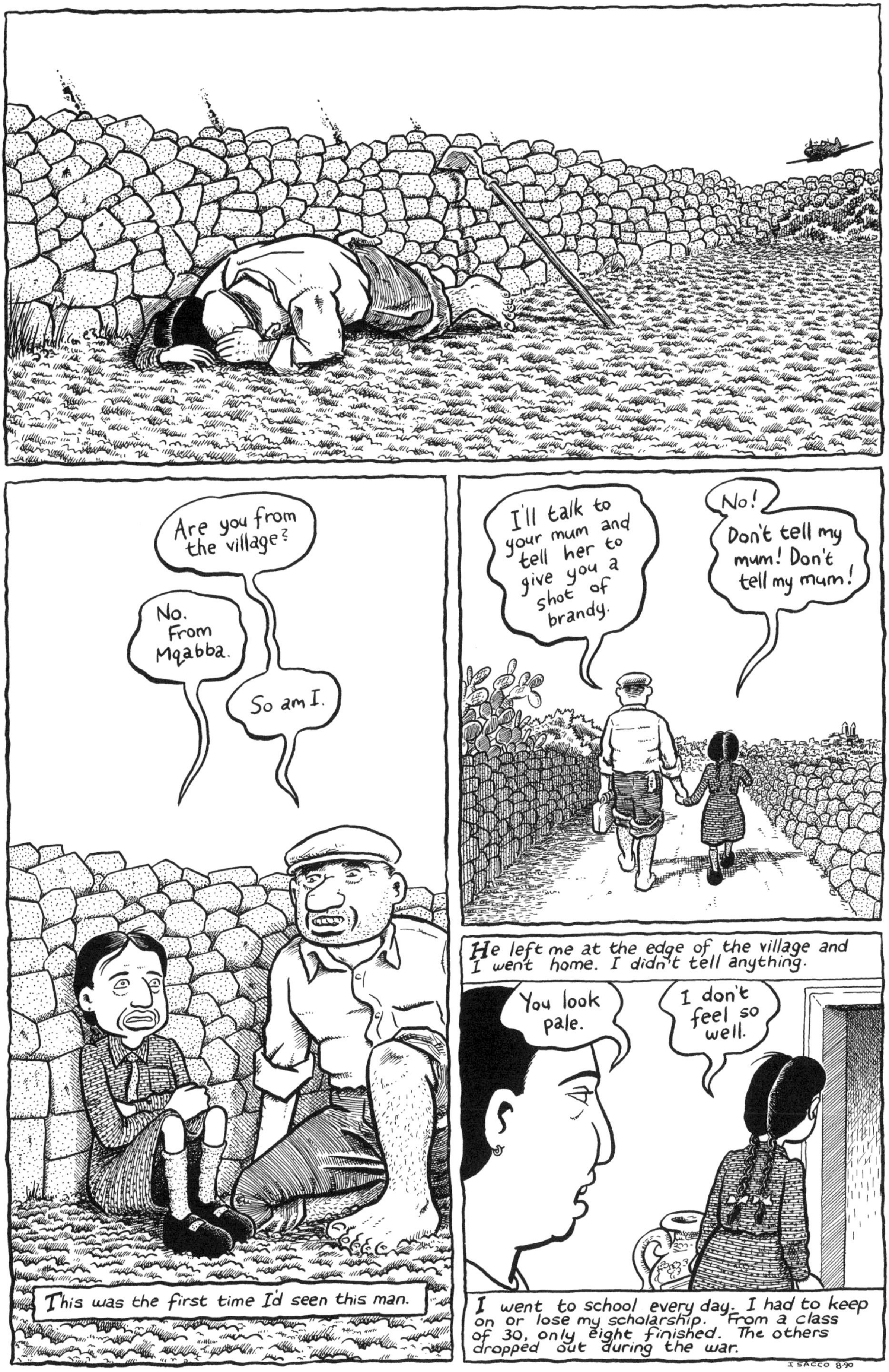

Are you from the village?
No. From Mqabba.
So am I.
This was the first time I'd seen this man.
I'll talk to your mum and tell her to give you a shot of brandy.
No! Don't tell my mum! Don't tell my mum!
He left me at the edge of the village and I went home. I didn't tell anything.
You look pale.
I don't feel so well.
I went to school every day. I had to keep on or lose my scholarship. From a class of 30, only eight finished. The others dropped out during the war.
J SACCO 8·90

PART NINE:

HOW I LOVED THE WAR

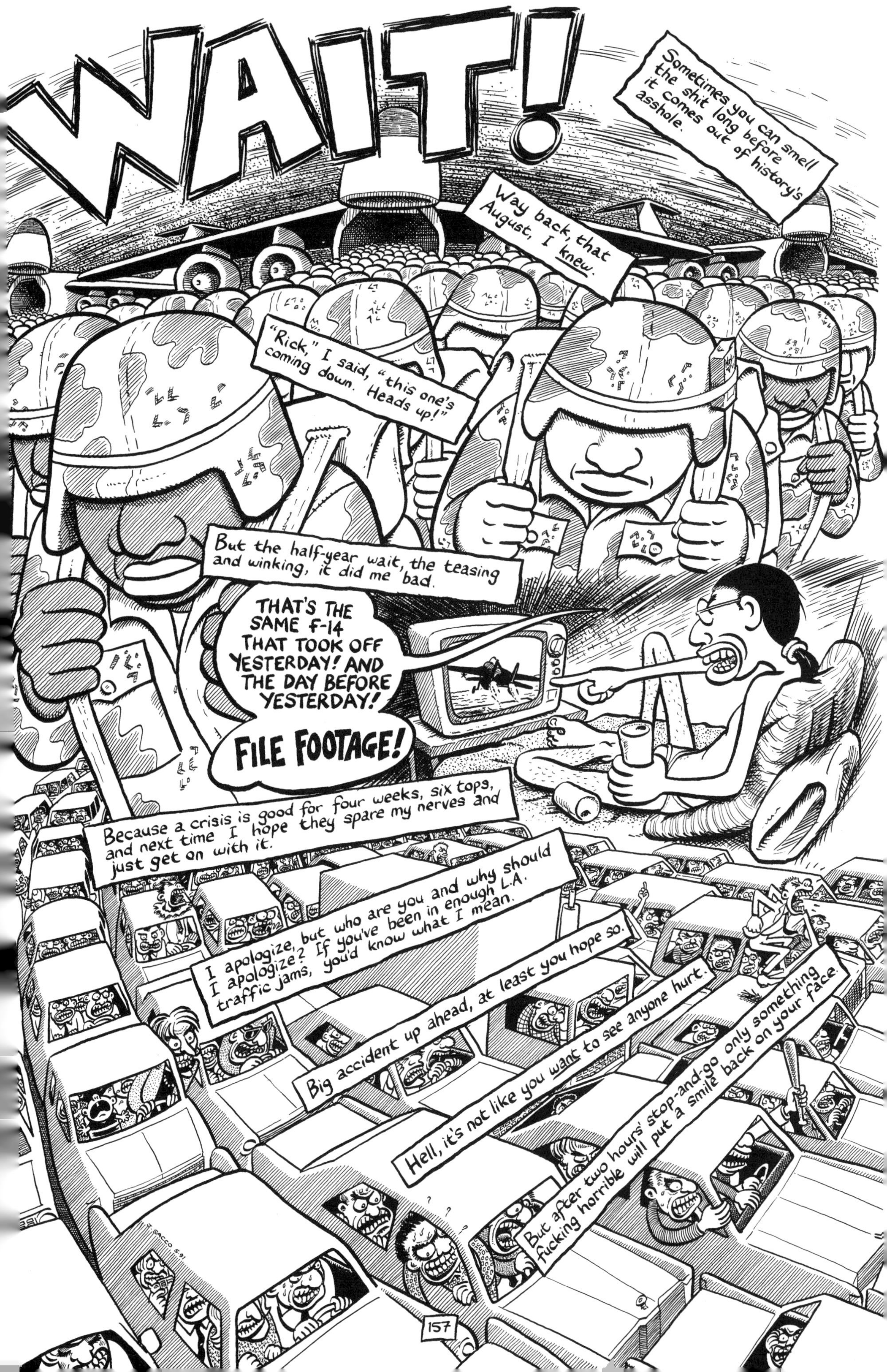
WAIT!
Sometimes you can smell the shit long before it comes out of history's asshole.
Way back, that August, I knew.
"Rick," I said, "this one's coming down. Heads up!"
But the half-year wait, the teasing and winking, it did me bad.
THAT'S THE SAME F-14 THAT TOOK OFF YESTERDAY! AND THE DAY BEFORE YESTERDAY!
FILE FOOTAGE!
Because a crisis is good for four weeks, six tops, and next time I hope they spare my nerves and just get on with it.
I apologize, but who are you and why should I apologize? If you've been in enough L.A. traffic jams, you'd know what I mean.
Big accident up ahead, at least you hope so.
Hell, it's not like you want to see anyone hurt.
But after two hours' stop-and-go only something fucking horrible will put a smile back on your face.

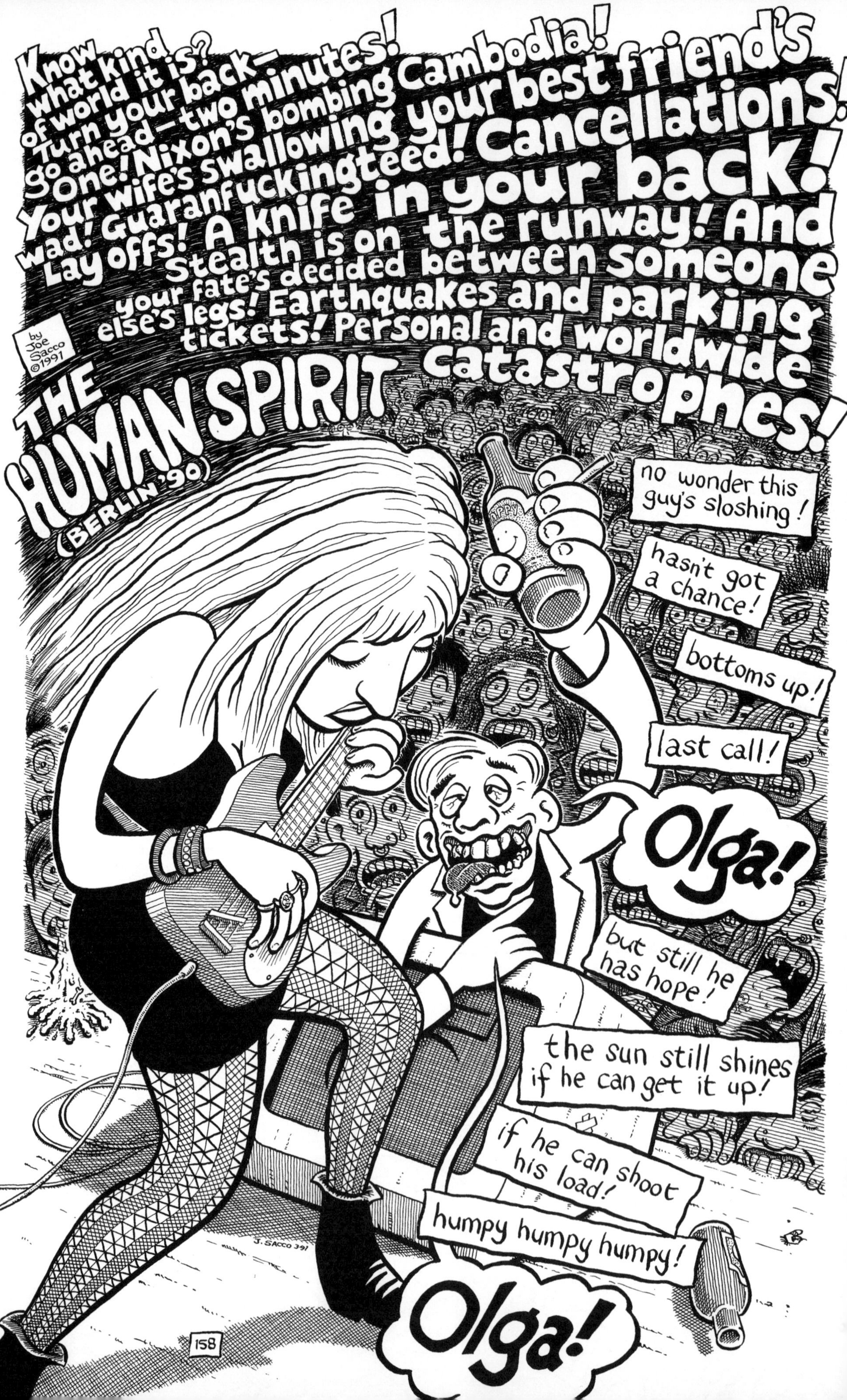
Know what kind of world it is? Turn your back— go ahead—two minutes! One! Nixon's bombing Cambodia! Your wife's swallowing your best friend's wad! Guaranfuckingteed! Cancellations! Lay offs! A knife in your back! Stealth is on the runway! And your fate's decided between someone else's legs! Earthquakes and parking tickets! Personal and worldwide catastrophes!
by Joe Sacco ©1991
THE HUMAN SPIRIT
(BERLIN '90)
no wonder this guy's sloshing!
hasn't got a chance!
bottoms up!
last call!
Olga!
but still he has hope!
the sun still shines if he can get it up!
if he can shoot his load!
humpy humpy humpy!
Olga!
J. SACCO 3.91

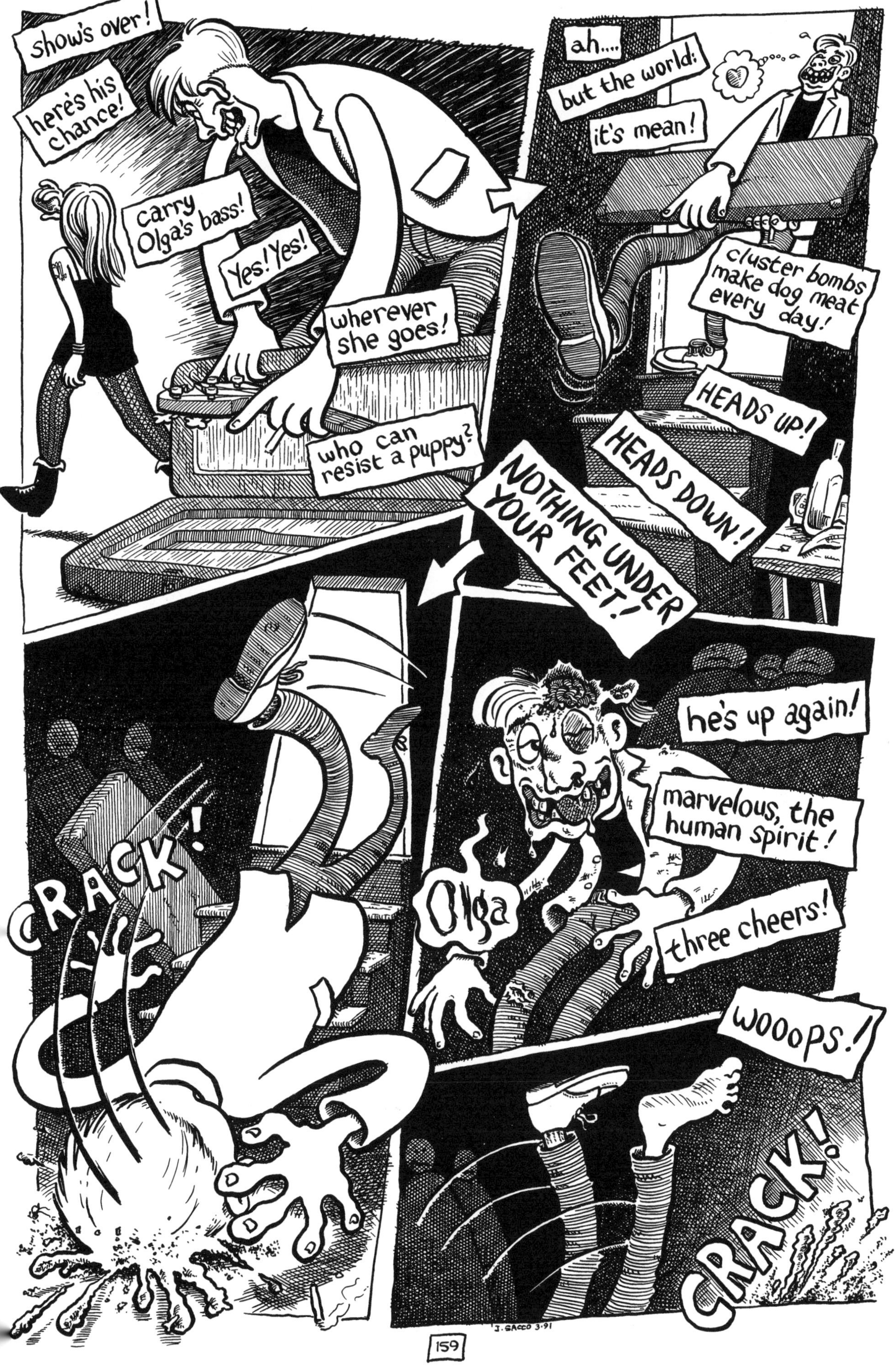
show's over!
here's his chance!
carry Olga's bass!
Yes! Yes!
wherever she goes!
who can resist a puppy?
ah....
but the world:
it's mean!
cluster bombs make dog meat every day!
HEADS UP!
HEADS DOWN!
NOTHING UNDER YOUR FEET!
CRACK!
he's up again!
marvelous, the human spirit!
Olga
three cheers!
WOOOPS!
CRACK!
J. SACCO 3·91

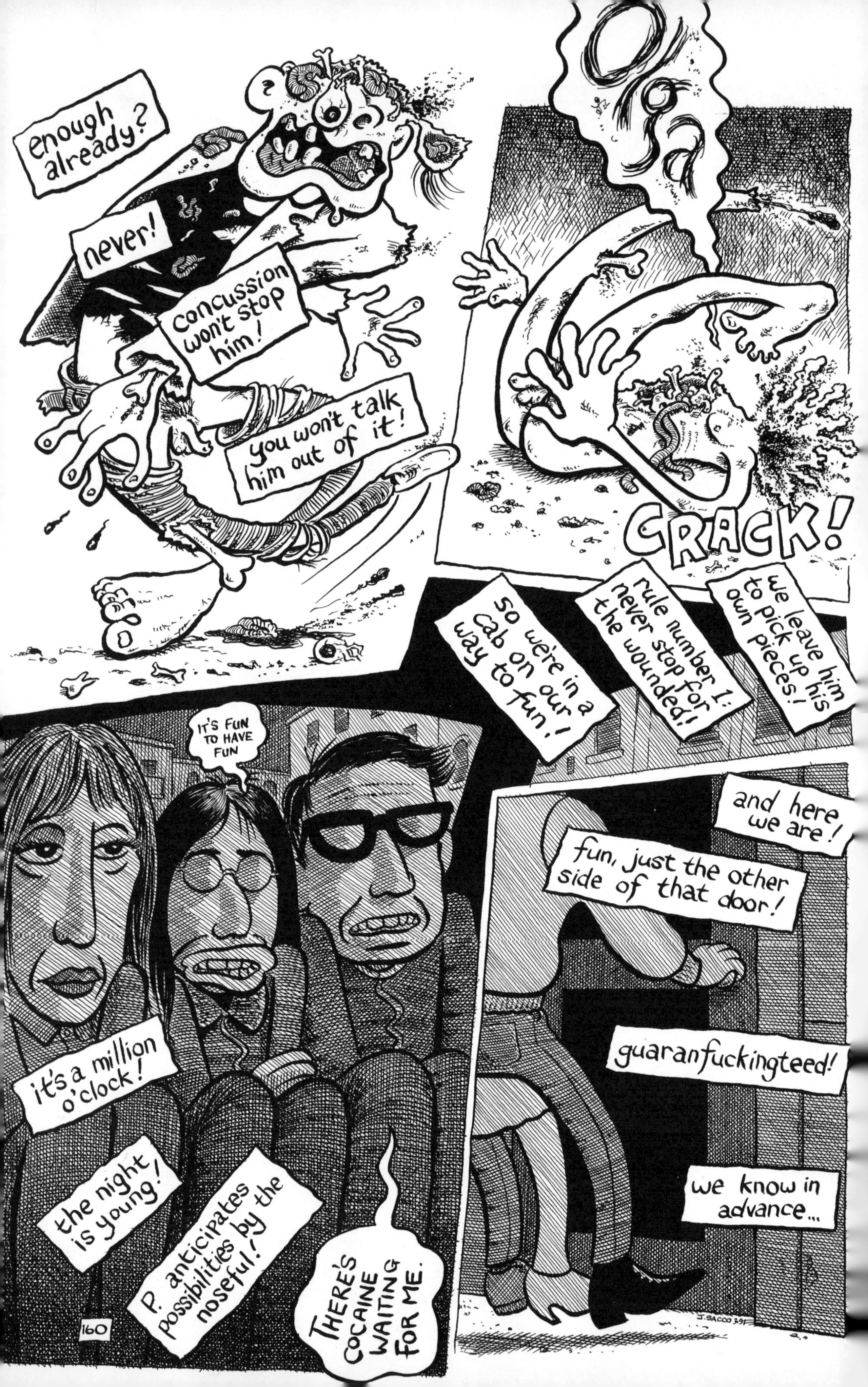
enough already?
never!
concussion won't stop him!
you won't talk him out of it!
CRACK!
we leave him to pick up his own pieces!
rule number 1: never stop for the wounded!
so we're in a cab on our way to fun!
IT'S FUN TO HAVE FUN
it's a million o'clock!
the night is young!
P. anticipates possibilities by the noseful!
THERE'S COCAINE WAITING FOR ME.
and here we are!
fun, just the other side of that door!
guaranfuckingteed!
we know in advance...
J. SACCO 3.95

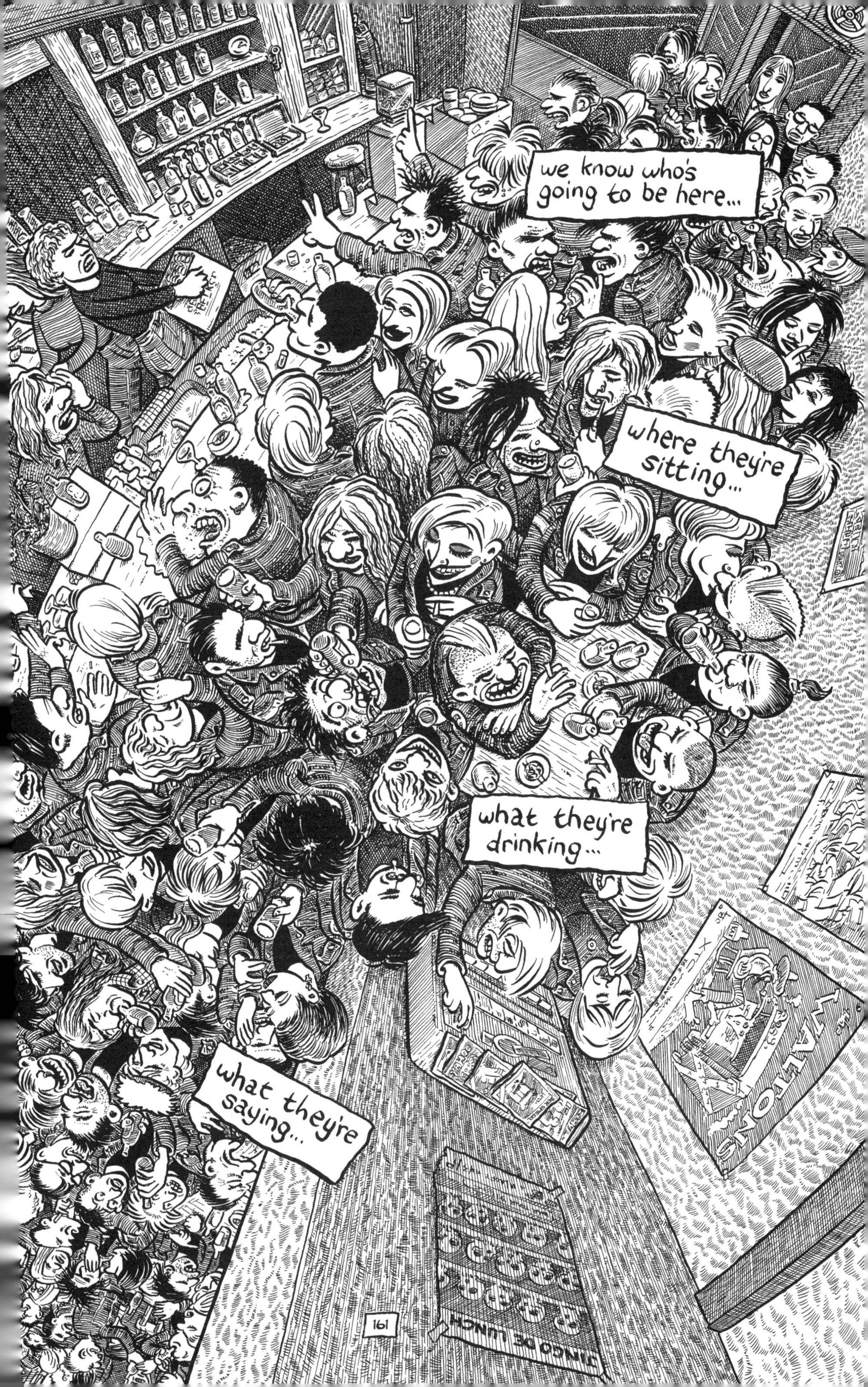
we know who's going to be here...
where they're sitting...
what they're drinking...
what they're saying...

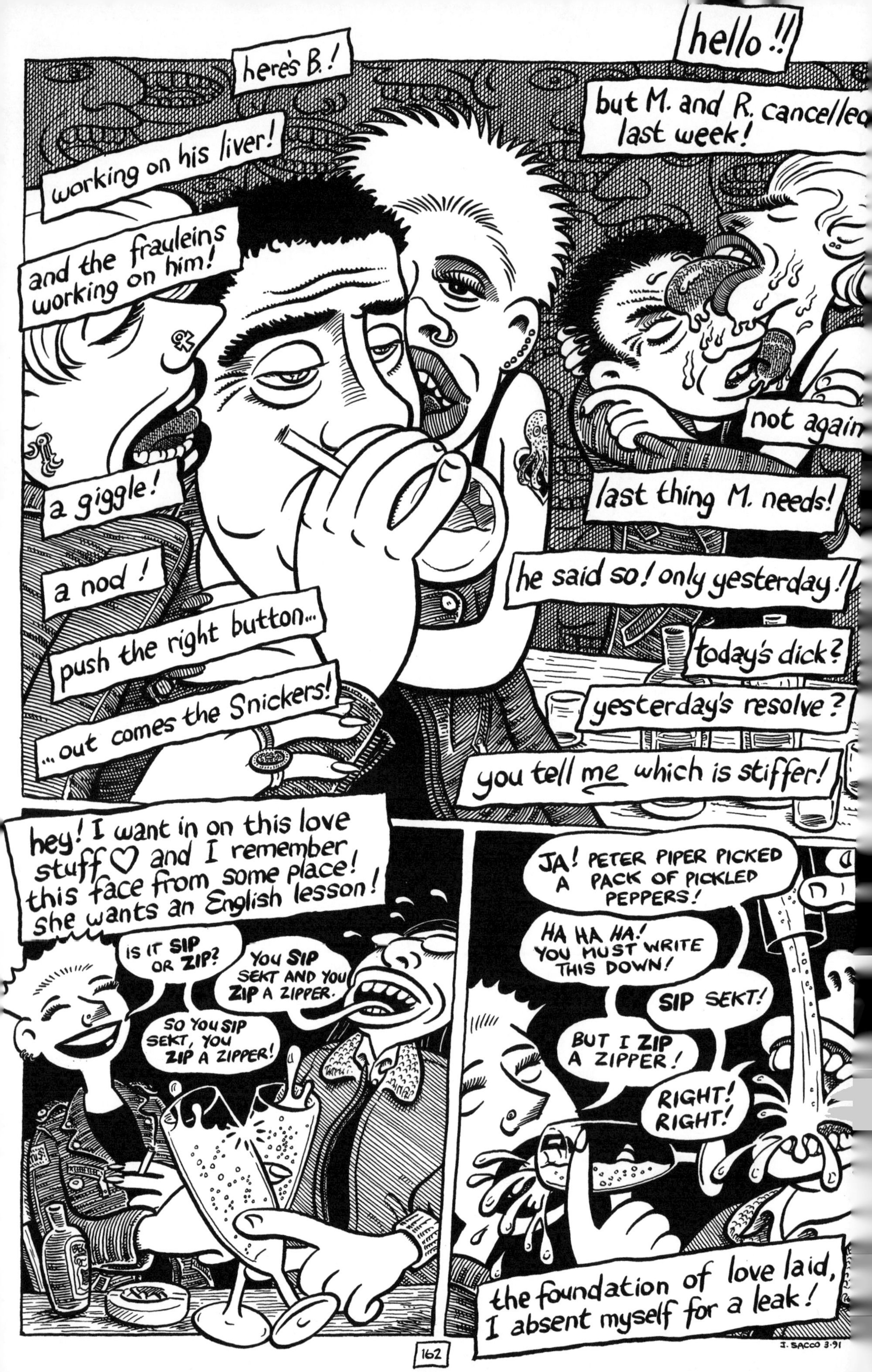
here's B.!
hello!!
but M. and R. cancelled last week!
working on his liver!
and the frauleins working on him!
a giggle!
a nod!
push the right button...
...out comes the Snickers!
not again
last thing M. needs!
he said so! only yesterday!
today's dick?
yesterday's resolve?
you tell me which is stiffer!
hey! I want in on this love stuff ♡ and I remember this face from some place! this face from some place! she wants an English lesson!
IS IT SIP OR ZIP?
YOU SIP SEKT AND YOU ZIP A ZIPPER.
SO YOU SIP SEKT, YOU ZIP A ZIPPER!
JA! PETER PIPER PICKED A PACK OF PICKLED PEPPERS!
HA HA HA! YOU MUST WRITE THIS DOWN!
SIP SEKT!
BUT I ZIP A ZIPPER!
RIGHT! RIGHT!
the foundation of love laid, I absent myself for a leak!
J. SACCO 3·91

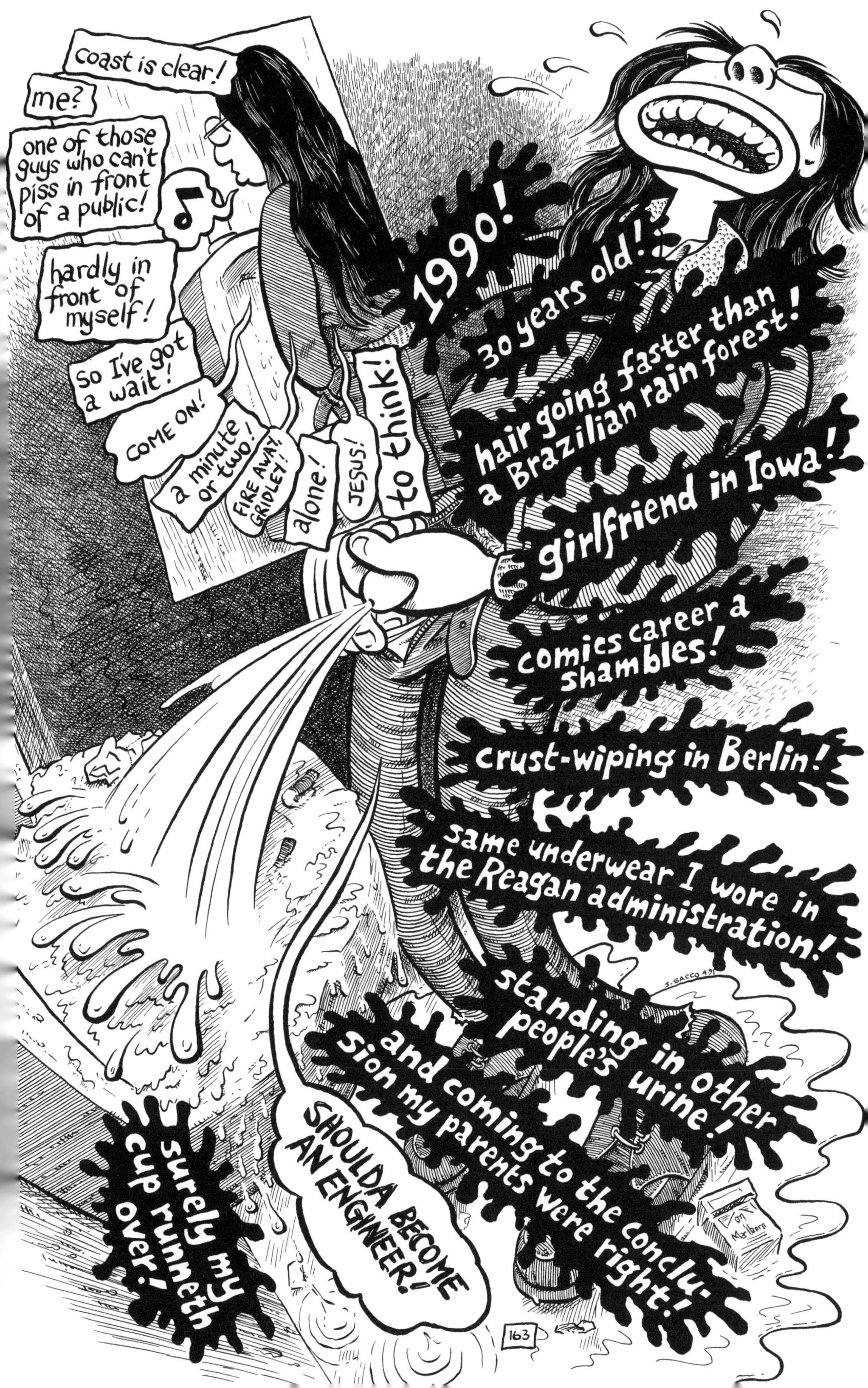

coast is clear!
me?
one of those guys who can't piss in front of a public!
hardly in front of myself!
So I've got a wait!
COME ON!
a minute or two!
FIRE AWAY, GRIDLEY!
alone!
JESUS!
to think!
1990!
30 years old!
hair going faster than a Brazilian rain forest!
girlfriend in Iowa!
comics career a shambles!
crust-wiping in Berlin!
same underwear I wore in the Reagan administration!
standing in other people's urine!
and coming to the conclusion my parents were right!
SHOULDA BECOME AN ENGINEER!
surely my cup runneth over!
J. SACCO 4.91

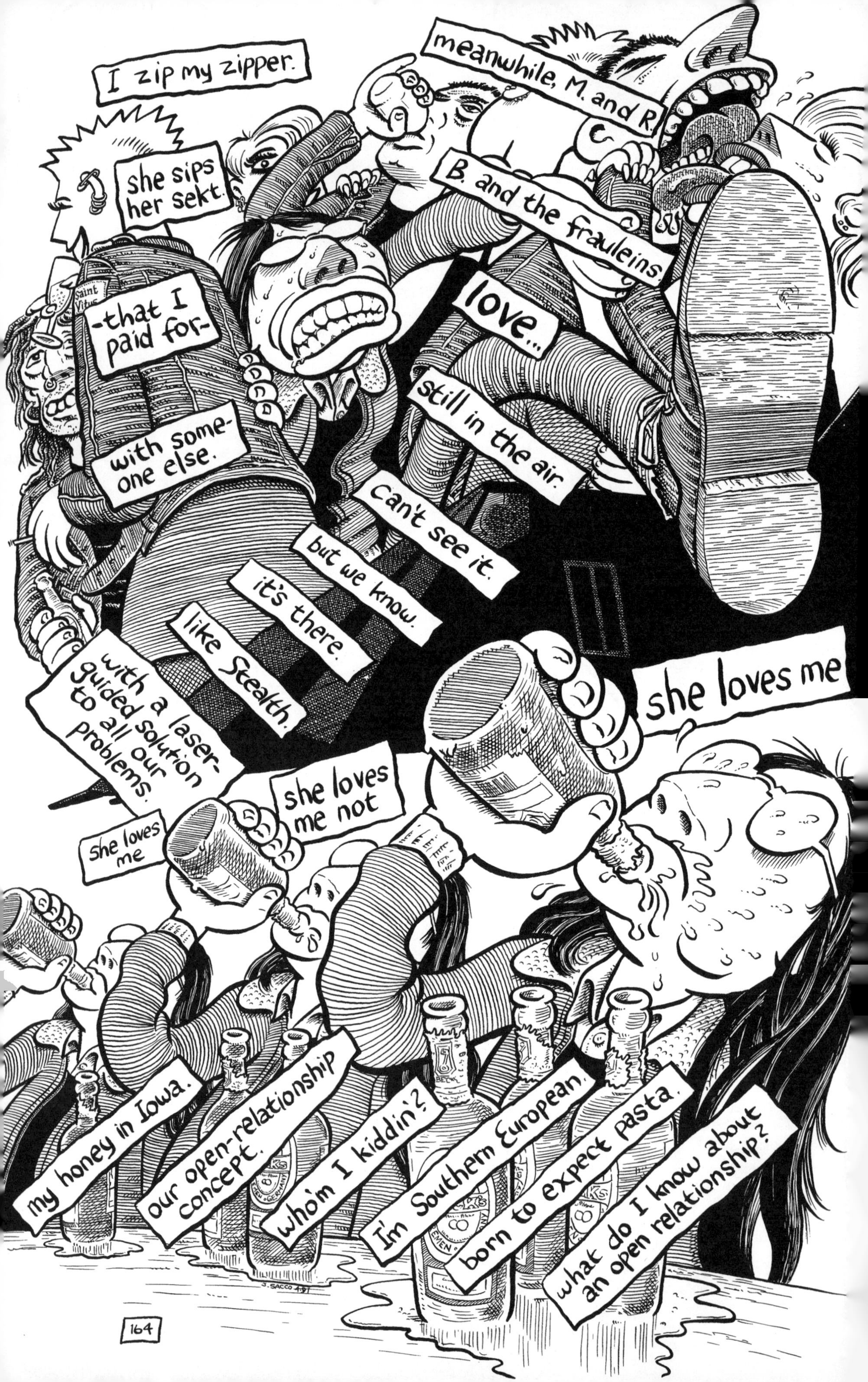
I zip my zipper.
she sips her sekt.
-that I paid for-
with some-one else.
meanwhile, M. and R.
B. and the frauleins.
love...
still in the air.
can't see it.
but we know.
it's there.
like Stealth.
with a laser-guided solution to all our problems.
she loves me
she loves me not
she loves me
my honey in Iowa.
our open-relationship concept.
who'm I kiddin'?
I'm Southern European.
born to expect pasta.
what do I know about an open relationship?
Saint Vitus
J. SACCO

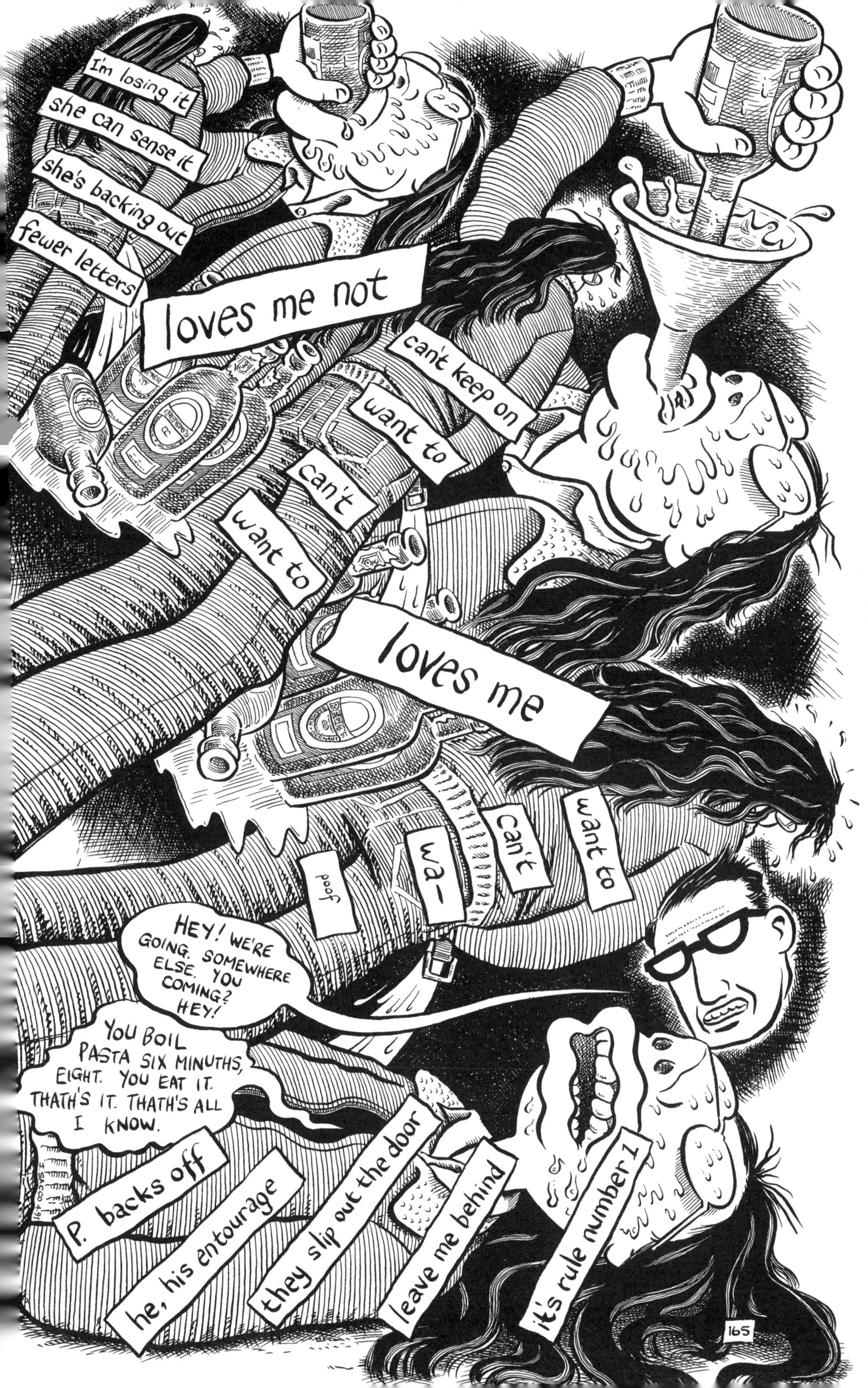
I'm losing it
she can sense it
she's backing out
fewer letters
loves me not
can't keep on
want to
can't
want to
loves me
want to
Can't
wa-
food
HEY! WE'RE GOING SOMEWHERE ELSE. YOU COMING? HEY!
YOU BOIL PASTA SIX MINUTHS, EIGHT. YOU EAT IT. THATH'S IT. THATH'S ALL I KNOW.
P. backs off
he, his entourage
they slip out the door
leave me behind
it's rule number 1

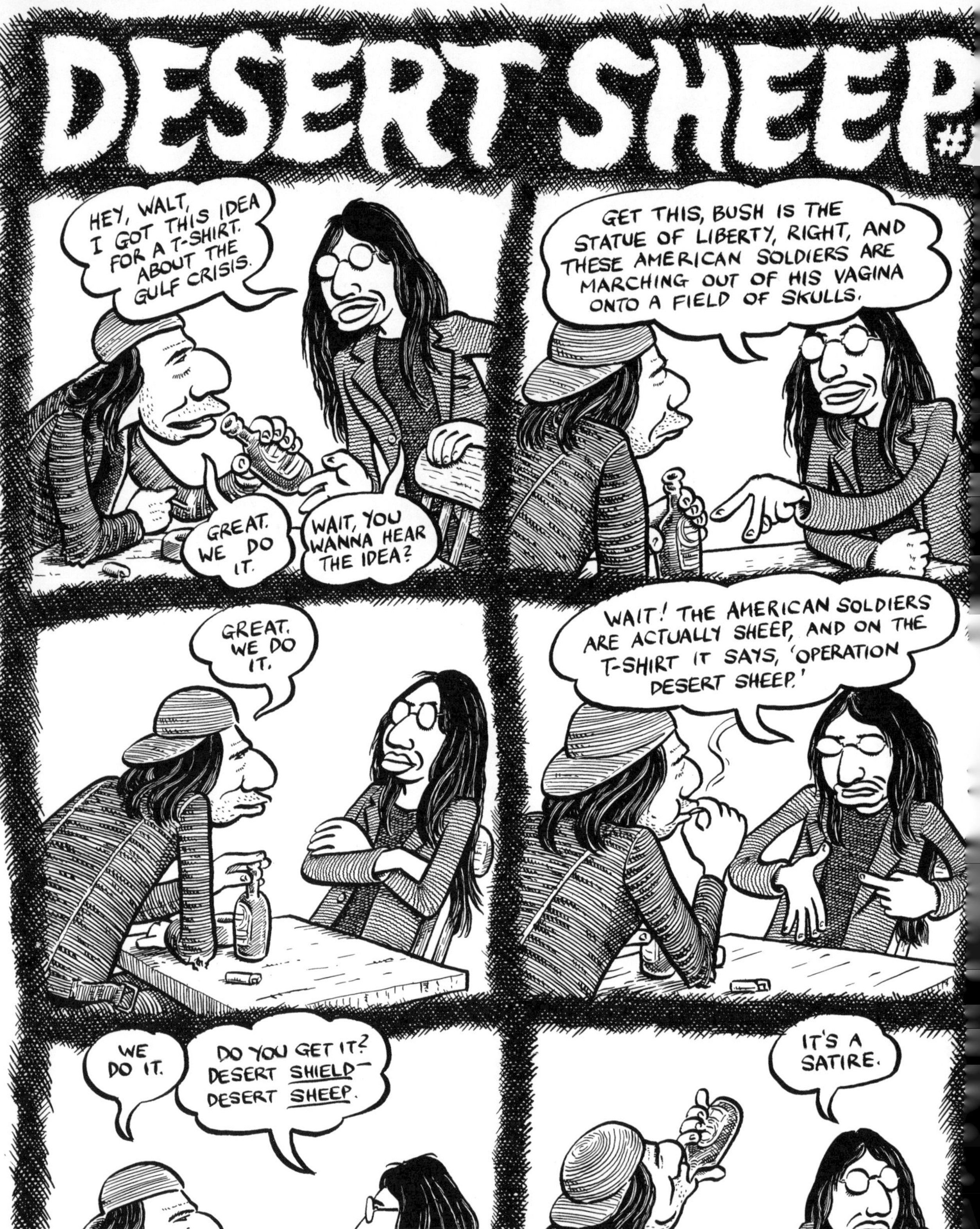
DESERT SHEEP
HEY, WALT, I GOT THIS IDEA FOR A T-SHIRT. ABOUT THE GULF CRISIS.
GREAT. WE DO IT.
WAIT, YOU WANNA HEAR THE IDEA?
GET THIS, BUSH IS THE STATUE OF LIBERTY, RIGHT, AND THESE AMERICAN SOLDIERS ARE MARCHING OUT OF HIS VAGINA ONTO A FIELD OF SKULLS.
GREAT. WE DO IT.
WAIT! THE AMERICAN SOLDIERS ARE ACTUALLY SHEEP, AND ON THE T-SHIRT IT SAYS, 'OPERATION DESERT SHEEP.'
WE DO IT.
DO YOU GET IT? DESERT SHIELD— DESERT SHEEP.
IT'S A SATIRE.
J. SACCO

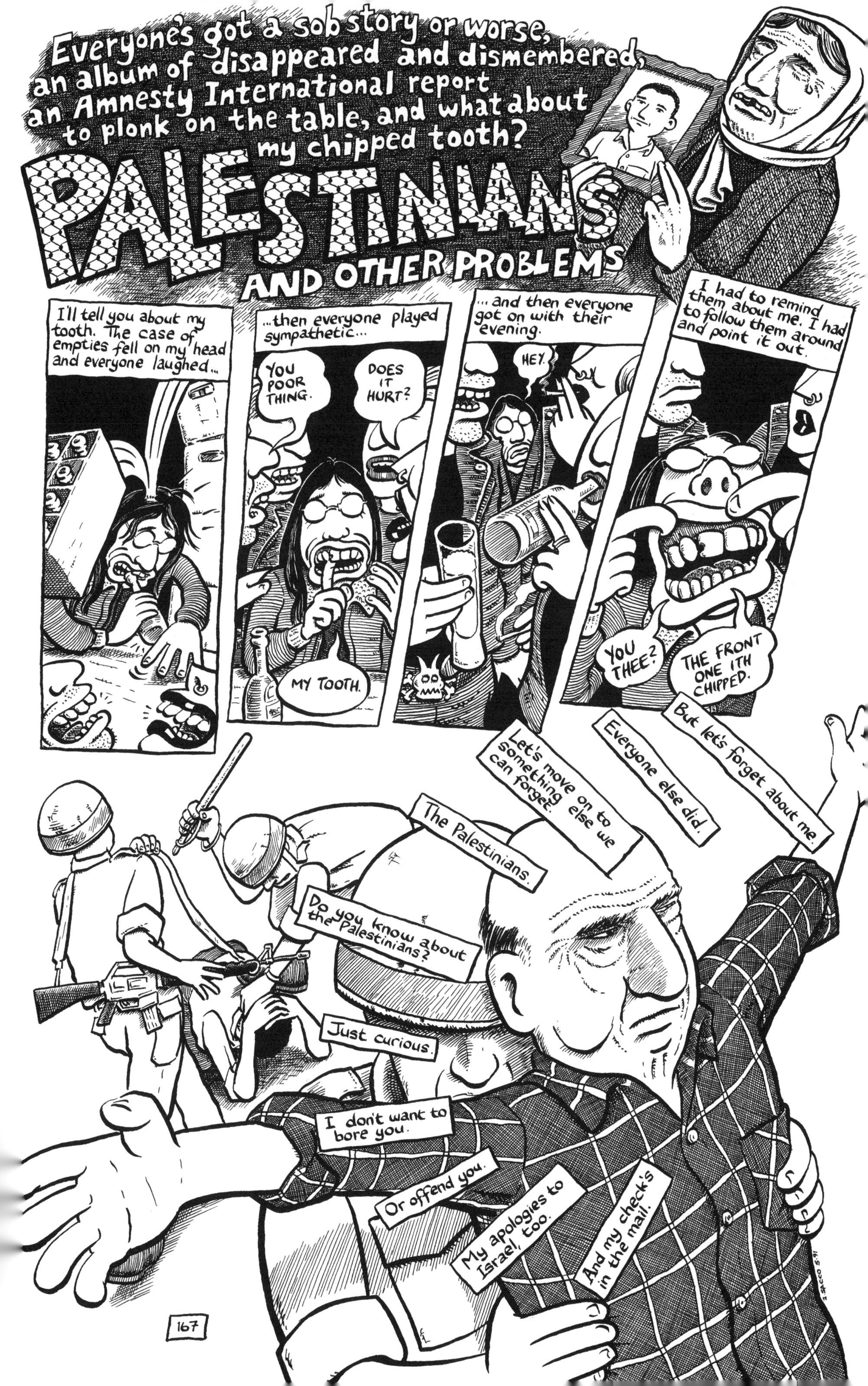

Everyone's got a sob story or worse, an album of disappeared and dismembered, an Amnesty International report to plonk on the table, and what about my chipped tooth?
PALESTINIANS
AND OTHER PROBLEMS
I'll tell you about my tooth. The case of empties fell on my head and everyone laughed...
...then everyone played sympathetic...
YOU POOR THING.
DOES IT HURT?
MY TOOTH.
...and then everyone got on with their evening.
HEY.
I had to remind them about me. I had to follow them around and point it out.
YOU THEE?
THE FRONT ONE ITH CHIPPED.
But let's forget about me.
Everyone else did.
Let's move on to something else we can forget.
The Palestinians.
Do you know about the Palestinians?
Just curious.
I don't want to bore you.
Or offend you.
My apologies to Israel, too.
And my check's in the mail.

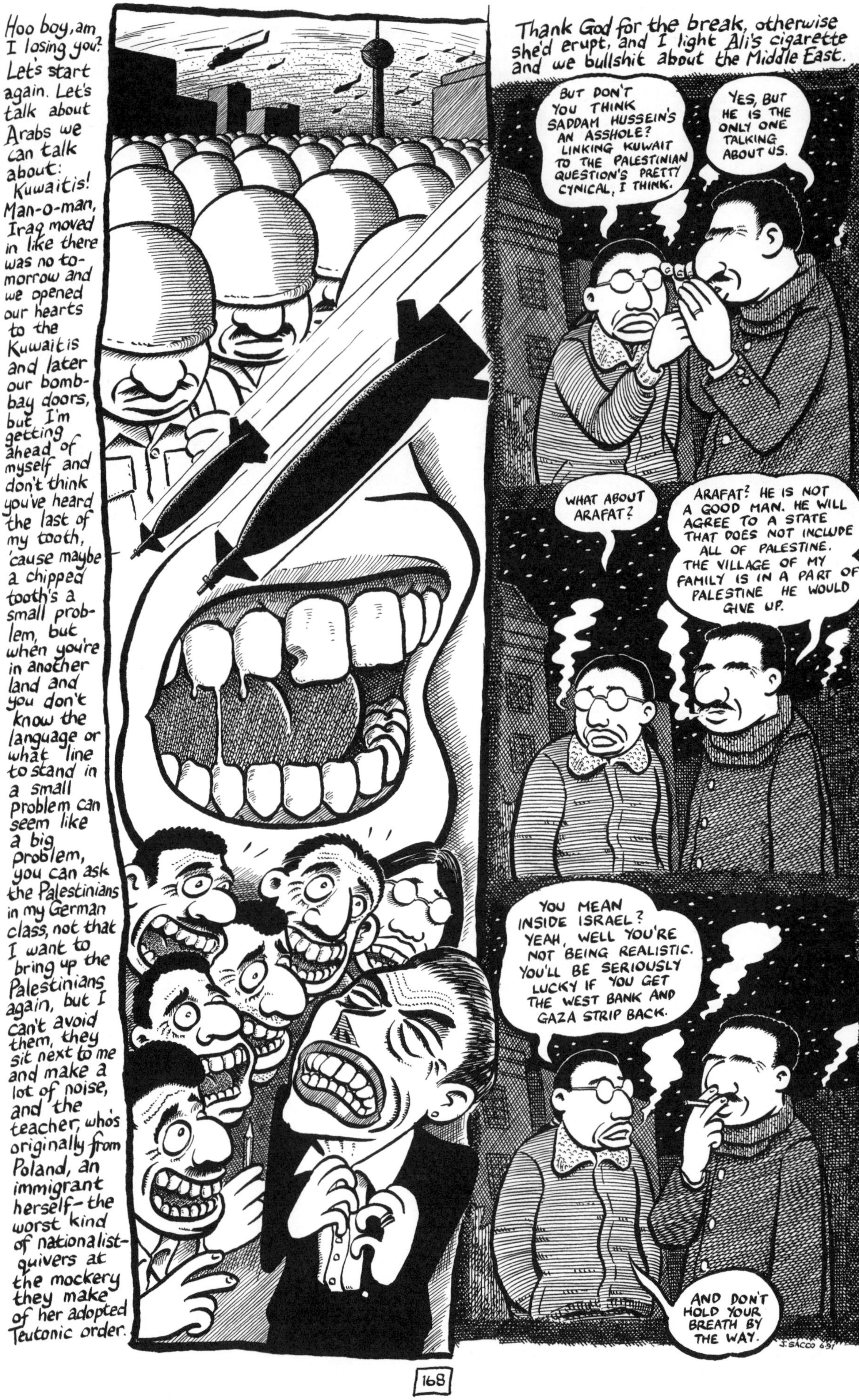

Hoo boy, am I losing you? Let's start again. Let's talk about Arabs we can talk about: Kuwaitis! Man-o-man, Iraq moved in like there was no tomorrow and we opened our hearts to the Kuwaitis and later our bomb-bay doors, but I'm getting ahead of myself and don't think you've heard the last of my tooth, 'cause maybe a chipped tooth's a small problem, but when you're in another land and you don't know the language or what line to stand in a small problem can seem like a big problem, you can ask the Palestinians in my German class, not that I want to bring up the Palestinians again, but I can't avoid them, they sit next to me and make a lot of noise, and the teacher, who's originally from Poland, an immigrant herself—the worst kind of nationalist—quivers at the mockery they make of her adopted Teutonic order.
Thank God for the break, otherwise she'd erupt, and I light Ali's cigarette and we bullshit about the Middle East.
BUT DON'T YOU THINK SADDAM HUSSEIN'S AN ASSHOLE? LINKING KUWAIT TO THE PALESTINIAN QUESTION'S PRETTY CYNICAL, I THINK.
YES, BUT HE IS THE ONLY ONE TALKING ABOUT US.
WHAT ABOUT ARAFAT?
ARAFAT? HE IS NOT A GOOD MAN. HE WILL AGREE TO A STATE THAT DOES NOT INCLUDE ALL OF PALESTINE. THE VILLAGE OF MY FAMILY IS IN A PART OF PALESTINE HE WOULD GIVE UP.
YOU MEAN INSIDE ISRAEL? YEAH, WELL YOU'RE NOT BEING REALISTIC. YOU'LL BE SERIOUSLY LUCKY IF YOU GET THE WEST BANK AND GAZA STRIP BACK.
AND DON'T HOLD YOUR BREATH BY THE WAY.
J. SACCO 6.91

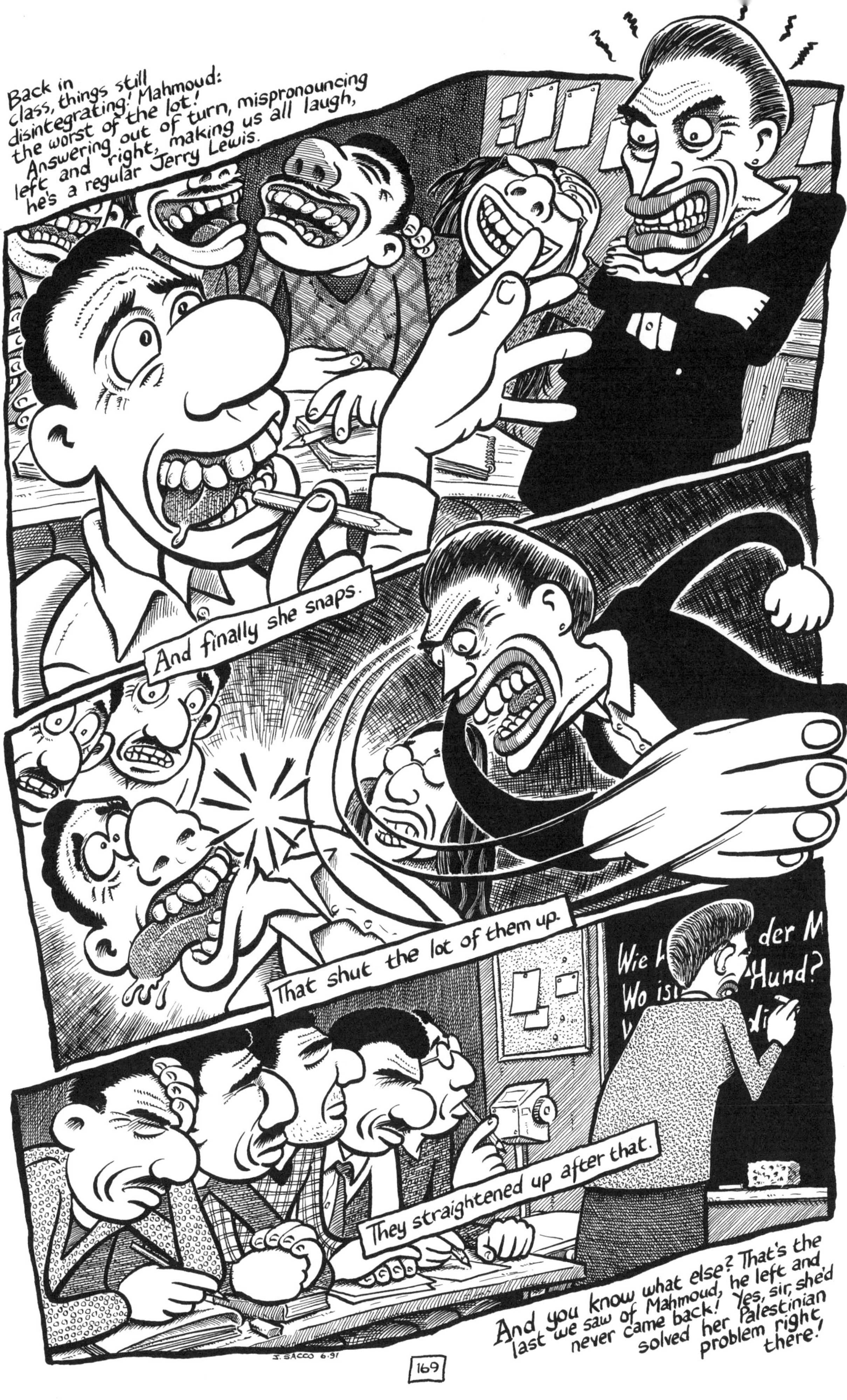
Back in class, things still disintegrating! Mahmoud: the worst of the lot! Answering out of turn, mispronouncing left and right, making us all laugh, he's a regular Jerry Lewis.
And finally she snaps.
That shut the lot of them up.
Wie
der M
Hund?
Wo ist
They straightened up after that.
And you know what else? That's the last we saw of Mahmoud, he left and never came back! Yes, sir, she'd solved her Palestinian problem right there!
J. SACCO 6.91

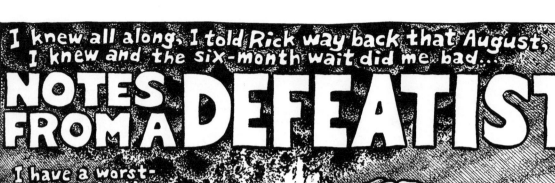

NOTES FROM A DEFEATIST

I knew all along, I told Rick way back that August, I knew and the six-month wait did me bad...

I have a worst-case imagination, and why not? It's been a bad century Sommes, Holocausts. Hiroshimas, what next?

I jumped to conclusions, I killed parties with extrapolations from Stalingrad, I dropped Cambodias between twitterings with girls I didn't know, I was really being a pest.

In 1917 French soldiers bleated on their way to the slaughter

BAAAAAAM BAAAAAAM

What about me, where was my sense of humor?

J. SACCO 8-91

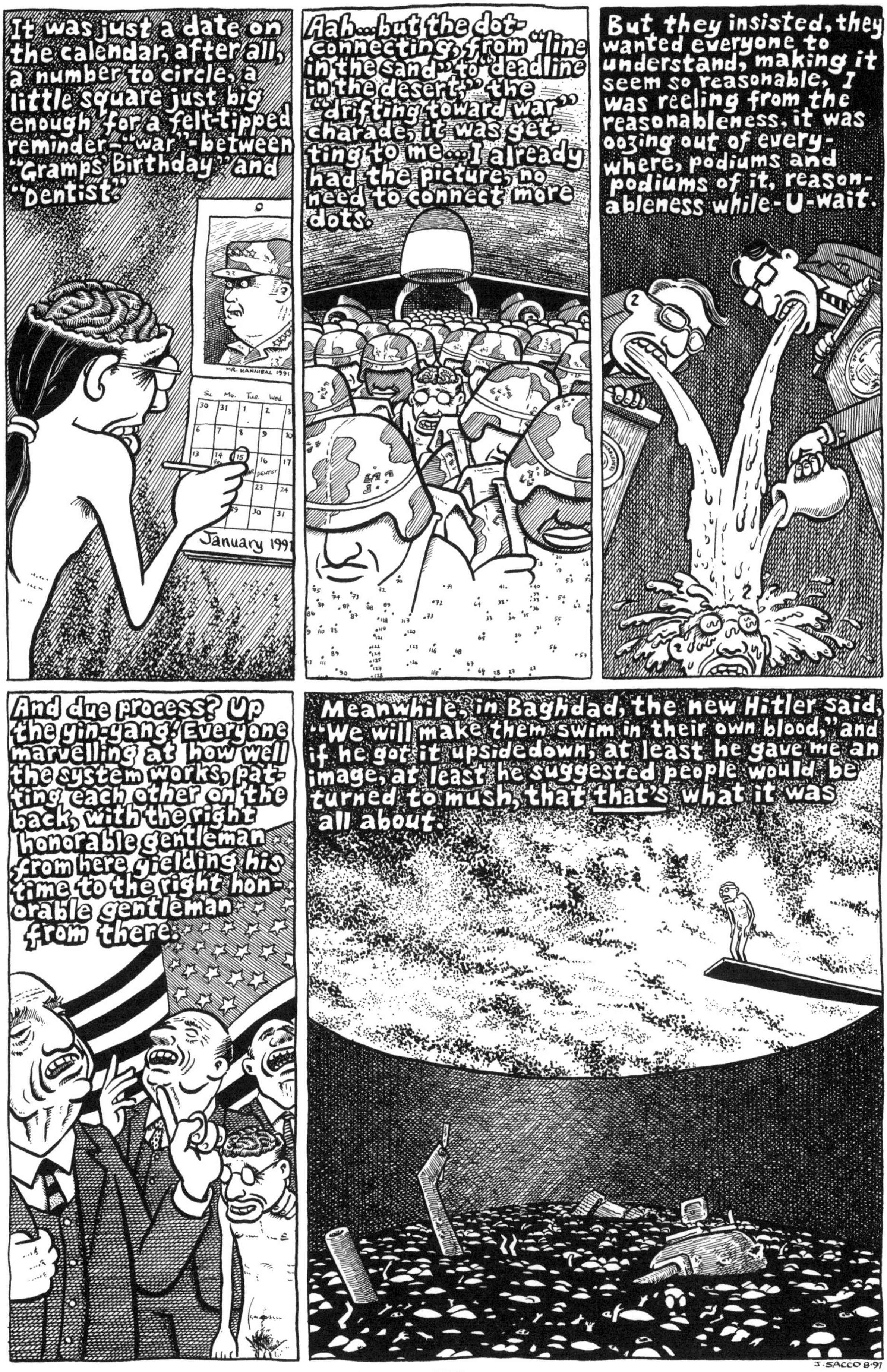
It was just a date on the calendar, after all, a number to circle, a little square just big enough for a felt-tipped reminder—"war"—between "Gramps' Birthday" and "Dentist."
MR. HANNIBAL 1991
January 1991
Aah...but the dot-connecting, from "line in the sand" to "deadline in the desert," the "drifting toward war" charade, it was getting to me... I already had the picture, no need to connect more dots.
But they insisted, they wanted everyone to understand, making it seem so reasonable, I was reeling from the reasonableness, it was oozing out of everywhere, podiums and podiums of it, reasonableness while-U-wait.
And due process? Up the yin-yang! Everyone marvelling at how well the system works, patting each other on the back, with the right honorable gentleman from here yielding his time to the right honorable gentleman from there.
Meanwhile, in Baghdad, the new Hitler said, "We will make them swim in their own blood," and if he got it upsidedown, at least he gave me an image, at least he suggested people would be turned to mush, that that's what it was all about.
J. SACCO 8·91

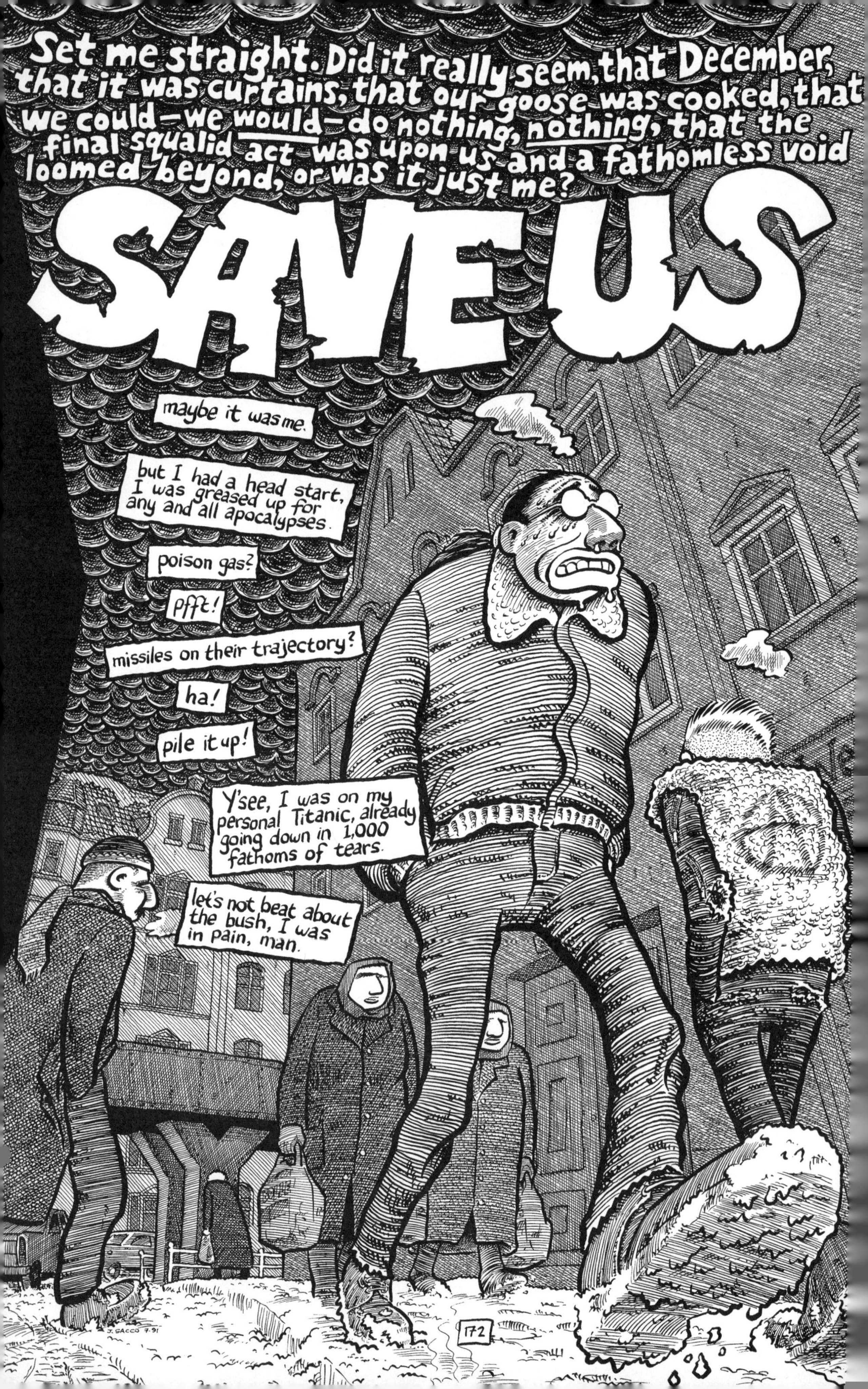
Set me straight. Did it really seem, that December, that it was curtains, that our goose was cooked, that we could—we would—do nothing, nothing, that the final squalid act was upon us and a fathomless void loomed beyond, or was it just me?
SAVE US
maybe it was me.
but I had a head start, I was greased up for any and all apocalypses.
poison gas?
pfft!
missiles on their trajectory?
ha!
pile it up!
Y'see, I was on my personal Titanic, already going down in 1,000 fathoms of tears.
let's not beat about the bush, I was in pain, man.
J. SACCO 7.91
172

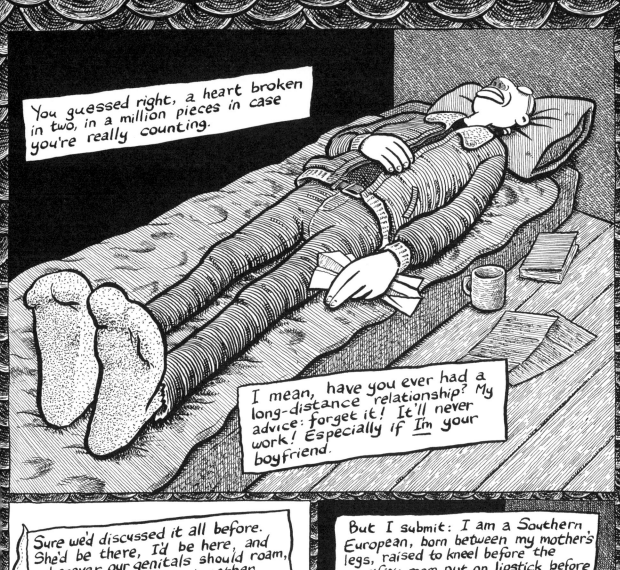

You guessed right, a heart broken in two, in a million pieces in case you're really counting.

I mean, have you ever had a long-distance relationship? My advice: forget it! It'll never work! Especially if I'm your boyfriend.

Sure we'd discussed it all before. She'd be there, I'd be here, and wherever our genitals should roam, in the end we'd be together.

First there is a mountain, then there is no mountain, then there is...

CONFIDENT PHASE

But I submit: I am a Southern European, born between my mother's legs, raised to kneel before the crucifix; mom put on lipstick before dad came home, dinner was on the table, and pasta the main course.

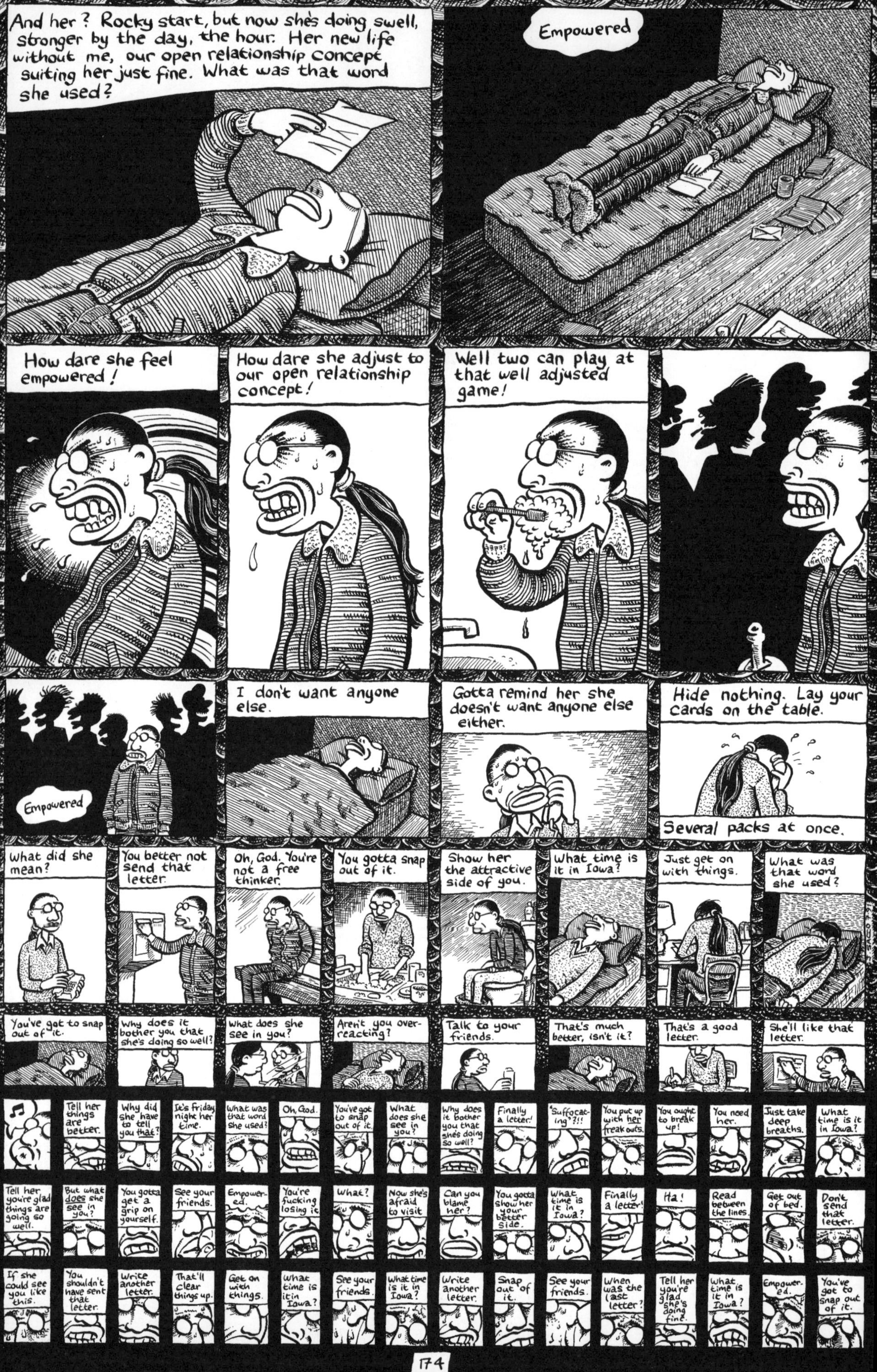

And her? Rocky start, but now she's doing swell, stronger by the day, the hour. Her new life without me, our open relationship concept suiting her just fine. What was that word she used?
Empowered
How dare she feel empowered!
How dare she adjust to our open relationship concept!
Well two can play at that well adjusted game!
Empowered
I don't want anyone else.
Gotta remind her she doesn't want anyone else either.
Hide nothing. Lay your cards on the table.
Several packs at once.
What did she mean?
You better not send that letter.
Oh, God. You're not a free thinker.
You gotta snap out of it.
Show her the attractive side of you.
What time is it in Iowa?
Just get on with things.
What was that word she used?
You've got to snap out of it.
Why does it bother you that she's doing so well?
What does she see in you?
Aren't you over-reacting?
Talk to your friends.
That's much better, isn't it?
That's a good letter.
She'll like that letter.
♫
Tell her things are better.
Why did she have to tell you that?
It's Friday night her time.
What was that word she used?
Oh, God.
You've got to snap out of it.
What does she see in you?
Why does it bother you that she's doing so well?
Finally a letter!
'Suffocating'?!!
You put up with her freak outs.
You ought to break up!
You need her.
Just take deep breaths.
What time is it in Iowa?
Tell her you're glad things are going so well.
But what does she see in you?
You gotta get a grip on yourself.
See your friends.
Empowered.
You're fucking losing it
What?
Now she's afraid to visit
Can you blame her?
You gotta show her your better side.
What time is it in Iowa?
Finally a letter!
Ha!
Read between the lines.
Get out of bed.
Don't send that letter.
If she could see you like this.
You shouldn't have sent that letter.
Write another letter.
That'll clear things up.
Get on with things.
What time is it in Iowa?
See your friends.
What time is it in Iowa?
Write another letter.
Snap out of it.
See your friends.
When was the last letter?
Tell her you're glad she's doing fine.
What time is it in Iowa?
Empowered.
You've got to snap out of it.

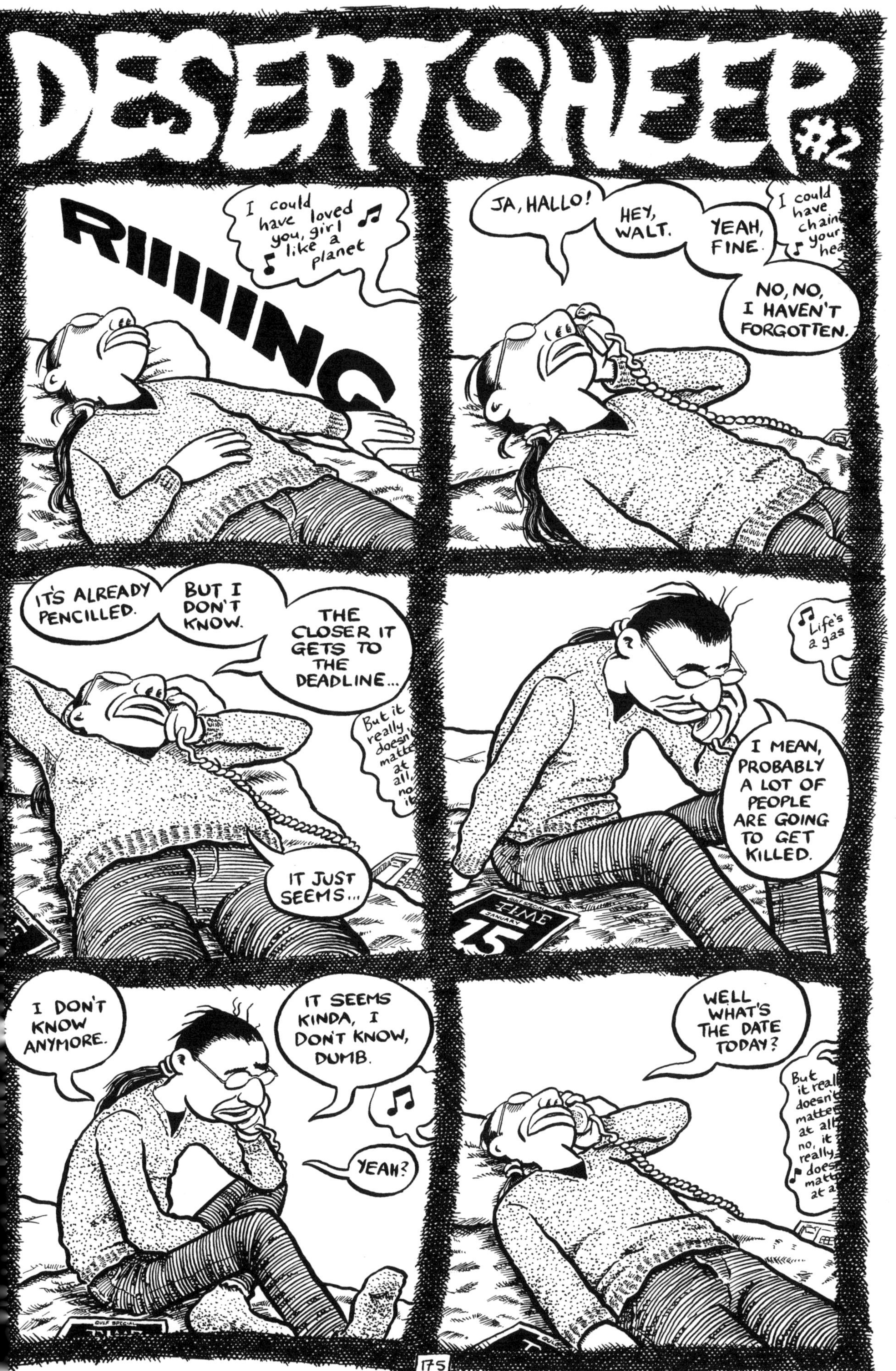
DESERT SHEEP #2
RIIIIING
I could have loved you, girl like a planet
JA, HALLO!
HEY, WALT.
YEAH, FINE.
I could have chain your hea
NO, NO, I HAVEN'T FORGOTTEN.
IT'S ALREADY PENCILLED.
BUT I DON'T KNOW.
THE CLOSER IT GETS TO THE DEADLINE...
But it really doesn' matt at all, no
IT JUST SEEMS...
Life's a gas
I MEAN, PROBABLY A LOT OF PEOPLE ARE GOING TO GET KILLED.
TIME
JANUARY
15
GULF SPECIAL
I DON'T KNOW ANYMORE.
IT SEEMS KINDA, I DON'T KNOW, DUMB.
YEAH?
WELL WHAT'S THE DATE TODAY?
But it reall doesn't matte at all no, it really does matt at a

J. SACCO 7-91

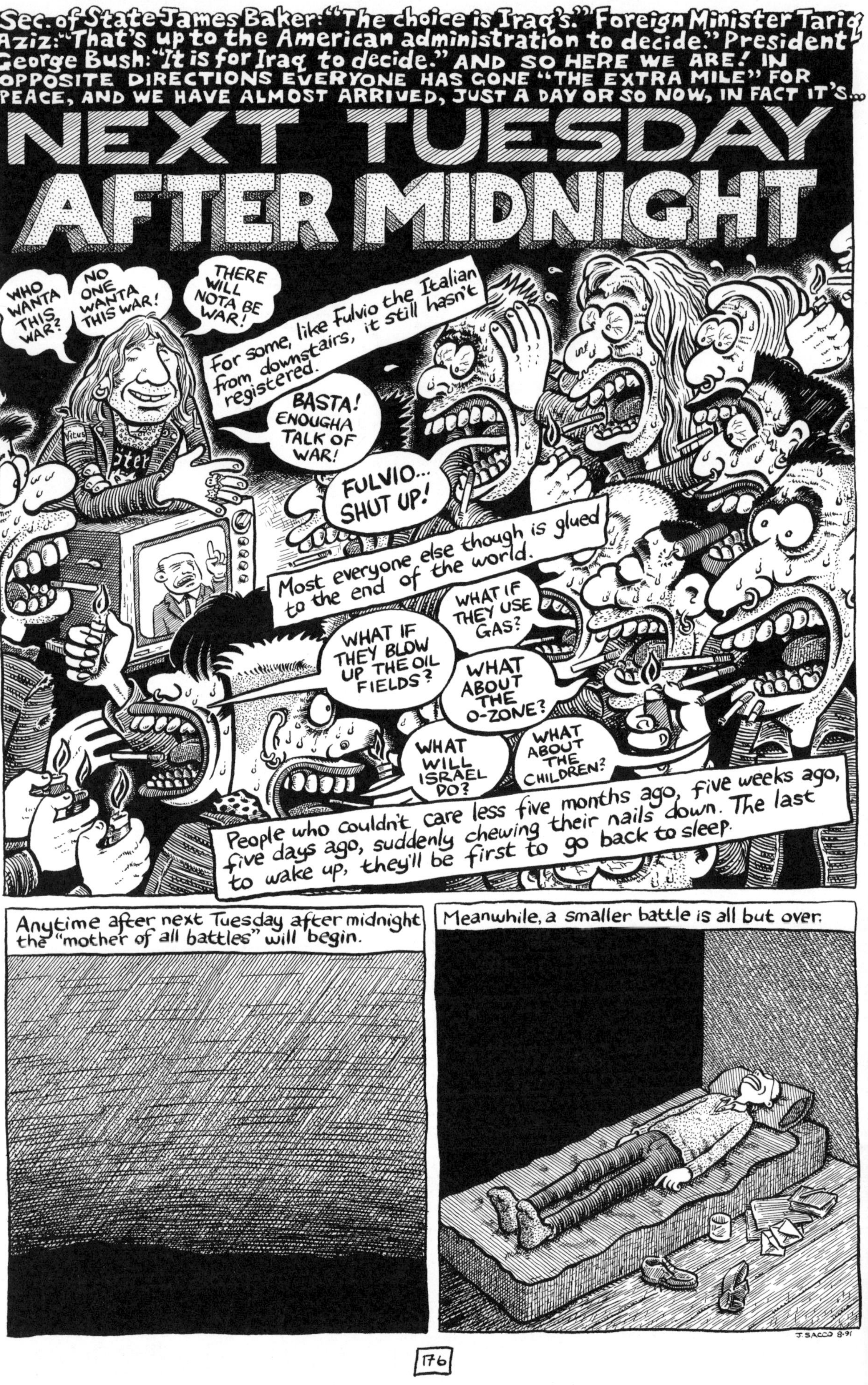

Sec. of State James Baker: "The choice is Iraq's." Foreign Minister Tariq Aziz: "That's up to the American administration to decide." President George Bush: "It is for Iraq to decide." AND SO HERE WE ARE! IN OPPOSITE DIRECTIONS EVERYONE HAS GONE "THE EXTRA MILE" FOR PEACE, AND WE HAVE ALMOST ARRIVED, JUST A DAY OR SO NOW, IN FACT IT'S...
NEXT TUESDAY AFTER MIDNIGHT
WHO WANTA THIS WAR?
NO ONE WANTA THIS WAR!
THERE WILL NOTA BE WAR!
For some, like Fulvio the Italian from downstairs, it still hasn't registered.
BASTA! ENOUGHA TALK OF WAR!
FULVIO... SHUT UP!
Most everyone else though is glued to the end of the world.
WHAT IF THEY USE GAS?
WHAT IF THEY BLOW UP THE OIL FIELDS?
WHAT ABOUT THE O-ZONE?
WHAT WILL ISRAEL DO?
WHAT ABOUT THE CHILDREN?
People who couldn't care less five months ago, five weeks ago, five days ago, suddenly chewing their nails down. The last to wake up, they'll be first to go back to sleep.
Anytime after next Tuesday after midnight the "mother of all battles" will begin.
Meanwhile, a smaller battle is all but over.
J. SACCO 8-91

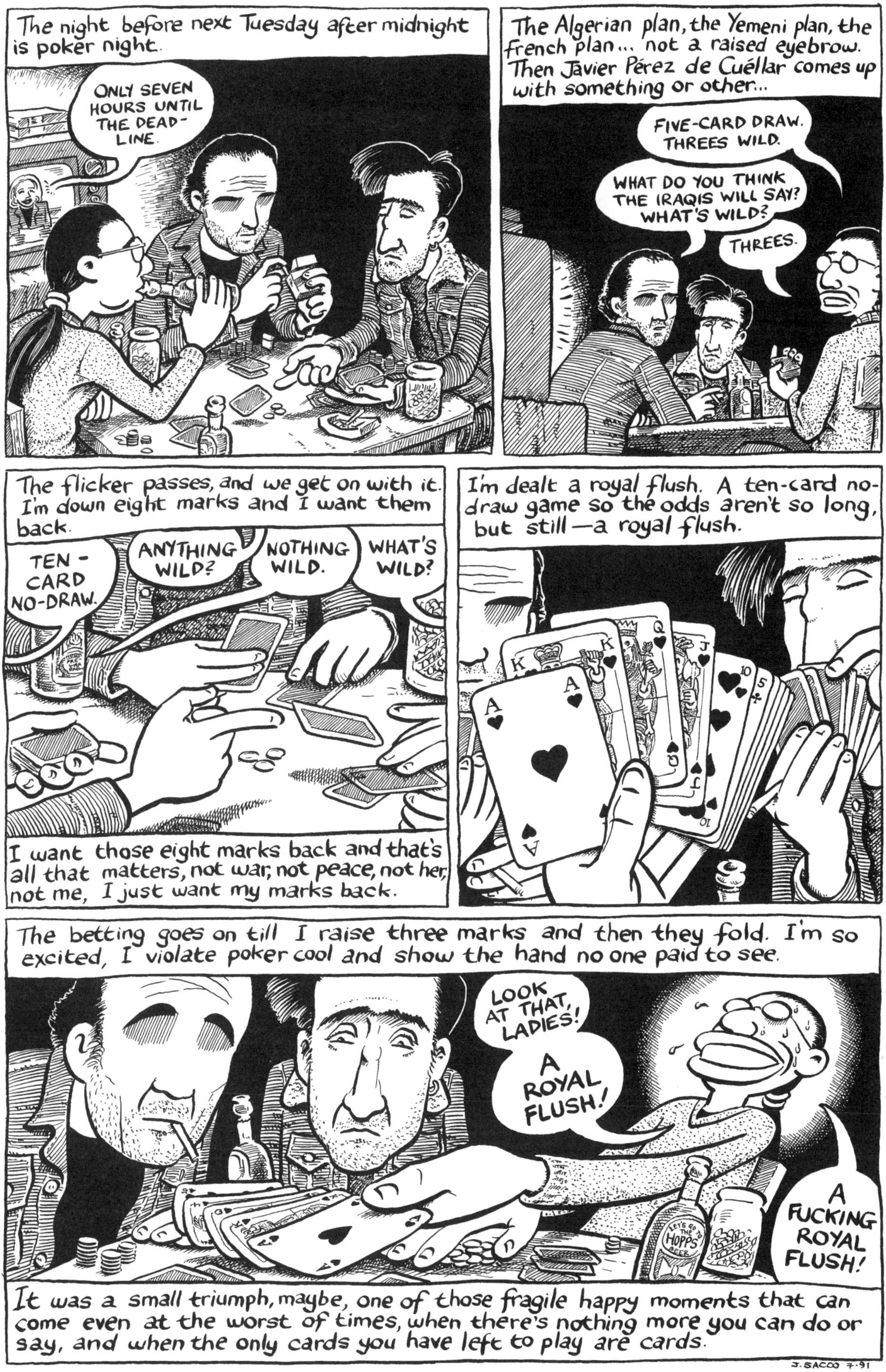
The night before next Tuesday after midnight is poker night.
ONLY SEVEN HOURS UNTIL THE DEAD-LINE.
The Algerian plan, the Yemeni plan, the French plan... not a raised eyebrow. Then Jávier Pérez de Cuéllar comes up with something or other...
FIVE-CARD DRAW. THREES WILD.
WHAT DO YOU THINK THE IRAQIS WILL SAY? WHAT'S WILD?
THREES.
The flicker passes, and we get on with it. I'm down eight marks and I want them back.
TEN-CARD NO-DRAW.
ANYTHING WILD?
NOTHING WILD.
WHAT'S WILD?
I want those eight marks back and that's all that matters, not war, not peace, not her, not me, I just want my marks back.
I'm dealt a royal flush. A ten-card no-draw game so the odds aren't so long, but still—a royal flush.
The betting goes on till I raise three marks and then they fold. I'm so excited, I violate poker cool and show the hand no one paid to see.
LOOK AT THAT, LADIES!
A ROYAL FLUSH!
A FUCKING ROYAL FLUSH!
LET'S GO TO THE HOPPS BEER
It was a small triumph, maybe, one of those fragile happy moments that can come even at the worst of times, when there's nothing more you can do or say, and when the only cards you have left to play are cards.
J. SACCO 7·91

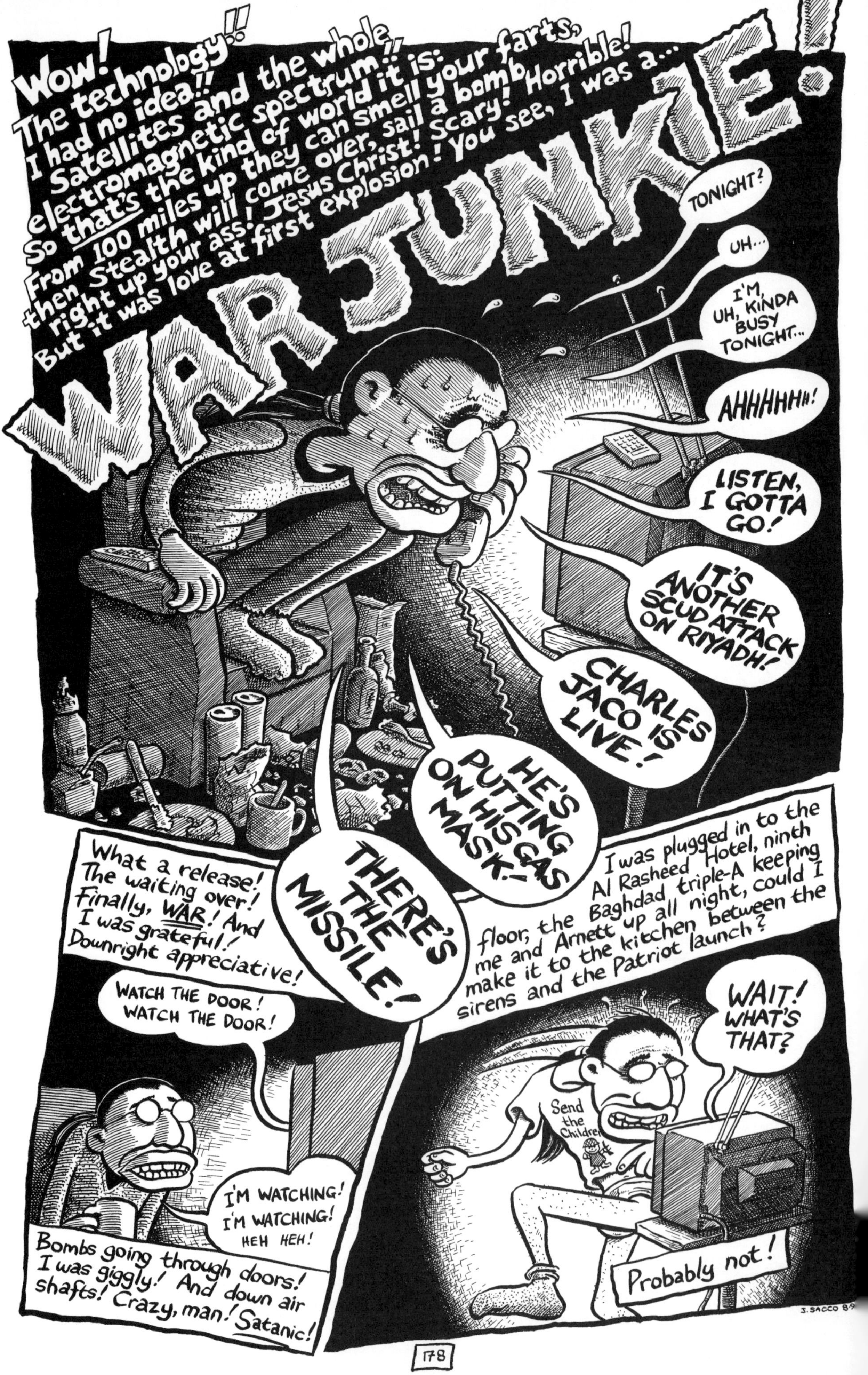

Wow! The technology!! I had no idea!! Satellites and the whole electromagnetic spectrum!! So that's the kind of world it is: From 100 miles up they can smell your farts, then Stealth will come over, sail a bomb right up your ass! Jesus Christ! Scary! Horrible! But it was love at first explosion! You see, I was a...
WAR JUNKIE!
TONIGHT?
UH...
I'M, UH, KINDA BUSY TONIGHT...
AHHHHH!!
LISTEN, I GOTTA GO!
IT'S ANOTHER SCUD ATTACK ON RIYADH!
CHARLES JACO IS LIVE!
HE'S PUTTING ON HIS GAS MASK!
THERE'S THE MISSILE!
What a release! The waiting over! Finally, WAR! And I was grateful! Downright appreciative!
I was plugged in to the Al Rasheed Hotel, ninth floor, the Baghdad triple-A keeping me and Arnett up all night, could I make it to the kitchen between the sirens and the Patriot launch?
WATCH THE DOOR! WATCH THE DOOR!
I'M WATCHING! I'M WATCHING! HEH HEH!
Bombs going through doors! I was giggly! And down air shafts! Crazy, man! Satanic!
WAIT! WHAT'S THAT?
Send the Children
Probably not!
J. SACCO 8.9

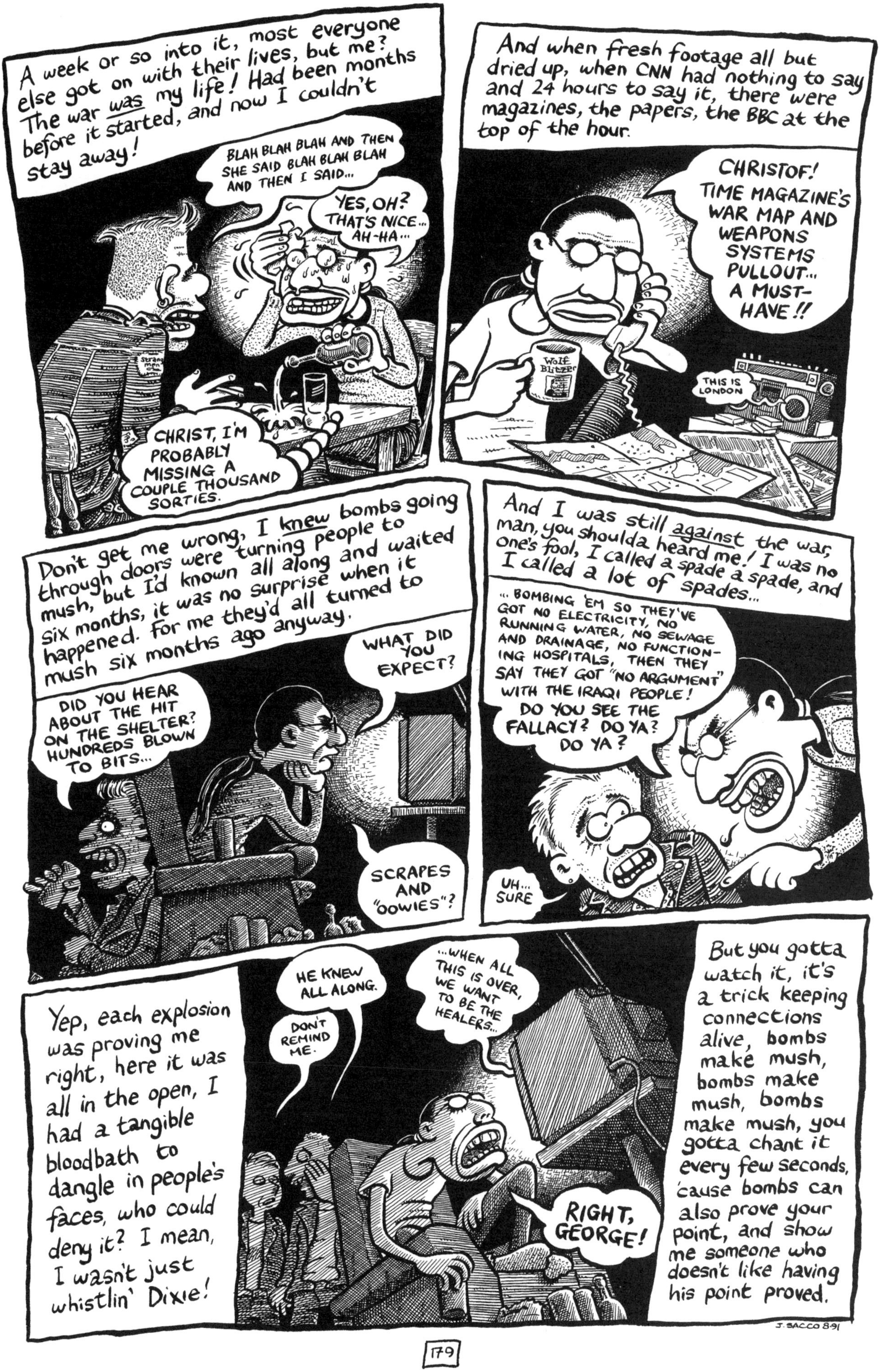
A week or so into it, most everyone else got on with their lives, but me? The war was my life! Had been months before it started, and now I couldn't stay away!
BLAH BLAH BLAH AND THEN SHE SAID BLAH BLAH BLAH AND THEN I SAID...
YES, OH? THAT'S NICE... AH-HA...
CHRIST, I'M PROBABLY MISSING A COUPLE THOUSAND SORTIES.
And when fresh footage all but dried up, when CNN had nothing to say and 24 hours to say it, there were magazines, the papers, the BBC at the top of the hour.
CHRISTOF! TIME MAGAZINE'S WAR MAP AND WEAPONS SYSTEMS PULLOUT... A MUST-HAVE!!
Wolf Blitzer
THIS IS LONDON
Don't get me wrong, I knew bombs going through doors were turning people to mush, but I'd known all along and waited six months, it was no surprise when it happened. For me they'd all turned to mush six months ago anyway.
DID YOU HEAR ABOUT THE HIT ON THE SHELTER? HUNDREDS BLOWN TO BITS...
WHAT DID YOU EXPECT?
SCRAPES AND "OOWIES"?
And I was still against the war, man, you shoulda heard me! I was no one's fool, I called a spade a spade, and I called a lot of spades...
...BOMBING 'EM SO THEY'VE GOT NO ELECTRICITY, NO RUNNING WATER, NO SEWAGE AND DRAINAGE, NO FUNCTIONING HOSPITALS, THEN THEY SAY THEY GOT "NO ARGUMENT" WITH THE IRAQI PEOPLE! DO YOU SEE THE FALLACY? DO YA? DO YA?
UH... SURE
Yep, each explosion was proving me right, here it was all in the open, I had a tangible bloodbath to dangle in people's faces, who could deny it? I mean, I wasn't just whistlin' Dixie!
HE KNEW ALL ALONG.
DON'T REMIND ME.
...WHEN ALL THIS IS OVER, WE WANT TO BE THE HEALERS...
RIGHT, GEORGE!
But you gotta watch it, it's a trick keeping connections alive, bombs make mush, bombs make mush, bombs make mush, you gotta chant it every few seconds, 'cause bombs can also prove your point, and show me someone who doesn't like having his point proved.
J. SACCO 8.91

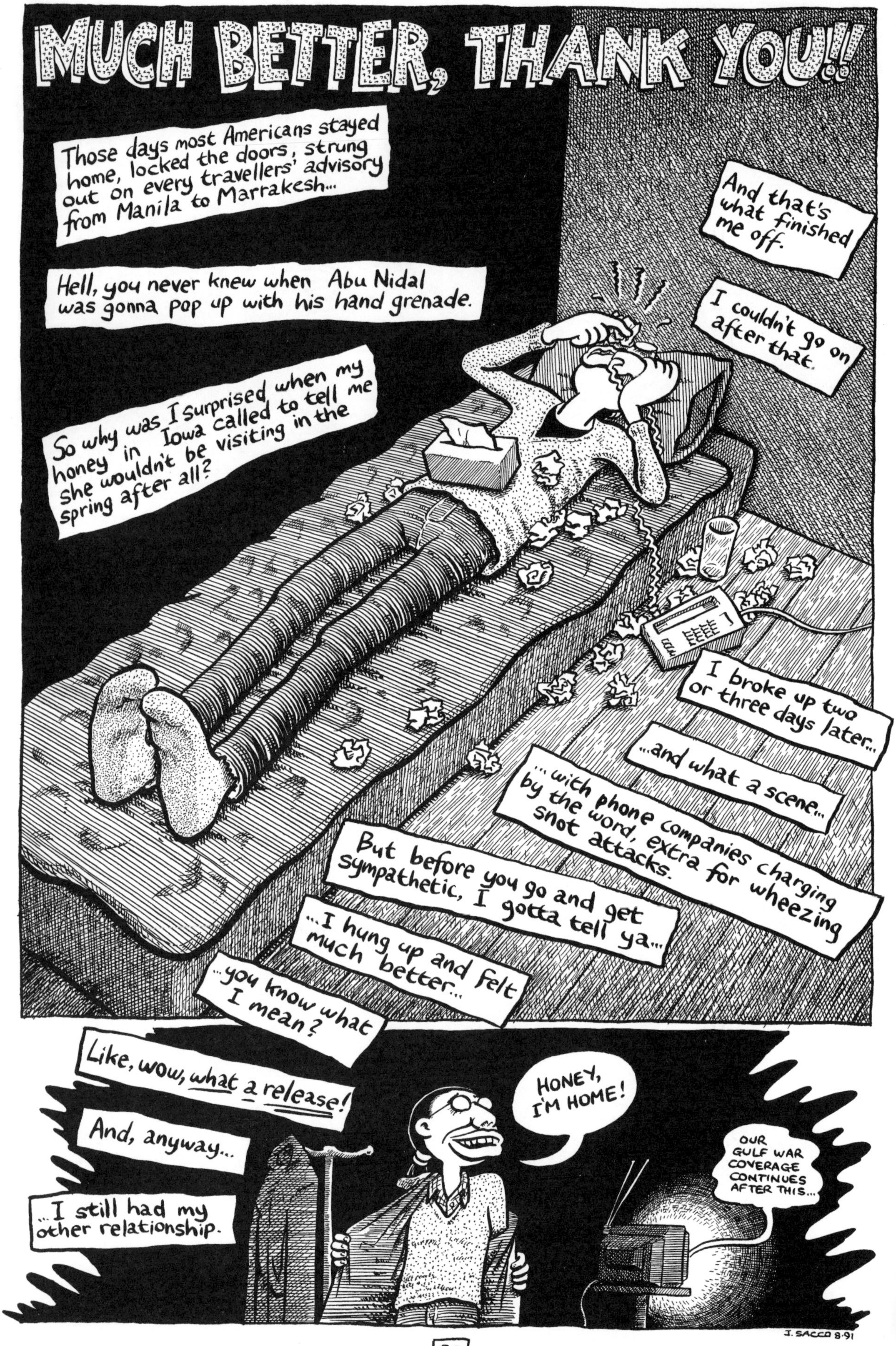
MUCH BETTER, THANK YOU!!
Those days most Americans stayed home, locked the doors, strung out on every travellers' advisory from Manila to Marrakesh...
Hell, you never knew when Abu Nidal was gonna pop up with his hand grenade.
So why was I surprised when my honey in Iowa called to tell me she wouldn't be visiting in the spring after all?
And that's what finished me off.
I couldn't go on after that.
I broke up two or three days later...
...and what a scene...
...with phone companies charging by the word, extra for wheezing snot attacks.
But before you go and get sympathetic, I gotta tell ya...
...I hung up and felt much better...
...you know what I mean?
Like, wow, what a release!
And, anyway...
...I still had my other relationship.
HONEY, I'M HOME!
OUR GULF WAR COVERAGE CONTINUES AFTER THIS...
J. SACCO 8·91

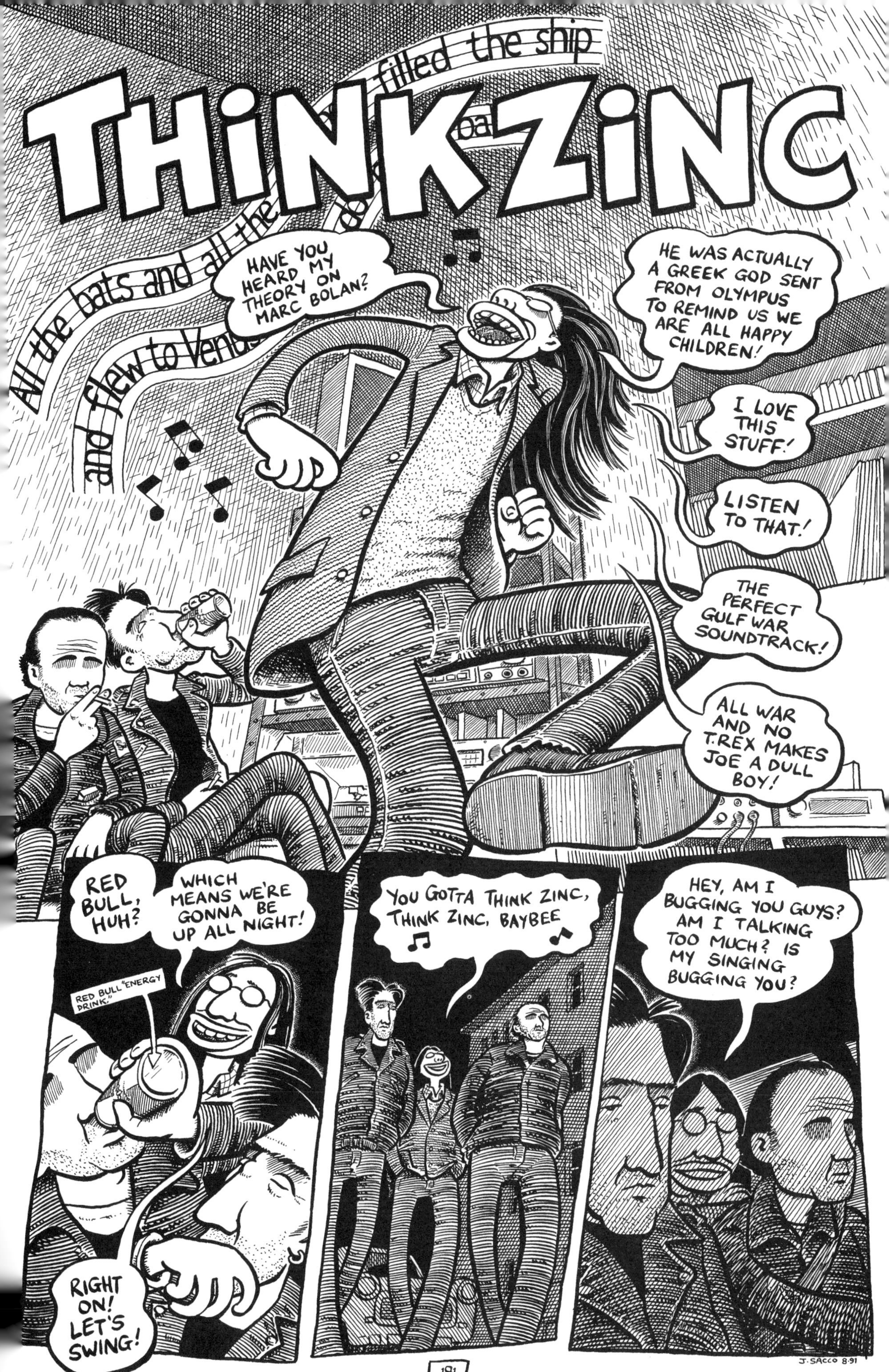
THINK ZINC
All the bats and all the ... filled the ship
and flew to Venus
HAVE YOU HEARD MY THEORY ON MARC BOLAN?
HE WAS ACTUALLY A GREEK GOD SENT FROM OLYMPUS TO REMIND US WE ARE ALL HAPPY CHILDREN!
I LOVE THIS STUFF!
LISTEN TO THAT!
THE PERFECT GULF WAR SOUNDTRACK!
ALL WAR AND NO T.REX MAKES JOE A DULL BOY!
RED BULL, HUH?
WHICH MEANS WE'RE GONNA BE UP ALL NIGHT!
RED BULL "ENERGY DRINK."
RIGHT ON! LET'S SWING!
YOU GOTTA THINK ZINC, THINK ZINC, BAYBEE
HEY, AM I BUGGING YOU GUYS? AM I TALKING TOO MUCH? IS MY SINGING BUGGING YOU?
J. SACCO 8.91

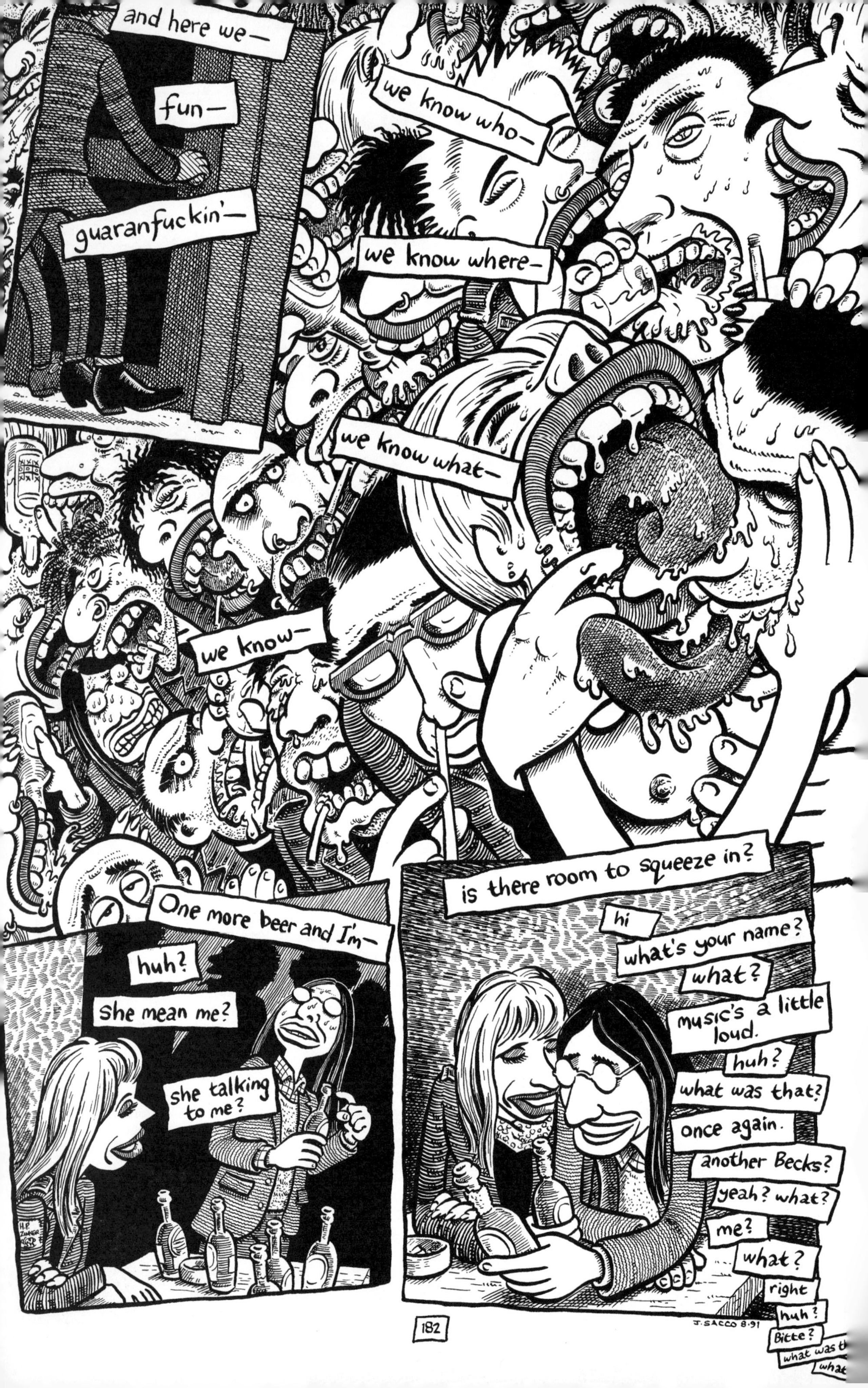

and here we—
fun—
guaranfuckin'—
we know who—
we know where—
we know what—
we know—
One more beer and I'm—
huh?
she mean me?
she talking to me?
H.P. ZINKER
is there room to squeeze in?
hi
what's your name?
what?
music's a little loud.
huh?
what was that?
once again.
another Becks?
yeah? what?
me?
what?
right
huh?
Bitte?
J. SACCO 8·91

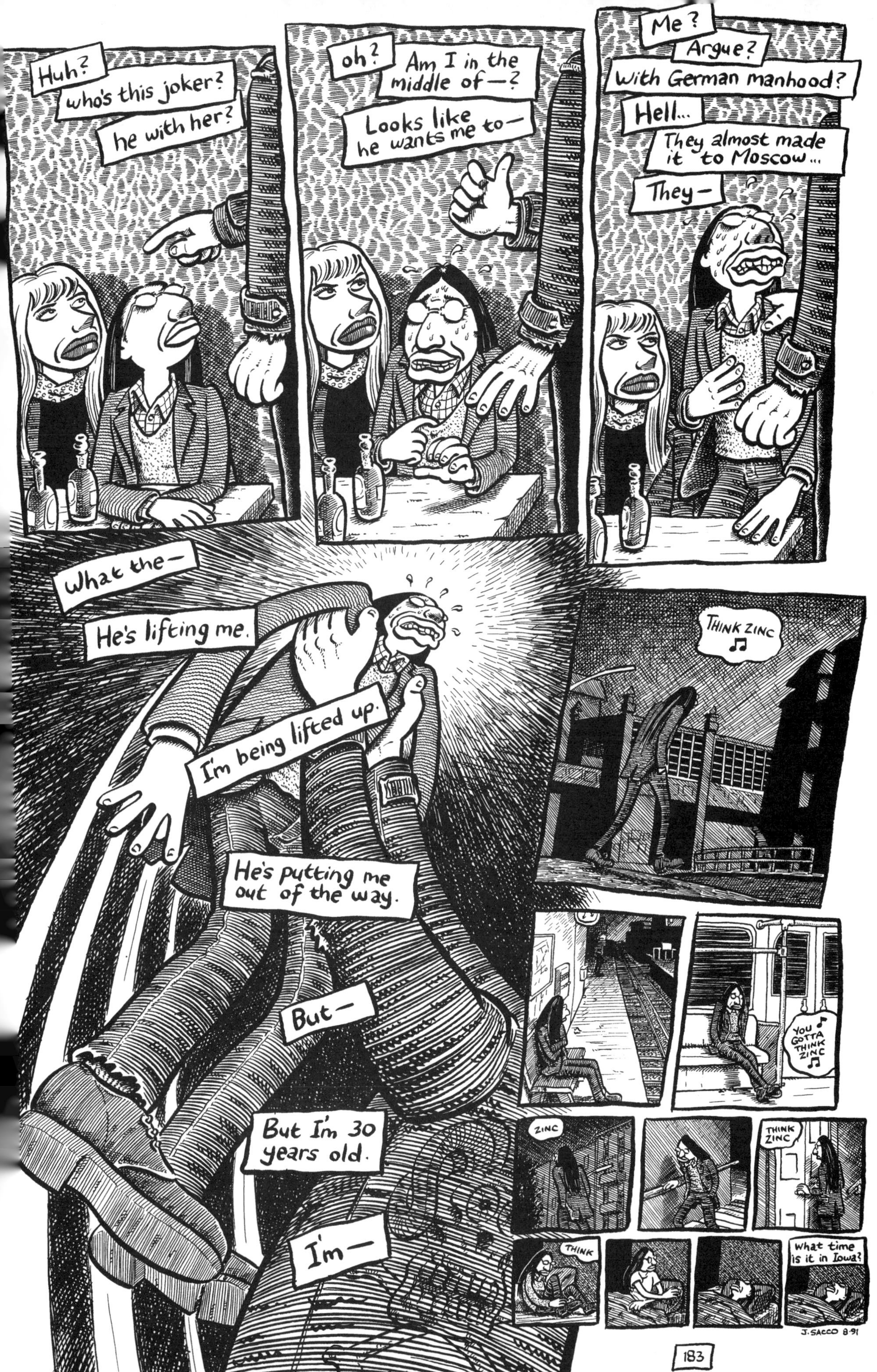

Huh?
who's this joker?
he with her?
oh?
Am I in the middle of—?
Looks like he wants me to—
Me?
Argue?
With German manhood?
Hell...
They almost made it to Moscow...
They—
What the—
He's lifting me.
I'm being lifted up.
He's putting me out of the way.
But—
But I'm 30 years old.
I'm—
THINK ZINC
YOU GOTTA THINK ZINC
ZINC
THINK ZINC
THINK
What time is it in Iowa?
J. SACCO 8·91

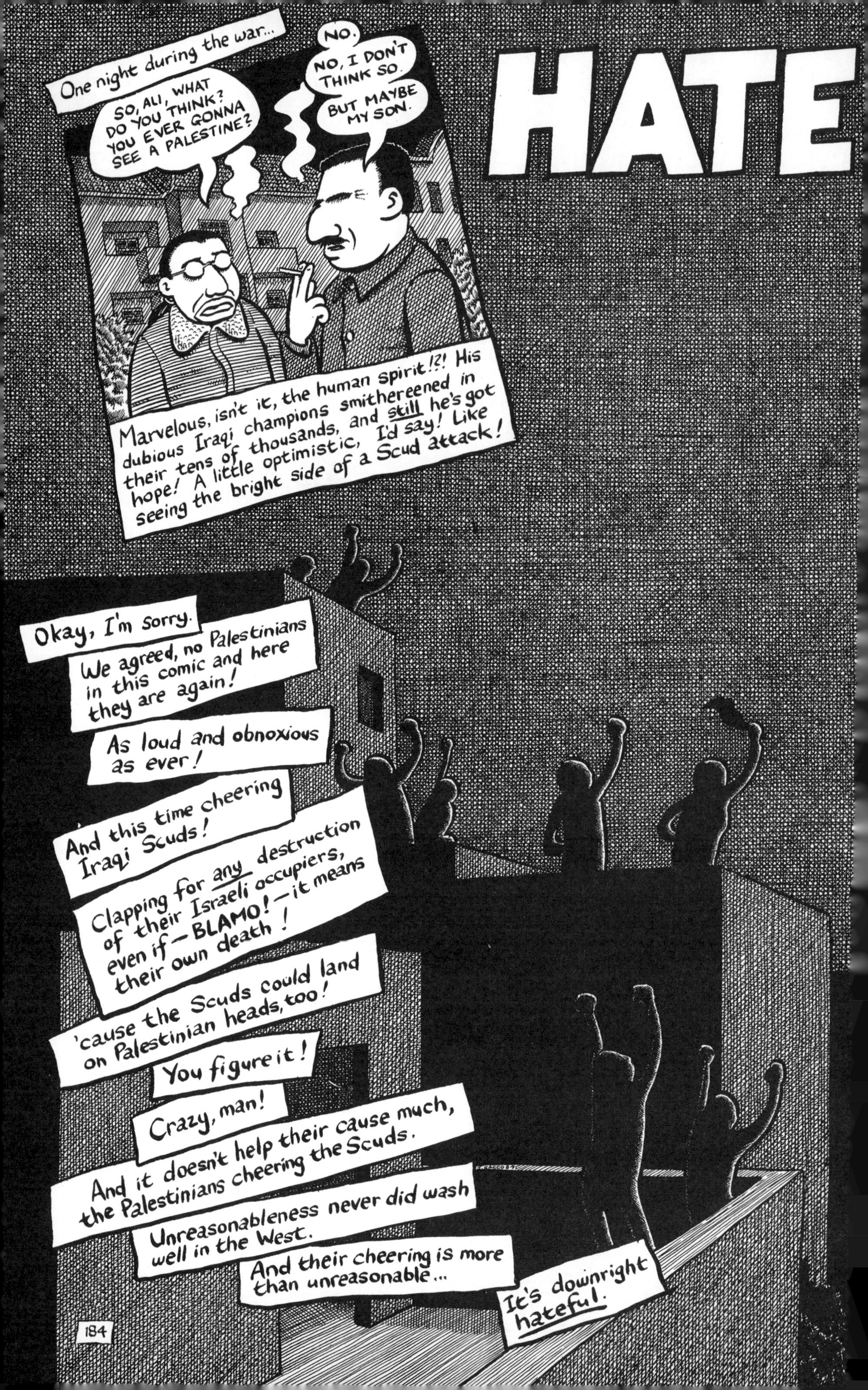
HATE
One night during the war...
SO, ALI, WHAT DO YOU THINK? YOU EVER GONNA SEE A PALESTINE?
NO.
NO, I DON'T THINK SO.
BUT MAYBE MY SON.
Marvelous, isn't it, the human spirit!?! His dubious Iraqi champions smithereened in their tens of thousands, and still he's got hope! A little optimistic, I'd say! Like seeing the bright side of a Scud attack!
Okay, I'm sorry.
We agreed, no Palestinians in this comic and here they are again!
As loud and obnoxious as ever!
And this time cheering Iraqi Scuds!
Clapping for any destruction of their Israeli occupiers, even if—BLAMO!—it means their own death!
'cause the Scuds could land on Palestinian heads, too!
You figure it!
Crazy, man!
And it doesn't help their cause much, the Palestinians cheering the Scuds.
Unreasonableness never did wash well in the West.
And their cheering is more than unreasonable...
It's downright hateful.

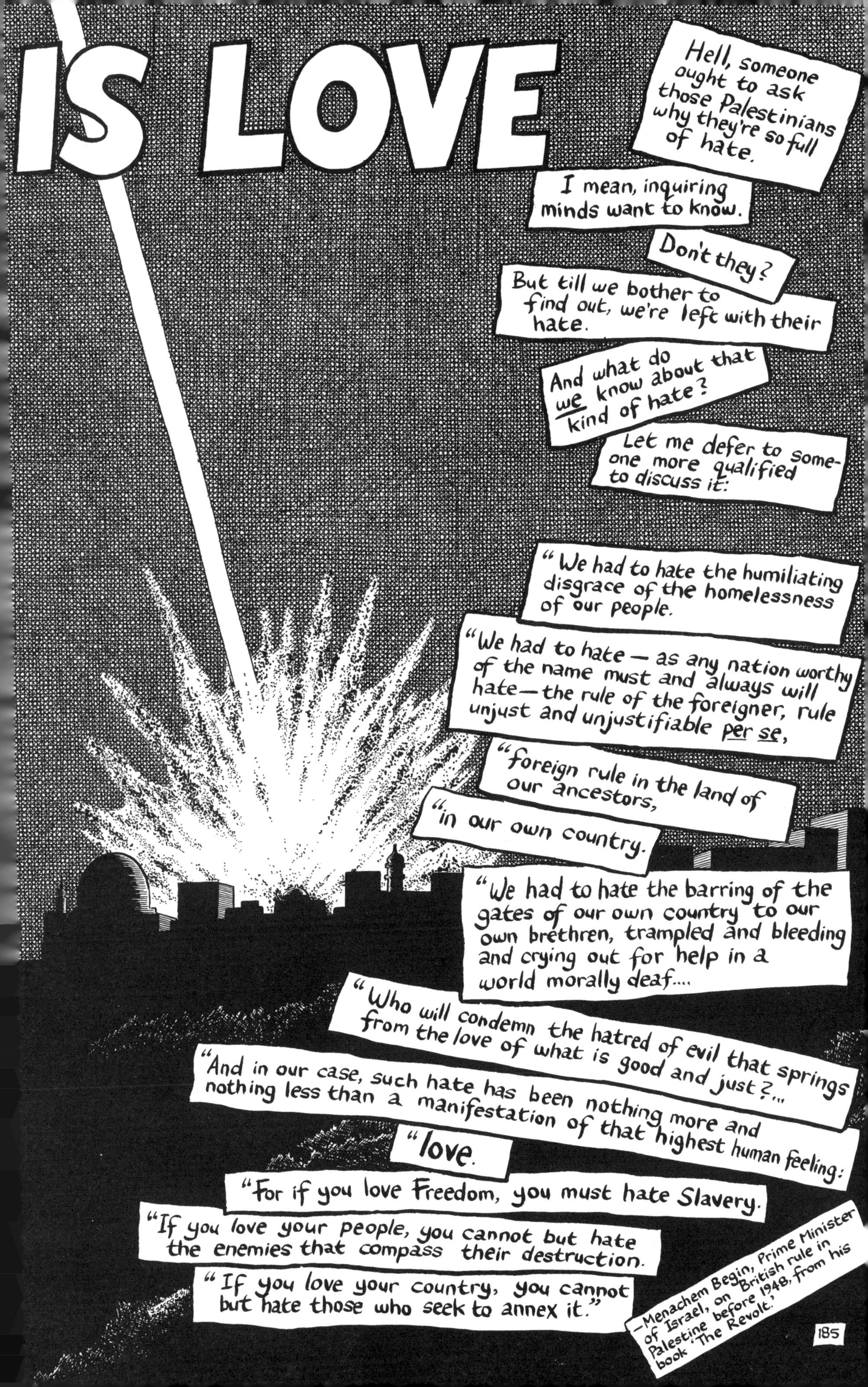
IS LOVE
Hell, someone ought to ask those Palestinians why they're so full of hate.
I mean, inquiring minds want to know.
Don't they?
But till we bother to find out, we're left with their hate.
And what do we know about that kind of hate?
Let me defer to someone more qualified to discuss it:
"We had to hate the humiliating disgrace of the homelessness of our people.
"We had to hate — as any nation worthy of the name must and always will hate — the rule of the foreigner, rule unjust and unjustifiable per se,
"foreign rule in the land of our ancestors,
"in our own country.
"We had to hate the barring of the gates of our own country to our own brethren, trampled and bleeding and crying out for help in a world morally deaf....
"Who will condemn the hatred of evil that springs from the love of what is good and just?...
"And in our case, such hate has been nothing more and nothing less than a manifestation of that highest human feeling:
"love.
"For if you love Freedom, you must hate Slavery.
"If you love your people, you cannot but hate the enemies that compass their destruction.
"If you love your country, you cannot but hate those who seek to annex it."
— Menachem Begin, Prime Minister of Israel, on British rule in Palestine before 1948, from his book 'The Revolt.'

In the end Bush could say, "Most Americans know instinctively why we're in the Gulf," and by then most Americans did, they figured the war was going so well it'd been their idea all along, but that's democracy, people bullshitted into thinking they think up the bullshit, satisfied it'd all been on the up 'n' up, nice and comfy in their support groups, with 'Sonja Live' helping them deal with it and tomorrow their weight problem.

WAS I RIGHT?

It's an old story, we've all got stories like this, you want out but there are certain formalities, certain annihilations that need to be concluded, a white flag won't help. You can accept all the Soviet peace plans you'd like, it's too late, the spokesperson says, "Meaningless," "An outrage," says the President, he promises more war "with undiminished intensity," leaving Kuwait is irrelevant, you are slaughtered on the highway home, where are your Scuds now? You are bumper to bumper and slaughtered with impunity, it's you versus the whole electromagnetic spectrum, and you are slaughtered until the slaughter stops.

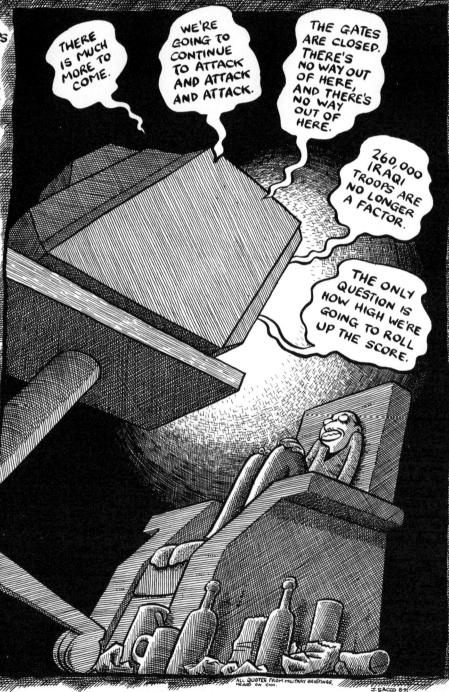

THERE IS MUCH MORE TO COME.

WE'RE GOING TO CONTINUE TO ATTACK AND ATTACK AND ATTACK.

THE GATES ARE CLOSED. THERE'S NO WAY OUT OF HERE, AND THERE'S NO WAY OUT OF HERE.

260,000 IRAQI TROOPS ARE NO LONGER A FACTOR.

THE ONLY QUESTION IS HOW HIGH WE'RE GOING TO ROLL UP THE SCORE.

ALL QUOTES FROM MILITARY BRIEFINGS, HEARD ON CNN.

J. SACCO 8-91

186

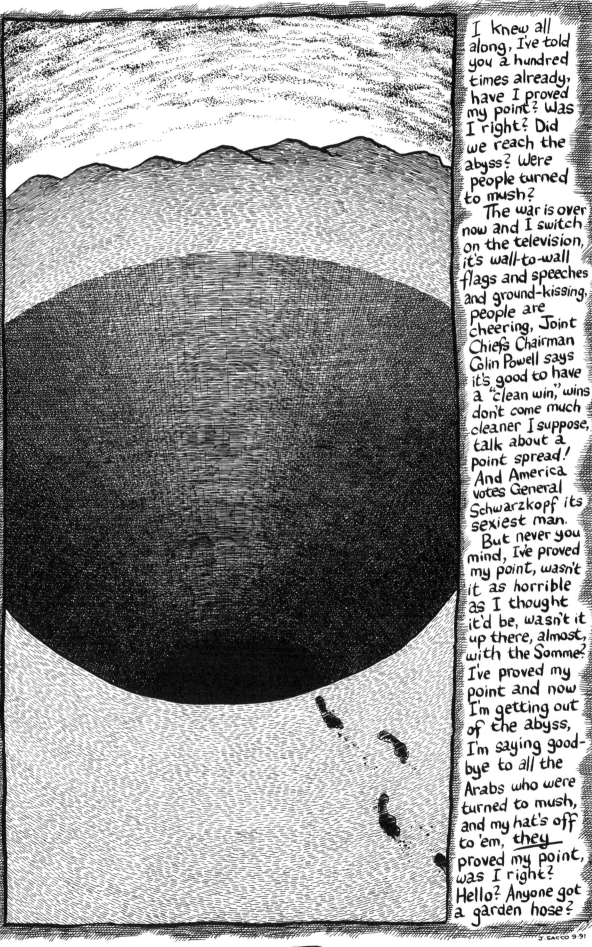

I knew all along, I've told you a hundred times already, have I proved my point? Was I right? Did we reach the abyss? Were people turned to mush?

The war is over now and I switch on the television, it's wall-to-wall flags and speeches and ground-kissing, people are cheering, Joint Chiefs Chairman Colin Powell says it's good to have a "clean win," wins don't come much cleaner I suppose, talk about a point spread! And America votes General Schwarzkopf its sexiest man.

But never you mind, I've proved my point, wasn't it as horrible as I thought it'd be, wasn't it up there, almost, with the Somme? I've proved my point and now I'm getting out of the abyss, I'm saying good-bye to all the Arabs who were turned to mush, and my hat's off to 'em, <u>they</u> proved my point, was I right? Hello? Anyone got a garden hose?

J. SACCO 9.91

People tend to prioritize catastrophes, a parking ticket can edge out 140,000 drowned Bangladeshis, some horrors make us cry while others make us cheer, and, incidentally, we're not all swimming in the same blood.

Goodbye to all that

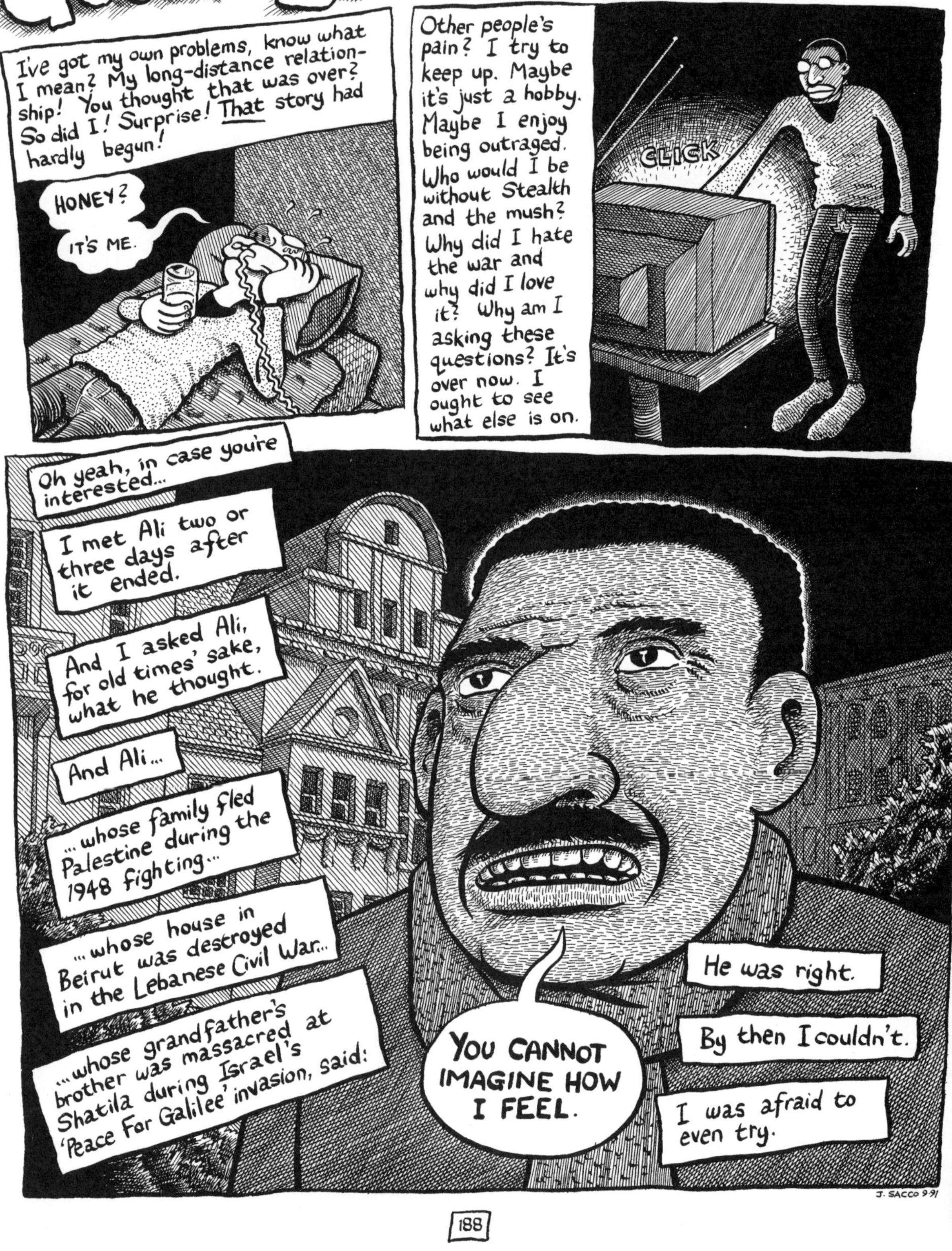

I've got my own problems, know what I mean? My long-distance relationship! You thought that was over? So did I! Surprise! That story had hardly begun!
HONEY?
IT'S ME.
Other people's pain? I try to keep up. Maybe it's just a hobby. Maybe I enjoy being outraged. Who would I be without Stealth and the mush? Why did I hate the war and why did I love it? Why am I asking these questions? It's over now. I ought to see what else is on.
CLICK
Oh yeah, in case you're interested...
I met Ali two or three days after it ended.
And I asked Ali, for old times' sake, what he thought.
And Ali...
...whose family fled Palestine during the 1948 fighting...
...whose house in Beirut was destroyed in the Lebanese Civil War...
...whose grandfather's brother was massacred at Shatila during Israel's 'Peace For Galilee' invasion, said:
YOU CANNOT IMAGINE HOW I FEEL.
He was right.
By then I couldn't.
I was afraid to even try.
J. SACCO 9·91

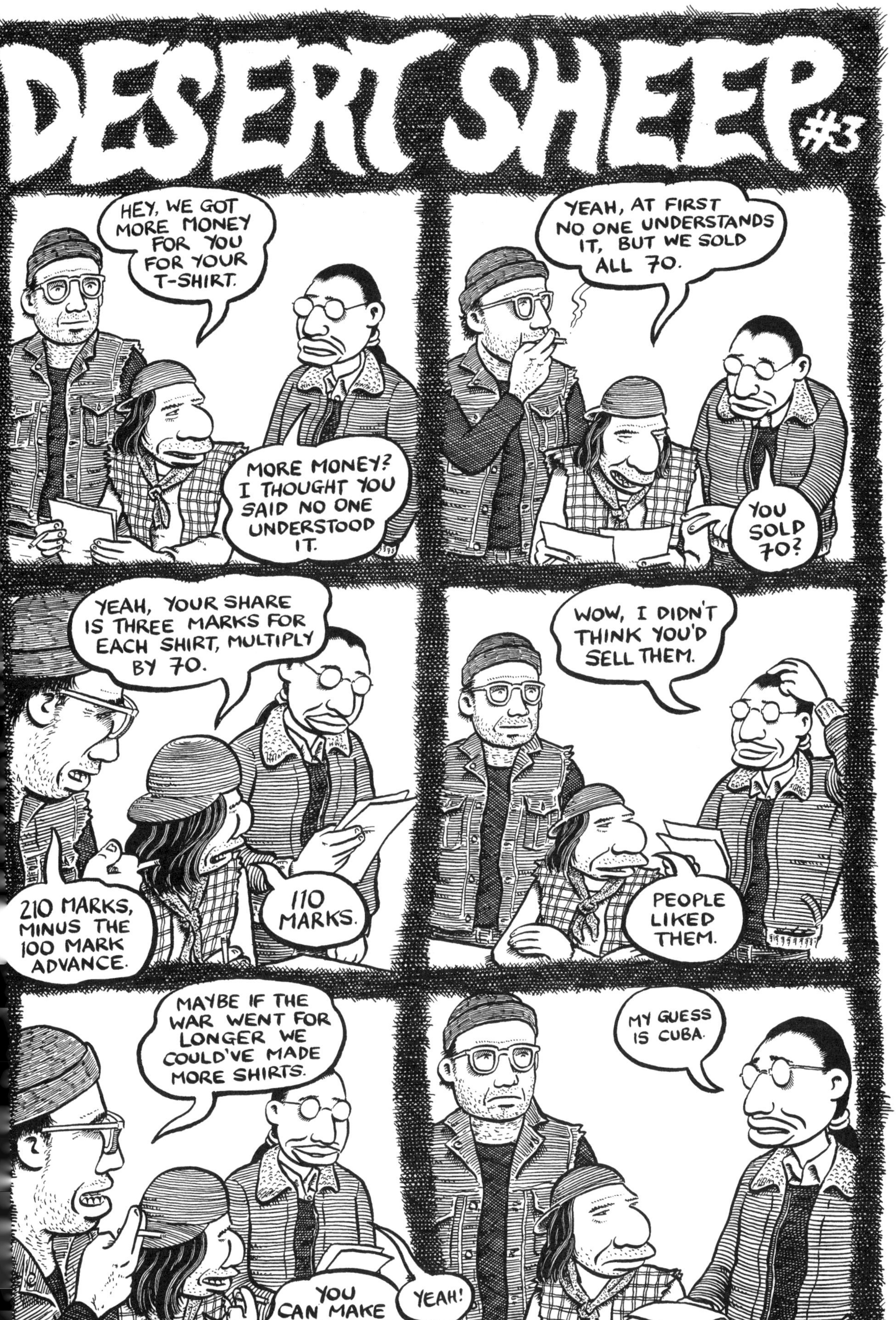
DESERT SHEEP #3
HEY, WE GOT MORE MONEY FOR YOU FOR YOUR T-SHIRT.
MORE MONEY? I THOUGHT YOU SAID NO ONE UNDERSTOOD IT.
YEAH, AT FIRST NO ONE UNDERSTANDS IT, BUT WE SOLD ALL 70.
YOU SOLD 70?
YEAH, YOUR SHARE IS THREE MARKS FOR EACH SHIRT, MULTIPLY BY 70.
210 MARKS, MINUS THE 100 MARK ADVANCE.
110 MARKS.
WOW, I DIDN'T THINK YOU'D SELL THEM.
PEOPLE LIKED THEM.
MAYBE IF THE WAR WENT FOR LONGER WE COULD'VE MADE MORE SHIRTS.
YOU CAN MAKE A SHIRT FOR THE NEXT WAR.
YEAH!
MY GUESS IS CUBA.
J. SACCO 9/91

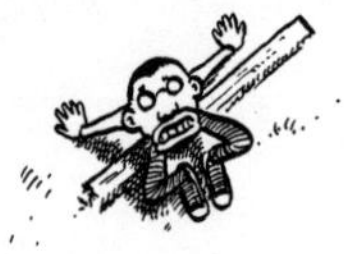

PART TEN:

EPILOGUE: ON MY DAY OFF

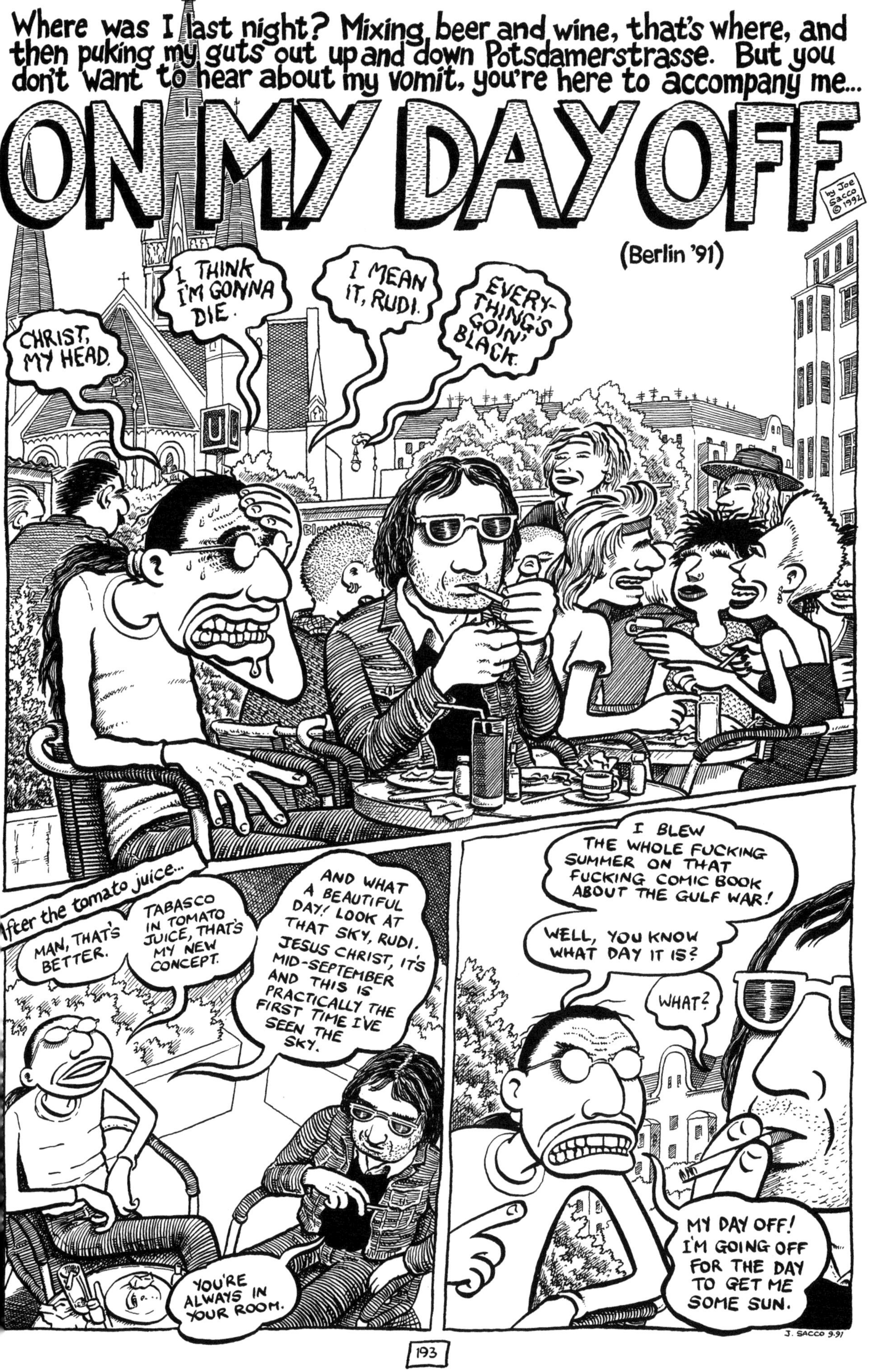
Where was I last night? Mixing beer and wine, that's where, and then puking my guts out up and down Potsdamerstrasse. But you don't want to hear about my vomit, you're here to accompany me...
ON MY DAY OFF
by Joe Sacco © 1992
(Berlin '91)
CHRIST, MY HEAD.
I THINK I'M GONNA DIE.
I MEAN IT, RUDI.
EVERY-THING'S GOIN' BLACK.
After the tomato juice...
MAN, THAT'S BETTER.
TABASCO IN TOMATO JUICE, THAT'S MY NEW CONCEPT.
AND WHAT A BEAUTIFUL DAY! LOOK AT THAT SKY, RUDI. JESUS CHRIST, IT'S MID-SEPTEMBER AND THIS IS PRACTICALLY THE FIRST TIME I'VE SEEN THE SKY.
YOU'RE ALWAYS IN YOUR ROOM.
I BLEW THE WHOLE FUCKING SUMMER ON THAT FUCKING COMIC BOOK ABOUT THE GULF WAR!
WELL, YOU KNOW WHAT DAY IT IS?
WHAT?
MY DAY OFF! I'M GOING OFF FOR THE DAY TO GET ME SOME SUN.
J. SACCO 9.91

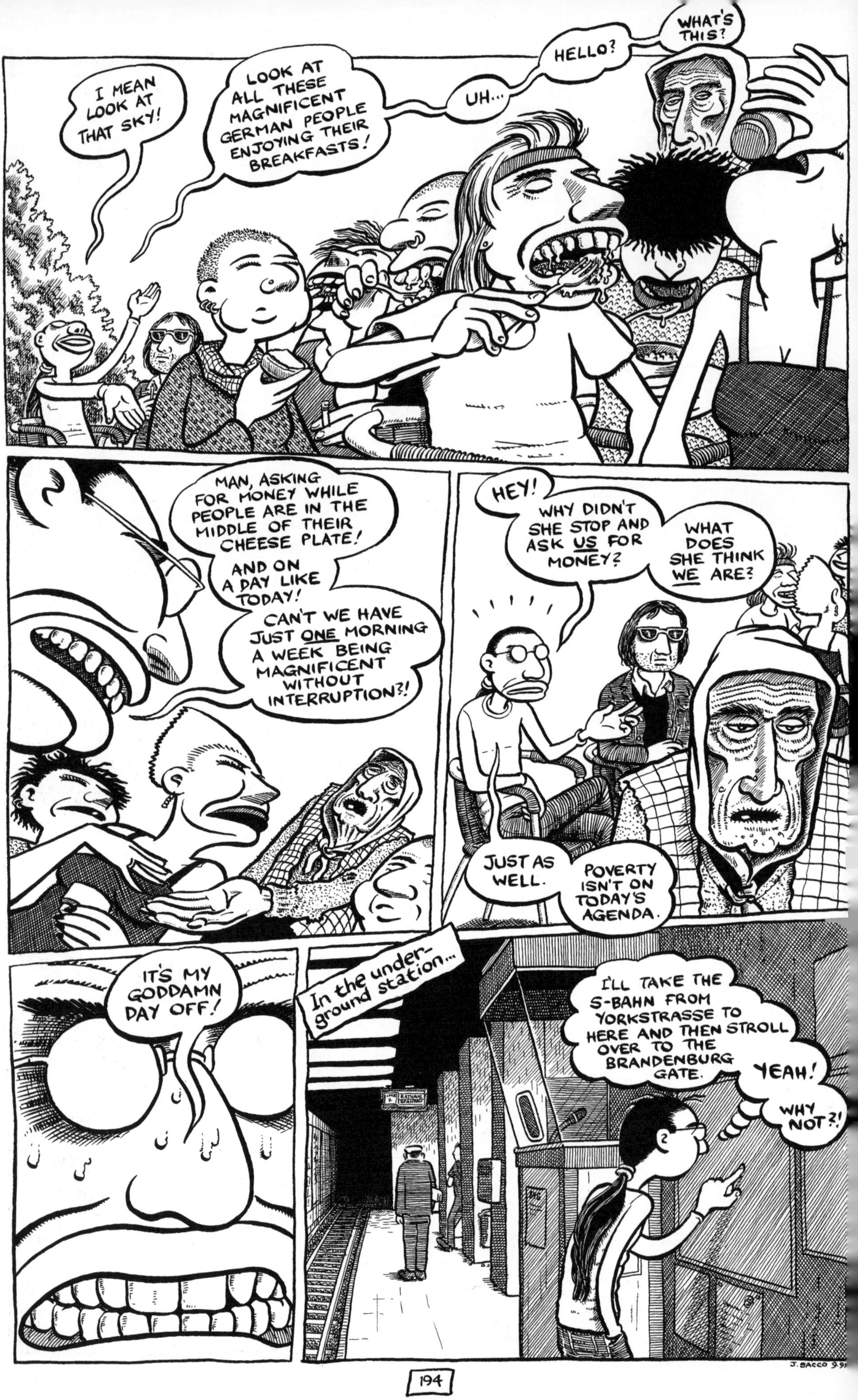
I MEAN LOOK AT THAT SKY!
LOOK AT ALL THESE MAGNIFICENT GERMAN PEOPLE ENJOYING THEIR BREAKFASTS!
UH...
HELLO?
WHAT'S THIS?
MAN, ASKING FOR MONEY WHILE PEOPLE ARE IN THE MIDDLE OF THEIR CHEESE PLATE!
AND ON A DAY LIKE TODAY!
CAN'T WE HAVE JUST ONE MORNING A WEEK BEING MAGNIFICENT WITHOUT INTERRUPTION?!
HEY!
WHY DIDN'T SHE STOP AND ASK US FOR MONEY?
WHAT DOES SHE THINK WE ARE?
JUST AS WELL.
POVERTY ISN'T ON TODAY'S AGENDA.
IT'S MY GODDAMN DAY OFF!
In the underground station...
I'LL TAKE THE S-BAHN FROM YORKSTRASSE TO HERE AND THEN STROLL OVER TO THE BRANDENBURG GATE.
YEAH!
WHY NOT?!
J. SACCO 9.91

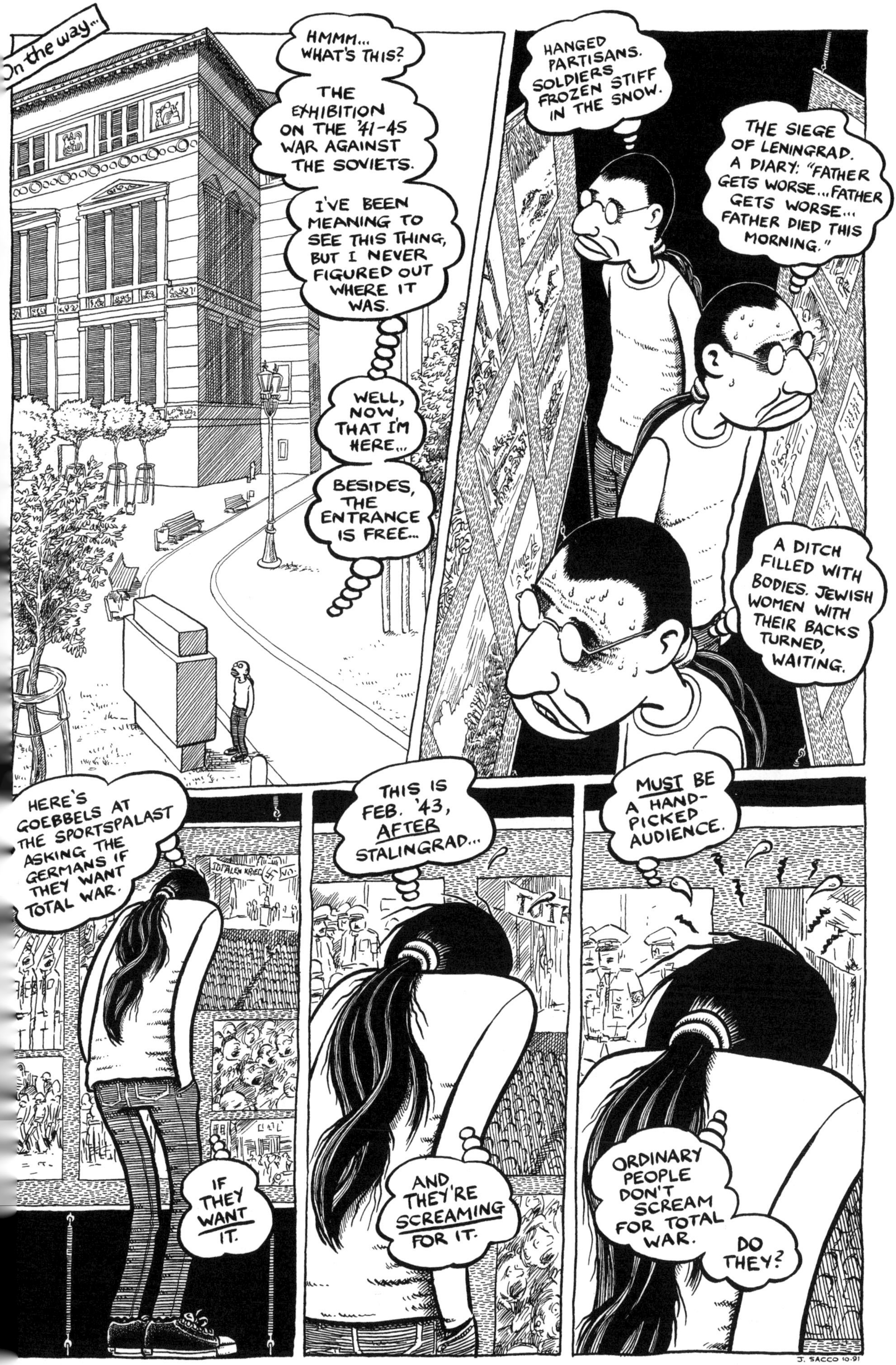
On the way...
HMMM... WHAT'S THIS?
THE EXHIBITION ON THE '41-45 WAR AGAINST THE SOVIETS.
I'VE BEEN MEANING TO SEE THIS THING, BUT I NEVER FIGURED OUT WHERE IT WAS.
WELL, NOW THAT I'M HERE...
BESIDES, THE ENTRANCE IS FREE...
HANGED PARTISANS. SOLDIERS FROZEN STIFF IN THE SNOW.
THE SIEGE OF LENINGRAD. A DIARY: "FATHER GETS WORSE... FATHER GETS WORSE... FATHER DIED THIS MORNING."
A DITCH FILLED WITH BODIES. JEWISH WOMEN WITH THEIR BACKS TURNED, WAITING.
HERE'S GOEBBELS AT THE SPORTSPALAST ASKING THE GERMANS IF THEY WANT TOTAL WAR.
IF THEY WANT IT.
THIS IS FEB. '43, AFTER STALINGRAD...
AND THEY'RE SCREAMING FOR IT.
MUST BE A HAND-PICKED AUDIENCE.
ORDINARY PEOPLE DON'T SCREAM FOR TOTAL WAR.
DO THEY?
J. SACCO 10.91

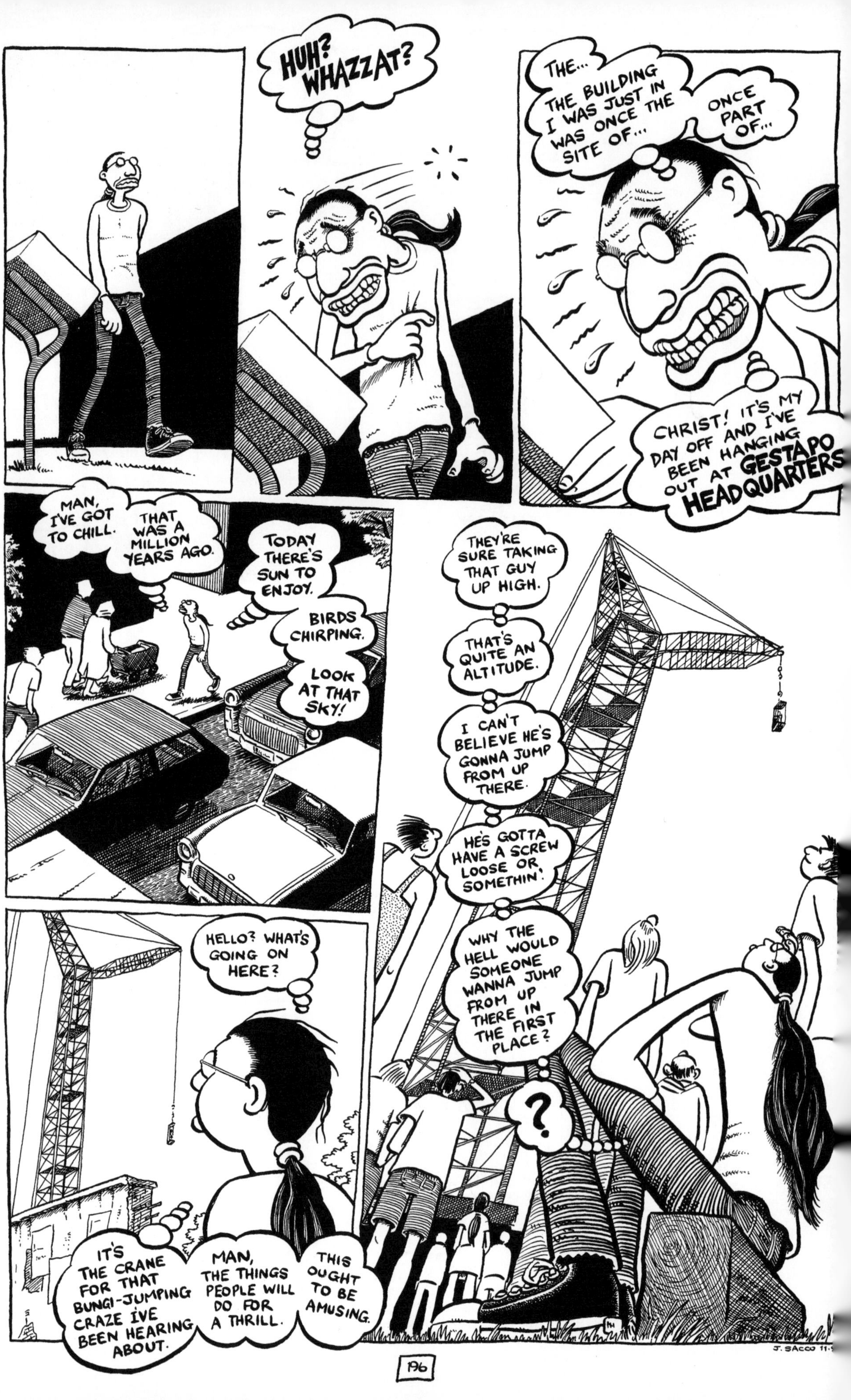
HUH? WHAZZAT?
THE... THE BUILDING I WAS JUST IN WAS ONCE THE SITE OF...
ONCE PART OF...
CHRIST! IT'S MY DAY OFF AND I'VE BEEN HANGING OUT AT GESTAPO HEADQUARTERS
MAN, I'VE GOT TO CHILL.
THAT WAS A MILLION YEARS AGO.
TODAY THERE'S SUN TO ENJOY.
BIRDS CHIRPING.
LOOK AT THAT SKY!
HELLO? WHAT'S GOING ON HERE?
IT'S THE CRANE FOR THAT BUNGI-JUMPING CRAZE I'VE BEEN HEARING ABOUT.
MAN, THE THINGS PEOPLE WILL DO FOR A THRILL.
THIS OUGHT TO BE AMUSING.
THEY'RE SURE TAKING THAT GUY UP HIGH.
THAT'S QUITE AN ALTITUDE.
I CAN'T BELIEVE HE'S GONNA JUMP FROM UP THERE.
HE'S GOTTA HAVE A SCREW LOOSE OR SOMETHIN'.
WHY THE HELL WOULD SOMEONE WANNA JUMP FROM UP THERE IN THE FIRST PLACE?
?
J. SACCO

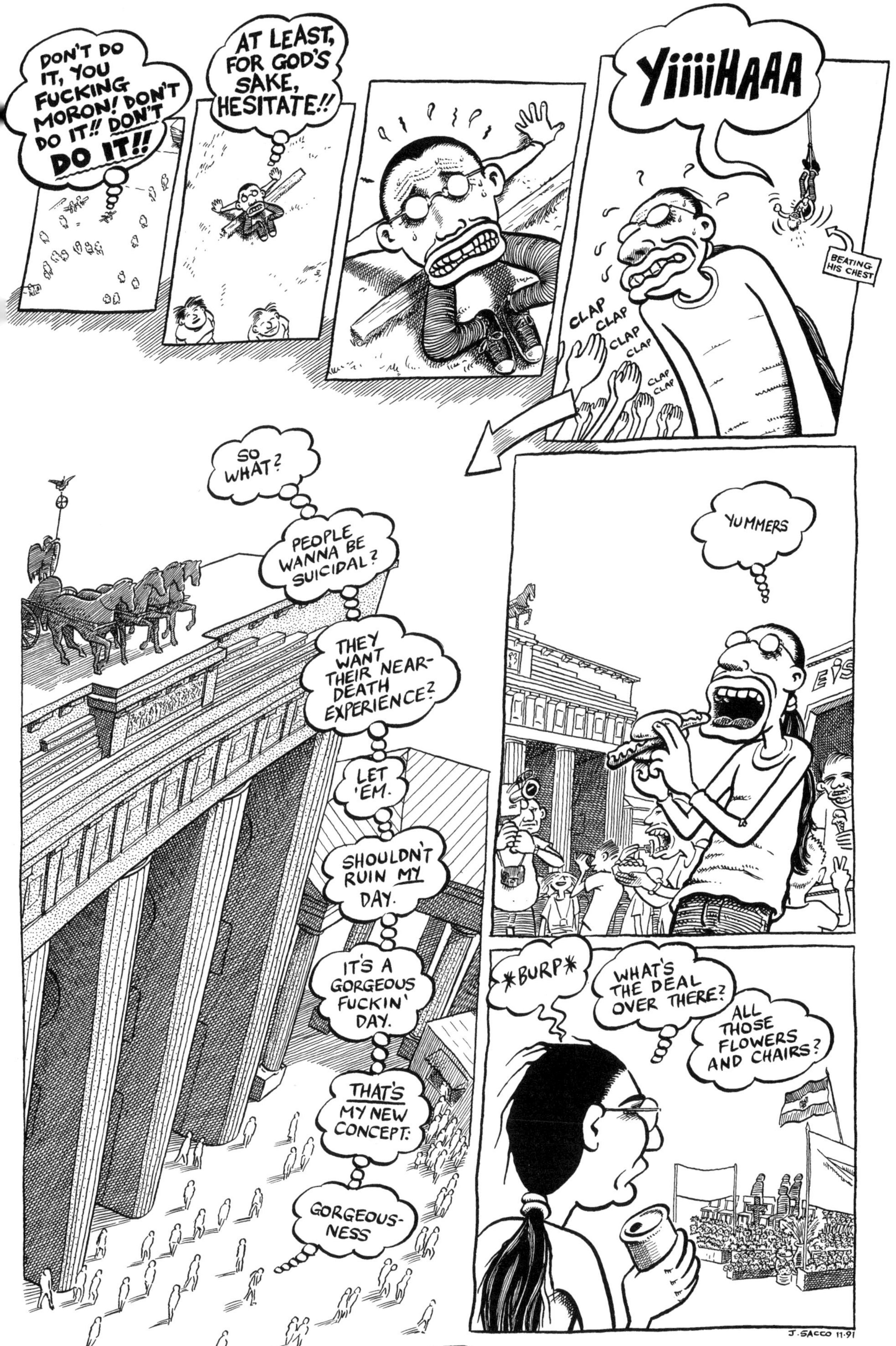
DON'T DO IT, YOU FUCKING MORON! DON'T DO IT!! DON'T DO IT!!
AT LEAST, FOR GOD'S SAKE, HESITATE!!
YiiiiHAAA
BEATING HIS CHEST
CLAP CLAP CLAP CLAP CLAP CLAP
SO WHAT?
PEOPLE WANNA BE SUICIDAL?
THEY WANT THEIR NEAR-DEATH EXPERIENCE?
LET 'EM.
SHOULDN'T RUIN MY DAY.
IT'S A GORGEOUS FUCKIN' DAY.
THAT'S MY NEW CONCEPT:
GORGEOUS-NESS
YUMMERS
BURP
WHAT'S THE DEAL OVER THERE?
ALL THOSE FLOWERS AND CHAIRS?
J. SACCO 11·91

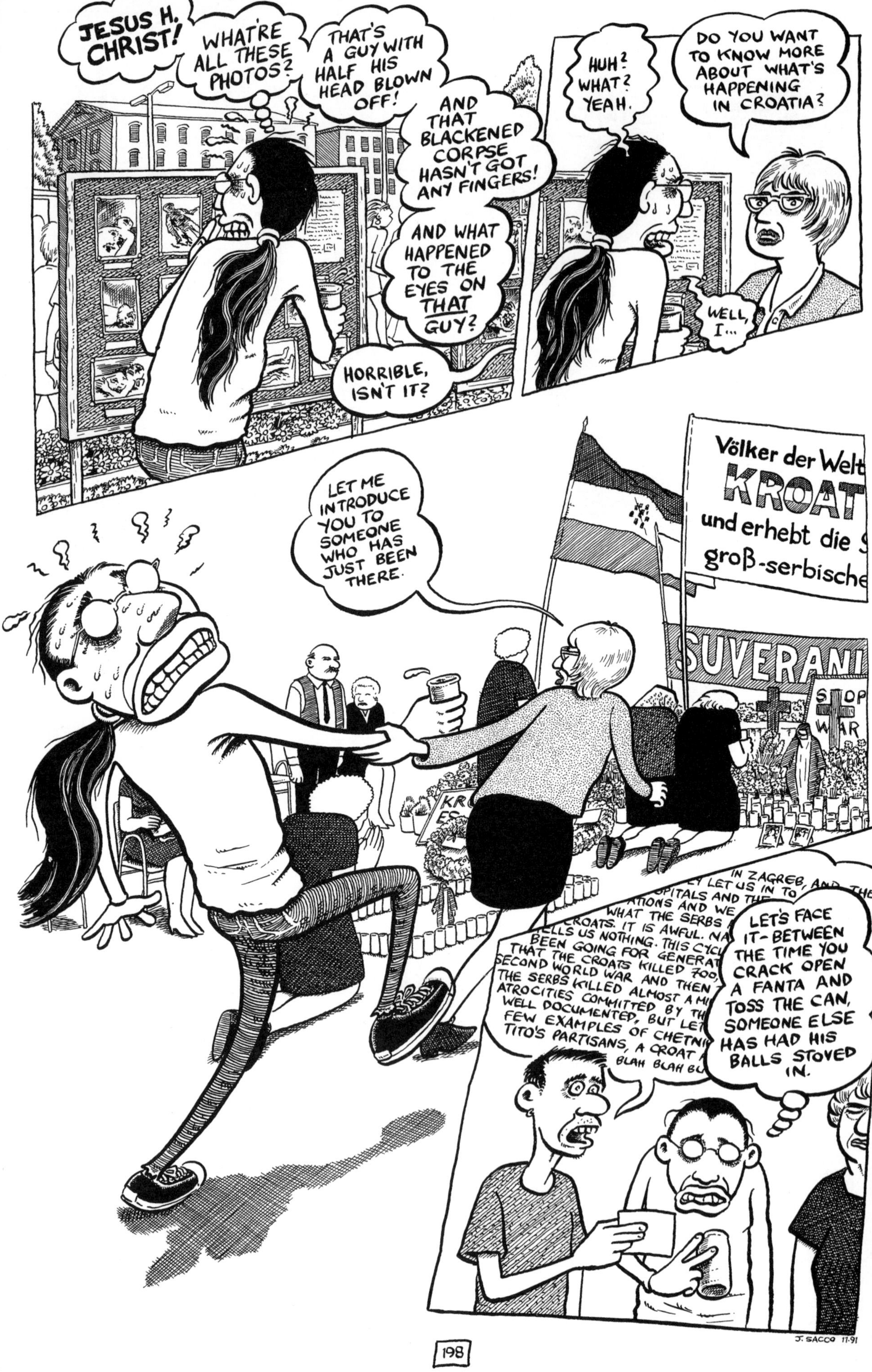
JESUS H. CHRIST!
WHAT'RE ALL THESE PHOTOS?
THAT'S A GUY WITH HALF HIS HEAD BLOWN OFF!
AND THAT BLACKENED CORPSE HASN'T GOT ANY FINGERS!
AND WHAT HAPPENED TO THE EYES ON THAT GUY?
HORRIBLE, ISN'T IT?
HUH? WHAT? YEAH.
DO YOU WANT TO KNOW MORE ABOUT WHAT'S HAPPENING IN CROATIA?
WELL, I...
Völker der Welt
KROAT
und erhebt die
groß-serbische
SUVERANI
STOP WAR
LET ME INTRODUCE YOU TO SOMEONE WHO HAS JUST BEEN THERE.
IN ZAGREB, AND
LET US IN TO
PITALS AND
ATIONS AND WE
WHAT THE SERBS
CROATS. IT IS AWFUL.
US NOTHING. THIS
BEEN GOING FOR
THAT THE CROATS KILLED
SECOND WORLD WAR AND THEN
THE SERBS KILLED ALMOST A
ATROCITIES COMMITTED BY
WELL DOCUMENTED, BUT
FEW EXAMPLES OF
TITO'S PARTISANS, A CROAT
BLAH BLAH
LET'S FACE IT- BETWEEN THE TIME YOU CRACK OPEN A FANTA AND TOSS THE CAN, SOMEONE ELSE HAS HAD HIS BALLS STOVED IN.
J. SACCO 11.91

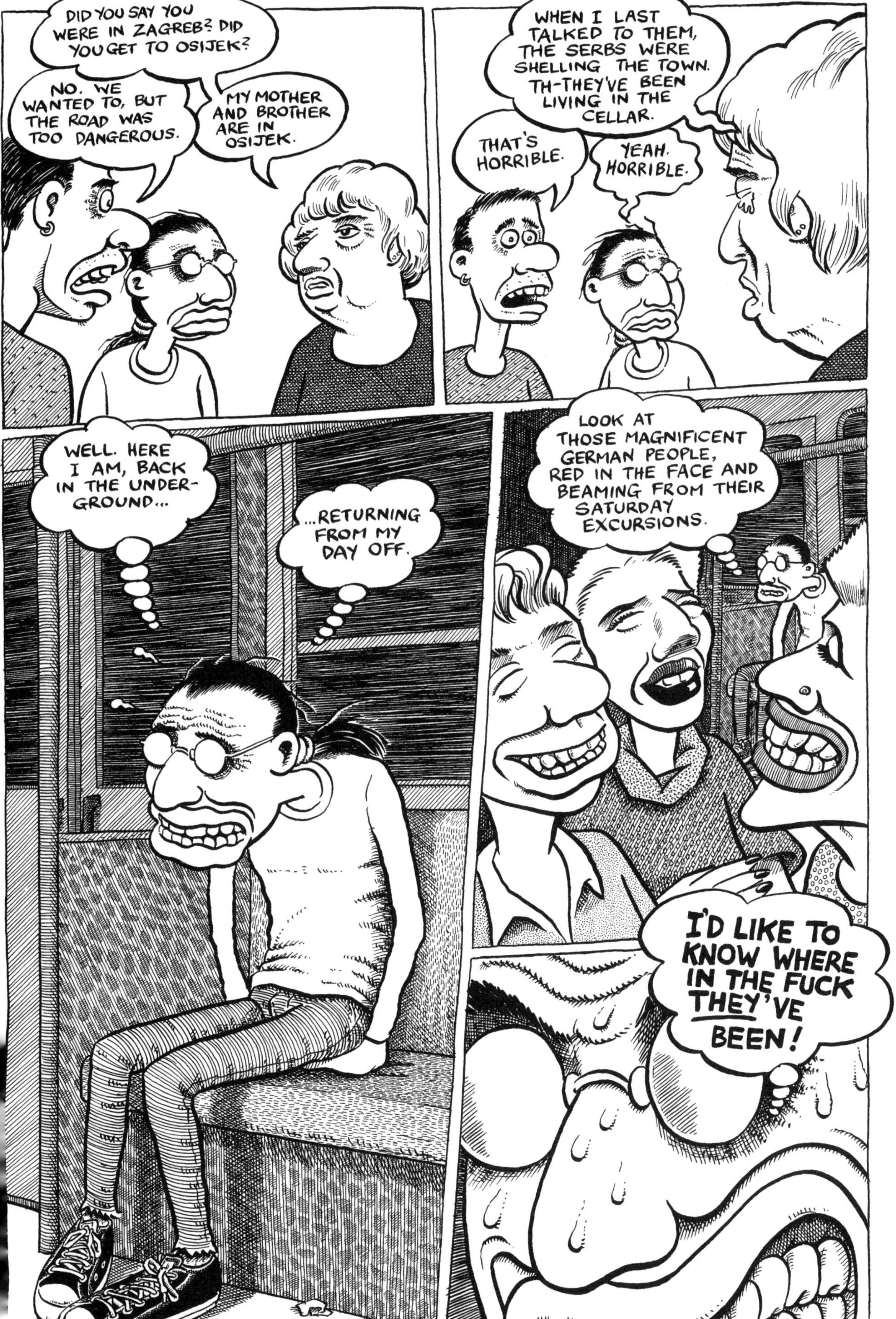
DID YOU SAY YOU WERE IN ZAGREB? DID YOU GET TO OSIJEK?
NO. WE WANTED TO, BUT THE ROAD WAS TOO DANGEROUS.
MY MOTHER AND BROTHER ARE IN OSIJEK.
WHEN I LAST TALKED TO THEM, THE SERBS WERE SHELLING THE TOWN. TH-THEY'VE BEEN LIVING IN THE CELLAR.
THAT'S HORRIBLE.
YEAH. HORRIBLE.
WELL. HERE I AM, BACK IN THE UNDER-GROUND...
...RETURNING FROM MY DAY OFF.
LOOK AT THOSE MAGNIFICENT GERMAN PEOPLE, RED IN THE FACE AND BEAMING FROM THEIR SATURDAY EXCURSIONS.
I'D LIKE TO KNOW WHERE IN THE FUCK THEY'VE BEEN!
J. SACCO 11-91

NOTE FROM A DEFEATIST:
APOCRYPHA

APOCRYPHA:
INTRODUCTION

I just got back from Paris. And I found things here at Fantagraphics Books in some disorder. I'd left the organization of this latest collection in what I thought were capable hands, but what do I find? Mutiny! My own publisher — Kim Thompson is his name — waits till I'm tied up in Paris to start rearranging things to his own liking, completely ignoring the instructions I'd left on several Post-It notes. He's gone and done things his own way. Now he tells me it's too late to switch things back because it would ruin something called "pagination." Since when does "pagination" stand in the way of art? But I'm having the last laugh. I'm including the following pages no matter what Mr. Kim Thompson says. Frankly, he wanted to drop the following pages because he thinks they stink. Well, what does it matter to me whether they stink or not? What's at issue here is power, and my First Amendment right to have things my way because I make more money than Mr. Kim Thompson does. I'm sure you agree.

Joe Sacco
Nov. 2002

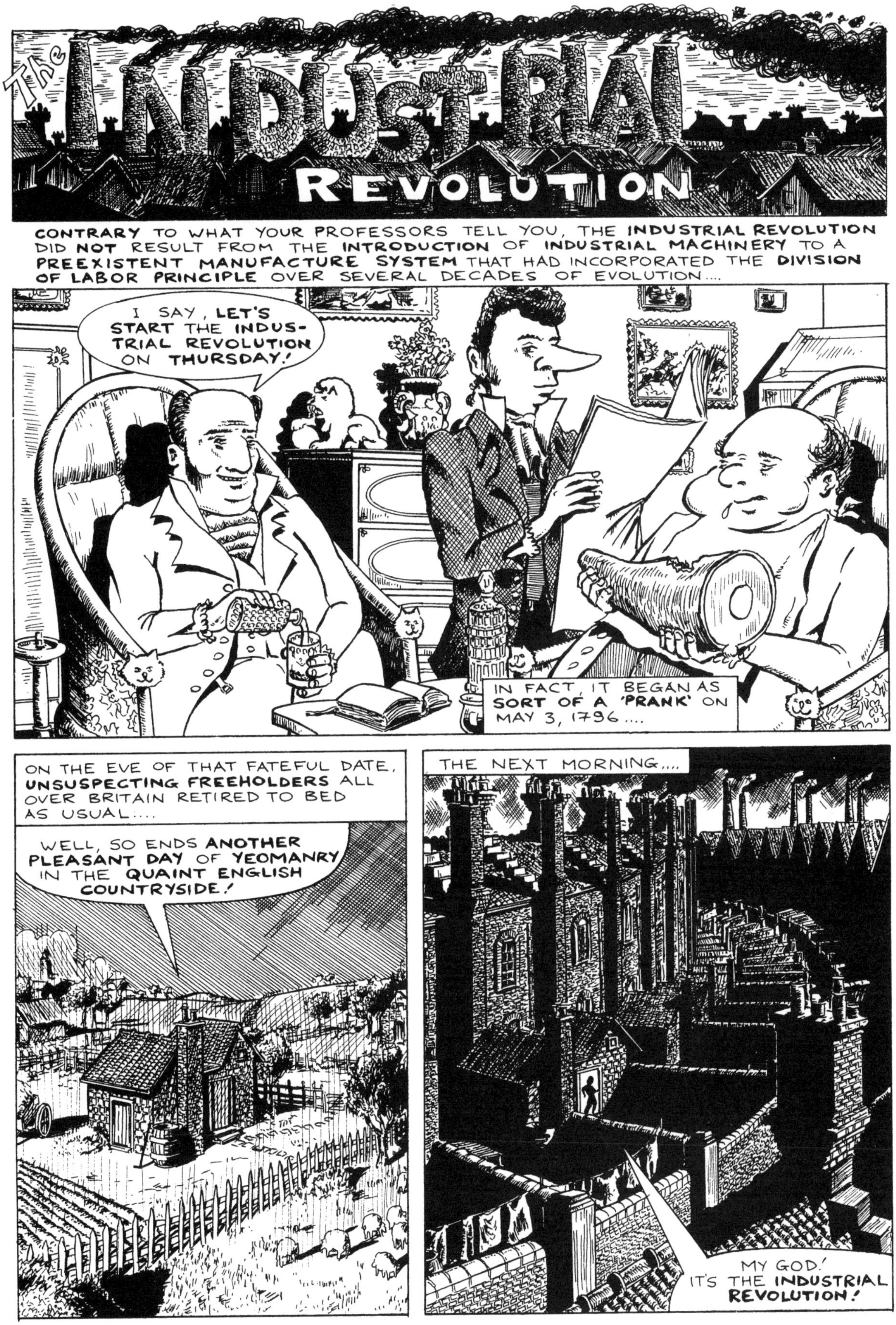
The INDUSTRIAL REVOLUTION
CONTRARY TO WHAT YOUR PROFESSORS TELL YOU, THE INDUSTRIAL REVOLUTION DID NOT RESULT FROM THE INTRODUCTION OF INDUSTRIAL MACHINERY TO A PREEXISTENT MANUFACTURE SYSTEM THAT HAD INCORPORATED THE DIVISION OF LABOR PRINCIPLE OVER SEVERAL DECADES OF EVOLUTION....
I SAY, LET'S START THE INDUSTRIAL REVOLUTION ON THURSDAY!
IN FACT, IT BEGAN AS SORT OF A 'PRANK' ON MAY 3, 1796....
ON THE EVE OF THAT FATEFUL DATE, UNSUSPECTING FREEHOLDERS ALL OVER BRITAIN RETIRED TO BED AS USUAL....
WELL, SO ENDS ANOTHER PLEASANT DAY OF YEOMANRY IN THE QUAINT ENGLISH COUNTRYSIDE!
THE NEXT MORNING....
MY GOD! IT'S THE INDUSTRIAL REVOLUTION!

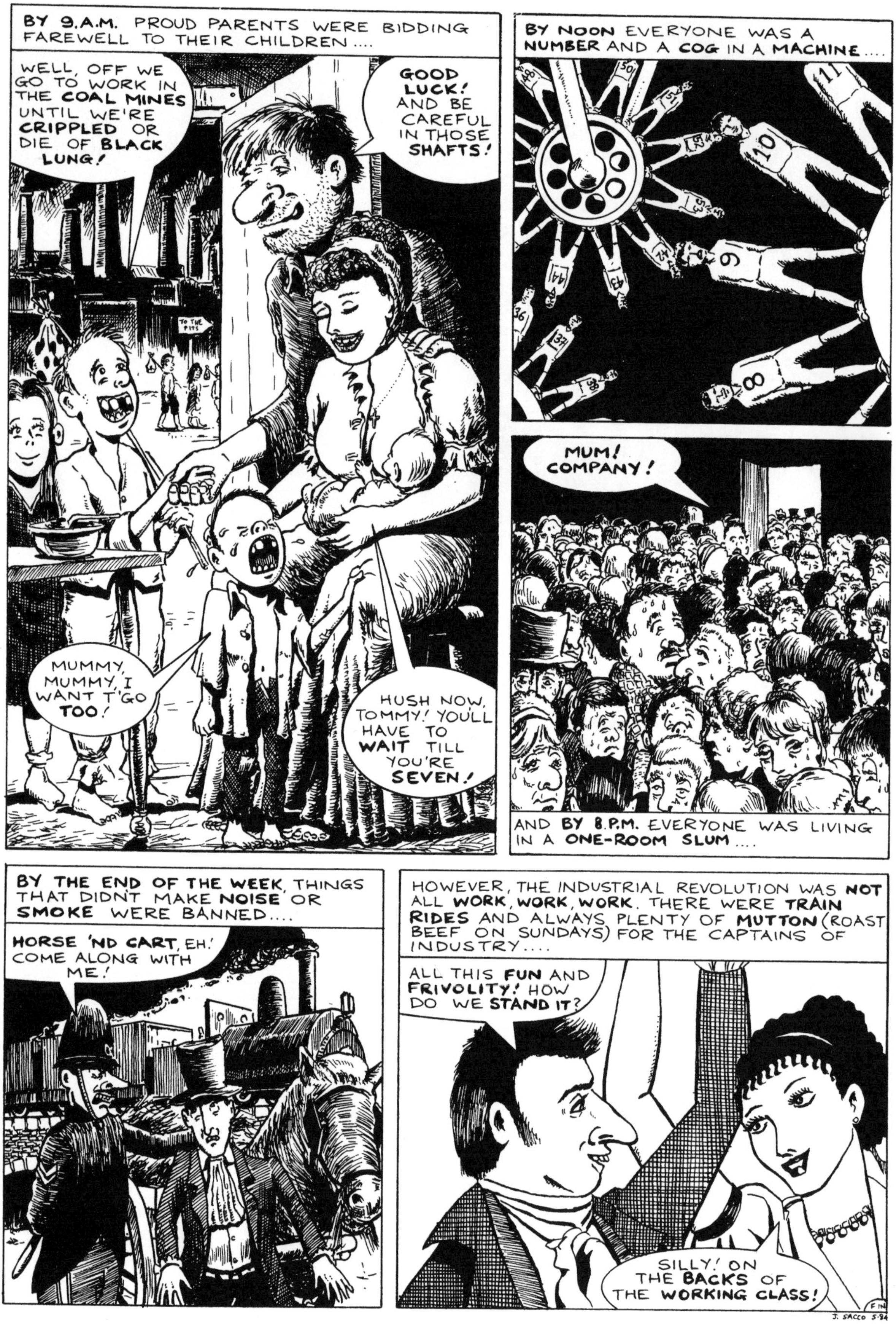
BY 9.A.M. PROUD PARENTS WERE BIDDING FAREWELL TO THEIR CHILDREN....
WELL, OFF WE GO TO WORK IN THE COAL MINES UNTIL WE'RE CRIPPLED OR DIE OF BLACK LUNG!
GOOD LUCK! AND BE CAREFUL IN THOSE SHAFTS!
TO THE PITS
MUMMY, MUMMY, I WANT T'GO TOO!
HUSH NOW, TOMMY! YOU'LL HAVE TO WAIT TILL YOU'RE SEVEN!
BY NOON EVERYONE WAS A NUMBER AND A COG IN A MACHINE....
MUM! COMPANY!
AND BY 8.P.M. EVERYONE WAS LIVING IN A ONE-ROOM SLUM....
BY THE END OF THE WEEK, THINGS THAT DIDN'T MAKE NOISE OR SMOKE WERE BANNED....
HORSE 'ND CART, EH! COME ALONG WITH ME!
HOWEVER, THE INDUSTRIAL REVOLUTION WAS NOT ALL WORK, WORK, WORK. THERE WERE TRAIN RIDES AND ALWAYS PLENTY OF MUTTON (ROAST BEEF ON SUNDAYS) FOR THE CAPTAINS OF INDUSTRY....
ALL THIS FUN AND FRIVOLITY! HOW DO WE STAND IT?
SILLY! ON THE BACKS OF THE WORKING CLASS!
FIN
J. SACCO 5·84

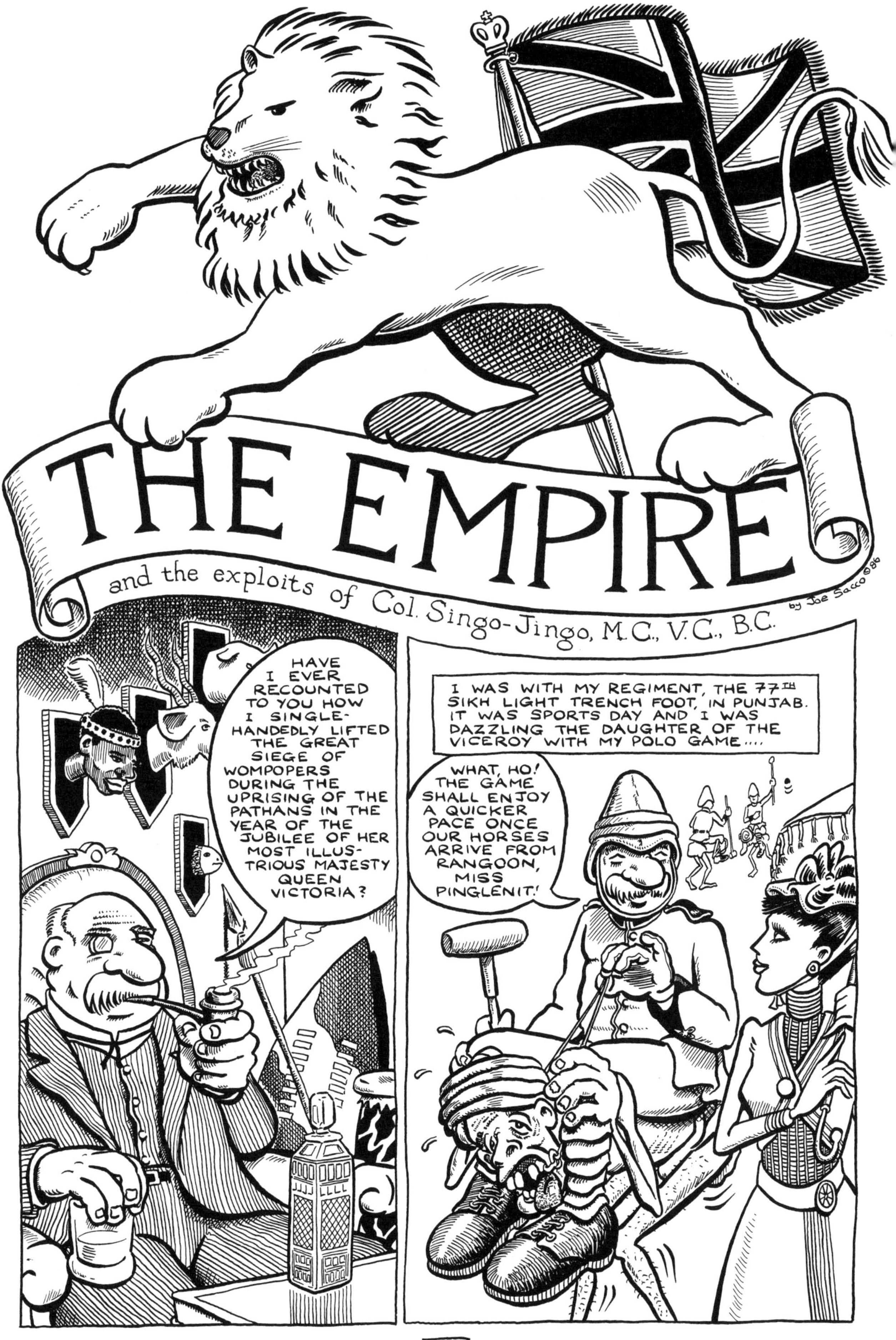
THE EMPIRE
and the exploits of Col. Singo-Jingo, M.C., V.C., B.C.
by Joe Sacco ©86
HAVE I EVER RECOUNTED TO YOU HOW I SINGLE-HANDEDLY LIFTED THE GREAT SIEGE OF WOMPOPERS DURING THE UPRISING OF THE PATHANS IN THE YEAR OF THE JUBILEE OF HER MOST ILLUSTRIOUS MAJESTY QUEEN VICTORIA?
I WAS WITH MY REGIMENT, THE 77TH SIKH LIGHT TRENCH FOOT, IN PUNJAB. IT WAS SPORTS DAY AND I WAS DAZZLING THE DAUGHTER OF THE VICEROY WITH MY POLO GAME....
WHAT, HO! THE GAME SHALL ENJOY A QUICKER PACE ONCE OUR HORSES ARRIVE FROM RANGOON, MISS PINGLENIT!

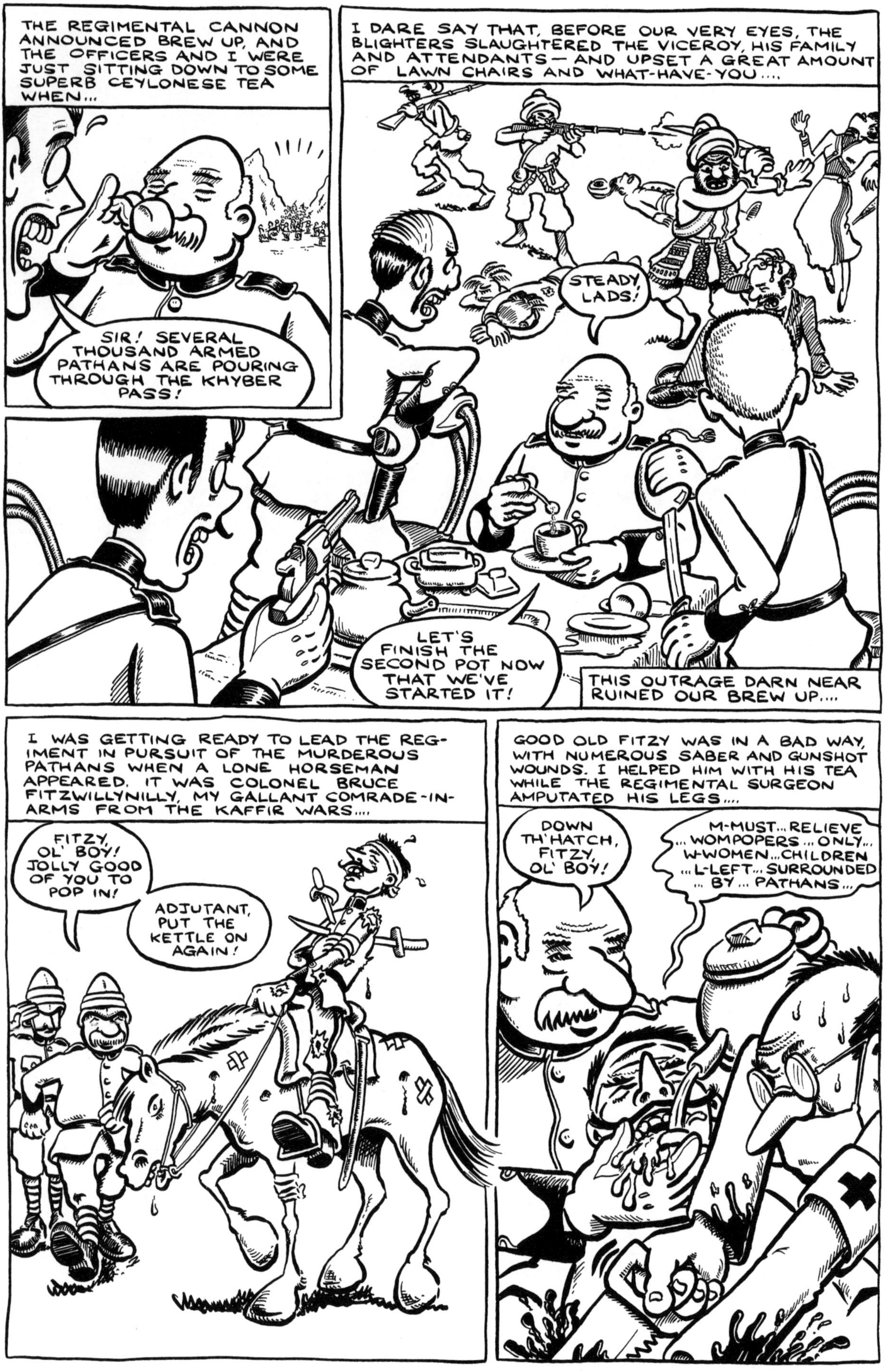
THE REGIMENTAL CANNON ANNOUNCED BREW UP, AND THE OFFICERS AND I WERE JUST SITTING DOWN TO SOME SUPERB CEYLONESE TEA WHEN...
SIR! SEVERAL THOUSAND ARMED PATHANS ARE POURING THROUGH THE KHYBER PASS!
I DARE SAY THAT, BEFORE OUR VERY EYES, THE BLIGHTERS SLAUGHTERED THE VICEROY, HIS FAMILY AND ATTENDANTS— AND UPSET A GREAT AMOUNT OF LAWN CHAIRS AND WHAT-HAVE-YOU....
STEADY LADS!
LET'S FINISH THE SECOND POT NOW THAT WE'VE STARTED IT!
THIS OUTRAGE DARN NEAR RUINED OUR BREW UP....
I WAS GETTING READY TO LEAD THE REGIMENT IN PURSUIT OF THE MURDEROUS PATHANS WHEN A LONE HORSEMAN APPEARED. IT WAS COLONEL BRUCE FITZWILLYNILLY, MY GALLANT COMRADE-IN-ARMS FROM THE KAFFIR WARS....
FITZY, OL' BOY! JOLLY GOOD OF YOU TO POP IN!
ADJUTANT, PUT THE KETTLE ON AGAIN!
GOOD OLD FITZY WAS IN A BAD WAY, WITH NUMEROUS SABER AND GUNSHOT WOUNDS. I HELPED HIM WITH HIS TEA WHILE THE REGIMENTAL SURGEON AMPUTATED HIS LEGS....
DOWN TH'HATCH, FITZY, OL' BOY!
M-MUST... RELIEVE ... WOMPOPERS ... ONLY... W-WOMEN... CHILDREN ... L-LEFT... SURROUNDED ... BY... PATHANS...

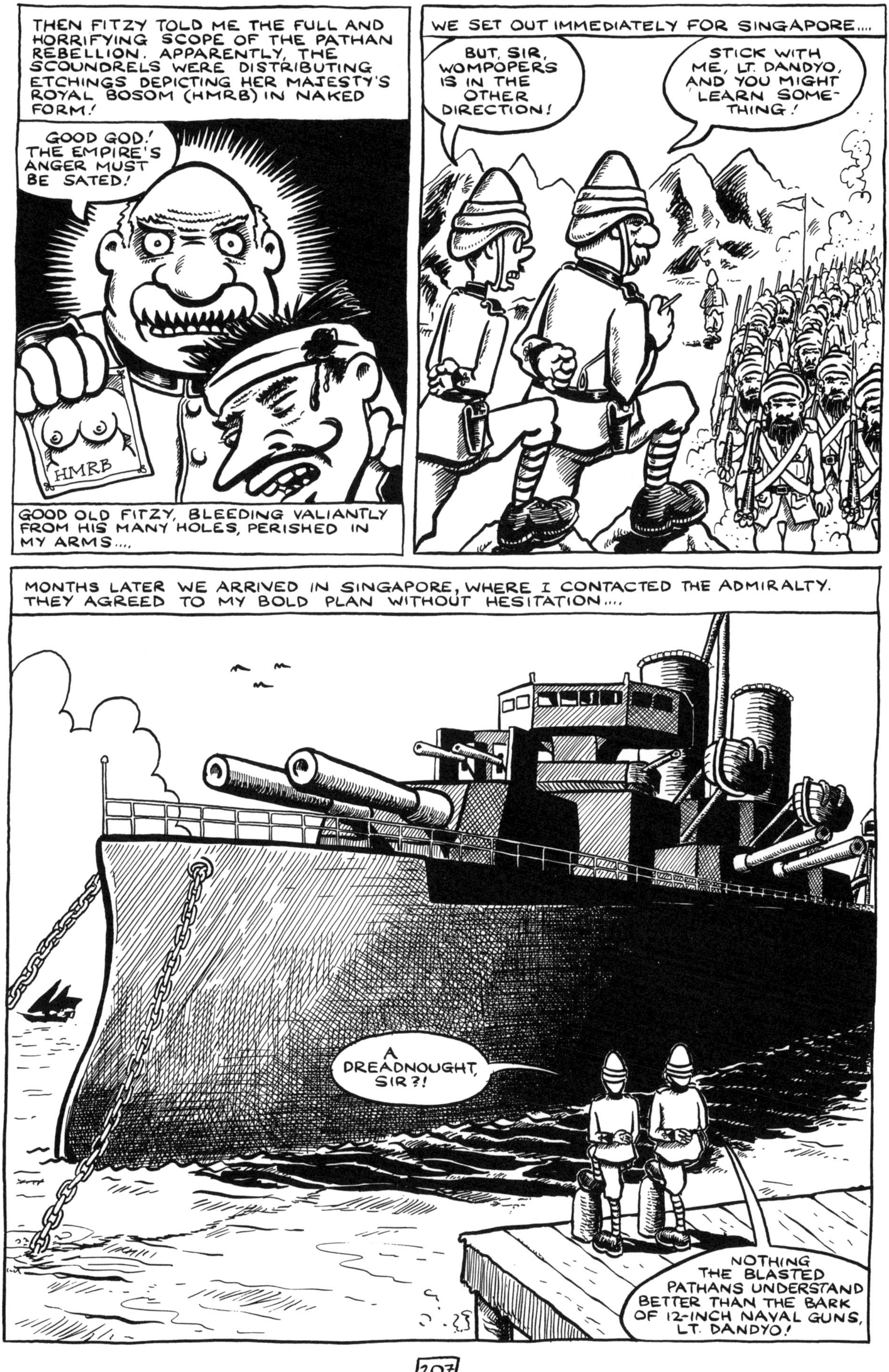
THEN FITZY TOLD ME THE FULL AND HORRIFYING SCOPE OF THE PATHAN REBELLION. APPARENTLY, THE SCOUNDRELS WERE DISTRIBUTING ETCHINGS DEPICTING HER MAJESTY'S ROYAL BOSOM (HMRB) IN NAKED FORM!
GOOD GOD! THE EMPIRE'S ANGER MUST BE SATED!
HMRB
GOOD OLD FITZY, BLEEDING VALIANTLY FROM HIS MANY HOLES, PERISHED IN MY ARMS....
WE SET OUT IMMEDIATELY FOR SINGAPORE....
BUT, SIR, WOMPOPERS IS IN THE OTHER DIRECTION!
STICK WITH ME, LT. DANDYO, AND YOU MIGHT LEARN SOMETHING!
MONTHS LATER WE ARRIVED IN SINGAPORE, WHERE I CONTACTED THE ADMIRALTY. THEY AGREED TO MY BOLD PLAN WITHOUT HESITATION....
A DREADNOUGHT, SIR?!
NOTHING THE BLASTED PATHANS UNDERSTAND BETTER THAN THE BARK OF 12-INCH NAVAL GUNS, LT. DANDYO!

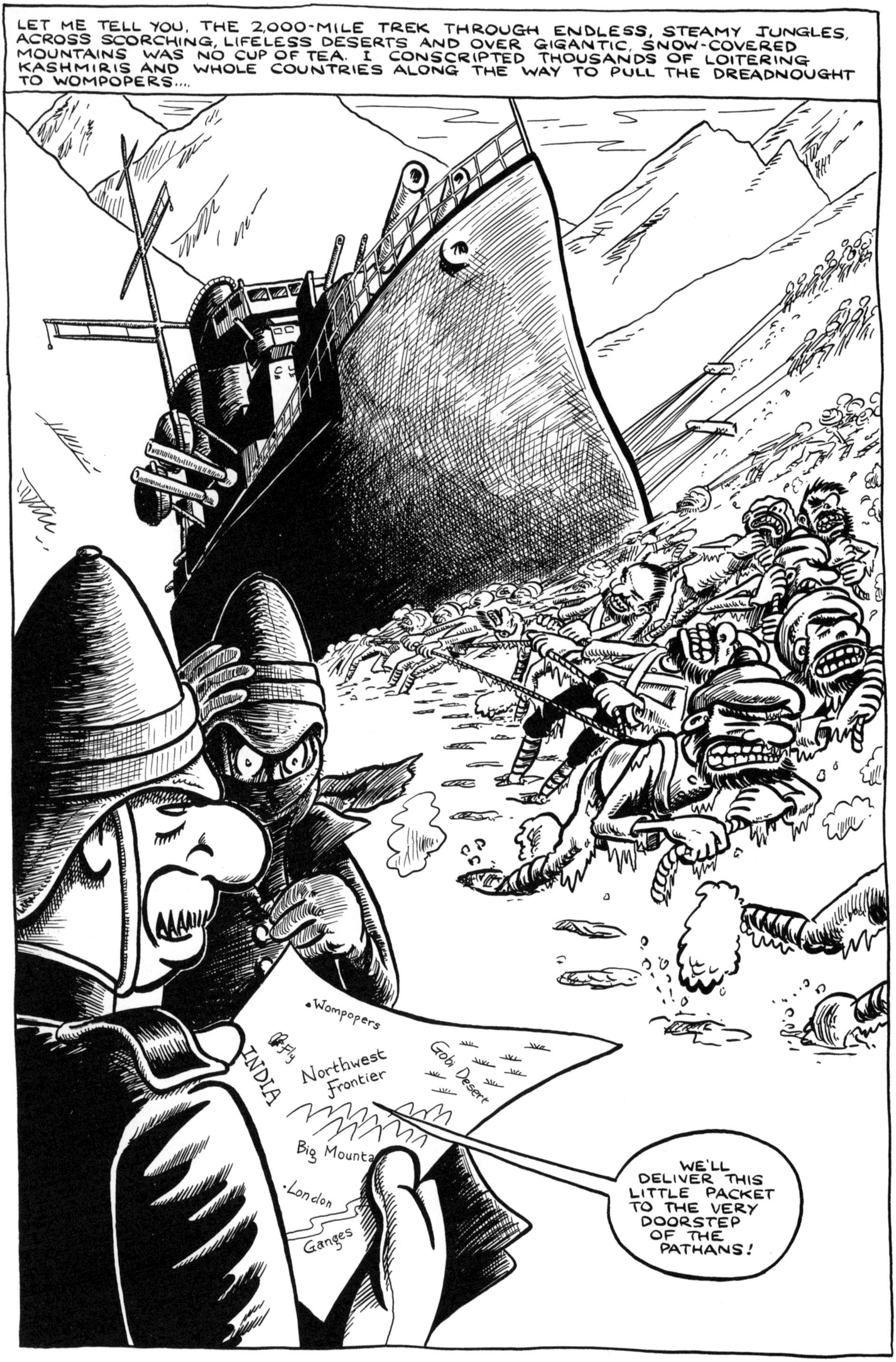
LET ME TELL YOU, THE 2,000-MILE TREK THROUGH ENDLESS, STEAMY JUNGLES, ACROSS SCORCHING, LIFELESS DESERTS AND OVER GIGANTIC, SNOW-COVERED MOUNTAINS WAS NO CUP OF TEA. I CONSCRIPTED THOUSANDS OF LOITERING KASHMIRIS AND WHOLE COUNTRIES ALONG THE WAY TO PULL THE DREADNOUGHT TO WOMPOPERS....
Wompopers
Fly
INDIA
Northwest Frontier
Gobi Desert
Big Mounta
London
Ganges
WE'LL DELIVER THIS LITTLE PACKET TO THE VERY DOORSTEP OF THE PATHANS!

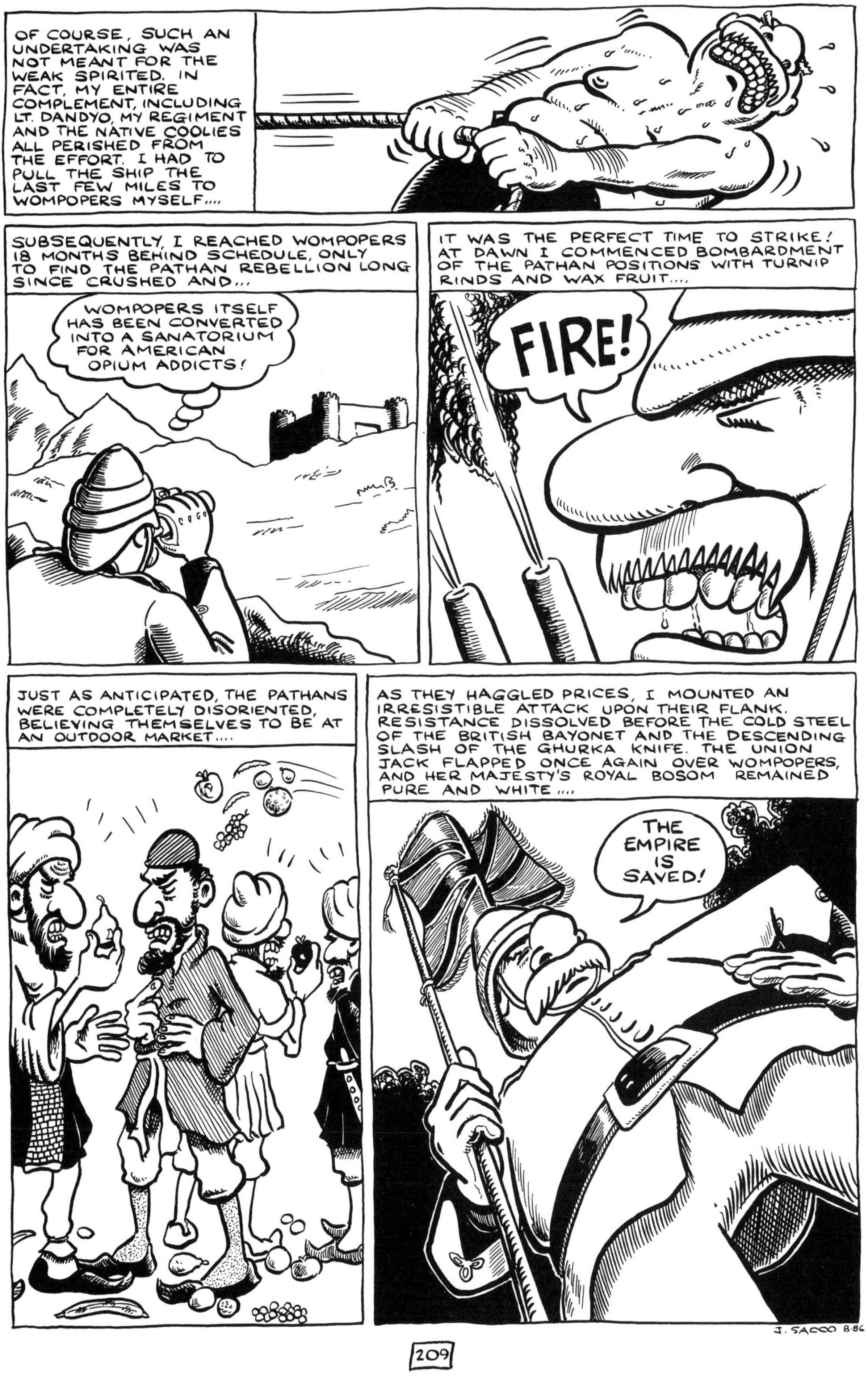
OF COURSE, SUCH AN UNDERTAKING WAS NOT MEANT FOR THE WEAK SPIRITED. IN FACT, MY ENTIRE COMPLEMENT, INCLUDING LT. DANDYO, MY REGIMENT AND THE NATIVE COOLIES ALL PERISHED FROM THE EFFORT. I HAD TO PULL THE SHIP THE LAST FEW MILES TO WOMPOPERS MYSELF....
SUBSEQUENTLY, I REACHED WOMPOPERS 18 MONTHS BEHIND SCHEDULE, ONLY TO FIND THE PATHAN REBELLION LONG SINCE CRUSHED AND...
WOMPOPERS ITSELF HAS BEEN CONVERTED INTO A SANATORIUM FOR AMERICAN OPIUM ADDICTS!
IT WAS THE PERFECT TIME TO STRIKE! AT DAWN I COMMENCED BOMBARDMENT OF THE PATHAN POSITIONS WITH TURNIP RINDS AND WAX FRUIT....
FIRE!
JUST AS ANTICIPATED, THE PATHANS WERE COMPLETELY DISORIENTED, BELIEVING THEMSELVES TO BE AT AN OUTDOOR MARKET....
AS THEY HAGGLED PRICES, I MOUNTED AN IRRESISTIBLE ATTACK UPON THEIR FLANK. RESISTANCE DISSOLVED BEFORE THE COLD STEEL OF THE BRITISH BAYONET AND THE DESCENDING SLASH OF THE GHURKA KNIFE. THE UNION JACK FLAPPED ONCE AGAIN OVER WOMPOPERS, AND HER MAJESTY'S ROYAL BOSOM REMAINED PURE AND WHITE....
THE EMPIRE IS SAVED!
J. SACCO 8.86

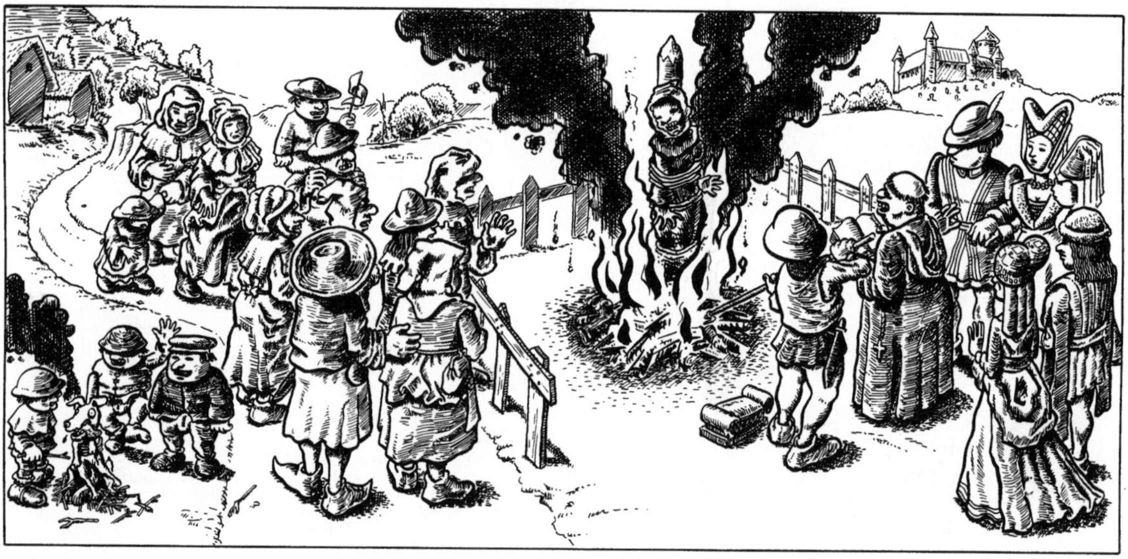

The Buffoon's Tale

BY SACCO
(AFTER BRUEGHEL)
© 86-87

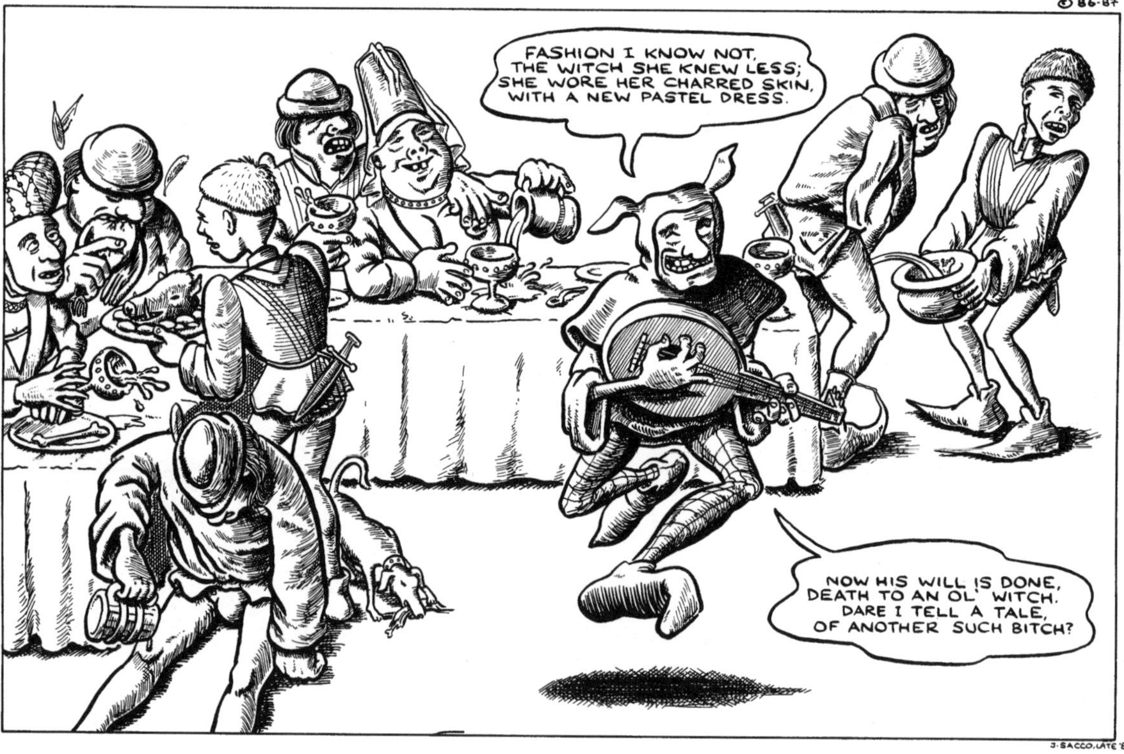
FASHION I KNOW NOT, THE WITCH SHE KNEW LESS; SHE WORE HER CHARRED SKIN, WITH A NEW PASTEL DRESS.
NOW HIS WILL IS DONE, DEATH TO AN OL' WITCH. DARE I TELL A TALE, OF ANOTHER SUCH BITCH?

J. SACCO, LATE '86

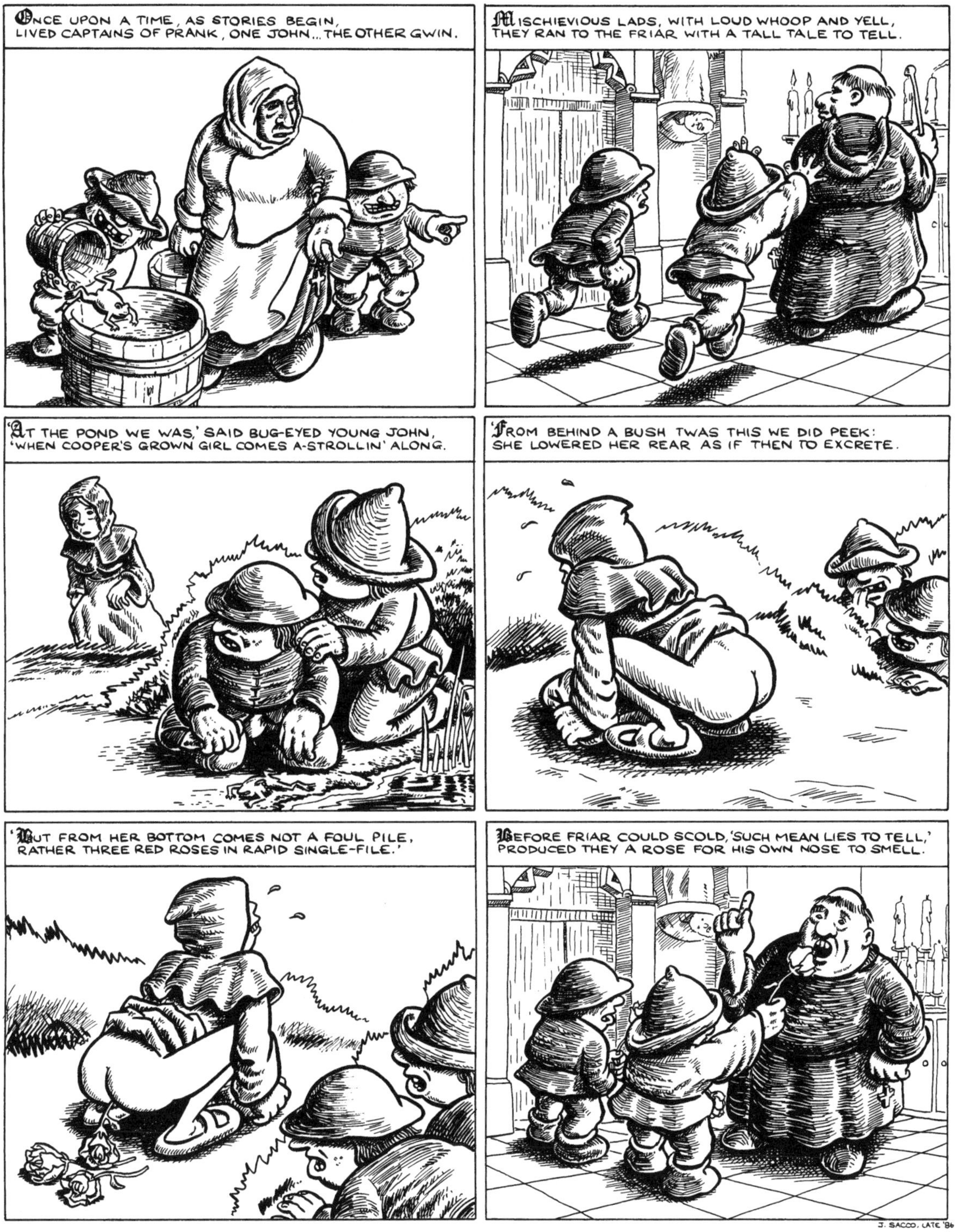
Once upon a time, as stories begin,
lived captains of prank, one John... the other Gwin.
Mischievious lads, with loud whoop and yell,
they ran to the friar with a tall tale to tell.
'At the pond we was,' said bug-eyed young John,
'when Cooper's grown girl comes a-strollin' along.
'From behind a bush twas this we did peek:
she lowered her rear as if then to excrete.
'But from her bottom comes not a foul pile,
rather three red roses in rapid single-file.'
Before friar could scold, 'Such mean lies to tell,'
produced they a rose for his own nose to smell.
J. Sacco. Late '86

'THEN METHINKS, I THINK,' THOUGHT FRIAR WITH ILL EASE,
THAT THIS TIME OF YEAR, BLOOMS NO FLOWERS LIKE THESE.'

CONCLUDED THE FRIAR, WITH SHAKE AND TREMBLE,
'THE COOPER'S DAUGHTER HAS LAIN WITH THE DEVIL.'

'ON TO THE COOPER'S,' FRIAR FLEW DOWN THE STREET,
AND FOUND HIM GORGING VARIETIES OF MEAT.

STOOD THE FRIAR IN SHOCK: SUCH HEARTY REPAST!
WHILE COOPER EXPLAINED, 'THE FOOD DROPS FROM 'ER ASS.'

FROM OUT OF HER HOME, DRAGGED BY HOLY FRIAR,
WHEN SERFS LEARNED THE EVIL, THEY SHOWED HER THEIR IRE.

ADMITTING THE WORST, SUCH INDISCRETION,
A TRIAL SHORT AND QUICK, THAT FOLLOWED CONFESSION.

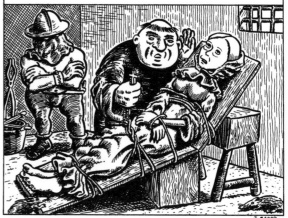

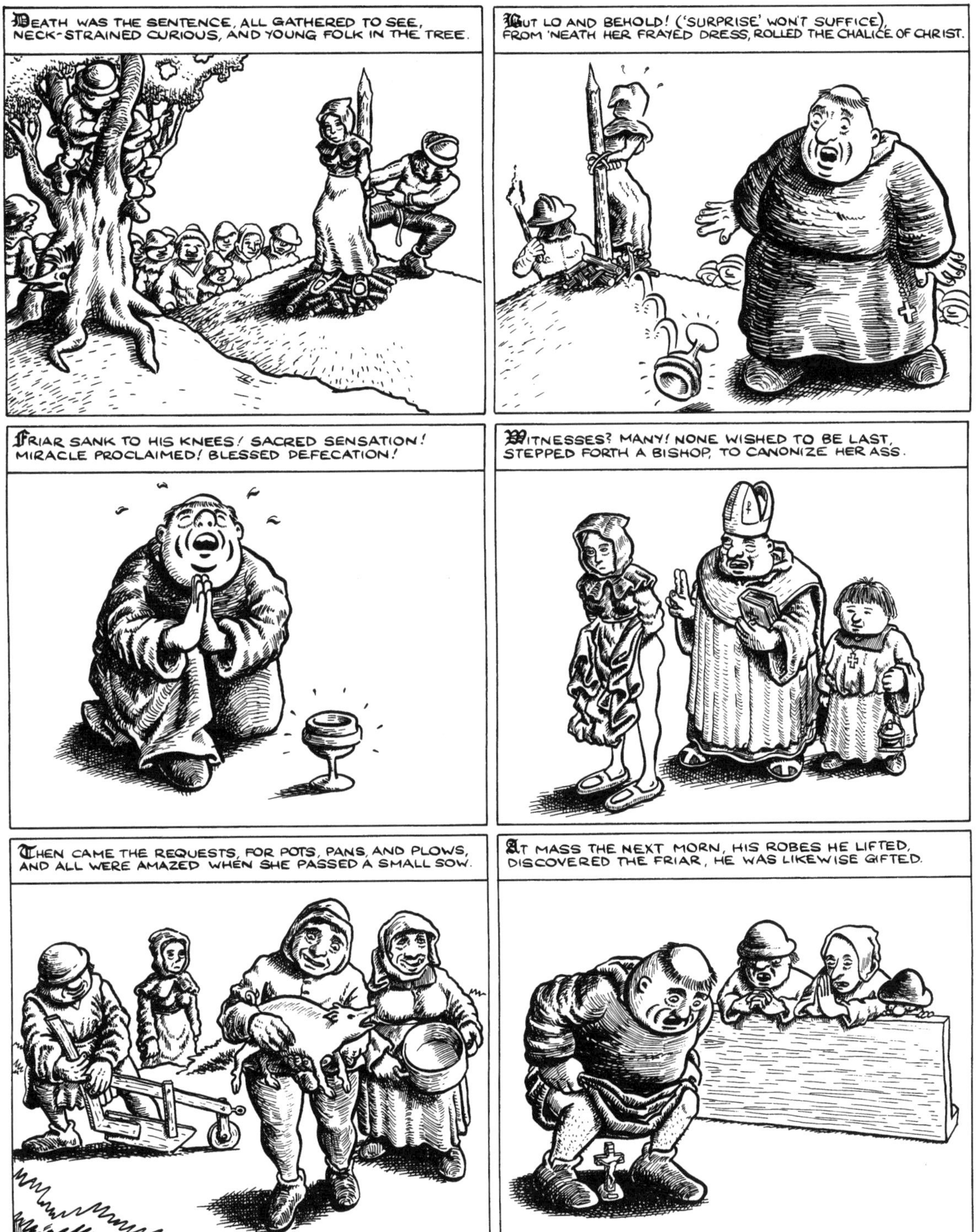
DEATH WAS THE SENTENCE, ALL GATHERED TO SEE,
NECK-STRAINED CURIOUS, AND YOUNG FOLK IN THE TREE.
BUT LO AND BEHOLD! ('SURPRISE' WON'T SUFFICE),
FROM 'NEATH HER FRAYED DRESS, ROLLED THE CHALICE OF CHRIST.
FRIAR SANK TO HIS KNEES! SACRED SENSATION!
MIRACLE PROCLAIMED! BLESSED DEFECATION!
WITNESSES? MANY! NONE WISHED TO BE LAST,
STEPPED FORTH A BISHOP, TO CANONIZE HER ASS.
THEN CAME THE REQUESTS, FOR POTS, PANS, AND PLOWS,
AND ALL WERE AMAZED WHEN SHE PASSED A SMALL SOW.
AT MASS THE NEXT MORN, HIS ROBES HE LIFTED,
DISCOVERED THE FRIAR, HE WAS LIKEWISE GIFTED.
J. SACCO, LATE 86

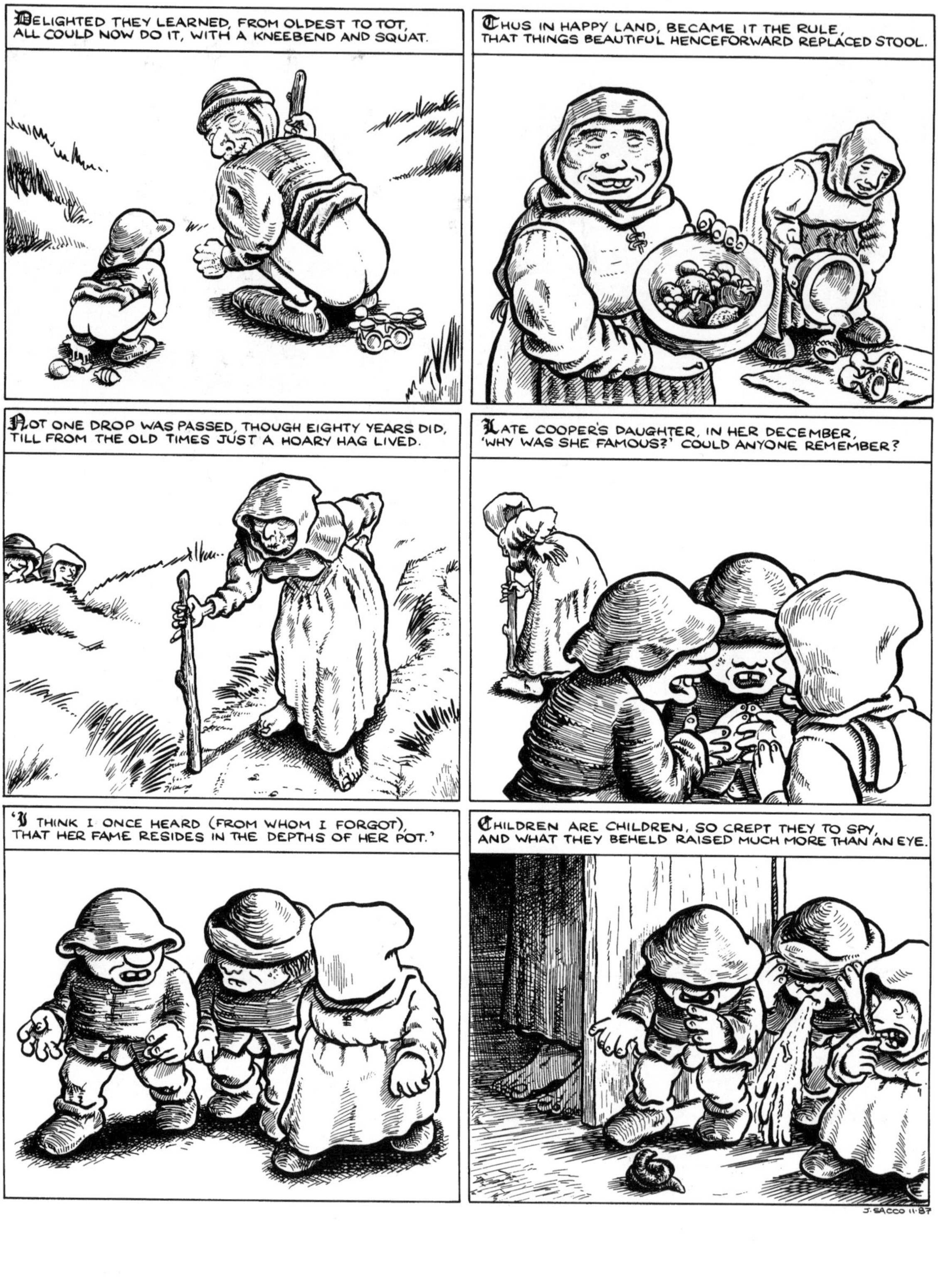
DELIGHTED THEY LEARNED, FROM OLDEST TO TOT, ALL COULD NOW DO IT, WITH A KNEEBEND AND SQUAT.
THUS IN HAPPY LAND, BECAME IT THE RULE, THAT THINGS BEAUTIFUL HENCEFORWARD REPLACED STOOL.
NOT ONE DROP WAS PASSED, THOUGH EIGHTY YEARS DID, TILL FROM THE OLD TIMES JUST A HOARY HAG LIVED.
LATE COOPER'S DAUGHTER, IN HER DECEMBER, 'WHY WAS SHE FAMOUS?' COULD ANYONE REMEMBER?
'I THINK I ONCE HEARD (FROM WHOM I FORGOT), THAT HER FAME RESIDES IN THE DEPTHS OF HER POT.'
CHILDREN ARE CHILDREN, SO CREPT THEY TO SPY, AND WHAT THEY BEHELD RAISED MUCH MORE THAN AN EYE.
J. SACCO 11.87

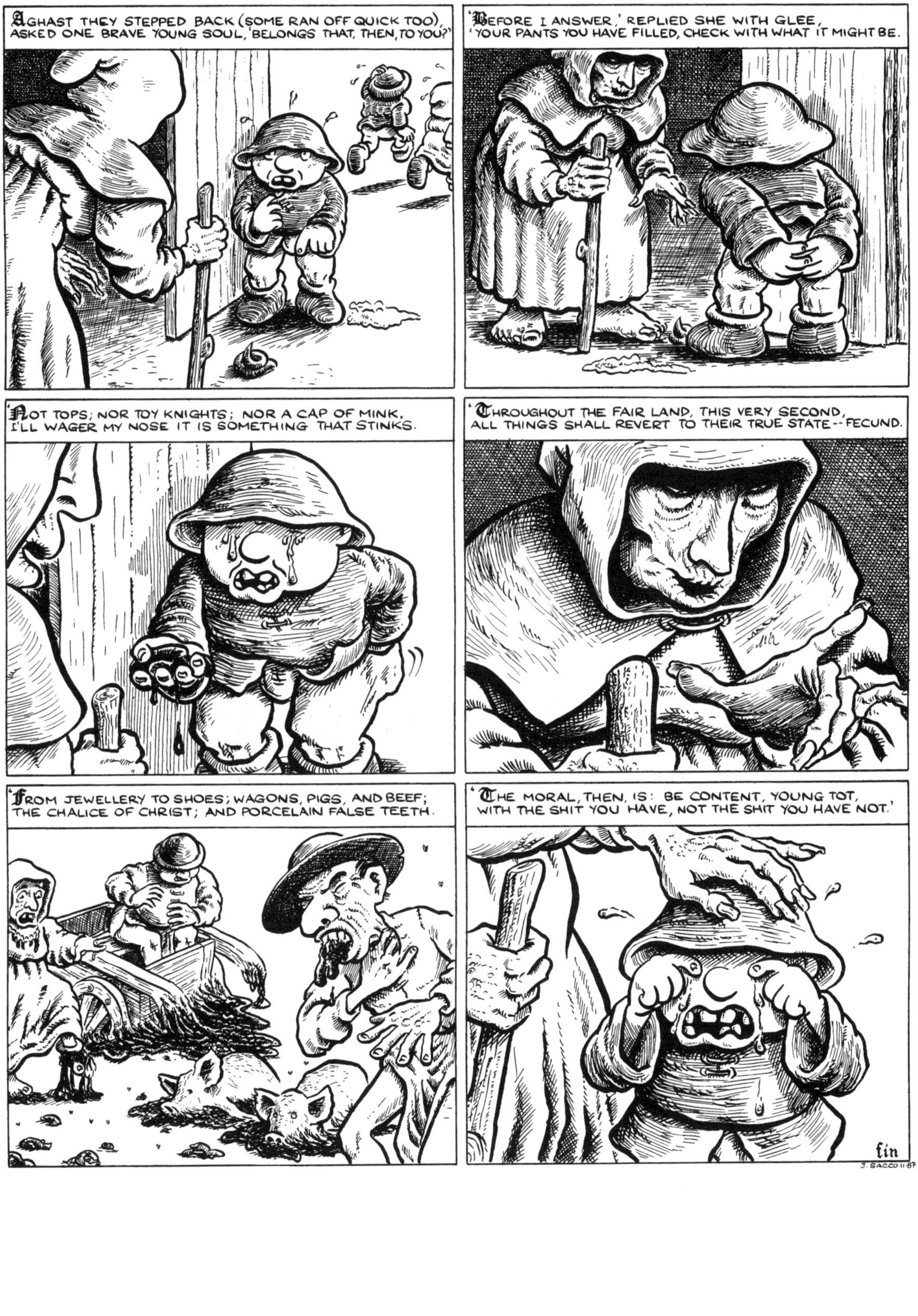
AGHAST THEY STEPPED BACK (SOME RAN OFF QUICK TOO), ASKED ONE BRAVE YOUNG SOUL, 'BELONGS THAT, THEN, TO YOU?'
'BEFORE I ANSWER,' REPLIED SHE WITH GLEE, 'YOUR PANTS YOU HAVE FILLED, CHECK WITH WHAT IT MIGHT BE.
'NOT TOPS; NOR TOY KNIGHTS; NOR A CAP OF MINK, I'LL WAGER MY NOSE IT IS SOMETHING THAT STINKS.
'THROUGHOUT THE FAIR LAND, THIS VERY SECOND, ALL THINGS SHALL REVERT TO THEIR TRUE STATE--FECUND.
'FROM JEWELLERY TO SHOES; WAGONS, PIGS, AND BEEF; THE CHALICE OF CHRIST; AND PORCELAIN FALSE TEETH.
'THE MORAL, THEN, IS: BE CONTENT, YOUNG TOT, WITH THE SHIT YOU HAVE, NOT THE SHIT YOU HAVE NOT.'
fin
J. SACCO 11 87

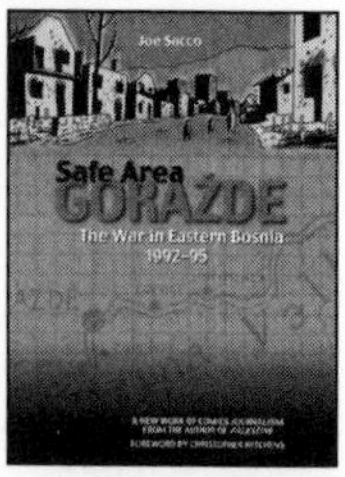
Safe Area
GORAZDE
The War in Eastern Bosnia
1992-95

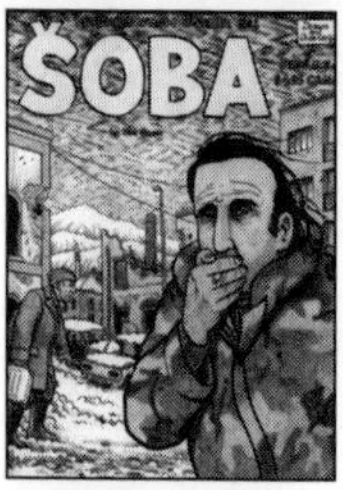
SOBA

SAFE AREA GORAZDE

AND OTHER STORIES OF THE BOSNIAN WAR

Safe Area Gorazde (2000, Fantagraphics Books, introduction by Christopher Hitchens), Sacco's stunning 228-page reportage on the Bosnian War.

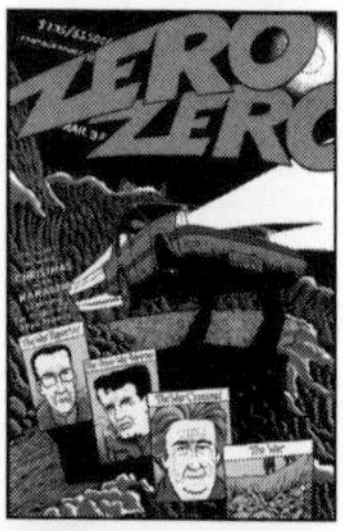
ZERO
ZERO

"Christmas with Karadzic" (1997, Fantagraphics Books, in *Zero Zero*).

Soba (1998, Drawn and Quarterly).

The Fixer (scheduled for Fall 2003, Drawn and Quarterly).

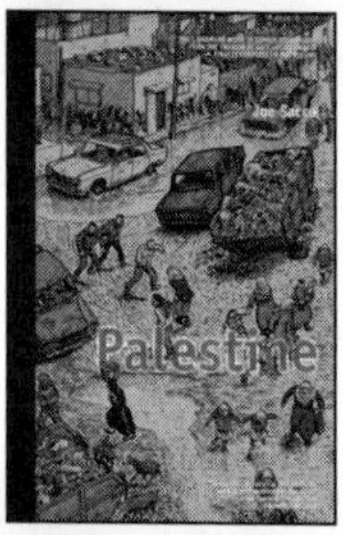
Palestine

PALESTINE

The 288-page *Palestine* (1992-1995, Fantagraphics Books) follows Sacco into the heart of the Middle Eastern conflict. With an introduction by Edward L. Said.

ALSO BY:

JOE SACCO

ORDERING INFORMATION:

Safe Area Gorazde (softcover): $21.95 postpaid
Safe Area Gorazde (hardcover): $29.95 postpaid
Zero Zero #15 (featuring "Christmas with Karadzic"): $4.95 postpaid
Soba: $4.95 postpaid
The Fixer: not yet released
Palestine: $27.95 postpaid

Available from Fantagraphics Books, 7563 Lake City Way NE, Seattle, WA 98115; Or call 1-800-657-1100 to order by phone; or order from www.fantagraphics.com

Bookstores please contact W.W. Norton and Company: 1-800-233-4830 for toll-free service in the contintental U.S., 212-354-5000 outside the U.S.; U.K. customers contact Turnaround Distributor Services at 208-829-3009.